Modern Political Parties

Modern Political Parties

Approaches to Comparative Politics

CONTRIBUTORS

Frederick C. Barghoorn

Samuel H. Beer

Gwendolen M. Carter

Andrew Gyorgy

Charles A. Micaud

Sigmund Neumann

Felix E. Oppenheim

Dankwart A. Rustow

Robert A. Scalapino

E. E. Schattschneider

EDITED BY

Sigmund Neumann

THE UNIVERSITY OF CHICAGO PRESS

Library of Congress Catalog Number: 55-10249

THE UNIVERSITY OF CHICAGO PRESS, CHICAGO 37
Cambridge University Press, London, N.W. 1, England
The University of Toronto Press, Toronto 5, Canada

Preface

The issue of the political party has entered, only of late and at last, the sphere of our professional concern; yet its discussion is still lacking in sharp theoretical concepts, historical depth, and the comparative data which alone could assure a substantial delineation of this crucial institution of modern political dynamics. It was out of this realization that the editor invited a number of proven area specialists to pool their substantive findings, which in turn could serve as a basis for a concrete theory and thus fill a long-felt need for an authoritative presentation of diverse political party systems.

The result is the panorama of studies presented in this volume. The separate researchers in the field who engaged in this co-operative enterprise, though they arrived independently at this juncture, found much in common. Viewing dynamic social forces rather than static constitutional structures as the key to an understanding of world affairs, they anticipated that their common study of political parties would yield a more realistic appraisal of comparative politics proper.

Purposely, no preconceived directives or definitions were proposed which would delimit the full flavor and fruitfulness of independent research into the character of contrasting political movements. The underlying expectation, however, was that a wider conceptualization would emerge out of the factual presentation of the various party systems. The result was a most rewarding experience of co-operation, doubly gratifying as, stretching over a number of years, it overcame the frustrating handicaps of time and space experienced by the contributing authors.

The project itself—the first of its kind —has certain limitations of which the editor is too well aware. It does not try to be up to date (which would be the safest way of being out of date by the time of publication). But the main purpose was, above all, to present in concrete form the persistent patterns and problems of major party systems. For another thing, this study does not claim any comprehensive coverage of its subject. Much as it might be desirable to include studies on less familiar areas like China and Latin America and the exciting developments among the formerly dependent peoples of India, the Philippines, and Indonesia, such an expansion would have made this text unmanageable, and thus it had to be left to the future. In fact, the purpose of this book is not to provide an encyclopedic panorama; it is not meant as a definitive study of political parties but proposes to be simply a preliminary pathfinder. It frankly raises more questions than it answers. It is, above all, an invitation to join in an exciting searching party through a virgin field that calls for inquisitive minds and many helping hands.

SIGMUND NEUMANN

Table of Contents

THE TOTALITARIAN COUNTERPART

PARTIES IN TRANSITION

TOWARD A COMPARATIVE STUDY OF POLITICAL PARTIES

FOR FURTHER STUDY

INDEX

Why Study Political Parties?

SIGMUND NEUMANN

Political parties are the lifeline of modern politics, yet they are largely forgotten as the main path to the study of political thought and practice today. Where is there an adequate theory to account for these crucial forces in our political life? More preconceived ideas— most of them essentially negative or naïve evaluations—are spread about these key instruments than about any other institution in politics. They have even been called the "villain" of public affairs and sneered at or ignored completely as unsuitable for serious speculation. In the United States especially, there has prevailed the underlying conviction that "the spirit of American government" can be found only at the grass roots of direct democracy; hence organized parties have been regarded merely as the fever curve in the pathology of politics, charting the growing morbidity of boss rule, "professional" politics, and party machines in the body politic, where the individuality of free citizens is suppressed. The political party, in the popular mind, is defined simply as something which someone else engages in, usually for personal profit and sometimes for graft. In view of this, it is not accidental that the most significant contributions to the theme were made by foreign observers of the American scene, like De Tocqueville, Lord Bryce, Ostrogorski, Max Weber, and Robert Michels, and by American students of foreign governments, like A. M. Lowell.

The interest in political parties now springing up among our political scientists and historians is a reflection of the silent revolution which has taken place in the modern study of politics. It has something to do with the fact that in our modern mass society, whether at war or at peace, in democracies no less than in dictatorships, the people have become potent participants and protagonists. They are wooed daily through the mass media of radio, television, press, and propaganda. Their actions and reactions, their direction and controls, become more significant for governments at work than constitutional structures and successions of cabinets. Our concern, therefore, has turned away from a merely formal, legalistic, and constitutional approach to a prime consideration of political dynamics and the processes of decision-making. We want to know where, when, and how politics is made in this constantly changing political scene. Such a new emphasis indicates that the instituted agencies, policies, and procedures must have undergone fundamental changes, too. This calls for reconsideration, reappraisal, and redefinition. The priority lists of the study of public affairs are properly spelled out in terms of the major concerns and critical areas of the body politic.

Political parties are indeed critically significant. In democracy's politics they are fought over not only in election years (and surely there is always an election year somewhere) but daily. Their very existence has been challenged by dictatorship's monolithic controls (though garbed in party disguise) in the Soviet system today, which is far more powerful than yesteryears' fascism and National Socialism. Moreover, in the twilight zones of a two-power world, political parties are being tested in numerous attempts at democratic renewal in areas as far apart as Germany

1

and Japan, Italy and India, Southeast Asia and Africa, the Near East and South America. It is through the nexus of political parties that the manifold character and dynamic life of the different continents can be constantly revealed. And while the innumerable and ever oscillating variations within the present-day party appearances and practices, in democracies and dictatorships, easily blur the lines of demarcation and rightly forewarn against quick generalizations, the overwhelming conflict between the two giant blocs in the bipolar world may well be epitomized in the two contrasting systems of party organization, the loyalties they command, the relationship they spell out between leaders and followers, and the policies they articulate on a world scale.

Such an extension of the restricted national arena of political parties to include the international scene demands no less the search for implications in our own personal life; for political parties, reaching out as they do into world affairs, still enter man's private existence, as the role of the Third International in the Czech Communist revolution of 1948 so amply proved. It is this simultaneous attack on all sides which gives twentieth-century politics its three-dimensional involvement—personal, national, and international—and its confusing complexity. National parties have become increasingly crucial factors on far-flung international fronts as well as in our more immediate personal activities, apart from their basic articulation of a state's political course. This widening of the political frontier requires continuous cross-referencing and synthesizing, in order to circumscribe the character and course, structure and strategy, of modern political parties. Such a definition by contrast, therefore, points the way to the rewards to be found along the way of a comparative approach to the study of the modern political party.

Within hardly a quarter of a century this nation has seen significant changes in the approach to political science, from political alchemy to political morphology to comparative government proper. The mere collection of haphazard, exotic facts out of curiosity was the stage for the beginner in world affairs only a generation ago. A more serious and systematic consideration of significant data became exciting to a young nation discovering the wide world at the eve of World War II. And now, in its aftermath, a purposeful comparison of alternatives in policy decision—the prerequisite for the maturing protagonists among the great powers—makes the demands on the academic discipline grow and entirely change in character.

If the comparative method is to fulfil its proper functions in this global world, where even internal national decisions are dependent on a continuous awareness of their international implications, it must enlarge its scope in area to include non-Western countries and so-called "primitive" peoples; deepen its attack through meaningful, historical analyses; and focus its evaluation on the dynamic forces within the communities. Moreover, it must constantly interrelate the available data and thus contribute to a genuinely comparative study. Only when reaching beyond a mere political morphology of legislative, executive, and judicial forms can the responsible citizen recognize the different nature, purpose, and direction of the political powers in being and in conflict.

"To know thyself, compare thyself to others." The comparative approach is, above all, an eye opener to a people's self-recognition and to its taking a stand. It is not accidental that the great civilizations, like that of the Renaissance, were developed at the crossroads of mankind and articulated by the meeting with contrasting systems. This encounter alone made an awakening western Europe fully aware of her own character and quality, apart from being naturally and fruitfully influenced by the impact of the strange, new forces.

We are again living in such a period of opening frontiers, which will force us to recognize the values and concepts we live by and to test them anew against their challenge from abroad. It is in this crisis of our own society that comparative government becomes a must for the mature citizen.

Beyond that, the intensive study of contrasting civilizations offers the necessary equipment for present-day policy decisions. While our planet is continuously shrinking, bringing the politics of far-distant areas into our compass, thoughtful students of public affairs have often been troubled by our limited "knowledge by experience." Its only substitute seems to be "knowledge by learning," which puts a great responsibility on our generation to make comparative government a live issue—comprehensive and contemporary.

Contemporary, indeed, it must be in a deeper sense than headline actuality. In the clash of these fast-changing systems, another fact becomes increasingly obvious: the need for a continuous conceptual housecleaning. One could well argue that a time lag usually exists between historical reality and its conceptualization, especially in a great age of transition when the political vocabulary is quickly outdated and thus full of misnomers. We are still living within an ideological framework of a hundred years back and naturally cannot master our present-day political conflicts with such obsolete and often romantic stereotypes. This is a time when a meaningful historical comparison is called for. More than that: a theoretical clarification becomes a paramount preliminary for appropriate strategies of this revolutionary age. All fundamental political concepts, like nationalism, sovereignty, imperial-

ism, socialism, and statism, must therefore be redefined in the light of a new reality. On this basis alone can theory become, as it should, a guide to proper political action, a compass through chaos.

The issue of the party is a perfect illustration of our changing approach to a meaningful comparative government and of this incessant metamorphosis of its concepts. What better key to an understanding of the vital processes among the great antagonists in world affairs can be found than in the political parties, reaching down to each citizen within each nation, focusing the interplay of national pressure groups, and affecting the international scene through their manifold organizations? What other agency can serve as a more pointed example of the continuously shifting meaning of our social concepts? And what other institutions can thus impress on us equally well the urgency of their ever renewed reappraisal?

Not only has the concept changed through the ages—and, indeed, at an accelerated pace in this twentieth century—but also different types of parties arise concurrently in our times. The loose application of the term to the most divergent phenomena has led to dangerous confusions; and revolutions, like military battles, national and international, have been lost through obsolete strategy. Is it not conceivable that much of the confusion and difficulty in present-day party struggle derives from the use of such an antiquated arsenal, refurbished though it be by the daydreamers of a glorified past? Yet does the proverbial and powerful "man in the street" recognize this significant shift in the character of modern political parties? Or does even the statesman?

Matters are further complicated on our shrinking planet by the fact that areas which once were worlds apart geographically and historically have now been pushed together. Now different ages and different party systems have become strange bedfellows; and, as in geological structures, dislocations have occurred in the continuous pattern of our societal structure. This coexistence in time of noncontemporaries has given our political life its complexities, its contrasting stratification, and its conflicting political generations—problems which can be mastered only by a rigorous re-examination of the multifarious mutations in the structure of today's political parties.

It is necessary that all our political science concepts be spelled out in time and space, both in their specific historical situation and in their local representation, for any premature generalization only tends to invalidate the genuine character of political forces.

The question of a proper approach to a meaningful theory of political party structure poses a dilemma because the overwhelming data of our material world fall into a conceivable pattern only if seen through the controlled order of a conceptual framework, which in turn can be conceived only in a full appreciation of the rich texture of reality. The task of attempting to systematize our knowledge, therefore, is confronted by almost overwhelming difficulties and can proceed only by a simultaneous attack on both theory and practice. Social concepts evolve by stages, remaining necessarily fragmentary and tentative, and, at best, present only a useful working hypothesis for a deeper penetration into an ever changing reality. Hence a conceptualization of political parties must be a constantly renewed effort. Most definitely it can never be a one-man job; it must be the work of proved experts, who by pooling their substantive findings in their special areas can contribute to the laying of the foundations for a concrete theory of the modern political party.

Political parties are the main agents of public affairs. For this very reason they must be seen within the complete settings of their own governmental systems. Only against this background of historical circumstances, institutional traditions, and national characteristics can the specific nature, issues, and contributions of the different party patterns be fully evaluated. Each national analysis, therefore, emphasizes different features (grown out of long-range experiences of the peoples' existence) and adds to the cumulative definition of modern political parties.

Our tour naturally starts out with a view of the British parties which in so many ways have been regarded—like the British political system altogether—as the prototype of democratic government. This inquiry, however, shows two significant facts: the specific conditions under which the British political parties unfolded and the significant changes which they underwent under the impact of ensuing social transformations. Thus from the outset the circumspect student is forewarned against any easy transfer of these indigenous organs of politics into other national patterns. The genius of Britain's unwritten constitution and its ever renewed flexibility is reflected in the successful transformation of its party system from a governing elite to the present-day organized mass parties.

The four selected Dominion states present a global transfer of the two-party theme and, at the same time, significant variations from the island's original pattern in the kaleidoscopic Empire turning Commonwealth.

The succeeding studies of France, Belgium, and Scandinavia introduce the vexing problems of modern multiparty systems. The French political scene illustrates the tensions and liabilities of ideological fronts in a complex social setting, emphasized by the still unfinished political revolution of 1789, the nation's coinciding economic transformations, and its deep resistance to the prevailing temper of encompassing world forces. The resulting instability of the party system, so often commented on, finds its counterbalance, however, in basic ideological traditions.

The Belgian case shows on a small canvas the cleavage of multifarious political forces of race, religion, and social classes and their eventual compromise in a two-and-a-half-party pattern.

Scandinavia presents probably the happiest solution of a functioning multiparty system. This fact may well be due to the relatively stable social order of a peninsula which, geographically removed from the center of world conflicts today, could preserve politically unambitious parties of representation so characteristic of the nineteenth-century state of balance and peace.

The concluding study on the democratic party systems shows the historical transformations of the United States from the limited political administration of early independence to the intricate responsibilities of a major world power. While this amazing maturing process of our nation can be assumed as a familiar tale and therefore is here drawn in bold strokes, emphasis is laid on the shifting functions of the equally changing political organs and the growth of modern party government. Its unique present-day character becomes increasingly recognizable in the daily encounters of the United States with our partners in world affairs. They in turn are deeply concerned about our ability to articulate clearly the responsible role of the American parties.

Democratic parties find an even more pressing need for self-articulation vis-à-vis the dictatorial challenge. The complex ramifications of the Soviet system demand a full exposition before their impact can be clearly grasped. After the demise of the Third Reich, the U.S.S.R. remains unquestionably the outstanding case of comprehensive controls and

their key instrument, the monolithic party. Its structure and functions, its sociology and psychology, must be understood in order to evaluate its persistent power at home and, even more, its fatal ambitions abroad. The elaborate study of the shifts in techniques of subversion from the Comintern to the Cominform points to the specific and crucial character of the Bolshevik party and its world drive, which transforms Russia's historical imperialism into a new, fierce force. The subsequent comparative analysis of the eastern European countries is a case study in Soviet satellite parties, in the true sense of the word.

The final section of the analytical studies presents two nations which, in the critical development of their parties, have run the gamut of practically all forms of government in the short span of hardly a century. Experimentation and cultural borrowing were the order of Japan's history from Prince Ito's importation of Prussian feudal institutions to the country's quick adaptation to Western democracy, its subsequent submission to militant autocracy and, after a crushing defeat, to military government controls and a new democratic beginning. Those abrupt changes may serve as a warning, however, that the amazing development of the post-dictatorial Japanese system will still have to undergo the test of time.

No less is such a careful consideration and tentative evaluation imperative for a full appreciation of Germany's future. Here, as in other countries, the political parties merely articulate the special features of the national life. No wonder, then, that in this *Land der Mitte* the political forces of the divided Reich reflect the tensions of the people between East and West, torn by lasting and contradictory traditions of the Bismarckian Reich, the Weimar Republic, Hitler's rule, the occupational interlude, and the competing images of a partitioned Germany—not to mention the more remote and yet ever present liabilities of a thousand years' Holy Roman Empire, heavily mortgaging the young party system even before it began. A full account of the German parties—their ideological intricacies, their sociological constellations, their international implications—is an appropriate forewarning against easygoing generalizations concerning the past, present, and future of political dynamics.

It is against such a colorful background of a wide party panorama that, finally, a tentative sketch of some persistent themes for a comparative analysis may be ventured. The concluding part presents nothing but preliminary propositions for further study, particularly in its attempt at a definition of modern political parties.

If any fundamental thesis evolves from this presentation of past and present analyses, it is the impression of the changing function and consequently shifting role of political parties in this century when politics—on the international, national, and personal plane—has become our fate. Putting it differ-

ently: We are living in a time of crisis and decision which naturally affects each people in different degrees and dimensions and consequently demands diverse party systems to respond to the needs of the nations.

Yet, granted those wide differences, the modern mass society in its global frame may well impose on all peoples a deeper involvement in the public domain, which, in turn, may be illustrated in a visible shift from loose parties of individual representation to powerful parties of social integration. Moreover, accepting such a fateful interpenetration of our personal, national, and international existence, it may be even more important to recognize that the future of the Western world will depend on our ability to conceive a concept of party that, while fulfilling this task of social integration, does not destroy the fundamental traditions of personal freedom and individual responsibilities. It is in the light of these crucial decisions of our time that the world conflict between the totalitarian and democratic societies reaches through the diverse party formations down to the very base of human existence.

DEMOCRATIC PARTY SYSTEMS

Great Britain: From Governing Elite to Organized Mass Parties[1]

SAMUEL H. BEER
Harvard University

I / BRITISH PARTIES AND THE PROBLEM OF DEMOCRATIC LEADERSHIP

"Nobody will understand parliament government," wrote Walter Bagehot, in *The English Constitution*, "who fancies it an easy thing. . . . You have not a perception of the first elements in this matter till you know that government by a *club* is a standing wonder." The same may be said of democracy in general as well as of parliamentary government. Consider any modern democratic state, with its millions of members divided into innumerable groups and separated from one another by occupation, education, economic interest, religion, and traditional attitudes. How can such a vast club govern itself at all, let alone govern itself well?

Democracy gives the people political power, but the people speak with many voices and have many wills. These many wills may push public policy first in one direction and then in another or even in different directions at the same time. American politics is not the only illustration of this. If we have our pressure groups, the Continental democracies of Europe have their multiparty systems. The classic example of the self-defeating democracy is Weimar Germany, for there in the last years of the Republic the division of views and interests reached the point where the Reichstag, faithfully reflecting the many wills of the people, could muster a majority *against* but not *for* any cabinet and any line of policy. And French democracy under the Third and Fourth Republic frequently verged on a similar state of paralysis.

Now between democracy and government there may be a certain opposition. Democracy requires that the people participate as fully as possible in the business of governing; government, on the other hand, requires that those who hold office deliberately decide what they will and will not do and pursue with vigor and consistency the action they have decided on. We ask of government that it should act on a policy—that is, a design for action deliberately adopted, consistently expressed in various spheres, and continuously pursued over an appropriate period of time.[2] The problem which any popular government faces is how to reconcile wide public participation with this need for policy.

---

1. Except for a few points of detail, such as the numbers of party members, this section on British parties, which was written in 1951, does not take account of changes since that year. I wish to thank the *Journal of Politics*, which published the section on the Conservative party in its issue of February, 1952, for permission to reprint. Tables 1 and 2, p. 57, summarize the results of British elections from 1900 to 1955.

2. The problem of "the formation of policy" was succinctly put in a statement submitted to the Tomlin Commission: "The business of government, if it is to be well done, calls for the steady application of long and wide views to complex problems: for the pursuit, as regards each and every subject-matter, of definite lines of action, mutually consistent, conformed to public opinion and capable of being followed continuously while conditions so permit, and of being readily adjusted when they do not" (Royal Commission on the Civil Service [1929–30], Appendix VIII).

9

How has Britain dealt with this problem in the past, and how does she deal with it today? If we look at popular government in Britain in the mid-nineteenth century through the eyes of Walter Bagehot, we see one possible solution of the problem—or, perhaps more correctly, an escape from it. Bagehot did indeed find that effective government was compatible with the widened suffrage created by the Reform Act of 1832 but only because the mass of newly enfranchised voters did not push their actual participation in politics too far. The shaping of programs, the choice of candidates, as well as the immediate business of lawmaking and administering, remained with "the educated ten thousand," who alone, in his opinion, had the requisite ability.

Writing a generation later and after the further extension of the franchise in 1867 and 1885, A. L. Lowell similarly concluded that in Britain "the national government is still mainly in the hands of the upper class." He wrote, in *The Government of England,*

The condition is one to which Professor Burgess alludes as "government of the people, for the people, by the best of the people." Without discussing in what sense they are the best of the people, it is clear that most of the seats of the House of Commons are still held by the members of a distinct social class. . . . The mass of the people prefer to be represented by men of social position, and the higher his social position, the better they like a candidate; provided, of course, that the party to which he belongs is prepared to carry out their wishes. . . . The sentiment of deference, or snobbishness, becomes, if anything, stronger as the social scale descends. The workingman, when not provoked by an acute grievance to vote for a trade-union candidate, prefers a man with a title, and thus the latest extensions of the franchise have rather strengthened than weakened the hold of the governing class upon public life.

How this deferential relationship, this ethos of "natural leadership," arose and managed to survive into modern times is one of the most important themes of English history. Its spirit, one hardly need point out, has a feudal tinge and a medieval background. But in what way did it help to protect government against the distractions of pressures and to maintain the conditions of policy-making? In the nature of the case it meant that a certain restraint, voluntary and uncoerced, was imposed upon the political activity of that part of the public not belonging to the governing class. To the extent that these other classes felt that governing was the task of their "betters," they did not themselves take the political initiative or urgently press their demands or raise up from their own midst leaders to dispute the claim of the governing class to political office. For the same reason, those who governed felt a certain aloofness, a sense of independence, toward those pressures and popular demands that did emerge. On some occasions, of course, political activity occupied large sections of the public—Chartism is the obvious example—and the deference which the masses accorded the governing class did not isolate it from their feelings and opinions—from the agitation of the Anti-Corn Law League or from the social unrest of the mid-eighties. The relationship between the masses and the governing class, however, opened an easy road to office to its members, freed them from popular demands, and gave them ample opportunity to govern according to their own judgment and standards.

That opportunity was often used to favor their own selfish interests. But this class was not simply an upper class —the rich, the educated, the fashionable; it was also a political class, as Taine and De Tocqueville observed and emphasized. That is to say, it was a group of persons who not only were engaged in politics but also, because of their values and training, had a strong sense of responsibility for politics. Wealth was by no means despised, but it was overshadowed by political power and frame as a definition of success in life. Moved by these values, the upper class had developed, through long practice in directing the civil and military organization of the community, what Mosca (in *The Ruling Class*) called "a real art of governing," which, he thought, had made British government "distinguished for carefully considered policies and for great steadfastness and sagacity in carrying them out." With these talents, guided by its not undemanding standards, and supported by popular deference, the upper class long continued to govern nation and empire—and, relatively speaking, to govern them well—even though the formal structure of power was becoming democratized.

Today that monopoly has been broken—or, rather, it has been so far whittled away over a long period of years that popular participation in politics is at least as wide and as intense in Britain as in any other Western country. But that participation differs in manner and spirit from the participation of, say, Frenchmen or Americans in their politics. Judged by any of the common indexes—percentage of eligible voters casting a ballot, numbers of dues-paying party members, activity of volunteer party workers, public knowledge of political questions—participation in Britain equals or exceeds that of other countries. How, then, we must ask, does Britain still manage to reconcile the conditions of popular government with the need for policy?

Let us consider some of the possibilities. One possibility is the great popular leader. Through his personal appeal to the electorate he may be able to influence the legislature as well as rebel factions and potential rivals in his own following so powerfully that a sphere of independent decision is maintained within which he and his lieutenants may rationally determine and co-ordinate policy. This is the solution that emerges at times under the United States presidential system. While in this instance the problem is solved through personal leadership, a similar effect may result from the leadership of a governing class, like that of nineteenth-century England. In the following pages it will be argued that there is a third means—an impersonal one—which may perform the function of leadership: the structures of action of political parties.

The President of the United States, we often say, is not just one man but an "institution." We mean, for instance, that a decision announced as coming from the President is not the product of the thought of a single individual but rather of a complex structure of agencies, staffs, and White House advisers. Likewise, in the field of economics Schumpeter has argued that the functions of the entrepreneur, the business leader, are becoming more and more institutionalized, as bureau and committee work in great industrial organizations takes the place of purely individual action. Leadership in British politics has developed similarly, becoming less a function of particular persons and the traditional governing class and more a function of the formal and informal structures of party. At the same time, popular participation in government through the party system has been greatly extended. Yet that system and its institutions of leadership have maintained the necessary conditions of policy-making.

We cannot, of course, expect to find in Britain or in any country equal participation by all citizens in government. If this is the "classical theory" of democracy—it would seem to be Rousseau's—then the classical theory is misleading and impracticable, and, judged in its light, the arguments of antidemocratic critics like Mosca and Michels must be accepted. There will always be different levels of public participation, for the ordinary voter has only limited time, inclination, and ability for politics. He does not enact the laws or administer the government services. Nor is it he who provides informed, daily criticism of the government, shapes alternative programs, or expounds these programs before the public. For such activities will be largely confined to professional politicians, journalists, spokesmen for interests, and the more active party members—in short, a minority of the state. Furthermore, the personal qualities—the values and abilities—of these leading minorities will always be of great importance. No democracy can do without gifted men offering some degree of personal leadership. And if these constitute a class in the sense of having in common a high standard of achievement and ethics and a strong sense of responsibility, the existence of such a class will be one reason for greater wisdom and justice in the state.

Personal leadership has not vanished from British politics, nor has a governing class. Yet, in its shift of emphasis from them, the development we shall trace has brought about a profound alteration in the real conditions under which Britain is governed.

II / British Parties Before World War I

In a famous essay ("Politics as a Vocation") Max Weber described three stages which in his opinion have marked the development of political parties. At first, parties were "pure followings of the aristocracy," changing their allegiance as the "great noble families" which led them changed theirs. The second stage was the "parties of notables." These arose with "the rising power of the bourgeoisie" and consisted of informal local associations of the propertied and cultured circles, held together in the nation as a whole not by a formal party machine but by the members of the party with seats in the legislature. The framing of election programs, the choice of leaders and candidates, and the general control of the party rested with these circles of notables, above all the parliamentary party.

With this structure Weber sharply contrasted the modern forms of party organization—"the children of democracy, of mass franchise, of the necessity to woo and organize the masses, and develop the utmost unity and direction and the strictest discipline." In these forms there is a large, formally organized national machine whose power rests not with the parliamentary party as such or with the formal party conventions and assemblies but with the party bureaucrats, organizers, and especially the party leader who has shown the capacity to win the support of a mass electorate. The party organization outside the legislature disciplines the party members in the legislature; in turn the leader, because of his demagogic ability, tends to dominate the machine while using it to rally the masses behind him. This is the stage, in Weber's terms, of "plebiscitarian democracy."

Party Structure: 1832–1867

Without examining the aristocratic origins of British parties, at this point it may be said that after the Reform of 1832 Weber's sketch of the structure of a "party of notables" applies to both the Conservatives and the Liberals. Within Parliament the parties had very little formal organization. By custom, ministers in the House of Commons occupied the front bench to the right of the speaker, leading members of the Opposition the front bench facing them, while supporters of each side ranged themselves on benches behind their respective leaders and below the gangway. The "Whips," dating from the eighteenth century—the chief government Whip in the House of Commons having the title of "Patronage Secretary to the Treasury," an office created in 1714—had, as their principal task within Parliament, to help party leaders muster their followers for divisions.

After the Reform of 1832, party organization outside Parliament, practically unknown before, grew rapidly, taking the form of local registration associations. The formation of these associations was sometimes instigated by the candidates, sometimes by local party "notables," sometimes by interested organizations—such as the Anti-Corn Law League—and sometimes by the Whip of the parliamentary party. Their membership seems to have been small, headed by the local notables, who provided the larger part of the funds. They were designed, it should be emphasized, not as a means by which the voters might nominate candidates but as a means of getting the names of local supporters on the electoral register and of canvassing the voters at election time. The local notables and the parliamentary leaders continued to have the controlling power. With their acquiescence, or possibly at their request, the candidate "offered himself" to the electorate of the constituency.

A link between the parliamentary and the provincial leadership was provided by the great political clubs—the Carlton, founded in 1831 by the Conservatives, and the Reform, founded in 1836 by the Liberals—to which belonged prominent local adherents as well as sitting members of Parliament and aspirants to a seat. In each there was a political committee, close to the Whip, which kept up relationships with the local associations or local party agents. Quite early, the Whip had a general agent of the party who watched the electoral situation in the constituencies with the aid of his correspondents. At his office in one of the clubs the Whip received requests from would-be candidates in search of constituencies and from constituencies in search of candidates. And if his party was in power, ministers looked to him for recommendations regarding the disposition of the not inconsiderable patronage—church livings, secretarial positions, Lords lieutenants' commissions—which still remained at their disposal and which was commonly used for political purposes.

In the course of time more formal arrangements were introduced. Around 1861 the Liberal Whip set up a central body, the Liberal Registration Association, composed of "gentlemen of known Liberal political opinions." The association promoted the organization of registration associations, assisted them in their work, and took over the important task of recommending parliamentary candidates to the local leaders. From the association and a similar body set up by the Conservatives in 1870 on Disraeli's initiative, the present central offices of these parties descended.

In this mid-Victorian period the social life of the aristocratic and wealthy classes in London and in the country merged naturally with their political life. Saturday evening gatherings at 94 Picadilly, Lord Palmerston's celebrated London residence, often settled the fate of men and measures. "In Lord and Lady Palmerston's hospitality," one contemporary (the Earl of Malmesbury) remarked, "there was from the outset something purposeful, a note of political value which not even the graciousness and geniality of the host and hostess ever quite concealed." Meetings of party members of both houses were sometimes held in the political clubs and sometimes at the London homes of leaders like Lord Derby and Lord John Russell. Party leaders were chosen in a most informal manner. It was at a dinner at Lord Derby's, for instance, that a group of the principal Conservatives decided in 1849 to make Disraeli the party leader in the House of Commons.

English society remained deferential, and the party structure reflected this fact. Organization grew from the top down, and authority in the choice of candidates and policies continued to rest with the parliamentary parties. By choosing between persons and policies so selected and presented to them, the newly enfranchised voters exercised their modest function in self-government.

That they should do no more was, in Bagehot's opinion, a prerequisite if British political institutions were to work. "I have said," he wrote, "that cabinet government is possible in England because England was a deferential country. I meant that the nominal constituency was not the real constituency; that the mass of the 'ten-pound' householders did not really form their own opinions, and did not exact of their representatives an obedience to those opinions; that they were in fact guided in their judgment by the better educated classes; that they preferred representatives from those classes, and gave those representatives much license." Such deference, in his view, was fortunate, since the mass of the electorate were incompetent to originate government policy. "Their own notions," he continued, "if they had been cross-examined upon them, would have been found always most confused and often most foolish. They were competent to decide an issue selected by the higher classes, but they were incompetent to do more."[3]

3. *The English Constitution,* pp. 263–65.

Party Structure: 1867–1914

The extension of the franchise in the latter part of the century led to great changes in the formal organization of the parties outside Parliament. Following the Reform of 1867 the local associations of both parties were reorganized and their membership greatly enlarged. In both parties they became democratic at least in form, admitting all adherents of the party or all who paid a small subscription. They also became representative in form, their affairs being managed by a series of councils and committees composed mainly of delegates chosen by meetings of the members. At the same time, national bodies based largely upon the local associations were set up. The National Liberal Federation, founded in 1877, federated the local associations of the party which had adopted a representative form. Its Council, a large assembly composed of delegates chosen by the local associations and in proportion to the population of their towns or districts, met annually. A less numerous body, the General Committee, consisting of local delegates, the officers of the federation, and certain co-opted members, chose a small executive committee. The National Union of Conservative and Constitutional Associations, dating from 1867, also had a large representative assembly, its annual conference. Its executive body, the Council, was smaller than the General Committee of the Liberal Federation and included not only the principal officers of the union and local delegates but also certain individuals who had made large subscriptions to party funds.

Conceivably, these changes in the formal structures of the parties might have revolutionized the way in which leaders were chosen and their policies when in power or in opposition were determined. As has sometimes happened on the Continent, party bureaucrats and professional organizers might have gained control over the extra-parliamentary organization and used this power to dominate the parliamentary party. Or perhaps the party organization might have become, in fact as well as in form, radically democratized. The latter seems to have been the purpose of Joseph Chamberlain and his radical followers when, independently of the parliamentary leaders, they founded the National Liberal Federation. "The essential feature of the proposed Federation," read the summons to the conference of 1877, "is the principle which must henceforth govern the action of the Liberals as a political party, namely, the direct participation of all members of the party in the direction, and in the selection of those particular measures of reforms and of progress to which priority shall be given." "We hope," said Chamberlain to the assembled delegates, "that the time is not distant when we may see a meeting of what will be a really Liberal Parliament, outside the Imperial Legislature."

Yet neither of these varieties of party government materialized. There were professional organizers of great ability. The general agents of the national parties and the candidates' paid election agents, who often doubled as secretaries to the local associations, were indispensable. But a striking fact about British politics, now as then, is that these highly professional operators never acquired independent political power comparable to the power of the American "boss" or the Continental "bureaucrat."

Nor did the new representative bodies take over direction of the parties. In accord with Chamberlain's hopes, the Liberal Council passed resolutions expressing party policy and thereby, so Lord Roseberry said, embarrassed the government of 1894–95 by forcing it to overplay its hand when it was supported by a precarious majority in Commons and opposed by a

resolutely hostile Lords. But by the end of the century the Council was, as Lowell puts it, "effectively muzzled." The Executive Committee controlled its agenda, determining what resolutions were to be discussed. Dissent was often voiced, but amendments could not be moved. Thus the Council became a vehicle for arousing enthusiasm and ratifying decisions of the leaders, but not for policy-making. When it came to a choice of election issues or government policy, the parliamentary chiefs freely selected from the large and rather miscellaneous collection of declarations compiled by the Council.

The Conservative Union had been conceived differently from the federation, its purpose being not to make policy but to strengthen organization and win elections, and demands for greater popular control were met by a reassertion of this principle. Policy, replied the chief Whip, when that demand was raised at the conference of 1906, must be initiated by the leaders. Conservative conferences passed resolutions, enjoying greater liberty of initiating them and moving amendments than the Liberal body. But as these resolutions were only advisory, the parliamentary chiefs retained the effective power of decision.

A third possible result of the structural changes in the party and the extension of the franchise was that "plebiscitary Caesarism" which Max Weber professed to find in modern parties. Gladstone, it is true, established over the leaders of his party a dominance resting largely upon his immense personal authority with the electorate—his "charismatic leadership," if you like. For example, his return from retirement to enter the campaign of 1880—"the pilgrimage of passion"—resulted in so great a personal triumph that his restoration to the leadership could not be resisted. Again in 1886 when the Home Rule question was presented to the

Council, the delegates voted by an overwhelming majority in favor of Gladstone's policy, despite their previous wavering and indecisiveness and despite even the appeal of Joseph Chamberlain, principal founder of the federation and leader of Home Rule's opponents. But after Gladstone, who were the "Caesars" of British politics? Roseberry, Harcourt, Campbell-Bannerman, Asquith—not until we reach Lloyd George do we find a candidate for the kingly crown, and he, instead of dominating his party, fatally divided it. Nor does the Conservative line—Salisbury, Balfour, Bonar Law, Baldwin, Neville Chamberlain—provide a "Caesar" until we reach Churchill, but he, while secure in control of his party, was rejected by the masses at the moment of his greatest triumph and personal popularity.

Looking at British parties from 1867 to World War I, one is struck by the toughness of the old forms shaped in the days of the "parties of notables," or, indeed, even earlier. The parliamentary parties remained at the center of authority; within them occurred the important intrigues and negotiations in the choice of leaders and the determination of policy. Under the control of their respective parliamentary chiefs, the old machinery of the Whips and the central offices continued to find, examine, and recommend candidates; to receive and hold the funds of the central organization; and to keep up communication with local leaders. The new representative organs outside Parliament greatly helped the parliamentary chiefs win votes from a mass electorate and maintain discipline among their parliamentary followers. Now, as before, the chiefs would at times respond to unrest and to the manifest wishes of voters. But whether they did and how they did was decided not by the new party organs but by the old proc-

esses of party government under parliamentary leaders.

III / THE CONSERVATIVE PARTY OF THE INTERWAR YEARS

How far have these old patterns been modified in recent years? Let us consider several incidents from the annals of the Conservative party between the wars, emphasizing two themes: the choice of a leader and the determination of policy.

The Revolt of 1922

Both themes are illustrated by the revolt of 1922. At that time the Conservatives had been in Lloyd George's coalition government since its formation in December, 1916, and had fought the "coupon election" of 1918 with great success. In March, 1921, upon the retirement of Bonar Law from leadership of the party for reasons of health, Austen Chamberlain had been unanimously chosen leader of the party in the House of Commons at a meeting of Conservative M.P.'s.[4] Hostility

4. In the Conservative party there is normally (1) the leader of the party (as a whole), who also, of course, leads the party in the house in which he sits and who, when necessary, appoints (2) someone to lead the party in the other house, at present always the Lords. In the past, when the leader of the party, not being prime minister, died or retired, as in 1921, the party provided a successor only to the extent of choosing a leader in the house in which the previous leader had sat. In such cases there was no leader of the party as a whole but only leaders in the respective houses. If the leader was prime minister, however, his death or resignation would be followed by the appointment from the party of a succeeding prime minister, who thereafter would be chosen leader of the party. Bonar Law, Baldwin, Neville Chamberlain, and Churchill were all chosen leader of the party after they had become prime ministers. The meeting at which the leader of the party was chosen included (before 1922) all Conservative M.P.'s and peers; since 1922, prospective Conservative candidates and, since 1937, members of the Executive Committee of the National Union have also been included.

to continuing the coalition, however, had been growing for reasons of both policy and party. The enemies of coalition included not only the die-hards, opposed to self-government for Ireland and "entrenched on the heights well-known of old—individualism, the white man's hard-won burden, armed nationality and the land"—but also a larger section of the party, less inflexible in policy but unwilling to risk further the party's individual life. Among the causes of the revolt, wrote Chamberlain later, were the Irish Treaty and "the consequent Die-hard movement which became formidable when it rallied around Salisbury and afforded an organization for the discontented" and "the growth of party feeling and party jealousy in the machine which is far too much run by old men and paid agents."[5] The supporters of coalition included some of the ablest leaders of the party: fearing socialism, some of them, like Chamberlain himself, were ready to see coalition develop into a new party.

Dissension was not confined to the parliamentary party. In the provinces similar disagreements were boiling up, and both sections of opinion were represented at the annual conference of the Conservative Union in November, 1921. There, after a bitter debate, the friends of Chamberlain carried a vote of confidence overwhelmingly in his favor. But the schism grew. "The prevailing feeling amongst Conservative M.P.'s," wrote a Tory "backbencher" in January, 1922, "and still more in the constituencies is that they will not have another Coalition election." By late summer, wrote Chamberlain, "some 80 members or candidates of our Party were already pledged against *any* Coali-

5. Most of the direct quotations which follow can be found in Keith Feiling, *The Life of Neville Chamberlain* (London, 1946), and Sir Charles Petrie, *The Life and Letters of Austen Chamberlain* (London, 1939).

tion and more would be getting pledged under pressure from their associations unless Ll.G. would retire and allow the Coalition to be reformed under a Unionist."

Nevertheless, in September the coalition leaders decided on an early dissolution and a united appeal to the country, holding unlikely Chamberlain's fears that he might not be able to carry his party with him. When informed of this decision, the party chairman, principal agent, and chief Whip were "frankly appalled" and "very disturbed," the Whip insisting that the question of coalition be referred to the party conference. To ward off this possibility, Chamberlain agreed to put the question to a meeting of Conservative M.P.'s. The Executive Committee of the party, slighted at this failure to consult it, resolved to call an emergency conference. But at the meeting of M.P.'s, held at the Carlton Club on the evening of October 19, 1922, Chamberlain's fears were realized: the opponents of coalition, led by Stanley Baldwin, clinched their victory when Bonar Law intervened on their side, and a resolution rejecting Chamberlain's views and proposing that the party fight the election independently was passed by 187 to 87 votes. Upon Lloyd George's consequent resignation, Bonar Law became prime minister and thereafter leader of the party.

This notable revolt suggests that the Conservative party is not a party of monolithic unity, autocratically ruled by its leader, and that pressures from the active members of the constituency organizations may have an important part in determining whether or not the leader will carry the party with him. It also suggests, however, that pressures from below, if they are to be effective, must find champions in the circle of parliamentary leaders among whom the decisive battles are fought.

The Shift of Conservative Policy to Protection

To elaborate this sketch of the party's structure of action, let us examine an event of considerably more moment— the shift of Conservative policy to protection during the interwar years. This shift was not simply a matter of proposing that free trade be abandoned and certain tariffs be raised. It involved an imperial policy and, even more important, a domestic economic policy. Tariff reform was proposed as a means not only of protecting the home market but also of promoting "industrial rationalization"—an objective that tended to become cartelism.

This shift in policy is perhaps important enough to be compared to the adoption of socialism by the Labour party and its development of a socialist program in the same period. From the later years of the previous century the doctrine of "fair trade" had been making headway among Conservatives, and there is a parallel between the efforts of the protectionists, such as the Tariff Reform League of Joseph Chamberlain, and those of the Socialists, such as the I.L.P. and the Fabians, within their respective parties. The Conservatives' tentative advances toward winning over the electorate to protection, however, had been sharply rebuffed, and in the campaign of 1922 Bonar Law had pledged the party not to introduce tariffs, if returned to power. Apparently his tactics were prudent. For the Conservatives returned with 347 seats against 118, evenly divided between the Lloyd George and the Asquith Liberals, and 142 for Labour.

In May of the following year Bonar Law, fatally stricken, resigned as prime minister, declining to follow the usual practice of recommending a successor to the king. Judged by seniority or accomplishment, the logical choice was Curzon, but he was a member of the House of Lords and, more important,

widely unpopular in the party, as the king learned upon consulting a few leading Conservatives. Acting upon this advice, the king sent for Stanley Baldwin, leader of the House of Commons, a protégé of Bonar Law and, like him, a businessman, who after accepting the office of prime minister was formally chosen leader of the party.

The new prime minister and leader faced two urgent needs: first, a policy to deal with mounting unemployment and declining trade and, second, a device to reunite the two factions of the party, still sorely embittered by the struggle over coalition. The obvious device—proffers of office to leaders of the factions—did not accomplish the latter purpose. But in the autumn, after "some private thinking," the new leader hit upon what seemed to be a solution to both problems: tariff reform. In the negotiations leading to the election of November, 1923, when the government appealed to the country for a mandate to impose taxes on certain manufactured goods, but not food imports, and to institute dominion preference, the formal organs of the party in and out of Parliament played an insignificant part. Baldwin himself largely made the decisions but always under limitations. One was the fact that, while protection would rally both die-hards and Chamberlainites, he could not adopt their extreme demands, such as the demand for a tariff on food, without alienating many voters, Another was the resistance to a general tariff presented by certain manufacturing interests strongly represented in the party—for example, the great textile industry, with spokesmen in Lord Derby and the Lancashire members.

In 1923, as in 1906, protection was emphatically rejected by the electorate. Defeat finally joined the two factions of the party. And while, curiously enough, it did not raise a rebellion against Baldwin, it did put protection on the shelf, for the next election, in 1924, was fought and triumphantly won on the more popular issue of opposition to bolshevism.

During the five years of Conservative rule from 1924 to 1929 the issue of protection languished. But the depression of 1929, the full force of which hit Britain after the party had gone into Opposition following their defeat in that year, brought it once again to the fore. This time it was not Baldwin who took the lead. In the press, campaigns for protection were conducted by Rothermere and Beaverbrook, both of whom had opposed it in 1923. Beaverbrook's "crusade" for empire free trade and protection against the foreigner met with a strong and sympathetic response in the party in Parliament and the constituencies, and in September, 1930, the principal agent reported that feeling against the hesitant Baldwin was rising. The architect of "the great policy," however, and the "general" of its final victory was Neville Chamberlain, Austen's half-brother, intimate of Stanley Baldwin and minister of health in his second government. In the autumn of 1930 he induced Baldwin to issue a statement (actually drafted by Chamberlain) committing the party to "the principle of imperial preference," which enabled the leader to pacify dissent and win a vote of confidence at a parliamentary party meeting called at the instigation of his opponents.

The opportunity for realizing "the great policy" did not arise until a year later after the formation of the National Government. That government, headed by Ramsay MacDonald and supported by Conservatives, Liberals, and a handful of Labour M.P.'s, was agreed on a dissolution but could not agree on a program. In these critical negotiations the stand of the Conservative party was determined by a small committee of parliamentary leaders first set up at

Chamberlain's instigation as "a sort of inner shadow Cabinet" while the party was in Opposition. This group agreed on a united appeal to the country but tried to have protection included in the program. Since their Liberal colleagues, however, would not go along, a program could not be agreed on and the prime minister made his unique appeal to the country for "a doctor's mandate." Protection, therefore, was not submitted to the voters as a direct issue. The most that can be said is that Baldwin and Chamberlain went out of their way during the campaign to free their party of previous pledges not to introduce the issue. Next year, in spite of the continued opposition of many of the Liberals, the Conservative leaders were able to push through the Import Duties Act of 1932 and later to negotiate the Ottawa agreements establishing imperial preference. Now, wrote Chamberlain, the government was provided with "such a lever as has never been possessed before by any government for inducing, or if you like forcing, industry to set its house in order."

In this shift of policy, although protection was never a widely popular policy, public opinion had some part, as did the interests standing to gain by protection which were influential in the party. On the whole, however, the story serves to illustrate an observation of a leading historian of the party: "Conservative annals," writes Keith Feiling, "are never intelligible unless it is recognized that the leaders skirmish far ahead of the rank and file."

The Choice of an Election Issue in 1935

"To skirmish far ahead of the rank and file" is a function of a democratic leader. While the average voter or party member has a role in initiating policy, he also needs the guidance of leaders who will direct his attention to emerging problems, even if they are unpleasant, and who will propose solutions, even if they are painful. How urgently the voter needs such guidance and how important personal leadership may be in a democracy appear from the story of how British foreign policy was made —or failed to be made—during the 1930's. The whole story cannot be examined here, but one spisode is revealing: the choice of an election issue by the Conservatives in 1935.

In the autumn of that year as the parliament of 1931 approached its last year of legal existence, the leaders of the government, in which Baldwin was now prime minister, faced the question of choosing a time and finding an issue favorable for an appeal to the country. Hitler was rearming, Mussolini's invasion of Abyssinia was afoot, and feeling in Britain was at a confused and difficult stage, inclining toward action against aggression and at the same time recoiling violently from rearmament and the prospect of war.

The situation demanded a statement of issues which would not merely reflect the confusion of public opinion but would set before the electorate the questions of policy which had to be decided. It is not unfair to say that neither party measured up to the situation. While Labour was more aware of the ultimate danger from fascism, most of its leaders were incapable of facing the need for rearmament, and until July, 1937, the parliamentary party continued to vote against the military estimates. In a single speech Mr. Attlee, the party's new leader, supported "effective sanctions, effectively applied" and opposed "piling up armaments."

The Conservatives had sizable plans for rearmament which they had already begun. But would they run the political risk of being quite frank about these plans with the electorate? Their Central Office proposed that the election be deferred until January, 1936, and that the party's success in dealing with unemployment be made the chief

issue. Against this, Neville Chamberlain objected that what was wanted was an issue that would put unemployment in the background and, "if possible, substitute for the hope of fresh benefits a fear in the public mind—always the strongest motive to induce people to vote." He proposed, therefore, that the party "take the bold course of actually appealing to the country on a defense programme."

A third course, however, was followed by Baldwin. On the one hand, he spoke strongly of the need for rearmament, and his principal speech was devoted to the unsatisfactory condition of the navy. On the other hand, in a speech to the Peace Society he declared: "I give you my word that there will be no great armaments." "A singular promise," comments Churchill in *The Gathering Storm,* "in the light of the knowledge which the Government had of strenuous German preparations." And in fear that the government would be labeled "warmongers," as indeed they loudly were by their Labour opponents, party leaders advised that Churchill not be taken into the government. In the face of Mussolini's invasion of Abyssinia the government in its election manifesto boldly proclaimed its support of collective action against aggression, promising that "we shall . . . continue to do all in our power to uphold the Covenant and to maintain and increase the efficiency of the League." Yet at Geneva, as Churchill observed, under the guidance of Britain and pressure from France, the league committee charged with devising sanctions kept clear of measures which would paralyze the aggressor, adopting "merely such half-hearted sanctions as the aggressor would tolerate, because in fact, though onerous, they stimulated Italian war spirit." And before the end of the year the Hoare-Laval agreement providing for the partition of Abyssinia had been arranged by the foreign secretary with the knowledge of the cabinet.

Politically, Baldwin's tactic was enormously successful. The election returned the government with a reduced, but still huge, majority. But other requirements of the democratic process were evaded. An editorial in the London *Times,* December 15, 1947, upon the occasion of his death summarized this criticism:

Democratic leadership required that he should go to the country with a frank acknowledgment of the dangers, challenging its illusions with inconvenient truth, and risking defeat. But he hesitated to take a course that might place the control of national policy in the hands of men who, in his view, were more likely to accelerate than retard the onset of war. He made the worst of two worlds. What he sacrificed to political expediency obscured the real issue, delayed the education of public opinion, and impeded the process of rearmament, on the speed of which the success of any conceivable foreign policy then depended.

In fairness one must ask: How often do democratic leaders in any country measure up to this exacting standard?

The Rise and Fall of Neville Chamberlain

The rise and fall of Neville Chamberlain, Baldwin's successor, illustrate how the Conservative leader may achieve his position—and how he may lose it. Unlike his half-brother, Neville Chamberain had not been destined by his father for a career in national politics. He did not enter Parliament until he was forty-nine and after a career in business and municipal politics in Birmingham. He rose rapidly, however, and by the later years of Baldwin's second government was, as his biographer writes, among "the select, impermanent class of *papabili,* or future prime ministers." In 1928 a triumphant reception at the party conference marked a first recognition that he might be the future leader.

For a time Churchill was a powerful rival for the succession, but his break with Baldwin over appeasement in India and in Europe failed to shake the leadership and merely isolated him with a small group of supporters. By 1936 it was agreed, at least between Baldwin and Chamberlain, that Chamberlain should be the successor, and in October of that year he took Baldwin's place at the mass meeting which it is customary for the leader to address after the party conference, "the main result" being, he wrote, "a general acceptance of my position as heir-apparent." By this combined process, then, of co-operation by the old leader and informal acceptance by the leading circles of the party, he became the obvious choice. Upon Baldwin's resignation as prime minister on May 28, 1937, Chamberlain was called by the king, and three days later he formally took over leadership of the party at the usual meeting.

His fall was precipitate, but it had been in preparation for some time. Even in 1936 Baldwin and Chamberlain were already being criticized for lack of vigor in rearmament by a group within the party, as yet small but highly officered and led by Churchill. This "party cave" grew and extended its attacks upon the "appeasement" policy. It was joined by Eden, who resigned as foreign secretary in February, 1938, and by Duff Cooper, who resigned as first lord of the Admiralty at the time of Munich. The vote concluding the debate on the Munich agreement provided a climax when, although the government's majority was large, thirty normal supporters abstained.

The outbreak of war in the following September rallied the party and the country, but complaints soon arose of lack of vigor and, more important, lack of understanding of the foe and the task. Chamberlain's fall was finally precipitated by the debate on the disastrous Norway expedition of April, 1940. It was not simply the failure of the expedition that was the cause nor, as Chamberlain himself thought, simply that "sudden and bitter disappointment . . . just boiled up, with the accumulated mass of grievances, to find expression." What moved the House, one feels when reading the debate, was the gross and apparently incurable misunderstanding and underestimate of Hitler and naziism which had very largely fathered appeasement and still persisted in Chamberlain's mind. In the vote following the debate the government still had a majority, but thirty-three Conservatives had voted against it and some sixty more had abstained. Chamberlain resigned in favor of Churchill, who, however, did not take over leadership of the party until Chamberlain's failing health forced him out of political life in the fall of the year.

The Role of Business Interests

The Conservative party of the inter-war years was not the party of Salisbury and Balfour. As these incidents indicate, however, the structure of action and policy-making was not greatly different from what it had been in their day. Nor can one say that the change consisted in a more reactionary and die-hard attitude toward social and economic policy. The Conservatives in these years pushed through severe taxation of the rich, large extensions of social security, and very substantial housing programs and provided practical examples of nationalization, later followed by Labour, by setting up the Central Electricity Board and the British Broadcasting Corporation. Neville Chamberlain himself was a creditable example of the Tory radical who did not disdain to use the weapons of socialism in the fight against it and for a positive social policy.

The change was of a more important, though less easily identified, kind: it was a decline in vigor, in foresight, perhaps also in self-confidence. The two main Conservative policies of this period—protection and appeasement—illustrate this decline. Both involved the surrender of the initiative. Both were attempts to save what was left of the past rather than to make a larger future. Both were policies of adaptation, of strategic retreat. Both, in short, represented a failure to do what a governing class is expected to do. Dissatisfaction with Conservative rule in those days was not simply the result of unemployment and trade depression. In dealing with such matters the Conservatives do not have a discreditable record. The resentment and distrust which today still cluster about references to "the bad old days" and Conservative rule are as much the reaction of British society to a failure of leadership, the failure of the Conservatives and of that governing class with which they had been closely associated, to "give the country a lead" as they had in the past.

Was this party, then, no longer a wing of the governing class? Or was that class in decline? Certainly, if one looks at the leading circles of the party, one sees that it was still a party of the rich. Of forty-three Conservative M.P.'s who died between 1931 and 1938, for example, thirty-three left estates averaging £218,156. It was also still the party of the better educated. Eighty per cent of the Conservative members in this period had gone to private schools, 40 per cent to Oxford or Cambridge. The corresponding figures for the Labour party are 4½ and 8 per cent. What is perhaps more significant is that it had become very largely the party of the businessman, as can be seen from the character of Conservative leaders. Between Balfour and Churchill, two leaders of aristocratic background, intervened three men—Bonar Law, Baldwin, and Neville Chamberlain—who were businessmen before they were politicians. There was a similar change in their followers, a change which led Lloyd George to refer to his largely Conservative majority in the House elected in 1918 as "the Associated Chambers of Commerce." In the parliaments of this period, about a third of all Conservative M.P.'s were directors of corporations. In the parliament of 1935, the percentage was higher: 44 per cent or 181 M.P.'s, who among them held 775 directorships.[6]

This change suggests an interesting question. Is there some connection between the rise of the businessman in the party and the tragic inadequacies of Conservative policy between the wars? Is there something about the occupation of the businessman that prepares him poorly for political leadership? Is it true, as Schumpeter says, that "without the protection of some non-bourgeois group, the bourgeoisie is politically helpless and unable not only to lead its nation but even to take care of its particular class interest"?

Whether or not Conservative businessmen could govern, they could at least influence government. Political pressures exist in Britain as in any democratic government, but they operate differently from the way they do in the United States, working largely through party and cabinet rather than through individual legislators, and evidence of their operation is harder to obtain. One example, however, which will be familiar to students of American politics may be cited: the withdrawal of a proposed national defense tax on business in May, 1937.

6. Much of the preceding data is from Simon Haxey, *Tory M.P.* (London, 1939), and J. F. S. Ross, *Parliamentary Representation* (London, 1943).

Britain at the time was slowly rearming, and to meet the new expenses Neville Chamberlain, then chancellor of the Exchequer, decided to levy a graduated tax on the profits of trade and business which he called the "National Defence Contribution." He realized that there would be resistance from the business community, for he described this proposal as "the bravest thing I have ever done since I have been in public life, for I have risked the Premiership." When the tax was announced on April 22 there was alarm in the City, and the measure was attacked by government backbenchers and certain prominent economists. Amid charges from Labour that the government was yielding to the pressure of vested interests, Chamberlain consulted with representatives of finance and industry, but the modifications he conceded did not still the protests.

On May 27, while the finance bill was pending in the House, the Federation of British Industries, together with the Association of British Chambers of Commerce, the Chamber of Shipping, the British Iron and Steel Federation, Lever Brothers, Imperial Chemical Industries, and similar bodies passed a resolution that the bill required "drastic amendment" to render it "acceptable to the tax-paying community," and it was decided "to bring this resolution to the attention of M.P.'s." Results were promptly forthcoming. On May 28 the finance committee of the Conservative parliamentary party begged Chamberlain to withdraw the tax. On May 31 and June 1, when the second reading of the finance bill was taken, many Conservatives spoke against the National Defence Contribution. Finally, on the second day of that debate, the withdrawal of the tax was announced. Chamberlain had yielded, accepting "the undertaking of the business world" that they would find a sufficient sum by some other means.

IV / THE STRUCTURE OF THE CONSERVATIVE PARTY TODAY

During the war the Conservatives, along with the other parties in Churchill's coalition government, observed an electoral truce, and their organization slipped badly. As victory emerged, however, Churchill's leadership rose invincibly over the party and, so it seemed, over the country as well. To both chief and followers, therefore, the defeat of 1945 was a staggering blow. It meant more than an ordinary defeat at the polls. It meant more than the introduction of the British version of socialism. The event was a revolution, as A. D. Lindsay observed, not because of Labour's legislative program but because it shattered the "calm assumption" that to rule the nation was the peculiar business of Britain's traditional governing class.

Yet in the postwar years the party made a rapid recovery and in its reaction to defeat again showed the resiliency that has enabled British conservatism to survive comparable disasters in the past. Organization was tightened and extended, paid party membership rising from less than a million to the unprecedented figure of two and three-quarters million by 1952. The Conservative appeal to the voter was "repackaged," and the substance of Labour's social revolution has been widely accepted in the party. But has the party's structure of action changed?

Constituency Organization

Unlike the Labour party, the Conservatives have no single document setting out the constitution of the party. Its formal organization comprises three elements: (1) the constituency organizations federated in the National Union of Conservative and Unionist Associa-

tions, (2) the Central Office, and (3) the parliamentary party. Membership is wholly individual and is organized in local associations based on the parliamentary constituencies. Anyone may join who signifies his agreement with the objects of the association and is prepared to pay an annual subscription, the amount of which is fixed locally, 2s. 6d. being a minimum figure. The associations have branches in the wards or polling districts, and it is there that the main work both between and during elections is done, especially the arduous labor of canvassing.

The governing body of the local Conservative association is the Executive Council. It includes representatives not only from the branches but also from the Young Conservatives and local Conservative clubs, as well as the officers of the association, elected at the annual general meeting, and a limited number of co-opted members. The Executive Council performs its work largely through a number of committees, the principal being an inner executive, the Finance and General Purposes Committee. Acting through these bodies, the association is considered to have "complete autonomy in the management of its affairs." It raises and administers its funds and, under the recently revised rules, subscribes a modest sum to the funds of the national party headquarters. It engages its own agent and staff, conducts local propaganda, and selects its parliamentary candidate.

In all these matters, however, there is guidance from the central agencies. The election agents are career officials. They must go through an intensive training program lasting eighteen months and be examined and certified by the party's Central Examination Board. Salaries are reasonable—£600–£800 per year after experience of a general election and not less than two years in charge of a constituency—and agents enjoy the benefits of a superannuation plan. In British politics the professional agent is a necessary complement to the often amateur candidate. He must be thoroughly acquainted with the complicated and, by American standards, somewhat austere election laws, as well as the technical devices by which voters may be influenced and elections won. He is not, however, a "boss," and policy is not his concern. His career lies in working his way up to a constituency offering better pay and conditions and ultimately achieving perhaps a position as chief agent for several constituencies or as a high official in an area office or in the organization department of the Central Office.

In selecting a parliamentary candidate, the Executive Council intrusts the first stage to a small selection committee. This committee normally considers local possibilities and also asks for suggestions from the Central Office in London, which, following ancient practice, keeps a long list of persons who have been interviewed by representatives of both the Central Office and the National Union and approved by the Standing Advisory Committee on Parliamentary Candidates. From the names recommended by the selection committee a choice is made by a meeting of the Executive Council, before which each aspirant appears and shows his paces in a short speech. The person so chosen is then formally adopted as prospective candidate at a general meeting of the association. Before adoption, however, the name of the recommended candidate must be approved by the Standing Advisory Committee on Parliamentary Candidates, which includes representatives of both the parliamentary party and the National Union. The association failing to get such approval will be denied the usual letter from the leader in support of its candidate, the assistance of parliamentary speakers,

and any help, financial or otherwise, from the Central Office.

This requirement of central approval, so foreign to American political practice and attitudes, puts a powerful weapon for enforcing discipline in the hands of party leaders. It is not, however, a weapon that often needs to be unsheathed, the general election of 1950 providing only one example. In that case, because of certain particularly demagogic appeals to prejudice in his speeches, an aspirant was denied recognition by the Standing Advisory Committee. Being, as one party official put it, "an orator," he was nevertheless adopted by the local association and, although defeated in the election, polled a heavy Conservative vote.

No less remarkable from an American viewpoint is the absence of open, public competition from the process of nomination in both the major parties. The structure of British parties is, in general, like that of American parties during the days of the delegate convention system. There is no structural reason why the open competition of aspirants for the nomination which characterized American party politics under that system, as well as the direct primary, should not occur. "Canvassing," i.e., the solicitation by a candidate of the support of important persons in the local party or of party branches in the wards or (in the case of the Labour party) of local trade-union branches, does take place but does not involve public campaigning and must be done modestly and quietly, as it is not a practice thought to be "good form." In either party an effort to get your supporters to attend a meeting in order to bring pressure to bear for your nomination is severely frowned on and rarely attempted. The result, again, in both parties is that nominations rest in the hands of quite small groups of active party members.

Above the local associations the constituency side of the Conservative party is organized at two levels—the area and the nation. The area organizations, of which there are twelve in England and Wales, act as co-ordinating agencies between the local associations and the central bodies of the party. Each has a council composed of representatives of the association and other party units, an executive committee with its sub-committees, a chairman elected by the council, and advisory committees corresponding to the central advisory committees of the National Union. At this level also there are strong links with the Central Office, which appoints the area agent, his deputy, and all other paid officials of the area office.

The Annual Conference

Embracing all units of the constituency side of the party, the National Union of Conservative and Unionist Associations[7] has as one of its principal duties the business of arranging the annual conference of the party. Under present rules the conference has a potential attendance of 5,600 but only 3,000 or 4,000 actually attend.[8] It is usually held in the early autumn and lasts about three days, its main formal business being to approve the annual report of the Executive Committee and Central Council of the union and to discuss motions relating to organization and policy submitted by area councils and constituency organizations.

The conference cannot, of course, be a policy-making body. Its great size alone would prevent this. Since only certain assembly halls in London and Blackpool can accommodate it, in recent years, when the conference has been held elsewhere, those attending had to be distributed through two or

7. The name "Unionist" derives from the accession of the Liberal opponents of Irish Home Rule formally consummated in 1912, although effective in practice for many years before that date.

more halls interconnected by a public address system and, in one case, television. Its main purpose, therefore, is to hear and cheer its leaders and, in general, as the London *Times* put it (October 12, 1949), "to raise the Conservative standard and to put its bearers up and down the country in good heart."

Yet the conference can provide the occasion for protests to be effectively uttered and the opinion of the lower levels of party membership to be heard and even enforced. In 1946, for example, there was a considerable demand in the party for a statement of policy defining the Conservative position toward the great measures of social reform inaugurated by Labour. At the conference that year an insurrection led by the Young Conservatives, whose objective had the sympathy of the more progressive party leaders, was an important cause of the issuance, the following year, of the *Industrial Charter*, in which the party in large measure accepted the social revolution of 1945.

8. Those entitled to attend are approximately as follows:

Seven representatives from each constituency in England, Wales, and Northern Ireland	3,878
Constituency agents from England, Wales, and Northern Ireland	554
Members of Parliament and candidates (U.K.)	625
Peers who are members of the Central Council	100
Representatives of areas, central associations of certain divided boroughs, and other organizations	320
Ex officio and co-opted members	70
Representatives from Scotland and Northern Ireland	43
	5,590

Although they send representatives to the conference, to the Central Council, and to the National Executive Committee, the constituency organizations of Scotland and Northern Ireland are not formally parts of the N.U.C.U.A. but have their own organizations —the Scottish Unionist Association and the Ulster Unionist Council.

An even more significant event occurred at the conference of 1950 when the delegates bolted from the party leadership and beat "the platform" on the crucial issue of housing. The resolution on this issue presented by the leadership was, one observer wrote, "pleasantly vague." But during the speeches—they could hardly be called a debate—"the magic target" of 300,000 houses a year was mentioned, and from then on the delegates were determined to get it into the resolution. The chairman of the party, Lord Woolton, "rose with outstretched hand. . . . 'This is magnificent,' he told the delegates, which is Lord Woolton's way of saying, 'This is confoundedly awkward.' Then to bloodcurdling yells of triumph from the floor, he accepted the target on behalf of the leadership—and, indeed, he could have done nothing else." "One feels after this week," wrote the same observer, "that the annual conference will never again relapse into its old passivity."[9]

Certainly this victory of the "floor" over the "platform" was not a mere paper victory. The target of 300,000 houses a year figured prominently in Conservative propaganda during the election of the following year. After the party took power, despite the acute economic problems it faced, Churchill's government excepted housing from its policy of deflation and austerity and, it is said, against the wishes of the chancellor of the Exchequer permitted the minister of housing to claim the resources for a program even larger than that of the Labour government.

The governing body of the National Union is not the conference but the Central Council, a smaller but still unwieldy body, consisting of the same membership as the conference, except that each constituency association sends only three instead of seven delegates or

9. *Observer* (London), October 15, 1950, p. 5.

"representatives," as the party wishes to have them called. Like the conference, it considers resolutions submitted by constituency organizations, its decisions being "conveyed to the Leader of the Party." It elects the officers of the National Union—a president, chairman, and three vice-chairmen—may make amendments to the "constitution" of the National Union, and receives reports from the National Union's Executive Committee.

This latter body has about one hundred and twenty members, consisting chiefly of area representatives and officers of the parliamentary party, the National Union, the Central Office, and associated organizations. At its monthly meetings it discusses organization, resolutions from constituency organizations, and the reports of its advisory committees. Its general purposes subcommittee is charged, among other things, with preparing the agenda of the conference and the meetings of the Council.

The Central Office and the Parliamentary Party

In contrast with the formal organization of the Labour party, the Conservative Executive Committee does not control the Central Office, which now, as in the past, is under the leader, who appoints its principal officers. At the head of the Central Office is the chairman of the party, usually a politician and occasionally a prominent one. With the organization and publicity of the party under his authority, his drive and ingenuity profoundly affect Conservative fortunes. Lord Woolton, who held this post from 1946 until 1955, was formerly manager of a huge London department store and during the war an immensely successful minister of food. While his weight in policy-making might have been greater, the impact of an able administrator was evident in the heightened effectiveness of the Tory machine during recent elections, and the great modern retailer's sense for mass opinion could be seen in the "repackaging" of Conservative propaganda, which was as striking a change as the shift in policy.

At the "official" level the senior permanent head of the Central Office is the general director, formerly known as the "Principal Agent," who has charge of the very sizable bureaucracy of the Central Office—running to about one hundred employees—and its area offices, and who is also honorary secretary of the National Union. Under him are two main departments, one for organization and another for publicity, as well as smaller departments for speakers, local government, trade-unions, and Young Conservatives.

The organization department stands at the head of the hierarchy of professional organizers extending down through the area and constituency agents. Modern in form, this hierarchy harks back in spirit to an earlier age. Here we are not likely to find members of the governing class or makers of policy but rather political descendants of the originals of Disraeli's Messrs. Tadpole and Taper. Publicity, while also no innovation, has changed greatly in quantity and style. Its quantity especially impresses an American. Leaflets, posters, and weekly and monthly publications pour forth, especially at the time of a general election, in hundreds of thousands, even millions, of copies. For example, two and a half million copies of the *Industrial Charter*, according to party officials, were sold at sixpence a copy during the first three months following publication. That was a sober, reasoned argument of forty pages, but the party does not neglect the simple and cruder devices of modern advertising. One of the postwar additions to its media, a tabloid called *Popular Pictorial*, uses them all—cheese-cake, comic strips, music-hall humor, prizes—and one issue which featured a front-page portrait of a bathing beauty in a white suit caused no little consternation in some quarters of the party.

Two other central agencies demand special attention, the Conservative Political Centre (C.P.C.) and the Research Department. The C.P.C., set up in November, 1945, by the Central Council but a part of the Central Office, is the secretariat and organizing body of the vigorous new political education movement in the party. While the publicity department of the Central Office directs propaganda aimed at the electorate as a whole, the C.P.C. is concerned with the more active party members, encouraging, supervising, and providing special publications for study groups and lecture courses in the constituencies. According to party officials, the weekly and fortnightly study and discussion groups had more than a hundred thousand participants during the four years before the election of 1950.

One part of these activities was an ambitious scheme inaugurated in 1946 and called the "Two Way Movement of Ideas," whose express purpose was "to enable all ranks of the Conservative Party to take an active part in forming the long-term policy of the Party." The formal arrangements of the scheme did indeed create this opportunity. The study groups discussed topics suggested by the C.P.C., such as housing, trade-unions, and bureaucracy, and drew up reports expressing their conclusions which were forwarded to the C.P.C., where they were analyzed and consolidated in a general report. Operating under the policy direction of the National Union's Advisory Committee on Political Education and in close liaison with the Research Department, to which the better reports were submitted, the scheme theoretically might have given substance to the democratic dream of a great political party informed and educated by ideas springing from the "grass roots." In some sense, no doubt, the masses in a democracy do at times originate the larger ideas on which policy is based; but, judging by the results of this Conservative scheme, the thinking that renews and adapts a party's policy must continue to be done at the top.

Yet if this scheme did not greatly enlighten the leaders, it did much to educate the more active members of the rank and file, strengthening and enlarging the circles that link the party leadership with the millions of Conservative voters. In the study groups taking part in the "Two Way Movement of Ideas" were found the more active party members—the sort who serve as specially trained canvassers, volunteer speakers, and unpaid officials of the constituency organizations and who as delegates to area and national meetings may press for statements of policy and more effective leadership. The growth in numbers and activity of this level of Conservative membership is a significant development in the history of the party and of British democracy.

Standing apart from the bureaucracy of the Central Office and yet closely linked with its departments is the Research Department. Here are "the back-room boys"—in the British sense—and, though not politicians, they have a very real part in preparing and shaping policy. The importance of the department is indicated by the fact that of the three chief appointments made directly by the leader of the party, the chairman of the Research Department is one, the other two being the chief Whip and the chairman of the party. Founded in 1929 by Neville Chamberlain, who remained its chairman until his death in 1940, it was used by him as a center for research to develop and buttress "the great policy" and was consulted by Conservative ministers who

desired expert but partisan advice on their schemes before taking them up with civil servants. Since 1946 the chairman has been R. A. Butler, who, as a minister in the wartime coalition, sponsored the great Education Act of 1944 and is a leading member of the progressive wing of the parliamentary party.

The department's staff consists of about sixty, twenty-four of whom are research officers. It is organized into five sections: External and Defence, Economics, Home Affairs, Political, and Editorial and Reference. Aside from getting out certain publications on policy and current problems for party members, its duties are to consult with leaders in the making of long-range policy and to brief Conservative M.P.'s on issues before Parliament, especially those who are to speak in debate. In one sense the department is to party leaders what the higher civil service is to ministers. Yet its members are not only partisan but often of parliamentary caliber, and some of the ablest new M.P.'s elected on the Conservative side in 1950 came directly from the department.

In the third element of the party— the parliamentary party—organization and activity merge with the familiar constitutional role of the "Opposition" or the "government," as the case may be, and therefore need be only briefly described. Consisting of the Conservative members of the House of Commons, the parliamentary party meets weekly as the Conservative and Unionist Members Committee—commonly called the "1922 committee"—to which the Conservative peers, who are separately organized, send a member or two for liaison. In contrast with the practice in the Labour party, ministers do not attend these meetings when the party is in power except by invitation. An Executive Committee, elected by this body and always composed of back-bench members, expresses the views of the parliamentary party to the leader, chief Whip, chairman of the party, and other leaders. While in Opposition in postwar years, the parliamentary party set up a number of committees roughly paralleling the principal ministries. Their chief officers met as the "Business Committee." Above this was the "shadow cabinet," formally entitled the Consultative Committee, whose membership, like that of a cabinet, was not elected but was chosen by the leader. The chief Whip, also appointed by the leader, and his assistants carry out the duties of "the usual channels." They also report to the leader on sentiment within the parliamentary party, advise him and his lieutenants on tactics, observe how members vote, and, where discipline mut be administered, consult with the leader, who may, as a last resort, "withdraw the Whip," thereby expelling the recalcitrant M.P. from the parliamentary party and almost certainly depriving him of his seat in the House at the next election.

The Process of Making Policy

What is the role of the various parts of the party in the process of policy-making? Formally the leader has overriding personal power in this sphere. Elected by a meeting which includes the Conservative members of both Houses, prospective candidates, and the Executive Committee of the National Union, he possesses, when once installed, complete formal authority over the parliamentary party and the Central Office. He selects the "shadow cabinet" and chooses the Whips, and directly and personally appoints the chairman of the party. In policy he is still emphatically declared to be supreme; as the official reports of the Committee on Party Organization (1948 and 1949) state, "endorsements [of the party program] and pronouncements

on Party policy are the prerogative of the Leader." Resolutions on policy may be passed by the conference or Council, and detailed programs may be adopted by them, but they are advisory only and not binding on the leader.

The formal organization of a party, however, like the written constitution of a state, may conceal more than it reveals. The elaborate representative apparatus set up by the nineteenth-century parties may have been largely "sham," as Lowell observed, not without satisfaction. But so also will be the formally "autocratic" powers of the Conservative party leader when the real forces within the party create conditions and demands to which he must accommodate his personal wishes.

In British constitutional history a voice in policy has followed the power of the purse. And while finance is one of the best-kept secrets of the Conservative party, there has clearly been a substantial shift in the source of party finance, as one would expect in a society where incomes are taxed with socialist severity while party activity is continuously heightened. Formerly, the Central Office could directly acquire resources sufficient both to finance its own activities and to extend help to the constituencies, but now it must ask for aid from the latter. In 1948 a quota system was established under which constituency organizations would ultimately contribute £200,000 per year to the Central Office. To the less prosperous associations the Central Office continues to extend financial aid, the need for which was increased by a complementary and radical reform. In the past, Conservative candidates have commonly made—and have been expected to make—heavy contributions to their local associations. Running sometimes to £5,000 or £6,000 during a five-year period, these have tended to make candidacies open only to wealthy men. Now, however, by a decision of the National Union, the amount which a candidate may contribute has been reduced to a nominal sum. But to shift the financial burden to a larger circle of party adherents is to provide these adherents with a new incentive to participate in party processes.[10]

Some opportunity for rather wider circles of the party to take part in policy-making was opened up, it might seem, when the party took to issuing elaborate statements of policy during the postwar years. In 1945 the closest thing to a program produced by the Conservatives was a brief message entitled "Mr. Churchill's Declaration of Policy to the Electors." In the course of adapting itself to defeat and to the social revolution of 1945, however, the party issued several statements of its program, the principal ones being the *Industrial Charter* (1947) and *The Right Road for Britain* (1950), the first running to forty pages and the second to sixty-five. The break which the issuance of such documents represents in Conservative tradition, always more inclined to put forward leaders rather than detailed programs to the electorate, is both a measure of the extent to which Labour had successfully conditioned the electorate to expect elaborate policy statements and an indication of the degree in which the electorate in turn influenced Tory policy-making.

10. At a meeting of the Central Council at which this matter was discussed, Sir David Maxwell-Fyfe made the connection explicit. The party's organization, he said, "must be such as to satisfy the constituencies which were raising large sums of money for their own work and for the party as a whole. There must be a method by which they were satisfied that the money was being well spent and that their representatives had a voice in the expenditure. The national union, through its executive committee, should have a voice in the formulation of policy without fettering the discretion of the leader of the party, who was the ultimate arbiter" (*Times* [London], July 16, 1949).

This vague but pressing demand among the electorate at large was reflected in the demands of party workers for statements of policy with which to reply to Labour's concrete acts. At the conference of 1946, for instance, delegates, among whom the Young Conservatives were particularly active, succeeded in having passed—not unanimously but by a large majority—a resolution that statements of the policy, principles, and program of the party should be promptly prepared and issued. The means by which the National Union might also have had a hand directly in shaping such statements was present in the Advisory Committee on Policy and Political Education which had been set up by the Central Council in 1945. The chairman and members of this committee, it is true, were appointed by the leader, but its membership was subject to the approval of the Executive Committee of the National Union.

In actual fact, however, this committee had no important part in framing either the *Industrial Charter* or *The Right Road for Britain*. On the contrary, in each case, it was merely "kept informed," while the main decisions were made by a small committee drawn from the parliamentary party and appointed by the leader. In the case of *The Right Road*, for instance, the initiative was taken when in the autumn of 1948 a committee of the shadow cabinet was appointed, nominally by Churchill, actually, it appears, by Eden, who was made chairman.[11] With respect to this statement, as well as the *Industrial Charter*, the staff work was particularly important, the new ideas of Mr. Butler's "backroom boys" being very much needed by a party attempting so radical an

11. Its members were Anthony Eden, Lord Woolton, Oliver Lyttleton, R. A. Butler, Harold Macmillan, Sir David Maxwell-Fyfe, Sir John Anderson, and Lord Salisbury.

adaptation of its policy and program. Material for the committee's deliberations was prepared by the Research Department, whose head served as secretary to the committee. Each section of the department compiled for its field a suggested statement, which was then submitted to the committee and finally combined in a general statement put into a publishable draft by the secretary. At this point, the approval of the leader, as well as the comments of other prominent Conservatives, was obtained. *The Right Road* was then published in July, 1949, and in October was accepted by the conference with only eight dissidents, their leader being the indomitable Sir Waldron Smithers, who sharply protested the program's promises of "a materialistic Utopia." From this junction of pressure from some, but not by any means all, sectors of the party with the initiative of certain parliamentary leaders issued the new Tory program. And from these decisions also followed the fact that a future Tory government could never have as free a hand as it had when men rather than measures were its pledge to the electorate.

That this statement should be issued and especially that it should take the form it did, committing the party in some detail to what Conservatives would do if given power, were not things initiated or supported with enthusiasm by the leader.

Churchill, even while accepting *The Right Road*, told the conference:

I have advised you consistently during these last four years not to commit yourselves to rigid detailed programmes. . . . All I will promise to the British electorate in your name, and the only pledge that I will give on behalf of the Conservative party is that if the government of Britain is entrusted to us at this crisis in her fate we will do our best for all, without fear or favor, without class or party bias, without rancor or spite, but with the clear and

faithful simplicity that we showed in the days of Dunkirk.

This is all in accord with the Conservatives' theory of the position of their leader and with their aversion to "caucus government"—that is, control of the parliamentary chiefs by bodies outside Parliament to which they accuse Labour of being subject. Yet when party and leader have gone to the country on such a program, distributed in millions of copies in the original and in a shortened version, it is doubtful that the theory of the leader's full powers can entirely withstand the pressures and expectations so aroused within the rank and file of the party and electorate. And, indeed, the record of the Conservative government after 1951 bore out this expectation. Labour's predictions of unemployment and of Tory attacks on the "welfare state" proved utterly wrong. Not only did the Conservatives expand the subsidized housing program; they also faithfully carried out the welfare promises of *The Right Road for Britain*, Tory budgets continuing the steady increase in the amounts spent on the social services.

The development should not be exaggerated, for neither Britain nor the Conservative party is governed in the manner of a Rousseauist democracy. The Conservative leader and his parliamentary lieutenants still carry the major responsibility for initiating action and move freely within a wide sphere of independent action. Yet the structure of action of the party has been perceptibly altered. The circles of participation within the party embrace a larger membership, and a heightened effort is being made to reach the minds as well as the wills of a wider public.

V / THE LABOUR PARTY BEFORE WORLD WAR II

The Conservative party grew from the top down, and its present structure is still strongly marked by its association with the governing class. Did the Labour party grow from the bottom up? Does its rise indicate that the initiative in politics can be taken by the ordinary voter or at least by leaders close to him in the social structure and in the scale of social evaluation? And today does Labour show how, independently of the traditional governing class, a party may be able to govern the nation and govern it well? Before turning to an examination of the structure of the party at the present time, three episodes from its history will be briefly considered: (1) the foundation of the party in 1900, (2) its adoption of socialism in 1918, and (3) the collapse of the second Labour government in 1931.

The Foundation of the Party

The party did not originate spontaneously as a mass movement of the rank and file of the working class. For years it attracted the allegiance of only a small fraction of the workers, organized and unorganized, and though the governing class of the time did not provide it with its chiefs, the leadership of other elites was important. Yet there was also a "grass-roots" movement. Behind the foundation of the party in 1900 lay a generation of rising interest in political action among certain sections of the working class. The conditions which stimulated this interest have their parallels in other countries at similar stages of economic development. Some, such as the discriminatory master and servant law, primarily concerned the individual worker; others, arising from legislation or judicial decision, hindered the activity of trade-unions.

Such conditions, coupled with the extension of the franchise of 1867, may sufficiently explain the heightened interest and activity of some workingmen in politics. The facts suggest that this interest was based on a tolerably ra-

tional calculus of advantage and disadvantage and do not at all compel us to seek an explanation in a Paretan theory of the manipulation of mass sentiments by elites. The common-sense grievances that people felt as workmen and as trade-unionists, however, do not explain the particular forms which their heightened interest and activity took, for that depended largely on the kind of leadership which was offered them.

Although the facts were far more complicated than this brief description can indicate, one may broadly distinguish three types of leadership, each proposing some degree of independent political action, which were offered to the working class in the last decades of the century. One favored what came to be known as "Lib-Lab" collaboration and was strongly represented among the chiefs of the Trades Union Congress founded in 1864 primarily for the purpose of urging trade-union views on members of the government and Parliament. Opposed to an independent party, the Lib-Lab leaders adopted the tactic of working with the more radical wing of the Liberals and inducing local associations of that party to accept as candidates trade-unionists sponsored by local trades councils. These candidates, when returned to Parliament, sat as members of the Liberal party, within which they gave a voice to the trade-union viewpoint.

At the opposite pole from Lib-Lab collaboration was the tactic of the Social Democratic Federation (S.D.F.), founded by H. M. Hyndman in 1881. The S.D.F. was one of the earliest societies with an outright socialist program and, though it had certain insular peculiarities, it is fair to characterize it as Marxist. But it was not the first exponent of Marxism in England, for the *Communist Manifesto*, after all, had been written and first published in London and Marx himself had lived there in exile while composing *Das*

Kapital. Yet a striking fact about the British working-class movement then as well as later was the failure of Marxism to make serious inroads on the rank and file or the leaders of the socialist Left. Hyndman's organization was wracked by bitter quarrels and reduced by periodic secessions, gaining no significant following and enjoying no electoral success. In 1900 it affiliated briefly with the Labour party, then went its way alone until Hyndman, having become violently nationalistic, led off some of them and formed the National Socialist party during World War I. The remaining fraction became in 1920 the Communist party, which in 1945 polled the largest vote in its history, some hundred thousand out of a total vote of twenty-five million.

The body which won the influence that the S.D.F. had hoped for and which in time weaned the Trades Union Council (T.U.C.) away from Lib-Lab collaboration was the Independent Labour party (I.L.P.), founded in 1893 by James Keir Hardie, a leader of the Scottish miners and in his early days a lay preacher and temperance advocate. The I.L.P. did not succeed in making itself the mass political organization of the working class and the trade-unions, but throughout the history of the Labour party it has had an influence greatly out of proportion to its numbers and has been the principal instrument in making socialism acceptable to the rank and file. The reasons why Hardie had such influence while Hyndman did not were partly personal but largely ideological and cultural. G. D. H. Cole writes (in his *British Working Class Politics, 1832-1914*):

It was not so much that Hardie's views were more moderate than those of Hyndman and his followers as that he spoke a different language. . . . Hardie, despite his public reputation for wildness, did not sound at all wild to a gathering of miners

or iron-workers or factory operatives who had been brought up on the Bible, and were much readier to accept Socialism when it came to them clothed in the garments of morality than when it was presented in economic terms or by means of slogans of class-war.

When one thinks of the spirit of the I.L.P. and its influence on the Labour party, a purely utilitarian explanation for the rise of the party strikes one as inadequate. The energy that first created the movement and then drove it on in the following generations flowed not only from the desire for material advantage and social justice—its real source was deeper and more difficult to analyze: a strong sense of solidarity which welded together the British lower classes in political action and was expressed in an evangelical belief in "The Movement" and its mission. What had produced the Labour party in one age had produced Methodism in another: what Keir Hardie was to his followers, John Wesley had equally been to his disciples. And even today it is such feelings, this sense of a "mission," and not primarily material and ethical concerns, which powerfully animate the party, constituting the underlying thematic emotions on which the skilful leader plays and from which the multitudes of individual party workers draw their inner strength.

On the one hand, then, Hardie and his lieutenants formed the ideas and shaped the actions of their followers. On the other hand, in responding to these men who spoke the same "language" as they did, rather than to others, their followers helped determine in general what strategy and what policy the political movement of the working class would adopt. Leadership played a creative role, but in responding to their immediate grievances as workers and trade-unionists and in "selecting" the kind of leadership they would follow, the rank and file also exercised initiative in the process that led to the foundation of the Labour party.

The efforts of Hardie and the I.L.P. bore fruit at the turn of the century. The immediate initiative was taken by the T.U.C., which, after defeating many similar resolutions over a period of years, in 1899 finally agreed by a slender majority to call a conference of representatives of trade-unions and socialist societies to devise ways and means "for securing the return of an increased number of Labour Members to the next Parliament." In the following year this conference created a federal organization that took the name "Labour Representation Committee," which was changed in 1906 to "Labour party."

The Adoption of Socialism

The organization formed in 1900 had no mass following and virtually no program; in the next two decades it acquired both. The causes of the party's growth were much the same as those that led to its foundation: immediate grievances calling for a political remedy; continuous propaganda by small but able socialist elites; and, most important, the steady rise of the trade-unions. As comparison with American experience shows, the growth of trade-unions did not in itself determine that there should be a labor party and that it should grow, but it provided the indispensable social base on which other influences might build. And the character of British trade-unionism—strongly bent on creating a mass organization and not simply a cadre of militants; insistent on the regular payment of dues and the accumulation of substantial funds; aiming at immediate benefits but capable of ideology in small and familiar doses—had, as it still has, a profound influence on the character of the party.[12]

Not until 1918 did the party acquire a program. In that year the annual conference adopted *Labour and the New Social Order,* a statement of the party's objects that clearly committed it to socialism and thereby definitively separated it from the Liberals. Why did the party become socialist? Or, to put the question another way: Why did it finally break with the Liberals?

On the face of it, this step was the triumph of the socialist elites, the principal immediate influence being the Fabian Society. *Labour and the New Social Order,* although nominally drafted by a committee of the party executive, was principally the work of Sidney Webb, the leading member of the society, and expressed throughout Fabian philosophy and policy. Founded in 1884, the society, though consisting only of a small number of intellectuals, had from the publication of the famous *Fabian Essays* in 1889 carried on with great success the "permeation" of public opinion with the socialist idea as they interpreted it. Their interpretation was so influential that socialism in Britain is sometimes characterized as Fabianism in contrast with the Marxist socialism of Germany or the syndicalist socialism of France. Ultimately the Fabians have perhaps been as important an influence on British socialism as the I.L.P. If British socialism derives its strong ethical and sometimes sentimental tone from the I.L.P., the heirs of nonconformist radicalism and, more distantly, Robert Owen and the Chart-

12. From 2 million in 1900, membership in all trade-unions grew to 4.1 million on the eve of World War I, then to a temporary postwar peak of 8.3 million in 1920. The growth of the party followed that of the unions. Membership rose steadily until it stood at 1.6 million in 1914; then during the war it doubled, reaching 4.5 million in 1920, practically all of which represented affiliated trade-unions. Representation in the House of Commons rose from two in 1900 to sixty in 1918.

ists, it also derives from the Fabians, the heirs of Bentham and the utilitarians, something equally important—an emphasis on "brass tacks," efficiency, concrete problems and practical solutions, verging at times on a cold technocracy.[13] The intellectual elite of British socialism, the Fabians, unlike the I.L.P., exercised their influence on the rank and file at a distance, directing their efforts at the leaders of opinion rather than the "average sensual man" —to use the Webbs' term—in whom, indeed, they had little faith.

How did the socialism of the I.L.P. and the Fabians win over the Labour party? Did their proposals promise something that could not be gained through co-operation with and seconded by pressure on the Liberals? The immense program of social, economic, and political reform pushed through by the "New Deal" governments of Campbell-Bannerman and Asquith before World War I accomplished a peaceful revolution comparable to those of 1832 and 1945. The measures advocated in *Labour and the New Social Order* went beyond these reforms, but they were of the same kind—for example, progressive taxation of large incomes, comprehensive social security, satisfactory maintenance of the unemployed, a generous system of education—save for one item, "the common ownership of the means of production." The program, to be sure, did not demand the nationalization of all industries, marking out specifically only certain ones, principally the land, railways, mines, and electric power. But this sufficed to put an abyss between Labour and the Liberals.

The consequences were immensely

13. "The perfect and fitting development of each individual," wrote Webb, "is not necessarily the utmost and highest cultivation of his own personality, but the filling, in the best possible way, of his humble function in the great social machine" (*Fabian Essays* ["Jubilee" ed.; London, 1948], p. 54).

important for British politics. For this step not only committed the Labour party to socialism but also marked the start of the precipitate decline of the Liberals. With the trade-unions throwing their support very largely to another party tied to a fundamentally different program, the Liberals lost their hold on the working class in the period when the franchise was radically democratized. At the same time many middle-class Liberals, confronted with the threat of socialism, moved over to the camp of their former enemies, the Conservatives. Special circumstances, such as the long and bitter quarrel between Lloyd George and Asquith, contributed to the Liberal decline. But the fundamental reason was the shift of the trade-unions and their working-class followers to the Labour party and socialism.

But was the adoption of socialism by the Labour party worth the loss of Liberal help in gaining further extensions of the program of social reform? The question itself suggests that, instead of thinking of this break between the two parties as an advance to a new position by Labour, perhaps it is more instructive to regard it as a halt by the Liberals. The new demands of the Labour party were largely of the same kind as those granted by the Liberal "New Deal." But it can be plausibly argued that they went beyond these reforms in a degree which made further co-operation by the Liberals very unlikely. Even before the war, while the Labour party on the whole still supported the Liberal government, there were already serious disagreements on policy, and in the constituencies collaboration had almost completely broken down. In the postwar years this divergence continued, as when, for example, in 1922 the coalition government, supported by the larger wing of the Liberals led by Lloyd George, carried through drastic cuts in the social services during a period of trade depression and unemployment. Some Liberals continued to champion further welfare measures, and on later occasions the party produced some of the most intelligent proposals for economic reconstruction of the interwar period. Yet, on the whole, as British capitalism passed into the straitened circumstances of the postwar decades, the party could no longer produce a united leadership and a large popular following to support the extension of the social program it had inaugurated before the war. The trade-unions, on the other hand, were bent on pushing forward such reforms, whether or not British capitalism could support them. Their adoption of socialism, it would seem, was more a symbol of this will than of a conversion to a clearly understood and practicable theory of socialist reconstruction.

The Liberals halted and the trade-unions pushed leftward: but this is again to imply that objective material interests played the major part in the development of the party. Ideas also had an independent influence not only immediately through the propaganda of the socialist intellectuals but also through the secular trends of certain basic themes of nineteenth-century liberalism. That political philosophy, like its party, had never been entirely at peace with itself. The program of a laissez faire and nationalist society which the early Liberals had designed with high hopes jarred against their fundamental conception of the nature of man and society, as the developing thought of John Stuart Mill exemplified. Conceivably, this Liberal conception itself could disillusion its adherents with the Liberal society of the twentieth century, even after the establishment of social insurance and the League of Nations, and persuade them that a socialist reorganization was necessary. Such apparently was the spiritual progress of many of the Liberals

who left their party for Labour during this time.

The Crisis of 1931

Although Labour may have had a philosophy, that it lacked a practicable theory of socialist reconstruction is suggested by the record of the two Labour governments of the interwar years, both of which were headed by Ramsay MacDonald, the first in 1924 and the second in 1929–31. On each occasion the program of the government was little more than to push ahead with typical Lib-Lab reforms. In each case, it is true, the government was in a minority and depended for its existence upon the support of the Liberals. But if the party had had a majority, would it have known what to do with it? Did it as yet have the ideas necessary for the construction of a viable socialist economy? The pronouncements of the leaders and the statements in the party program make it hard to think so.

This lack of ideas lay behind the severest crisis in the party's history, the collapse of the second Labour government in 1931, an incident that is also worth examining for the light it throws on the role of personal leadership in the party and the forces determining the party's stand on policy. In the general election of 1929 Labour had been returned as the largest party in the House, winning 288 seats to the Conservatives' 260 and the Liberals' 59. While that election occurred at a time of relative prosperity, unemployment stood at 1,163,000 or 10 per cent of the insured population, and the party had made this the principal issue. Its election program, however, did not differ greatly from that of the Liberals, who at the time were showing the effects of a renewed radicalism on the part of Lloyd George. The legislation of the government, in addition to typical welfare measures, also included large programs of public works, housing, and slum clearance. But since these programs were planned to extend over a long period of time, their effect on unemployment was negligible, and the incapacity of the government to deal with this major problem was increasingly emphasized as the world-wide depression following the Wall Street crash of 1929 spread to England and unemployment rose rapidly, reaching 2.5 million by the end of 1930.

The interesting question is whether socialism as it was conceived by any of the factions in the party at that time provided the basis for a policy which would have enabled the government to deal adequately with this familiar movement of the capitalist economy. The chiefs of the party were severely criticized for failing to carry out a "constructive socialist policy." But precisely what form would such a policy have taken, and how far would it have succeeded in solving the economic problem? Could socialism as it was then understood have dealt with the problem without the "know-how" of economic planning later provided by Keynesian economics and the experience of World War II?

Certain groups in the party did propose other programs of action. Sir Oswald Mosley, then a member of the government and a leader of the left wing, early in 1930 produced a program that in many respects—for example, import control, development of British agriculture, rationalization of industry—strongly resembled the "neomercantilist" policy later carried out by the "National" government with considerable success. The government was also urged by the I.L.P. to adopt "socialist remedies," by which was meant shorter working hours, a larger housing program, and especially nationalization. But within the cabinet such proposals were coldly received. Philip Snowden, then chancellor of the Exchequer, a leading member of the I.L.P. and a rigid socialist in doctrine, was quite as rigidly devoted to free trade, the gold standard, and a balanced budget. Far from having a socialist specific to apply, "most of the Cabinet," writes G.D.H. Cole in his *History of the Labour Party from 1914,* "never came near to understanding the crisis, or to having any notion of how to deal with it." When a run on sterling precipitated a financial crisis in the summer of 1931, the cabinet followed Snowden's thoroughly orthodox proposals, which included large cuts in social services to balance the budget, and split only when he proposed to reduce unemployment benefits. Under these circumstances MacDonald offered his resignation to the king, who, acting on the advice of Baldwin and Samuel, the Conservative and Liberal leaders, suggested that MacDonald form a National government, a suggestion that he was easily persuaded to adopt.

The National government tactic, in which Neville Chamberlain was the "constructive engineer," is reminiscent of a similar tactic after World War I in which the Conservatives' acceptance of Lloyd George's leadership for a short time helped to widen the schism among Liberals and hasten the decline of that party. In 1931, however, this tactic did not have the same success. For a generation MacDonald had been the outstanding popular leader of the party and, with Snowden and J. H. Thomas, both of whom he carried with him into the new government, constituted the Big Three in Labour party leadership. As Chamberlain had anticipated, MacDonald brought over many Labour voters, and in the ensuing general election the Labour poll fell by two million. But in contrast with what probably would have happened in either of the older parties and what certainly would have happened in a nineteenth-century party, the Labour organization was not split. The party expelled MacDonald and his handful of supporters among the Labour M.P.'s, and not a single constituency organization or prominent trade-union leader followed the "National Labour" line.

As these events indicate, the party had attained an unusual degree of independence of personal leadership. Within the party organization a "public opinion" which the elites could not manipulate at will had developed and had sent roots down deep into the rank and file. While MacDonald and the Right could not disregard or manipulate this opinion, neither could the leaders of the Left. In the previous year Mosley, who had found considerable support for his proposals at the annual conference, had seceded in hopes of forming a new left-wing party, only to find his following reduced to five M.P.'s. Similarly the I.L.P., which had had such an immense part in founding and educating the party, upon "dis-affiliating" in 1932 because of its disgust with "gradualism," failed to break off any significant section and instead succeeded merely in reducing its own membership.

Yet the "opinion" of the Labour party, while strong in resisting the blandishments of its elites, was incapable of initiating a practicable policy. What that "opinion" came to, one may suspect, was a widespread commitment to socialist declarations, largely verbal and without much operational significance, and a stubborn insistence on immediate economic benefits. The threat to unemployment payments—which was also, of course, a threat to existing wage rates—was the concession the party would not make to Snowden and MacDonald. In essence the party's "opinion" meant the immediate interests of the trade-unions.

VI / THE STRUCTURE OF THE LABOUR PARTY TODAY

The triumph of 1945 gave Labour the solid majority its prewar governments had lacked. For the use of this majority the party had been prepared by two generations of socialist and especially Fabian thought. But in making the policies that would carry out their program, while governing the country in a difficult time, the Labour government received indispensable assistance from two other sources: the development of Keynesian economics and the wartime practice of physical planning and control. These gave the party's dogma hands and feet and enabled its leaders to frame and stand for policies that were more national than trade-union demands and more practicable than doctrinaire socialism. In the framing of these policies the machinery of the party continued to provide wide opportunities for participation by its lower ranks. At the same time, their hands strengthened by the new approach to economic planning and control, the parliamentary leaders of the party claimed and enjoyed a sphere of independent action probably as great as that of the Conservative leadership. The wide authority of Labour leadership is as notable a feature of British politics in these postwar years as the extension of participation on the Tory side.

Affiliated Membership

As in the Conservative party, one may broadly distinguish three elements in the formal organization of the Labour party: (1) the organization of the party membership, (2) the party headquarters, and (3) the parliamentary party. The first of these, however, is rather more complicated than in the Conservative party, since membership is of two kinds: affiliated and individual. The affiliated members are organizations—trade-unions, socialist societies, and certain professional and co-operative societies—although the local Labour parties in the constituencies through which individuals belong to the party are also considered affiliated members for some purposes. In a total of 6.1 million in 1953 the affiliated membership accounted for 5.1 million, the individual membership for 1 million.

The great bulk of the affiliated membership is provided by the trade-unions. They do not, of course, include the whole of the British working class or, indeed, the whole of British organized labor. In a total of well over twenty million wage- and salary-earners, only some nine million are members of trade-unions, while rather more than half the latter number constitutes the trade-union membership of the party.

Furthermore, Labour party sentiment varies considerably from one union to another. The strength of this sentiment could be roughly measured while the Trades Disputes Act of 1927 was in effect, since under its provisions a union member could be assessed for the political levy from which affiliation fees are paid only if he individually "contracted in" to pay it. While this procedure prevailed, affiliated trade-union membership in the party never rose above the figure of 2.6 million reached in 1946. In 1945 the percentage of trade-union members affiliated to the party ranged from 70 per cent in cotton textiles and 67 per cent in mining and quarrying to 16 per cent in the building, woodworking, and furniture trades and 20 per cent among the shipbuilders. Since the repeal of the act in 1946, "contracting in" has no longer been required, and the figure for trade-union membership in the party cannot be considered as representing so many individual declarations of political belief. Nor does that figure represent the total membership of all affiliated unions, since each union's contribution to the affiliated membership and its voting power in

the annual conference are measured only by the proportion of its membership—which may be considerably less than the total—on which it chooses to pay affiliation fees. In short, neither the working class nor the trade-unions form a single monolithic body solidly lined up behind the party.

How far does affiliation signify participation by union members in the political activities of the party? Since the unions differ greatly in their internal political structures as well as attachment to the party, it is very hard to generalize. The general opinion is that "the sense of political responsibility among the members of the unions is not very great."[14] While not concerned precisely with this problem, a recent study of the levels of active membership in British unions tends to confirm this view.[15] Its findings are that within the branches only some 15–25 per cent of the members participate actively in the government of their organizations. This group, which varies in size from one union to another, is the hard core of active members who regularly attend meetings, provide candidates for union office, discuss policy, pass resolutions, and largely conduct the political and nonpolitical business of the branch.

Such apathy on the part of the rank and file may shock the classical democrat and gratify the elitist. Yet it should also be pointed out, as this study indicates, that the rank and file are not so uninfluential or so easy to "manipulate" as their ostensible inactivity would suggest. They accept the leadership of the active members until that leadership runs against strongly held ideas and sentiments; then they show sudden and vigorous activity. For example, prac-

14. N. Barou, *British Trade Unions* (London, 1947), p. 136.

15. *British Trade Unionism: Six Studies by P.E.P.* [Political and Economic Planning] (London, 1948).

tically all strikes in the period 1945–48, which cost the economy some seven million working days, were unofficial and largely the consequence of the initiative of the rank and file.

In the government of a union, as in democratic politics generally, the existence of this "veto power" in the hands of the apparently apathetic rank and file may greatly affect the general course of policy, even though that power is rarely exercised. One of the functions of the democratic leader is to anticipate the exercise of this power, although his success in anticipating and so preventing its exercise may seem to confirm the existence of an oligarchy ruling over a mass of inert followers. Yet one can hardly call these processes of anticipation marked by occasional revolt the perfect practice of democracy. While their big battalions are not wholly composed of ardent and politically conscious warriors, the trade-unions very largely provide the party with the sinews of war. The central party organization is financed mainly by them, its financial statements for 1953 showing trade-union affiliation fees amounting to nearly five times those received from the constituency organizations. They also make heavy contributions in other ways. Practically the whole of the general election fund reported in the financial statement for 1951 came from trade-unions. Through the local branches, which are affiliated with the constituency organizations, they help support the local activities of the party, and at the time of general elections some of the national trade-union bodies assume responsibility for the larger part of the campaign expenses of their nominees who have been adopted as candidates by constituency organizations.

While the trade-unions preponderate in membership and in financial contributions, it would seem, if one takes the proportion of trade-union nominees among all Labour M.P.'s as an index, that their influence has been considerably moderated over the years. From 86 per cent in 1918, that proportion fell to 53 per cent in 1935 and 29 per cent in 1945, a year in which the Labour M.P.'s elected included a greatly enlarged group of people of middle-class origin and occupation, 25 per cent having been educated in "public" schools as compared with only 9 per cent in the average interwar House.[16] Though proportionately smaller, the trade-union group in absolute numbers, however, was larger than ever before, standing at 121, of whom 35 were nominees of the miners' union, while in the Labour cabinet of 20, 9 were active trade-unionists. In the election of 1951, 139 candidates were put forward on the financial responsibility of the trade-unions and 436 by constituency parties; of the former, 105 were elected; of the latter, 173, the relative "safety" of the seats held by the trade-union nominees being reflected in these figures.

Of the other affiliated organizations, the most important is the **Fabian Society**, whose membership, never large, stood at some twenty-three hundred in 1953. After a period of eclipse in the twenties and thirties, the society was revived in 1938 by amalgamation with the New Fabian Research Bureau, founded in 1931 by a group of younger Socialists, including Attlee, Cripps, Dalton, and Bevin. The society's work is to propagandize not simply for the party but rather for its version of socialism. And through its Socialist Propaganda Committee it has attempted to stimulate propaganda by the more ardent socialists in the local party organizations and in local Fabian groups. Sober, intelligent, factual, the society's tracts and research publications, each dealing with some special subject, such

16. J. F. S. Ross, "The New House of Commons," *Pilot Papers*, II, No. 1 (March, 1947), 33.

as the health services, colonial policy, full employment, or the nationalization of a particular industry, have done a good deal to educate some of the more active members of the party and indirectly to mold party opinion and policy in general. While the society has never recovered the influence it seemed to have when the Webbs were at the height of their power, it has successfully "permeated" the party, and in 1945 practically all the members of the new government and nearly half the Labour M.P.'s were members.

While not in the strict sense affiliated with the party, the Co-operative Movement is a powerful ally. Originating in the inspiration of Robert Owen, an ancestor also of the Labour party, consumer co-operation grew in the nineteenth and twentieth centuries until at present some ten million persons representing over half the families in Britain are members of the various societies. Although its members have been very largely of the working class and many have been committed to the socialism of a "co-operative commonwealth," the movement has resisted formal affiliation with the Labour party. Instead, when the co-operatives surrendered their traditional doctrine of political neutrality in 1918, they founded a separate organization, the Co-operative party, based principally on the affiliation of local societies and including comparatively few individual members.

As one would expect, the consumers' interest has not provided a firm base for political action in comparison with the producers' interest, which Labour embodies through its connection with the trade-unions, and the political future of the Co-operative Movement seems to lie in a subordinate partnership with the Labour party. Within that party, however, the co-operatives form an effective pressure group. Nationalization of industrial assurance, proposed in the party program issued in 1949, was watered down to a proposal of mutual ownership by policyholders largely because of pressure from Co-operative leaders, and it may be that, as in Sweden, their resistance to further nationalization has been one cause of Labour's recent moderation on the subject.

Local co-operative societies have for a long time affiliated with local Labour parties, and in recent years the movement has established closer relations with the national Labour organization. In 1941 the Co-operative Union, representing the societies, formally joined the National Council of Labour, a body of twenty-one members which includes equal representation from the Co-operative Union, the T.U.C., and the Labour party and which from time to time issues pronouncements on general political questions. Local co-operative parties may offer their candidates for adoption by local Labour parties, but in the special agreements regulating these arrangements the Labour party has won its point that such candidates, if adopted, must abide by the rules of the Labour party and submit to its discipline. In the 1951 election local Labour parties adopted thirty-eight Co-operative party candidates, of whom sixteen were elected, while one member of the cabinet, Viscount Alexander of Hillsborough, had been a leader in co-operative politics.

Constituency Parties

The political shock troops of the party are the individual members, who in 1953 numbered a million and were organized in 613 local parties in the constituencies.[17] Before 1918 the party was strictly federal, and an individual could win a voice in its councils only

17. The Labour party limits its organization to Great Britain but has close contacts with the small Northern Ireland Labour party, whose vote the Labour party includes in its total poll.

as a member of an affiliated body. By establishing individual membership and local parties, the way was opened for utilizing the energies of people who might not have been able or willing to join an affiliated body. Women, who first received the vote in the year this change was made, could now participate and at the present time carry an equal burden with men in local party activity. The local Labour parties have also provided a means by which socialists of middle-class origin can participate in the party.

The form of the local organizations is similar to that of the Conservatives. Any person may join who agrees to accept and conform to the constitution and policies of the party. He must, if eligible, be a member of a bona fide trade-union. Annual dues are usually 6s., of which 6d. goes to the national party organization. In an urban area the members of the local party are grouped in wards. Meetings open to all members in the ward are held periodically, as in the case of trade-union branches. However, only a small fraction regularly attend such meetings. The governing body of the local party is a committee, usually called the General Management Committee, consisting of delegates from the ward committees, from the special women's sections, and from other organizations, such as trade-union branches and co-operative societies, which are affiliated with the local party. This committee elects an executive committee and other officials, including a secretary, who is often also the election agent.

The paid bureaucracy of the Labour party, however, is smaller than that of the Conservatives. While both parties have greatly improved the recruitment and training of constituency agents— "probably the most important development in party organization in 1950," according to H. G. Nicholas—Labour has lagged behind the Conservatives. According to officials of the Conservative Central Office, the party's associations in 1950 had nearly 580 full-time paid officials in charge of constituency organizations. The Labour party, on the other hand, reported 279 full-time agents and 350 part-time agents employed at the time of the general election that year.

Selection of a parliamentary candidate, while initially in the hands of the General Committee, is subject to stricter and more explicit control from above than in the Conservative party. Under the party Constitution the selection of a candidate "shall not be regarded as completed until the name of the person has been placed before a meeting of the National Executive Committee, and his or her selection has been duly endorsed." And indorsement by the National Executive Committee carries with it certain stringent conditions. The candidate must include in his election address and must advocate in his campaign "the issues for that Election as defined by the National Executive." He must "accept and conform to the Constitution, Programme, Principles and Policy of the Party" and must "undertake to accept and act in harmony with the Standing Orders of the Parliamentary Labour Party." Breach of these conditions may lead to withdrawal of the indorsement and possibly expulsion from the party. The National Executive, however, exercises its powers with restraint, and the local parties have considerable freedom in the choice of candidates. After the collapse of 1931, for example, they very commonly passed over the names of ex-ministers recommended by the committee, and at the election of 1950 the Labour minister of town and country planning failed to secure adoption by a local party.

The process of selection itself resembles in its main features the procedure followed by the Conservatives. A selection committee in consultation with central officials puts together a list of possible candidates from which it selects a "short list" of aspirants to be heard and judged by the General Management Committee. Canvassing on the quiet is fairly common, as a result of which delegates may come to the selection meeting with their minds already much inclined toward a particular aspirant. In some cases delegates from trade-union branches may have been instructed by their higher offices to support a fellow-unionist seeking the nomination. Public campaigning for the nomination, however, is unknown in the Labour as in the Conservative party. Indeed, in some local parties the meeting, after hearing the speeches of aspirants, goes directly to the vote without discussion of their merits, the theory being that discussion might enable some members unduly to sway delegates.

As in the Conservative party, there is a level of organization intervening between the national and local bodies. Most of the constituency parties are grouped in county federations. Above these are ten regional councils covering the whole country except for London County, where the huge London Labour party includes forty-three constituency parties. The councils are federations of trade-unions, co-operatives, and constituency parties, and each has its permanent officials and executive committee to conduct propaganda, hold rallies, and supervise local organization.

The Annual Conference

In contrast with the Conservative party, the formally sovereign body is the Annual Conference.[18] Its voting members, who usually number over one thousand, are delegates from the constituency organizations, federations, national trade-unions, and other affiliated bodies, each delegation having voting power proportional to the number of members on whom its organization has paid affiliation fees. Ex officio members of the conference, principally the members of the National Executive Committee, members of the parliamentary party, and indorsed candidates, may not vote.

The main business of the conference is to debate the reports of the National Executive Committee and the parliamentary leaders, consider resolutions on policy and party organization, adopt a program when an election impends, and elect a National Executive Committee for the ensuing twelve months. These proceedings are colored by the usual self-congratulation and ideological cant of the partisan political gathering. Yet compared to the proceedings of most mass organizations, they are often impressive, showing at times intelligence and a sense of genuine deliberation.

Unlike speakers at the Conservative conference who speak only for themselves, the delegates who come to the rostrum at the Labour conference have in many instances been instructed by their organizations and therefore may bring to the assembly the fruits of some previous deliberation and decision as well as their own views. In the debates on workers' participation, nationalization, food and clothing subsidies, equal pay for women, and other points of policy, foreign and domestic, the opinions of different sections within the party are vigorously expressed, often differing sharply from one another and from those of the National Executive and the parliamentary leaders. The views of the leaders are not often rejected: they could not be without disastrous effects on the policy and government of the party. Yet these debates and the votes following them are emi-

18. "The work of the Party shall be under the direction and control of the Party Conference which shall itself be subject to the Constitution and Standing Orders of the Party."

nently effective means for informing the leaders of the extent and intensity of support for divergent views and for warning them of the forces to which they must comply if they are to continue to lead. In this sense the debates are not sham but a real part of the process of policy-making.

The resolutions submitted to the conference come largely from the local parties,[19] and it is their delegates who commonly voice the protests and proposals of the left wing.[20] The trade-union vote, on the other hand, can usually be relied upon by the party leaders to override too ardent constituency delegates. In this division within the party one can see the two main streams, still not perfectly merged, from which the movement flows: trade-union interests and socialist ideology.[21] But the trade-unions, while less articulate, are by no means at one on all

issues, nor are they passive followers of the party leaders. Their delegates can deliver sharp attacks on the leadership—for example, over the question of workers' control or the wage freeze—which are the more ominous because of the immense economic power of the organizations whose views they represent.

The conference performs the functions of a deliberative assembly by providing a forum where ideas are presented for consideration and forces are weighed against one another. But it is also much more. Within the assembly hall, aspirants to a seat in Parliament go through their paces before delegates whose parties may be looking for candidates, while M.P.'s who feel the call of ministerial office demonstrate their power with the party to parliamentary chiefs. Outside, the social life of the conference, heavily charged with politics, spreads through the town, affording to the ambitious an opportunity to have a word with a party leader and to the rank and file at least a chance to see the prime minister doing the "hokeypokey" at the mayor's reception.

Apart from these satisfactions, there is also, as one intimate observer has put it, "the warmer glow of contiguity."

We know that we are 5 million strong, but when that is reduced to the active membership and dispersed among a 50 million population, the really active people are almost isolated and sometimes lonely. From being one who cares and thinks amongst thousands who don't seem to bother, the delegate from a local party finds himself at Conference among hundreds who feel very much as he does. Here is the movement in the flesh, keen and talkative.

Here the devoted Labour partisan imbibes "the feeling of belonging, along with many others, to something that is big and important." In addition to being an organ for deciding policy, the

19. Of the 362 resolutions on the preliminary agenda for the 1950 conference, only 17 came from trade-unions. While undoubtedly the constituency parties are more articulate than the unions, these figures do not fairly measure the political consciousness of the two sections because nearly all the trade-union resolutions came from national organizations embracing many local branches, while the constituency resolutions for the most part came directly from local labor parties.

20. The left tendency of the constituency delegates can often be traced in the vote for the seven members of the National Executive Committee elected by the constituency delegates. At the conference of 1952, for example, the whole Bevanite slate of six candidates was elected from a field of twenty-seven candidates which included prominent moderates and former ministers like Herbert Morrison and Hugh Gaitskell.

21. A vote at the party conference of 1949 illustrates this division. For left-wing breaches of discipline two Labour M.P.'s, Konni Zilliacus and L. J. Solley, had been refused indorsement by the National Executive Committee. When the conference was asked to vote on a resolution to "refer back" the executive's report on this subject, the tally for and against reflected almost exactly the division between the constituency and trade-union delegates.

conference, like the representative gathering of any great organization that is socially alive, is also a cult celebrating the sacred rites through which solidarity is expressed and reinforced.

The National Executive Committee

Between meetings of the conference the government of the party is vested formally in the National Executive Committee. This body has twenty-eight members: twenty-five elected by the conference; the party treasurer, also elected by the conference; and, ex officio, the leader of the parliamentary and, since 1954, his deputy. Because the choice of the elected members by the conference at large seemed to give too much weight to the trade-unions, since 1937 twelve have been elected by the trade-union delegates, one by the delegates of the other affiliated bodies, seven by the constituency delegates, and the remaining five, all women, by the conference as a whole. The committee chooses a chairman from its members. By custom, however, the chairman is chosen according to seniority of service on the committee and holds office for only a year—a convention reflecting the fact that the post is not of pre-eminent political importance.

The National Executive Committee, which meets about once a month for two or three days at a time, has wide powers in policy-making, maintaining discipline, and supervising party organization. Acting jointly with the Executive Committee of the parliamentary party, it decides what items from the party program shall be included in the manifesto issued prior to a general election. It convenes the annual conference and while it does not fix its agenda, which is controlled by a committee elected at the previous conference, its report and the other resolutions that it may submit set many of the issues for discussion. Its powers in

enforcing discipline extend not only to withdrawal or refusal of indorsement of candidates but also to expulsion of individuals from the party and "dis-affiliation" of organizations.

These powers may assist parliamentary chiefs in maintaining discipline in the House. During the parliament of 1945 five Labour M.P.'s were expelled by the National Executive Committee, four for left-wing breaches of discipline and one for opposition to the nationalization of the iron and steel industry, with the result that in all cases they suffered crushing defeat by official Labour candidates when the rebels stood for re-election in 1950. The Committee can be brought to use its powers even against leading figures in the party, as when, for example, it expelled Sir Stafford Cripps in 1938 for continuing to advocate, against the decision of the conference, a Popular Front with the Communists.

With the general problem of Communist infiltration the party, under the guidance of the National Executive Committee, has dealt effectively. The threat has waxed and waned from time to time since the foundation of the Communist party in 1920. While the fellow-traveler influence is strong in some local parties and Communist party members are prominent in a few unions, Labour has resolutely and successfully resisted "boring from within." The Communists have consistently been refused affiliation, and a list of "proscribed organizations," including some dozen Front organizations, has been drawn up to which neither a member of the Labour party nor a parliamentary candidate nor a delegate to the conference may belong. The Communists are more important than their negligible vote of 92,000 in 1950 would indicate,[22] but

22. A rough measurement of their strength in the trade-union movement was provided in September, 1950, when the T.U.C. indorsed the United Nations action in Korea by a vote

the problem they present to the country and to the socialist movement in Britain in comparison with that in other countries is very slight indeed.

While the Conservative party has experienced some difficulty in linking the general constituency organization and the Central Office, a similar problem can hardly arise in the Labour party, since the party bureaucracy, with headquarters in Transport House, is directly under the National Executive Committee. The subcommittees through which the Committee does most of its work receive secretarial and technical assistance from the bureaucracy, much as the ministerial committees of the cabinet are assisted by officials from the cabinet office and the departments of state. The plausible fear that the permanent officials of the party machine, who are always "on the spot" and at the center of day-to-day activities, might dominate the party has not materialized. The secretary of the party, who is the chief permanent official of the bureaucracy, may be a person of considerable political importance, as he was, for example, when Arthur Henderson held the post from 1911 to 1934. Otherwise the bureaucrats, while important advisers of the party leaders, have been kept in the position of respected subordination that the British civil servant occupies in relation to a minister of the Crown.

Under the secretary are six departments. The Organization Department is headed by the national agent, who is also secretary to the organization subcommittee of the National Executive Committee. At each of the regional headquarters this department has professional organizers, through whom it maintains liaison with the regional councils. It prepares manuals on the conduct of elections for the local parties, arranges elaborate courses of study for organizers, reviews the rules of local parties (which must have the indorsement of the National Executive Committee), handles relations with the League of Youth, a large ancillary organization of the party with some five hundred and sixty branches, and inaugurates special membership drives in the constituencies.

The principal task of the Press and Publicity Department is to prepare and direct the vast flood of printed material which goes out from Transport House. Its regular publications include the *Socialist Advance,* a sixteen-page illustrated magazine for the League of Youth, the *Labour Organizer* for key party workers, and clipsheets for the local party journals. Its special publications grow in number as local or general elections approach. In 1949, for example, they reached a total of sixty-one and ranged in character from short popular leaflets on subjects like rent control or housing to the massive *Speakers' Handbook,* which ran to nearly five hundred pages and included critical statistics, succinct partisan arguments, choice quotations from the Opposition, and other ammunition for the continuous party warfare of British politics. Though not owned by the party but by Odhams Press and the T.U.C. jointly, the *Daily Herald,* Britain's second largest newspaper, is regarded in the party as "our daily" and plays a major role in presenting the Labour case and conducting party publicity.

The other four departments are the Women's Department, which maintains liaison with the eighteen hundred women's sections in the local parties and holds an annual conference of Labour women; the International Department, which keeps up extensive relations with socialist parties in other

---

of 6,942,000 against 595,000. "The opposition to the reports," wrote the London *Times,* "was almost entirely Communist, so that the vote of nearly 600,000 probably represents about the present strength of Communist-dominated unions" (September 7, 1950).

countries; the Research Department, which performs preparatory work for the party program and the frequent policy reports of the National Executive Committee and provides information in response to individual inquiries and for use in the regular and occasional party publications; and the Finance Department, which administers receipts and expenses in connection with the various party funds.

The third element in the party organization, the parliamentary Labour party, consists of Labour members of the House of Commons and also nominally the sixty or so Labour peers. While Labour was in power from 1945 to 1951 the formal organization of the parliamentary party in the House of Commons differed considerably from what it had been when the party was in Opposition. During its prewar days of opposition the decisions on policy arrived at by its regular weekly meetings were binding on all members, leaders and backbenchers alike. Its Standing Orders provided that, while members might abstain from voting in matters of conscience, such as religion and temperance, they were otherwise obliged to vote in accord with the decisions of the party meeting, which might punish recalcitrant members by "withdrawing the Whip"—i.e., expelling them from the parliamentary party— and reporting this action to the National Executive Committee for consideration of further penalties.

The meetings of the parliamentary party continued during the parliament of 1945, and ministers regularly attended to explain and often to defend their policies. But the decisions of the party leaders, which were now the decisions of the government, were made in the first instance in the cabinet. On the other hand, the Standing Orders were suspended. And not only did backbenchers very commonly attack the government with vehemence, they also

frequently abstained or voted against it. The party, however, retained the power of withdrawing the Whip, and a Liaison Committee, established to maintain contact between ministers and backbenchers, also considered voting records. In addition to this committee, which included the chairman and vice-chairman of the parliamentary party, the leader of the House, the chief Whip, and a Labour peer, further provision for contact with the government was made by the establishment of twenty study groups of backbenchers, with which ministers met for "the interchange of views."

When in Opposition, the party in the House had elected at the start of each session a chairman who was also leader of the parliamentary party. On coming to power in 1945, the party separated the two offices, the chairman now being chosen from the backbenchers. After the general election of 1950, a joint meeting of the parliamentary party and the N.E.C. went through the motion of re-electing Attlee "Leader of the Party." The functions of leader of the House were intrusted to an important cabinet member, Herbert Morrison, under whom the Whips, twelve in number, performed their traditional duties.

Upon again going into Opposition after its defeat in 1951, the party once more combined the office of chairman and leader, vesting it in Clement Attlee, but attempted for several months to continue the suspension of the Standing Orders. The growth of the left-wing group, led by Aneurin Bevan, however, severely strained party unity in the House as well as in the country. Discipline reached a low point during the divisions following the debate on defense policy in March, 1952. Defying a three-line Whip, the Bevanites, some fifty-five in number, abstained from supporting the Opposition motion agreed on by the party meeting and voted against the government motion on which the party meeting had decided to abstain. At a subsequent meeting the parliamentary party imposed Standing Orders which bound members to accept "the decisions of the Party Meeting" while recognizing "the right of individual Members to abstain from voting on matters of deeply held personal or conscientious conviction."

Social Bases of British Parties

The formal organization of Labour differs radically from that of the Conservatives. But does this reflect a difference in the social bases of the two parties? Can we say that the Conservatives, as the party of the middle and upper classes, follow the old pattern of British politics, vesting the principal power in the parliamentary party, where the traditional governing class predominates, while Labour, as the party of the working class, has broken with this pattern and radically democratized its party processes in fact as well as in form?

The social bases of the two parties do indeed differ. The most striking instance is the organic connection of British trade-unions with Labour. Yet, as we have seen, this does not mean that all trade-unionists can be counted as party members, and, if we look at analyses of how the electorate votes, we must qualify still further our estimate of the allegiance of the working class to the Labour party. The British Institute of Public Opinion divides the voting population into four groups: the well-to-do, comprising 5 per cent of the population; a "middle class," comprising 21 per cent; a large lower stratum, comprising 59 per cent; and a fourth group of the "very poor," comprising 15 per cent. Its polls in recent years show that the two upper strata are preponderantly Conservative, the two lower strata preponderantly Labour. But they also show a substantial portion of the very poor—about a third—and of the third stratum—about a third—with Conservative affiliations. On the other hand, among the two upper strata a tenth of the well-to-do and a fifth of the middle class declare for Labour. In each stratum the Liberal party, which in the election of 1950 won 9 per cent of the total vote, has followers, with the middle class being slightly more inclined to it than the others.

Labour, it is often remarked, cannot win an election without some support from the middle class. No doubt, as Labour opinion is now distributed among the electorate, the party could not dispense with the sizable fraction of that group supporting it. But it is dependent upon that support precisely because it has not won a larger following among the two lower strata, which between them include nearly three-quarters of the electorate. Within these two lower strata the agricultural laborers have been a particularly difficult group to win over to Labour. While, according to the institute's polls, about a third to a quarter of them support Labour, nearly half have announced they would vote Conservative —the remainder consisting largely of those who declared themselves undecided. Furthermore, even in those groups where one might expect an almost unanimous Labour following there is a substantial Conservative vote. Among weekly wage-earnaers in factories, heavy industry, transport, and mining, although more than half are for Labour, around a fifth support the Conservatives. Perhaps the most interesting division indicated by the institute's polls is that among trade-union members. A majority support Labour, and there is a sprinkling of Liberals, but a fifth to a quarter have declared themselves for the Conservatives. Even today, it appears, Disraeli's belief that the working class is naturally conservative is not wholly illusory.

The highly industrialized areas are the strongholds of Labour and the rural areas the strongholds of conservatism. But in each type of area there is a substantial group of dissidents from majority opinion. In the 1950 election, for instance, the mining country in Glamorgan and Monmouth in Wales returned twenty-one Labour M.P.'s and only two Conservatives, but the popular vote in that area included a little more than 26 per cent for the Conservatives. Similarly, in the industrial area around Durham and in the Yorkshire coal and steel district, the Conservatives managed to win more than 30 per cent of the popular vote, and in the Black Country around Birmingham nearly 40 per cent. In the strongly Tory regions of the southern counties and northern Scotland, on the other hand, Labour polled from a third to two-fifths of the vote. Only in Northern Ireland was the Labour poll relatively insignificant, amounting to about a fifth of the vote for the Conservatives. Neither on sectional nor on class lines is Britain sharply divided into "two nations."

Clearer signs of class division appear if we look at the circles of active politicians in the two parties. Of the 621 Conservative candidates in 1950, for example, 274 can be identified as businessmen and only 7 as manual workers. In contrast, among the 617 Labour candidates were 92 manual workers and 91 others, mostly trade-union officials, who formerly belonged to that occupational group. Also, on the Conservative side, Nicholas points out, were 39 candidates "whom it was not possible to allocate to any category more meaningful than 'private means' and who, under that designation, may serve as not unjustifiable reminders of the party's historic associations with rank and wealth." Yet Labour included a substantial number identified with business: 92 engaged in profit-making and

21 salaried managers. And in each party by far the largest group—258 for Labour, 308 for the Conservatives—came from the professions, a social category whose class affiliations are notoriously difficult to define or predict.

Of the statistics on education, the most striking is the number of Old Etonians among the Conservatives: 107 as compared with only 5 on the Labour side. Three hundred and sixty-four Conservatives had gone to "public" schools, but only 108 Labourites, while of those whose education had stopped at the elementary grade, 184 were on the Labour side and only 21 on the Conservative. About half the Conservatives had been to a university as compared with two-fifths of the Labourites, but the older universities, Oxford and Cambridge, claimed 247 Conservatives and only 98 Labourites.

In terms of occupation and education the Conservatives exhibit a strong connection with the well-to-do and more expensivly educated classes, while in numerical proportion Labour is more representative of its own social base and, indeed, of the society as a whole. Yet other classes besides the working class provide not only substantial electoral support for Labour but also and in still greater degree active politicians and leaders of the party. Labour ministers with an Oxford or Cambridge education are by no means rare—they were nearly a third of the sixty-five Labour ministers between 1945 and 1951—and the public schools are well represented among the leaders of the party. Indeed, Winchester, one of the more distinguished public schools, had educated all three ministers who presented the Labour budget of 1950–51, a fact which they showed they were not unmindful of by presenting to the school library a specially bound volume of Hansard "as a memorial of an unique event never likely to be repeated."[23]

23. *The Wykehamist,* July 18, 1950, p. 154.

The Process of Making Policy

The obvious danger of a formal organization like that of the Labour party is "caucus government"—rule by an extra-parliamentary body. The National Executive Committee controls the vast bureaucracy of the party and under the party constitution could legally use its wide disciplinary powers even against a Labour prime minister or the members of his cabinet. The opportunity to govern a Labour government might also tempt the annual conference with its power to elect the National Executive Committee and its large, though not unlimited, authority in policy-making; beyond the conference lies the threat of the trade-unions, embracing the great mass of party membership and wielding immense financial and economic power. Whether one considers the terms of formal organization or the "real forces" involved, interference of this kind would certainly not be surprising, and it has occurred often enough in socialist parties on the Continent. The Labour party, however, has avoided "caucus government" and has kept in the hands of its parliamentary leadership the chief role in deciding essential matters of policy, discipline, and ministerial office.

The National Executive Committee has been not a rival but a co-operative and even a subordinate partner, one reason for which, as is often mentioned, is the committee's and parliamentary party's overlapping membership. For example, of the twenty-eight members of the committee in 1954, seventeen were M.P.'s. But this, rather than a cause, is a symptom of the informal authority which the parliamentary party enjoys within the party. The hand of parliamentary leaders is strengthened further by the fact that, under the Standing Orders of the Labour party, members of the General Council of the T.U.C.—that is, many of the ablest and most powerful Labour leaders—are in-

eligible for election to the National Executive Committee. But that would not account for the responsibility and self-restraint shown in recent years by the General Council of the T.U.C. and most higher union officials. Electoral necessities are important: if Labour is to win a majority, it must not be merely a doctrinaire party and must be more than the instrument of the trade-unions. Most important are the necessities of the British constitution: "caucus government" is incompatible with cabinet government and with the conventions, attitudes, and values which cabinet government has bred into the British voter and politician.

The long and detailed programs which Labour is in the habit of presenting to the country would seem to provide a particularly tempting opportunity for extra-parliamentary control. Certainly, they do permit the many vigorous wills of the party to be expressed and also to have effect—within limits. The procedure by which the party drew up the program of 1949, *Labour Believes in Britain,* will illustrate this. Under the party constitution "the Conference shall decide from time to time what specific proposals of legislative, financial or administrative reform shall be included in the Party Programme." But obviously its formal sovereignty cannot be allowed full sway if a coherent statement of national policy is to be produced. Speaking for the National Executive Committee at the 1948 conference, therefore, Herbert Morrison, also a member of the "inner" cabinet, asked the organizations which had submitted policy resolutions to remit them to the National Executive Committee for consideration without debate at the conference. Later these resolutions were considered by seven subcommittees set up by the Policy Committee of the executive committee. That committee, of which Morrison was chairman, included several of the leading members of the cabinet, and a slight majority were from the parliamentary party. All the chairmen of the subcommittees were members of the government.

Staff work was thorough and extensive. Working closely with the Fabian Society, the Research Department of the party provided technical assistance to the subcommittees, its research papers for this purpose running to some 500,000 words. Reports were submitted by the subcommittees of the Policy Committee, and in February, 1949, at a "house party" on the Isle of Wight attended by members of the National Executive Committee and a number of ministers, a draft statement of policy was prepared. After representatives of trade-unions and the co-operatives had been consulted, the statement was circulated among constituency and other affiliated organizations and in June submitted to the annual conference.

But there was still to be no "lawmaking from the floor." Many organizations had submitted resolutions calling for amendments. Over some strong protests, however, the National Executive Committee succeeded in persuading delegates to rule that such resolutions were to be remitted to the committee without debate. To the conference was left the right of criticizing, which it vigorously exercised in a two-day discussion, and of approving, which it did with little dissent, being faced with the alternative of either accepting or rejecting the statement as a whole.

Even granting that it has been drawn up under the guidance of party leaders, a program committing a government in detail to a line of action may seriously embarrass it and harm the country. That the voter should be fully informed what party leaders will do with power before a mandate is given them is one interpretation of democracy. But often the course of events at home and abroad cannot be accurately forecast,

and the leaders of the "programmatic" party, confronted with an emergency or unforeseen turn in foreign affairs, may lack the flexibility of mind and the freedom of maneuver within their mandate to cope with the new problem.

In a sense this is what happened when the economic crisis of 1947 broke over the Labour government. Coming to power in 1945 and committed to the long and detailed pledges of *Let Us Face the Future,* ministers vigorously plunged ahead with their respective schemes, maintaining what was for a group of self-proclaimed planners remarkably little co-ordination. The resources of the economy were overstrained, and the further burden undertaken by the government when it agreed to make sterling freely convertible promised a crisis by midsummer of 1947. Early in the year storm signals were hoisted in the appropriate place: letters to the London *Times* from prominent economists warned the government. Perhaps also the Treasury sounded an expert alarm, although higher civil servants differ on this question. The government, however, remained complacent, from which state it was in no way helped to rouse itself by the annual conference that spring or by the National Executive Committee, even in the face of rising and intelligent criticism by some of the Opposition and certain Labour backbenchers. Not until the autumn and two months after the sterling crisis had broken did the government have in hand a program radical enough to meet the problem.

Yet its slowness in facing the facts— a trait which Labour certainly has no monopoly on—is not so worthy of note as its vigor and flexibility in action when it finally faced them. The policy of deflation and radical austerity inaugurated by Sir Stafford Cripps as chancellor of the Exchequer and minister in charge of central planning trenched deeply on cherished objectives of the party program—housing, subsidies, wage raises—and ran counter to powerful pressures in party and trade-unions. Yet party and interest groups were convinced, or resisted, or sometimes appeased by moderate concessions, and a government which was committed by its principles to large-scale spending carried out one of the most successful fights against inflation of any country during the postwar period.

One essential of the new policy was the so-called "wage freeze" of February, 1948. This was not a law, or a decree, or, indeed, a "freeze," but a statement by the prime minister "requesting" trade-unions and the public generally not to seek increases in personal incomes except in special cases. This step did not halt wage raises, but it did moderate them very considerably during the succeeding two and a half years —and did so, it may be added, much to the surprise of many observers, who regularly prophesied that the line on wages was about to be broken through. Ministers were in continual negotiation with trade-unions, but success was won not by ministers alone but also by the efforts of a number of hardheaded labor leaders in the General Council of the T.U.C., who in this instance showed a sense of responsibility worthy of a model governing class.

The Role of the Parliamentary Leaders

While tension with the trade-unions has represented a greater threat to the government's economic policy, its sharp and frequent clashes with the left wing of the party in parliament have been more in the public eye. Yet in spite of them and Labour's strong tradition of back-bench participation in policy-making, the parliamentary leaders have maintained a sphere of independent action probably as wide as that of the Conservatives' leadership when in power. In the parliament of 1945 the left wing, while not Communist, consisted of a score or so of fairly faithful "fellow-travelers" as well as a much larger number of left-center M.P.'s, led by the chiefs of the "Keep Left" group, R. H. S. Crossman, Michael Foot, and Ian Mikardo. Mustering a strength of seventy to eighty and utilizing the study groups to organize their efforts, the left wing conducted a lively campaign, attacking especially the government's foreign policy during the opening phases of the "cold war." The study group concerned with foreign affairs sent delegations to Foreign Secretary Ernest Bevin and letters to Prime Minister Attlee, demanding changes in British policy toward Spain, Indonesia, and Greece, finally obliging Bevin to bring the issue to a head by demanding and winning what was in effect a vote of confidence at a party meeting. Pressure was also turned on the minister of defense over the question of conscription. In April, 1947, a revolt organized by another study group obliged the government to retreat on this issue by cutting the proposed term of service from eighteen to twelve months, after seventy-two Labour M.P.'s had voted against the government and seventy others had abstained or failed to attend the sitting. Early in the following year, however, the government returned to the attack and put through its original proposal.

Alarmed at this use of the study-group structure, the party leaders attempted to shift the emphasis of back-bench activity to the area groups, whose members consisted of M.P.'s drawn from the various regions of the country and in which the more active leftists were swamped by the loyal majority. Formal disciplinary powers were also used. At the time of the Italian general election in April, 1948, when the government was officially supporting the non-Communist parties in that election, a telegram of encouragement signed by thirty-seven Labour M.P.'s was sent to the left socialist allies of the Communist party of Italy. One of the signers, John Platts-Mills, was expelled from the party by the National Executive Committee, after which the parliamentary party withdrew the Whip. Fifteen of the signers, when approached by the National Executive Committee, declared they had not signed or had signed under a misunderstanding or had since retracted. The remaining twenty-one were warned against acting "as a group in organized opposition to Party policy" and informed that "unless they individually undertake by first post Thursday, May 6, 1948, to desist in future from such conduct they are excluded from membership in the Labour Party." All gave the required assurances.

These measures and the approach of the general election of 1950 tightened party discipline and damped down rebellion. Equally important, however, was the shock to left socialists as in 1948 the news transpired of the "cannibalization" of the Social Democrats of Czechoslovakia by the Communists after the Communist coup early that year. Party unity was maintained during the campaign, and Aneurin Bevan, minister of health, to whom the Left looked for a champion in the cabinet, was given only a minor role in the appeal to the country.

Against pressure from within and without a leading role has been retained for Labour's chiefs in parliament. And among them, in terms of the real political forces as well as constitutional conventions, the "first among equals" is Clement Attlee. In its mixture of the new and the old in the British party system Attlee's leadership is a crucially important subject for analysis. To recount the way in which he achieved his position is to suggest that he may be merely a functionary, a person set at the head of the party simply to carry out assigned tasks and to quote approved policies. Middle class in origin, educated at one of the better public schools and Oxford, converted to socialism through his experience as a social worker, he exemplifies in his political views the leftward evolution of certain humanitarian and egalitarian principles of nineteenth-century liberalism. Entering the House in 1922, he served in noncabinet posts in the first and second MacDonald governments. Almost by default he became deputy leader of the party when in the debacle of 1931 most of the more prominent Labourites were defeated at the polls. Four years later the new leader, George Lansbury, was obliged to resign because of his excessively pacifistic views, and Attlee succeeded him. Not brilliant service in politics or administration or wide electoral appeal had given him the leadership but principally the elimination of more logical candidates in 1931 and the fact that during this time bitter divisions within the party prevented a "strong man" identified with one of the factions from being accepted by the others. Indeed, it is as if the party, having recently escaped the jaws of King Stork when the "charismatic" MacDonald tried to swallow it up in his coalition with the Tories, preferred to subject itself to an unexciting but safe King Log. And today, if it is his personal qualities that account for his primacy in the party, these qualities are certainly not the dramatic traits of character and action usually associated with the eminent political leader. Slight of build, plain, aloof, almost shy, and certainly no orator, his appearance and behavior suggest Churchill's cruel and inaccurate taunt, "a sheep in sheep's clothing."

Yet Attlee, particularly while in office, had a hold on his party comparable to that of the traditional British political chief, as he showed when, in the closely divided House elected in

1950, tensions mounted within the party following the outbreak of the Korean War. Outwardly the parliamentary party approved almost unanimously the government's support of the United Nations action, but in the House and in many constituency parties there were strong currents of dissatisfaction. These grew when Communist China intervened—the "New China" for which many Labourites and not merely "fellow-travelers" had expressed the warmest sympathies—and when the rearmament figures, having already been raised in the summer, were again raised early in 1951. At the same time the balance of personalities in the cabinet was radically altered when Sir Stafford Cripps, who had held a high place in the conscience of the nation, if not in the passions of the party, retired from politics because of illness and Ernest Bevin, whose massive character and immense trade-union following had led some to speak of him as the "King maker," died after a long period of failing health. Seizing these opportunities, Aneurin Bevan resigned from the cabinet in April not only as an act of protest against the government's policy but also as a major step in a campaign to wrest leadership from Attlee and to re-make the party in a more suitable image. Faced with these pressures and threats, Attlee, however, was not swerved from his path. Under his direction British policy faced the harsh consequences at home and abroad of rearmament and a heightened "cold war."

Personal qualities go far to explain Attlee's authority with party and electorate. He is a shrewd politician and often a skilful "trimmer." But in certain essentials he has profound moral integrity. When, for instance, the Korean issue was being discussed by the cabinet during the summer of 1950, according to one irritated leftist, Attlee could see only "the moral issue"—"as if a little man had been hit by a big man and a British policeman had to step in." But also the institution of leader of the Labour party has played a part. Technically no such office exists. Under the constitution of the party Attlee is only "Leader of the Parliamentary Party." Yet in spite of the absense of the title and his formal subjection to re-election by the parliamentary party, Attlee is as truly leader of the whole party as the Conservative chief normally has been of his. This is not inevitable, but the tendency of the basic conditions of British politics works powerfully for such a result, particularly when a party is in power. If Labour is to govern, discipline is mandatory; and in the House elected in 1950, in which Labour enjoyed a majority of only six, the party, in spite of serious divisions, showed formidable loyalty. Even the Bevanites, while vigorously pressing their attack in the spring of 1951, did not dare run the risk to themselves of overturning the government. In great measure the loyalty enjoyed by Attlee has similar roots. If Labour is to govern, a principal instrument of its power is the office of prime minister. But that office, while dependent in some degree for its authority upon personalities and special political conditions, also bestows a large, hard core of power upon the man who is His (or Her) Majesty's first minister. The two parties, differing greatly in their social bases and formal organizations, have been molded into not dissimilar structures by the constitution in which they operate. Similarly, the same basic constitutional framework from which Conservative leadership originally emerged shaped leadership in the Labour party and the authority of Clement Attlee.

A remark attributed to Churchill is relevant. Early in the parliament of 1945, against an onslaught of the Conservative leader, Attlee counterattacked with vigor and effect. As Churchill was leaving the House, someone remarked to him that Attlee's powers were a surprise. "Feed a grub royal jelly," he replied, "—bound to make a Queen."

"I have said," wrote Bagehot, "that Cabinet government is possible in England, because England was a deferential country."[24] This statement still holds good, but not in the sense that Bagehot intended. The deference to a social class to which he referred, if it has not entirely vanished, has at least been greatly weakened. Yet a sentiment and attitude persist which it is not inaccurate to call by the same name but which are directed toward a different object, the political party. Supported by such sentiments and attitudes, the ordered structures of party politics in Britain have extended the scope of popular participation and yet maintained the conditions of policy-making. In this development of the British party system appears a familiar theme of British constitutional history: the democratizing of once aristocratic attitudes and structures.

For example, in the early nineteenth century, as we have observed, the mass of the voters did not feel that it was their role to nominate the gentlemen who "offered themselves" as candidates. Today, though their social origins are far more various, candidates still "offer themselves" in the sense that both voter and candidate act on the assumption that the function of the voter is to choose between candidates nominated by the parties, not to nominate them himself. In the process by which a candidate is nominated, the voter, if he is an active party member, may have some part, subject to the party structure, which gives great influence to local and central leadership. Against the official candidate so chosen, the independent

rarely has a serious chance of success at the polls and, indeed, in spite of the ease of nomination under British electoral laws, rarely attempts to fight "the system."[25]

Few features of British politics are more remarkable to an American than this absence of what one might call the Jacksonian attitude underlying the American primary, viz., that it is for the mass of the voters to nominate the candidates as well as choose between them. In this respect the manner and spirit of British democracy strongly contrast with the manner and spirit of American democracy. An attitude originally formed in an age of aristocracy has been handed on to an age of democracy and bureaucracy and fitted into the British version of popular government. Now, as then, this attitude helps protect the process of government from the disruptive impact of pressures. Today, however, while the thrust of will from below is diverted from expressing itself in local and sectional independence, it is no longer muffled by a governing class but channeled into the structures of party action, where it is expressed but also in some degree disciplined and rationalized.

The large sphere assigned to the upper levels of the party structure, however, does not mean that the lower levels are restricted to a merely passive role. To conceive of British parties simply as the elite on top and the mass following below is misreading the facts. For in these structures the more or less active rank and file and the intermediate as well as the higher levels of leadership all participate substantially in actual policy-making. Great Britain is vigorously democratic—after her own fashion.

24. *Ibid.*, p. 13.

25. Of the 1,867 candidates in the election of 1950, only 56 ran as independents.

TABLE 1

RESULTS OF GENERAL ELECTIONS, 1900–1955: NUMBER OF SEATS IN THE HOUSE OF COMMONS

Year	Labour	Ind. Labour	Communist	Ind. Lib.	Lib.	Lib. Nat.	Cons.	Coalition Labour	Irish Nat.	Sinn Fein	Others
1900....	2	....	....	....	184	....	402	....	82	....	....
1906....	30	....	....	....	397	....	132	....	83	....	....
1910 (Jan.).	40	....	....	....	275	....	273	....	82	....	....
1910 (Dec.).	42	....	....	....	270	....	273	....	84	....	1
1918....	60	....	....	34	....	137	374	15	7	73	7
1922....	142	....	1	59	....	59	347	1	2	1	3
1923....	191	....	....	....	158	....	258	....	....	....	8
1924....	152	....	1	....	42	....	415	....	....	....	6
1929....	288	....	....	....	59	....	260	....	....	....	8
1931....	46	6	....	....	72	....	475	13	....	....	3
1935....	154	4	1	21	....	33	390	8	....	....	4
1945....	394	4	2	12	....	13	202	....	....	....	13
1950....	315	....	....	9	....	2	296	....	....	....	3
1951....	295	....	....	6	....	1	320	....	....	....	3
1955....	277	....	....	6	....	2	343	....	....	....	2

TABLE 2

VOTING AT GENERAL ELECTIONS, 1900–1955*

Year	Electorate	Labour	Liberal	Lib. Nat. or Coalition	Conservative
1900.......	6.6	0.06	2.1	......	2.6
1906.......	7.3	0.3	2.7	......	2.6
1910 (Jan.)..	7.7	0.5	2.8	......	2.9
1910 (Dec.).	7.7	0.4	2.3	......	2.5
1918.......	21.4	2.2	1.4	1.4	4.2
1922.......	21.1	4.2	2.6	1.5	5.5
1923.......	21.3	4.3	4.2	......	5.4
1924.......	21.7	5.5	3.0	......	7.4
1929.......	28.9	8.4	5.3	......	8.7
1931.......	30.0	6.6	1.5	0.8	11.9
1935.......	31.4	8.5	1.4	0.9	10.5
1945.......	33.2	12.0	2.2	0.8	9.2
1950.......	34.4	13.3	2.6	0.04	12.5
1951.......	34.9	13.9	0.7	0.02	13.7
1955.......	34.8	12.4	0.7	0.04	13.3

* Votes in millions. Figures for electorate refer to registered electorate.

The Commonwealth Overseas: Variations on a British Theme

GWENDOLEN M. CARTER[1]
Smith College

I / INTRODUCTION

Rarely have transplanted institutions grown with such vigor and fidelity to the parent-stock as in the older overseas members of the Commonwealth of Nations—Canada, South Africa, Australia, and New Zealand.* The characteristic features of the parliamentary system—the fusion of legislative and executive powers, cabinet solidarity, the power of dissolution, the active role of the Opposition—are as evident at Ottawa, Cape Town, Canberra, and Wellington as at Westminster. Although each of these overseas countries necessarily has a written constitution (though New Zealand only a rudimentary one), their framers took the parliamentary system too much for granted to circumscribe its growth by definition. Thus flexibility in operation is the distinguishing feature of the system abroad, as at home, while continuity in tradition and acceptance of the spirit underlying the system provide its most significant safeguards.

1. Appreciation is expressed to the Rockefeller Foundation, the Social Science Research Council, the Canadian Institute of International Affairs, and the International Secretariat of the Institute of Pacific Relations for grants which enabled the author to study these party systems at first hand during an extended study tour of Commonwealth countries during 1948–49 and a year of field research in South Africa, 1952–53.

* Tables 1–4, indicating for these countries the seats won, the percentage of popular vote polled by each party, and the percentage of enrolled voters participating in general elections, can be found on pp. 103–5.

Under such circumstances it is not surprising to find here also the characteristic features of the British party system. Although like Great Britain itself these overseas countries from time to time have had three or even more political parties, each country has basically a two-party system. That is, there are usually two major parties, one of which can win an absolute majority of seats in Parliament and thus provide the responsible, effective leadership so requisite to the parliamentary system. In preparation for such opportunities, conservative parties in the Dominions, like that in Great Britain, have increasingly developed the closely knit organization which labor adopted early in response to its common purposes and its dependence on unity for success.

Not only history but also continuous contacts and a sense of common interests have kept the political traditions of these overseas countries in close touch with those of Great Britain. The stream of migration, the bonds of sentiment, the material advantages of close economic, financial, and defense arrangements, and constant interchanges of information made significant through intimate consultation at every level not only explain the maintenance of the Commonwealth association but also have their impact on internal political developments.

Important as are these links and similarities, the sharp contrasts that we find between Great Britain and these overseas members of the Commonwealth are no less significant for the understanding of their characteristics. Unlike Great Britain, with its long, continuous constitutional and social evolution, these four countries—Canada, Australia, New Zealand, and South Africa —developed within the last century from small, struggling frontier communities into unified, organized modern states. Of necessity, they were experimental, using the means at hand to develop new, often inhospitable lands. If in so doing they developed new forms of co-operative or state action, it was circumstance rather than concept which gave the spur.

Many of the people in these countries, however, differed in attitude from those at home. They faced hardships abroad because they wished to break away from set social patterns and lack of material opportunities. They were equalitarian in attitude, interpreting equality variously according to their particular circumstances: where conditions were good, they saw it as freedom to make what they could from the land and its resources, and where conditions were bad, they saw it as the right to demand protection and improved conditions through government aid.

At the same time, in all four of these overseas Commonwealth countries there has always been basically an acceptance of the democratic capitalism characteristic of the period in which they have developed. Equally strong has been a general suspicion of theoretical ideas (which contrasts with English attitudes and experience) and a mistrust of intellectuals, even though, paradoxically, their ideas have often been followed. Where apparently radical measures have been adopted in these countries, their purpose has been not to overthrow or even fundamentally change capitalism but to provide the palliatives necessary to insulate living standards against capitalism's vagaries or to use state resources for projects, like the building of railways, for which there were insufficient incentives to attract private capital.

It is now necessary, however, to differentiate among these overseas countries, whose particular characteristics strongly influence their party structures. The most obvious difference is that Canada and South Africa both include two different European races, while Australians and New Zealanders are overwhelmingly British in origin. Such a loose generalization neglects the fact that nearly 20 per cent of Australians are Irish Roman Catholics and ignores New Zealand's 6 per cent of Maoris, who elect their own representatives to Parliament. It is perhaps even more misleading to emphasize the similarities between Canada and South Africa, for there are good reasons in their histories and the distribution of their populations to explain why the party structure of Canada has only once, and briefly, under the stress of the conscription issue in World War I, divided between the English-speaking and the French-speaking peoples, whereas in South Africa the characteristic demarcation is between the alliance of moderate Afrikaners and English-speaking inhabitants and the "pure" nationalistic Afrikaners. Biracialism nevertheless complicates many of the issues of South African and Canadian politics, a problem which Australia and New Zealand do not have.

More than racial composition, however, lies behind the most striking difference between the Pacific Dominions and the others—namely, the early rise of labor to political self-consciousness in Australia and New Zealand and its later emergence and less important political influence in Canada and South Africa. Confronted by a non-European population which outnumbers five to one those of European origin and supplies the basic labor force in all fields, the white trade-unions in South Africa have been too self-centered in their interests to develop a powerful labor movement. Canada's scattered communities, the ethnic division between French, English, and European Canadians, the agrarian structure of the country, the influence of the United States, and characteristically American stereotypes about the limitless range of economic opportunities slowed the growth of an organized Canadian labor movement and its entrance into politics until the depression of the 1930's. In contrast were the early preoccupation of Australians and New Zealanders with economic conditions and the geographical concentrations of their working-class groups—in Australia because the land could not support the small farmer and in New Zealand because the Wakefield land-settlement system sought deliberately to provide a large labor force for the relatively few landowners. Out of the spirit of "mateship" among Australian workers in the mines and the shearing sheds (often the same men in both), the long depression in the 1870's and 1880's in New Zealand, and the disastrous industrial conflicts in 1890–91 in both countries, Australian and New Zealand labor turned to political action in the latter decade and never withdrew.

Other significant causes of difference are not hard to find. Canada's proximity to a large and dynamic country of similar culture contrasts sharply with the isolation of the other three. Canadian and Australian federalism makes a political division of authority which is reflected in their party structures. New Zealand remains largely dependent for exports on primary products, while Canada, Australia, and even South Africa are developing heavy industries, which in varying degrees make them exporters of manufactured goods as well as of primary products.

It is perhaps too soon to say that these four countries have developed distinctive cultures reflecting separate self-consciousness and individualities. Moreover, they are more unified in opposition to outside pressures than in response to domestic issues. This is because they are still in the process of growth.

Yet at the same time the peoples of these countries have some of the qualities of maturity. They have chosen to work their way to independence within the Commonwealth, rather than take the more orthodox and simple, though less rewarding, road to separation; they have wrestled with the problems of opening huge countries and exploiting vast resources with relatively small numbers; they have depended almost invariably on constitutional means to solve their internal disputes. Broadly speaking, their evolution has reflected the practical, immediate purposes of growing communities which are basically conservative in attitude and traditional in approach, yet responsive to the needs of their people.

Political parties have been the instruments through which these communities have pursued their purposes. Thus the history and analysis of their parties provide the best understanding of their growth and present circumstances. At the same time, the very fact that issues have been sifted through the mesh of party politics has had its effect upon these issues—ameliorating them in some cases, intensifying them in others—and on the communities themselves. Thus the study of parties in these four countries, which so nearly meet the ideal criteria for constitutional democracies—almost universal literacy, widespread economic prosperity, a balance between industry and agriculture, social mobility,[2] and relative immunity from external pressures—throws light

2. None of these criteria holds true, of course, for South Africa's non-European population, but they are valid for the European minority, which has the monopoly of political power.

also on the character and effect of political parties themselves.

II / CANADA

Canada, the first in settlement, is naturally the oldest in parliamentary experience among the overseas members of the Commonwealth. The principle of responsible government—that the executive is responsible to the local legislature—was first enunciated there in 1838 and applied in 1848; it has made possible the achievement of independence within the Commonwealth. Here, too, in 1867, the first great experiment in nation-making in the British Empire brought into existence the Dominion of Canada, with a federal constitution drafted by Canadians themselves. In a short time this new country stretched from the Atlantic to the Pacific, occupying in the northern half of North America an area larger, though far less richly endowed, than that possessed by the United States.

Nowhere else in the Commonwealth overseas were the forms of British institutions so faithfully copied as in Canada. Even the names of its major parties—Conservative and Liberal—are patterned on those of Great Britain. Yet to mistake the form for the fact is to misunderstand the character of Canadian political life. Its temper, like its setting, is American. More favorably situated geographically than Australia, New Zealand, or South Africa, closer to centers of world trade, with a variety of resources—agricultural, mineral, industrial—and a moving frontier, Canada has experienced the social mobility, optimism, and economic advance which reduce class stratification and work against class alignments in politics. Thus Canadian institutions have been affected by an attitude of equalitarianism only less marked than that in the United States, and the major Canadian political parties bear far more resemblance to those of the United States than to those of Great Britain: that is, they are great holding companies, incorporating conflicting interests and maintaining their cohesion through the struggle for political power rather than through principle or class interest. Only the minority Cooperative Commonwealth Federation (C.C.F.) party, which came to birth in the 1930's with the depression as its midwife, resembles the labor parties so influential in Great Britain, Australia, and New Zealand.

The task of bridging the divisions in Canadian life which the major Canadian parties have consciously assumed is still more difficult than the similar task performed by American political parties. Although the nearly eight million persons of Anglo-Saxon descent and Protestant faith, concentrated in Ontario, the Maritime Provinces, and British Columbia, have put their stamp on much of Canadian life, including that of the three million European Canadians, the fierce opposition to assimilation of over five million Catholic French-speaking Canadians centered in Quebec makes impossible any Canadian parallel to the American "melting pot." Moreover, the great majority of Canadians live perforce in the more temperate areas of their country, within a hundred and fifty miles of the American border. This long ribbon of population stretching more than three thousand miles between the two oceans is sliced by rocky wastes or mountains into four great regions: the Maritimes and Newfoundland, with their own regional outlook shaped by history and strategic position; the rich agricultural and industrial St. Lawrence Valley of Quebec and Ontario; the wheat-growing Prairies; and British Columbia, separated from the rest of Canada by the Rocky Mountains. Because of the division in language and race between Ontario and Quebec, it is necessary for a truly national political party in Canada to win substantial representation in all five major areas or at least in the three most important—Quebec, Ontario, and the Prairies.

One further fact: Canada's continent-wide frontier with a dynamic world power helps shape its national life. With more people, trade, literature, and radio programs crossing the American-Canadian frontier than any other in the world, Canada is inevitably "Americanized" in outlook. Yet the very effort to maintain a distinctive national life despite these pressures helps to strengthen Canada's ties to the Commonwealth and to emphasize those qualities in its society which differ from those of the United States. Thus it has long been easier to distinguish a Canadian nationalism which is directed against undue external influences, British or American, than one which springs spontaneously from a sense of inner Canadian unity.

The Golden Age of the Two-Party System

In the face of the obvious divisive factors within Canada, it is not surprising that its earliest political parties were loose coalitions of sectional groups based on race, geography, and, to some extent, class. What is remarkable is that these sectional groups were shaped into two great national political parties in the quarter-century following confederation in 1867. This was due partly to skilful compromises, partly to a shrewd use of political patronage, but largely to the consummate skill of two great Canadian politicians—Sir John A. Macdonald, who created the Liberal-Conservative party, which dominated Canadian politics for forty years, and Sir Wilfred Laurier, who weaned Quebec away from its allegiance to the Conservatives at the end of the century and forged the modern Liberal party, which has been in power in Canada throughout most of this century.

Macdonald's aim was to build Canada into a united whole, capable of existing side by side with the vigorous, expanding United States. Dedicating the Liberal-Conservative party to a Hamiltonian federalism, he sponsored the Canadian Pacific Railway to link all parts of the country and he favored the exploitation of Canada's natural resources, immigration to fill its empty spaces, and protective tariffs to encourage commercial and industrial interests. Nation-building, protection, and, in addition, imperial patriotism became standard parts of Conservative platforms, although, with the possible exception of protection, the Conservatives, like their political opponents, have been largely opportunistic in their approach to issues.

While the Liberal-Conservative party took shape as early as 1854 and governed the new Canadian federation from 1867 to 1873 and again from 1878 to 1896, the opposition party developed more slowly. Its original nucleus—the "Clear Grits" of Ontario and the "Rouges" of Quebec—stood for local autonomy in contrast to Macdonald's centralizing drive. When in power, the Liberals have maintained a distinctive emphasis on provincial autonomy, freer trade, and national autonomy. But by the time Sir Wilfred Laurier brought the Liberals undisputedly into office in 1896, the party had curbed its earlier distrust of economic interests and learned the importance of associating government with big business, notably the C.P.R.'s competitors, the Grand Trunk Railway (subsequently absorbed in the Canadian National Railway) and the Bank of Commerce. Thereafter the contest between the Conservatives and the Liberals was not over what attitude should be adopted toward business and commercial interests but for the support of such interests. Moreover, in external trade Laurier took the edge off the insistence of the Liberals on Canada's autonomy in imperial relations by producing the brilliant compromise of imperial preference, under which special rates, lower than those accorded under most-favored-nation agreements, were granted to British importers.

The year 1896 marks the most significant watershed in Canadian politics: the winning of French Canada from its support of the Conservatives to a new and, as it proved, permanent allegiance to the Liberal party. Laurier, originally a member of the anticlerical "Rouge" group, smothered its radicalism, made peace with the Roman Catholic church, and captured the allegiance of French Canada through the appeal of sentiment, personality, matchless oratory, and an unimpeachable liberalism of the English rather than the Continental variety. Thereafter, only local nationalism and on one occasion depression have been able to shake the Liberal hold upon Quebec, whose quarter of the seats in the House of Commons is a powerful factor in any political contest.

The Liberals developed steadily the alliance between Quebec and Prairie Liberalism which has proved an invincible combination in Canadian politics. But the groups on which it chiefly depended were those most susceptible to the claims of sectional interest. The first challenge to Liberal unity came from the Quebec nationalist movement under Henri Bourassa, a fiery, eloquent dissident who opposed Laurier's dispatch of Canadian forces to fight in the South African war and subsequently sought to extend Quebec's special educational and religious privileges to French Canadian minorities in other provinces. Western sectionalism focused in farmers' movements seeking lower tariffs in an effort to free the newly developed Prairie Provinces from the domination of eastern interests.

The Liberals' answer to western demands was the Reciprocity Agreement of 1911, under which Canadian primary producers would be permitted to sell their products duty-free in the American market. Unexpected opposition to reciprocity from established Canadian interests fearful of unrestricted American competition joined paradoxically with a Quebec nationalist revolt against Laurier's Naval Bill of 1910, to push the Liberals out of office in 1911. Few events better illustrate the difficulties of balancing the conflicting attitudes and interests of Canada's diverse groups. On the one hand, it highlighted the divergent interests of established business in the east and prairie farmers in the west; on the other hand, it pointed out the contrast between the spirit of national pride, which was an element in the defeat of the Reciprocity Agreement, and Bourassa's opposition to the Naval Bill for fear the building of a Canadian navy might embroil Canada in Britain's wars.

The Test of War and the Rise of a Third Party

World War I provided a still more acid test of Canada's thinly knit unity. Originally, Canada's participation received the wholehearted support of every section in the population, including that of the Quebec nationalists. But within a year, a dispute over the use of French as a language of instruction in Ontario schools touched Quebec nationalism in its most sensitive spot, roused animosity against English-speaking Canada, and undercut earlier enthusiasm for the war effort. When Sir Robert Borden, the Conservative prime minister, decided to introduce conscription for overseas service in the crucial period of 1917, he met irreconcilable Quebec opposition. The Liberal party split:

those from the west and Ontario accepted the verdict of the majority and voted almost unanimously for conscription; the conservative French Canadian Liberals, insisting that their people had a contractually protected position dating back to the Quebec Act of 1774 and having a more limited sense of civic obligation, voted against the measure.

The general election of 1917 followed the same line of division. For the first and only time in Canada's history, politics split on racial lines, with an English-speaking Union government facing a predominantly French-speaking Opposition. Increased racial tension climaxed in riots and bloodshed in Quebec city during the Easter week end of 1918. But under the restraining influence of the Roman Catholic church, French Canada's innate sense of law and order reasserted itself. Moreover, it was apparent that its sense of separate "nationality" was passive rather than active. No less important, the rest of Canada learned the wisdom of letting Quebec go its own way rather than try to coerce it. The glorious, though costly, Canadian contribution to the last hundred days of the war, in which the French Canadian battalion played a brilliant role, climaxed Canada's distinguished military record and paved the way for reuniting the country's major elements. The potential threat to Canadian unity remained; but the very closeness of an open break in the spring of 1918 shocked both English- and French-speaking Canada into a determination to avoid in the future so dangerous a situation.

Abroad, Canada's nationhood was abundantly demonstrated. Its share in the strategy of the war and peace through organs like the Imperial War Cabinet was followed by separate membership in the League of Nations and the International Labour Organization. In addition, the Conservatives favored a close working-together with Great Britain to give Canada the chance to influence the foreign policies by which it would inevitably be affected. The Liberals put more weight on autonomy than on collaboration. Yet there is much sense in Henri Bourassa's quip in the 1920's that the Conservatives were "in favor of the unity of the Empire and the autonomy of Canada," while the Liberals supported "the autonomy of Canada and the unity of the Empire." The proof was to come in 1939, when the Liberals brought a united Canada into World War II.

Though the Liberals and Conservatives have remained the two most important parties in Canada, their golden age of undisputed prominence ended with World War I. As Conservative opposition to reciprocity had undercut that party's influence in the Prairie Provinces, so Liberal opposition to conscription weakened its hold in that area. In the general election of 1921, a reconstituted Liberal party under a new English Canadian leader, William Lyon Mackenzie King, and based mainly in Quebec and the Maritimes, defeated the Conservatives, who suffered to the full the unpopularity of a coalition and wartime government and won seats only in their industrial and traditionally Tory Ontario strongholds and in Vancouver Island. Startlingly, a third party, the Progressives, emerged out of radical agrarian discontent to carry the Prairies and twenty-four seats in Ontario and temporarily to outnumber the Conservatives in the House by fifteen members.

The threat of the Progressives to the older parties was, however, less dangerous than it seemed. The party lacked organization; in practice, it never unified its traditionally minded Manitoba members, who still hoped for a free world market, and the radically tempered Albertans, who envisaged a managed society in which all classes would receive economic justice through state-directed co-operation. The force of progressivism was spent by 1926, leaving its legacy chiefly in the political temper of the west, out of which sprang the socialist CCF in the depression period, and in the provincial organizations of Manitoba and Alberta, destined in their diverse developments to become associated, respectively, with the Conservative and the Social Credit parties.

Before their demise, however, the Progressives temporarily held the balance of power between almost evenly matched Liberal and Conservative parties following the 1925 elections. Withdrawing their support from the Liberals over a vote on irregularities in the Customs Department, they temporarily put the Conservatives into office, only to desert them within a short time. The governor-general then granted the Conservative leader, Arthur Meighen, the dissolution refused earlier to the Liberals.

The Liberals Regain Their National Position

With consummate shrewdness, Mackenzie King campaigned on the issue of whether or not the governor-general should have refused him a dissolution. National pride reacted against this apparent (though constitutionally justified) intervention in Canadian politics by an English representative. King had found a unifying formula of Canadian political nationalism, magic in its appeal alike to conservative Quebec, the radical Prairies, and the independent reformers of Ontario and the Maritimes. When he swept back into power, the schism of 1917 had been largely healed, and the Liberal party had a majority drawn from every province and based firmly once more on Quebec and Saskatchewan.

Within the British Commonwealth, Canadian, Irish, and South African nationalism combined at this time to demand definition of the imperial relationship. In the Balfour *Report,* drafted at the imperial conference of 1926, the independence of the individual members of the Commonwealth was given classic expression. "Great Britain and the Dominions are autonomous communities within the British Empire," read the *Report,* "equal in status, in no way subordinate one to another in any aspect of their domestic or external relations, though united by a common allegiance to the Crown and freely associated as members of the British Commonwealth of Nations." Full legislative independence came with the Statute of Westminster in 1931 (by which time the Conservatives were in power in Canada), which opened the way for each Dominion to acquire full powers of sovereignty in internal and external affairs. The year of the Balfour *Report* (1926) also saw the establishment of a separate Canadian legation in Washington (since raised to the status of an embassy), the first step toward Canada's world-wide diplomatic service and the necessary corollary to its assertion of separate national status.

The election of 1926 marked an apparent return to the traditional Canadian two-party system, both parties once again national and composite in character. When the depression came, the economic nationalism of the Conservatives had more appeal than the political nationalism of the Liberals. Even Quebec broke its solid front and returned twenty-four Conservatives among its sixty-five members, the highest proportion since 1911 or, before that, 1891. Ontario and Manitoba went overwhelmingly protectionist. In response, the new Conservative leader, R. B. Bennett, an eloquent and dominating figure, embarked on a vigorous program of securing markets through tariff bargains, culminating in the Ottawa Agreements of 1932, which made the largely unsuccessful attempt to turn the British Commonwealth into an economic unit. Bennett also attempted to introduce a

"New Deal" program of social welfare under federal powers, which he vainly hoped might be acquired through adopting International Labour Organization conventions. In a similar, last-hour effort, the government threw its weight behind rapid, effective enforcement of League of Nations sanctions in the Italo-Ethiopian campaign. But even without this, the Conservatives' temporary popularity in Quebec had come to an end. The Liberals began their long period of office in 1935 with a virtually solid French Canadian bloc once more intact, which they have maintained in the federal sphere through the four succeeding elections—1940, 1945, 1949, and 1953.

The most serious problems faced by the Liberal government between 1935 and 1939 were those of foreign policy, and its greatest danger was that of an internal split within its stronghold of Quebec, which was strongly isolationist. Thus the Liberals opposed further league sanctions against Italy, notably oil sanctions, and subsequently enacted neutrality legislation in connection with the Spanish Civil War.

It was impossible, however, to disregard the threat offered by Nazi Germany, and in 1937 King personally told Hitler that if the latter should precipitate war, Canada would support Great Britain. In the spring of 1939, after the fall of Czechoslovakia, Ernest Lapointe, King's chief lieutenant, warned French Canada that if Britain was attacked, English-speaking Canadians would insist on entering the war. The visit of the king and queen roused French Canadian enthusiasm, while the Soviet-German pact in August, 1939, brought their hatred of materialistic communism into play. The deciding factor in the French Canadian attitude to the war, however, was the pledge of Prime Minister King and the Quebec members of the federal cabinet that there would be no conscription for overseas service. On Sep-

tember 10, after extensive debate in Parliament, ending with a virtually unanimous vote, Canada by its own action entered World War II, in which it made a spectacular contribution, little less in some fields than that of the three great powers.

The Strains of World War II

Almost at once, however, the war policy of the Liberal government was challenged in Quebec by Maurice Duplessis's Union Nationale. Duplessis had once been leader of the Quebec Conservatives; in 1936 he had defeated the provincial Liberal party on the twofold platform of French Canadian nationalism and social reform. Once in office, Duplessis turned sharply to the right, supporting big business, particularly the power interests, and curbing labor unions. Growing labor opposition in Quebec led him to appeal to French Canadian nationalism by challenging the federal government's War Measures Act as a violation of provincial autonomy. In the face of this open threat to federal authority and the war effort, Liberal cabinet ministers from Quebec, notably Lapointe, gave unprecedented help to secure a victory for the local Liberal party (under Adelard Godbout), which reflected Quebec's unwillingness to be isolated from the rest of Canada.

In the spring of 1942, when the ever widening war had created the same pressures as in 1917, King instituted a nation-wide plebiscite asking release from the "no conscription" pledge to which Quebec voted "No" as resoundingly as the other provinces voted "Yes." Moving cautiously, the Liberal government secured power to institute conscription by order-in-council if and when it should find this imperative. Despite pressure from English-speaking Canada and from his own minister of war, Ralston, who was peremptorily replaced, King doggedly refused to institute conscription for overseas service until the second front was opened in 1944. Temporarily it looked as if Quebec might then withdraw its support from the Liberal government, but the federal party remained intact and won a substantial vote of confidence in the 1945 elections, reaffirmed still more strikingly in 1949.

In Quebec, however, the feeling that King had broken his pledge against conscription became fuel to the nationalist movement from 1942 on. Despite the efforts of the local Liberals and a new and extreme antiwar party, the Bloc Populaire Canadien, which sought the support of organized labor through its program of economic and social reform, the Union Nationale swept triumphantly back into power in 1944 on the issues of conscription and provincial autonomy, built a powerful party organization, and overwhelmingly maintained its control of Quebec in the provincial elections of 1948 and 1952.

Although the Union Nationale has made no open attempt to enter federal politics, its antagonism to the Liberals, coupled with its economic policies, opened the way for a tacit alliance with the Conservatives reminiscent of the one between Borden and Bourassa in 1911. Forged originally between George Drew, then Conservative premier of Ontario, and Duplessis, on the basis of a common opposition to the extension of federal authority under war emergency powers, this alignment seemed to offer hope of national success when Drew was chosen national Conservative leader in 1948. This perennial hope had no better results, however, than those achieved under John Bracken, former premier of Manitoba, whose election in 1942 as leader of the Progressive Conservatives (the addition of the word "Progressive" was in response to his wishes) carried the expectation of bringing the west back into the fold. Although the Conservative party has

consistently remained the official Opposition and polls about 30 per cent of the national vote, it has not yet regained its earlier position of a national party capable of securing substantial representation in all major sections of the country.

New Third Parties

The relative weakness of the Conservative party after 1935 turned attention on two third parties which entered the federal field in the 1930's: the Co-operative Commonwealth Federation (CCF) and the Social Credit party. Both arose out of the depression and were successors to, rather than descendants of, the Progressives. They built on the tradition of progressivism but found their drive in the radicalism of despair, as Bennett's tariff and currency depreciation measures intensified the effects of the depression in the Prairies.

The first of these parties to take form —the CCF, founded in 1932—has attempted with varying success to unite agrarian interests and urban labor, a task which the Progressives had hardly tried to perform. Its program, outlined in the Regina Manifesto (1933), is similar to that of the British Labour party in emphasizing economic planning, nationalization of monopolistic industries, social security, and a comprehensive labor code, all to be achieved by constitutional means. The CCF does not indorse nationalization of land, however, but, because of its agrarian base, supports the family farm as the basic unit of production.

Under its first leader, J. S. Woodsworth, a veteran parliamentarian of saintly character, indomitable will, and great ability, the federal CCF tended to turn away from its agrarian base and to come increasingly under the influence of urban labor and socialist intellectuals. Although Woodsworth, a convinced pacifist, opposed participation in World War II, the majority of the party stood firm behind M. J. Coldwell, a man of great integrity, social idealism, and subsequently Woodsworth's successor, who supported the declaration of war but opposed sending Canadian troops overseas. As Canadian trade-union membership doubled between 1939 and 1943 under the vigorous leadership of the Canadian Congress of Labor (founded in 1940 as an extension of the CIO), which by 1948 accepted the CCF as its political party, the latter made impressive gains, polling over 15 per cent of the votes in the 1945 election. Moreover, the CCF had become the official opposition in every provincial legislature west of the Ottawa River except Saskatchewan, where it was in power.

From this high-water mark, however, the CCF steadily receded in strength. Only in the predominantly agricultural province of Saskatchewan, whose tempered radicalism had been forged in nine years of drought and depression in the 1930's, has the CCF maintained its political position. Moreover, it has governed this province since 1944 less as a socialist party than as a true descendant of the liberal agrarian protest movements of the twenties, stressing social services (notably education and socialized medicine), security of landholding, and stable wheat prices. Thus the CCF is far from having achieved the position among the Canadian working classes that the British, Australian, and New Zealand Labor parties established long ago.

Both the relatively late rise in Canada of a political party representing organized labor and its failure to become a dominant political influence stem from the slow development of class consciousness in Canada and the weakness of its trade-union movement. The expanding Canadian frontier, far more hospitable to the small farmer than that in Australia, stopped the rise of an agricultural proletariat in Canada comparable to that on the huge Australian sheep runs. Heavy immigration of non-British groups prior to 1914 brought elements unfamiliar with trade-union organization. Social mobility in the period of nation-building limited class stratification. Moreover, the Canadian population is scattered far more widely than the Australian, where the concentration of nearly half the population in two major and not distant cities—Sydney and Melbourne—gives a cohesion to organized labor unmatched in Canadian cities. In addition, the attraction of American unionism has constantly embroiled Canadian English-speaking unions in jurisdictional disputes between national and international unions and has reproduced in Canada the split between craft and industrial unionism. Even more serious for the strength of unionism in Canada is the division between English- and French-speaking unions, the latter, under clerical influence, customarily maintaining isolation from those in other parts of the country.

Another problem for the growth of a Canadian labor party dedicated to constitutional principles is that a revolutionary Communist party was organized still earlier. This took form after World War I out of small Marxist groups of European immigrants, but it soon acquired English Canadian members and leaders and became intrenched in the larger industrial and mining centers. In 1931 the party was declared illegal, and its principal leaders were imprisoned for more than two years. Subsequently, the Communists organized again as the Labor Progressive party, a small but potent group. Throughout its history, therefore, the CCF has had to fight against both the "fellow-travelers" in its own ranks and the Labor Progressives' efforts to join it in a common front.

Not only has the CCF found it difficult to keep the public aware of its fundamental difference from the Communists; it has found its appeal to collectivism undercut by the readiness of the older parties to establish public ownership where the situation seemed to demand it. As the Liberals have introduced a program of social security since 1942, there have been few distinctive issues for the CCF to campaign on except national health insurance. Thus, while Canada maintains its current prosperity, it seems unlikely that the CCF can noticeably increase its political strength.

In marked contrast to the CCF stands the second of the minor parties—the Social Credit party—which has held Alberta since 1935 and which won British Columbia in an unexpected electoral victory in 1952. Out of the drought, depression, and debt of the early 1930's developed an irresistible mass movement led by the evangelistic William Aberhart and devoted to the thesis that the economic system can be reformed through providing the people with credit based on the potential goods and services of society. To do this, the state should control the monetary system and establish fair prices for all goods.

Under pressure from within the movement, Aberhart introduced social credit legislation in 1937 and, later, mortgage and debt legislation. The program perished, however, through the federal power of disallowance and rulings by the courts that parts of the bills were *ultra vires*. With the outbreak of war, Aberhart gave a tacit agreement not to introduce further social credit legislation; at the same time, the small federal Social Credit party strongly supported the war effort.

Within Alberta, those who desired more basic changes than were yet instituted began to desert to the CCF, which emerged as the major challenge to the Social Credit party's hold on power. In response, at first tentatively under Aberhart and more decisively under Ernest C. Manning, who became leader on Aberhart's death in 1943, the Social Credit party turned sharply to the right. It became the vigorous opponent of socialism and the defender of individualism, while capitalism was declared to be the ideal form of economic organization if only its monetary system were changed.

Thereafter, both within Alberta and in the House of Commons, where it is now called the "New Democracy," the Social Credit party became a highly conservative and at times reactionary party, with little else to distinguish it except its sectionalism. When it scored its success in British Columbia in 1952, it was noticeable that its leader and many of its supporters were former Conservatives. Thus in the far west, free-enterprise orthodoxy and Social Credit emotionalism have combined to bring political success to a *de facto* conservatism. There now seems more chance that the parties of the right— the Progressive Conservatives and Social Credit—may together provide an effective opposition to the Liberal party than that a challenge to its position will come from the CCF on the left.

Liberal Strengths and Leadership

At the same time, only the federal Liberal party has proved capable since 1935 of commanding substantial support in every major region of Canada. In part this support, particularly in the election of 1953, has been in response to the national leadership and personal charm of Prime Minister Louis St. Laurent, who succeeded Mackenzie King in 1948. The national position of the Liberals rests still more, however, on what may be called a national policy in the grand style of earlier days: development of natural resources, relatively successful efforts to control inflation and at the same time to promote Canadian trade, and a substantial program of social security. Hardly less important is the appeal of what might be considered the constructively negative aspects of the Liberal program. In its lack of clear-cut ideology, class basis, sectionalism, or dominant economic interest, the Liberal party is the one which divides Canadians least. In a country whose inner unity is not yet knit, this virtue outweighs whatever faults of inconsistency it may embody. Moreover, now that the Soviet Union is the potential enemy, Catholic French Canada no longer opposes an active international policy. Even if war should come, Canada would fight more unitedly than ever before.

For more than a quarter of a century Mackenzie King was the leader of the Liberal party and for most of that period prime minister of Canada. A man of natural warmth, great sensitivity, and quick temper, he early schooled himself to caution and control. His political philosophy was in a sense negative: that it is better to avoid crises than to press issues or principles. But it was combined with an awareness of currents of opinion in the major areas of Canada that made them feel he understood their needs and problems. In practice, he defeated his critics from within the party and his opponents outside; he won back the Progressives into the Liberal fold, prevented the CCF from becoming a major party in Canada by taking over much of its social welfare policy (which, incidentally, fitted his own humanitarianism), and kept the Conservatives from regaining their power by securing their support against the challenge of the CCF. In the process Canada remained united and developed along the lines which he foreshadowed. So, too, did the modern Commonwealth and Canada's partnership with the United States.

What were the secrets of Mackenzie King's political leadership? Not orthodox ones. He was no brilliant orator like Laurier or a masterful figure like Macdonald, nor was he a distinguished parliamentarian. His gifts lay outside the immediate political arena, in his sense of timing, his endless patience in seeking compromise, his ruthlessness (as with Ralston), his ability to attract talent to politics and administration and to infuse a sense of teamwork.

King worked on two fundamental assumptions in domestic affairs: that French-speaking Canadians form a special group within Canada whose consent and co-operation were necessary for every major policy, and that this was true only to a lesser degree of every important area of Canada. In a sense, this was bringing federalism into the party system. It meant keeping the Liberal party an association of representative groups rather than turning it into a highly centralized structure. This suited King's rather devious approach. Its phenomenal success suggests that it also suited Canada.

Party Organization

THE LIBERAL AND PROGRESSIVE CONSERVATIVE PARTIES.—Both these parties have long been characterized by loose organization and an insistence on the autonomy of local units. But the Progressive Conservatives are normally so dormant between elections that party organization performs the functions of selecting candidates and getting out the vote rather than exercising any continuing influence on party policies and strategy.

The units of organization are the poll, the riding or constituency, the province, and the nation. In Ontario and a few of the large cities in other provinces, regional or district associations form an intermediate grouping between the constituency and the province. Young people and women are also organized separately along similar lines.

In this hierarchy it is anticipated that the poll organization will maintain immediate contact with the voters, the constituency organization select the candidates (usually done through a convention composed of delegates from the polling subdivisions), the provincial association provide the leadership, and the national organization form a superstructure frankly dependent on the provincial organizations. Except that constituency organizations are always jealous of their prerogative of selecting candidates and resent interference or even suggestions from the provincial organizations, local conditions determine the effectiveness of particular units.

At the provincial level, the Liberal and Progressive Conservative parties each has an association whose voting members include delegates from each constituency, members of the provincial and national parliamentary parties, and also candidates defeated at the previous election. In practice, the association has relatively little influence, however, as the actual control of party affairs is in the hands of the Executive Committee of fifteen to twenty members and a representative Management Committee of about fifty members. The Liberal association in Ontario, a politically active province, did not even meet for a period of eleven years, because the Executive Committee was unwilling to face hostile criticism from the rank and file.

At the national level the major task is to maintain co-ordination between the various provincial organizations and liaison between the parliamentary group and the rank and file throughout the country. The national Liberal Federation, like the comparable Conservative organization, has the same type of membership as the provincial organizations, the representatives in the national group coming from the provinces instead of from the constituencies.

Being dependent on the provincial organizations for work in the field, the Federation can do little more than test opinion, offer a forum for grievances,

and distribute information. It has no formal authority over the parliamentary members, but the latter often heed its information and moral pressure—the national Liberal Federation being responsible, for example, for the introduction of family allowances into the Liberal program.

By and large, however, there is only one time when the rank and file of the Liberal or Conservative party are associated actively with the formulation of policy at a high level, and that is in the party convention called to select a new platform, organization, or, more commonly, a new leader in the provincial or national sphere. This adoption of an American device in place of the British practice of having the parliamentary members choose their own leaders arose out of the need to awaken widespread popular enthusiasm, and it has now become standard practice in both parties. The party convention was first used by the Liberals in 1893 to re-establish unity in the party, again in 1919 when Mackenzie King was chosen Laurier's successor, and in 1948 to select St. Laurent when King retired after being prime minister longer than any other person in British history.

In all these cases the convention awakened fresh enthusiasm and was soon followed by national success. The Liberals' experience persuaded the Conservatives to adopt the practice in 1927, when R. B. Bennett was chosen national leader in a party convention. The subsequent success of the Conservative party in 1930 seemed proof of the magic of the device. But the party's experiences in 1938, 1942, and 1948, when Manion, Bracken, and Drew, respectively, were chosen national leaders at party conventions, only to face sweeping electoral defeats, have done much to destroy this illusion. In fact, there is now relatively little enthusiasm in either party for this method of selecting a leader, although by this time it is too well established as a democratic and representative institution to be challenged with impunity.

The composition of party conventions gives an important role to the official element, made up of members of provincial and federal legislatures, but also includes delegates-at-large chosen by the provincial and special (e.g., youth) associations and delegates from each federal constituency. Any party association may send in resolutions as a basis for the platform, but the latter, in practice, is the creation of the Resolutions Committee, a widely representative body, and its adoption is rather perfunctory, the more so because the parliamentary members of a party rarely consider themselves bound by its vague generalizations. The focus of interest in the convention is the selection of a leader, and this proceeds in a rather more sober atmosphere than is common in similar sessions in the United States. Voting is by secret ballot, and the successful candidate must receive a majority of the votes. Generally his election is then made unanimous. The delegates return home fired, it is hoped, with enthusiasm for the party's cause, and their role as determinants of party policy is suspended until it becomes necessary once more to seek a new leader.

Part of the reason why the ordinary members of the Liberal or Progressive Conservative parties exercise, at best, only an occasional direct influence is because the fees (twenty-five cents to a dollar annually) of the small proportion who are enrolled members total only a very minor part of the funds on which the party depends for its paid workers and elaborate pre-election propaganda. Large contributions from business and industrial interests have always been common. Frequently, these are given to both parties, sometimes in the proportion of 60 to 40 to the party

in power and the Opposition, respectively; occasionally, as with some breweries, in equal shares. Scandals are not unknown, but heavy giving to one party or the other is rarely to secure particular privileges but rather to induce a generally favorable attitude.

Both the provincial and the national parliamentary leaders of the Liberal and Progressive Conservative parties play the dominant role in determining party policies in their particular spheres. When the party is in office, the prime minister chooses his cabinet ministers and can even virtually ignore the wishes of the caucus (the parliamentary members of his party). King at times also backed his own judgment on policy against that of the caucus, and his extraordinary ability to sense trends of thought made his followers reluctant to stand against him, for example, on determining the date of an election. In practice, the leader of the Conservative party, whether in or out of office, has proved even more ready to enunciate a personal policy. Thus, despite the obvious looseness of organization, there is an effective centralization of power in both parties, restrained only by the leader's need to retain unity and support.

This fact is as true in the provincial sphere as in the federal, however, and has resulted sometimes in bitter rivalry between the leaders of the provincial and federal branches of the same party. The most notable example of this was the antagonism between Mitchell Hepburn, Liberal premier of Ontario, and Mackenzie King; but there was also a good deal of feeling between George Drew, Progressive Conservative premier of Ontario, and Bracken, when the latter was national Progressive Conservative leader. In fact, it has become almost axiomatic that when the same party is in power in one of the major provinces as well as in the nation, the provincial administration attempts to prove its independence by emphasizing different aspects of the program from those stressed in Ottawa. The importance of this for survival was demonstrated when Adelard Godbout's admirable administration of Quebec Province in the early years of the war was attacked chiefly on the grounds that it was subservient to the federal Liberal party. Thus does Canadian federalism exhibit one of its most paradoxical features.

THE CCF.—In its early days the CCF successfully tackled the perennial problem of political parties—how to insure interest and a continuous supply of enthusiastic volunteer workers—by making its basic unit the club, whose members pay an annual fee of $3.00, carry on study as well as social activities, and disseminate political propaganda. Enthusiasm in the clubs has now diminished noticeably, however, in the east. The remarkable degree of mass participation in Saskatchewan is built now, as earlier, on the ready-made base of participation in co-operatives and other self-help groups.

Constituency, provincial, and youth organizations differ little in form but considerably in spirit from those of the older parties. In particular, greater emphasis is laid on research and dissemination of information. The provincial council, a representative body of about fifty members which meets five times a year, and the provincial executive committee of thirteen members are responsible to the provincial convention which meets once a year. In one respect—its power to suspend or expel an individual, group, or organization which violates the principles of the CCF—the provincial council has authority not possessed in the older parties which have not had to face the same threat of Communist infiltration. But the general authority of the provincial convention is evidenced by its annual election of the leader and close supervision of the administration of party affairs.

Approximately the same arrangements exist in the federal sphere. The national convention is held every two years, elects or re-elects the national leader of the party and the national executive council, and passes on the party's platform. Here, as in the provincial sphere, the control is direct and detailed.

The overdetailed resolutions of the provincial convention which have complicated Premier Douglas' administration of Saskatchewan from time to time suggest the possible penalty for this active participation of the rank and file in the affairs of the CCF. Part of the reason, nevertheless, why the CCF has been able to carry through such a far-reaching program in that province is that in few places have so high a proportion of people continuously engaged in political discussions on the work of their government.

The chief weaknesses of the CCF are lack of money and the limited appeal of its platform, particularly in times of prosperity. Although dependence on regular membership fees and small contributions is thoroughly democratic, it limits in practice the propaganda work on which the party places so much stress. The CCF has a weekly or fortnightly newspaper in every province from Ontario west; carries on research continuously through paid and voluntary channels; and is responsible for more books and pamphlets than any other political party in Canada's history. Nevertheless, it aspires to a still broader educational program through which to overcome the resistance to its ideas, which is still its greatest handicap. It is less ignorance, however, than prosperity, a dislike for class-based parties, and satisfaction with the integrating role of the Liberal party which limit the appeal of the CCF in Canada.

III / SOUTH AFRICA

While Canada exists side by side with a dynamic world power, South Africa is the only independent state in Africa which is the home of peoples of European ancestry. Although this might seem to afford South Africa a chance to develop in comfortable isolation, in fact, it has had to struggle with a much more complicated racial pattern and a far more difficult political evolution than Canada has. In the nineteenth century, when Canadians won the battle for responsible government, established their federation, and built their basic party structure, English- and Afrikaans-speaking South Africans were still seeking a way to live harmoniously together, an effort vastly complicated by the inconsistencies of British imperial policy. At the end of the century the two peoples were ranged against each other in the Boer War. The subsequent history of South Africa is marked by efforts, none wholly successful, to establish a basic unity between them.

Within six years of their defeat and annexation in 1901, the two former Boer states—the Transvaal and the Orange Free State—were given full responsible government under their two outstanding leaders, General Louis Botha and General Jan Christiaan Smuts, who accepted the British flag wholeheartedly because they regarded the grant of self-government as the finest act in British history. In the same forward-looking spirit, Afrikaans- and English-speaking leaders in the four colonies—the Transvaal, the Orange Free State, Cape Province, and Natal—drafted the South Africa Act (1909) which created a new Dominion with the same status as Canada, Australia, and New Zealand. Thus South Africa was free to work out its own destiny within the British Commonwealth. Yet the very lateness of the unification, only five years before the outbreak of World War I, created problems for the new country which can hardly be overestimated.

Although the form of the constitution, a close union and not a federation on the Canadian or Australian model, showed the expectation that former divisions had been bridged, the distinctiveness of the provinces has remained. In the Cape, site of the mid-seventeenth-century Dutch settlement, English- and Afrikaans-speaking settlers have intermingled since the early nineteenth century in a liberal atmosphere which accepted political rights for non-European males who could meet educational and property qualifications (notably the Cape Colored). Subtropical Natal on the Indian Ocean is the most predominantly English part of the country—the only part, in fact, where there is a substantial English-speaking farming community. Here reside almost all South Africa's Indians, brought as indentured labor in the 1860's to work the sugar plantations, persuaded to remain when their term of service ended, but increasingly unpopular. The predominantly agricultural Orange Free State is largely Afrikaans-speaking and is the center of a historic Afrikaner nationalism. The Transvaal, with its industry and its great gold mines along the ridge of the Witwatersrand, is more cosmopolitan in population, but its Afrikaans-speaking citizens possess an intense sense of nationalism. Throughout all the provinces are scattered the Bantu or Africans, dominant in numbers but lacking effective influence, either pinioned on inadequate reserves of land or serving as the basic labor force in every sphere of life.

Summarizing the complexity of the total racial picture at the present time, it will suffice to say that, of South Africa's thirteen million people, two and a half million are of European ancestry—nearly a million and a half Afrikaners, descended from the original Dutch, Germans, and French Huguenots of the days of the Dutch East India Company, and outnumbering the million or so of English descent—and over ten million are non-European, including more than eight and a half million Bantu of pure African ancestry, over one million Colored of mixed descent, and three hundred and eighty-five thousand Indians. But even these facts hardly begin to indicate the extent of the racial complexities in South Africa, for the Bantu are divided into many tribes, and the Indians into Hindus and Moslems.

The salient fact in the racial situation, however, is that those of European descent are politically, economically, and socially dominant. No non-European, for example, is eligible to sit in Parliament; the only non-Europeans who can still vote on the common roll with Europeans are Colored and Indian males in Cape Province. In the political sphere, therefore, it is the Europeans who maneuver for control. Those who are wise know that the most significant question in South Africa is the native problem. But it is the issues and attitudes of immediate concern to the Europeans which dominate politics.

When South African union was consummated, the memory of the Boer War was so immediate that the crucial question was whether mutual respect and compromise would govern the relations of Afrikaners and English South Africans or whether one or the other would try to force its pattern of life upon the whole country. In large measure the shifting alignments of South African political parties have always reflected this issue, rather than those of economic, social, or foreign policy. The advantage, in so far as there is one, is that issues of race and nationalism have been debated in the tempering atmos-

phere of Parliament and that the need to secure political power has sometimes aided compromise. The danger is that every issue in the country has been injected with Afrikaner or English South African nationalism, thereby intensifying the threat of these forces to the unity of the state and to South Africa's relationship to the Commonwealth.

Even before union had been achieved, two factors had operated to create an exclusive Afrikaner nationalism: their self-consciousness forged in the struggles of the late nineteenth century and their belief that a party stands for the whole nation and exists to express its traditions. This belief finds no parallel in French Canada, where the solid support for a single party has arisen out of the feeling of need to protect contractual and minority rights. But although the sense of exclusive Afrikanerdom has always animated some of those who speak Afrikaans, it has been counterbalanced by those Afrikaners who repudiate so narrow a nationalism in favor of a South Africa built on the united efforts of two peoples.

The Rise of National Political Parties

In the first Union Parliament in 1910, General Botha united in the South African party the ministries from the four former colonies, thus bringing together the Afrikaners and the moderate English South Africans. Ranged against them were a purely English-speaking opposition known as the Unionists and a weak Labor party. But within a short time a more fundamental division appeared as the result of a challenge to Botha's policy of national unity by General James Barry Hertzog, who feared that the Afrikaners would lose their separate identity through such a development. Hertzog created the Nationalist party, dedicated in internal affairs to the "two-streams" concept—that Afrikaans- and English-speaking groups must develop separately until each reached its full realization—and, externally, to placing the interests of South Africa before those of the empire. Thus emerged almost from the beginning the split between those Afrikaners, like Botha and Smuts, who felt South Africa could best develop through the joint efforts of English and Afrikaners and within the Commonwealth, and those like Hertzog who stressed Afrikanerdom and South African interests.

World War I, in a measure, strengthened both parties. Hertzog and his eleven parliamentary followers opposed entry into the war but held aloof from the abortive rebellion by old Afrikaner nationalists which broke out shortly thereafter. It was put down firmly but without retribution by Botha, who subsequently led South Africa in a united war effort which included capturing South-West Africa. When Hertzog increased his support, especially in the Free State, in the 1915 election so that the South African party lost its absolute majority, Botha reached an understanding with the Unionists under which he governed until his death in 1919.

This agreement with the Unionists was made permanent after the war, when Smuts, as Botha's successor, failed either to gain a majority of the seats in the 1920 election or to make an agreement with Hertzog, who insisted at that time that South Africa must become a republic. Thus appeared a more or less permanent alignment in South African politics in which all the English South Africans except those in the Labor party merged their fortunes with the moderate Afrikaners and stood opposed to militant Afrikanerdom.

The reason why the predominantly English-speaking Labor party acted differently from other English elements in South Africa at this time arose out of its particular purpose: the protection of the interests of white labor against both the capitalists and the competition of native labor. Thus in the great Rand strike of 1922 the Labor movement (exclusively white) fought to prevent an increase in the proportion of native to white labor and to exclude natives from skilled occupations, policies which were favored by the mine-owners to reduce costs. Although organized white labor has succeeded in maintaining its monopoly of skilled employment throughout South Africa, it was defeated in this particular strike when the government used force to stop disorder. Out of bitterness, the Labor party turned so much against Smuts that in 1923 it entered into an agreement with Hertzog's Nationalists that they would not oppose each other in any constituency. In 1924, when for the only time in its history it held the balance of power, the Labor party formed a coalition with the Nationalists based on a common antagonism to Smuts, a common belief in white supremacy, and an agreement by the Nationalists that they would not break the existing constitutional relations of South Africa with the British Commonwealth.

Hertzog in Power

For fifteen years, from 1924 to 1939, Hertzog was prime minister of South Africa, depending at first on this coalition with the Labor party, then for three years with an absolute majority of his own, then from 1933 in coalition and ultimately fusion with Smuts's South Africa party in what became known as the United party. It was a period of great significance for South Africa, for it saw the working-out of Hertzog's "two-streams" concept to the point where he himself believed that the equality of the Afrikaner with the English South African had been achieved. Thus he was ready in the period after 1933 to concentrate upon united efforts. But he was to be no more successful than Botha had been in holding together Afrikanerdom and the moderate English in a common program of action.

The Nationalist-Labor coalition carried through two types of policies between 1924 and 1927 that were characteristic of the future course of South African development. One placed a legislative seal of approval on the so-called "civilized labor policy," which extended the white monopoly of certain skilled and unskilled jobs from the mines to other occupations. In point of fact, however, trade-unionism and the industrial "color bar" remained more significant means of achieving this purpose. The other policy emphasized the "two streams," as through requiring bilingualism for government service. The adoption of separate symbols of the nationalisms within South Africa resulted in the anthem "Die Stem van Sud Afrika" being given equal place with "God Save the King," while a separate South African flag (including, after a bitter struggle, a small Union Jack) was devised which ultimately superseded the Union Jack.

Internationally, Hertzog retained his nationalist aspirations, though he shelved the idea of a republic as the price of labor's support. But the course of development within the British Commonwealth was running with him. The Balfour *Report* of 1926 satisfied Hertzog that South Africa was now independent in fact and would soon be in form. In the Status of the Union Act of 1934 the Union Parliament itself decreed the provisions of the Statute of Westminster. South Africa also acquired its own Great Seal and Signet, so that the authority of the Crown could be exercised within the country itself.

These South African acts formed the necessary prelude to the fusion of Hertzog's and Smuts's parties into the United party in 1934, but there remained significant differences of interpretation between the two men about South Africa's relationship to the Commonwealth. Hertzog emphasized the divisibility of the Crown and therefore the right to secession (obviously now a legal possibility) and to neutrality in British wars. While Smuts did not deny the constitutional points, he did repudiate these implications. They fitted ill with his conception that membership in the Commonwealth, with its mutual benefits and responsibilities, was a greater freedom than insistence on narrow national purposes, a view which came from his philosophy of holism, that all entities tend to seek larger groupings within which to realize themselves. Thus fusion of the nationalists and moderates meant, in fact, an agreement to overlook differences in the interests of joining forces to deal with urgent economic issues.

The Rise of "Purified" Nationalism

Fusion brought new confidence and prosperity to South Africa, raising the hope that concentration on problems of development might submerge racial lines of division in party politics. Yet both the extreme Afrikaner and the extreme English elements greeted fusion with equal suspicion. A small minority of English left Smuts's South Africa party before fusion and formed the Dominion party, preaching against the now fully accepted doctrine of the independent status of South Africa. More serious was D. F. Malan's break from Hertzog on the eve of fusion, to form the "purified" Nationalist party (HNP), which preached a more virulent nationalism than that of Hertzog and encouraged a new withdrawal of the Afrikaner people from the community as a whole. Afrikaner Boy Scouts seceded to form their own association; Afrikaner student groups did likewise. In 1938 a nation-wide commemoration of the Great Trek was turned into an exclusively Afrikaner pageant. Out of it sprang the Ossewa-Brandwag (the "ox-wagon" guard), initially an organization to promote Afrikaner culture but soon transformed into a Nazi pattern and preaching the merits of the one-party state. More insidious was the secret society of the Broederbond, which sought to penetrate the administration, politics, and education and pattern them on the ideal of Christian Afrikaner nationalism.

For six years, from 1933 to 1939, Hertzog and Smuts worked together by concentrating on those questions, like economic and native policy, on which they could agree. In 1936 they took the fateful step of removing the Bantu from the common roll in Cape Province and placing them on a separate roll to elect three Europeans to represent them. They sponsored a South Africa development that resulted in unprecedented prosperity for the *platteland* as well as the cities. The tense issue of war and peace on which they were bound to differ was left on one side until, in September, 1939, it could no longer be ignored.

Wartime Divisions and the Search for Afrikaner Unity

When the Nazis attacked Poland, Hertzog counseled neutrality; Smuts and his followers felt that South Africa should not stand aloof. The cabinet split; the governor-general refused Hertzog a dissolution. In a tense parliamentary session, Smuts's stand was indorsed by 80 votes to 67. Just one day after Great Britain declared war on Germany, South Africa too was at war.

This time there was no rebellion, as in 1914. South Africa participated actively in the war through volunteer forces in which Afrikaner and English South Africans served side by side. But on the home front, party alignments gave grim evidence that separate nationalisms still held South Africans apart from one another.

Smuts formed a coalition consisting of about two-thirds of the members of the United party, the Dominion party, and the Labor party, now only a shadow of what it had been in the 1920's, thus uniting behind him all English-speaking South Africans and a substantial group of moderate Afrikaners. Opposed to him stood Malan's HNP and Hertzog, with about one-third of the former United party members.

The most significant party maneuvers during the war were not those of the government, which showed overwhelming strength in the 1943 election—89 seats for the United party, which was supported by all others except the 43 HNP—but of that substantial portion of Afrikanerdom represented in the Opposition. Efforts to re-establish unity between Hertzog and Malan, though apparently successful in January, 1940, foundered on the unwillingness of Malan's more extreme followers (such as Strijdom and Swart) to guarantee equality of civil and political rights to English South Africans, which Hertzog insisted must be in any program he supported. Defeated in his own province of the Orange Free State, Hertzog withdrew from public life. The extremists had won the first round of their struggle to keep the HNP "pure."

Another type of challenge to the HNP came from nationalistic Afrikaner organizations like the Ossewa-Brandwag, whose leader, Van Rensberg, began to challenge Malan's predominant position. In the July, 1943, election, however, the HNP proved decisively its undisputed control of the hard core of Afrikanerdom and also increased its quantitative Afrikaner vote. In fact, the most significant feature of this election was not the heavy parliamentary majority which Smuts gained but the fact that the Afrikaner vote supporting him was cut from 40 to 32 per cent.

This shift toward the Nationalists continued almost unperceived during the succeeding period. It gained from Smuts's policy toward the Indians in South Africa, perhaps the most unpopular of all racial groups in that much-divided country. In the Asiatic Land Tenure and Indian Representation Act (1946), restrictions on landownership and occupation by Indians in Durban, Natal's chief port, were accompanied by provisions for communal representation of Indians in the Union Parliament and the Natal Provincial Council, the latter by their own people. The Indians themselves indignantly rejected the offer of political representation so long as they were discriminated against in other ways.

The Labor party split on the question: its leader and a minority of its members opposed the grant of political rights to the Indians and were ejected, while the majority accepted Smuts's proposal. The Dominion party likewise split: its leader and the majority opposed the measure, ejected their liberals, and confusingly changed their name to the South African party. The United party did not split obviously, but its Natal members were particularly bitter about the measure, which heightened the tension between the illiberal and the liberal wings of the party. Thus the only party benefiting from the tension arising out of the Asiatic legislation was the HNP.

The Election of 1948

The attitude toward non-Europeans became the major political issue in the election of 1948. Jan Hofmeyr, Smuts's chief lieutenant, asserted the necessity for giving every group in South Africa a chance for free development in terms of its potentialities. The HNP, in contrast, preached *apartheid* (racial segregation). Coupled with their anti-Communist, anti-Indian propaganda, it succeeded, to everyone's surprise, in bringing them into political power.

The distribution of seats was striking-ly even. The United and Labor parties, which had an election pact, secured only 71 seats, though they polled a majority of the votes, but they had the support of the three native representatives. The Nationalists won 70 seats, making them dependent initially on the nine votes of the Afrikaner party, led by N. C. Havenga (formerly Hertzog's lieutenant) and with its ranks open to members of the OB, whom the HNP refused at that time to accept. Despite the earlier hostility of both Havenga and the OB to Malan, the Afrikaner party had an electoral pact with the Nationalists in 1948, joined with them in a governing coalition after the election, and were absorbed in a fusion after the Nationalists organized and won all six new Assembly seats in elections in 1950 in the mandated territory of South-West Africa.

The most disturbing aspect of the election, as of succeeding developments, was the sharpness of the cleavage between nationalistic Afrikanerdom, on the one side, and English-speaking South Africans and moderate Afrikaners, on the other. The two nationalist parties won practically every seat in the predominantly Afrikaans-speaking areas, while the United party and labor gained nearly every seat in the English-speaking areas. The United party, true to the tradition of Botha and Smuts, ran both Afrikaans- and English-speaking candidates (in this election in about equal numbers) and secured 20–25 per cent of the Afrikaners, as well as almost all the English-speaking vote. The Nationalists, in contrast, had not a single predominantly English-speaking candidate, and their cabinet naturally was composed exclusively of Afrikaners. For the first time in the history of the Union the government was composed of only one of its two European peoples. Moreover, the party in power had gone through a long period in the wilderness for the sake of its convictions and had emerged triumphant from opposition within the ranks of Afrikanerdom itself as well as from wider-looking elements outside.

Malan's Nationalists in Power

Once in power, the Nationalists proceeded systematically to implement their program of strengthening Afrikanerdom within the country and drawing more sharply the lines of division between Europeans and non-Europeans. Their first move in the former program was to withdraw support from the program of government-assisted immigration from Great Britain. Shortly thereafter, they passed by a slim majority the hotly contested South African Citizenship Act of 1949, which placed British immigrants on virtually the same basis as non-British in securing citizenship in the Union.

Still more drastic were the measures to separate non-Europeans from Europeans. *Apartheid*, in practice, means social, residential, and political segregation on grounds of race. Such segregation is traditional in South Africa, but the Nationalists made it more rigid and reinforced it by legislative enactment. The Immorality and Mixed Marriages Acts placed heavy penalties on miscegenation. Under the Population Registration Act, everyone in the Union has a card specifying his or her race, thus making it easier to enforce the acts already mentioned. The Group Areas Act permits the designation of residential areas for the exclusive use of Europeans or one of the non-European groups, while the Bantu Authorities Act is an attempt to bolster the badly shaken tribal structure.

Another Nationalist measure, the Suppression of Communism Act (1950), declared illegal the small Communist party, which had worked in the Union since 1921 and had gained a certain following among non-Europeans. Under this act, Sam Kahn and subsequently Brian Bunting, successively elected as native representatives, were ejected from their seats in the House. Furthermore, over fifty labor leaders were "named" as Communists and removed from their union offices, while a number of non-European leaders were convicted of so-called "statutory communism," that is, of taking measures in support of "economic, political, or social change," and were immobilized from political action for two- or three-year periods. This latter action played a considerable role in curbing the defiance campaign against unjust laws which the African National Congress and Indian National Congress undertook in 1952 in opposition to the native pass laws and certain *apartheid* legislation.

The only *apartheid* measure which roused widespread opposition among Europeans, however, was the attempt to take the Colored off the common roll in Cape Province, as Hertzog and Smuts had earlier removed the Bantu. Partly the opposition was because of earlier pledges that the Colored, whom Hertzog designated as "an appendage of the white race," would be left on the common roll; but more particularly because the Nationalists, not having the two-thirds majority of votes specified for such action under the entrenched clauses of the South Africa Act (1909), attempted to remove them through simple legislative enactment, on the ground (supported by some eminent constitutional lawyers) that the Statute of Westminster (1931) removed the restrictions of the entrenched clauses.

In opposition to what they termed "unconstitutional action," an association of war veterans, the Torch Commando, sprang into existence. Comprising both Afrikaners and English South Africans under the leadership of a former ace, Group Captain A. G. Malan, the Torch Commando, through its colorful torchlight parades and organization, performed a significant task in rousing the politically apathetic English South Africans to a realization of the potential dangers of Afrikaner nationalism. The United party also fought the Separate Representation of Voters bill, and both found justification for their attitude when the Supreme Court declared the measure unconstitutional in March, 1952. When the Nationalists refused to accept the verdict of the court and passed legislation (also declared unconstitutional) to make Parliament itself a high court superior to the Supreme Court, the United party, the Labor party, and the Torch Commando grouped themselves into the United Front for a common effort against the Nationalists.

The Election of 1953 and New Party Developments

For the election of April, 1953, both the Nationalists and their opponents exerted their full strength. On the crucial question of non-European policy there was little difference, though the United party, because of the urging of its liberal wing and the needs of secondary industry, supported vocational training for the Bantu and Bantu rights to buy land in the native townships. While the more intransigent attitude of the Nationalist party may have been an element in its political success, it was largely the intense sense of devotion to the party on the part of *platteland* Afrikaners and the Afrikaans working class that brought it back into power with a vastly increased parliamentary majority.

No Nationalist party has ever won a popular majority of the votes in South Africa, and 1953 was no exception. The United and Labor parties, working together in an electoral pact, polled something over 100,000 more votes (depending on the calculations for the unopposed seats) than did the Nationalists. The latter, however, won an over-all majority of twenty-nine seats. This paradoxical result stems not only from the overrepresentation of rural areas but also from the solid concentrations of United party supporters in the big cities and in Natal, neither of which is likely to be reversed in the future. Moreover, the Nationalists increased their total votes over 1948 more than did their opponents and made important new inroads in the industrial and mining suburbs of Johannesburg.

The opposition had been held together before the election by the hope of defeating the Nationalists. Within a few weeks of its results, two new parties were formed, the Liberal and the Union Federal party. The Liberal party, under Mrs. Margaret Ballinger, a native representative since 1938, Alan Paton, the novelist, and Leo Marquard, is South Africa's first party to support "equal rights for all educated men" and, late in 1954, universal suffrage to be achieved by stages. Its backing is largely among urban intellectuals and professional people, and it has no mass following. The Union Federal party, uniting some liberals from the Torch Commando with a predominantly Natal-based following under Senator Heaton Nicholls (formerly leader of the United party in the Senate), aims to safeguard provincial autonomy and the English language and tradition in South Africa and favors a limited liberalism, including votes on a communal roll for Indians. In trials of strength with the United party, neither the Liberals nor the Union Federalists have yet shown any promise of becoming major political factors.

The United party, itself, moreover, suffered revolt late in 1953 against the leadership of J. G. N. Strauss, an able but only occasionally forceful figure, who succeeded the brilliant, world-renowned Smuts in 1950. This led to the expulsion of six members, who now call themselves the Conservatives. They reject as impractical Nationalist-indorsed objectives of ultimate territorial segregation and maintain a traditional attitude on racial issues. In contrast, the United party in November, 1954, formally indorsed the process of economic integration of the non-Europeans which is so obvious a feature of recent South African development, but it has taken no steps to develop a dynamic policy based on this declaration.

The Objectives of Afrikaner Nationalism

The Nationalists continue to press ahead with *apartheid* in every sphere. After the election, they passed the Bantu Education Act providing for a separate educational system for Africans organized under the central Department of Native Affairs; the Native (Settlement of Disputes) Act, which left African trade-unions unrecognized and African strikes illegal and established a largely white conciliation machinery to deal with disputes affecting natives; the Unequal Amenities Act; and a new Industrial Conciliation Act which empowers the minister of labor to establish a vertical as well as a horizontal color bar, i.e., between industries as well as between skilled and unskilled jobs. Behind this legislation lies the hope of the Nationalists that they can gain the advantages of non-European labor without allowing it either to compete harmfully with white (largely Afrikaans) labor or to secure rights in the European areas.

At the same time, the Afrikaner Nationalist sees votes and political power as the means to counterbalance the superior economic position of English South Africans. Although it is true that South African politics do not have so markedly an economic base as do Australian or New Zealand politics, it is important to realize that the United party includes all the big financial, commercial, mining, and industrial interests in the Union and that its agricultural

support is mainly from wealthy farmers. The Nationalists, on the other hand, have won the Afrikaans working class away from such allegiance as they had in the late 1920's and 1930's to the Labor party, leaving the latter largely an intellectual group. Thus the economic configuration of political allegiance intensifies the division between Afrikaners and English South Africans, as it spurs the Nationalists to enforce their non-European policy despite the fact that it is bitterly resented by that politically impotent but numerically significant group.

Internationally, the threat of the Soviet Union is felt with equal sharpness by the two European peoples of South Africa. Thus, as in Canada, a war against this enemy would find European South Africans united as never before in their history. Nevertheless, there might well be differences of opinion on the character of participation in a future war, with the United party urging active aid in Europe or North Africa and the Nationalists emphasizing responsibilities in the southern half of Africa. Only after strong United party pressure did Malan agree, for example, to send a fighter squadron to Korea.

Since the intense and forceful Hans Strijdom succeeded Malan as prime minister late in 1954, more is heard of a republic, and one ultimately outside the Commonwealth, though the party is still pledged not to establish a republic in South Africa without a special vote in support of it. Moreover, so long as the Nationalists do not command a majority of the votes in the country, they would hardly want to put the election of a president to popular vote. Commonwealth membership is not irksome, although the admission of the Gold Coast to that group would be still more unpalatable to South Africa than is the membership of the Asian Dominions. Generally speaking, the Nationalist government has co-operated well with Great Britain, particularly in economic issues like the supply of gold. At the same time, British public sentiment is openly critical of Nationalist racial policies. Thus while self-interest tends to hold the two countries together, the intangible but powerful Commonwealth bonds of sentiment and sympathy are largely lacking so long as the Nationalists stay in power—which may in fact be very long indeed.

Party Leaders

Characteristic of all South African parties is their dependence upon a leader. In the history of the Union only five men have been prime minister—Botha, Smuts, Hertzog, Malan, and now Strijdom—all Afrikaners but differing widely in approach and appeal. All have had in common, however, the assurance of their own vision, the ability to impose their personal program on the party, a sense of political strategy, and (although this is less true for Malan and Strijdom) a concern with issues rather than organization.

Louis Botha was the most farsighted, generous, and wisest of all South Africa's leaders. To a degree unmatched by any of the others, Botha maintained a world view and at the same time remained in touch with the sentiments of the *platteland*. Jan Christian Smuts, a world figure, was never accepted so completely within South Africa itself. His rapier-like mind, his distantness from people despite his interest in them, led many to find him "too clever." But Smuts's strength was his far-ranging vision, vigor, and greatness of character, which led him to work under Hertzog in the thirties rather than claim the highest office for himself. Despite his bitter disappointment at his electoral defeat in 1948, he went on fighting to the end, not in any spirit of bitterness but out of devotion to his friends. The legend of Smuts may in time be as important for South Africa as was his life.

James Barry Hertzog was less of an international figure than Smuts but closer to his own people. He had an instinctive feeling for their aspirations and great vigor in expressing them. He was a fighter who was wise enough to know when he had won his point. He became a supporter of the British Commonwealth after the Balfour Report of 1926 and worked for a South Africa built on the equal rights and responsibilities of English- and Afrikaans-speaking peoples, once he believed the Afrikaner had achieved his due position in the country. Hertzog's tragedy, like that of South Africa itself, was that the forces of nationalism which he encouraged for justifiable ends refused the limits which those ends implied.

Malan was less dynamic than his predecessors but no less dominant. He welded the Nationalists into a far more cohesive unity than had Hertzog and gave them both a more exclusive and a more potent faith. Of the first four prime ministers of the Union, he was the least impressive nationally and internationally. It has yet to be proved, however, that his influence in shaping South Africa may not have been the greatest, for he represented a limited outlook which the other three strove against but which may yet—to its peril —characterize the South Africa of the future.

Party Organization

The development of highly organized, efficient party structures is relatively recent in South Africa. The United party, in particular, paid little attention to party organization until after it lost the 1948 election. A remarkable amount was done, particularly in the highly important Witwatersrand area of the Transvaal, in the period immediately preceding the 1953 election, but its major effect was to get out the vote on election day rather than to make converts for the party. The internal struggle within the party since the election has kept active certain constituencies, especially in Johannesburg, but this is still the exception rather than the rule.

The Nationalists, in contrast, evolved a tightly knit and highly disciplined party structure in each province except Natal well before the 1953 election. Under a professional staff of ardent young organizers, each responsible for several constituencies, a volunteer staff organized on the block system keeps constant touch with the people in their immediate vicinity. Moreover, the extraordinary cohesiveness of nationalistic Afrikanerdom means that to a considerable extent the Afrikaans schools, the Dutch Reformed church, the Afrikaner economic associations like the Reddingsdaadbond (which gives advice to Afrikaans businessmen and makes contacts), and cultural societies co-ordinated by the FAK (Federasie van Afrikaanse Kultuurvereinginge) act to supplement the formal efforts of the Nationalist party organizers. Nothing quite like this is found anywhere else in the Commonwealth except perhaps in the rural areas of Quebec.

The Nationalists are organized by provinces and have only an advisory body at the national level. Since this body includes the four provincial leaders, however, its decisions are tantamount to national ones. The annual provincial conferences are said to be the supreme organs, and certainly they play an important role in providing a sense of participation to the local representatives who come for the two- or three-day series of meetings. Group singing, placards, vigorous and very lengthy speeches by the leaders, numerous resolutions which are voted on formally, all contribute to the enthusiasm of the party workers. The leaders receive great respect and are followed far more faithfully than in other parties, like the Australian Labor party, where there is a similar amount of local participation.

It is also true, however, that certain of the Nationalist policies such as taking the Colored off the common roll have been voted year after year by provincial conferences and that the leaders maintain that they have an obligation, therefore, to institute them.

The United party has annual provincial congresses and a biennial Union congress, which has become increasingly important since the party improved its national organization. None of these gatherings, however, exhibits the same degree of enthusiasm or participation by local representatives as do the Nationalist meetings.

As a matter of form, party leaders are re-elected every year by the Nationalist party. Strijdom, long the party's leader in the Transvaal, was chosen Malan's successor by the parliamentary caucus and confirmed by provincial congresses. Mr. Strauss was selected in the same way by the United party after General Smuts's resignation.

The United party has depended for funds largely on donations and relatively little on membership fees. Widespread criticism of the way in which funds had been used for unproductive ventures before the 1948 election led to the setting-up of the United South Africa Trust Fund, which received substantial contributions from business and industry and gave extensively for the reorganization of the party machinery and to the Torch Commando before the 1953 election.

The Nationalists depend to a far greater degree than the United party upon the fees collected from party members, partly because there are few large Afrikaner businesses on which to draw for contributions and partly because of the sense of participation induced by this means. In the Cape, for example, no one may vote in a nomination campaign unless he has paid his party dues. While Nationalist leaders are prone to say that their lack of financial resources handicaps them, it seems likely that the emphasis on small personal contributions reinforces the active membership on which successful parties depend so much.

IV / AUSTRALIA AND NEW ZEALAND

Off the coast of Asia lie Australia and New Zealand, outposts of Western civilization in the southwest Pacific. Neither faces the racial complexities which mark Canadian and South African politics; on the contrary, their people are overwhelmingly British in origin. Moreover, their very isolation, being as far from their original homeland as is possible, reinforces their ties to Britain of sentiment and culture.

Yet Australia and New Zealand are no less distinctive in their own ways than is Canada or South Africa. A continent in its own right, equal in size to the United States, Australia is permanently handicapped by its lack of rainfall and its dead center of sandy waste, which takes three days to cross by train. Even today, Australia's nearly nine million people are mostly concentrated around a few large centers, mainly in the southeast. Similarly, many of New Zealand's two million people are found in the four large cities of its two long and narrow islands.

Both countries were initially inhospitable to the small settler, though New Zealand today has a far higher proportion of family farms than has Australia. Lack of the necessities of life and land hunger created intense class bitterness in the first decades of both Australia and New Zealand, a bitterness directed chiefly against the wealthy landowners whose fortunes from sheep raising for wool were shared with English as well as local financial interests. It was in this atmosphere that the labor movements, in particular the Australian, so early acquired both their cohesion and their strength.

The Australian Pattern

THE AUSTRALIAN LABOR MOVEMENT.— Australian workers had organized in trade-unions even before the planned settlement of New Zealand took place in 1840. In the 1850's, an industrial struggle fought under the slogan of "Eight Hours Work, Eight Hours Leisure, Eight Hours Sleep" was on its way to success. Already the Australian labor movement was acquiring some of its most characteristic features. It united agricultural workers like the sheep shearers with coal miners and those in the towns. It had no quarrel with the capitalist system as such but aimed to insure good conditions of work, a moderately high standard of living, and a feeling of independence for its members. Its leadership was generally English or Scotch, but among its members was a plentiful sprinkling of impoverished, discontented, anti-English Irish Catholics who still form one-fifth of the Australian people and remain faithful adherents of the Labor party.

Even before Australian confederation in 1901, the class divisions in the country had become reflected in the structure of political parties. When the great depression-induced strikes of 1891 were crushed, Australian labor decided that its hope lay not in direct action but in political participation. What is most striking is the rapidity of its political success. In 1891 Labor took one-third of the seats in New South Wales, the most populous and prosperous of the Australian colonies. To the first federal parliament, Labor elected nearly one-quarter of the members of each house. In 1904, only three years after federation, the Australian Labor party formed the government for a brief period, by many years the first labor party to acquire national political power in a British Commonwealth country.

The strength of the ALP and the disappearance as a live issue of the initial political division over protectionism versus free trade soon produced the typical alignment in Australian politics of labor versus non-labor parties. Labor emphasized improvement of the condition of the workers through social welfare measures, raising of tariffs to protect wage standards from outside competition, and exclusion of the colored races from the country for the same reason. Labor was also nationalistic, favoring compulsory military training for home defense and the creation of an Australian navy, to be kept in Australian waters except in case of war. Already it was choosing the major theme songs of Australian politics, and the ALP had become the decisive political force in the country.

Characteristic of the Australian Labor party has been the breadth of its membership and therefore the variety of opinions it has included. Centered in the trade-unions, it has also attracted small shopkeepers, small mining proprietors and prospectors, and other comparable groups which feared the domination of big business or big landowners. Despite the suspicion of intellectuals by the rank and file, the ALP has always included members of the professional classes, particularly ardent democrats and nationalists. Local conditions secured it the adherence of the liquor trades. Most of its members have had a middle-of-the-road, practical approach to issues, but others express views as varied as theoretical radicalism and conservatism. This span became the more marked after the Communist party was organized in 1921, exerting a competitive influence on the left wing of the ALP, and it is not without significance that the ALP formulated socialist objectives in that same year. More important, however, is the fact that little was done to realize these objectives until after World War II and that these subsequent efforts threw into high relief the divergent attitude on the issue

of the Irish Roman Catholics who form so substantial and, on occasions, conservative a right wing of the party.

Not only on internal issues but also on foreign policy the ALP has found sharp differences of views among its members. In World War I, after organizing a striking war effort the ALP split disastrously in 1916 over conscription for overseas service and expelled its leader, Prime Minister William M. Hughes, who then became prime minister of a "Nationalist" party made up mainly of the former opposition. When Labor once again acquired political power in 1929, the depression hit Australia with catastrophic effect. A rigorous and ultimately successful deflationary policy caused such internal dissension in the Labor government that it collapsed, and once again a Labor leader, this time J. A. Lyons, deserted the party to head a non-Labor administration.

Then shortly before Pearl Harbor, as attention was focusing increasingly on the Pacific, the Australian Labor party took over political responsibility from the fumbling and divided non-Labor parties. Under their inspired, half-mystical, sensitive leader, John Curtin, who had welded the party into a whole again in the years just before the war and who, more than any other person, expressed both its strengths and its weaknesses, the ALP directed with a sure hand the ever increasing Australian war effort. With less than seven and a half million people, Australia had nearly a million in uniform in the course of the war. Conscription for limited overseas service provided the most touchy of the issues that Curtin had to handle, but Labor maintained its solidarity when the area of service was extended to cover General MacArthur's Southwest Pacific zone. This greater maturity of approach among Labor's adherents was coupled with an independent approach to Pacific problems, which sometimes caused friction with Great Britain but reflected Australia's coming of age in international affairs.

In internal affairs Labor's program met with less wholehearted support. Both in 1944 and 1946 the ALP unsuccessfully sought a substantial extension of federal powers with which to insure "full employment." Returned to office in 1946 with a slightly reduced majority, the Labor party embarked for the first time on a considerable program of nationalization, indorsing a state medical scheme and attempting to nationalize all transportation and the banks. There was widespread opposition to extension of state control not only from the Opposition but also from Labor's own somewhat conservative right wing and Catholic elements. Moreover, the Communist-led coal strike of 1949 severely damaged the government despite its firm handling of that crisis, and the ALP was defeated in the 1949 elections for the first time as the result of a straight fight. What was clear by this time was that the ALP is a liberal party with a strong socialist wing and is fundamentally dedicated to the interests of the working class. Because of its widely varied elements, however, it remains subject to internal dissensions, as shown by further intra-party struggles in 1954 and 1955.

THE NON-LABOR PARTIES.—For all its problems in maintaining unity, the ALP has shown qualities of resilience and cohesion which Australian non-labor parties may well envy. The relatively small, though influential, Country party which developed at the end of World War I had the positive aim of promoting the particular ends of agriculturists. But the other non-labor party, which has gone variously under the name of National, United Australia, and Liberal party, has found difficulty in establishing a positive focus for its activities other than providing an alternative to Labor. Naturally enough, it has appealed to the banking, commercial, manufacturing, and large-scale mining interests and found fair support among professional groups. But it has had the not surprising difficulties of a moderately liberal party with a conservative wing operating in a country where conservatism is generally dubbed reaction, and against a party, the ALP, which expresses a largely liberal emphasis. To maintain itself, the Liberal party also has to follow middle-of-the-road policies, often not so different from those sponsored by Labor.

Policy toward Australian Communists was one of the most controversial and troublesome problems faced after 1949. The Liberals came into office pledged to eliminate Communists from public life and from important posts in the trade-unions. Their far-reaching Communist Party Dissolution bill, introduced in April, 1950, was opposed at first on general principles by the ALP parliamentary party and the federal executive committee. Following the outbreak of the Korean War, pressure from Catholic members in Victoria and realization that the stand was generally unpopular in the country led the Executive and subsequently the parliamentary party to reverse themselves, and the bill was allowed to pass. In March, 1951, however, the High Court declared it invalid. Fortified by his success in winning a majority in both the House and the Senate in the April, 1951, election (held ostensibly over Labor's opposition to the government's banking bill), Prime Minister Menzies then held a national referendum in September, 1951, on an amendment to the constitution to provide the necessary powers. The ALP unitedly opposed the amendment as providing too sweeping powers to the federal government and it was defeated by a margin of 52,082 votes. In the meantime the unions themselves, in particular the coal miners, had curbed their Communist members and the issue ceased to have such urgency, though the Liberals have continued to use it in electoral propaganda.

Much credit for the Liberal successes in 1949, 1951, and 1954 must go to R. G. Menzies, a genuine liberal and a man of brilliant talents, though sometimes overly clever for his own good, who courageously fought his way back into office after a long period of unpopularity following his ouster from the prime ministership in 1941 by a palace revolution in his own party. Menzies is an individualist who has to force himself to work in a team; he is a star who prefers not to be outshone. But he is also unsparing of himself, learns by experience, and has been a more decisive, wiser prime minister since 1949 than in 1940.

The most obvious comparison with Menzies is Stanley Bruce, who headed a United Australia (Liberal) and Country party coalition in the 1920's. Urbane, steady, effective, Bruce carried Australia through an important formative period of growth, working closely with Great Britain throughout. He subsequently represented his country in London with distinction and success and crowned his career with a peerage and seat in the British House of Lords.

To a certain degree the comparison of these men with typical Labor leaders dramatizes the social divisions within the country. The Liberal leaders have a broader background, more contact with Great Britain, and greater sympathy for its imperial policies. Menzies, for example, has sent Australian troops to Malaya to help fight the Communist guerrillas. For these reasons they inspire confidence in many Australians who fear the limited vision of Labor, however much they trust its basic sincerity. From the side of the working class, there is often a grudging respect for Liberal leadership but little belief in its understanding of their basic sentiments.

The Country party leader, Sir Arthur

Fadden, represents still another type. He is an able, energetic politician of the back-slapping variety. He and Menzies have little in common; moreover, he helped to oust Menzies from his position as prime minister in 1940. That they work together in coalition is good evidence that they realize that only through unity can they keep political power.

LABOR LEADERS.—On the whole, the leaders of the ALP have been sound rather than brilliant, with a gift for conciliation rather than vision. This is not wholly true, however, of John Curtin, leader of the ALP from 1935 and prime minister from 1941 to 1945, who had inner sources of strength that grew more apparent with responsibilities. He had a gift for language, persuasiveness, and a deep sense of historic British values. His appeal to the United States after the fall of Singapore, his request for General MacArthur as commander-in-chief in the Pacific area, and his insistence on a Pacific Council in Washington were interpreted by many as a shift away from Great Britain. But no one can believe this who has heard his wartime broadcasts (fortunately preserved by the Australian Broadcasting Corporation) and marked the growing warmth of sentiment, culminating in his stirring Guildhall speech in London in 1944. It was Curtin, too, who fought so strongly, if unsuccessfully, for an empire secretariat. In all these moves, Curtin was inspired by the needs of the time, by practical common sense, and by farsightedness. That he was able to weld the ALP into unity in the difficult years before 1939 and then to conduct a great war effort bespeaks outstanding qualities of imagination and leadership as well as an understanding of the rank and file.

Joseph Chiffley, who succeeded Curtin as leader of the ALP and was prime minister from 1945 to 1949, had very different qualities. He was a straightforward, shrewd, genuine man of the people with a lack of eloquence which at first jeopardized his chances to be chosen leader. He won his place through competence, hard work, and demonstrated mastery of detail. When prime minister, he spent hours on the telephone every day keeping in touch with Labor sentiment throughout the country. While he lacked Curtin's spark and vision, he won universal respect in office. Perhaps more than Curtin did, he dominated party councils through weight of knowledge, persistence, and decisiveness.

"Solid, faithful, conscientious and able," L. F. Crisp has characterized the leaders of the ALP. One further thing can be said. They were men who for the most part reflected in themselves both the strengths and the weaknesses of the party: its close touch with the rank and file, on the one hand, and its lack of expert knowledge, on the other. There is no intellectual leadership in the ALP comparable to that of the Fabian Society in the British Labour party. Labor's intellectuals, like H. V. Evatt, the present brilliant, self-assertive leader, are looked on with mixed pride and a suspicion that personal interests will be put above party and class interests. The result is, however, that the ALP has its greatest successes when, as before World War I or during World War II, its aims accord with those of the community as a whole, and its greatest difficulties when, as in the depression of 1930–32, it faces crises for the handling of which it lacks both experience and knowledge.

The Pattern in New Zealand

THE RISE OF MODERN PARTIES.—Although the timing was similar to that in Australia, partly because of the mutual experience of disastrous strikes crushed in 1891, the initial alignment of forces in New Zealand was less clear-cut and permanent than in the other country,

though immediately more effective. In 1891 a great Liberal victory resulted from the union of the landless, the unemployed, the trade-unions, and the liberal middle class, temporarily united against the landed interests and in support of a tariff to protect the standards of local factories. Under the leadership of Richard John Seddon, a rough, vigorous, autocratic humanitarian, who was premier from 1893 to 1906, and through the vision of William Pember Reeves, a scholarly intellectual, the Liberal party carried through a spectacular program of land reform, social legislation, and compulsory arbitration of industrial disputes. This temporarily focused the attention of a surprised world upon New Zealand and was dubbed by outsiders "socialism without dogma," as was the somewhat less spectacular but similar development in Australia under labor. In both countries the real force behind social legislation was not any particular doctrine but the hard conditions of life, the practical nature of the people, and the determination to use the authority and financial power of the state to insure the interests of individuals and particular groups. So well did these measures satisfy the workingmen who had seats in the New Zealand House of Representatives that, although they did not share in political power, they gave unfailing support to what was in fact a liberal-labor administration.

New economic developments, however, put an unbearable strain on this combination soon after the turn of the century. The trade-unions, spurred by the growth of towns and factories, organized their own political party, the New Zealand Labor party, which had members in Parliament from 1908 on. The Labor party found difficulty, however, in holding together its moderate and radical groups and wasted much of its energies in internal dissension.

Much more successful at that time

was the agricultural group, which broke away from the Liberals to form a new political party on the right, the Reform party. The small farmers were ready to support a radical program until their hunger for land was satisfied; thereafter their natural conservatism reasserted itself. They became reluctant to support further expensive social legislation and clamored for freeholds. Gradually they coalesced with the disorganized and dwindling remnants of the Conservative party of the landed interests, under the leadership of William F. Massey. In 1912 the Reform party came into office; the following year it used hastily recruited forces from the countryside to crush militant syndicalist-minded trade-unions in the waterside workers' strike. Rural conservatism was in the saddle.

REFORM AND LIBERAL PARTIES IN POWER.—From 1912 to 1928 and from 1931 to 1935 the Reform party, either alone or in coalition with the Liberals, remained in power, seeking the interests of the farmers at home and the Empire abroad. It took New Zealand into World War I and organized an impressive national front. It introduced conscription for overseas service, despite the opposition of part of the Labor party, which split seriously over the issue, though not over participation in the war. Massey also participated in the imperial war cabinet and the Paris Peace Conference, and separately signed the Treaty of Versailles, as did other Dominion leaders. To Massey, however, these acts evidenced imperial unity rather than the emergence of separate status—at least he tried to persuade himself that they did.

The characteristic line of New Zealand external policy prior to World War I had been staunch allegiance to and support of Great Britain, arising out of a deep sense of unity and common purpose. In place of building a separate navy like its neighbor Australia, New Zealand contributed a battleship to the British Navy. After the war New Zealand "dragged its feet" as the British Commonwealth consolidated its distinctive features. New Zealand statesmen of both the Reform and Liberal parties almost universally exhibited dread of the steady progress toward decentralization, spoke of the Statute of Westminster as "the damned Statute," and gloomily felt that change was leading to disruption.

Within New Zealand itself, however, the Reform and Liberal parties were not reluctant to approve radical measures which benefited the groups whose interests they had closest at heart. Thus were established machinery for marketing agricultural produce (in the early twenties); substantial legislative interference with fixed contracts affecting rents, interest, and mortgages (during the depression); and the New Zealand Reserve Bank with only a minority of private shareholders. "Conservatism," in fact, is a relative term in New Zealand as in Australia and by no means excludes radical, experimental measures which the times and particular interests may demand.

The Reform and Liberal parties continued as separate entities throughout the 1920's. The Liberals, although temporarily successful in 1929, lacked creative liberalism and were supported mainly by commercial and manufacturing interests to whom neither the Reform party nor Labor appealed. In World War I the two parties had formed a coalition; in 1931 they did so again in the face of the depression and increasing Labor strength. In 1935, when Labor swept triumphantly into power, they adopted the name National party, and a year or two later formed a unified organization. Thus New Zealand achieved the typical two-party alignment of the parliamentary system, a division which can be described as labor versus non-labor or, more accurately, a social reformist or humanitarian party with a fairly large socialist wing versus a conservative party with a liberal wing.

LABOR ACHIEVES OFFICE.—The striking Labor victory of 1935 brought a Labor party into undisputed political control for the first time in the history of the British Commonwealth. (In Australia, Labor has never controlled the federal and all the state administrations at the same time.) The basis of its support, however, was an alliance between the trade-unions and many of the small sheep and dairy farmers, not unlike that of the Liberals in Seddon's day. Soon after the 1935 election the farming interests, which were initially attracted by plans for guaranteed prices for agricultural products and credit reform, began to return to their former allegiance. In 1938, Labor lost most of the dairy seats; in 1943 it lost almost all the rest of the farmer constituencies it had gained in 1935. But what defeated Labor in New Zealand in 1949, as in Australia, was the so-called floating vote: in New Zealand this included the office workers, government employees, and small retailers. As between the party of the trade-unions, the Labor party, and the party of the farmers, the National party, it is the tertiary workers of the service occupations who now hold the balance of power.

Labor's first years were its best. The far-reaching Social Security Act of 1938 built on earlier legislation but instituted free medical services and old age pensions regardless of income, a program not unlike that of Great Britain's later Beveridge Plan. Labor also stimulated secondary industries, now far more important in the total life of the country than is generally realized because New Zealand's exports are nearly all primary products: butter, cheese, and frozen meat. Internationally, Labor adopted a favorable policy toward the League of Nations, resting on principles of international morality which led New Zealand to be one of the two countries (South Africa was the other) which were willing to continue sanctions in the Italo-Ethiopian conflict. Even more remarkable was the unswerving stand against aggression maintained by its representative on the League Council from 1936 to 1939, even when this stand led to obvious divergencies from British policy.

New Zealand's response to war in September, 1939, was immediate and wholehearted. Moreover, when war came to the Pacific and Australian troops were withdrawn from the Middle East to defend their homeland, New Zealand troops in the European and African zones were not brought back. With rare vision, New Zealanders accepted the fact that the war and the British Commonwealth could continue if New Zealand were occupied but that both would be lost if Great Britain went under.

But Labor's drive at home was spent long before it went out of office in 1949. What lost Labor that election was its inability to compete with the fresher, more vigorous appeal of the National party. The unattached voters of the office and retail group were tired of controls, irritated by the left-wing trade-unions, with their intrenched Communist members, and found little that was forward-looking or essentially liberal in Labor's electioneering.

The leaders of the New Zealand Labor party have been men who care about the everyday affairs of simple people and are not afraid to use the same directness in their approach to international affairs. Harry Holland, who shaped the party, had great integrity and fighting spirit. Michael Savage, their first prime minister, was distinguished less for ability than for his simplicity, directness, personal charm, and perhaps too abundant optimism. Peter Fraser, prime minister from 1940 to 1949, was a shrewd and kindly politician as ready to listen to the troubles of a man in arrears with his rent as to criticize the veto power in the Security Council. The very smallness of the population made their personal touch possible; it did not limit their international vision. It must also be said, however, that Fraser and his successor as party leader, Walter Nash, a man strongly influenced by Christian socialism and one of the relatively few intellectuals in the party, grew autocratic as they aged, did not develop younger men, and lost the ability to awaken the enthusiasm of the rank and file of the party. Because of this, they contributed to the failure of their party in 1949, but it would be too much to say that they caused it.

THE NATIONAL PARTY IN OFFICE.—The National party, which has been in office since 1949, illustrates the degree to which diverse groups can work together and even moderate their particular interests if this offers the only road to political office. Although the groups which provide its nucleus of support— the farmers and the manufacturing, commercial, and financial interests—are essentially conservative in attitude, the party campaigned itself into power in 1949 by its liberal emphasis on releasing controls along with reassurances that it regarded the "welfare state" with as much tenderness as did Labor. In power, the National party has maintained a lavish social security program and the same policy of restricted hours of work and high wages as the Labor opposition stands for.

In 1951 Prime Minister Sidney Holland, an affable businessman of great vigor and considerable persuasiveness, guessed shrewdly that the country was behind him in the government's firm handling of the dockworkers' strike that was tying up New Zealand's external trade. In a surprise move he accepted a Labor motion of no confidence and, in an election marked by unusual bit-

terness, was returned to office with an increased majority of four and a higher percentage of votes.[3] In 1954 he again retained his position.

Traditionally, the groups that now unite in the National party have followed the British lead implicitly in international affairs. Under their guidance, New Zealand has taken a less active role in international affairs and Commonwealth conferences than under Labor. Essentially, however, both parties strongly support Great Britain at all times, even when they may be critical of its actions behind the scenes. Since New Zealand has never felt as engaged in Asian affairs as does Australia, the fact that the National party did not offer anything like as decisive leadership in the Korean crisis as the Liberals in Australia is only suggestive. It is more important that both parties finally indorsed sending a contingent to Korea in line with the action of the other, older members of the Commonwealth.

Party Organization

THE LABOR PARTIES.—In both Australia and New Zealand, as in Great Britain, the Labor party draws the bulk of its membership and financial support from the trade-unions. Yet in none of the three countries is it an exclusively one-class party. Of the three parties, that in Australia has consistently attracted the widest variety of groups. The New Zealand Labor party is far more the party of the organized working class than is its Australian equivalent.

Compulsory arbitration has led both countries to become highly unionized,

3. The Labor party retained the four Maori seats. It has often been said in the past that the Maoris follow the election trends, but this seems now to have been contradicted as, for the first time, the Maoris voted on the same day as European New Zealanders in this election.

since only registered unions can claim the benefits of the system. Trade-unions are the most reliable sources of income for the two Labor parties, although big business in both countries has tended over the years to distribute its contributions between the two major parties in order to have good relations with both, a fact made possible by the generally nonsocialistic policies of Labor when in office.

Although the trade-unions are the backbone of the Australian and New Zealand Labor parties, it is a mistake to look on them as wholly unified groups. Historically the great difficulty in establishing a strong Labor party in New Zealand lay in the split between the more radical unions, which resented the restraints of compulsory unionism and engaged in often disastrous direct action, and the more conservative craft unions, which favored industrial harmony. Even the amalgamation, begun in 1937 under the Labor government's sponsorship, of the industrial unions' Alliance of Labor and the craft unions' Trades and Labor Councils into the Federation of Labor failed to establish a genuine basis of unity. The more radical unions—like the "wharfies," the "trammies," and the carpenters—continued to nourish a not unjustified suspicion that the leadership of the Federation of Labor was not only conservative of view but also somewhat unresponsive to pressure from the rank and file. In consequence, there were unauthorized strikes in 1948 and 1949 and vigorous intra-federation disputes, culminating in a split between the aggressive Trades Union Congress under the leadership of the wharfsiders and the more moderate Federation of Labor, from which it seceded in 1951.

Although divisions between the more radical and the more conservative trade-unions have not been so obvious or so detrimental to the growth of the Labor party in Australia as in New Zealand, they do exist. Moreover, as the strikes of 1949 prove, the trade-unions are in a relatively stronger position within the community at large in Australia than in New Zealand. It is significant, however, that at that time it was a Labor government which supported the compulsory arbitration system against the radical trade-unions (many of which had Communists in leading posts) and eventually forced the end of the strike.

The greatest contrasts between the ALP and the NZLP, however, lie in organization. These arise partly out of history and partly out of the difference between a federal and a unitary structure. For all its tendencies toward centralization when in office, the Australian Labor party has strictly adhered to an internal federalism for itself, which provides the state organizations with considerable power. Thus there are two major centers of authority in the Australian Labor party: the state executives and conferences and the parliamentary members or caucus. In New Zealand, the national executive and the parliamentary leaders are the chief centers of power and work closely together. Naturally, they often provide more effective leadership than the ALP customarily enjoys, but at the expense of the influence of the rank and file, which plays such a role in the ALP.

It is the combination of democracy and discipline in the Australian Labor party organization that is so striking. From its earliest days, even before the Commonwealth had been established, the "movement" wrestled with the problem of how to keep its parliamentary representatives responsive to the will of the members as a whole. To secure the principle stated in the present constitution of the New South Wales Labor party, "The collective membership is sovereign," the party developed "the pledge" by which parliamentary candidates agreed to accept the interpretation of the party's program laid down by the representative state conference. Throughout its history the party has not hesitated to expel even its most prominent members, like W. M. Hughes, prime minister in World War I, when they refused to follow the will of "the collective membership," as over conscription in 1917.

This discipline is combined with a tightly knit, hierarchical organization in the individual states and a much looser federal party organization to co-ordinate them. The basic unit is the local party branch, which may be formed by as few as fifteen members. It must conform to written rules and accept the supervision of the state central executive. On the vitality of the local branches depends the health of the party, for their biweekly meetings are the channel through which trade-unionists and others make their individual influence felt. The next level of organization is the "electorate councils" in state and federal electorates, to which local branches send representatives. The ruling authority in the state is the annual conference, in which affiliated trade-unions and electoral councils are directly represented, and, between its sessions, the central executive (numbering about thirty in New South Wales, the most populous of the states), elected by conference but relatively stable in membership and correspondingly powerful. Between them, they determine policy, control membership dues, watch party loyalty, pass on local candidates, and do publicity and educational work.[4] In comparison, the triennial federal conference and national executive are relatively weak because they lack significant powers and duties and large independent funds.

In New Zealand, the organization is, of course, unitary, and thus power centers in the national conference and more particularly in the national executive. On the local level are branches and trade-union affiliates, the latter of which are more numerous and thus dominate in the national conference. The national executive consists of seventeen members, five resident in the area of party headquarters, and twelve divisional representatives. The resident members naturally have a great influence over the formulation of policy, since the executive not only supervises the local branches (which, in consequence, have lacked vitality, especially since about 1938) but also controls party finances and campaign funds, selects the parliamentary candidates from a panel proposed by the branches, and applies party discipline, as in the expulsion of John A. Lee, a prominent party member who challenged the "orthodoxy" of the leaders and par-

4. In five of the six Australian states—New South Wales, Victoria, Queensland, South Australia, and Tasmania—Labor's industrial and political wings are organized separately. Thus there is both a state executive heading the political organization and a statewide trades and labor council. Naturally, there is close working together between the two groups in each state, and in Queensland, South Australia, and Tasmania they may almost be said to form interlocking directorates. The state executive in New South Wales has been notoriously unstable and subject to a variety of influences of special interests as well as the trades and labor council. In Western Australia, the political and industrial wings are fused, and industrial labor rarely attempts to act independently of the state executive. On the other hand, it is almost impossible to "pack" the state executive (as has happened, for example, in New South Wales), since all trade-unionists participate in the ballot. The reason for the difference between Western Australia and the other states is that the former has had such difficulties of isolation to overcome that it could be developed only by the government, which has built the railways, docks, etc., and controls a considerable proportion of industry. Thus what has been important in Western Australia has been to exert pressure directly upon the government, whereas in other states most of the industry is privately owned, and direct action may therefore be a more effective approach.

ticularly the fitness of the then leader, Michael Savage. As in Australia, Labor candidates in New Zealand are pledged to accept the official interpretation of the program, but this means in practice the interpretation of the parliamentary leaders and resident members of the national executive.

Thus while the state conferences and state executives wield decisive power in the Australian organization, the central executive is the most important nonparliamentary unit in the New Zealand party. An even more significant contrast between the centralization of authority in the New Zealand Labor party and the decentralization in the Australian Labor party lies, however, in the relationship between the party organization and the parliamentary members and in the way in which the caucus operates.

The New Zealand structure is relatively simple. Caucus (the parliamentary members of both Houses) designates the leader, who becomes prime minister when the party is in office. The prime minister nominates the members of his cabinet, subject to approval by the caucus, which is, however, not always perfunctory. Thereafter, the closest relationship is maintained between the prime minister, the national executive, and the executive of the Federation of Labor. The cabinet and caucus are continually consulted, but the tendency is for "orthodoxy" to be the prerogative of the relatively small number of people in the groups cited above.

In comparison to the NZLP, the ALP is markedly decentralized. In the first place, the caucus chooses not only the prime minister but all the other cabinet ministers. The most important ministers are chosen first; a minister must get more than half the votes cast, and there is generally a regional distribution of offices. One result of the practice of caucus selection of ministers is

that the prime minister cannot force his policy by demanding the resignation of a minister, as in the United Kingdom or Canada. On the other hand, prime ministers, like Chiffley, have dominated their cabinets under most circumstances; the cabinet generally presents a united front in caucus; and the latter almost invariably follows the lead of the cabinet except when their own interests are concerned, as, for example, in the raising of parliamentary salaries. Thus although there is more decentralization of authority within the caucus in Australia than in New Zealand and far more than in the parliamentary Labor party in the United Kingdom, a Labor prime minister can make himself an effective leader, as both Curtin and Chiffley demonstrated.

More serious difficulties arise in the ALP through differences between the caucus and the state conferences and executives. The degree of power residing in the latter, taken in conjunction with the responsibilities of the former, has led to conflicts of loyalty not easily reconciled. Federal caucus has favored centralizing measures, like standard gauges for the railways and extension of wartime powers after World War II, which state Labor groups have frequently opposed. Quite apart from obvious splits like that of 1917 when the federal caucus voted in support of Hughes's proposal for conscription and five out of six state conferences and executives rejected it, there may well be differences of opinion as to the interpretation of the platform. In that case, "the collective membership," as represented by the annual state conference, traditionally claims final right of decision. There are still many resources open to an acute party politician like Chiffley to prevent differences from coming to an open break, but it is significant that, as noted, the parliamentary party bowed to the decision of the representatives of the state executives in October, 1950, and withdrew its opposition to the Suppression of Communism bill. Some outsiders have challenged this action as a violation of the responsibilities of members of Parliament to their constituencies and the country at large.

The degree of decentralization of the ALP, together with its stringent discipline, throws considerably more weight to the rank and file than is true in the New Zealand party. One of the penalties has been the splits of the past, but there is a counterbalancing advantage in the tremendous resilience of the ALP. In the legislation of its first four years in office the NZLP demonstrated the advantages of more unified direction in a unitary country than the Australian party can enjoy; its ultimate parliamentary defeat in 1949 reflects some of the dangers of overcentralization and lack of rank-and-file enthusiasm for the "orthodoxy" preached by the older members of the party.

THE NON-LABOR PARTIES.—While the Labor parties in Australia and New Zealand both have a solid core of trade-union support reflected in their characteristic programs and activities, the non-labor parties are less clearly defined. It is true that the Country party in Australia and the earlier Reform party in New Zealand have rested on the support of certain agricultural interests and found their programs and cohesion therein. But the Liberal party in Australia and the present National party in New Zealand secure their unity chiefly through their opposition to the Labor party and mold their platforms by the necessity of presenting attractive alternatives to Labor at election times. Increasingly, however, they have sought also to build party organizations with vitality comparable to that of the Labor parties.

Of all the non-labor parties in Australia and New Zealand, the Australian Liberal party has had the greatest difficulty in maintaining its cohesion and developing a distinctive program. Although conservative business and commercial interests have been the most constant groups supporting the Liberal party in one or another of its manifestations over the years, they have not had a dominant effect on its program. On the contrary, the Liberal party has sponsored measures of social legislation, such as old age and invalid pensions between 1902 and 1908 and child endowments in 1941, and accepted a substantial framework of governmental regulation for the system of private enterprise, which it favors. Thus, historically, as already suggested, the policies of the Liberal party when in office have differed more in detail than in general character from those of the Labor party.

One reason for its success as a "liberal" party in 1949 was that the Liberal party convinced the public that it was financially independent of big business, with which, regardless of its policies, the party has been associated in many minds. The constitution of the reorganized Liberal party specifically forbids accepting contributions from trade groups or associations. To replace these sources, a great deal of effort has been put into extending the basis of contributions, chiefly through monthly door-to-door collections and by making party units raise their own funds. This policy has not only greatly increased the sources of financial support but has also reinvigorated the local areas.

This dependence on personal canvassing for funds was only one evidence of the fact that the Liberal party, for the first time in its history, developed a truly popular organization throughout the country prior to the election of 1949. It is true that in certain of the individual states, notably South Australia, there has long been a strong Liberal party organization working for state elections through branches, district committees, and a large council and executive which are assisted by several committees to assure spreading responsibility among a large number of people. In this state it has been abundantly evident that vigorous leadership could turn the Liberal Federation into an effective instrument for political propaganda and managing state electoral campaigns. The new development was that the Liberal party in other states, notably New South Wales (which now elects 47 members to a house of 123), adopted similar organizational techniques before the 1949 election and used them for the federal and not merely state elections. No nonlabor party had ever been so well organized before on both the professional and the voluntary levels, New South Wales alone having some four hundred and sixty branches dotted throughout the state and, in addition, numerous youth clubs. Moreover, in the 1949 election they had the telling support of the staffs of the private banks, bitter over the proposed nationalization, and the medical profession, at loggerheads with Labor over its state health plan.

Although on paper the organization of the Liberal party has long looked not unlike that of the Labor party, it operates in a very different way. The structure is federal in character, with a triennial national convention and an executive chosen from the state organizations. Technically each of the states is represented equally, but in the past the smaller states, South and Western Australia, Queensland, and Tasmania, have had almost no chance to influence policy. It has yet to be seen whether new developments will decisively affect this situation.

Moreover, the Liberal Federation does little or nothing to influence the parliamentary policies of Liberal members in either the state or the federal legislature. The state organizations select the candidates and exact a mild pledge to support the principles of the federation but, in fact, leave the parliamentary members complete liberty. Thus there is nothing of the rigid discipline of the Labor party, as in the "pledge" and the doctrine of "the sovereignty of the collective membership." On the contrary, the parliamentary leaders of the Liberal party control both the party program and its organization.

In Parliament, too, there is a marked difference between the Liberal and Labor parties in the relation of the parliamentary members to the prime minister. The Liberal prime minister chooses his own cabinet and may dismiss its members, who are personally responsible to him. Moreover, in the selection of cabinets Liberal administrations have been less careful to secure regional representation than has Labor. A notable example was Menzies' cabinet in 1939, which was composed almost entirely of Victorians. This is less likely to be repeated, however, since it proved a serious source of weakness in Menzies' administration, by antagonizing members of his party who felt they had a right to be included in his cabinet, thus causing in some measure the party intrigues which led to his resignation in 1941. The Liberal-Country party cabinets of 1949, 1951, and 1954, it may be noted, had substantial geographical representation.

Despite the fact that it is an "interest" party, the Country party has never developed the momentum of a "movement" as Labor has done. The interests of its supporters tend to be too particularized, while distance complicates the discussion of common problems. Hence although the programs of the Country party—such as fixed home prices for primary products, rural credits for co-operative marketing, and state-financed soil-erosion programs—are those which aid agriculturalists generally, they tend to be the creation of individuals rather than any mass sentiment. This is perhaps the more necessary, since the party's basic aim of low tariffs is so out of step with everyone else in Australian politics that it has to seek its ends through expedients.

Although it is difficult to secure information about Country party finances, the big landowners and wool brokers probably supply a substantial proportion of its funds. This, together with the difficulties of small-scale farming in Australia, helps to explain why the Country party is not primarily a small farmer-owners party even to the degree which was true for the Reform party in New Zealand.

The Country party has attempted to pattern its organization and discipline on that of the Labor party, but without much success. State organizations select candidates for the federal parliament and also send delegates to a national conference. Since the Country party's strength lies in its bargaining power, however, its leaders have had great freedom in interpreting the program and are little more responsible to the rank and file of their members than is true of the Liberal party.

The National party in New Zealand does not depend on such diverse groups as the Liberal party in Australia, because the country is more homogeneous in activities, but it faces perhaps a more difficult problem: holding together city businessmen and prosperous farmers. Moreover, neither group is unified in itself. Manufacturers' interests differ from those of importers; while the battle between the sheep and the cows is not only economic but also indicative of the class structure (suggested by Oliver Duff's quip, "Sheep make gentlemen and cows unmake them") reflected in politics. It also has regional implications, for the South Island thrives on wool exports, while the North Island is the center of the prosperous dairy industry.

The secret of the cohesion of the National party is that it offers the only alternative to the Labor party. In the interests of getting into power, the older antagonisms reflected in the Liberal and Reform parties have been subdued into a workable combination which steadily gained increasing support throughout the latter part of the 1940's until it swept into office in 1949.

The National party can draw for financial support on both the wealthy farmers and the manufacturing, financial, and commercial interests. A new development since 1949 has been widespread canvassing for subscriptions, especially in the wealthy suburbs and among farmers.

In organization the National party also showed some developments prior to the 1949 election similar to those of the Liberal party in Australia. It encouraged some active junior groups and increased the number of both professional and voluntary workers. In general, however, the National party has always been more loosely organized than the Labor party and has allowed greater autonomy to its local branches. These features, and less emphasis on party orthodoxy, are not surprising results of the great variety of opinions and attitudes found within the National party, particularly when it comes within reach of political power.

The local unit of organization in the National party is the electorate, whose committee (to which branches send representatives) has the right in theory, although not always in practice, to choose parliamentary candidates. The electorates are grouped into three divisions in the more populous North Island and two in the South, to aid campaigning. Above this level is the annual conference made up of four representatives from each electorate. Its officers, together with twenty-six members—twenty-one selected by the divisional committee and five by the parliamentary members—form the national executive, or Dominion Council. A standing committee on policy consists of three nominees of this council and three members of Parliament appointed by the parliamentary leader, who acts as chairman of the body. Thus the hierarchy finds its logical peak in the parliamentary leader of the party.

As is true of the Labor party in New Zealand, the parliamentary leader frequently consults more with powerful nonparty interest groups, e.g., representatives of the Manufacturers' Federation and other business interests, than with members of his party organization. There is not quite the same degree of centralization in the National party, however, as in the NZLP, in that the local units' control of funds (although these are sometimes passed on to the central office when seats seem "safe") together with their diversity gives them somewhat more independence than is true of the Labor party. Since the local units of the National party, however, make little or no effort to influence the policies of parliamentary members, once they have been elected, this greater independence, which may help to maintain their enthusiasm, does little to aid transmission of rank-and-file ideas to the party's leaders.

V / CONCLUSION

In all four of the older overseas members of the Commonwealth, parties form the dynamic of the political process. In South Africa, it is true, other groups like the Ossewa Brandwag, the Broederbond, and the Torch Commando have operated outside the regular party structure to promote ends peculiarly their own. Even there, however, the tendency has been for these groups, particularly the Ossewa Brandwag and the Torch Commando, to be drawn into politics and increasingly associated with one or the other recognized political party.

Also, the logic of the alternation of political power has provided a strong imperative toward a two-party system in each of these four countries. Though this showed signs of breaking down in Canada with the progressive weakening of the Conservative party, no other party has yet been able to threaten its position as the official opposition. The principal weakness of the Conservatives in Canada is their inability to secure a strong foothold either in the Prairies (apart from Manitoba) or in Quebec. Only the Liberals have consistently been able to secure strong support in every major section of the country in federal elections.

The strength of the two-party system in these four countries has been the more remarkable because each has a distinctive regionalism. This is the most obvious in Canada (where it is reflected in the distinctiveness of provincial party alignments), but it is also noticeable in all the others. Moreover, their regionalism is accentuated by the smallness of their populations as compared to the areas they occupy. Even New Zealand is more than a thousand miles from tip to tip of its two islands, and its relatively small population is grouped mainly around its four major cities, two in the North Island and two in the South. Not the least of the contributions of political parties to nation-building in these countries has been that they have only rarely concentrated on sectional interests but instead have placed their main emphasis on the big issues of national policy, both domestic and external.

In regard to the racial divisions so obvious in Canada and South Africa, the record is less clear. With the single exception of the struggle over conscription during World War I, when Canada's political parties divided largely along racial lines, the Canadian party system has been a solvent, rather than an intensifier, of racial feeling. This remains true, despite the fact that nearly all of Canada's French Canadians work within the Liberal party in federal politics.

In South Africa, however, the picture is far from reassuring at the present time. In the past Hertzog used the Nationalist party to improve the position of Afrikaners to the point where they could co-operate on equal terms with English-speaking South Africans. Thus its racialism had an ultimate objective of national unity. Botha and Smuts, in contrast, believed that the best way to build South African unity was for English- and Afrikaans-speaking peoples to work together in a single party. Hertzog himself joined in this program after 1933, by which time he felt that the "two-streams" policy had worked itself out; and the United party, which is the creation of both Hertzog and Smuts, continues the tradition. In contrast, the Nationalists of Malan and Strijdom seek to establish, if not impose, the values of one of the two European peoples of the Union on the whole country. In so doing, they have roused fears among the English-speaking (and some moderate Afrikaners) that are seriously exacerbating racial feeling.

South African experience thus demonstrates that political parties with an exclusively racial base tend to intensify racial divisions and could widen them through selfishly oriented policies to the point where the parliamentary system itself may be endangered, as it will always be when it ceases to provide adequate opportunities for the safeguarding of minority rights. At the same time, political parties which include racial minorities (as do the Liberal party in Canada and the United party in South Africa) but associate them with other elements in the population act both to safeguard the minority and to reduce the intensity of racial divisions.

As to the economic and social divisions within the community, the party system in these countries has been both a reflection and a modifier. In Australia and New Zealand, where these divisions are most strongly felt, working-class self-consciousness developed early under the spur of harsh conditions and is still obvious today. Yet the very fact that this self-consciousness adopted a political manifestation through the organization of Labor parties may well have taken the edge off its bitterness and certainly made possible a much earlier adoption of its programs than would otherwise have occurred. In both countries Labor in office proved itself to be far more than a supporter of partisan interests. This may be partly because it has always had to appeal outside its safe centers of support to unattached voters and partly because Labor was largely empirical in office, as in opposition, and only occasionally doctrinaire. The net result has been to associate a class-conscious group with national policies and responsibilities which have had a broadening effect. The same can also be said of the non-labor parties in these countries, which have had to modify their natural class interests to achieve electoral success.

In certain ways these four countries —Canada, Australia, New Zealand, and South Africa—have had unusually favorable conditions for developing their party and parliamentary structures. They inherited a strong tradition from Great Britain, and they have had conditions of relative peace, prosperity, and freedom from outside interference within which to develop. That the characteristic temper is one of moderation was demonstrated after the bitter election of 1951 in New Zealand, when the Labor party accepted the verdict of the electors with good grace and sportsmanship.

Yet at the same time such a temper will persist only so long as the political system appears to provide relatively equal opportunities to both sides. In South Africa the Nationalist party used a slim parliamentary majority during its first term of office to push through a measure affecting citizenship which was resented by one of its two European peoples. It attempted to remove the Colored from the common roll in Cape Province by means which the Opposition—and subsequently the courts—declared to be unconstitutional. In the face of such tactics, even a tradition of moderation may not be sufficient to restrain a frustrated Opposition from unparliamentary methods.

What is obvious, then, is that the successful working of the parliamentary system depends on a considerable degree of restraint on the part of political parties. This restraint is the more necessary when parties represent a particular region, racial group, or economic class, for it then demands that particular purposes shall not be pressed to the exclusion of programs that can secure wider support. On the whole, political parties with bases so narrow and exclusive have been rare in these countries, and even when they have represented such interests predominantly (as do the Labor parties in Australia and New Zealand), they have not promoted programs so narrow as to violate the rule. Only the present South African Nationalist party seems in danger of doing so. The major Canadian federal parties, in contrast, are so broadly based that moderation develops, as in American parties, through the interaction of different interest groups within the parties themselves.

Some observers of recent political trends in Australia, New Zealand, and Great Britain have gone beyond these generalizations, however, to suggest that the defeat of the Labor parties in all three countries between 1949 and 1951 points to a basic dilemma for parties which have adopted socialist programs, whether or not they plan immediately to implement them. This dilemma arises from the incompatibility of these socialist aims with the capitalist system so firmly rooted and widely accepted in their communities. It is true at least in Australia and New Zealand that their Labor parties have had their greatest periods of success when they were tackling conditions which offended the equalitarian views of the community. Once this is done, more serious difficulties arise. The party must decide whether it intends to introduce more than palliatives to ease the dislocations and inequalities inherent in capitalism. If it does not do so, it tends to lose its momentum, alienate its own more radical wing, and have little to offer but a good record in the past as a reason for returning to office. If the party makes a more frontal attack upon capitalism, however, it risks alienating its own right-wing followers and even more the middle-class groups on which it inevitably depends for electoral success. Neither of these alternatives offers a substantial basis for long-range success in countries so strongly committed to the system of democratic capitalism as Australia and New Zealand are.

One answer to this dilemma may be that, paradoxically, the Labor parties in Australia and New Zealand will continue to have their greatest success in the future, as in the past, when they differ least in basic objectives from their political opponents. Under these circumstances they can profit from the mistakes of their opponents and take advantage of the tendencies of parliamentary democracies to replace parties in office by their opponents. This generalization, of course, assumes the continuation of relative prosperity at home and abroad. Violent economic dislocation leading to widespread hardships might well shake the abiding faith in the existing economic system and open the way to the more radical policies demanded by the left-wing groups of the Labor parties. In an earlier period, a further alternative might have been an increase in popularity for Communist parties, but this now seems unlikely unless the latter can pose more convincingly than at present as national parties, free from the suspected subordination to the interests of the Soviet Union which is their greatest handicap.

It has been seen that political parties in Canada, Australia, New Zealand, and South Africa fulfil more or less adequately the major criteria for political parties: to offer the people a meaningful and adequate choice both of policies and of leaders; to reflect the desires of the people and of the members of the parties themselves; to assist in the process of arriving peacefully at a settlement of controversial issues (although this is not certain in South Africa at the present time); and to provide an effective instrument for carrying out the judgment of the voters, once they have made their choice of parties. One further question remains: How far do the parties in these countries provide a channel for active political participation by the rank and file of the membership, not merely in promoting the victory of the party but in determining its policies and choosing its leaders?

Of all the parties considered in this section, the Australian Labor party is the one which most satisfactorily provides this intimate interplay between the rank and file of its members and the leaders and programs of the party. In its earlier days the Canadian CCF had much of the same active participation by its members. Subsequently, however, there has been less activity by the rank and file of party members in the east, and, partly as a conse-

quence, the federal CCF has yielded somewhat, although not to the same degree as the New Zealand Labor party, to the trend toward party oligarchy which Robert Michels' *Political Parties* prophesied to be inevitable, particularly for socialist parties. In Saskatchewan, in contrast, the ready-made base of agricultural co-operation has made possible striking and fairly constant mass participation in the formulation and consideration of programs.

It is significant that reinvigorated local branches played a considerable role in the electoral successes in 1949 of both the Australian Liberal party and the New Zealand National party. In comparison, neither the Liberal nor the Conservative party in Canada nor the United party in South Africa had shown much evidence of this kind of activity by the rank and file up to early 1953. More constituency participation within the United party, however, preceded its electoral fight in 1953 and subsequent internal struggles. The South African Nationalist party is *sui generis* in this regard: generating intense interest and support in the Afrikaans-speaking *platteland* and urban working class, responsive to the sentiments and, in particular, the prejudices of its most intense members, yet with a much more authoritarian leadership than is found in the Australian Labor party.

What seems clear is that intra-party democracy of the type exhibited by the Australian Labor party has provided in the past an impressive degree of resilience in the face of internal divisions which might well have wrecked another party. At its worst, the dominance of "the collective membership" may threaten the parliamentary system by making an extra-parliamentary body superior to the elected representatives; at its best, it provides the interplay between the members of the community and their elected representatives which is an ideal of democracy.

Political parties are the means through which modern electorates maintain their contact with and influence over the governmental machinery. Such a survey as has been undertaken here demonstrates that there is nothing stereotyped about the ways in which they operate or the purposes for which they may be used. In the end, political parties are the vehicles of political purposes, capable of infinite variety, like the democracy which they serve. What can be said, however, from the experience of these four countries is that political parties can help to bridge the economic, social, regional, and even racial divisions which threaten national unity. Furthermore, political parties make the issues of public policy dramatic and intelligible. Through the alternatives they offer, they make popular control possible. Thus they are not only an aid to democracy but an essential element in making it possible.

TABLE 1

UNION OF SOUTH AFRICA: SEATS WON AND PERCENTAGE OF POPULAR VOTES POLLED
BY EACH PARTY DURING PERIOD 1938–53*

PARTIES	1938		1943.		1948		1953	
	Seats	Per Cent Votes	Seats	Per Cent Votes	Seats	Per Cent Votes	Seats	Per Cent Votes
Nationalist........	27	29.56	43	33.66	70	36.37	94	45.50
Afrikaner..........	......	......	......	......	9	3.59	......	......
United............	111	54.42	89	53.18	65	50.38	57	51.62
Labour............	3	5.06	9	4.12	6	2.76	5	2.78
Dominion..........	8	6.28	7	3.53	......	......	......	......
Others............	1	4.68	2	5.51	......	6.90	......	0.10
Total.........	150	100.00	150	100.00	150	100.00	156	100.00

PERCENTAGE OF ENROLLED VOTERS PARTICIPATING IN GENERAL ELECTIONS

1938	1943	1948	1953
86.46	81.81	79.90	87.23

* The returns are taken from the *Government Gazette*. The party affiliations of the successful candidates for 1938 and 1943 have been secured from M. P. A. Malan and M. C. van Rensburg. *Verkiesingsuitslae, 1910–1943;* for 1948 and 1953 from M. P. Bernon and G. Krog, *The Facts, Figures, and Guide for the General Election.* Where seats were uncontested, 85 per cent of 85 per cent of the number on the rolls has been given to the unopposed candidate. Fifteen per cent of 85 per cent of the number on the rolls has been given to the major opposing party. Number of unopposed seats: 1938: 4 United party; 1943: 1 Nationalist, 16 United party, 1 Dominion party; 1948: 1 Nationalist, 11 United party; 1953: 2 Nationalist, 18 United party.

TABLE 2

New Zealand: Seats Won and Percentage of Popular Vote Polled by Each Party during Period 1935–51*

Parties	1935 Seats	1935 Per Cent	1938 Seats	1938 Per Cent	1943 Seats	1943 Per Cent	1946 Seats	1946 Per Cent	1949 Seats	1949 Per Cent	1951 Seats	1951 Per Cent
National.....	19	32.8	25	41.0	34	43.5	38	48.5	46	51.9	50	53.99
Labour......	55	46.1	53	56.1	45	47.6	42	51.3	34	47.2	30	45
Others......	7.8 (Democrat)				4.3 (Democratic Labour)							

PERCENTAGE OF ELECTORATE VOTING†

1935	1938	1943	1945	1949	1951
90.75	94.34	83.39‡	93.46	93.53	88.83 89.08 (including Maori electorates)

* Figures through the courtesy of the New Zealand Embassy.

† These percentage figures are for European electorates only, as Maori rolls are a new departure.
   Maori electorates: In 1951, there were 49,487 on the roll, and 37,933 votes were cast. In 1949, 35,196 voters were enrolled and 38,749 votes were cast. Declaration votes were permitted.

‡ Percentage only of civilian votes cast. Military personnel were not listed on rolls but were often included on civilian rolls, so it is impossible to obtain current percentage.

TABLE 3

Canada: Seats Won and Percentage of Popular Vote Polled by Each Party during Period 1935–53*

Parties	1935 Seats	1935 Per Cent	1940 Seats	1940 Per Cent	1945 Seats	1945 Per Cent	1949 Seats	1949 Per Cent	1953 Seats	1953 Per Cent
Liberal..........	176	46.5	181†	54.8	125†	41.4	194†	50.0	172†	49.9
Progressive Conservative......	39	29.8	39‡	30.7	66‡	27.7	41‡	29.8	51‡	31
Cooperative Commonwealth Federation........	7	8.7	8	8.5	28	15.7	13	13.4	23	11.2
Social Credit.....	18	4.1	10§	2.6	13§	4.0	10§	3.8	15§	5.4
Others..........	5	10.8	7	3.4	13	11.2	4	3.0	4	2.2

PERCENTAGE OF ENROLLED VOTERS PARTICIPATING IN GENERAL ELECTIONS*

1935...................	75	1949...................	74
1940...................	70	1953...................	67
1945...................	76		

* Compiled from figures in *Reports of Chief Electoral Officer* (1935–54).

† Including Independent Liberal.

‡ Including Independent Conservative.

§ In 1940, New Democracy including Social Credit; thereafter including Independent Social Credit and, in 1949, Union des Électeurs, the Quebec version of Social Credit.

TABLE 4

AUSTRALIA: SEATS WON AND PERCENTAGE OF POPULAR VOTE POLLED BY EACH PARTY DURING PERIOD 1937–54*

PARTIES	1937		1940		1943		1946		1949		1951		1954	
	Seats	Per Cent	Seats	Per Cent	Seats	Per Cent	Seats	Per Cent	Seats	Per Cent	Seats	Per Cent	Seats	Per Cent
A.L.P.	29	42.5	36	40.2	48	50.0	43	49.9	48	46.0	54†	42.6	59†	49.7
Liberal	28	35.9	23	30.5	12	19.4	18	33.0	57	39.7	52 }	46.1	47 }	47.5
Country	17	13.3	14	13.7	13	12.2	11	10.9	17	10.6	17 }	11.2	17 }	
Others	1	8.3	2	15.6	2	18.4	3	6.2	1	3.7	.....	.....	.....	2.7
	(Ind.)		(Ind.)		(Ind.)		(1 Ind. Lab.) (1 Lang. Lab.) (1 Ind.)		(Ind.)					

PERCENTAGE OF ENROLLED VOTERS PARTICIPATING IN GENERAL ELECTIONS FOR HOUSE OF REPRESENTATIVES, 1937–54

1937.................	96.13	1949.............	97.93‡
1940.................	94.82	1951.............	97.87‡
1943.................	96.32	1954.............	97.08
1946.................	93.97		

* The figures for the elections, 1937–49, are taken from Louise Overacker, *The Australian Party System* (New Haven, 1952), p. 331. They do not include the voting for the Northern Territory member, the Independent. The figures for the votes cast in the 1940 and 1943 elections as recorded by the *Sydney Morning Herald*, October 2, 1943, differ considerably from those given here. The figures for the 1951 election are taken from the *Australian Parliamentary Handbook* (1952), p. 235, and those for 1954 from the *Sydney Morning Herald*, June 24, 1954.
† Including two from Northern Territories who vote only on issues affecting their constituencies.
‡ Includes 1.9 per cent of informal votes in 1949 and 1951 and 1.3 per cent in 1954.

French Political Parties: Ideological Myths and Social Realities[1]

CHARLES A. MICAUD

University of Virginia

The most spectacular weakness of the French parliamentary system has been the fragility of her successive governments, for since her liberation France has had some twenty cabinets with an average life-span of less than six months. And it has been aptly said that one day out of every four France is either waiting for a ministerial crisis, is having it, or is convalescing from it. Thanks to the rapid rotation of ministries, one deputy out of four is entitled to put on his visiting card the title of "Ancien Ministre."

But governmental instability does not necessarily mean total discontinuity and incoherence, and permanent officials are always there to carry on the routine of administration. Two men belonging to the same party—Robert Schuman and Georges Bidault—have (until 1954) monopolized the ministry of foreign affairs and assured the continuity of French foreign policy. If, by contrast, France has had during that time eleven different ministers of fi-

nance and fourteen of economic affairs, this does not imply that there are radically different solutions to France's economic and financial problems. Since 1947, in fact, the government has been following a consistently conservative policy, despite the presence of the Socialist party in the coalition; and following the elections in 1951 this conservatism has been more solidly intrenched than ever.

More dangerous than instability and stemming partly from it is immobility, that is, the absence of dynamic leadership capable of facing important economic and social issues, of adopting a program of necessary, even if unpopular, reforms, and implementing it. No government is given enough time to adopt a long-range program, and the very survival of each government demands that it avoid dangerous issues.

The French party system is largely responsible for this instability and immobility. It is characterized mainly by the weak structure and consequent lack of discipline of the parties of the Center and the Right. Other characteristics are the heterogeneity of party followings, making each political formation extremely sensitive to any shift in public opinion and to any organized pressure, and the "intellectualism" of the parties, that is, their incapacity to present a concrete program that would be the basis of responsible action and of a lasting contract between the members of a coalition. Above all is the absence of incentives to action that normally would result from the presence of an

1. Parts of this chapter were taken from the author's contributions to the following publications: "The Third Force Today," in E. M. Earle's *Modern France* (Princeton, 1951); "Organization and Leadership in the French Communist Party," in *World Politics* (spring, 1953); "French Intellectuals and Communism," in *Social Research* (fall, 1954); "Social Democracy in France," in *World Politics* (summer, 1955); and "The Bases of Communist Strength in France," in *Western Political Quarterly* (summer, 1955). The author also wishes to express his gratitude to the Social Science Research Institute at the University of Virginia for a grant-in-aid which made this study possible.

alternative coalition, ready to take over.

This leads us to the second characteristic of French politics: the presence of a strong totalitarian party at the Left and of an authoritarian party at the Right. From 1947 to 1951 these parties' dual challenges to parliamentary democracy forced a heterogeneous coalition for defense of the Republic, including Socialists and conservatives, that by its very composition was incapable of a constructive and forceful policy. The electoral system of 1951 was designed to save the Republic by weakening the parliamentary representation of the two extremes. Although it allowed the Socialists to pass on to the opposition and although the De Gaulle RPF came in due time to support the government, the presence of a strong Communist party continues to prevent an acceptable alternative to the present Center-Right coalition. Because of this lack of alternative, there is no incentive to embark upon reforms and no responsibility toward the electorate. The underlying tensions keep on accumulating, thus adding to the appeal of the extremes. There is today an unwritten and unholy alliance between communism and reactionary conservatism. By keeping the trade-unions divided and weak and by preventing the merging of left-wing political formations, the Communist party creates an imbalance of social and political forces that directly benefits the partisans of the status quo.

French politics thus suffers from a double handicap: the character of French parties—weak structure, lack of discipline, heterogeneity and fickleness of clientele, absence of concrete programs—and the lack of consensus on institutions and values that was dramatized in the conflict of the three forces of communism, de Gaullism, and "republicanism." The latter may well have been the greater handicap, as it prevented the process of peaceful change that alone could re-create the lost consensus.

I / THE BASES OF THE FRENCH PARTY SYSTEM

In order to put the parties of the Fourth Republic in proper perspective, it is necessary to examine, first, the conflicting ideologies which have divided France since the inception of the Third Republic and which underlie the party division of today. This lack of consensus is in turn both cause and consequence of the underlying tensions in the economic life and social structure of the country. To these ideological and social factors must be added the political developments that helped shape the party system of today.

Ideological

According to the classical interpretation of French politics during the Third Republic, France was divided into two blocs: Right and Left, reactionaries and republicans, the party of resistance and the party of movement. The main criterion of reaction appeared to be a clerical stand; that of republicanism, an anticlerical one. This division was hardly satisfactory to explain the political dynamics of the Third Republic, especially after 1918. It roughly corresponded to the phenomenon of the two blocs at the second ballot of the elections but had no continuous basis of fact in parliamentary life. It put the liberal Catholic Démocrates populaires near the extreme Right and the Radical Socialists at the Left, although the first was often more sensitive to the claims of the working class than was the second. It had to ignore the left-wing Catholic Jeune République and, more important, to place the Communists among the stern defenders of the ideals of 1789.

A more satisfactory grouping of the basic tendencies in French politics may be found in a triangular pattern: in the Third Republic, as in the Fourth, the libertarian Center was faced with the double challenge of an authoritarian Right and an egalitarian Left. If in normal times the two extremes were not a major threat to the Republic, they would gather great strength in time of crisis and would be a constant handicap to the successful working of the parliamentary system.

During the first decades of the Third Republic the main threat came from the Right. The issue of republican defense, justified during the period of consolidation of the regime, prevented a realignment of parties on economic and social issues that had become of paramount importance after the turn of the century. When a new challenge came from the Marxist Left, French politics took on the aspect of a double conflict between partisans and opponents of the republican ideology and between partisans and opponents of the economic status quo.

The Radicals and a few smaller groups at the Center were rightists in economic problems and leftists in political outlook. They could side alternately with the Right and the Left. Generally, republican solidarity led to an electoral alliance with the Socialists against the threat of "reaction." But soon after victory was won at the polls, as in 1924, 1932, and 1936, the Center would shift its support from Left to Right.

The presence of the two extremes prevented an acceptable alternative to the rule of the Center, since the Right was unreliable and the Left unco-operative. It gave the parties of the Center a quasi-monopoly of power and the possibility of maintaining it without attempting to deal with the cause of social unrest. They could capitalize on the fear of reaction and revolution in order to remain in power. Republican defense was their main *raison d'être*, a negative outlook which, in turn, benefited the two extremes.

As Katherine Munro expressed it:

The Right wing parties never quite forgot the possibility of a counter revolution while the Left wing parties revived the Revolution militant in their Marxism or Communism; each side suspected the other of using the Republic to achieve its own ends and of being legal only so far as it suited it. This suspicion threatened time and time again to make the Republic unworkable, since it led to obstruction in both the political and the economic sphere, and difficulties of government in turn undermined confidence in the regime and its rulers.

THE AUTHORITARIAN IDEOLOGY.—The authoritarian ideology followed two main currents: (1) the traditionalist aristocratic and monarchist current from De Maistre to Maurras and (2) the Caesarian or Bonapartist current, which, while lacking the philosophical underpinning of the first, nevertheless had its own ethos of charismatic leadership. Both currents more or less merged in the twentieth century when integral nationalism furnished an emotional and philosophical basis for an authoritarian movement of mass appeal. In the name of national survival, the leader, supported by an elite and a *mystique*, could impose a much-needed unity on the threatened country, keep the traditional order, and check the advance of socialism which was beginning to terrify many of the bourgeoisie and the peasantry.

A large section of the bourgeoisie came to adopt a frozen oligarchical outlook similar to that of the old aristocracy, according to which rights and privileges were based on birth rather than on function and merit. As Julien Benda remarked shortly before World War II, the bourgeoisie had abandoned the doctrine of the rights of man and equality of opportunity—the basic ideas of the French Revolution—for the thesis of the "rights of the elite," not *l'élite-individu* but *l'élite-classe*, whose foundation was heredity and no longer personal ability.

In normal times the authoritarian movement appeared relatively weak, but in times of crisis, when people were insecure, it would grow to threatening proportions. In 1848 millions had already gathered behind Louis Napoleon and a few years later behind the Empire. If a leader was present, large numbers were ready to follow, as the Boulanger episode clearly showed. After World War I had added to the general insecurity, the appeal of authoritarianism began to grow under the double impact of international communism and fascism. Fortunately, the divisions among the leagues, the absence of an undisputed leader, and the indifference of most *petits bourgeois* and peasants saved France from fascism, if not from defeat. The temptation had been strong to back Mussolini, Franco, and even Hitler in the crusade against communism and democracy. After the defeat Pétain appeared as a savior, and the myth of the "National Revolution" united most rightist factions behind his leadership. They remained quiet and fearful for a time after liberation, only to find in De Gaulle the charismatic leader who would save them from real and imaginary perils.

The main motivation behind the authoritarian movements seems to have been insecurity—hence the appeal of an immutable order. The policy of the "return to the land" advocated by Vichy and the outlook of technocrats and corporatists have in common the fear of a possible social upheaval and the will to establish firmly the foundations of the unequal society. Privileges have to be maintained by force in proportion as the elite appears less capable of creative leadership for the good of the whole community. This reactionary position could only encourage the revolutionary movement, which in turn justified the premises of the authoritarian ideology. Each extreme found in the presence of the other sufficient food for its own growth.

If a deep sense of insecurity may explain the survival of the authoritarian outlook, it remains that security itself is a relative value. Perhaps the French bourgeoisie, along with the peasantry, showed an exaggerated concern for security which created conditions leading to even greater insecurity. Obsession with security can be traced outside the political sphere in such things as the choice of careers and investments or the conduct of business: there the main concern was to save as much as possible and risk as little as possible. In the bourgeois pattern of culture, high value was put on caution and foresight. The ideal was to obtain absolute guaranties that present conditions would never be upset, that the status quo would remain forever. This ideal of a static order in which the dynamic forces of life are kept leashed was translated into a narrow conservatism and, in times of danger, into a taste for an authoritarian form of government.

THE EQUALITARIAN IDEOLOGY.—The equalitarian ideology can be defined as the revolutionary creed which sacrifices everything to the goal of equality. It is as doctrinaire as authoritarianism and as inimical to the libertarian view of man, for it is also anchored on the emotional basis of a frustrated need: emphasis on equality betrays a deep sense of injustice, just as emphasis on authority betrays insecurity. The appeal of Marxism in France and its lack of appeal in England should not be interpreted as a sign of a French intellectual propensity toward beautiful constructions of the mind. It was not that Marx was intellectually convincing—most Marxists had not read Marx, and those who did often could not agree on the interpretation of the master—but rather that his moral appeal, his call for justice in the classless society, was pregnant with meaning for people who felt unjustly treated by society. Marxism was necessary both as a dream of what ought to be and as a weapon to bring it about.

In its various forms it holds equality in the classless society as the supreme good. Until equality becomes effective, one cannot speak of freedom—it is only hypocrisy, a "bourgeois luxury." Since the state is, by definition, the dictatorship of a class, formal democracy is only an institutional device to protect the bourgeois monopoly of power. Peaceful change is obviously impossible; only catastrophic change can bring about the good society. Then the state will wither away, either immediately, as some syndicalists believed, or after a period of dictatorship by the proletariat, as most Marxists thought.

Trade-unions existed less as means for obtaining immediate and tangible advantages for the workers than as instruments for the conquest of power. It was better to keep the unions lean and fit for battle than prosperous and contented. If this concept discouraged employers from accepting trade-unionism—collective bargaining was practically unknown until 1936—it was all to the good, since it created conditions that appeared to justify the revolutionary premises.

This dialectical process applied to the Socialist party as well. Although it was hesitating between a strategy of gradualism and one of revolution, it was prevented by Marxian symbolism from co-operating with bourgeois parties. The famous controversy between Guesde and Jaurès during and after the Dreyfus affair illustrates the dilemma of the Socialists and foreshadows the coming divorce of Social Democrats and Communists. World War I and the death of Jaurès perhaps prevented the birth of a genuine French labor party. Instead, the SFIO (the Socialist party) split between its reformist and humanistic wing under Blum's leadership and its revolutionary wing, the new Communist party. The CGT—the major trade-union organization—did likewise. The brief reconciliation of 1935 and 1936, dictated as it was by the threat of fascism, could not be more than a temporary alliance.

While the Labour party in Britain, through its alliance with the Liberals, obtained many advantages for the workers, the French Socialist party until 1936—and to a greater extent the Communist party—have prevented the working class from having a voice in the determination of national policies. The conservatism of the Right and the Center could continue to leave unsolved the problems presented by modern technology. The French economy remained relatively backward, and social security and labor legislation were not prominent on the program of any government until 1936. Meanwhile the revolutionary temper kept feeding on this indifference of the middle classes, for which it was partly responsible.

If the revolutionary ideology seems to answer deep-seated emotional needs, it also creates conditions that frustrate those needs, stimulate discontent, and prevent the reaching of a new consensus. It organizes resentment and hatred; it indirectly feeds the reactionary position, which in turn increases its own dynamism. Organizations influenced by ideological considerations become a major obstacle to peaceful change; each side interprets a concession as a defeat. Each situation becomes charged with ideological significance and is interpreted in terms of its strategic consequences. The premise of enmity develops an emotional and intolerant outlook. Compromises become a

question of reconciling not only conflicting interests but conflicting sets of
values, which are, by definition, incompatible.

THE LIBERTARIAN IDEOLOGY.—To understand the libertarian ideology, it
must be remembered that France passed
abruptly from royal absolutism to the
dictatorship of the Comité du Salut
public and later of Bonaparte. Freedom, as soon as proclaimed, had to
be sacrificed for the sake of republican
defense. Expectations had been created
that were frustrated and excesses committed that were not forgotten, both
of which made the ideals of the Revolution suspect for many generations. Institutional continuity had been abruptly ended, and 1789 had started the
cycle of revolution-reaction which dominated the nineteenth century. The
attempts made by the Restoration and
the July Monarchy to reconcile authority with freedom and equality failed.
For with each try the ruling class was
persistently indifferent to the claims of
its rivals, and the barricades took the
place of reform bills as instruments of
change.

When the Third Republic came to
life, lack of consensus was evident. The
workers, having just suffered a bloody
defeat, were bitter. The aristocracy and
clergy, as well as an important section
of the bourgeoisie and the peasantry,
had no love for the Republic. Only
the division of Monarchists and Bona-
partists, among the ranks of the majority, allowed the Republic to be born.
In order to survive, the new regime had
to use the weapon of the state against
its enemies: the concept of a strong and
centralized state remained unchallenged except by the extremes.

Paradoxically, the strong state which
was necessary to protect the Republic
made for a weak government, necessary
to protect the individual against possible abuses of power. The main duty
of the deputy was to keep watch over
the government and, through it, over
the permanent officialdom. Old memories refreshed by unpleasant incidents
—MacMahon, Boulanger, the Dreyfus
affair—kept as an article of faith the
principle of the supremacy of the legislature over the executive. To overthrow the government periodically, to
prevent it from effectively ruling
France, became a republican duty. The
multiparty system itself was reassuring,
since it prevented a possible concentration of power and made the coalition
government harmless.

The rich and many-sided liberal democratic movement of the mid-nineteenth
century, in which Catholics like Lammenais and Montalembert shared with
the Socialist Proudhon and the bourgeois liberals De Tocqueville and La-
martine a faith in the importance and
dignity of the individual, in the Third
Republic became frozen into a *mystique républicaine*. It had its positive
aspects: the belief that man is his own
ruler, free to think and behave according to his own judgment; a passionate
faith in the sovereignty of the people;
and a strong belief that progress was
inevitable. Its devotion to the cause of
individual justice was proved at the
time of the Dreyfus affair. But the negative aspects of the republican faith
dominated.

Freedom came to be equated with
defense of the Republic, threatened by
reaction, and defense of the individual,
threatened by possible abuses of power
and the resurgence of a hierarchical
system. The keynote was vigilance. The
main function of the deputy was his
control of the ministers, who, in turn,
controlled the permanent officials in
order to prevent or correct abuses of
power. In Paris the temptation was
great for the latter to forget his mission
and to become a tool of the elite, which
was in permanent conspiracy against
the Republic.

"Where does democracy reside,"

wrote Alain, one of the high priests of the republican faith, "if not in a third power that political science has not described and which I call the *contrôleur?* It is nothing else than the continually effective power of deposing kings and specialists the very moment they no longer manage affairs according to the interests of the greatest numbers." Is the function of the parties to create a strong government? "Not at all!" answers Alain. "The elector does not choose a king; he chooses a *contrôleur.*" Parties are dangerous, since they seek power and since vigilance cannot be delegated. A strong government is not wanted; on the contrary, it is to be avoided. The role of the minister is not "to administer and command . . . but rather to oppose further advance by the powerful and voracious administration."

It must be admitted that this system worked well as a protective device and that it admirably answered the age-long mistrust of the little man against the administration and the "important people." Lack of organization was an essential prerequisite that fitted a traditional inability to organize. That it prevented effective leadership, adaptation to fast-changing conditions, and necessary reforms was no sin for people who were deeply satisfied with their way of living. French politics could remain in the realm of abstractions and general principles and be indifferent to specific programs. The good republicans could continue to think of themselves as progressives and to believe in the eternal virtue of their principles. They conformed to Bertrand de Jouvenel's saying: "La stagnation est peut-être la seule forme pratique de la fidélité aux principes."

Economic and Social

Economic considerations alone cannot explain the divisions among parties. In the Third Republic only the Social-

ists and later the Communists drew heavily on the support of one class and openly defended its interests. The differences among other parties concerning economic and social problems as well as the composition of their electoral following were not significant enough to justify a clear-cut division between a conservative Right and a progressive Center. It would be misleading to consider the parties of the Right as exclusive champions of the plutocracy and those of the Center as the protectors of the *petits bourgeois*. The interests of big capital were perhaps more effectively represented by the Alliance démocratique than by the Fédération républicaine that stood at its right. If most people of the upper middle classes voted Right and perhaps most *petits bourgeois* voted Center, all classes, and particularly the peasants, spread their votes from extreme Right to extreme Left.

In his study of political geography François Goguel reaches the conclusion that social structures are less important in determining party divisions than political and ideological factors. Left-wing parties do not recruit equally in all industrial regions, any more than do right-wing parties in regions of religious observance. The only tentative generalization Goguel allows himself is to point out that votes for the Center parties come mainly from regions of static economy, while urban regions with a modern and complex economic structure gave the Communist party and the de Gaullist RPF their largest number of votes. It would be difficult, however, to see a lasting trend of political allegiances dividing "static" and "dynamic" France. The fact that communism is strong in urban areas explains the strong vote for the most outspoken anti–Communist party. In less troubled times this anti–Communist vote may well go to another party. Thus in 1951 many "indépendants" succeeded in getting the support of voters who had followed De Gaulle in 1947, the year of crisis.

The most significant characteristic of the French social structure is the large proportion of nonsalaried people—independent producers, including peasant proprietors and middlemen (41 per cent of the active population in France, as against 20 per cent in the United States, 10 per cent in Great Britain, 22 per cent in Sweden, and 32 per cent in West Germany). This fact has important consequences for the character of the French party system. It explains partly the consistently large vote for the conservative parties as well as their weak structure and lack of discipline. Independent producers are more difficult to organize in a mass party than are salaried people and particularly wage-earners.

But, more important still, the large number of independent producers is a characteristic of a semiartisan economic structure, which, in turn, has a vital effect on political orientation. In agriculture more than one-third of the farms are exploited by one person, 60 per cent by less than three persons, and only 8 per cent by five or more persons. In industry 70 per cent of the plants have less than five workers, 90 per cent less than ten, and under 1 per cent have more than one hundred. In trade the number of employees per unit of distribution is 0.74 as against 5.8 in the United States.

This semiartisan economy is characterized by high costs of production, low productivity, and consequently low wages. French agricultural productivity, or output per man, is only one-half that of Denmark. Industrial productivity is one-fourth that of the United States and about half that of Sweden. French wages are correspondingly lower. More than half the salaried people earn less than 25,000 francs a month ($75 at 1955 rates of exchange).

Here is an essential factor in determining the vote of French industrial workers for the Communist party, particularly if linked with the small chances of promotion in a rigid, departmentalized social structure.

Salaried people are not the only ones to suffer from low productivity. The middle classes see their living standards deteriorate, partly as a consequence of the war and of inflation. Lack of competition has kept alive many marginal farms, shops, and plants which give their owners very meager profits. It has been estimated that 40 per cent of French peasants have a submarginal living standard. Shopkeepers receive a declining part of the national income. The middle classes no longer enjoy the privileged position that they used to have, and their resentment has been a factor in the trend to political extremism, particularly during the years of rapid inflation.

French parties, on the other hand, are not adequate instruments for economic transformation and do not present a clear-cut choice to the electorate. There is a divorce between politics and economics that encourages the voter's ignorance of economic problems, the *immobilisme* of the government, and the general irresponsibility and demoralization that follow.

No French party represents the interests of a particular social group, with the exception of the Communist party. The followings of the parties are essentially heterogeneous. According to a study made in 1952 by the French Institute of Public Opinion on the social composition of the party electorates, the only generalization that can be made is that many industrial workers follow the Communist party, a large proportion of white-collar workers (including government employees) follow the Socialist SFIO and the Catholic MRP, while the largest number of independent producers seem to vote for the political formations of the Right and Center-Right.

The heterogeneity of party followings goes a long way toward explaining the divorce of politics and economics; for a concrete economic and social program would be a handicap more than an asset. Reluctance to face important issues is joined with the sensitivity of parties to the manifestation of displeasure by any occupational group—wine growers, shopkeepers, or schoolteachers—and to their vulnerability to any organized pressure. Above all, a political party is anxious not to displease anyone; the vaguer its program, the safer it is. The lowest possible common denominator reached by each party is further multiplied by the need to find agreement among parties in a coalition government.

The ignorance of economic facts by the public at large—which the parties encourage—makes for resentments directed at the wrong causes and breeds escapism and demoralization. Goldhoarding and tax evasion are among the consequences of a growing sense of futility as the economic situation deteriorates and the government seems as incapable as the opposition to show the way out. Even the middle classes, securely in power, are dissatisfied and bitter. Political apathy or open cynicism gives the measure of the growing unconcern for a political game that is divorced from reality.

Political

In the Third Republic only the leftist parties—first the Socialist SFIO, then the Communist party—were well organized and disciplined. They possessed a strong structure, effective leadership, and large numbers of active party members. In the new mass parties the permanent "section" replaced the *ad hoc* electoral committee; its main function was to recruit party members in order both to spread the doctrine and to sell

party cards, the only way to finance elections. Discipline was as essential as numbers in the struggle for victory, and party headquarters were in a position to present candidates and a program and to organize an efficient electoral campaign on a national scale.

Elsewhere, with the possible exception of the Radical Socialists, parties were more or less volatile organizations of electoral committees, over which headquarters had little or no authority. Local committees or self-appointed groups of "notables" would select their own candidates and choose a proper party label in almost complete independence of the central organization of the party. Once elected, the successful candidates chose the parliamentary group to which they wished to belong. Parties and groups did not coincide. The members of the same group could belong to different parties and vice versa. This divorce between the electoral functions of the party and the parliamentary functions of the group explains why the deputy had little reason to remain loyal to either. Between elections the party lost its reason for being and its touch with the deputy, while the group had no effective sanctions against a rebel, since other groups were ready to welcome him and since it played no role in his re-election.

This weak structure of the "bourgeois" parties of the Center and the Right may have corresponded to the anarchical individualism of the Frenchman, particularly the independent producer. It also resulted from the fact that electoral funds came easily from well-to-do supporters, making a strong organization unnecessary to finance elections. Local notables, moreover, were reluctant to identify themselves with a party and to work for it in between elections.

The French concept of the state, indivisible and sovereign, was inimical

to the role of the party as an intermediary between the citizen and the
state, particularly if it should represent
sectional interests. Parties began as
coalitions for the defense of ideological
principles. As the Republic became
more solidly intrenched, the Right and
the Center inherited the abandoned
shells of formerly left-wing parties as
the Left moved on to new formations.
Confusion resulted from misleading
labels and frequent splits, which tended
to multiply the parties and to keep
them poorly organized. Electoral fickleness and lack of cohesion followed.

The impact of the electoral system
—the *scrutin d'arrondissement* in which
deputies were elected from single-member constituencies—is also important
in explaining the weak structure of the
parties. Under this system an absolute
majority was required for election. If
it was lacking, a second runoff ballot
was held, at which a relative majority
was sufficient to be elected. In practice the second ballot was needed in
most districts. The system allowed the
electors to vote the first time for the
man who best represented their own
nuance of opinion, thus encouraging
a varied expression of political views.
The second time, electors voted less for
the man or party close to their heart
than against the one they disliked most.
Generally the field was left to two
candidates, one representing the Right,
the other the Left; the less successful
candidates had by then withdrawn in
favor of one or the other. The resulting
duel kept alive the old ideological divisions between rightists and leftists.
Radicals and Socialists maintained republican solidarity against the "reactionary threat" and the "clerical menace," thus helping in no small measure
to keep clericalism and reaction alive.
The second ballot also facilitated the
cuisine électorale—deals among candidates, favors, and compromises. More
important, perhaps, it kept the parties

weak as electoral organizations, since
coalitions were often inevitable in order
to insure victory.

The electoral system put the premium
on the man rather than the party. His
personality and his connections were
more important than the label he wore
and the support he got from the party
machinery. He owed little to the party
organization, except perhaps to its local
committee, and felt no obligation toward it. If he was diligent in forward-
ing the interests of the community,
ready to shake hands and dispense
small favors, he was solidly intrenched
in his district. The system had definite
advantages for both citizens and deputies. It allowed the former to pick and
choose and later to keep close watch
over a man who needed the good graces
of the "citizen-king" and often had to
be his errand boy. It also gave the
successful candidate real power and
independence of action. At home even
the prefect respected him. In Paris he
was a personality courted by cabinet-
wreckers and cabinet-makers as well
as by the ministers, who had to spend
much time examining his complaints or
his claims concerning local conditions
and influential electors. Being relatively independent of party or group leadership, he had opportunities to navigate
on the parliamentary sea toward the
haven of a ministerial post. There were
conveniently located groups in the
Chamber and Senate whose main purpose seemed to gather the *ministrables*.
To them governmental instability was
less an evil than a welcome opportunity.

This electoral system was deeply
satisfying to the individualistic turn of
mind of the Frenchman. Typical is the
approving tone with which Alain quotes
the remark of a good republican pressed
to become a candidate at the next election: "I am willing to say that I am
a Radical, because, all in all, it is true.
But I will tell you how I interpret it,

and you will take me just as I am. I am not a child to submit to the Koran of this or that Mohammed." Electors undoubtedly appreciated this proof of independent thinking. The republican *mystique* offered powerful support to the independence of the deputy, whose primary role was to protect citizens against possible administrative abuses and the Republic against the conspiracy of the elite in Paris. Vigilance was the main virtue, and vigilance could not be delegated to party bureaucracies. On the contrary, it would continue only so long as there existed "the Idealist of the province, the formidable man who is stopped neither by promises nor by threats because he feels intrenched and invincible in the fortress of his *arrondissement,* as the feudal lord of old days in his castle."

Perhaps the large number of parties and their lack of organization were also due to the absence of a sufficient incentive for a regrouping and reorganization of existing parties. The Center coalition was normally in power and not seriously threatened by either leftist or rightist opposition. There was no organized opposition united on a positive program and ready to take over. The absence of an alternative allowed periodic reshuffling of the cabinet that did not substantially alter its composition or its policy. The game could go on with no risks and with some advantages.

The Center could maintain itself in power, since the Right was untrustworthy and the Left unwilling to come in. Since the Dreyfus affair, the Radicals could govern France with the support of either Center-Right or Center-Left. They were in a convenient position to play the Left against the Right when at election time they appealed to republican solidarity, and the Right against the Left when, once elected, they appealed to the defense of the franc. The anticlerical issue had proved its electoral usefulness; it was unnecessary to face the dangerous economic and social issues. The *raison d'être* of the Radicals was republican defense; it was sufficient for the party to exist and therefore unnecessary, even dangerous, to create. The peasant proprietors and *petits bourgeois* who voted Radical were profoundly uninterested in the problems created by the machine and deeply suspicious of both capital and labor. The workers, whose votes were not sought for, had no way of having their demands realized. The French economy suffered because the Center was anxious to protect agricultural interests at the expense of the industrial development of the country and the living standards of the whole population.

If the party system made for ministerial instability, this did not unduly irritate the good republicans. They could point to the real continuity of policy and administration despite frequent shifts. A new cabinet would often have a high percentage of men who had belonged to the defeated team. Important cabinet posts, such as foreign affairs, often saw the same leader survive a number of crises. Permanent officials were there to carry on the routine of administration. In spite of the odds against him, a skilful diplomat could put together a coalition government supported by a workable majority. In times of crisis there would emerge a capable leader with enough prestige—a Waldeck Rousseau, a Clemenceau, or a Poincaré—who would bring about sufficient unity. In other times a shrewd manipulator, a Briand or a Laval, would be on hand. If the new team did not last, the consequences did not appear very grave.

The criticism of the parliamentary system as it operated could be dismissed by the Left and Center as another manifestation of the Right's ill will toward democratic institutions.

Characteristically, the attacks of the Right on the evil of ministerial instability took the form of a demand for a strong and independent executive rather than of strong and independent parties capable of forming a lasting coalition.

Unfortunately, lack of executive leadership continued to undermine confidence in the regime. Unstable and ineffective governments kept adding to the appeal of the authoritarian and equalitarian ideologies. As David Thomson said:

The Center parties . . . although disagreeing among themselves about domestic issues, were forced to shuffle and reshuffle in a series of uneasy coalitions in order to carry on the government. Constant compromise was unavoidable if they were not to risk the whole regime being defeated and overthrown, and positive legislation could be no more than the highest common denominator of their agreement. The system survived and worked only so far as these Center groups could agree to make it work; and perpetual half measures were the price paid for making it work. Every government and every measure which got through both houses of parliament had to be a half-way house.

The result was that "the general atmosphere of politics and the tone of nearly all legislation was one of half-hearted, timid compromise of which the fruits were usually too little and too late."

Frenchmen have often stressed their political intelligence, as contrasted with the muddleheaded and opportunistic outlook of the British. If the test of political intelligence is the ability of a people to face new realities, discuss them in a realistic manner, and take steps accordingly, then the British, it must be said, have shown greater political intelligence than the French. The principles to which the French are attached reflect both an intellectual propensity—partly the influence of the educational system—and emotionalism, a consequence of the conflict described here. It would be legitimate to talk of an "escapist" outlook, for the principles were often irrelevant and no longer fitted new conditions. They belonged to an electoral vocabulary that was expected from every candidate and had the dual advantage of reassuring the voters while not binding the candidate to a specific course of action. The Right-Left division had kept alive old myths and slogans and continued to feed political oratory to the satisfaction of all. Except for the Marxist parties, the "doctrine" of a political party remained sufficiently vague and confused to allow for all kinds of interpretation by both candidates and electors. Yet principles could be conveniently recalled at the proper time to justify any vote in parliament.

Perhaps this "intellectualism" of French parties was due to the poverty of French communal life, from social and cultural organizations to local self-government. As early as the seventeenth century the artificial centralization of the state imposed by Louis XIV led the "bourgeois" to lose interest in the affairs of the town. The Revolution and the Empire accentuated this indifference, and the Third Republic continued to discriminate against possible rivals to the sovereign state and to strengthen its highly centralized administrative apparatus. The Frenchman lacked the school of realism provided for by the practice of self-government in a pluralistic society. He was led to consider national problems, quite remote from his immediate experience and competence, in the light of abstract speculations and systems of thought and morals.

For him a party was, first of all, a doctrine, a system of morals, or simply a *tendance,* a vague outlook for which he felt sympathy. Ideas could easily remain divorced from realities, since he was basically satisfied with his way of life and had no interest in economic or social reforms. But abstract verbalism could not sustain a solid political organization, produce a concrete program, and present a clear choice to the electorate. A lasting contract between parties in the government was impossible, since they lacked the necessary discipline of vote, pragmatic outlook, and sufficient incentive to keep the coalition together. Irresponsibility was the rule, since people voted not for a government team, as in Great Britain, but at best for part of a team the composition of which was unknown at election time. The apparently greater choice offered by the many parties in France was not an effective choice, since they remained in the stratosphere of principles and since the program of the government-to-be was established not before the elections for the people to decide upon, but afterwards, among parliamentary groups without direct responsibility to the electorate. At the next election the parties could find good excuses for their past record and continue to offer slogans rather than programs.

One result was a general indifference toward the business of government in spite of the national habit of discussing political principles. Politics had a bad name, since it involved compromises which clashed with the principles proclaimed at election time. The citizen felt that his entire civic duty was discharged by going to the polls every four years. Having done his duty, he was free to criticize a government— never of his own choice, since he had not voted for that particular coalition— and even to cheat the state to the best of his ability.

II / The Parties in the Fourth Republic

In 1945 and 1946 seventy-five per cent of the electorate was grouped into three strong and well-disciplined parties. The Fourth Republic was differentiated from the Third less by the new institutional framework than by the new electoral system and the character of the parties. "In some respects," wrote A. Siegfried in *L'Année politique* (1946), "the new regime is but a continuation of the old. There is, however, a fundamental difference: Yesterday the party was weak, without organization and without authority; it has become disciplined, of rigid structure, of independent power."

A few years later this diagnosis appeared somewhat less convincing. Besides the Communist party, only the Socialist SFIO and the Catholic MRP were well organized and able to maintain voting discipline. Elsewhere a confusion very reminiscent of the Third Republic reigned. The smaller parties and groups were unable to maintain discipline even on all-important issues. New groups and intergroups were formed that gave a fluid and unpredictable picture of parliamentary divisions as well as of electoral realities. In 1947 the MRP saw two-thirds of its followers abandon it for the new de Gaullist RPF, while the SFIO was losing considerable strength at each election. At the same time the Radical Socialist party, the pillar of the Third Republic, was regaining power and prestige, as were the rightist formations, only temporarily discredited—a trend confirmed by the elections of 1951. Ministerial crises followed one another in the best tradition of the Third Republic.

The evil of monolithic parties dominated by their respective bureaucracies, described daily in the papers of the smaller parties in the first year of the new Republic, proved to be a temporary one. Today the Republic suffers less from the "dictatorship of the parties" than from the divisions and impotence of most of them. If there was some reason to guard against the rule of the party machines at the time of the tripartite coalition, there is now ground to worry about a return to pre-war conditions. Despite the solid phalanx of Socialists and MRP, one of the main weaknesses of the so-called "Third Force" coalition was its inability to establish a cohesive bloc based on party discipline. It had to rely on the votes of individuals more than on the ability of the leaders to keep the various groups united behind a common program.

An even greater source of weakness has been the continued and aggravated lack of consensus. At the time of the *tripartisme*, when the government was made up of three large and well-disciplined parties in apparent agreement over a program, the presence of the Communists in the coalition condemned it to vacillation and inefficiency in the implementation of policies. After the Communists had been ousted in May, 1947, the double challenge of the extreme Left and of a new extreme Right under Charles de Gaulle prevented the new coalition from giving France imaginative and effective leadership; for it suffered, above all, from the lack of an acceptable alternative and the resulting enforced cohabitation of parties with different economic and social programs. Two conditions were lacking that would have made for a cohesive and effective coalition government: agreement on major issues and party discipline. In turn the relative lack of success of the government by the Center facilitated the appeal of the two extremes, which benefited from their strategic position and demagogic methods. In 1951 a new electoral system had to be devised to prevent these extremes from gaining a majority of seats in the National Assembly and to give parliamentary democracy a new lease on life.

The Electoral Systems of 1946 and 1951

The municipal elections in the spring of 1945 saw the rebirth of organized parties. At the general elections of October three large parties—PCF, SFIO, and MRP—obtained three-fourths of the vote and four-fifths of the seats; the Radical Socialists and *Modérés* of various labels divided the rest. All hopes had ended of creating a mass party based on the various resistance movements; only two small resistance organizations, the UDSR and the MURF, were left in the field, the first gravitating around the Socialist orbit and the second around the Communist one.

The success of the three large parties and particularly of the MRP can be explained partly by the new electoral system of *scrutin de liste* with proportional representation. Each department was treated as a single electoral district. Seats were distributed according to the complicated rule of the "highest average." No splitting of the ticket was allowed: the elector had no choice but to vote for one list. He could alter the order of the names on the ballot, but the change was effective only if more than half the voters did likewise—a purely hypothetical situation.

The system with its local distribution of the remainder of the votes favored the large parties which were nationally organized and had relatively strong and evenly distributed representation. A Radical candidate needed almost twice as many votes to be elected as a Communist or MRP candidate.

A second consequence was the tightening of party discipline. Since the elector cannot split his ticket or choose his favorite candidate, he has to vote for a party and not for a man. This gives the party headquarters the power of electoral life and death over the candidate. A man who is placed third or fourth on the list has little chance of being elected, while the No. 1 man is practically certain of his election, particularly if his party is one of the "big three." Once in parliament, he will have a strong incentive to respect party discipline, since it is up to his party to have him re-elected. Fear of such a sanction, however, does not seem to have prevented nonconformity within the smaller groups, which are less effective electoral agents, often in coalition with other groups and dependent on the local appeal of their candidates. The efficient electoral machines of the large parties allowed them to choose their candidates more freely and to expect more from them.

The electoral law of May, 1951, which made possible a coalition of the Center parties, was an attempt to diminish the parliamentary representation of extreme Left and extreme Right and allow the Third Force coalition to obtain a majority of seats. It was no longer a question of encouraging the formation of large, disciplined parties for the purpose of governmental stability but of preventing the extremes from obtaining too many seats in the Chamber. Republican defense had become the paramount issue: the regime could survive only if its supporters obtained enough seats to form a viable majority.

The new electoral law encountered much opposition. The Communists saw it as directed mainly against themselves, while the de Gaullists wanted a list system with two ballots that would allow them to lead an anti-Communist bloc on the second ballot. The smaller parties—Radicals, UDSR, and Independents—wanted the old uni-nominal system of the Third Republic. Socialists and MRP's finally succeeded in having the complicated and unrepresentative system of *apparentements* adopted for the June elections.[2]

Thanks to the new electoral system, the Communists and the RPF obtained only one-third of the seats in the new National Assembly, though they had gathered 48 per cent of the votes. Under the 1945 system of proportional representation they would have had a majority of the seats and made the parliamentary system unworkable.

The Communist Party (PCF)

The Communist party is the largest party in France. Although it lost in June, 1951, some 8 per cent of the votes it had obtained in 1946, it still holds the allegiance of almost one-fourth of the French people. An electoral map shows its strength distributed throughout France, with three major strongholds in the northern, central, and southeastern parts. The loss of votes at the election of 1951, particularly among peasant and middle-class elements, did not affect its major strongholds in industrial areas and in some agricultural regions. The continuous hold of the party on the Confédération générale du Travail, by far the largest trade-union organization, is still a great asset. Communism in France remains a major political force, in a position to threaten both political stability and capacity for effective military defense.

Although chances of its seizing power through an electoral victory, the reconstruction of a popular front, or insur-

2. Except for the departments of the Seine and Seine-et-Oise, where proportional representation under the law of 1946 continued to apply, the new system allowed electoral lists in each department to be presented to the voters as a coalition and to form a single electoral pool. If the pool of *listes apparentées* should obtain more than 50 per cent of the total votes expressed, all the seats in the department would be attributed to the pool and then distributed among the allied lists through proportional representation and the rule of the highest average. If no list and no pool obtained a majority, seats would be distributed according to the system of 1946; however, the allied lists would be considered as a single list for the distribution of the seats and thus would continue to benefit by their alliance.

rection are remote, it is in a position to prevent any effective solution of French social and political problems. Born in part of the inability of French society to furnish a sense of national community, communism tends by its very presence to perpetuate and aggravate the weaknesses of French democracy. It prevents the working class from exercising effective pressure in the determination of national policies. It profits by the demoralization and defeatism that it creates. The absence of national unity engenders a passionate desire for unity that contributes to the appeal of both communism and de Gaullism, the latter being essentially a consequence of the former.

The paradox of the continued strength of a totalitarian party among one of the most individualistic peoples in the world deserves, therefore, special consideration—the more so since the Communist party has at its disposal in an effective organization many thousand fanatical *militants* and several thousand well-trained leaders, a human capital that gives it an enormous advantage over other parties.

HISTORICAL SKETCH.—The Communist party was created by the Socialist Congress of Tours in December, 1920, when three-fourths of the delegates voted to join the Third International. Shortly before the congress, two Socialist leaders, Cachin and Frossard, had returned from the Soviet Union convinced that the new revolution was in the best tradition of the revolutions of 1793, 1848, and 1871.

Two main factors explain the mass exodus of left-wing Socialists and revolutionary syndicalists to communism. The first was pacifism. Socialist leaders had been discredited for their participation in the war effort, and an active antiwar minority had been spreading its propaganda with great effectiveness. The second factor was the immense prestige of the Russian revolution.

There was tangible proof that the revolution was possible: if it had happened in precapitalist Russia, it was bound to come soon in highly industrialized western Europe. The reformist Socialists were proved doubly wrong; they had underestimated both the warlike character of capitalism and the revolutionary potentialities of the workers.

The Third International had made it clear that the creation of the French section was contingent upon acceptance of the famous twenty-one conditions, the most important being the subordination of the French party to all decisions of the congress and executive committee of the Third International and the principle of "democratic centralization," which meant, in fact, complete subordination of party members to the central organization. These conditions were accepted by the Congress of Tours. It did not mean, however, that most of the new Communists took them seriously; they thought that while discipline might be good for the Russians, it was not for French consumption. Within a few months there developed within the new party a right, center, and left in accord with well-established French traditions.

In 1924 the party was reorganized on the basis of the cell in the plant or in the shop, with the idea of enforcing discipline, of shaking off the inertia of party members, and of establishing close contact with the workers. Unity of doctrine and of action was established in a party in which the *Cahiers du bolchevisme* saw "20 per cent Jaurésisme, 10 per cent Marxism, 20 per cent Leninism, 20 per cent Trotskyism and 30 per cent confusionism."

The conquest of the working class meant an all-out war with the Socialists. The advice of Trotsky was to be closely followed: "We must unmask without out pity the policy of the dissidents. We must ridicule their leaders in the eyes of the people and make it hate them." Thorez launched the formula: "Poing brandi pour les chefs, main tendue aux masses." The battle raged during the elections of 1928 and 1932, in which the Communists lost some 200,000 votes. Duclos had defeated Blum; at a partial election a few months later Thorez was defeated by a Socialist-Radical coalition. *L'Humanité* and the Socialist *Populaire* exchanged daily insults.

Soon after the riots of February, 1934, Socialists and Communists began to operate a *rapprochement* against the rising threat of fascism which led to the creation of the Popular Front. The party became a pillar of the Republic and ardently patriotic; it advocated vigorous resistance to Hitler, Mussolini, and Franco and pressed for an effective Franco-Soviet alliance. Two years after its inception the Popular Front had disintegrated; the party was still vigorous in its attack on the appeasement policy of Daladier and Bonnet and, in protest against it, launched a general strike on November 30, 1938.

A third and more spectacular shift was to follow the signing of the German-Soviet nonaggression pact of August, 1939. It was hailed by the party as a great achievement of Soviet diplomacy and as serving the cause of peace. The war became a conflict of rival capitalistic systems which should leave the working class indifferent. The government had the party outlawed and started it on a long period of clandestine existence.

After the German attack on the Soviet Union in June, 1941, came the fourth shift; the party was now ready and eager to lead the resistance. It emerged from the war with an impressive list of martyrs and a new prestige. National unity appeared to have been sealed in blood, the party reintegrated in the national community. It had also acquired great power, had seized many newspapers, and had appointed new mayors, prefects, and justices for the trial of collaborators. Above all, its men held key positions in most trade-unions. The passionate desire for national unity and the knowledge of the economic difficulties ahead made Communist cooperation in the government appear necessary. The party was preaching loyalty to the Republic, hard work and patience, and love for France. Its appeals to national solidarity seemed to many a decisive proof of a change of heart.

A fifth shift came in the spring of 1947, when a wave of strikes threatened the party with being outflanked at its left. The Communist support to the Renault strikers gave Socialist and Catholic ministers a welcome opportunity to oust their Communist colleagues from the cabinet. Within a few months the party had reversed its policy of collaboration. It openly resumed the tactics of class war and political strikes. The main reason for this about-face had been the deterioration of the international situation. In the fall of 1947 the new Cominform had urged an all-out struggle against American imperialism camouflaged behind the Marshall Plan. The struggle for peace and opposition to American imperialism became the main concern of the party.

STRATEGY AND TACTICS.—The Communist party is no ordinary party. It is first an instrument for the conquest of power and next an instrument for the exercise of the dictatorship of the proletariat. To understand its character, organization, and tactics, one must proceed from a few simple propositions: class war is inevitable, reforms inoperative, and a revolutionary upheaval necessary to bring about the classless society. The struggle is an international one, and the Soviet Union is the leader in the battle for the liberation of mankind; its interests are necessarily those of France, since they inevitably serve the cause of the revolution.

In order to reach this goal, the French Communist party, as its statutes direct, must subordinate itself to the decisions of the Third International and in practice to the government of the Soviet Union. Everything must be sacrificed to the defense of the U.S.S.R. In his famous declaration to the National Assembly on February 24, 1949, Thorez admitted the role that the party would play in case of war: "If the Soviet army came to pursue an aggressor on our soil, the workers and the people of France could not act toward the Soviet army otherwise than the workers and the people of Poland, Rumania, and Yugoslavia." During the German occupation the slogan was circulated among Communist youth: "France is our country but the U.S.S.R. is our fatherland." Musmeaux, a Communist deputy, could tell the French National Assembly on March 3, 1950: "When you say to us that the U.S.S.R. is our fatherland, it is not an insult to us. We are proud of it. We glory in it."

The instrument for the transformation of society is the party—"the party first." To serve it is the single duty and absolute discipline, the first virtue; as in war, no moral scruple should interfere with victory; all tactics are good that weaken the enemy; doctrinal rigidity and tactical elasticity are not incompatible. According to circumstances, the party can alternate a policy of revolutionary action demanding an elite of shock troops and one of mass recruiting, parliamentary action, and co-operation with other parties.

The constant preoccupation of the party in the period between the wars was to increase its working-class support, without which no revolution could succeed. This meant the elimination of the Socialist rival, for which end all means were good. The conquest of the peasantry and middle classes was not a dominant concern before World War II. To gain, or at least to neutralize, the peasantry became an all-important goal only after the liberation. For this end tactics were devised that proved very successful; the increase in party membership and votes has been many times greater among nonworkers than among workers. The proportion of *militants* to the population is now as great in some agricultural regions as in industrial ones, and there were for some years more rural cells than factory cells. The policy of gaining the peasantry and middle classes was in line with the new tactics of mass recruiting and peaceful seizure of power. It also corresponded to the fact that propaganda among the workers was now subject to the law of diminishing returns.

ORGANIZATION.—The organization of the PCF conforms to the Marxist-Leninist doctrine that demands a dialectical relation between theory and practice as well as between the party and the masses. The party must keep in close touch with the proletariat, which it is to educate, guide, and, when possible, stir into action. The *militants* must at all times be in a position to appraise the possibilities of revolutionary mass action and to send a stream of information to the leader-theorists, who establish the party line on the basis of the "objective situation." Once the line is established, the party organization furnishes an excellent instrument for its prompt implementation.

Through its propaganda and recruiting agencies—the most important of which are the 20,000 cells—as well as through its many newspapers and periodicals, the Communist party reaches everywhere. It is in a position to keep in close touch with the grievances of most localities and occupational groups, to organize them, spread its slogans, and recruit new members. Para-Communist organizations, the most important of which is the CGT, include all types from peace movements to women and youth groups, war veteran organizations, and associations of specific occupational groups such as artists, intellectuals, sportsmen, housewives, and concierges.

The hierarchical structure of the PCF permits immediate and efficient execution of orders coming from above. It allows the various echelons direct and constant control of the units below them. Opposition is prevented from developing, since no contact is allowed between cells or sections; communications are possible only through the medium of the echelon above. Elections are controlled similarly and permit the party bureaucracy to eliminate doubtful candidates. Opposition is thus easily prevented, and, when it manifests itself, it can be quickly detected and suppressed through this effective chain of command. Thus the party possesses a magnificent instrument for maintaining the efficiency and orthodoxy of its cadres and *militants*.

At the same time, military efficiency is combined with an appearance of democratic rule. The members of the cell do not feel themselves to be under the yoke of party officialdom. They elect their officers, discuss the issues, and vote to approve policy decisions. Since those decisions are made by the top echelons, only the manner of implementing them is a matter for discussion. In that sense, the local organizations are allowed a certain degree of initiative.

The basic unit is the cell, which is the keystone of the Communist organization. It includes at least three members either in the place of work (factory, office, department store) or in the place of residence (city block, town, or village). The party has always attached fundamental importance to the factory cells, since its main concern is with the urban proletariat, the "only truly revolutionary class." There are some 20,000 cells for about 400,000 party members, as against 30,000 cells and 600,000 party members in 1947. Above the cell is the section, which directs the work of the cells of a large factory, a town, or a district. Its role is to execute the decisions coming from the echelon above and to control the work of the cells below. The section secretary, who is, in fact, chosen by the officers of the departmental federation, is supposed to know all the officers and most of the party members of the cells under him. He is required to make frequent visits to the local units, and if opposition develops in any of the cells, his role is to intervene, explain, and, if necessary, have the rebels expelled. Since there exists no communication among cells, organized opposition is impossible.

Above the section is the departmental federation. In some industrial departments of France the region is the intermediate unit between the section and the federation. The elected departmental secretary, who holds a post of great importance, must be acceptable to the Central Committee. The role of the federation is to execute the decisions of the Central Committee and to organize the work of the sections. The secretary is, at all levels, the important man in the chain of command. In practice, he selects his fellow-officers and is himself nominated by the secretary immediately above him.

Every two years there is a meeting of the national Congress of the party, made up of delegates elected by the federal assemblies. In theory, it is the highest authority of the party. In practice, it rubber-stamps decisions reached by the party leadership. The Congress elects, by show of hands and in an atmosphere of enthusiasm, the members of the Central Committee, the list having been established by the party leaders.

Above the Central Committee of some forty regular members are the Political Bureau and the Secretariat, which are in fact selected by the inner group of top leaders. The Political Bureau comprises some ten members, including the members of the Secretariat, Duclos, Billoux, Servin, and Fajon. These men, along with the general secretary of the CGT, Benoît Frachon, form the general staff of the party.

"MILITANTS" AND LEADERS.—The real strength of the party resides in its large number of devoted *militants* (perhaps as many as 50,000 of them) and well-trained and efficient local leaders. They form the best recruiting agents and, if necessary, the shock troops for revolutionary and underground activities.

To attain the maximum degree of revolutionary efficiency, the party has striven to create a closed society impermeable to outside influences and in a constant state of tension with the larger national society which it aims to destroy. "The party," wrote Rossi, "for the Communist is his country, his order, his fatherland; *l'esprit de parti* is the supreme value both ideally and practically, a value that must be developed unceasingly." Through the establishment of this closed society, the PCF has succeeded in creating a new type of Frenchman: obedient, politically efficient, and, above all, fanatical. Real *militants* show a humble devotion and a willing acceptance of any amount of work and sacrifice. By joining the party many of the new converts have committed their whole lives.

For most believers the doctrine is limited to a series of simple articles of faith and a few basic assumptions that are untouchable. The process of reasoning and the admission of evidence apply only within the charmed circle. The simple and effective mythology teaches that capitalism is the source of all evils: poverty, war, the alienations and the humiliations of man; that it is doomed by its inner contradictions; that the laws of history make it inevitable that the proletariat, led by the Communist party, will overthrow bourgeois rule and establish the classless society that will transform man; that the struggle will be a hard one, and absolute discipline, dedication, and faith in leaders are necessary; but that victory will come through the enlightened leadership of the powerful Soviet Union, the fatherland of socialism. Thus the interests of mankind are equated with those of the proletariat, which in turn are equated with those of the party and ultimately with the interests of the Soviet Union, the necessary leader in the struggle for the liberation of mankind.

Doctrine is linked to action. It is not abstract speculation, but a "guide to action." As such it cannot be separated from organization and leadership. The leaders are the ones who interpret the doctrine and establish the "line." They are the men who know how to read the scriptures and have a monopoly of correct interpretation. Their function as high priests adds to their prestige as political leaders and justifies the admiration and obedience due to them.

Understanding the role of the cell is of the utmost importance in any effort to account for the number and quality of the *militants*. Through it, party members are held tightly within a new and exclusive primary association. The cell is, first of all, a school for *militants*. There doctrine is taught at an elementary level and thoroughly digested. The party line is expounded and justified. When faced by hesitation or opposition, the cell secretary must convince the nonconformists and, if necessary, have them expelled. Conformity is further enforced by mutual vigilance.

Dangerous readings and dangerous friendships are forbidden.

The cell is also a politico-military organization and can be compared to a company or a section of an army in combat. It has a sector of the front assigned to it and within the limits of the general directives can use a great deal of initiative in developing local strategy. The party member thus acquires a sense of importance; he is a planner, a conspirator, and a soldier at the same time. Efficiency is one of the main qualities stressed; it is maintained by example, praise and criticism, promotion and demotion. As in the army, discipline is the major virtue. Good fellowship and selflessness, the willingness to accept tasks, and especially courage are qualities that are encouraged and rewarded.

The cell is the center of the whole life of the *militant,* including his affective life. Friendships and often love affairs gravitate around the party. Through the cell families meet. But friendships acquired through the party are conditional, almost functional. A friend is immediately rejected when there is good reason to question his loyalty; for personal values and the strongest emotions are subordinated to party values. The net result is the creation of a new type of man, totally dependent upon a party that shapes his personality. The fear of being rejected by his community is a source of great anxiety and the strongest negative tie that attaches a man to the party.

The Communist cells form the best recruiting agencies. No opportunity must be neglected to convert people. A *militant* must be a constant and alert teacher. He is also a fighter, the champion of the little people, always ready to redress grievances. Perhaps the main contribution of the cell has been the organization of grievances, the struggle for even the smallest demands of various occupational groups and particular-

ly of the workers. The party has had very little competition from other quarters in this respect, and this policy has contributed materially to its prestige as the champion of the underprivileged.

The backbone of the party is made up of the *permanents* or paid functionaries. They are the elite of professional revolutionaries, the officer corps, the men who have the greatest interest in the party. There are thousands of them in the regular organization of the party, in the secret apparatus, the para-Communist organization, the newspapers and periodicals, the municipalities, and particularly the CGT.

Party leaders are on the lookout for capable young men and women, especially workers, who are active and popular, have given guaranties of reliability, and have shown qualities of leadership. Promising young people are sent to party schools, both national and regional, that turn out thousands of students every year. There they acquire both theoretical knowledge and practical skills.

The two main criteria for promotion appear to be efficiency and docility. Local leaders must have enough intelligence to take the initiative in the carrying-out of orders but not enough to question these orders. Emphasis is put on youth, especially in the middle echelons, and, whenever possible, workers are given preference over members of the middle classes.

Several techniques insure docility, such as the use of lengthy questionnaires and the habit of self-criticism and mutual vigilance. Leaders are made to realize that their prestige and power are purely functional and in direct proportion to their place in the hierarchy. No one is safe from the possibility of demotion or elimination, as the recent demotion of Marty and Tillon proved again. Most *permanents* are anxious to hold on to their jobs; the fear of losing their new style of life and of being thrown back to the drudgery of factory work is a powerful incentive. Such is the satisfaction of holding a position of power and of being shown respect and admiration by the rank and file.

THE APPEAL OF COMMUNISM.—In the election of June, 1951, the PCF obtained 26.5 per cent of the effective votes. The loss of 8 per cent (450,000 votes) over the previous election was particularly evident in the Paris area and in the rural departments, where the Communist vote had already been substantially lower than the average electoral strength of the party. The three strongholds remain in the north, center, and southeast.

The appeal of communism to large strata of French society may be attributed partly to the superiority of the party in organization and leadership and partly to receptivity to the Communist mythology stemming from the old French revolutionary tradition.

In short, the Communist mythology is effective in proportion as the "revolution" appears likely to succeed in the near future; most people do not want to fight for a losing cause. Thus the PCF has had its greatest appeal whenever expectations of victory were high, as in the year following World War I, when the Russian revolution appeared to be the prelude to world revolution; in the early days of the Popular Front, when the depression and the struggle against fascism polarized political forces and offered new opportunities for revolutionary action; and again in 1945, when the war had weakened the capitalistic structure and opened a perspective of victory to the proletariat through its strong Communist party and the powerful external support of the Soviet Union.

World War II allowed the party to mobilize many people in resistance organizations and to benefit from its prestige in the struggle for liberation. The liberation allowed it to seize important posts of command. To many it appeared as the irresistible wave of the future. It could capitalize both on the early hopes for a better democracy and on the following disappointments, particularly when it dissociated itself from the coalition government in 1947. Socialists and Catholics could again be presented as the enemies of the workers.

Besides these several factors applicable to the whole clientele of the PCF, the appeal of communism among workers, peasants, and intellectuals involves different criteria, since situations and motivations are far from identical among these three groups. Let us examine them separately.

The appeal of communism to the French workers is relatively easy to interpret as the result of long-standing grievances against the French capitalist system. The revolutionary temper of French workers was kept alive by the long discrimination of the state and of employers against labor, by the lack of opportunities for the sons of workers, by the relative failure of French capitalism to expand production and improve distribution, and, above all, by the lack of effective instruments in the hands of the working class to improve its economic and social conditions. Until 1936 social reform and labor legislation lagged far behind those of most western European countries. Collective bargaining was practically unknown. The trade-unions were weak, and the working class was not represented in the determination of national policies.

After the liberation, high expectations were created which were soon frustrated. Structural reforms of the economy, an elaborate program of social security, and participation of labor in the management and profits of industry were to take place. After a brief period of sacrifices that were to be shared by all, higher living standards were to bring the good life. Socialism was around the corner. These hopes were not fulfilled, as inflation kept prices well above wages and business showed no intention of relinquishing its privileges. Workers became convinced that their real wages remained far below those of 1937, despite accrued social security benefits and family allowances. Resentment was directed at employers, who, it was widely believed, established prices and wages on the ability of the marginal plants to pay, thus fixing high profits to the more efficiently managed ones. It was directed also at the state as the largest employer of labor that kept wages low and prices high and at the Socialist party as a member of the government coalition, especially after the PCF passed into the opposition in 1947. To most workers the SFIO certainly did not appear as a satisfactory alternative to the PCF.

On the other hand, French society continued to furnish inadequate outlets to the more energetic and gifted members of the working class or to their children. Only 7 per cent of the students in secondary education and 3 per cent of university students are of working-class origin in a country where diplomas are essential for obtaining even mediocre positions. Professor Collinet has shown that the normal process of promotion takes two generations: children of workers become shopkeepers or petty functionaries, and their children in turn have a chance at higher education. Promotion within the plant is also extremely difficult past the position of foreman. The PCF profits from this lack of promotion, both directly by offering the most ambitious young men positions of prestige and power within the party or the CGT and indirectly by feeding on the accumulated resentment of the underprivileged.

If individual promotion is limited, the same is true of class promotion, that is, the ability of the working class to obtain satisfaction for their demands either through powerful trade-unions or through a political party that plays a role in the determination of national policies. On the one hand, the PCF as the party of the working class stands in systematic opposition to other parties. On the other hand, the division of organized labor, its lack of numerical strength, the revolutionary character of the CGT, and the weakness of non-Communist trade-unions add up to a very inefficient instrument for obtaining better wages and working conditions, particularly since trade-unions are not geared to obtain results at the plant level but are content with pressing for minimum conditions through nationwide collective agreements. At the same time the prestige of the CGT as the oldest, largest, and most dynamic labor organization is a great asset to the PCF, which uses the appealing argument of working-class unity to criticize its smaller rivals.

If individual and class promotion is wanting, the same goes for what may be labeled "national promotion," the expectation of higher living standards through a rapidly expanding economy. After a few years of rapid expansion, the French economy in 1954 stands at about the level of production and productivity of 1929, the highest prewar year. The old age of French machinery (despite significant progress in many plants), antiquated methods of production and distribution, and the survival of thousands of poorly equipped and inefficient plants do not give the workers the feeling of a dynamic economy promising lower prices and higher wages.

Another factor of importance in explaining the continuous revolutionary reflexes of the working class is the traditionally poor state of labor-management relations, despite many isolated efforts at improving them. French management is too often content with accepting class struggle as an unfortunate fact and using it as an excuse for authoritarian and oppressive treatment of the personnel. By contrast with the United States or Sweden, human relations within the plant have always been a neglected aspect of the science of management. Little effort is made to understand the psychology of the workers and to interest them in the production processes through information, promotion, or collective premiums. Instead of collective methods for increasing productivity while reducing physical effort, piecework remains the rule and is a source of continuous irritation and nonintegration. The shop committees established in 1945 to give workers some voice in the conduct of business have remained paper organizations. Management is generally satisfied with the rivalry of competing trade-unions and has little desire to see a vigorous and nonpolitical trade-union movement weaken its strong bargaining position.

It must also be kept in mind that modern technology has shaped a new type of worker, unskilled and semi-skilled, an insecure and unhappy automaton who is easily the victim of the techniques of mass manipulation of the PCF. Finally, in many industrial towns or neighborhoods the pressure of social conformity plays in favor of the PCF, which often controls the trade-unions, the municipality, the social security agencies, jobs, and leisure. It takes courage to oppose local public opinion and the determined local leaders of a party which does not tolerate any opposition.

The heaviest rural Communist vote comes from some of the most backward agricultural sections of central and southern France, made up of peasant proprietors who work hard for a marginal living. It has been estimated that 40 per cent of the French rural population have an annual income of less than $300. The discrepancy between the productivity and incomes of farmers in northern and southern France is in the proportion of 3 to 1.

A purely economic interpretation of the success of communism in the countryside, however, is far from satisfactory. Not all backward agricultural regions give the PCF a heavy vote but only those which have traditionally voted for the "Left." Nor are Communist electors in rural areas necessarily peasants. Artisans, small bourgeois, and pensioned people often constitute the bulk of Communist voters in the village. It has also been observed that the most economically weak people—sharecroppers, agricultural workers, and domestics—perhaps because of their very insecurity and dependence on patrons, generally do not vote for the PCF.

Whole regions or isolated villages have traditionally voted for the extreme Left. Memories of past abuses from the feudal lord, the church, or the administration may often be the determining factor in establishing reflexes that have become solidly intrenched. A vote for the PCF often is a transfer of the old habit of voting against the government whatever it may be, for it is held responsible for low agricultural prices and high industrial ones, for taxing the peasant, and for taking his son away in the army. This vote of protest is not to be interpreted as a desire to see a Communist regime installed in Paris. Personal factors such as family rivalries or the prestige of an individual may be more important than ideological considerations in determining voting habits. Completely irrational behavior is often the case as communism is interpreted through the prism of rural values such as property, thrift, and family. Thus a Communist candidate for the municipal council had cards printed that presented him as an "independent Communist and property-owner." Sympathy with the PCF may be found in a staunch friend of the

United States who opposes trade-unions and social expenditures by the government.

In some regions the resistance has played a role in converting peasants to new values through contact with the Communist underground and in creating new political divisions. After the liberation, the PCF had effective means for convincing people. It had also become legitimized and had lost much of its revolutionary aura. Above all, the party made a special effort to convert the rural population, in line with its new tactics of mass recruiting. Cells multiplied, and party workers became active. *La Terre,* a competent Communist weekly, became the most widely read paper in the countryside.

Propaganda concentrated on absentee owners, who were resented as parasites by all the tillers of the soil, and on the middlemen and the trusts, held responsible for the high prices of industrial goods. After 1947 it was directed especially at the state, accused of discrimination against the farmer. The party had an appealing program to offer: revaluation of agricultural products, extension of social security benefits to the rural population, defense of peasant property, modernization of methods of production. Once in power, it would coerce no one into joining collective farms, although it implied that most peasants would gladly take the initiative and abandon an outworn system of exploitation. Propaganda was directed at specific grievances fitting the local conditions, at giving useful advice and offering a pragmatic program for improving the lot of the peasants. It avoided Marxist doctrines and sang a very different tune from the one destined for the consumption of the workers. Finally, the well-orchestrated pacifist campaign of the last few years seems to have found some response, particularly as the rearmament program is deemed responsible for the de-terioration of economic conditions in the countryside.

Analyzing the political outlook of the Paris students, this writer was struck by the fact that communism, along with left-wing Catholicism, is the only pole of attraction for the politically conscious minority. Although somewhat on the decline, the influence of communism among left-wing intellectuals is still great, as they see no alternative to the vigorous proletarian party. Socialism is out of the question. As in 1946, it is still for them "communism or despair."

The fascination exercised by communism on the intellectuals is complex. The party has known how to play on the sense of guilt of those who feel responsible for being members of the accursed bourgeoisie and must expiate this original sin. It has presented itself as the heir of the "enlightenment," the successor of the eighteenth-century materialist philosophers, the only party of "movement," of youth and progress. It has used the prestige of Marxism as a system of integration applicable to all sciences and offering a total explication of the universe. It has capitalized upon the intellectuals' deep resentment of a moral and social order in decomposition, incapable of furnishing the security and sense of purpose for which they yearn. Many are also attracted by the strength and efficiency of the party and by the prospects of victory.

The party offers certainty, purpose, and active participation in a common cause to men who suffer from doubt and isolation. This is perhaps the stronger motivation among intellectuals, who as "professional doubters" have an appetite for certainty and a nostalgia for action. Here is a dynamic organization offering a simple set of propositions and a call for common endeavor that allows the individual to transcend himself and to reintegrate himself in a pattern of purposeful action. Monnerot explains that, once adopted, the new religion has a therapeutic effect, as if individual neuroses, now exteriorized and projected into a collective neurosis, had lost their harmful effects. The collective intoxication of the secular religion liberates; it creates a world where dreams and action are intertwined, where no sense of guilt exists. The strong demands made by party discipline are not too high a price to pay for security and certainty.

The Socialist Party (SFIO)

Formerly a revolutionary party with almost exclusive working-class support, the Socialist SFIO in the twenties was already supported mainly by *petits bourgeois* and peasants, who saw in it a progressive republican party. André Siegfried commented about the election of Narbonne in April, 1929, which saw the victory of the Socialist leader Léon Blum in one of the strongholds of the Radicals, that if the Socialist party had conquered the agricultural south, it might well be that, in fact, the south had conquered the Socialist party. The election was not to be interpreted, he explained, as a victory for Marxism but as another manifestation of *sinistrisme*. For the voters it was not a question of reforms to realize so much as a question of proving the quality of one's republicanism by choosing the "most advanced" candidate. In the southern provinces of Languedoc and Provence each generation had moved further to the left: "The Radicals are sixty years old, the Socialists are forty, and the young men are beginning to become Communists."

A study of electoral geography made by Ernest Labrousse confirms the existence of this *sinistrisme*, this tendency toward the Left. By comparing the map of the election of 1849 with that of 1946, he shows that the regions which had voted for the leftist Montagne in 1849 were those which voted for the

Socialists and Communists in 1946, with the only difference that the Red zone was substantially larger in 1946. The slow electoral growth of the "Marxist" parties from 1 per cent of the total vote in 1881 to 17 per cent in 1914, 30 per cent in 1932, and 50 per cent in 1945 can be attributed less to the impact of Marxism than to the old tradition of "red republicanism." In 1889 the extreme Left was still represented by Clemenceau. It was not until the formation of the united SFIO in 1905 that there emerged a strong Socialist party able to steal votes from the Radicals at a time when the latter became a party of government. In 1910 the SFIO already had a million votes, and in 1914 it could elect 103 deputies.

After the war the process continued, with the Socialists losing working-class support to the new Communist party and gaining *petits bourgeois* votes at the expense of the Radicals. It is significant that the Communist vote almost doubled between 1932 and 1936, while the Socialist vote remained stationary and the Radicals lost one-fourth of their following. The Socialists had lost votes to the Communists and gained at the expense of the Radicals. The Communists were already outvoting the Socialists in the Paris suburbs and gaining strong support in other industrial areas. The main electoral strength of the SFIO came from the rural regions of southern France.

Inevitably, the party was influenced by its new clientele. It was, however, the prisoner of its Marxist tenets and of the reluctance of its *militants* to accept the new situation. The party continued to refuse to abandon revolutionary symbols and, until 1936, to enter a coalition government. Perhaps the main reason for this refusal was the need to compete with the Communists for working-class support by insisting on principles that no longer corresponded to electoral realities or to the reformist outlook of the leaders. The result was that the absence of the Socialists from the determination of national policies contributed to the discredit of the regime and to the growth of the extremes. A policy that was neither effectively reformist nor genuinely revolutionary combined the disadvantages of each approach to social change and was a major handicap to the growth of democracy.

Today the Socialist party is a mirror of French democracy; its weaknesses and contradictions reflect the weaknesses and contradictions of the regime. In a sense it is the most French of all parties. It is revolutionary in principle, yet is made up of people who cherish security. It is collectivist and prides itself on being a working-class party, but its clientele is largely made up of *petits bourgeois*, artisans, shopkeepers, white-collar workers, peasant proprietors, and public servants. It talks equality but believes in freedom; it demands a unity of doctrine and of action that is prevented by the conflicting outlook of its *militants* and electors; it glorifies change and progress but is deeply traditionalist in its outlook. It is both self-critical and self-indulgent, both doctrinaire and easy-going.

In spite of the wishes of most party members, it was forced to remain in the government until 1951 and in so doing to compromise with its principles and to weaken its electoral appeal, particularly among the workers. Its centrist position obliged it to take the role of the Radical Socialists in the Third Republic and to appear as a party of "tired revolutionaries." There was no way out of the dilemma: effective resistance to communism and later to de Gaullism as well implied continued participation in the government and the adoption of measures that could easily be exploited by the Communist demagogues. This unhappy situation and the successive electoral defeats

have produced resentment and a deep inferiority complex among many followers, which may in turn account for the hesitation and contradiction in its strategy and tactics.

The SFIO was, from its inception in 1905, a merging of several trends. If the original Congress of Tours proclaimed it a "party of class war and revolution," orthodox Marxism had not eliminated the influence of early utopian socialists and reformers. The party was divided over a number of important issues, and it took the authority of Jaurès to make way for a reconciliation of apparently irreconcilable goals such as pacifism and patriotism, revolution and peaceful change, historical materialism and belief in moral ideals, the dogma of class war and the faith in liberal democracy, all-out opposition to the bourgeois regime and co-operation with bourgeois parties.

Party discipline was maintained at the price of individual defections and splits within the party. Thus in 1919 the Parti socialiste français was formed, which rejected orthodox Marxism and favored participation in the government; in 1921 it was the turn of the Communist party; in 1932 thirty deputies left the SFIO to form the Union socialiste républicaine and a neo-Socialist movement was created which favored a nationalistic and authoritarian course of action. After 1935 the partisans of collective security behind Blum clashed with the pacifists behind Paul Faure. Again after the defeat of 1940 the party was divided over the Vichy regime. If only thirty-seven out of the one hundred and seventy-five deputies and senators voted against the granting of plenary powers to Pétain, actually few Socialists of the pacifist and violently anti-Communist wing followed him or the all-out collaborator, Marcel Déat.

Many thousands of party members were active in the resistance. The party was the first to organize for clandestine action against the Germans. Some of its leaders played a major role in the creation of the National Committee of Resistance and in the recognition of De Gaulle as the leader of the resistance. During this period the party acquired new blood; the old *militants* were outnumbered by younger and more dynamic elements, who seemed united behind a bold, if somewhat vague and optimistic, program of political, social, and economic renovation. After the liberation the party had acquired new prestige and opportunities. The bourgeois was discredited, and in the new balance of social forces the Socialists appeared destined to play a leading role. "Socialism is the master of the hour," Blum could tell the first congress of the party in August, 1945.

A few months later the elections showed that the prognostications of an overwhelming Socialist victory had been too optimistic. The party came in third, after the Communists and the new MRP. It had gained at the expense of the Radicals but had lost votes to the Communists in the industrial centers and in some agricultural areas. The next two elections were serious defeats: the Socialist vote fell from 24 per cent of the effective votes in 1945 to 21 per cent in June, 1946, 18 per cent in November, 1946, and 15 per cent in the election of 1951. Yet the defeated party became the pillar of the government coalition, the axis of the tripartite coalition, and, until 1951, one of the two main components of the Third Force coalition. The new constitution was largely molded by the Socialists, who gave the Fourth Republic its first president and the government some of its premiers and the holders of the most important ministerial seats. Without the SFIO no government could live, for it had become the center of gravity of French politics. This new strength was also a basic weakness, particularly after

the Communists had left the government, since the need for defense of the Republic prevented the party from choosing its partners in the coalition.

STRUCTURE.—The SFIO has the most democratic organization of the three parties which succeeded in keeping unity and discipline in their ranks. This democratic character is reflected in the emphasis put on free elections and free discussions of all issues, in the importance given to local organizations in the selection of candidates for election, in the imposition of sanctions, and particularly in the special effort made to allow the will of a changing majority to prevail even over the policies adopted by the parliamentary group. The outlook of the *militants,* however, has not been that of the majority of the voters; a more representative and more efficient democracy might have been served better by allowing the parliamentary leaders, as the representatives of the electors, greater freedom of action.

The basic unit of the party is the section; its membership varies from ten to several hundred, with an average of about fifty. It is left free to establish its internal organization and the methods used for implementing the decisions of the higher authorities. The sections of a department form a federation; a federal congress, made up of the delegates of the section, once a year elects an executive committee, which in turn selects a secretariat. Delegates of the federation, in proportion to the number of paid-up members, are sent to the National Congress, which is the supreme authority of the party. Proportional representation is used, so that minority opinion can be expressed at the congress.

Every deputy is careful to maintain sound relations with the local section and federation. He makes frequent visits to his fellow party members, where he answers their criticisms and tries to oppose their vigilant mistrust—altogether not an easy task. The fear of possible desertions has led to an effort to bar opportunists from positions of responsibility; only a long-standing party member can become a candidate for election. This procedure has prevented the party from acquiring the services of able and popular men, particularly at the liberation, and has put a premium on past performance rather than on capabilities.

Besides the National Congress of the party that meets at least once a year, there is a National Council made up of one delegate of each federation, that meets whenever new developments warrant it. Its role is to oversee and advise the Comité directeur or Executive Committee, elected by the congress, and further to guarantee the expression of the changing majority will. The Comité directeur executes the decisions of the congress and council, appoints an administrative bureau, directs press and propaganda, and, most important, controls the parliamentary group. Since it is made up of representatives of the *militants*, it often clashes with the parliamentary leadership, which represents the voters and is inclined to look at policy decisions with greater restraint and realism. Not until December, 1949, was a mixed commission, in which both the Executive Committee and the parliamentary group participate, instituted to avoid divided authority in case of a ministerial crisis.

In principle, party discipline is maintained by allowing free deliberation but by insisting on unity of action, once a decision has been reached. Every party member from prime minister to simple *militant* is under the control of his federation, which inflicts disciplinary action through a Commission des conflits. A similar committee exists at the national level for cases involving a federation; it also functions as a court of appeal. Penalties ranging from warn-

ing to exclusion are relatively effective in extreme cases of disobedience, but frequently the principle of unity of action cannot be implemented against important personalities. Léon Blum's editorials in *Le Populaire* often contradicted the decisions taken by the competent authorities of the party.

The party has attempted, with little success, to rival the Communist cells by creating in 1945 the *groupes socialistes d'entreprise,* grouping workers in factories and artisans in localities, with the aim of extending Socialist influence, gathering information on present trends, and educating the workers for their future participation in management. By August, 1947, only some fifty thousand had entered the groups, of whom only one-third were party members. To rival the Communist-controlled CGT, the CGT—Force ouvrière was launched in 1947 with the support of the SFIO. It is nominally independent but is led by Socialist sympathizers. Its strength lies largely among government workers, and it has not been able successfully to challenge the Communist hold on industrial workers.

Incidentally, the formal independence of the trade-union movement has become largely nominal, now that the three large parties have their own labor confederations: CGT for the Communists, FO for the Socialists, and CFTC for the MRP. Political independence may no longer be possible, since the state is the main employer of labor and determines wage rates and conditions of work. Political pressure brought about by trade-unions has become an important characteristic of the new parliamentary system; it underlies the difficulties met by the Socialist party in attempting to remain in the government while satisfying the legitimate grievances of labor.

The structure of the SFIO is relatively strong if compared with that of the Radical Socialists but weak if compared to the Communist party. It is characterized by a semicentralized organization, in which federations and sections have a certain autonomy, and by a constant concern for democratic processes. This concern has weakened the SFIO, since it has resulted in the competition of different *tendances* within the party; in divergences coming from regional, occupational, and even personal factors; and in frequent rifts. The most important source of tension— the conflict between doctrinaire *militants* and opportunistic parliamentarians —is a serious element of weakness. Lack of homogeneity and frequent shifts in tactics have led to the widespread belief that the party lacks effective leadership and efficacy.

It is difficult to evaluate the degree of militancy of the party members. Except in the north and in a few departments such as the Haute Vienne, the organization appears quite weak, and its activity is rather sporadic. Besides the workers, the most active *militants* appear to be the many schoolteachers, who play an important role as local cadres. In any case the SFIO lacks the large number of devoted and active party members, the main asset of the PCF. Neither young workers nor young intellectuals are attracted by a party that seems to lack the vigor and efficacy of its rival.

Party membership has gone down from 350,000 dues-paying members— the figure officially given by the party and probably inflated—to 160,000 in 1950 and to probably no more than 110,000 today. Turnover is relatively high. It has been established that the membership has been more fickle than the electorate from 1919 to 1939: from 1919 to 1926 alone, 46.6 per cent of the party members were lost, probably most of them to the PCF.

STRATEGY AND TACTICS.—Back in 1945 the SFIO was prevented by old mistrusts from joining hands with the Catholic MRP. But past experience had also taught it to be well aware of the Communist threat. *Tripartisme* was born from this reluctance to make a choice.

The divisions within the party have involved strategy and tactics rather than doctrine. It is true that the left wing under the leadership of austere and doctrinaire Guy Mollet professes its faith in orthodox Marxism, while the right wing, which includes most of the parliamentary leaders, believes in *socialisme humaniste*. To them, class struggle is not inevitable; they believe that human sympathy and solidarity, rather than economic determinism, will progressively bring about the just society. But both wings would agree with Jaurès that "without socialism democracy is imperfect, but without democracy socialism is powerless." They would agree that democracy comes first and that gradual change can be obtained through education and persuasion rather than organized violence. Both sides heartily dislike communism for its totalitarian goal, its unethical methods, undemocratic organization, and dependence upon a foreign government. It is significant that at the congresses of 1945 and 1946 less than 1 per cent of the delegates favored organic unity with the Communists or even unity of action. If a Comité d'entente between the two parties was created in the early days, growing Socialist mistrust prevented it from establishing an acceptable program.

If the left wing refused to let Léon Blum alter the revolutionary symbols of the party and replace *lutte de classe* by *action de classe*, the reason was to be found largely in electoral tactics, for the central problem of the party is how to fight communism more effectively. Unlike Italy, France has very few Socialists in sympathy with the Communists and only two schools of thought concerning the best means of answering their threat. They stood in clear-cut opposition at the congress of August, 1946. For Blum and most of the leaders—Philip, Mayer, and Le Troquer—the Socialist electoral defeat was due to past collaboration with the Communists; an all-out opposition against them and an open *rapprochement* with the MRP were essential. Guy Mollet, the leader of the left wing, who was to replace Mayer as the general secretary of the party, explained the stand of the other school: "I am against all participation in a government that would permit the Communists to enter into more or less systematic opposition and thus to regain an influence that they are in the process of losing. . . . For as soon as our party loses the audience of the workers, as soon as socialism becomes compromised or discredited, it will be no longer a question of democracy or republic in our country. . . . It is the party which must first be saved." No collaboration should develop with the parties of the Center, and participation in the government should be on the basis of a minimum program destined to protect the interests of the workers. This position corresponds to the Jacobin outlook of the *militant*, often a poorly paid schoolteacher or minor public servant, and meets the acute embarrassment of the Socialist campaigner in the working-class districts who finds himself unable to explain the position of his party. These *militants*, infuriated by two successive defeats, took the offensive at the congress of 1946 and won a majority in the Comité directeur. A few months later the party suffered another electoral blow, and at the next congress the majority imposed conditions upon continued participation in the government that amounted to a break with the MRP and the Radicals. But the new threat created by the RPF of De Gaulle and the new revolutionary tactics of the Communists soon

persuaded even the left-wingers that the party no longer had a choice, that it was in no position to leave the coalition government.

The continued hesitations and shifts in tactics gave the impression of a party without strong and resolute leadership. Whenever it appeared friendly to the MRP, it would lose anticlerical electors; and whenever it relaxed its attacks on the Communists, it would lose the support of its right-wing and anti-Communist elements. Many defections followed within the party membership, including the Jeunesses socialistes and the pro-Communist Bataille socialiste. Successive defeats demoralized many followers; one of the leaders even referred to the "masochism" of the party.

Being a pillar of the government, the SFIO was identified with its mistakes and shortcomings. It was accused equally of conservatism and of collectivism and became the scapegoat for the orgy of bureaucratic red tape, for high, unfair, complicated taxes, and for the deficits in the nationalized enterprises.

In conclusion, it can be pointed out that the SFIO is only in part the helpless victim of its totalitarian rival. Its lack of efficacy is due partly to its heterogeneous following, defective organization, and frequent tactical shifts. It is due also to lack of imaginative leadership and to the difficulty in which it finds itself in evolving a new doctrinal approach and a realistic program conforming to the actual needs of the less fortunate members of French society.

It is difficult to reconcile the Marxist tenets, to which many *militants* cling, with a realistic appraisal of foreign experiments and new economic and social facts. The lessons to be obtained from British or Swedish experiments or from the evolution of modern capitalism in the United States are necessarily colored by doctrinaire *parti-pris* and categories of thought inimical to pragmatic evaluation. It is, for instance, most difficult for a Socialist *militant* to admit that increases in production and productivity and the cutting-down of industrial and agricultural costs are more important for obtaining higher living standards than is the partial application of the principles of planned economy and nationalization.

Doctrinal fuzziness and attachment to principles more appropriate to another age are serious handicaps. It may explain why socialism holds so little attraction for the intellectuals. The sad comment made by a student to *Espirit* back in 1946 is still relevant today: "It is just as ridiculous and impossible to be a Socialist in 1946 as it was to be a Radical in 1936"; for the Socialist party of today, being neither fish nor fowl, is very much like the Radical Socialist party of yesterday. To some extent it is the prisoner of static France—the France of the small towns and villages—rather than of dynamic France, which still seeks her way.

The "Mouvement républicain populaire" (MRP)

The greatest surprise of the general elections of October, 1945, was the spectacular success of the new Catholic MRP, which obtained 25 per cent of the effective votes. For the first time, France had a large and disciplined non-Marxist party, and for the first time Catholics had voted en masse for a party that was not identified with the right.

The intellectual origins of the new party, born in November, 1944, go back to the two currents which in the nineteenth century opposed the dominant authoritarian trend within the church: liberal Catholicism, spearheaded by Montalembert and Dupanloup, and the democratic and social movement behind Lammenais, and later *Le Sillon* of Marc Sangnier. More recently it stemmed from the Parti démocrate populaire created in 1924 and the smaller and more genuinely prolabor Jeune République. Both these parties stressed their loyalty to the Third Republic and their desire to bring about social reforms along the lines of the papal encyclicals *De rerum novarum* and *Quadrigesimo anno,* which condemned the abuses of capitalism as well as the atheistic materialism of Marxism. The first party was rather vague in its advocacy of social justice; it looked for a solution to class struggle outside capitalism and Marxism in some form of corporativism that would keep "free trade-unions within the organized profession." The second was more explicit and favored a nationalized and co-operative sector of the economy in addition to the private one.

Besides these two small parties there existed a Catholic trade-union movement, the CFTC, which rallied mainly white-collar workers in addition to industrial workers in predominantly Catholic areas; its democratic and Socialist left wing was making steady progress over the corporativist and paternalistic outlook of the right wing. These organizations, as well as various Catholic movements for the study of social conditions such as the Semaines sociales and several youth organizations, prepared the ground for the coming success of the MRP.

If the Vichy regime had had the support of most of the church hierarchy, many Catholics had played an important role in the resistance. Georges Bidault had become the president of the National Council of the Resistance. Other prominent leaders of the MRP had had brilliant records. Clandestine activity brought together men who formerly were divided by their political and religious outlook; the anticlericalism of many Socialists and the anti-Marxism of many Catholics melted away in the common struggle. Catholics and Socialists often found themselves in agreement over the purposes of the new *socialisme humaniste* and its attempts at reconciling freedom and social justice and at allowing maximum self-realization of individual capabilities against the double threat of capitalism and totalitarianism. Both could agree on the new "Charter of the Resistance," prepared co-operatively by the National Council of the Resistance; it asked for true political and social democracy, structural reforms of the economy, an expansion of social services, and the participation of workers in the management of industry.

The first congress of the MRP in November, 1946, stressed its goal of political, economic, and social democracy, the conjunction of Christian values and the desire for liberation and renovation born of the resistance. Each successive congress continued to emphasize the double aim of democratic freedom and social justice. At the congress of 1950, Teitgen, one of the leaders, told the delegates that the party refused the destiny of an "intelligent conservative party"; and Bidault, its new president, used the formula, "gouverner au centre avec des moyens de droite pour atteindre des buts de gauche ('govern in the Center with the means of the Right to meet the needs of the Left')." Despite the invitation of the *Modérés* to abandon the Socialists and lead a coalition of the Center and the Right, the MRP steadily adhered until 1951 to its alliance with the SFIO. It has also been consistent in its opposition to neo-Gaullism, which Teitgen accused of aiming at a *République des notables*.

Yet for two years the MRP had prided itself on its loyalty to General de Gaulle; it was "the party of fidelity." To this identification it owed part of its early electoral successes. Its main appeal perhaps came from the belief on the part of many that it presented the best protection against communism at a time when the rightist parties were discredited, the SFIO unreliable, and the small parties of the Center without sufficient strength and dynamism. The new party appealed not only to the Catholic progressives but to the traditionally conservative masses, particularly of the western and eastern provinces; it was supported by the clergy, out of either conviction or necessity. It appealed also to many non-Catholic elements who saw in the strengthening of the church a necessary element of order and discipline in a troubled world. To some it appeared as the left-wing of the Right, to others as the right-wing of the Left. Even the Communist campaign against the MRP was an asset. So was the new electoral law and the reflex of *voter utile*.

By the time of the municipal elections in the fall of 1947 the party had lost its major electoral assets. It was no longer De Gaulle's party, it no longer appeared effective in the struggle against communism, and it had become identified with the failures and shortcomings of the past governments. Some two-thirds of its electors abandoned it for the new RPF. In Paris it had lost four-fifths of its following. In spite of grave electoral risks, the party had remained in the government in January, 1946, along with Socialists and Communists after the departure of De Gaulle, had accepted a constitution of leftist inspiration, and had continued to be friendly to the Socialists, much to the scandal of the *bien-pensants*. The second constitutional referendum in June, 1946, made clear that they had not followed the party's advice to vote for the new constitution.

Yet, despite the electoral disaster of 1947, party discipline was maintained, for only a handful of MRP deputies followed the RPF, most local organizations remaining loyal. The party membership acquired new homogeneity and strength. At the cantonal elections of the spring of 1950 and the general elections of June, 1951, the MRP regained some lost ground.

One reason for this success in keeping discipline is the organization of the party; another is the character of the membership and leadership. The formal organization resembles that of the SFIO: it provides for a National Congress and Council, an Executive Committee, as well as local sections and federations. It is, however, devised to produce more effective leadership. In the first place, the system of representation to the National Congress prevents the larger federation from running the show, which indirectly strengthens the authority of the Center. In the second place, the Executive Committee is made up of a majority of parliamentarians and of a minority of representatives of party members elected by regional councils. This provides for effective control of the party by the parliamentary leadership, which allows for continuity of policy and greater elasticity of tactics, since the leaders are not at the mercy of a change of directives by the *militants*. It may be added that the Executive Committee has more control over the electoral lists than the Comité directeur of the SFIO, another advantage in maintaining discipline. This advantage may partly explain the attachment of the MRP for proportional representation, for a return to the single-member district would weaken the party both electorally and organizationally. It is to be noticed, however, that since its inception the MRP has manifested its concern with the "organization of democracy" through both the strengthening of the parties and the increased role to be played by "natural" communities in a pluralistic society; for it was anxious to avoid a return to the mores of the Third Republic, to its dangerous ideological split into a Right and a Left, and to the old dichotomy of "sovereign individual" and "sovereign state."

Another factor that explains the continued cohesion of the party is the homogeneity of its membership, which contrasts with the heterogeneity of the electorate. The MRP has recruited its *militants* largely among practicing Catholics, most of whom have a common political and social outlook anchored on common religious convictions. Added to this binding force is the fact that this is a young party, which, unlike the SFIO, has had no time to develop competing sects. Its young men and women are eager for service and trained to respect their leaders and doctrines. They have formed teams, *équipes ouvrières,* and *équipes rurales,* which effectively reach various occupational groups and take their educational role seriously. Perhaps the religious background of the *militants,* often trained in the Catholic-sponsored youth groups, explains their willingness to accept discipline and group action, as well as the earnestness of their efforts.

As in the PCF, emphasis is put on giving workers—general white-collar workers and artisans—priority over the bourgeois in positions of responsibility. It has also a larger percentage of women both in parliament and in party organization than any party except the Communists. Although not a "confessional" party under the direct influence of the clergy, the MRP is essentially a party of Catholics; it is identified with a faith rather than with a class. It recruits among all occupational groups, particularly among the lower middle classes.

It has often been observed that the MRP lacks the brilliant stars of the SFIO or the Radicals. Party members put high valuation on hard work, earnestness, reliability, and teamwork. The ideal leader was Robert Schuman —serious and hard-working rather than brilliant. It is perhaps characteristic that the more magnetic Maurice Schumann, "the voice of London" and the first president of the party, disappeared for a time from the party firmament. Besides the new president, Georges Bidault, former college professor and editorialist of *L'Aube,* Teitgen, a vigorous and outspoken foe of the Communists, and Pfimlin, there are few really outstanding personalities; but there is a large number of competent men.

It is difficult to ascertain the relationship of the party with the church; there are no formal ties, and the party has been careful to stress its independence from the hierarchy. Informal advice and pressure, however, are probably felt. It has been said that the influence of the priest is comparable to that of the schoolteacher in the SFIO, but it is certainly less vocal.

The party has stressed its role in educating the citizen, and its *bureaux d'études* have been active in spreading information on administrative, economic, and social problems. The emphasis has been on the immediate and practical rather than on the theoretical. This is in line with the proclaimed aim of the party to seek a large basis of agreement among Frenchmen concerning the solution of the concrete problems that face them rather than adding to fruitless ideological controversies.

The continuous participation of the MRP in the coalition government has left it open to the accusation of opportunism, particularly since the SFIO has passed to the opposition. Its left-wing *militants* have lost their initial enthusiasm, and many of them are accusing the party of betraying its original ideals. A number of them look to a merging with the SFIO with longing. Their criticism was especially strong after the MRP joined the Laniel government and when it refused later to support the Mendès-France cabinet. It appeared to them that the party had given up any pretense at being a left-wing organization and was now content with being identified with the Center-Right, letting even the Radical Socialists outflank it on its left.

The Leftist Union

The Rassemblement des gauches républicaines, which obtained about one hundred seats at the election of 1951, is not a party but a coalition of parties, grouping chiefly the Radical Socialists and the UDSR (Union démocratique et sociale de le Résistance). It constitutes a general staff that coordinates the electoral tactics and the parliamentary action of the two parties.

THE RADICAL SOCIALIST PARTY.— Through its long acquaintance with the duties and privileges of government, the Radical Socialist party had become sedate and cautious and had opened its ranks to many opportunists during the last decades of the Third Republic. Originally a truly progressive party, the Radical Socialists had become to a large extent an opportunist coalition; its clientele, originally urban, had become largely rural. If the old radical spirit was still represented in its left wing, the majority of its deputies were in sympathy with the conservatism of leaders like Chautemps, Malvy, and Caillaux. In the center of the party the libertarian Édouard Herriot had a rival in the more authoritarian Édouard Daladier, both men being convinced that they were the true interpreters of Jacobinism. Some Radicals favored a continued alliance with the SFIO; a majority was opposed to it, yet unwilling to sign a lasting contract with the Right.

These divisions made discipline of vote impossible; often the Left wing of the party would side with the Socialists, while the majority would vote with the Right and a sizable group would abstain. The *militants* would add to the confusion by opposing the parliamentary alliances of their deputies. Thus the National Congress of the party in 1928 forced the withdrawal of Herriot from the Poincaré cabinet. Now that the franc had been saved, it was time to reassert the republicanism of the party by ending its collaboration with the Right. Republican conscience prevented a long alliance with the parties of reaction and demanded another *rapprochement* with the Socialists under the slogan, "No Enemy at the Left." The myth of being leftist may have corresponded to an electoral necessity. In the long run it worked to the advantage of the parties at the left of the Radicals, which became, by definition, more "republican."

The Radical Socialists and their allies represented *la démocratie des petites gens*. The rank and file was made up largely of *petits bourgeois*—peasant proprietors, shopkeepers, small businessmen, public servants, and professional people. They were against reaction and against revolution. Satisfied with their civilized way of living, they wanted to be left alone. Often ignorant of the new conditions created by modern technology, they had no desire to see their way of life upset for the sake of efficient production. "It is a good thing to talk about reforms," said the monarch of Pierre Mille, "but it is dangerous to make them."

Although the largest party in France before World War I, the Radical Socialists were considerably weakened by the war. Their anticlerical platform no longer had the same electoral appeal, and their inability to choose between a lasting alliance with either the *Modérés* or the Socialists contributed to their discredit. World War II was a greater blow than World War I. The party was compromised by collaboration with Vichy on the part of a number of its leaders and newspapers and by the conspicuous lack of resistance ac-

tivities among most of its members. It also suffered from the general discredit of the Third Republic and the desire to bring new blood into French politics.

The Radicals also made tactical errors. Their opposition to a new constitution was not in accord with the public desire for new institutions, and their flirtation with the Communist party—Edouard Herriot became the honorary president of the Jeunesses républicaines de France, the former Communist youth organization—did not reassure non-Communists. These tactics were soon abandoned. While continuing to oppose the rule of the Big Three and the new electoral system, the Radicals participated in the government from 1947 on and made the best of their dual tactics of cooperation and opposition. In the spring of 1946 the extreme left wing, along with Pierre Cot, Albert Bayet, and their pro-Communist friends, left a party that had become ardently *antidirigiste* and continued its militant opposition to the rule of the Big Three. It demanded a return to economic liberalism, with minimum interference on the part of the state and lower taxes.

The party was more successful at the local elections and at the election for the Council of the Republic in 1948 than in the general elections. Undoubtedly the electoral system of 1945 and 1946 was a grave handicap for a relatively small party whose success in the past had been based on the local appeal of individual candidates rather than on the ability of the party itself to gather votes. Its stand in favor of a return to the *scrutin d'arrondissement* is thus understandable. It is significant that the system of indirect elections to the Council of the Republic, which favored rural voters at the expense of urban ones, allowed the Radicals to become the stronger group in France's second chamber. In 1949 the party benefited also from a general swing away from the Left and from planned economy. At the elections of 1951 it profited by the system of *apparentement*. Although it lost some 200,000 votes, it managed to increase its representation in the National Assembly from 48 to 76 deputies.

When it comes to specific financial, economic, and social problems, the party has been unable to maintain unity of vote. The first split found a majority behind Herriot, to accept compromises with Socialists and Catholics in order to keep the Third Force coalition alive, and a minority behind Daladier that was opposed to this collaboration. Another split occurred on economic matters, the majority following the conservative policies of most of the leaders, while a small minority favored the New Deal approach of Mendès-France. Similarly, the party was split in two over the issue of the European Defense Community and the concept of European Union.

These divisions and the inability to maintain party discipline have been major drawbacks for the coalition government. The necessity of relying on Radical votes to obtain a majority, however, has put the party in an excellent strategic position and allowed it to exact a price for continued collaboration. Radicals have been premiers seven times, and almost consistently since 1947 have held important cabinet positions, particularly the ministry of finance.

The loose organization of the party explains in part its inability to exact discipline, the continued conflicts within its ranks, and its tactical suppleness. Its structure resembles that of the other parties: it is comprised of local committees, departmental federations, an Annual Congress, an Executive Committee, and a bureau. In fact, everything contributes to give a few personalities and coteries effective power within the party. The members of the

bureau—a president and sixteen vice-presidents—can direct the decisions of the heterogeneous congresses and of an executive committee made up of several hundred members. Any party member, besides the regular delegates, can participate in the Annual Congress, a situation that can profit any faction willing to pay the cost of its sympathizer's journey.

On the other hand, the departmental federations and local committees remain autonomous in their choice of candidates and electoral tactics, a fact which makes the Radical deputies quite independent of the leadership of the party. It is significant that the party refused to forbid its candidates to ally themselves with the RPF, although the Radical Socialist party was theoretically opposed to de Gaullism. At the municipal elections in 1947 and again at the elections for the Council of the Republic in 1948, hundreds of Radicals presented themselves on common lists with the de Gaullists, only to reassert their independence from the RPF, once elected. In 1951 they no longer needed to ride the de Gaullist crest; the conservative wind was strong enough to lead them to port.

At the Annual Congress in September, 1953, at the watering place of Aix-les-Bains, good food and drink helped prepare the atmosphere of optimism and of proper appreciation of eloquence. The congress applauded with equal enthusiasm Paul Faure; the economic liberal, Mendès-France; the New Dealer, Daladier, who opposed the European Union; and René Mayer, its staunch partisan. It applauded with greatest admiration the "synthesis" presented by Herriot, the great star of the show, although, or perhaps because, it cleverly avoided the issues. For it was the performance and eloquence of the stars rather than ideas that were at stake. By contrast, at the Congress of 1955, the younger delegates carried

Mendès-France to a noisy triumph over the conservative leadership of Martinaud-Deplat, perhaps the sign of a definite revival in a party that had long since lost its claim to genuine leftism.

The Union démocratique et sociale de la Résistance (*UDSR*).—The UDSR was created in June, 1945. It was originally a federation of resistance organizations in close alliance with the Socialists and did not become a formal political party until July, 1946, when it was already a member of the Leftist Union. In 1946 it succeeded in electing twenty-two deputies.

The UDSR started its career as an appendix to the SFIO but soon moved closer to the Radicals. The original purpose, still emphasized at the congress of May, 1947, was to form the core of a large French labor party which would unite MRP, Radicals, and Socialists. Actually, it has few active *militants* in the provinces; it has many generals and a few sergeants. Its heterogeneous elements and lack of organization prevented the adoption of a forceful policy. Party discipline was even less possible than within the ranks of its Radical neighbor. In spite of the efforts of its capable leader, René Pleven, to keep together the *pressés* and the *prudents*, the twelve deputies who belonged to the de Gaullist intergroup broke loose from the party in July, 1949.

As in the case of the Radicals, the strategic position of the UDSR allowed it to play a political role out of proportion to its numerical strength; it was Pleven and his friends who in March, 1948, saved the Schuman cabinet, and it was he who killed another Schuman cabinet in September of the same year and forced the creation of the Queuille cabinet. Finally, it was Pleven who became premier in 1950.

The "Modérés."—In the Third Republic the parties of the Right formed an electoral mass of almost constant strength. In 1936 the parties opposed to the Popular Front obtained almost 43 per cent of the effective vote. They had lost only 126,000 votes from 1928 to 1932 and 178,000 from 1932 to 1936. This compact electoral bloc was not translated into unity of action in parliament except in a negative way. When the Bloc national won the elections of 1919, it could not realize a permanent alliance and was divided into parliamentary fractions without unity of policy. It took the defeat of 1924 to group the various parties and organizations of the Right again in a campaign against the cartel.

Two main tendencies that often overlapped were expressed at the Right: the counterrevolutionary position of the extreme rightists and the conservative republican outlook of the *Modérés*. The authoritarian trend found expression largely outside parliament in the *Ligues*, the most important of which were the Action française, the Jeunesses patriotes, and the Croix de Feu. Most of the parliamentary formations represented the outlook of the *Modérés*. The most important was the Fédération républicaine, which championed social conservatism, clericalism, and nationalism. The second largest party, the Alliance démocratique, was divided into a number of parliamentary groups, and differed from the Fédération only by a greater indifference toward the rights of the church and by a less narrow nationalist outlook. The *Démocrates populaires* were a small Catholic party which accepted the République laïque (if not its anticlerical philosophy), favored international organization, and in theory accepted the need for social reforms. In practice it generally voted with the other rightist groups and was elected with rightist support.

The electoral strength of the Right was distributed throughout France, with strongholds in the west, in parts of the south, and in the northeast, both

in Lorraine, where nationalist sentiment was high, and in Alsace, where
the clergy was influential. In a study
of electoral geographiy Gabriel le Bras
shows a definite relationship in many
regions between a rightist political
orientation and the surviving influence
of the church. The trend toward the
Left is obvious in those regions where
the large majority of the population
has abandoned religious practice. A
recent trend toward the Right, however, is to be found especially in Bur-
gundy, formerly Radical Socialist, where
religious attendance is not the rule.

At the elections of 1946 the old rightist parties suffered a crushing defeat at
the hands of the new MRP, which captured the greater part of their conservative clientele, particularly in western and eastern France. Even more
than the Radicals, the parties of the
Right suffered from the pro-Vichy
policy of many of their leaders and
from the general trend toward new
institutions, new formulas, and new
men. The municipal elections of 1947
saw the principal party of the Right,
the PRL, swallowed up by the new
RPF of De Gaulle. It was not until the
elections of June, 1951, that the *Modérés* reasserted themselves as an electoral force. They succeeded in increasing their electoral strength and especially their representation in the assembly
by their extremely supple tactics: although generally in coalition with the
lists of the Third Force, they allied
themselves with the de Gaullists in a
number of departments and in others
refused any *apparentements*. They benefited, above all, from a growing reaction against *dirigisme*.

The general swing to the Right in
the election of 1951 gave the *Modérés*
an important strategic position in the
new chamber. They could either form
the right wing of a new Third Force
coalition or the center of a coalition
including the RPF and excluding the

Socialists, which came to be the formula adopted as the Socialists left the
government and the RPF gave it their
support.

Three main groups have represented
the *Modérés* in the National Assembly:
the Parti républicain de la Liberté,
the Independents, and the Peasants;
they represent the outlook and clientele of the old Alliance démocratique
and the Fédération républicaine. These
parties never succeeded in the Third
Republic in establishing a real organization of local committees, departmental federations, and central committees; they were general staffs made
up of actual and potential parliamentarians incapable of co-ordinating electoral tactics and parliamentary action.
Today their successors suffer from the
same organizational weakness, and all
attempts to unite rightist elements in a
single organization have failed.

THE PARTI RÉPUBLICAIN DE LA LI-
BERTÉ (PRL).—The PRL was created in
December, 1945, by a group of deputies who belonged to various segments
of the Right, in an attempt to form a
large party able to compete with the
Big Three. Among its founders were
former leaders of the *Fédération républicaine*, the *Alliance démocratique*,
and the PSF of Colonel de la Rocque.
It did not succeed in grouping more
than half of the rightist parliamentarians and was unable to set up an
efficient network of local committees
and federations.

The electoral strength of the PRL
came mainly from the prosperous
classes and the conservative regions.
It is characteristic that the PRL gained
half a million votes between the elections of June and November, 1946, a
rise which corresponds almost exactly
to the decline of the MRP, at that time
its major competitor among the conservative voters. The surprising show
of strength of the *Modérés* at the election of 1951 indicates the reluctance

of many French conservatives to follow an authoritarian movement and at the same time their unwillingness to identify themselves with a Third Force that is leftist in its orientation. Hence the attempt to create the so-called "Fourth Force."

Overshadowed by the RPF in 1947 and abandoned by many of its deputies for the de Gaullist intergroup, the PRL made room in 1951 for the Independents and the Peasants, who are now playing an important political role in the new assembly.

THE INDEPENDENTS AND THE PEASANTS. —By definition, the Indépendants républicains cannot form a real political party. They are a parliamentary group made up of deputies elected with the support of *ad hoc* electoral committees and are, in fact, independent, as the name indicates. It is unlikely that their electoral alliance with other rightist groups will lead to organic unity in parliament. In the past they have been totally unable to maintain any discipline within their ranks. If one of their leaders, Paul Reynaud, was inclined to back up the Third Force, a number of others favored De Gaulle.

The Parti paysan d'Union sociale benefits by a rather solid organization in some departments in central France and claims 25,000 dues-paying members. Its parliamentary group, however, has shown the same lack of discipline as have the other groups of the Right. It is as vulnerable as they are to the pressure of vested interests.

These groups benefited in the elections of 1951 from the discredit of other and better-known political formations held responsible for past mistakes and shortcomings. They have become essential in the formation of any government, as the center of gravity is moving to the Right. They seem to have succeeded in attracting enough RPF deputies to allow the formation of a lasting Center-Right coalition, which further di-

minishes the appeal of the De Gaulle formula. The success of M. Pinay, Independent, in getting twenty-seven de Gaullist deputies to support his cabinet proved to be a turning point in the consolidation of the French parliamentary system. Should the political, economic, and financial crisis deepen, however, the attraction of the *Modérés* toward an authoritarian formula may again prove strong.

The Rally of the French People (RPF)

The Rassemblement du Peuple Français was created on April 14, 1947, following De Gaulle's speech at Strasbourg. Soon afterward the new RPF organized throughout France local, departmental, and interdepartmental committees. The general toured the country, delivering impassioned speeches against the *régime des partis*. Common electoral lists were established with the parties of the Right and Center-Right, and the municipal elections of October, 1947, were a triumph for the RPF, which obtained 35 per cent of the total vote. In Paris it controlled fifty-two municipal councilors out of ninety. Most of the thirteen largest cities were given de Gaullist mayors. Immediately afterward De Gaulle demanded dissolution of the National Assembly and new elections; he sarcastically called the Third Force a *combinaison politicienne* and "general staffs without troops," and his lieutenant, Jacques Soustelle, even accused it of being "the Vichy of today." According to the leaders of the RPF, the French people had clearly repudiated their rulers, and new general elections were in order.

The challenge was taken up. Léon Blum told the assembly on November 21 that the Republic was in danger, threatened not only by international communism but by a new formation whose aim was "to deprive popular sovereignty of its fundamental rights";

and *Populaire* accused De Gaulle of aspiring to personal power and of leading an antidemocratic crusade. The MRP leaders somewhat reluctantly came to express similar views and exchanged bitter words with the spokesmen of the RPF. As for the Communists, they were quick to capitalize upon the opportunity by creating "committees of vigilance" for the protection of the Republic.

The elections had made it clear that De Gaulle had succeeded in mobilizing the forces of the old Right. The RPF had gathered most of the votes of the PRL and smaller rightist parties, a large percentage of the following of the Radicals and UDSR, and perhaps two-thirds of the MRP. The latter practically disappeared as a political force in Paris and in most of the larger cities. De Gaulle, who had been the leader of a predominantly leftist resistance, was now followed by the rightist supporters of Pétain and lost most of his former friends. The new rally appeared as a general mobilization of all antiparliamentary forces.

The appeal of De Gaulle was undoubtedly that of the charismatic leader, and the success of the RPF came from the conjunction of a crisis situation and the presence of a self-appointed, self-assured savior.

That the crisis was real needs little elaboration. The year 1947 was perhaps the worst postwar year; it found France in an almost desperate economic and financial situation. Inflation had ruined or demoralized large sections of the middle class. Those who benefited from it shared in the general feeling of insecurity and resented controls. The very vagueness of the economic program of the RPF was an asset, since people could see in it whatever they wanted to see. The Fourth Republic appeared to millions to be incapable of bringing back prosperity or insuring security from the growing fear of war and revo-

lution. Communism, expanding and militant, was threatening a government that seemed powerless to assert the authority of the state against the new revolutionary tactics.

If the crisis was real, it was also played up by De Gaulle, who needed to impart a sense of urgency in order to appear as the only alternative to chaos and disaster. The impotence of the regime and the impending catastrophe were the main themes of his speeches. The Communist threat was particularly helpful, for the political problem could be reduced to the presence of two competitors for power. There were only two camps: "good Frenchmen," who ought to unite behind the banners of the RPF, and the *séparatistes*. There was no room for a third solution. The crisis was not only dramatized but to a large extent aggravated by the presence of the savior, who divided rather than united and who prevented the adoption of more prosaic but also more effective measures for dealing with a difficult situation and complex problems.

De Gaulle is a controversial figure. In a series of books and articles written before the war he traced the portrait of the ideal leader—strong, silent, unbending, who, "confident in his own judgment and conscious of his strength, makes no attempt to please." There he revealed a certain contempt for man and his ability to govern himself: "Men are political animals who need organization, that is, orders and leaders." Humanity is divided between leaders and followers, and history is made not by anonymous forces but by the thought and actions of great men. His dominant passion seems to have been his faith in the destiny of France coupled with an equal faith in his own destiny. Confident in the infallibility of his mission, his sarcastic humor did not spare those who happened not to agree with him, and, as leader of the provisional government, he proved temperamentally unfitted for the give-and-take of parliamentary democracy.

The authoritarian character of his movement can be gathered from the centralized organization of the RPF. Unlike the Communist party, the de Gaullists frankly admitted the leadership principle as their basis of organization. The only concession to democratic procedures was the election of the president; and, since the general was the *raison d'être* of the RPF, his election to the presidency was an obvious choice. After June, 1949, the president appointed a *conseil de direction* to replace the former executive committee which had been elected by the party congress. A national council of 150 members had purely advisory functions. The same leadership principle was applied to the organization at the local level; an appointed representative ruled in fact, and the elected body only advised.

The constitutional program of the RPF also reflected an authoritarian bias. The reform of the constitution would have allowed a president elected by a broad suffrage to choose ministers responsible both to him and to parliament. In case of a conflict with the latter, the president, armed with the power of dissolution, would refer the dispute to the people. Unfortunately, "historical memories" preclude a division of power between the executive and the legislature in France. The criterion of democracy has traditionally been the effective control of the government by the representatives of the people, that is, by the parties. Faced with the determined opposition of a large percentage of the population, a strong president would probably have to rely on force as a substitute for consent, thus only increasing the opposition and the need for coercion. In a multiparty system where there is no clear-cut alternative to the present coalition government, the right of dissolution is either meaningless or a dangerous weapon for strengthening personal rule: the president could choose the proper time and the proper issue and use the dissolution as a device for having himself plebiscited. For he would offer a simple and fatal choice to the voters: Will they support him as the symbol of order, unity, and continuity, or will they invite the adventure represented by the rebellious parties?

The political structure destined to end the rivalry of the parties was to be completed by a social and economic structure destined to end class struggle. Trade-unions would continue to exist but would be deprived of their "political" character; compulsory unions would operate at the plant level, with leaders elected exclusively from among the workers. A system of "association" of capital, management, and labor would settle disputes peacefully within each industry, while an economic chamber would be the over-all co-ordinator. It is difficult to see how this new corporative system could have had a different fate from the Charter of Labor organized by Vichy.

At the elections of 1951 the RPF refused *apparentement* with other parties, except in a few departments, although the tactics of common lists had paid dividends in the municipal elections of October, 1947, and in the elections to the Council of the Republic. Coalitions with other parties would have brought about the election of more de Gaullist deputies but at the expense of the discipline of the parliamentary group. At first, the tactics of the RPF were those of open obstruction, in the hope that the parties of the Center would prove unable to govern and that new elections would give the party a large representation and perhaps a majority. These tactics largely explain the defection of some thirty RPF deputies who in July, 1952, created a new parliamentary group, the ARS (Action républicaine et sociale), in order to support the Pinay government. The temptation to participate in a Center-Right government had been too great.

In May, 1953, De Gaulle disowned his supporters in parliament. The RPF, now divided between the two groups of ARS and URAS (Union des Républicains d'Action sociale), had lost its reason for being. By supporting the government, it destroyed the possibility of the thorough revision of the constitution that had been the basis of De Gaulle's program.

He had had on his side the old anti-parliamentary bias of the rightists and the growing fear of communism. As the parliamentary system appeared able to deal with the Communist threat and as the economic situation improved, the solution that he proposed lost much of its appeal to most of his conservative followers, who preferred normalcy to adventure. Only a minority continued to believe in the myth of the Leader and the cure-all virtue of a mechanical rearrangement of institutions.

III / THE PARTY SYSTEM IN ACTION

Four types of coalition government ruled France after her liberation: the government of National Union, under De Gaulle, until January, 1946; the tripartite coalition of Communists, Socialists, and Catholics until May, 1947; the so-called "Third Force" coalition following the municipal elections of October, 1947; and the Center-Right government in power since 1951, except for the short interlude of the Mendès-France cabinet in 1954.

Whether the formula of a broad coalition under a leader of great prestige could have continued, had De Gaulle remained at his post, is open to question. It was, above all, a temporary solution dictated by the urgent need of reconstruction and the need of giving France a government "above the parties" while a constitution was being framed. As Siegfried wrote in *L'Année politique* (1946): "The personality of the general had dominated French politics since the liberation. . . . The De Gaulle regime was by a sort of logic essentially personal. Once he had left politics, temporarily or permanently . . . we came to a normal political or parliamentary life that recalled something already known."

The passage from the *régime personaliste* to the *régime des partis* was facilitated by the presence of three large and disciplined parties that appeared to be in agreement over the "Charter of the Resistance" and the ways of implementing it. Except for the hurdle of the constitution, there appeared to be a broad basis of agreement on most issues, particularly economic and social ones. Yet, despite this common outlook and program, the tripartite coalition obviously lacked cohesion. Mutual trust was wanting, and collective responsibility absent. Socialists and Catholics were faced with the tactics of division used by the Communists to discredit them and prevent their close co-operation. A struggle for power went on within the government; the Communists succeeded in occupying key positions in the administration and nationalized enterprises and in using their ministerial posts to distribute jobs and favors with an eye to the next elections. Nor was the new spoils system their monopoly; executive power became partitioned among parties intrenched in their own domains and interested mainly in increasing their respective strength.

In May, 1947, the Communist ministers were unceremoniously ousted from the Ramadier government following their position on the Renault strike and the wage policy of the cabinet. With the revolutionary strikes in the fall of 1947 the Communist party passed to the stage of violent opposition and directly threatened the regime. Another threat came from De Gaulle, who in the summer launched a vigorous campaign against the new constitution and formed his RPF. Its victory in the municipal elections of October gave some plausibility to his demands for dissolution of the National Assembly and new elections. The new challenge was met again, and the Third Force, as a coalition for Republic defense, came into official existence.

The fact that the Third Force was born in defeat and in danger explains its character. The Communist-inspired strikes in the fall of 1947 threatened the French economy and the life of the Republic. The government had to act vigorously to crush the offensive. Thus the Third Force had to be primarily a coalition against the Communist menace, which forced the government to make advances to the hesitant deputies in the no-man's-land between neo-Gaullism and the Third Force. The *travaillisme* dear to many Socialists and MRP's had to yield to the need for defense of the Republic; a positive program of reconstruction and social justice gave way to a negative program of survival. This meant in practice a forced cohabitation between people of opposed economic and social doctrines.

The conflict between liberalism and *dirigisme*, between Center-Right and Center-Left, led to lack of continuity, to contradictions, and to inefficiency— above all, to lack of active popular support. A surreptitiously conservative policy was adopted for which the Socialists got the blame from the workers and none of the credit from the investors. There was no way out for the Socialists: Republican defense demanded a sacrifice of principles and of votes. The *cure d'opposition*, about

which many Socialists dreamed, would have produced a crisis which was insoluble by any means short of De Gaulle's return on his own terms.

The small, but strategically essential, support given by some Radicals, UDSR's, and Independents, such as Paul Reynaud, allowed them to press successfully for a financial and economic policy distasteful to most Socialists and many Catholics. The situation was complicated by the inability of the smaller parties to keep discipline of vote. If before 1951 the government could always count on some 150 MRP deputies and 100 Socialists, it was fortunate to have on its side a majority of Radicals, half of the UDSR, and a few Independents, depending on the issues at stake. The government, pressed by the challenge of the extremes, was incapable of vigorous action against inflation. It could not afford to step on too many toes if it wanted to survive. Farmers, middlemen, and public servants were among its supporters, and the Communists and the de Gaullists were ready to comfort them and to excite them, as they showed early in 1948 when the Mayer Plan was launched.

By increasing the parliamentary representation of the Center parties, the elections of June, 1951, allowed the formation of a more homogeneous Center-Right coalition. It permitted the SFIO to pass to the opposition and succeeded in getting the support of the RPF, thus ending the antiparliamentary threat of de Gaullism. The Pinay government in power for ten months managed to stop inflation but followed the practice of preceding cabinets by avoiding dangerous issues and neglecting the long-range aspects of French economic recovery. A recession took place that added to the insecurity and resentment of wage-earners.

In spite of the greater homogeneity of the new coalition—only the MRP does not feel quite at ease in it—the lowest common denominator had to be found between parties basically attached to the status quo and vulnerable to pressures from any quarter, whether sugar-beet interests, wine growers, or big or small businessmen. No long-range program of economic expansion could be expected from a government pressed hard by mounting financial difficulties, having to face problems in a piecemeal manner, and divided over the diagnosis of the ills. Pressure from the outside was lacking, since public opinion was largely ignorant of the broad issues at stake and since no sanction existed in the form of a Center-Left coalition ready to take over.

The first time a left-wing alternative almost took shape was during the "New Deal" government of Mendès-France from June, 1954, to February, 1955. The "Mendès-France experiment" marks an attempt by a dynamic personality to reassert the authority of the executive at the expense of parliamentary and party leadership. Disregarding the wishes of party leaders, the new premier molded a governmental team of younger men, imposed his authority in initiating and implementing his program, and forced votes of confidence, relying on *ad hoc* majorities, the composition of which varied according to the issue at stake. His unorthodox approach included direct appeals to the electorate as a means of pressure on the parliamentarians. It was bound to create resentment, a resentment deepened by the gravity of the issues at stake. Most groups were dangerously split over European unity, German rearmament, North African policy, and economic and social reforms. Held responsible for the death of the EDC, Mendès-France brought upon himself the stubborn hostility of the MRP and was unable to hold behind him his "New Deal" majority, although many had expected

him to become the leader of a new Left made up of groups and individuals all the way from the Socialists to the left-wing de Gaullists. Ostensibly defeated over the North African issue, the "dynamic personality" had to make way for the "talented conciliator," Edgar Faure, who fell back once more on the support of the Center-Right. The personal prestige that Mendès-France had acquired, especially among the younger generation, proved, however, the widespread desire for a strong leadership and a new policy.

By 1948, and especially after the elections of 1951, the Fourth Republic had already come to look strangely like the Third. Not only were the social ideals of the resistance forgotten, as the political center of gravity moved well to the Right, but France came again to be governed by fragile majorities resting on the support of ill-disciplined groups divided among and within themselves. Old issues reappeared as a source of further division. It is significant that in 1951 the clerical issue of state support to Catholic schools again set the MRP and the *Modérés* in opposition to Socialists and Radicals, at the same time as the social issue of the sliding wage scale grouped Socialists and MRP against Radicals and *Modérés*. Soon afterward EDC and the North African problems split most of the groups, while economic and social policy and the issues of electoral, constitutional, and fiscal reforms created other fractions within each party. Even the most talented negotiators could not maintain any coalition for more than a few months. Would-be ministers were ready to precipitate new crises. Commenting on the twenty ministerial crises in ten years, veteran Paul Reynaud went so far as to say: "The assembly can overthrow as many governments as it pleases without any other motive than the opportunity of its members to satisfy ambitions overstimulated by the very frequency of the crises."

The frequent turnover of cabinets is closely linked to the weakness of executive leadership. "Governments are short-lived," wrote Philip Williams, "because they are weak, so that everyone speculated on the succession, and weak because their expectation of life being brief, they are always tempted to avoid dangerous and unpopular choices and to postpone decision; greater stability would make for greater responsibility." Inability to make prompt decisions and to adopt a long-range program and implement it with measures which are bound to be unpopular with some groups and for some time is a major drawback at any time. This relative paralysis of government is particularly grave now that the state must assume growing responsibilities and is faced with a lasting crisis situation. The weakness of the executive contributes to the discredit of parliamentary democracy and to the appeal of the authoritarian and totalitarian solutions. The presence of powerful extremes in turn adds immensely to the difficulties of government.

Its short life-expectancy forces each government to face problems as they come up in a haphazard fashion, to find a convenient and temporary solution, or to delay action and pass on the responsibility to the next cabinet. The situation makes for irresponsibility at all levels. The permanent officials feel independent of the ministers and carry on their own policies and their petty wars within the bureaus. The cabinet can act in relative independence of the National Assembly by railroading legislation through the procedure of urgency and by using its decree powers to modify and suspend existing laws in economic and financial matters. The assembly in turn acts in an irresponsible

way vis-à-vis the government: it can prevent governmental initiative in bills dealing with complex problems in which the administration should have a large amount of initiative and independence; it can delay or turn down important reforms and harass the government with criticisms on details of administration. Political parties feel no responsibility toward the electorate either for the collective policy of the government or for a decision to leave the coalition, since there is no electoral or parliamentary sanction attached. Opposition parties can be completely irresponsible in their criticism and promises, since they will not form the next government. The public itself has no party loyalty and no sense of responsibility to the government and to the state. Under these conditions vested interests of all types have a field day; they can successfully exercise discreet or open pressure on parliament or the government. The recent scandal of the Poujade-led organization of tax dodgers is only the most blatant manifestation of growing *incivisme*.

To restore effective leadership—and, with it, responsibility—the government needs, first of all, some guaranty of tenure. Since the presidential form of government is objectionable to a majority of Frenchmen, the problem of executive stability has to be faced within the framework of the parliamentary and multiparty system. Perhaps a solution can be found in constitutional reforms giving adequate weapons to the government (such as the unconditional right of dissolution or the adoption of the clause in the constitution of West Germany preventing the overthrow of the premier until his successor is already accepted by a majority). Perhaps a better solution exists in the adoption of a new electoral system designed to bring about a more coherent majority and at the same time to diminish the parliamentary representation of the Communist party.

But time and cohesion may prove insufficient if there is no incentive for responsible and dynamic leadership. And the incentive may exist only if there is an alternate coalition presenting an alternate program and ready to come in. Responsibility comes from the sanction of the polls. For this sanction to be effective, the electorate has to be presented with a relatively clear-cut choice of policies in a relatively balanced contest of power. If the two-party system is an ideal instrument for clear choice

and efficient government, the example of the northwestern European countries indicates that a multiparty system can also present alternative coalitions and a sufficiently clear choice of realistic programs for the electorate to decide upon. Whether this solution is possible in France, given the characteristics of the party system and the lack of consensus described earlier, is another matter. So long as the Communist party remains strong, the left-wing alternative is not likely to be found which alone could create the conditions needed to bring back the lost consensus.

APPENDIX

FRENCH ELECTORS AND THEIR PARTIES

The following summary is based on the inquiry made in 1952 by the Institut Français d'Opinion Publique, published as "Les Attitudes politiques des Français," *Sondages,* special number, Vol. III (1952).

THE COMMUNIST VOTER

The PCF is essentially a party of workers. According to the *Sondages* study, the proportion of workers among the Communist electors is twice that in the total population. In all other occupational groups it is below this average. Along with the RPF, the PCF has the smallest proportion of rural votes. Statistics also indicate that it has more men and more young people voting for it than for any other party and that the average Communist elector is more active than others in attending meetings, converting people, and contributing money.

His motivation in voting for the PCF seems to be, first of all, economic: low living standards, the defense of the interests of the working class, the fight against capitalism. Also important seems to be the defense of peace against the "war policy" of the government and the United States. The Communist voters are the only ones to believe in overwhelming majority (83 per cent) that rearmament and the presence of American troops in Europe contribute to the danger of war. For them it is the United States and not the Soviet Union that has aggressive intentions.

The cohesion of the party appears in the confidence of the voters in the leadership, in the faith, in the doctrine, and in the belief

in ultimate victory. Sixty-seven per cent of the people interviewed believe that the party will some day obtain a majority of votes and that communism will one day rule the world.

The revolutionary spirit of the voters is clearly shown in the *Sondages* poll. A majority stands against participation in the government, which many consider to be made up of dishonest men, traitors to the interests of the French people. Forty per cent believe that the party should take power by force if circumstances are favorable. On the other hand, 32 per cent believe that the PCF is the strongest support of the parliamentary system, while 46 per cent point to the RPF as the worst enemy of parliamentary institutions. It appears that about half the Communist electorate favors revolutionary action, while the other half stands for continued legality, perhaps in the certitude that some day the PCF will be in a position to seize power legally.

THE SOCIALIST VOTER

The SFIO is not a class party but has a very heterogeneous clientele which includes all the strata of French society. If anything, it is the party of the civil servants, either active or retired, and more generally of salaried people. It is characteristic that the SFIO has more success among older people and that it is stronger in small towns than in large cities. Of all parties, it has the largest proportion of electors in towns from 5,000 to 20,000 inhabitants, while the Communists and de Gaullists dominate the cities, and the Radicals the villages. Thus the SFIO has lost its character of a mass urban party.

Socialist voters, according to the *Sondages* study, show some political independence and are often in disagreement with the political line of the party. They have a certain lack of confidence in their leaders and are much less inclined to be politically active than the Communists. A large majority of them favor SFIO participation in the government (61 per cent for, 16 per cent against). In foreign policy the outlook is one of cautious sympathy for the United States and of guarded support of the Atlantic system against a Soviet threat, which many seem to ignore. Pacifism remains an important motivation for Socialist voters.

The MRP

The vote for the MRP is as heterogeneous as the vote for the SFIO. The proportion of white-collar workers is the highest of all parties. It seems that MRP voters are largely lower-middle-class people of Catholic convictions motivated often by Christian ethics and the goals of peace and greater social justice. They show greater confidence in their leaders than the electors of most parties.

The Radicals

Public opinion polls show that the Radical Socialist party is today followed mainly by peasant proprietors, tradesmen, and *rentiers*. Half of the voters live on their income from business or property, and their average income seems only slightly smaller than that of the *Modérés*. The party has very few sympathizers among industrial and white-collar workers. It has also fewer women and young people than other parties and is strong mainly in small towns and villages. Although the average voter is not inclined to proselytize, admits of little activity for the party, and shows little confidence in it, he is more constant than the followers of other parties. The Leftist Union gathered as many votes in 1951 as in 1946 (11.5 per cent of the effective national vote). Its support seems to come mainly from a realistic, tolerant, and somewhat skeptical *petit bourgeois* interested, above all, in security and stability, particularly in monetary terms. He is not much interested in ideas and has lost even his traditional anticlericalism. All he wants is peace and order and to be left alone.

The Modérés

The *Sondages* study indicates that the *Modérés* voters—comprising about 15 per cent of the electorate—form a heterogeneous group of people, sincere and less sincere republicans, interested, above all, in a conservative economic and financial policy. They are electorally fickle, as many voted first for the MRP, then for the PRL, RPF, or Independents. By contrast with the Radicals, the *Modérés* have more women electors than men, and more younger people. The largest occupational group following them is made up of peasant proprietors (about a third of the voters), followed by tradesmen and industrialists. There are more businessmen and fewer industrial and agricultural workers among them than in any other political formation. The living standards of the *Modérés* are also the highest of all parties (58 per cent are proprietors and own an automobile; a third have servants). They are not active politically except at election times. They show confidence neither in their party nor in the leaders, and, though they want continued participation in the government, they are highly critical of it. They worry less about political instability and the "incompetence" of rulers than about economic and financial matters such as inflation, taxes, and budgetary deficits. They admit that they vote as they do to protect their interests. More sympathy is expressed among the *Modérés* for the RPF than among the followers of any other party. Anticommunism led 70 per cent of the people interviewed to advocate the dissolution of the PCF.

The RPF

The RPF voters (22 per cent of the total electorate in 1951) came from all walks of life, with proportionally more industrialists, tradesmen, and white-collar workers than peasants and industrial workers. Their average living standard was somewhat below that of the *Modérés* and Radical voters.

The cult of the leader appears to have been the main incentive in voting for the RPF. Sixty-eight per cent of the people polled gave their total confidence to the general—the highest percentage of confidence given to the leader of any party—while characteristically only 12 per cent gave it to his lieutenant, Soustelle, and only a few mentioned

Malraux, Koenig, and Palevski. In other words, it was De Gaulle alone and not the collective leadership of the rally that inspired confidence. His prestige went even beyond the limits of the RPF, and it has been estimated that about 30 per cent of the electorate would have accepted his leadership.

Another and related motive in voting RPF was an antiparliamentarian stand: 62 per cent of the voters polled opposed a regime of unstable and incompetent governments; yet 56 per cent stood for participation in the govern- ment, and only 30 per cent for opposition. Anticommunism was another important factor in the appeal of the RPF: 77 per cent of the interviewees stood for the outlawing of PCF. Nationalism appears to be a lesser factor. If RPF voters favored the policy of rearmament in the Atlantic system and advocated the continuation of the war in Indo-China, it is interesting to note that they also favored the European Defense Community and German rearmament, contrary to the views of their leader.

Belgium: Party Cleavage and Compromise

FELIX E. OPPENHEIM
University of Delaware

I / IDEOLOGICAL BASES OF BELGIUM'S PARTY DIVISIONS

The geographical area which in 1830 became the kingdom of Belgium has been from medieval times a focal point for all major European ideological and political movements. A brief consideration of the political parties in Belgium is therefore of greater interest than the size of that country might warrant.

When studying the Belgian party structure, one has to keep in mind that it reflects not only the gradations of political opinion from Right to Left but also the linguistic differences between the French- and the Flemish-speaking peoples and the religious differences between the Catholics and the free-thinkers.

Another distinguishing feature of Belgian political parties is their pervading influence on the everyday life of the population. A Belgian who votes for the Catholic party not only will be a member of a Catholic manufacturer's organization or trade-union and send his children to Catholic schools but will usually also patronize a Catholic club, a Catholic bank, and a Catholic co-operative store. Similarly, every town has its Socialist "people's house," very often complete with theater, club, department store, and even a bakery. There are Catholic and Socialist sickness-benefit and mutual-aid societies with their own hospitals, sanatoria, and vacation camps. This characteristically Belgian combination of "politics through the mind" with "politics through the stomach," the origin of which has been traced back to the guilds of the medie-

val cities, has become part and parcel of Belgian folklore.

Catholics and Freethinkers

Belgium is historically a Catholic country and was not permanently affected by the Reformation. Although the Belgians joined the Dutch in the revolt against Philip II of Spain, they did not achieve political independence but remained under Catholic (Spanish, later Austrian, and finally French) rule until they were united with the Netherlands in 1815.[1] Fifteen years later the Catholic Belgians freed themselves from Protestant Dutch rule to form the independent kingdom of Belgium.

Catholicism in Belgium has always had to contend not so much with Protestantism as with a strong agnostic tradition rooted in the French Enlightenment. At present Belgium is about equally divided between Catholics and freethinkers.[2]

1. Following are the pertinent dates in this period of Belgium's history:
1566. Beginning of the revolt by the Belgians and Dutch against Philip II of Spain.
1579. Treaty of Arras: the southern (Belgian) provinces are restored to the Spanish Crown.
1713. Peace of Utrecht: the Spanish Netherlands come under Austrian (Hapsburg) rule and become the Austrian Netherlands.
1792. The Austrian Netherlands are conquered by the armies of the French Revolution.
1815. Congress of Vienna: Belgium is united with Holland to form the Kingdom of the Netherlands.
1830. Belgian revolution and independence.

2. There are no relevant statistics, as Belgians would not readily answer questions re-

Flemings and Walloons

The cleavage between Catholics and freethinkers tends to coincide with and is deepened by the language division. The Flemings, who speak Dutch dialects, are predominantly practicing Catholics, while the Walloons speak French (or French dialects) and incline toward agnosticism. Since one or the other language has enjoyed a privileged status at different times, Belgium, unlike Switzerland, has always had to cope with a language problem. During the nineteenth century the French language predominated, in part as a reaction against Dutch rule and in part due to the fact that French was at that time spoken by the wealthy class even in Flanders. And it would have been contrary to the prevailing laissez faire philosophy to attempt to change this situation through legislation. At the turn of the century the Flemish movement emerged as one of the many nationalistic currents of the period. Finally in 1932 Flemish and French were declared by law to be the only two official languages, each in its respective area, while the Brussels region was declared bilingual. Because of the steady increase of the Flemish over the Walloon population, the Walloons have tended since World War II, like the Flemish before World War I, to consider themselves a threatened minority.[3]

Conservatives and Progressives

During the first sixty years of Belgium's independence the party struc-

lating to their religious beliefs. The equal division between Catholics and freethinkers is evidenced by the fact that half the pupils go to Catholic elementary schools, while the other half attend public schools, which provide no religious instruction.

3. In 1947, of a total population of 8.5 million, 50.2 per cent lived in Flanders, 34.5 per cent in Wallonia, and 15.3 per cent in the Brussels area.

ture corresponded to the religious division. The Catholics adhered to the Catholic party, or the Right; the freethinkers to the Liberal party, or the Left. Catholics and Liberals, while divided over the question of public education, were united in their advocacy of laissez faire and in their defense of the interests of the wealthy, whom alone they represented.

In 1870 little more than 100,000 of the 5 million Belgians had the franchise. In 1893, under the pressure of the rising working-class movement, qualified universal suffrage was established (one or two additional votes were given to those meeting special requirements as to family status, education, and income). Thus the Socialists were able to gain representation in parliament and to emerge as a new, progressive party of the Left. When the Socialists finally won the struggle for unqualified universal male suffrage[4] in 1919, their share of the total vote was so great that it was impossible for either the Catholics or the Liberals ever again to gain the allegiance of the majority of the voters.

From 1847 to 1914 Liberal and Catholic cabinets alternated, according to whichever of the two parties had the majority in the lower house. In 1914 the Socialists for the first time participated in the government. Since 1919 unstable coalition governments have been the rule as a consequence of the absence of any majority party in the House of Representatives.[5] This has resulted in frequent and often extended cabinet crises, the common defect of cabinet and multiparty systems based on proportional representation. Since proportional representation, however, insures adequate representation of the Liberal

4. Women's franchise was not established until 1949.

5. Tables 1 and 2, on p. 167, summarize the percentage of the total vote and the number of seats in the House of Representatives, by party, from 1919 to 1954.

and Socialist minorities in Flanders and of the Catholic minority in Wallonia, this institution, like the monarchy, seems indispensable to the preservation of Belgium's unity.

Pro- and Anti-democrats

With the exception of its two periods of German occupation, representative government has functioned continuously in Belgium. The great majority of the people have adhered to the three "traditional" parties—Catholic, Liberal, and Socialist—all of which stand for parliamentary democracy and constitutional monarchy.

While Belgium has not remained free from the inroads of antidemocratic movements of the extreme Right and Left, the followers of such extremist parties have always been comparatively few. This is due not only to the strong democratic tradition but also in part to the fact that Belgium is the only country in which compulsory voting is enforced.

From 1925 on, the Communists have held a few seats in parliament; their following was sizable only during the three years following World War II. Two extreme rightist movements existed during the intrawar period—the Flemish Nationalists and a similiar party in Wallonia, the Rexists. Like totalitarian movements in other countries, both these parties advocated replacing existing parliamentary institutions with an authoritarian regime. The Flemish Nationalists attacked not only Belgian democracy but, as the extreme wing of the Flemish movement, the very existence of the Belgian state.[6] During the depression of the 1930's both parties became strong enough to constitute a real menace to democracy, but by the time of the German invasion their following had declined to such an extent that the Germans were unable to establish a quisling government there. Unlike the Netherlands, occupied Belgium

was, together with northern France, under a military government; both extreme rightist parties were outlawed after Belgium's liberation in September, 1944,[7] leaving postwar Belgium divided into Catholics (now again the only party of the Right), and Liberals, Socialists, and Communists (the parties of the Left).

II / THE CATHOLICS

Origins

The Dutch regime (1815–30) had suppressed religious as well as political freedom; consequently, Belgium's independence from the Netherlands was achieved by the combined efforts of Belgian Catholics and Liberals. The constitution of the new Belgian monarchy was also the work of both these parties, the Catholics willing to meet the Liberals' demands for freedom of opinion in exchange for freedom of education. The Belgian Catholics thus deemed it advantageous to support the constitution with its liberal bill of rights.[8] Unlike France, Belgium has no group which has continued to look back with nostalgia to the era preceding the French Revolution.

6. A similar Walloon separatist movement favoring Wallonia's incorporation into France arose after World War II but did not become sufficiently important to form a separate party.

7. This is not to say that fascism is dead in Belgium. By 1949 the former Flemish Nationalists had regained sufficient strength to compete again in the elections (under the name of "Flemish Concentration"). A serious depression might well give renewed impetus not only to communism but also to such latent neofascist currents.

8. The publication by Pope Pius IX of the *Syllabus* in 1864 made certain Catholics hesitate whether to support a constitution based on "freedom of evil." These doubts were dispelled by a letter of Pope Leon XIII in 1878 which stated that although the Belgian Constitution "contains some principles which I could not approve as Pope . . . , the Belgian Catholics should not only refrain from attacking it, but defend it."

It was the difference in the interpretation of "freedom of education" which, around 1848, brought an end to the cooperation of Catholics and Liberals. The Catholics held that religiously neutral schools were, by their very nature, anti-Catholic and that therefore the secular state had no right to organize, at the expense of the Catholic taxpayers, schools for the sole benefit of the freethinkers. The "school question" constituted the main political issue during the second half of the nineteenth century and has continued to divide the Right and the Left up to the present day. As late as 1948 a cabinet crisis occurred over the question of government subsidies to certain private Catholic schools.

Divergent Opinions

With the gradual awakening of political consciousness in the masses toward the end of the nineteenth century, a split occurred within the Catholic ranks. The conservative wing, which defended the interests of industry, the aristocracy, and the army, attempted to prevent the shift from laissez faire liberalism to modern democracy. Even after losing the battle against universal suffrage, minimum wages, and maximum hours, the rightist Catholics have continued to this day to stress the conservative values of tradition, authority, and hierarchy to the extent possible within the framework of democratic institutions.

Unlike the Catholics in Spain, Portugal, Italy, and Austria, most Belgian Catholics, including the conservatives, did not espouse fascism between the two world wars. Having backed the constitutional monarchy from the start, they continued to hold parliamentary democracy a sufficient bulwark against the threat of communism. Those among the Belgian Catholics who were swayed by totalitarian ideas withdrew from the Catholic party and formed the two dissident fascist parties. That both the Flemish Nationalists and the Rexists were originally Catholic groups is indicated by the Nationalists' watchword, "Everything for Flanders, Flanders for Christ," and by the Rexists' name, which was an abbreviation for "Christus Rex."

A number of Catholic leaders whose social philosophy was derived from the papal encyclical *Rerum Novarum* (1890) foresaw that the trend toward political equality and economic security could not be reversed and that they could not gain the masses for the Catholic party unless they themselves advocated electoral and social reforms. Since this potential mass following was predominantly Flemish, their leaders naturally supported the Flemish movement.[9] This left-wing Catholic current found expression in the Christian Democratic wing within the Catholic party and in organizations such as the Christian trade-unions and youth organizations.

Like the Flemish Nationalists and Rexists before World War II, some Catholic progressives seceded from the Catholic party after liberation, to form the Union Démocratique Belge (UDB), which, like the French MRP, was opposed to "political Catholicism," though "based on the spiritual values of Christianity," and favored "social and economic, as well as political, democracy." The UDB did not survive its defeat in the first postwar election.

The Christian Democrats have always accused the right-wing leaders of using religion for political purposes and the Catholic party for the defense of vested interests, although many Christian Democrats concede that they vote Catholic rather than Socialist only because of the latter's "materialistic philosophy."

9. An added reason for their support may be found in the fact that the Flemish movement was one of Catholic mysticism as opposed to French agnosticism and rationalism.

Struggle for Party Control

In spite of the growth of the Christian Democratic wing, the conservatives were, on the whole, able to maintain control of the party during the period between the two world wars and during the first year after liberation. The principal means by which they endeavored to preserve the party's conservative character after liberation was their support of King Leopold III's return to the throne, a policy which was opposed by all other parties.[10] The Catholic party attempted not so much to justify Leopold's acts and attitudes during the occupation as to make him the symbol of the status quo opposition to social change.

On August 15, 1945, however, an event occurred which made it appear as though the progressives had suddenly wrested all control away from the conservatives. On that day the Catholic party decided to dissolve itself and to reorganize under the new name of "Parti Social Chrétien" (PSC) as "a new party, with a new doctrine and a new cadre." In substituting "Christian" for "Catholic" in its name, the PSC apparently wished to indicate that it was "nonconfessional" and hence not linked to the church but rather that it represented the "human values on which our Western civilization is based." The

10. On May 28, 1940, the king, who is also commander-in-chief of the armed forces, capitulated to the Germans and gave himself up as prisoner of war. He thereby placed himself in a situation which Article 82 of the Belgian Constitution qualifies as "incapacity to reign." On June 7, 1944, Leopold was deported to Germany; in May, 1945, he was freed by the Americans in Austria. On July 19, 1945, the Left majority in parliament passed a bill according to which the king's "incapacity to reign" had not ended automatically with his liberation but was to continue until parliament itself declared its end. This device enabled the Left to prevent Leopold's return to the throne until after the election of 1950, which gave the Catholics a majority in both houses of parliament (see n. 13).

PSC's program thus resembles that of the Union Démocratique Belge; it was founded two months after the latter. The term "social" was incorporated in the name in order to give the party the appearance of a *progressive* Christian movement. The PSC's present platform contains such leftist slogans as: "The old liberal and capitalist world lies in ruins, hence we must build a new society, in which the individual is no longer a slave of money interests." "We are against a regime which gives political influence to the financially powerful." "The working class must have a greater share of the goods it produces." The most striking evidence of the PSC's break with its predecessor's conservatism was its coalition with the Socialists, whom the old Catholic party would have considered too strange to have as bedfellows without the Liberals in between. This government, which remained in office for over two years (March, 1947–June, 1949), under the premiership of the Socialist Paul-Henri Spaak instituted "structural reforms" which the old Catholic party would hardly have approved.

The leftward shift of the party's direction was not so radical, however, as these changes in name, program, and alignments seemed to indicate. Although the PSC's leadership did constitute, on the whole, a "young cadre," some of the old guard still remained on its national committee and subsequently won re-election. The party program, which on the whole reflected the "new doctrine," was interspersed with slogans attempting to bridge the gulf between progressives and conservatives such as: "The PSC repudiates Marxism no less than liberalistic capitalism. [It advocates applying] formulae which reconcile private initiative with public control." Nor could the PSC repudiate the pro-Leopold plank to which it had been committed by its predecessor, even though many PSC leaders gradually cooled toward the idea of Leopold's resumption of the throne. As soon as the PSC gained the majority in both houses (June, 1950), it voted for the king's return; but an all-PSC cabinet did not hesitate to draw up Leopold's act of abdication in favor of his son shortly thereafter.

On the whole, the Christian Democratic influence on the PSC's policy since 1945 seems to have been less than that of the conservatives' on the old Catholic party. There is no doubt that the PSC, which continues to be popularly known as the "Catholic party," is essentially the same Catholic party with a new façade.

Sources of Strength

Since the beginning of universal male suffrage in 1919 more Belgians have voted for the Catholic party than for any other,[11] and in Flanders the Catholics have held the absolute majority.[12] The vote for the Catholic party and the parties of the extreme Right, taken together, remained around 44 per cent during that whole period (see Table 1). Whenever there has been an increase in the support for the extreme rightist splinter parties, the vote for the Catholic party has decreased to that extent, and vice versa. The Catholic party's strength is likely to remain around 44 per cent, barring a revival of dissident Catholic movements. Because of their numerical strength, the Catholics have been continuously in power from 1884 to 1954, with the exception of the period August, 1945–March, 1947, when

11. Only in the elections of 1936, held at the height of the depression, was the Catholic party's following substantially smaller than that of the Socialists because of the defection of one-third of the Catholic voters to the Rexists and Flemish Nationalists (see Table 1).

12. For example, in 1946, 56.2 per cent of the Flemish, 35.5 per cent of the Brussels, and 27 per cent of the Walloon voters voted Catholic.

they voluntarily played the role of opposition party. Because of their lack of an absolute majority in parliament, however, they have been governing in coalition, usually with the Liberals or with both the Liberals and the Socialists.[13]

Like the Christian Democrats in Italy or Germany since the end of World War II, the Catholic voters in Belgium have, since the end of World War I, represented a conglomeration of disparate economic strata and political opinions and have little in common other than their allegiance to the Catholic church. Party leaders share only the common desire to keep dissidents from forming splinter parties and to prevent the one Catholic party from being split into rightist and leftist factions.

The main technique by which Catholic leaders have, on the whole, succeeded in maintaining the unity of the party has been the use of ambiguous terminology in its platforms, thereby making room for as many interpretations as there are shades of Catholic opinion. Unlike the other parties, the Catholic party has no official press. Each Catholic newspaper adapts the party platform to fit its readers' views and feels free even to attack the party's policies. Thus the conservative Catholic press emphasizes that the PSC is the "party of order" and has criticized its leadership for its "strangely advanced opinions," for its lukewarm defense of Leopold, and for its "alliance against nature" with the Socialists. This flexibility may be partly the unintended consequence of the fact that the struggle for power within the party has never resulted in a definite victory for

13. From June, 1950, to April, 1954, an all-Catholic cabinet was in office because of the exceptional circumstance that the Catholics had obtained an absolute majority of two seats in the House of Representatives, even though they had polled not more than 46.7 per cent of the total vote.

either rightists or leftists. To a large degree, it certainly is the result of a conscious compromise on the part of the leaders for the sake of holding the party together.

The Catholic party's ability to maintain the allegiance of a most diversified following may also be attributed to its powerful propaganda apparatus, which comprises not only its own organization but also the Catholic schools, the Catholic youth organizations, the Christian trade-unions, and the church hierarchy itself. Even though the Catholic party is organizationally independent of the Catholic church and claims to be "nonconfessional," Belgian Catholics ordinarily follow church directives in political, no less than in religious, matters, and the church usually expects the faithful to vote for none other than the Catholic party. In 1936 the archbishop of Malines voiced his disapproval of Catholics voting Rexist. In the following elections the Rexists lost seventeen of their previously held twenty-one seats. Similarly, the defeat of the Union Démocratique Belge in the 1946 elections may be due primarily to a speech of the archbishop on October 26, 1945, in which he stressed "the necessity of unity among Belgian Catholics, who have a basically different outlook on life than non-Catholics."

III / THE LIBERALS

Ideology

Spiritual heirs of the Enlightenment and of the French Revolution, the Liberals originally stood for the individual's liberation from the domination of both church and state. At first they were not antireligious but merely anticlerical in that they wanted public authority to be independent of the church in practice as well as in theory. Under the influence of the natural sciences and Comte's positivism, they tended gradually to become agnostic and anti-

religious and hence more antagonistic toward Catholicism. The seriousness of this rift is illustrated by the decision taken by a Liberal cabinet on June 5, 1880, to break off Belgium's diplomatic relations with the Vatican.

Because of their leanings toward French rationalism, the Liberals had little sympathy with the Flemish cause. Even though they became divided into a more conservative and a more progressive wing, the Liberal party as a whole continued, together with the rightist Catholics, to defend the interests of the wealthy by invoking the principle that government should protect individual rights but not insure satisfaction of needs. The Liberal party has continued after World War II to oppose government regulations of economic matters, however lenient these measures may have been in Belgium, as compared with those of the Dutch or British governments. Since the Catholic party, at least according to its platform, has now turned away from unrestricted laissez faire, the Liberals are by this standard the most conservative Belgian party, and it is only by tradition that they continue to be classified among the parties of the Left.

Party Strength

Unlike the French Radical Socialists, the Belgian Liberals failed to secure the allegiance of the rural masses, who turned to the Catholic party. This was primarily due to their failure to adapt classical liberalism to changing conditions. For the same reason, they could not compete with the Socialists for the vote of the industrial workers. Hence the Liberal party's following has remained confined to freethinkers among the urban bourgeoisie, the manufacturers, the liberal professions, and the café owners (cafés being more numerous and conspicuous in Belgium than even in France). In fact, liberalizing liquor-concession laws constituted for a long time one of the main planks of the platform of the "party of tavern keepers." The Liberals have ranked third in numerical strength after the Catholics and Socialists since the latter's accession to parliament in 1894.[14] Moreover, the Liberal vote has declined steadily from 1914 (25 per cent) to 1950 (11.5 per cent). The original aims of the Liberals, namely, the separation of church and state and compulsory education, have long been achieved. Today the once revolutionary ideas of freedom of thought, free enterprise, and agnosticism can no longer attract a mass following in Belgium. Because of the Liberal party's key position between the Right and the parties further to the Left, its political importance and influence have nevertheless remained greater than its numerical strength.

IV / THE SOCIALISTS

Platform and Alignments

The Belgian Socialist party has long been one of the most vital links in the international socialist movement. Émile Vandervelde, Louis de Brouckère, Henri de Man, Paul-Henri Spaak, and other Belgian Socialists have exercised a decisive influence on socialist thought and policy throughout Europe.

Belgian socialism from the start has been one of the most moderate labor movements. When the "Belgian Labor Party" was founded in 1885, socialism had already lost much of its initial revolutionary impetus, and the new party had to concentrate its efforts during a longer period than in most other western European countries on such "minimum demands" as unqualified universal suffrage, the eight-hour working day, and a graduated income tax. By the time these goals were realized after World War I, the Belgian Labor party had shifted from an opposition to a government party. From 1914 on, the Socialists have been in power most of the time. Too numerous to remain in the opposition but not strong enough to govern without the Liberals and the Catholics, the Socialists have had to relegate the building of a socialist society to the future and to uphold the existing political and economic system against the threat of authoritarianism from the extreme Right and Left. Even after World War II, they have not advocated nationalization of any industry but have limited themselves to demanding reforms which could be realized under conservative partnership, such as an enlarged social security system, labor-management committees, and vacations with pay.

During the years preceding World War II the Belgian Labor party, while willing to share governmental responsibilities with the two other traditional parties, was able, unlike the French Socialists, to resist the Communists' pressure to form a popular-front government. Only after liberation did the Belgian Socialists agree with the Liberals and Catholics to give the Communists some cabinet posts in an all-party government. The Socialists even went so far as to accede to the Communists' demands for the establishment of a "single," "nonpolitical" trade-union organization. Thus on April 15, 1945, the Socialist and the Communist labor unions merged into the General Labor Federation of Belgium.[15] Before the war the Socialist trade-unions had been a subdivision of the Socialist party and whoever had been affiliated with the former automatically became a party member. After the founding of the

14. There were two exceptions: in 1914 the Liberals polled more than the Socialists; in 1946 the Catholics, Socialists, and Communists had a larger vote than the Liberals.

15. The Christian trade-unions, which comprise about half the unionized workers in Belgium, refused to join the "single" General Labor Federation.

General Labor Federation, a member who wanted to join the Socialist party had to apply separately. By consenting to set up this new organization, the Socialists thus made a major concession to the Communists. On the party level itself, the Socialists were able to resist similar Communist pressures and to turn down the latter's demands for establishing a "united democratic party," common electoral lists, or a common platform. Earlier and more forcefully than in most other liberated countries, the Belgian Socialists had denounced the Communist party as a tool of Soviet Russia. Officially the Socialist party refused "to choose between the Soviet Union and the United States, as Socialist opinion admires without reservation neither Russian communism nor American capitalism." In fact, the Socialists realized as well as the Liberals and Catholics that they had to choose between the two great powers, and they chose the West.

Right Wing and Left Wing

The Socialist party's moderate policies have not always met with the unanimous approval of socialist opinion. The Socialists, too, are divided into rightists and leftists. The rightists, who have determined the party's policy most of the time, are inclined to subordinate socialist doctrine to political expediency, a pragmatic outlook found primarily, but not exclusively, among Flemish Socialists. Henri de Man, who was the party's president during the 1930's, went so far to the Right as to advocate an authoritarian brand of socialism, and his theories were largely responsible for the doctrinal crisis of Belgian and European socialism during that period.[16] Since the German invasion, Paul-Henri Spaak, De Man's long-standing rival, has been the most prominent Belgian Socialist. Even in physical appearance, Spaak,

the Socialist, resembles Churchill, the Conservative. Spaak, too, is a statesman of international influence, a middle-of-the-roader, a crusader for European unity and against extremism of the Right and the Left, yet a supple politician rather than an idealist. Like Churchill, Spaak is an excellent orator, endowed with biting humor and an epicurean outlook on life.

The Walloon Socialists, on the whole, tend to adhere more strictly to the Marxist and anticlerical tradition. Between the two world wars they frequently accused the Socialist party and trade-union leaders of having become bourgeois. Left-wing Socialists were less adamant than those of the right wing in their opposition to a popular-front government and more skeptical than the latter of the government's policy of neutrality. On the whole, left-wing Socialists have remained no less hostile to the Catholics than to the Communists;[17] yet they never went as far as did the Nenni Socialists in Italy or even the Bevanites in England. Neutralism has not become a noticeable current in Belgium even among left-wing Socialists.

Socialist Following

The Socialists' potential following is, on the whole, limited to the fixed-

16. These theories were expounded in his book *Beyond Marxism* (1927). Shortly before the outbreak of the second World War, De Man declared: "We are no longer a class party but a people's party which stands for order, authority, and nation." He welcomed the German invasion as beneficial to the Belgian working class but fled to Switzerland when the German defeat appeared inevitable.

17. On March 18, 1947, a minority of 65 of the 187 members of the party's executive committee voted against allowing Socialist ministers to join forces with "clericals, Leopoldists, and reactionaries" of the Catholic party. A few days later, Spaak introduced his Socialist-Catholic coalition cabinet with the words: "The future of Europe lies in an alliance of Socialism and Christianity."

income group among the freethinkers,[18] the very stratum which the Communists are always trying to attract. In this competition the Socialists are at a disadvantage because they cannot make tantalizing promises but must, when in power, defend such unpopular governmental measures as the freezing of wages. Furthermore, the Socialist party's organization, being more democratic, is also less efficient than the more authoritarian structure of both the Communist and the Catholic parties.

In spite of these handicaps, the Belgian Socialists have since 1919 polled, on the average, 34 per cent of the total vote. This percentage is far higher than in France, where the Socialists are proportionately weaker than the Radicals (which can be compared to the Belgian Liberals) and the Communists. It is true that after liberation the Socialists could not prevent the formation of the General Labor Federation; but, unlike the French CGT, the Belgian trade-union federation did not come under Communist domination and has since 1948 become an essentially Socialist organization independent of the Socialist party in name only.

The Belgian Socialists' steadfast refusal to give in to Communist bids for "unity" has contributed greatly to their relatively high numerical strength over the Communists as compared with France or Italy. The principal cause for the rapid revival of Socialist strength since the end of World War II, however, is to be found in the more rapid rise of Belgium's standard of living after liberation than that of most other former German-occupied countries. With the Liberals' strength declining and the Catholic progressives adhering to a party whose direction is,

18. It was mainly for the purpose of attracting intellectuals that the party after liberation changed its name from the Belgian Labor party to the Belgian Socialist party.

on the whole, conservative, the Socialists remain the most important "third force" in Belgium.

V / THE COMMUNISTS

Phases

Like Communists everywhere, a typical Communist in Belgium in 1933 considered the Socialists a greater curse than Hitler. In 1936 he volunteered for the Spanish Civil War, side by side with Socialists, as a crusader against fascism; in 1939 he approved of Belgium's neutrality in the war against Fascist Germany; after June, 1941, he risked and perhaps lost his life as a leader of the Belgian resistance movement against "the Fascist invaders."

The Belgian Communist party, which had never participated in any government, entered the first postliberation cabinet and shared governmental responsibilities with Socialists and Liberals, and for a time even with Catholics, until March, 1947. During that period the Belgian Communists endeavored to gain a mass following by adopting such slogans as "democratic solidarity," "increase of production," "a decent share of profit for small business," and "national independence." While branding the Catholic party in both its old and new forms as the seat of reaction, they carefully refrained from attacking the Catholic religion. They tried to outdo the Socialists in their attacks on Leopold but without questioning the monarchy itself any more than did the former; they attempted to increase their power through front organizations. Their most important effort in this direction, i.e., to dominate the General Labor Federation, met with failure.

Whether or not the Belgian Communists expected at any time to win over a majority either for themselves or for a Communist-dominated "democratic front," such hopes vanished when the

United States inaugurated its policy of restraining Soviet Russia by combating communism in western Europe. The Belgian Communist party was actually the first to shift to a new phase when it decided, on the very day of the announcement of the "Truman Doctrine" (March 12, 1947), to resign from the government. The Communists now attacked the European Recovery Program, the Brussels five-power pact, the Atlantic Pact, the projected European Defense Community, and even the Belgian-Dutch economic union as stratagems to make western Europe in general and Belgium in particular subservient to the United States. They claimed that "official Belgium has, more than any other country, become the agent of Yankee Imperialism."[19] They stopped wooing the Socialists and began to accuse them of having become "subservient to the forces of reaction." After having lost all control over the General Labor Federation to the Socialists, they criticized this organization for "collaborating with the AF of L" and for "seeking to destroy labor unity rather than to displease Washington."

Numerical Strength

The Belgian Communist party, which had been an insignificant group up to 1936, emerged from the German occupation as a mass party. They capitalized on their resistance record, on the news reports of the steady advance of Russian troops when the Anglo-Americans were visibly stalemated on Belgian soil in the Battle of the Bulge, and on the widespread discontent due to the shortages of the first postliberation

19. Following the line laid down by Thorez and Togliatti, the Belgian Communist party declared on March 5, 1949, that "Should the servants of American Imperialism who govern our country drag Belgium into an aggressive war against the USSR, the Communists would combat those who would be unmasked as the worst enemies of our people."

winter. Thus they were able to make a great number of Belgians believe that their coming into power would mean increased material well-being, personal freedom, and national independence from Soviet Russia as well as from the Anglo-Saxon powers. With the gradually rising standard of living in Belgium after the spring of 1945, their following fell off. In the first postwar election of February, 1946, they polled 12.7 per cent of the total vote, only half as much as the number of Communists in France and Italy at that time, where economic recovery had not made a comparable advance. Even so, the Communists made by far the greatest gain of all parties, as compared with their prewar strength, almost tripling their number of deputies and displacing the Liberals as the third largest party. Had the elections been held a year earlier, their strength would have been still greater. From 1945 on, their following has declined slowly but steadily; by 1950 their number had fallen below their prewar strength. Efforts at proselytizing farmers have remained unsuccessful; even among organized labor they have lost much ground, as shown by the history of the General Labor Federation. This trend might be reversed, however, in case of renewed economic instability or increased international tension.

VI / THE PARTIES AND FOREIGN AFFAIRS

In spite of their many differences on domestic issues, the three traditional parties of Belgium have been in general agreement on foreign affairs, and matters of international politics have seldom become campaign issues. During the intrawar period Belgium's policy of neutrality met at first with general approval. As Nazi Germany grew stronger, skepticism increased as to whether this policy would be effective in deterring German aggression. Some open criticism developed, especially among left-wing Socialists, against maintaining the appearance of neutrality in a changed political situation. To take an example from the writer's own experience while serving with the Belgian army: At the outbreak of the war in September, 1939, some artillery guns were pointed southwestward to protect Belgium against invasion—by France!

After liberation public opinion had no difficulty in adjusting to Belgium's new foreign policy of close alliance with the other democracies of western Europe and with the United States. The lowering of the iron curtain consolidated the feeling of solidarity with the Western bloc. If Benelux[20] has made little progress, the Schuman Plan, involving a larger geographical area but a more narrowly defined economic sector (coal and steel), has met with general approval, and similar projects would in the future undoubtedly be backed by the three traditional parties.

On the military level, the Atlantic Pact has been indorsed by all parties except the Communists and even the controversial European Defense Community was ratified by a great majority of the Belgian parliament. This is not to say that Belgians are less fearful than Frenchmen of German rearmament, even within a European army, or less skeptical about American ability or willingness to defend all of western Europe against Soviet attack. Yet in spite of these doubts neutralism has not become sufficiently important to influence party policy.

This sober outlook on foreign affairs is due in part to Belgium's tempered

20. "Benelux" is the name of the economic and customs union between the Netherlands and the former Belgian-Luxembourg customs union. The slowness of its implementation is due to opposition of vested interests among businessmen, labor, and farmers in the three countries concerned.

nationalism as compared with that of its neighbors, including the Netherlands. This tendency can, in turn, be explained by the fact that Belgium is divided into two language and culture groups. Furthermore, the events connected with World War II did not hurt national pride in Belgium as much as in those countries which suffered the loss of their status as great powers. Again, because it is a small power, Belgium has always put more trust in international organization than in national sovereignty. Finally, Belgians, more than citizens of the formerly great European powers, are aware that they can exercise but little influence on international politics and that the major decisions are being made in Washington and Moscow. Realists by temperament, Belgians consider it good politics to adjust with good grace rather than to submit grudgingly to what seems inevitable.

VII / Conclusion

Slowly and hesitatingly the Catholics and the Liberals, pressured by the Socialists, traveled the road from classical liberalism to modern democracy. As soon as all three parties had finally become united on democratic principles after World War I, they were put on the defensive by new, antidemocratic parties of the extreme Left and Right. Democracy was finally overthrown not by these movements but by the military might of Germany. After liberation the Belgian people again almost unanimously rallied to the basic tenets of democracy. There were no more Fascist parties; the Catholics adopted a more progressive platform; and even the Communists had to formulate a democratic program to gain a mass following, which they lost when their connection with Soviet totalitarianism became more manifest.

A deterioration of the living standard

TABLE 1

Percentage of the Total Vote in the General Elections from 1919 to 1954

Party	Nov. 16, 1919	Nov. 20, 1921	Apr. 5, 1925	June 2, 1929	Nov. 27, 1932	May 24, 1936	Apr. 2, 1939	Feb. 17, 1946	June 26, 1949	June 4, 1950	April 11, 1954
Flemish Nationalists	3.2	3.4	3.9	5.9	5.7	7.0	7.9	......	2.2*	......	3.0
Rexists						11.5	4.4				
Catholics	37.4	39.7	38.4	37.9	38.7	28.7	32.7	42.5	43.5	46.7	41.1
Total Right	40.6	43.1	42.3	43.8	44.4	47.2	45.0	42.5	45.7	46.7	44.1
Liberals	17.7	18.2	14.7	16.6	14.4	12.4	17.4	9.4	15.3	11.5	13.1
Socialists	36.7	35.0	39.5	36.0	37.1	32.1	30.2	32.7	29.7	35.8	38.3
Communists			1.6	2.3	2.8	6.0	5.4	12.7	7.5	4.6	3.6
Total Left	54.4	53.2	55.8	54.9	54.3	50.5	53.0	54.8	52.5	51.9	55.0
Splinter parties	5.0	3.7	1.9	1.3	1.3	2.3	2.0	2.7	1.8	1.4	0.9

*Flemish Concentration (see n. 7).

TABLE 2

Number of Seats in the House of Representatives from 1919 to 1954

Party	Nov. 16, 1919	Nov. 20, 1921	Apr. 5, 1925	June 2, 1929	Nov. 27, 1932	May 24, 1936	Apr. 2, 1939	Feb. 17, 1946	June 26, 1949	June 4, 1950	April 11, 1954
Flemish Nationalists	5	4	6	11	8	16	17	......	......	......	1
Rexists						21	4				
Catholics	73	80	78	76	79	63	73	92	105	108	95
Total Right	78	84	84	87	87	100	94	92	105	108	96
Liberals	34	33	23	28	24	23	33	17	29	20	25
Socialists	70	68	78	70	73	70	64	69	66	77	86
Communists			2	1	3	9	9	23	12	7	4
Total Left	104	101	103	99	100	102	106	109	107	104	115
Splinter parties	2	1	......	1	......		2	1	......	......	1
Total	184	186	187	187	187	202	202	202	212	212	212

in western Europe might, however, cause a resurgence of extreme leftist or rightist movements in Belgium. The defense of democracy would then fall once more upon the three "traditional" parties. These parties are likely to continue to exist as independent organizations, even though the division between Catholics, Liberals, and Socialists has never adequately reflected the ideological divisions among their voters. Divided between and within themselves, combining into unstable coalitions, these parties might be faced with the difficult problem of how to unite into a dynamic center group against the threat of totalitarian forces from within or without.

Scandinavia: Working Multiparty Systems

DANKWART A. RUSTOW
Princeton University

I / PARTY ORGANIZATION*

A political party is sometimes defined as an organization founded and maintained for the purpose of getting candidates elected to public office. This definition applies as much to Scandinavian[1] parties as it does to the parties of other countries governed by ballot; yet vote-getting is not the only function of parties in Sweden, Denmark, and Norway. The first modern parties in Scandinavia originated toward the middle of the nineteenth century as groups of like-minded representatives eager to obtain majorities for their legislative proposals. But even the most brilliant legislative victories may come to naught if the victors are defeated in a subsequent election. It was natural, therefore, that these parliamentary factions should proceed to establish constituency organizations that would insure a steady stream of recruits for their caucuses. Other political organizations were formed in the late nineteenth century among the disfranchised workers and small farmers. These mass movements agitated for far-reaching constitutional and social changes; they

became electoral organizations only to the extent that their demand for a democratic franchise became a reality. The introduction of proportional representation in elections throughout Scandinavia (1909–19) gave the parties a central role in the nomination of candidates, and the adoption of the principle of parliamentary cabinet government (1884–1917) brought the highest level of the executive branch within the reach of the parties.

Scandinavian parties organize voters, nominate and elect candidates, formulate legislative programs, muster parliamentary majorities, and form cabinets; but even this long list of purely political functions does not exhaust their activities. A Scandinavian party is not only a political apparatus, it is also a civic club, a pressure group, and an organization for the pursuit of a variety of leisure-time activities. All the major parties today have women's and youth organizations operating side by side with the vast network of local and regional associations that make up the party, properly speaking. The parties and their affiliates sponsor boy-scout groups, summer camps, civic training centers for party workers and others interested in public affairs, and adult-education classes in nonpolitical subjects such as foreign languages. Nearly all the daily newspapers are closely identified with one of the parties, and a large number of political and literary magazines either are published by the parties or give them consistent editorial support. The parties also have established intimate ties with economic and

* Table 2, indicating the popular vote in Scandinavia from 1920 to 1950, appears on p. 193.

1. Scandinavia, in the wider sense, includes Sweden, Denmark, Norway, Iceland, and Finland. While party developments in the last two countries present many interesting aspects, limitations of space have made it impossible to include them in this brief survey. Throughout the present essay "Scandinavia" and its derivatives are therefore understood to refer only to Sweden, Denmark, and Norway.

other interest groups. Officials of the national employers' associations sit in parliament as Conservatives, prominent union leaders are elected on Socialist tickets, farm producers' co-operatives lend solid support to the Agrarian parties, and many nonconformist sects and temperance societies recruit followers for the Liberal movement. In Norway and Sweden one-half to two-thirds of the Labor parties' membership consists of workers collectively affiliated through their trade-unions. Thus when the prime minister of a Scandinavian country confers with the chairmen of the major parties, he has before him a forum not only of political leaders but also of prominent and authorized spokesmen for industrial, agricultural, and labor interests.

A Scandinavian party consists not merely of professional politicians. The parties, to be sure, have elaborate hierarchies with full-time salaried personnel at the highest levels, but these rest on a broad base of common party members. At least every third voter in Denmark and every fourth in Norway and Sweden is a card-holding member of one of the parties and pays his annual dues of twenty-five cents to one dollar into the party treasury. Furthermore, nearly every party has developed a distinct and well-defined political philosophy, a Weltanschauung—and those few parties that have not done so tend to be apologetic about this deficiency. A politically conscious citizen of a Scandinavian country does not just "vote for" or "register in" a party at stated intervals, he *is* a Socialist, or Agrarian, or Liberal, or Conservative.

While party organization has spread out in many directions, the leadership in this vast array of expanding groups has become increasingly concentrated in a few hands. Fifty years ago party groups in the legislature had only loose and informal ties with the constituency organizations which conducted their campaigns; in the two bicameral countries, Denmark and Sweden, every party had separate caucuses for each legislative chamber. Today the parliamentary and national parties in all three countries are two branches of a single integrated organization, and a typical party executive committee includes ex officio representatives of the party's youth, women's, and other affiliates. Unification of party leadership has gone farthest in Sweden. Here the leader of a national party is at the same time the chairman of its parliamentary group and its floor leader in the chamber to which he has been elected (usually the lower); whenever his party is in office, he combines these functions with the powers of the premiership. The Norwegian parliament, on the other hand, jealously guards its traditional independence of both the executive branch and outside influence. A Norwegian party, therefore, generally has separate chairmen for its national and parliamentary organization, and a third person may be its candidate for the premiership. The Danish parties occupy a middle position between these two extremes.

Whether or not a party has cumulative leadership posts at the highest level, its followers still recognize and accept the need for discipline and concerted action. A parliamentary group that is divided on a major issue is likely to undermine its bargaining position in negotiations with other parties, both in the committee room and at decisive informal conferences in the lobby.[2] A parliamentary group which fails to maintain intimate contact with its own

2. It is true that in exceptional situations, where support of a small group is indispensable in order to secure a majority for a government, a party's reputation for poor discipline may strengthen the leader's hand. "Unless you grant this demand," he may argue, "I can't vouch for my followers." But even such tactical lack of discipline requires close teamwork.

cadres in the constituencies or with the organized interests it represents risks a serious setback at the polls. Once the official party leader has taken a position on a major question, the rank and file will stand with him. Most parties try to avoid frequent changes in leadership, and leaders are generally re-elected as often as they wish. On the rare occasions when a leader cannot carry along his followers, he is likely to be replaced by someone who can.

Thus leadership, at least in the democratic parties, is a two-way process. The leader will not commit his party to a new policy without having conferred with other high party officials. Many prospective premiers, especially those of the Socialist parties, consult the party executive committee before taking their list of ministers to the royal palace. An elaborate system of representation insures responsibility of leadership throughout the party hierarchy. The highest official authority on all party matters is the national convention, which is composed of delegates from the local districts and which meets at regular intervals of from one to four years. The convention, as a rule, has exclusive jurisdiction over the official program; it also elects the national executive committee and the party leader. The leader, the committee, and any party members who may happen to sit in the cabinet, of necessity have full discretion in carrying out the party's policy in the interval between conventions; yet their instructions are far more explicit than the glittering generalities found in American party platforms. The authority of the leader varies from party to party and with his personality. The Social Democratic parties have produced a number of outstanding leaders such as Hjalmar Branting, first representative of the Swedish Socialists in the Riksdag and their leader for nearly three decades (1897–1925); his successor, Per Albin Hansson (1925–

46); and Thorvald Stauning, chairman of the Danish party from 1909 until 1942. All three combined a deep sense of commitment to fundamental purposes with great tactical skill, and their patriarchal stature won them profound respect even among their opponents. Other parties, notably the Swedish Agrarians in their early days, have been jealous of strong leaders and have tended to reduce their chairmen to the position of mere figureheads.

Candidates for public office are nominated by local party organizations in the districts where they are to run. Most parties give their rank and file some voice in the nominating process, but as a rule the final decision is in the hands of the district committee or of a special nominating convention. The by-laws of the Swedish Labor party, however, provide that one-fourth of the delegates may appeal the decision of a nominating convention to the party membership in the district; in that case, party members voting by mail may add to and delete from the convention slate or rearrange the sequence of candidates, and their vote determines the final composition of the list. Norway is the only country in Scandinavia (and Europe) that has attempted to regulate nominations by statute. The purpose of the Norwegian Nominations Law of 1920 is to insure equal representation at the district nominating conventions for all district party members. The law is not mandatory, but parties that choose to abide by it are reimbursed from the public treasury for the travel expenses of their convention delegates—an inducement sufficiently attractive to guarantee general observance. Thus officially nominations are a purely local matter, although the central party leadership may influence to some extent the selection of candidates. Voters in all three countries have the right within wide limits to revise a party's list of candidates or vote for independents.

Although few of them do so, the voters' freedom to make up their own lists serves as a valuable check on the party's nominating procedures.

Discipline in the major parties is achieved through a minimum of compulsion and leaves ample leeway for disagreement on minor questions and discussion of major ones. The equivalent of the party whip in the Swedish Riksdag is known as the "pair secretary" whose chief function, as his title implies, is to alert members for important votes and to arrange pairs for those who cannot be on hand. In 1915 the Social Democratic group in the Riksdag, faced with the constant threat of rebellion by a radical minority, adopted a rule under which the caucus majority could indorse a policy and require all members, under penalty of exclusion, to refrain from speaking or voting against that policy. This "gag rule," however, was never enforced; it was repealed four years later after the rebels had seceded. No other Swedish party has ever attempted to tighten its discipline by laying down this kind of formal rule. While members of parliament are generally free to follow their own judgment and conscience on a wide range of questions, no party will tolerate within its ranks systematic opposition to its major policies. Penalties, as a rule, range from exclusion from committee assignments to a refusal to renominate the recalcitrant member at election time. The severest penalty—expulsion from the party—is usually reserved for those who work against the party's candidates in an election campaign.

Party cohesion is put to the severest tests at times when major political realignments are shaping up. One particular turning point in Swedish party history—the enactment of what has been called the "Swedish New Deal" in 1933—provides an excellent illustration of the variety of devices by which parties insure both internal discipline and responsibility of leadership. Early in 1933 a Social Democratic minority cabinet presented to the Riksdag a series of bills designed to combat the effects of the economic depression through increased unemployment assistance, large-scale public works expenditures, and relief to indebted farmers. In view of traditional alignments and of the announced policies of the several parties, the Socialists had hopes of winning Liberal support for some parts of their program, whereas the Agrarians and Conservatives could be expected to put up determined resistance to these reflationist policies. The negotiations with the Liberal leaders, however, dragged on without result, and the Socialist premier at last broke the deadlock by working out a deal with an insurgent group among the Agrarians who offered to support the government's program in return for a promise of substantial subsidies for agricultural production. This surprise move inaugurated a new era of fruitful cooperation between the Socialists and the Agrarians. At the time, however, it caused tensions in each of the four larger parties, which precipitated the following reactions: (1) The Agrarian party refused to re-elect its aging chairman, who had denounced the Socialist-Agrarian agreement as a horse-trading deal, and replaced him by the chieftain of the very faction that had negotiated this deal behind his back. (2) In the fall of 1934 a senate election in the central Swedish district of Örebro developed into a minor test of strength between the supporters and the opponents of the government's crisis policy. One of the candidates was a Conservative who had defied his party by supporting the New Deal, had been denied his old committee post by the Conservative caucus, had thereupon resigned his seat, and was now seeking re-election on an Agrarian ticket. At the same time, one of the few Socialist opponents of the government's depression policy was running for re-election with the official indorsement of his party. Faced with this choice, four of the Socialist electors in the district repudiated their party's anti–New Deal candidate and joined with four Agrarians to elect the ex-Conservative New Dealer. (3) Two left-wing Social Democrats who had opposed the government's policy joined with a group of ex-Communists in a new party venture shortly afterward; one of these was formally expelled by the Social Democrats at their next convention. (4) The Liberals, who had been almost evenly split for and against the New Deal, acknowledged this rift by appointing a member of each faction as joint chairmen of the party. Two years later, however, unity was restored under a new leader.

II / The Origins of the Present Party System

Before proceeding to a description of the individual parties and their policies, a summary of the origin and development of the present parties and a brief sketch of the electoral system may be in order.

The two most important factors in the emergence of modern European parties have probably been, first, the establishment of legislatures elected at frequent intervals and, second, the fight for universal and equal suffrage and its eventual adoption. In Scandinavia these developments occurred later than in many other parts of the Continent. The twin waves of revolutionary armies and revolutionary ideas which swept Europe between 1789 and 1814 had little direct impact on the countries of the far north. In Denmark the absolute rule of the monarch continued; in Sweden a Riksdag composed of the four traditional estates (nobility, clergy,

burghers, and peasants) was precariously pitted against a king with strong autocratic leanings. Only Norway took a first hesitant step toward popular government during this period. Using a brief interval of independence in 1814 —while their crown was changing hands from the Danish to the Swedish monarch—the Norwegians gave themselves a constitution which provided for a unicameral legislature or Storting and a limited franchise. In 1849 Denmark, in the wake of the second democratic revolution on the Continent, instituted a bicameral legislature or Rigsdag based on an even wider electorate. Seventeen years later, in 1866, the Swedish estates finally abdicated in favor of an elective bicameral parliament, and that same year Denmark revised its constitution. By this time the democratic movement in Europe had spent much of its original force, and a conservative reaction, symbolized by such figures as Louis Napoleon and Bismarck, had set in. The Conservative sponsors of the Danish and Swedish parliamentary reforms of 1866—Jacob Estrup and Baron Louis De Geer—took their cue from these developments and established upper chambers which represented only the wealthiest strata of society—large landowners, industrialists, and high civil servants. In Sweden the suffrage for the lower chamber was tied to an income and property qualification which excluded nearly two-thirds of the adult male population, thus giving the large farmers and the upper middle class in the cities control over that body. In Denmark the lower-house franchise of 1849, which included all but domestic servants, remained in effect. While the establishment of representative bodies encouraged the formation of political groups, the introduction of annual parliamentary sessions during this same period (Denmark, 1849; Sweden, 1866; Norway, 1869) made it possible for these nascent parties to retain their identity over the years.

The first well-organized parties in Scandinavia were formed toward the middle of the nineteenth century by representatives of the farmers and the urban middle class, who opposed the prevailing tendency toward plutocracy and royal government. The chief beneficiaries of the oligarchic regime, by contrast, were slow to follow suit. They tended to look upon any form of partisan organization as unpatriotic, if not downright treasonable; they could, moreover, well afford to remain unorganized so long as they felt secure in their control of the Danish and Swedish senates and in their close association with the monarchy in all three countries. In Denmark an antioligarchic party, known as "The Left" and supported by both rural and urban opposition forces, emerged as early as the 1840's. In Sweden a Ruralist party was formed in the first bicameral Riksdag of 1867. The Norwegian equivalent of these groups, also known as "The Left," was formed in 1884 by the merger of two separate opposition groups, one urban and one rural, both of which had been in existence for some twenty years. The foremost aim of these leftist groups (or Liberal-Agrarians, as we may call them) was to subject the cabinet to parliamentary responsibility; in addition, the more radical elements within or outside these parties insisted on a substantial widening of the franchise. Although the Liberal-Agrarians soon mustered solid majorities in the Norwegian Storting and in the Danish and Swedish lower chambers, it was nearly half a century before the change from oligarchy to democracy was completed. In Denmark and Sweden the transition was delayed partly through the intrenched resistance of the Conservatives in the senate, of the monarch, and of the ministry and partly through the halfheartedness of the reformers.

In Norway, where the fight for democracy became closely linked with that for independence of Sweden, the change came more quickly.

When in 1876 the Danish Left refused to pass the government's budget requests, the Conservative cabinet governed for nearly two decades without parliamentary appropriations. The opposition itself was weakened by recurrent tensions between its radical urban wing and its moderate rural supporters. During the nineties the leftist leaders finally came to terms with the Conservatives. In 1901 the king, in return, appointed one of them to the premiership, thus inaugurating a regime of cabinet government based on lower-chamber support. The tensions within the Left led in 1905 to the secession of the radical wing, which formed a separate Liberal party; and the moderate elements five years later reconstituted themselves as an Agrarian party (which, however, retained the official designation "The Left"). In 1915 a Liberal government finally obtained the adoption of universal suffrage in both houses.

The Swedish Ruralists in their perennial fight to subject the cabinet to control by the lower chamber developed a strong internal organization and discipline. But when the king in 1880 called upon their leader to form a cabinet, they refused to uphold the very principle of parliamentary government which they had championed while in opposition. A spokesman for the Ruralist rank and file is said to have declared that they would follow their leader to the threshold of the cabinet room but no farther. In the next two decades the Ruralist right wing gained complete control of the party, which increasingly aligned itself with the Conservative senate. The fight for parliamentary government and suffrage extension was resumed by a new movement, the Liberal party, which had originated in the suffrage societies formed in the 1880's among the disfranchised small farmers and lower middle class. In 1895 a number of advocates of suffrage extension founded the "People's party" in the lower chamber, and four years later these merged with a number of left-wing Ruralists in the Liberal party. Under Liberal and Socialist leadership, Sweden in 1917–20 finally completed the transition to democracy.

In Norway the liberal and agrarian opposition forces gained wide support in their patriotic struggle against Swedish predominance. In 1882 they won a parliamentary majority sufficiently large to assure them of control of the Impeachment Tribunal, which, under the Norwegian constitution, is made up in part of members of parliament, and thereupon proceeded to impeach and convict the Conservative, pro-Swedish ministry. The Swedish monarch, in order to avoid an open break, asked the leftist leader, Johan Sverdrup, to form a new cabinet. Norway thus became the first Scandinavian country to assert the principle of parliamentary cabinet government. Under the leadership of the Left, the suffrage was extended first to all adult men (1898) and later to all men and women over twenty-five (1913). After renewed conflict with Sweden, Norway declared herself independent in 1905 and elected a monarch of her own after centuries of rule by Danish and Swedish kings.

The Liberal-Agrarians of the late nineteenth century were the first group to organize as a political party, but others were soon to follow. In response to the growing menace from the Left, a number of separate Conservative groups in the Danish Rigsdag organized a joint caucus and a common electoral organization in 1883. An Independent Conservative faction, which split off in 1902, rejoined the parent-group in 1915 when the present Conservative party was founded. A Conservative electoral

alliance in Sweden was formed in 1904; and in 1912 various Conservative factions in the Riksdag, including remnants of the old Ruralist party, merged to form two Conservative groups, one in each chamber. Although these groups acted as two branches of a single party and were supported by the same constituency organizations, the formal dualism persisted until 1935.

Toward the end of the nineteenth century a third political group took its place by the side of the Liberal-Agrarians and the Conservatives. The rapid growth of the German Socialist movement inspired the formation in 1871 of a Danish Social Democratic party; the Danish example, in turn, was imitated nearly two decades later in Norway (1887) and in Sweden (1889). Unlike the two older political movements, these parties had set up a network of popular organizations long before they entered the national parliaments. In Denmark, where suffrage restrictions for the lower chamber were insignificant, the Socialist party elected its first candidates as early as 1884; in Sweden the first Socialists entered the Riksdag in 1896; while in Norway the Socialists remained unrepresented until after the advent of manhood suffrage in 1898. All three parties joined the Second (Socialist) International.

The youngest of the major political movements in Scandinavia is the Agrarian party. Toward the turn of the century the Scandinavian countries were still overwhelmingly agricultural. In Denmark, as we have seen, toward the beginning of this century the urban and rural elements of the old Left organized into separate Liberal and Agrarian parties. In Sweden, on the other hand, the Ruralist party had been replaced by a purely Liberal movement and its remnants absorbed into a Conservative party increasingly dominated by industrial interests. Politically orphaned, the farmers formed party organizations of their own, and two such groups, founded in 1913 and 1915, were merged in 1921 to form the present Agrarian party. In Norway several independent farmers' representatives were elected to the Storting in 1918; three years later these formed a Norwegian Agrarian party.

Since the early 1920's there have been only four major parties in Scandinavia, and these have been the same in each country—Conservatives, Agrarians, Liberals, and Socialists. Unlike any of the minor parties, these have been represented in the three parliaments continuously for over thirty years, usually polling a total of 90 per cent or more of the national vote. Until World War II they were the four largest parties in size of both popular vote and parliamentary delegation in each country, and the task of forming cabinets has rotated among them. In the immediate postwar elections of 1945 the Communist vote in Denmark and Norway surpassed that of the smallest of the four major parties; yet the defeat of the Communists in the next election —when their strength was cut in half— indicated that they held no serious threat to the four-party system. Recently, however, two new challengers have entered the ring. The groping for new ideals following the trying wartime experiences in Denmark and Norway gave a strong impetus to two parties that had hitherto led only a precarious existence. Both the Danish Justice party and the Norwegian Christian People's party are democratic, antitotalitarian, and strongly ideological movements. The vote for the Christian party in three postwar elections has equaled or exceeded that for the two smallest of the older parties, the Agrarians and the Liberals. If this situation persists, Norway may now be said to have a five- rather than a four-party system. The Justice party, on the other hand, reached its peak in 1950, only to de- cline sharply in the two elections of 1953. In Denmark, as in Sweden, the four-party system, therefore, appears to have lost none of its vitality.

The persistence of the four-party pattern throughout Scandinavia is to be attributed primarily to the fact that it closely reflects the social structure in each country and that social and economic differences today provide the main stimulus for party division. The Conservatives, Agrarians, and Socialists represent the interests of employers, farmers, and workers, respectively. Those middle class elements not readily identified with any of these groups have provided the chief support for the Liberal parties. Nevertheless, electoral procedures have contributed appreciably to the stabilization of the four-party system.

The struggle for universal suffrage was a major factor in the development of organized parties in Scandinavia; today universal suffrage has become the cornerstone of the electoral system in all three countries. By 1921 the right to vote had been extended to adult men and women throughout Scandinavia; the lower age limit for voters in Norway and Sweden was recently reduced to twenty-one, and in Denmark to twenty-three. An effective system of permanent registration makes it possible for every citizen to exercise his suffrage if he wishes to do so. Registration frauds and stuffed ballot boxes are unknown. Scandinavian experience contradicts the common assumption that high voting participation is a symptom of disease in the body politic, just as high fever is in the human body. In recent parliamentary elections the turnout at the polls has been over 80 per cent, and participation in local and provincial contests has been only slightly lower. In Sweden, where detailed statistics are available, participation has been consistently greater in the cities than in the rural areas; among men than among women; among the age groups from thirty-five to fifty-five than among either the young or the aged; among married persons than among the single, widowed, or divorced; and in the higher- rather than in the lower-income groups. Some of these differences in voting behavior, especially those between the sexes and among the social classes, have recently diminished and may eventually disappear.

Since Denmark's transition to unicameralism in 1953, only Sweden retains an upper chamber. But in Sweden, as in Denmark previously, both houses represent the same electorate, and there is no likelihood that the bitter feuds between the chambers which were so common during the oligarchic period will recur. The smaller size of the Swedish senate and the former Danish upper chamber have put small parties at a relative disadvantage. Moreover, Swedish senators are elected for staggered eight-year terms, with the result that party alignments may lag several years behind those in the lower chamber.[3] The Swedish constitution,

3. The Norwegian Storting (150 members), the Danish Folketing (175 members plus 2 each for the Faeroes and Greenland), and the lower house of the Swedish Riksdag (230 members), all are elected in direct proportional elections for four-year terms. General elections in Sweden are held every leap year, in Norway the year after that. Because of frequent dissolutions, few Danish Folketings have served more than three years, and the provincial and municipal assemblies, themselves popularly elected for four years, serve as electoral colleges. These are divided into eight groups, one of which elects one-eighth of the senate every year. (Thus only every other assembly in any given province gets a chance to elect its senators, barring the rare case of a senate dissolution.) The Danish senate, until its abolition in 1953, consisted of 76 members, also serving for eight-year terms. Three-eighths of these were elected every four years by special electoral colleges representing half the population. Every eighth year the outgoing senate itself chose the remaining fourth of the senators before adjourning for the popular senate elections.

however, provides both a preventive and a remedy for possible deadlocks which might result from this minor discrepancy: all bills are considered in joint committees before they reach the floor for a vote; if the houses disagree on any measure concerning revenue or expenditure, a joint vote of the two houses is taken, and the total of yeas and nays decides. While Norway's parliament is unicameral, it divides into two sections which debate and vote separately whenever nonfinancial bills are under consideration; a vote of the plenum decides in cases of disagreement.

Comparative studies have shown that the number of parties in a country is to some extent a function of the prevailing electoral system. Scandinavian experience indicates, however, that the connection between plurality elections and a two-party system, on the one hand, and proportional elections and party proliferation, on the other, though close, is not so automatic as is sometimes assumed. Legislators throughout Scandinavia were chosen by plurality until proportional representation was introduced in the early decades of this century (Sweden, 1909–19; Denmark, 1915; Norway, 1919), but only in Norway did something like a two-party system of Liberals and Conservatives emerge in the latter part of the nineteenth century. In Denmark and Sweden a similar development was prevented by the sharp cleavage between a plutocratic senate and a more popular lower chamber. Whenever a twofold alignment resulted, it was one of chamber against chamber rather than party against party, and political groupings in each chamber remained fluid.

Through the democratization of the franchise in the period from 1898 to 1921 large masses of new voters were admitted to the political arena, and the representatives of these new voters did not readily fit into either of the two political groups which had come down from oligarchic days. It is likely, however, that (had plurality elections continued) a two-party alignment would eventually have resulted—as it did in both Britain and the United States a generation or so after each widening of the franchise. But the adoption of proportionalism supervened, and the new system left room for a greater number of parties. The Danish Conservatives, for instance, were on the verge of extinction when the introduction of proportional representation gave them a new and indefinite lease on life, and it seems highly improbable that the separate Agrarian parties that were founded in Sweden and Norway around the time of World War I would have flourished under plurality elections.

While proportionalism has enabled four major parties to exist side by side, the Scandinavian versions of that system have tended to limit the number of parties and to prevent an endless multiplication of political groups. The effect of proportional representation on the number of parties in a country depends on many details too complex to relate here. Suffice it to say that no electoral system can insure perfect proportionality between votes and seats—at least (to quote Karl Braunias) so long as "representatives cannot be divided into fractions"[4]—and that any deviation from perfect proportionality tends to increase the delegations of the larger parties and reduce those of the smaller ones. The obstacles in the path of minor and especially of extremist parties today are greatest in the Swedish senate and next in the Swedish lower chamber. They were even greater in the Danish senate, which was

abolished as a result of the complete constitutional revision of 1953. The electoral law for the new unicameral Danish parliament favors small parties with solid local anchoring but discriminates heavily against splinter groups which are dispersed throughout the country.[5] The Norwegian law until 1949 also discriminated strongly against small parties; since then, however, a somewhat more proportional system has been adopted. The practical significance of these varying degrees of proportionality may be gathered from Table 1 (p. 192), which compares the percentage of votes and of seats obtained by the Communists in recent elections in the three countries. It will be noted that the party, despite a sizable following in the Danish and Swedish senate elections, received only an insignificant representation, and in the Norwegian elections of 1949 went unrepresented altogether. In the Danish lower chamber and unicameral elections, on the other hand, its share of parliamentary seats roughly equaled, or even surpassed, its share of the popular vote.

III / The Present Parties and Their Policies

The Liberals

The Liberal parties were the leaders of the constitutional reform movement which in the period from 1880 to 1920 transformed the three northern countries into full-fledged democracies. One by one, their major demands—universal and equal suffrage, recognition

4. Or, we might add, so long as parliamentary elections are not replaced by an elaborate system of procuration similar to that used at stockholders' meetings. The quotation is from Karl Braunias, *Das parlamentarische Wahlrecht* (Berlin: DeGruyter, 1932), I, 219.

5. The Danish electoral law also provides that any group not already represented in parliament at election time may not compete unless it presents a petition signed by 10,000 voters, or about as many as it takes to secure one seat. Just how effective this hurdle is in keeping out new parties is doubtful, for repeatedly nascent parties have gathered the requisite number of signatures without receiving anywhere near that number of votes in the subsequent election.

of the principle of parliamentary cabinet government, parliamentary control of military and foreign affairs, and, in Norway, national independence—became the law of the land. But their very success became their weakness. In their youth the parties had rallied many divergent groups—urban agnostics and rural nonconformists; landowners, farmers, and tenants; industrialists, merchants, and artisans—around the banner of liberal democracy. With the realization of their program, however, these groups were left without a unifying cause. On three occasions (in 1888, 1903, and 1908) the Norwegian Left lost substantial numbers of its moderate supporters, including many of its prominent leaders, who first formed independent parties but eventually joined the Conservatives. As a result of these successive splits, the party had become a purely Liberal movement by about 1910, and we shall therefore discuss it here as one of the Liberal parties.

In Sweden a group of prominent right-wing Liberals, on the eve of World War I, joined the Conservatives in protest against a Liberal defense budget which they warned would be inadequate to safeguard national security. A nation-wide referendum in 1923 on the question of liquor prohibition, which the prohibitionists lost by a narrow margin, brought on an even more serious split within the party. When the Liberal leadership, supported by a majority at a party convention, decided to call off any further prohibitionist propaganda, a number of leading prohibitionists and with them a majority of the rank and file seceded from the party. There had long been considerable distrust between the urban and the rural Liberal groups which had merged to found the party in 1899. The former supported democracy and parliamentarism on secular, rationalist grounds and believed that the consumption of li-

quor was, like religion, a purely private matter; the latter were steeped in the ardent faith of the Protestant nonconformist sects, and to them liberty, equality, and temperance were so many corollaries of the principles of Christian ethics. Their partnership in the fight for constitutional reform had allowed these groups to postpone their fundamental differences; now that the constitutional goals had been attained, a seemingly trivial incident was enough to cause an open break. Although both the prohibitionist Liberals and the urban Liberal party suffered setbacks at the polls throughout the next decade, they did not merge again until 1934.

The Danish Liberal party, unlike its two sister-groups, originated as a small offshoot from the large leftist or Liberal-Agrarian party. While it never attained the strength of the Norwegian and Swedish Liberals, it was spared the splits and secessions that weakened these groups; recently, however, it has found a serious competitor in the expanding Justice party.

Not only did the adoption of the democratic reforms of the early twentieth century deprive the Liberal parties of their *raison d'être;* the reforms in themselves strengthened their rivals both directly and indirectly. Universal suffrage for the first time gave the Socialists a chance to compete on equal terms with all other parties; and proportionalism, as we have seen, encouraged the formation of separate Agrarian parties in two of the three countries. Moreover, under the old plurality system of elections, the Liberal position at the center of the party spectrum had brought with it a substantial advantage: Liberal candidates could often count on Socialist support in Conservative strongholds and on Conservative support in working-class districts. Under proportionalism, however, every voter gave his ballot to the party of his first choice. The middle-of-the-road course of the Liberal parties, as we shall see, continued to be a major asset in parliament, but increasingly it became a liability in the hustings. Social and economic questions were now the order of the day, and, unlike the three other parties, the Liberals appeared to lack any solid identification with one of the major economic interests in society. As a result, the Liberal parties everywhere in Scandinavia have declined almost continuously since the end of World War I. Only the Swedish Liberals, under the ambitious leadership of Professor Bertil Ohlin and with a new program of "social liberalism," show signs of resurgent vitality. Ohlin's party today is the major opposition group in Sweden, but in Denmark and Norway the Liberals hold third and fourth places, respectively.

The Socialists

The Social Democrats, unlike the Liberals, have increased their following at almost every election since their beginnings in the 1870's and 1880's. For a quarter of a century or more (in Sweden since 1914; in Denmark since 1924; in Norway since 1927) they have been the largest single party in each of the Scandinavian countries. The Swedish Socialists won an absolute majority of the popular vote in three successive general elections (1938, 1940, and 1942) —probably a unique accomplishment among parties competing in proportional elections in any country. In Norway the Socialists won a majority of the Storting seats in 1949 and 1953, although their popular following fell slightly short of 50 per cent.

Fully as impressive as the rapid expansion of the Scandinavian Labor parties has been the ideological transformation they have undergone in the last fifty years. Their original programs were largely an adaptation of the program of the German Social Democratic party and revealed strong Marxist influences.

Their aims included the nationalization of all private property in the means of production, the abolition of the monarchy, demilitarization, and complete separation of church and state. While the Socialists did not advocate an immediate violent revolution, these demands implied a complete remodeling of the existing social, economic, and political order. One by one, however, radical aims have been abandoned in practice, if not in theory.

Many factors have contributed to this change of heart. Although Marxist doctrine has continued to inspire many of the intellectual leaders of the movement, it was never embraced by its mass following. Except for a short-lived attempt by the Danish police to suppress the nascent Socialist movement, the Scandinavian Socialists were never subjected to the kind of systematic persecution that did so much to embitter the Socialists of Germany and Russia. In their early electoral campaigns many Socialists received support from Liberal voters; once in parliament, they in turn co-operated closely with the Liberals, whose concern for universal suffrage they fully shared and who were sympathetic to many of their demands for immediate alleviation of social ills. The Scandinavian Socialists, unlike their colleagues in other countries, were thus, almost from the start, given an opportunity to co-operate in the solution of concrete political problems.

In the years immediately preceding and during World War I a marked tension developed between the Socialist leaders, who expected socialism to emerge as the mature product of gradual evolution, and a group of youthful radicals, who were impatient to speed up that process by means of violent revolution. The vast majority of the Danish and Swedish parties followed their moderate leaders, Stauning and Branting, while the radicals formed their own organizations, known first as "Left Socialist" and later as "Communist" parties. In Norway, on the other hand, the radicals gained control of the Labor party, which shortly thereafter became a member of the Third (Communist) International. It was not long, however, before disputes between the headquarters of the International in Moscow and its Norwegian affiliate caused a series of splits within the party. A substantial moderate wing broke off in 1921 under the name "Social Democratic party"; and the Labor party itself in 1923 severed all ties with the International, causing a small revolutionary minority to found a separate Communist party. Strong pressure from the Norwegian trade-unions in 1927 brought a merger among the Labor party, the Social Democrats, and a group of dissident Communists under the traditional Labor party label. Through a process of gradual sifting, a clear separation had thus taken place throughout the Scandinavian labor movement between a democratic majority and a small revolutionary minority.

Governmental responsibility further served to confirm the Social Democrats in their cautious reformist policy. In Sweden a Liberal-Socialist coalition in 1917–20 obtained the introduction of universal and equal suffrage for both chambers and an eight-hour workday in industry, and Socialist minority cabinets during the twenties worked for higher unemployment compensation and reduction of military expenditures. During the thirties the Socialists in all three Scandinavian countries developed a program of fighting unemployment with large-scale public works expenditures, subsidized agricultural production, and expanded social insurance. Socialist premiers have been in office in all three countries with little or no interruption for about two decades (in Denmark from 1929 to 1945 and from 1947 to 1950; in Sweden since 1932,

with a short interruption in the summer of 1936; in Norway since 1935). While the Socialists retain the demand for nationalization of industry in their official programs, they first postponed its realization indefinitely and then discarded it altogether as an aim of practical policy.

The hard core of the Scandinavian Socialist parties is still made up of industrial workers; yet they have in the last two decades successfully appealed both to professional and intellectual groups and to the rural vote, especially that of agricultural laborers and tenant farmers. The Socialists in Sweden and Norway today are equally strong in rural and urban districts; in Denmark, where the Agrarians have more extensive control of the rural vote, they remain a predominantly urban party. Statistical data from Denmark and Sweden indicate that among the four major parties the Socialist is the only one which has a stronger appeal to voters in their twenties and early thirties than to middle-aged and older voters; and the same is probably true of Norway.

The Conservatives

The Scandinavian Conservative parties were first organized in an effort to ward off the Liberal attack on the plutocratic-oligarchic constitutions of the late nineteenth century. The Conservative stand on constitutional matters, however, has never been one of indiscriminate hostility to any form of change. At various points in the Danish and Swedish constitutional debate they proposed far-reaching reforms in order to forestall other changes which they considered even less desirable. In both countries they agreed to manhood suffrage on condition that it be combined with proportional representation, which (as they correctly estimated) would prevent or delay the emergence of Socialist majorities in the legislature. In

1918 the Swedish Conservatives agreed to the introduction of universal and equal suffrage for both chambers rather than risk the abolition of the senate or a serious curtailment of its powers. In the late thirties the Danish Conservatives supported the Socialist-Liberal demand for a thoroughgoing reform of the upper chamber, hoping thereby to win an ear for their pleas for strong national defense. More recently the Swedish Conservatives have proposed that the constitution be amended so as to allow for popular referenda on legislation, which they think is the best permanent guaranty against any socialist experiments with nationalization of industry.

In the last thirty years the Conservatives have come to accept democracy and parliamentary government without reservation. During the 1930's individual Conservatives showed marked sympathy for the rising German National Socialist movement; yet the party organizations resolutely repudiated these tendencies. In 1934 the Swedish Conservatives, at the insistence of their veteran leader, Arvid Lindman, severed all ties with their own youth movement because it had advocated a reorganization of the Swedish state along "corporative" lines and had refused to join in a declaration condemning naziism. During World War II the chairman of the Danish Conservative party, Christmas Møller, escaped to Britain to head a Free Danish movement. On the other hand, the Conservatives have been the chief spokesmen in Scandinavia of a tempered form of nationalism. In Denmark they vigorously protested the sale of the Virgin Islands to the United States (1916) and the granting of autonomy to Iceland (1918); in 1920 and again in 1947 they favored the incorporation of any German-speaking parts of Slesvig that would declare for Denmark in a referendum. In all three countries the Conservatives have consistently advocated higher military and naval appropriations than any of the other parties. In Sweden, where they were originally opposed to joining the League of Nations, they later insisted that arrangements for collective security sponsored by the League were far too unreliable to justify unilateral disarmament. More recently, however, the Scandinavian Conservatives have supported their countries' entrance into the United Nations.

In their early days the Conservative parties were predominantly rural; since then they have lost a large part of their farm support to the Agrarians, and today they are much stronger in the cities than in rural areas. In both Denmark and Norway their main strongholds are the capital cities. Since 1914 the Conservative share of the national vote has shrunk to about one-half its former size in Norway and to about one-third in Sweden. Only the Danish Conservative party, which started out in 1915 as the smallest of the three, has very nearly held its own.

The Agrarians

The Agrarians in Sweden and Norway were the latecomers among the major parties, entering the political arena at a time when the major constitutional questions had finally been settled. It is not surprising, therefore, that they stated their programs largely in terms of economic interest. The Norwegian party had its origin in an economic pressure group which, after several futile attempts at getting individual farmers' candidates elected, finally reconstituted itself as a political party. The Swedish Agrarians announced frankly that their major purpose was "to advance the social, political, and economic interests of the agricultural population." On the other hand, the new parties stood uncommitted on many matters in the foreground of political attention which did not directly affect the farm economy; hence they were free to throw their weight behind whatever group came forth with the most attractive bid for Agrarian support. Throughout the 1920's they generally associated themselves with the non-Socialist parties and, above all, with the Conservatives. The depression of the early thirties, however, revealed a potential community of interests with the Socialists. In 1933 the Swedish Agrarians, in a complete about-face, agreed to vote for the Socialists' crisis policy in exchange for an extensive program of support for farm prices. A similar agreement was concluded in Norway two years later. On other questions such as those of national defense and regulation of labor disputes, the Swedish Agrarians continued to cooperate with the right-wing parties. Thus the Swedish Agrarian party has held a middle position between the Socialist and the non-Socialist camps since the early thirties, a position not unlike the one occupied earlier by the Liberals—except that the Socialists, having meanwhile gained in popular votes, were now less dependent on outside support than they had been in the twenties.

The Danish Agrarians, unlike their counterparts in the other two countries, continue a long historical tradition, being the direct successors of the oldest surviving party in Scandinavia. Since the split of the old Left into a Liberal and an Agrarian group, the Agrarians have increasingly aligned themselves with their former antagonists, the Conservatives, against the Liberals and Socialists. Like the Conservatives, they have favored the incorporation of southern Slesvig into Denmark. In the debate on the bicameral question in the thirties their position was more conservative than that of the Conservatives themselves, and the failure of the proposed parliamentary reform scheme at

that time was due largely to their opposition. In economic matters the Danish Agrarians long pursued a policy of laissez faire and of a balanced budget; they agreed only reluctantly to some parts of the Socialist-Liberal antidepression program in the early thirties. While the Agrarian parties in Norway and Sweden draw their strength almost exclusively from rural areas, the Danish Agrarians receive additional support from the smaller towns and some scattered votes from the big cities.

Other Parties

The Scandinavian Communists, as we have seen, split off from the larger Social Democratic parties toward the end of World War I. Throughout the 1920's they were weakened by recurrent splits and purges, most of them brought about by conflicts between their leaders and the central committee of the Third International in Moscow. Since the late twenties loyal Muscovites have been firmly in control in all three parties, and many of the original Communist leaders have eventually found their way back into the Socialist fold. Recent expulsions from the party of "Titoist" and "Trotskyite" deviationists, however, indicate that the era of purges is not yet over. In the last two decades Communist propaganda in Scandinavia has closely followed every turn and twist of Soviet foreign policy, and the electoral success of the Communists has been largely a function of popular reaction to that policy: in Sweden their vote dropped to an all-time low in 1940, shortly after the Russian attack on Finland. Following Hitler's invasion of Russia in 1941, Danish and Norwegian Communists joined the underground resistance against the German occupation, and for a few months after liberation they were included in the government coalitions of these countries. The Communist vote in Scandinavia reached a record high during the period of Western-Soviet unity in 1944–46; after the Communist coup in Czechoslovakia (1948), however, a substantial proportion of their followers went over to the Socialists. While the greatest single concentrations of Communist strength today are found in the big cities, about half the followers of the party in Norway and Sweden live in rural areas. One of their traditional strongholds in Sweden is the iron-ore mining district in the arctic province of Norrbotten. Because of the great value of Swedish iron to any potential belligerent and because of the strategic importance of this area (which is on the direct land route between Russia and the Atlantic coast of Norway), the presence of a strong Communist organization in this area has been a source of constant concern to Swedish government authorities.

The last of the dissident factions which split off from the Swedish Communist movement maintained its independent existence much longer than any of its predecessors. After a purge in 1924 Karl Kilbom and Nile Flyg emerged as the Moscow-accredited leaders of the Swedish Communist party, but five years later they themselves were repudiated by the Kremlin. They maintained control, however, of the party organization, forcing the Stalinists to set up a new party apparatus of their own. The Kilbom-Flyg group, reinforced by a number of dissident Social Democrats, in 1934 adopted the name "Socialist party." Two years later, Kilbom fell out with Flyg and, together with half the "Socialist" delegation in the Riksdag, joined the Social Democratic party. Flyg and the remaining "Socialists" increasingly injected a note of intransigent nationalism into their criticism of parliamentary government, and soon their position became undistinguishable from that of National Socialism; in 1940 the group lost its remaining seats in the Riksdag.

National Socialist parties were formed in the three northern countries in 1932 and 1933 and at times brown-shirted columns were seen marching through the streets of the Scandinavian capitals. The Nazis never gained a significant following; like the Communists, they too were plagued by internal squabbles. Neither in Sweden (where two Nazi factions, each claiming authenticity, competed with each other) nor in Norway did they manage to elect a single candidate. During the German occupation the Norwegian Nazis, headed by the ill-famed Vidkun Quisling, were in charge of a puppet government. Apparently the Danish Nazi movement was too badly disorganized to permit a similar venture. In 1939 three Danish Nazis were elected to the lower house, but the next year one of these founded a new party of his own. Then, too, a small group which had split off from the Danish Agrarians in 1934 (and which successively went under the name of "Independents," "Free People's party," and "Farmers' party") showed definite pro-Nazi leanings and expressed its eagerness to form a collaborationist government. The 1943 elections, which were conducted under the occupation and produced a record turnout, brought what amounted to a crushing defeat of the Nazis and their sympathizers. The National Socialists barely maintained their strength, whereas the "Farmers" lost two of their four mandates. After the liberation the leaders of the National Socialist movement in both Denmark and Norway were arrested, and the "Farmers'" delegates resigned their seats. Today little, if any, trace remains of these movements in Scandinavia.

In the last three decades several other minor parties have appeared on the Scandinavian scene. Most important among these are the Justice party in Denmark and the Christian party in Norway, both of which have already been mentioned. The Justice party was founded in the early twenties by a group of intellectuals previously associated with the Liberal party. Its program reveals the strong influence of Henry George's thinking: Politics is a struggle between justice and injustice; the most flagrant injustice in present-day society is the private ownership of land; it will be remedied by making all land the property of society as a whole; a tax to be collected from the possessors of land will provide the main source of government revenue in a just order of society. Like the Danish Liberals, the Justice party is strongly pacifist, although recently its Rigsdag delegation split almost evenly for and against the Atlantic Pact, a circumstance which may have contributed to the party's sharp decline after the 1950 elections.

The Norwegian Christian party was also founded by dissident Liberals; its program records its belief that the Golden Rule and other precepts of Protestant ethics are fully applicable to public affairs and hence should provide the main yardstick for political action. More specifically, the party favors national ownership of transport and communications but otherwise indorses private enterprise; it urges abstinence and the strengthening of Protestant religious education in the schools. Before World War II the followers of this movement were largely concentrated in the region around Bergen in western Norway; since the war, however, the party has spread to the rest of the country. Its greatest gains have been registered in rural areas, apparently at the expense of the declining Agrarian party.

Several other groups in Norway and Denmark should be mentioned. For many years the Norwegian Storting included a small number of representatives of factions which acted as auxiliaries to one of the larger parties. One of these groups, the Labor Democrats, was founded in 1905 by a number of

prominent left-wing Liberals and later called itself the "Radical People's party." While it maintained its own electoral organizations in a small number of constituencies, its parliamentary representatives at first sat with the Liberal party. In 1914, however, the Labor Democrats left the Liberal group in protest against a Liberal proposal for indirect taxation, and from then until their extinction in 1936 the rapidly dwindling Radicals formed their own parliamentary group. Another small party known as *Frisinnade* (a Germanic synonym for "Liberals") broke off from the Liberal party in 1908 and co-operated closely with the Conservatives. In most districts it put up joint candidates with the latter group, while in others its followers ran as independents. By 1936 the group had disappeared, and its supporters had been absorbed within the Conservative party.

An urban middle-class group in Denmark known as the "Economy party" won a number of seats immediately after World War I but disappeared after the 1924 elections. In 1939 a group of right-wing Socialists founded the Danish Rally, which, according to its program, proposed to find a middle way between socialist collectivism and liberal individualism. It left no doubt about its opposition to totalitarianism and during the war was recognized by the Free Danish Radio as one of the "decent" parties (the Nazis and the "Farmers" being the "indecent" ones). Unlike the four major parties and the Justice group, however, it freely expressed its criticism of specific policies of the national coalition government; as a result, the coalition parties denounced it as the "Danish Splintering" and heaped upon it much of the abuse that, but for occupation censorship, would have been directed against the "indecent" parties. After the war the Danish Rally gained considerable publicity through its ultranationalist stand on the Slesvig question, but it disappeared completely after the 1947 elections. During the interwar period the Slesvig party, representing the German-speaking minority on the southern Danish border, elected one representative in every lower chamber election. During World War II, however, the Slesvig Germans, refusing to recognize Danish sovereignty, abstained from voting and for some time thereafter failed to muster sufficient strength for separate representation. Finally, delegates for the Faeroe Islands, a Danish possession halfway between Scotland and Iceland, have at times represented a "unionist" and a "separatist" faction on the islands; at other times Agrarian or Socialist candidates have been returned.

IV / CONTROVERSY AND AGREEMENT AMONG THE PARTIES

The area of party controversy has narrowed considerably during the last half-century. Fifty years ago the Conservatives were steadfastly defending an oligarchic system of representation and the traditionally independent power of the crown against the onslaught of democratic forces. The Liberals were demanding universal suffrage and parliamentary government; the Socialists, in addition, were also advocating the abolition of the monarchy, while some of their more radical followers were looking forward to a social revolution which would transform the bourgeois order into a classless society. Although this constitutional struggle became extremely bitter at times, it never erupted into violence. In Denmark and Sweden the retention of the senates and the adoption of proportionalism represented important concessions to the Conservatives; on the whole, however, the Liberal program provided the basis of agreement upon

which the controversy was settled. Former aristocrats and former revolutionists thus have met on the middle ground of democratic parliamentarism. The monarchs have intrusted their power to cabinets which acknowledge the supremacy of the parliaments; in return they have gained the loyal respect of former republicans. The fact that the Norwegian people in 1905, after decades of fighting the rule of the Swedish monarch, elected a new hereditary king by an overwhelming majority is eloquent testimony to the vitality of the monarchic tradition in Scandinavia.

Since the end of World War I major constitutional questions have all but disappeared from the Scandinavian political agenda. There have been continual revisions of some of the details of parliamentary and administrative organization as well as of the minutiae of electoral procedure. Reform of the upper chamber was a lively issue in Danish politics on the eve of World War II, but the compromise painfully worked out by the Socialists, Liberals, and Conservatives fell just short of the requisite majority in a popular referendum. In 1953 the same question was linked with an issue more appealing to popular imagination—whether women, and specifically the king's eldest daughter, Princess Margaretha, should be eligible to succeed to the throne. This time the constitutional revision providing for a one-chamber parliament and a lower voting age as well as the full incorporation of Greenland into the realm passed by a narrow margin. Again recently prominent political leaders in various Swedish parties have suggested that the traditional cabinet system be replaced by a collegial government of the Swiss type combined with popular referendum. None of these changes or proposals, however, can compare in magnitude with the momentous transformations which took place in the preceding era, and none has stirred political emotions to such a degree.

In the absence of constitutional issues of the first order, the political debate in Scandinavian parliaments ·has turned increasingly to matters of economic and social legislation. Here again a broad consensus on fundamentals has evolved. The Scandinavian states for centuries have owned a large portion of their countries' timberlands, mineral resources, and water power, and modern means of communication have been developed largely under state ownership. The Scandinavian economy has thus always included both a public and a private sector, and this fact has undoubtedly made it easier for economic liberals and economic collectivists to transfer their arguments from the dogmatic to the pragmatic plane. Although the Socialists have on occasion reasserted their demand for nationalization of industry in principle, they have rarely pressed this demand in practice. The non-Socialists no longer oppose every extension of government control over the economy: The program of the Swedish Conservatives, for instance, states that the question of public or private management of a particular branch of production should always be answered on the merits of the case. The Socialists during their long tenure in office since the early thirties have concentrated on measures designed to insure full employment; on equalizing incomes by steeply progressive taxes; and on expanding such social benefits as unemployment and old age compensation, national health insurance, free vacations, and free maternity care. Some of these benefit schemes, however, were initiated decades ago under Liberal and Conservative aegis, and the question at issue today is not so much whether these benefits should continue or cease but rather on what

scale they should continue. The non-Socialists warn that a broad social program such as that advocated by the Socialists entails an excessive tax burden which is bound to stifle private initiative throughout the economy. The Conservatives, in particular, have insisted that expenditures for welfare purposes should not be allowed to impair military preparedness.

International events since the 1930's have helped to close the gap that once separated the parties on questions of defense and foreign policy. Throughout the twenties the Liberals and the Social Democrats favored reductions in military spending or even complete disarmament. In view of the rising menace of Fascist aggression during the thirties, however, the Socialists revised their thinking on military questions. In Sweden they sponsored a rearmament budget in 1938, and a Danish Socialist party convention in 1939 belatedly stressed the need for strong defense. In none of the three countries has there been any opposition to participation in the United Nations, and all parties, with the exception of the Communists, have supported recent measures of economic co-operation in western Europe. In Norway and Denmark there has been overwhelming support for the North Atlantic Defense Pact, although the Danish Liberal party and a number of antimilitarists in the Justice party joined the Communists in voting against its ratification. Swedish sentiment on the pact has been divided, but the matter has never become an issue among the parties: a majority in each of the four larger parties supports the government in its determination to stay aloof from any military alliances, while vocal minorities have urged Sweden to join the pact.

As the focus of political attention has shifted from one type of issue to another, the parties have grouped and regrouped themselves in a variety of patterns. The usual classification of parties along a continuous spectrum from Right to Left has retained much of its validity. Nevertheless, because of a constant tendency known in French politics as *sinistrisme,* the dividing line between Left and Right has shifted from time to time. The voters have steadily flocked toward the Left, and most new parties have formed at that end of the spectrum; as a result, older parties have been crowded toward the Right. The Danish Agrarians and the Norwegian Liberals, both of whom retain the official party name "The Left," today are right-of-center parties; in Sweden the Ruralist "Left" of the 1870's became the ancestor of today's Conservatives. In the great constitutional debate around the turn of the century, the Liberal-Agrarians, first by themselves, later reinforced by the Socialists, were aligned against various shades of Conservatives. Later, in the early days of the four-party system, the usual constellation was one of Liberals and Socialists against Conservatives and Agrarians, the two offshoots of the old Liberal-Agrarian group thus finding themselves on opposite sides of the political fence. More recently the major contrast in Scandinavian politics has been that between Socialists and non-Socialists (the latter—Liberals, Agrarians, and Conservatives—are commonly and without opprobrium referred to as "bourgeois" parties). In the last two or three decades, however, party groupings have become increasingly fluid.

The gradual reconciliation of fundamental differences among the major parties has made it easier for old antagonists to join hands in common endeavor. For long periods of time (in Sweden from 1888 until 1940 and again since 1944; in Denmark since 1905; and in Norway from 1919 to 1945) no single party has had a majority in any of the three legislatures. Scandinavian parliamentary practice makes it possible in such situations for a minority government to take office; as a result, most legislation in recent decades has been passed by ad hoc majorities rather than by stable government coalitions—a practice which has further contributed to a loosening of traditional alignments. A Liberal-Socialist government coalition in Sweden that had formed in 1917 broke up in 1920. For more than a decade after that the Liberal party held the position of a "balancer" between Right and Left, since no cabinet formed by any other party could obtain a legislative majority without its support. Under the adroit leadership of Carl Gustaf Ekman the Prohibitionist Liberals co-operated with the Socialists on foreign and military questions, while on questions of social legislation they formed a bourgeois bloc with the Conservatives and Agrarians. The large Socialist and Conservative parties each in turn watched helplessly as Ekman's small phalanx amended their government bills into Liberal party motions; yet fear of appearing unco-operative and negativistic kept the two parties from joining forces in voting down Ekman's compromise proposals. This Liberal predominance in Swedish politics came to an end in 1933, when the Socialists, who by then were close to having a parliamentary majority, succeeded in enlisting Agrarian support for their New Deal policy.

In Norway the radical attitude of the Labor party in the early twenties tended to weld the three bourgeois parties into a solid bloc. During the next decade, however, Norwegian developments followed a pattern similar to that established earlier in Sweden. A Liberal ministry which ruled by "balancing" the Right against the Left was replaced in 1935 by a Socialist minority cabinet supported alternately by Agrarians and

Liberals. Since the end of World War II the Norwegian Socialists have had a majority in the Storting; as a result, the Socialist-Bourgeois alignment has re-emerged, although on many major issues there is broad agreement among all the democratic parties.

In Denmark the older pattern of Socialists and Liberals versus Agrarians and Conservatives has prevailed. A Socialist-Liberal coalition was in power from 1929 to 1940—a record tenure among Scandinavian cabinets—and an Agrarian-Conservative coalition from 1950 to 1953. On other occasions the Socialists or the Agrarians have formed minority cabinets which received additional support from the Liberals or the Conservatives, respectively. At times, however, this constellation has given way to others. The Conservative party, discontented with a bloc pattern which relegated it to the role of an adjunct to the Agrarians, has periodically lined up with the parties of the Left. Under the dynamic leadership of Christmas Møller (1928–39) they tried to make good their claim that they were a middle-of-the-road party in economic and social matters, while avowedly remaining a party of the Right in questions of national defense. In the discussions on parliamentary reform the Conservatives outflanked the Agrarians both in 1919–20 and in 1937–39 by suggesting compromises which the Socialists and the Liberals accepted and the Agrarians turned down. In 1931 they backed the antidepression program of the Socialist-Liberal coalition in return for government concessions on military appropriations. Other points on the government crisis program were indorsed by all four parties or passed with Agrarian support over Conservative opposition.

At times of crisis in foreign policy all these shifting party constellations have regularly given way to a broad national front, including all parties except small groups at either extreme of the spectrum. When the long-smoldering dispute between Norway and Sweden came to a head in 1905 (and war between the two countries seemed a remote possibility), a broad coalition representing all shades of Liberal and Conservative opinion and excluding only a handful of Socialists was formed in each country to cope with the emergency. The Norwegian coalition, unlike the one in Sweden, remained in office even after the union between the two countries was peaceably dissolved. The Norwegian premier, Christian Michelsen, evidently hoped that the party truce of 1905 would be but the first stage in the gradual disappearance of all party distinctions. Shortly after the parties had announced their respective platforms for the 1906 elections, he issued a separate election manifesto that was to provide the basis for such nonpartisan unity. The attempt failed. Far from causing all parties to rally around his program, Michelsen succeeded merely in splitting his own Liberal movement, thus adding a new faction to the existing ones. Eventually his followers were absorbed into the Conservative party.

There was little danger that the Scandinavian countries would be drawn into World War I against their will. Politics, on the whole, continued as usual except that a Liberal government in Denmark agreed to take the leaders of the three opposition parties into the cabinet as "control ministers." World War II, on the other hand, brought about a truce among all democratic parties in the three northern countries. In Sweden a national coalition of Socialists, Agrarians, Liberals, and Conservatives was in power from December, 1939, until July, 1945. A similar coalition was formed in Denmark after the German invasion and remained in office as long as the Germans allowed a Danish cabinet to function. After liberation the same coalition was widened to include representatives of the Communists, the Danish Rally, the underground resistance, and the Free Danish movement; it resigned shortly after the first peacetime elections in the fall of 1945. The hasty departure of the Norwegian monarch, his ministers, and many Storting members left no time for a reconstruction of the Socialist cabinet in office at the time of the German invasion; yet the government co-operated closely with the leaders of other parties who had joined it in exile. In Norway, too, the first postwar elections were conducted by a coalition government including the four major parties which had agreed to campaign on the basis of a joint program of political and economic reconstruction. The task of carrying out this program fell to the lot of the Socialist majority cabinet which was formed late in 1945.

In conclusion, some of the factors which have created the atmosphere of moderation and conciliation so characteristic of Scandinavian politics may be briefly summarized. Although democracy in Scandinavia is a comparatively recent phenomenon, the tradition of popular representation and of government by law dates back, with some interruptions, to the early Middle Ages. The recent transition from oligarchy to democracy was accomplished peacefully, and the circle of politically active citizens was enlarged gradually. As a result, Scandinavian parliamentary government retains much of the intimacy typical of the earlier oligarchic period when the rulers were members of a small, closely knit, hereditary elite. From 1814 to 1940 the Scandinavian countries enjoyed a long period of peace interrupted only by the Austro-Prussian attack on Denmark in 1864. The effects of the great depression on

Scandinavia, though severe, were far less devastating than on many other countries. Historical circumstances thus have created conditions favorable to the smooth operation of modern governmental institutions.

Other factors have contributed to the same result. Each of the three countries has a small and remarkably homogeneous population. Nearly all the inhabitants speak the same native language and belong, at least nominally, to the same Lutheran state church. Among the small ethnic minorities in Scandinavia, only the Germans of north Slesvig have formed a nationality party, whereas the nomadic Laps in northern Sweden and Norway and the Finns on the Swedish-Finnish border have never become minorities in the political sense. The only sizable denominational minority groups—the Protestant dissenters in Sweden and Norway—have been very active in politics and especially in such movements as the Prohibitionist Liberal party in Sweden; yet high-churchmen, sectarians, and agnostics are to be found in each of the major parties, and religious questions have never precipitated partisan controversy. Scandinavia is thus free from the ethnic and religious cleavages which have exacerbated party feeling in other countries. Nor are there any regional contrasts of major political significance in any of the three countries. With the exception of North Slesvig, which was reincorporated into Denmark following a referendum in 1920, the territories now included in each of the three northern countries have been continuously under the same government for three centuries or more. A small group on the distant Faeroe Islands has been advocating greater independence from Denmark, but majority sentiment seems to favor continued Danish rule. Outside of these two areas there have never been any regional parties: a party founded in a distinct locality has always either expanded into a nation-wide movement or become extinct after a few years.

In the favorable climate produced by these historical and demographic conditions, political institutions have further tended to attenuate partisan antagonism. The constitutions of the three countries as they operate today are almost entirely devoid of any mechanical checks and balances which would encourage obstruction of the governmental process by a determined minority. The electoral system, as we have seen, discourages both the growth of extremist groups and an unlimited fragmentation of parties. While nearly all questions of policy are decided by simple majority, legislative procedure insures that expert opinion be consulted and dissenting voices heard. In the absence of a majority party, decisions have generally been the result of co-operation among two or more distinct parties. The executive branch is fully responsible to the legislatures; yet so long as there is no majority against them, cabinets can govern without the paralyzing need for continuous formal indorsement by parliament. Cabinets, therefore, have held office for periods long enough to allow for constructive, long-range planning. Political patronage is virtually unknown; even the undersecretaries in Swedish cabinet departments, who in the eyes of the constitution are political appointees, have generally been civil servants and have held their posts during good behavior.

In each of the three countries the monarch provides a stable and neutral point of reference at the center of the political arena and, in times of emergency, a potent symbol of national unity. While the monarchs no longer hold any power of political decision, they have on occasion had some discretion in selecting a prime minister and have at all times been free to advise the cabinet. In exercising these latter functions they have as a rule striven to temper partisanship and to reconcile conflicting points of view.

Among the parties of the Western world, those of the Scandinavian countries hold a unique position. The four-party system which has predominated during most of the twentieth century closely reflects the socioeconomic divisions of the population. Party organization is firmly intrenched and at once more extensive and intensive than in other democratic countries. Yet Scandinavian experience belies the frequent generalization that political stability can result only from a two-party system. In a highly homogeneous group of societies the parties could afford to be moderate as their strength increased. Party discipline is effective but voluntary, and the debate among the parties has centered upon concrete pragmatic issues—a tendency reinforced by the prevalence of material decisions in a growing welfare state.

Few countries approximate the singular combination of physical environment, social structure, and historical tradition characteristic of the Scandinavian countries, and few, if any, will ever reproduce the Scandinavian party system. In the three northern countries themselves, however, the system of four to five parties, all alike inclusive, strong, pragmatic, and conciliatory, has shown great vitality and stability. The vicissitudes of political leadership, the success and failure of specific policies, and slow changes in social structure may increase or reduce the strength of individual parties and lead to periodic shifts in the pattern of party alliances. One or another of the established parties may even disappear, and a few newcomers may enter the arena. Barring foreign invasion or other catastrophe, however, the party system itself can be expected to survive with minor variations for many decades to come.

Note on the translation of party names.— A few remarks on the translation of party names used in this study may serve to clear up possible confusion. Authors dealing with individual countries have translated the names of Scandinavian parties in a variety of ways; it has seemed desirable, in a comparative study, to give the same labels to analogous parties in each country, even though this does some violence to official party names. The most confusing circumstance is that the same name (*Venstre*, literally "Left") serves as the official appellation for both the Norwegian Liberals and the Danish Agrarians. Other writers have referred to the Danish Agrarians as the "Agrarian Left" or, rather confusingly, "Moderate Liberals" or just "Liberals," and to the Danish Liberals (officially *Det radikale Venstre*, or "Radical Left") as "Radical Liberals" or "Radicals."

The Swedish and Norwegian Agrarian parties have also been called "Farmers'" or "Peasants'" parties—a fairly literal translation of their official names (*Bondeförbundet* and *Bondepartiet*, respectively). When the Swedish liberals in 1923 split into a sectarian-prohibitionist and an urban minority faction, the latter retained the Latin name "Liberals," whereas the former adopted for its name a Germanic synonym *Frisinnade* (which is sometimes inaccurately rendered as "Independent"). Only the Danish Conservatives have officially embraced that name; their Swedish and Norwegian counterparts call themselves "The Right" (*Högern* in Sweden, *Høyre* in Norway).

The Labor movement goes under the name of the Social Democratic party in Denmark, Labor party in Norway, and Social Democratic Labor party in Sweden; in this study the terms "Social Democrats," "Socialists," and "Labor party" have been used interchangeably for all three. It should be noted, however, that there was a separate "Social Democratic" party in Norway (1921–27) and a "Socialist" party in Sweden (1934–40), as explained in the text. The Danish Justice party (*Retsforbundet*), finally, has also been called "Land Tax" or "Single Tax" party after one of its outstanding program demands.

TABLE 1

REPRESENTATION OF COMMUNIST PARTY IN
SCANDINAVIA, 1946–53

COUNTRY	CHAMBER	ELECTION YEAR	COMMUNIST PERCENTAGE OF		DIFFERENCE BETWEEN PERCENTAGE OF VOTE AND SEATS
			National Vote	Parliamentary Seats	
Denmark.....	Parliament	Sept., 1953	4.3	4.6	+0.3
Denmark.....	Lower	1950	4.6	4.7	+0.1
Denmark.....	Lower	April, 1953	4.8	4.7	−0.1
Sweden......	Lower	1952	4.4	2.2	−2.2
Sweden......	Lower	1948	6.3	3.5	−2.8
Norway......	Storting	1953	5.1	2.0	−3.1
Norway......	Storting	1949	5.8	0	−5.8
Sweden......	Upper	1946–51	11.2	2.7	−8.5
Denmark.....	Upper	1947	10.3	1.3	−9.0

TABLE 2
The Popular Vote in Scandinavia, 1920–53*

Election Year	Communists	Socialists	Liberals	Agrarians	Conservatives	Justice and Christian Parties	Nazis	Others
				Sweden				
1920.........	6.4	29.6	21.8	14.1	28.1	....	....	0.0
1921.........	7.8	36.2	19.1	11.1	25.8	....	....	0.0
1924.........	5.1	41.1	16.9	10.8	26.1	....	....	0.0
1928.........	6.4	37.0	15.9	11.2	29.4	....	....	0.1
1932.........	3.0	41.7	11.7	14.1	23.5	....	0.6	5.4
1936.........	3.3	45.9	12.9	14.3	17.6	....	0.7	5.3
1940.........	3.5	53.8	12.0	12.0	18.0	....	....	0.7
1944.........	10.3	46.6	12.9	13.6	15.9	....	0.1	0.6
1948.........	6.3	46.1	22.8	12.4	12.3	....	....	0.1
1952.........	4.4	46.0	24.6	10.7	14.2	....	....	0.1
				Denmark				
1920†........	0.4	32.2	12.1	34.0	17.9	....	....	3.4
1924.........	0.5	36.6	13.0	28.3	18.9	1.0‡	....	1.7
1926.........	0.4	37.2	11.3	28.3	20.6	1.3	....	0.9
1929.........	0.2	41.8	10.7	28.3	16.5	1.8	....	0.7
1932.........	1.1	42.7	9.4	24.7	18.7	2.7	0.05	0.65
1935.........	1.6	46.1	9.2	17.8	17.8	2.5	1.0	4.0
1939.........	2.0	42.9	9.5	18.2	18.7	2.0	1.8	4.9
1943.........	§	44.5	8.7	18.7	21.0	1.6	2.1	3.4
1945.........	12.5	32.8	8.1	23.4	18.2	1.9	....	3.1
1947.........	6.8	40.0	6.9	27.6	12.4	4.5	....	1.8
1950.........	4.6	39.6	8.2	21.3	17.8	8.2	....	0.3
1953, April....	4.8	40.4	8.6	22.1	17.3	5.6	....	1.2
1953, September	4.3	41.3	7.8	23.1	16.8	3.5	....	3.2
				Norway				
1921.........	21.3‖	9.2	22.6	13.1	33.4	....	....	0.3
1924.........	6.1	27.2#	20.4	13.5	32.5	....	....	0.3
1927.........	4.0	36.8‖	18.7	14.9	25.5	....	....	0.2
1930.........	1.7	31.4	21.0	15.9	30.0	....	....	....
1933.........	1.8	40.1	17.7	13.9	21.8	0.8**	2.2	1.7
1936.........	0.3	42.5	16.4	11.6	22.6	1.4	1.8	3.4
1945.........	11.9	41.0	13.8	8.0	17.0	7.9	....	0.3
1949.........	5.8	45.7	14.1	7.4	17.8	8.5	....	0.7
1953.........	5.1	46.7	10.0	9.2	18.4	10.5	....	0.5

* Figures represent percentages of national vote in general elections to the lower houses and the Storting.
† September 6, 1920 (third election of that year).
‡ Justice party. ‖ Labor party. ** Christian party.
§ Not allowed to compete. # Labor and Social Democratic parties.

United States: The Functional Approach to Party Government

E. E. SCHATTSCHNEIDER
Wesleyan University

I / THE RISE OF PARTY GOVERNMENT

Competing theories of party organization attempt to explain the nature of party systems in terms of the governmental structure in which they operate or the social structure in which they are imbedded. Both explanations are so reasonable that they have caused students of politics to overlook the proposition that the form, scope, and focus of party organization may also be understood in terms of the *function of politics* at any given time and place.[1]

It is doubtless unintelligent to insist on a single explanation of anything so complex as the American party system, and it is difficult or impossible to assign relative weights to all the factors that must be taken into account in a general explanation. The hypothesis that the function of politics has an influence on the nature of party organization is formulated here merely as a corrective for the overemphasis on traditional explanations, not as an exclusive determining principle. Explanations of the nature of the party system are important, in that every explanation implies a theory of political action and an atti-

tude toward the dynamics of politics. Since formal governmental structures are relatively rigid and the social structure is not readily responsive to efforts to change it, the implication of traditional explanations of the party system is that very little can be done to adapt political organizations to the needs of the community. The tendency of traditional explanations of the party system is therefore to produce static concepts of political organization. In view of the crisis in modern politics, the practical consequences of static ideas of political organization may be so great that a reconsideration of the subject seems desirable. The virtue of a functional theory of party organization is, first, that it helps to account for changes in the form, scope, and focus of the system and, second, that it provides an opportunity to re-examine pessimistic generalizations concerning the rigidity and immobility of the system.

Political scientists have produced no significant body of theory or techniques for the analysis of the functions of politics. Perhaps a good beginning might be made, however, by first finding out what the government is doing. What is American government about, and why would anyone want to get control of it? Even if we assume that parties are organized primarily to get control of the government, is it not likely that the kind of political organization produced by the nation and the kind of effort made by the people who participate in politics have something to do with the role played by the government in the com-

---

1. The controversy between adherents of the governmental and social explanations is summarized by Leslie Lipson in his article, "The Two-Party System in British Politics," *American Political Science Review*, XLVII (June, 1953), 337–58. Lipson attacks the idea that the party system is shaped chiefly by the governmental structure and argues that the formative influence is primarily the social structure. He makes no reference to the function of the political system as a factor to be considered.

munity and in the world? To understand the function of politics, it may be useful, therefore, to take a look at the total operations of the government at all levels of its activity. This approach to the study of politics relates the political system to the size of the government, its capacity to act, its resources, its productivity, the scale of its operations, and the direction in which it is moving. The nature of our involvement in politics can therefore be understood in these terms.

The functional concept of politics conveys a dynamic interpretation of the political system, because our governmental institutions have been profoundly affected in recent years by a peaceful revolution in public policy which has greatly altered current concepts of the management of American society and imposed upon the government a great, new, and unfamiliar role at home and abroad. It is usually assumed that every successful attempt to change the functions of the government or to carry through a major new governmental program implies some corresponding change in the organization of politics because government and politics are inseparable.

The relevance of political organization to the function of politics is easily demonstrated. Political organization is a cultural product of mature civilizations and societies.[2] Like factories, hospitals, and schools, political parties can be produced only by sustained and purposeful efforts of many people working together. It is unthinkable, therefore, that these organizations can be understood without examination of the objectives of the participants in the enterprises: What do people want to accomplish?

When looked at in this way, it becomes evident that there has been a different theory of political organizations for every major concept of public policy; that new policies have inevitably produced new kinds of politics. The nature of the political system is related by the *uses to which political organization is put:* What are the available resources of political action; what is the nature of the resistance to be overcome; what is the scale and intensity of the effort required; what concepts of power are implicit in the political action contemplated?[3]

A historical perspective of theories of party organization in the United States will show how closely these concepts have been related to the changing function of American politics. The Federalists sought to perpetuate the power of a relatively small group of men of position and property, who attempted to monopolize public office permanently and who were therefore opposed to efforts to organize the masses. These ideas and attitudes had

2. Malinowski defines culture as "an organized system of purposeful activities," *A Scientific Theory of Culture* (Chapel Hill: University of North Carolina Press, 1944), p. 52.

"One of the inadequacies of the definition of politics as a struggle for power is that it obscures, if it does not obliterate, the *purposes* in terms of which power is sought and used and the conflict of purposes out of which politics emerges. For it is the conflict of purposes that characterizes politics—not the struggle for a 'power' divorced from all purposeful motivation" (John H. Hallowell, *Religious Perspectives of College Training in Political Science* [New Haven: Yale University Press, 1950], p. 8).

3. The emphasis here is not on "getting"—as in Lasswell's famous description of politics as "who gets what, when, and how"—in that politics is here conceived of as a process of working with other people to accomplish things that cannot be accomplished alone. The dichotomy is not simply that between "selfish" and "unselfish" objectives but between different ways of sharing purposes or not sharing them. Political organization contemplates conflict, but it is a great oversimplification to suppose that the basis of conflict is merely the acquisitive instinct, or self-aggrandizement. Every society, group, faction, or party involves some kind of sharing of purposes.

a bearing on the Federalists' conviction that their position in society and their control of the economy were dependent on their permanent control of the government. They developed anti-party ideas, or, more precisely, they were opposed to a competitive party system in which an organized popular opposition might challenge the supremacy of the Federalist oligarchy. For this reason they refused to think of themselves as a party, denied the right of the opposition to organize and agitate, and generally refused to compete for popular support. The failure of the Federalist party to develop an organization in the electorate at large can be attributed to its objectives. The circumstances suggest that the Federalist party was a special kind of political organization designed for a particular purpose.

The Federalist system was vulnerable to Jeffersonian ideas of political organization intended to broaden the popular base of American politics. As the sponsor and owner of a political movement, Jefferson was able to extend his loose and sketchy organization widely among social strata never before exploited by the parties. The Jeffersonian system was so successful and the Federalist competition so feeble that an intensive and elaborate organization was not necessary.[4]

4. John Quincy Adams, in his *Parties in the United States* (New York, 1941), pp. 9, 105–6, and 125, commented on the position and the role of the Jeffersonian Republican party: "The anti-Federalists had always the advantage of *numbers*. Their principles, being those of democracy, were always favored by the majority of the people." Of Jefferson's influence in the Senate, Adams wrote: "There was scarcely an attempt made in the Senate for seven years to oppose anything he desired." Concerning presidential succession, Adams declared that the results would have been the same if the Constitution had authorized Jefferson to appoint his successor. According to Adams, Jefferson's personal influence within the party was so great as to be almost dictatorial.

Jefferson's Republican party was a personal political movement in which the congressional caucus ratified Jefferson's designation of Madison as his successor and in turn ratified Madison's choice of his own successor. On the other hand, the common understanding on which Jefferson's party was based was disrupted when the collapse of the Federalist party left the country without an organized alternative *because the Jeffersonian system contemplated the existence of the Federalist party*. With the disintegration of the Federalist party, an attack on the authority of the Republican caucus was inevitable. Thus only a very simple kind of party system existed at the end of the second decade of the nineteenth century. The Federalists had not yet learned to run an opposition, and the Republicans had not yet learned how to institutionalize presidential nominations in an expanding electorate. Whatever its deficiencies, however, the Jeffersonian party organization seems to have been able to meet the expressed needs of the people in control of the movement for two decades. On the face of the evidence, what the Jeffersonians did about political organization made sense in terms of what they were attempting to accomplish.

Jacksonian ideas of political organization were closely related to the circumstances under which Jackson came into power. The attack on "King Caucus," the "democratization" of the party structure, the idea of the plebiscitary presidency, and even the spoils system were designed to implement the campaign of a rank outsider for the presidency but reflected also the drive of a new social class for recognition and power. The development of the convention system indicated the supremacy of the local party organizations that had grown up in the electorate with the extension of the suffrage during the first three or four decades of the nineteenth century. The decentralization of the party structure created by the Jacksonians was appropriate to the overwhelming localism of American life at a time when the central government was microscopic and remote, in advance of the development of a national system of transportation and communication and the rise of a national economy. The whole Jacksonian apparatus reflected the function of politics at a stage in the growth of the country.

The salient characteristics of the party system after the time of Jackson were instability of national party leadership, the maximum possible rate of turnover in the presidency, and the ascendancy of the national convention as an arena for state and local party leaders. It seems likely that the best explanation for the condition of the national party leadership during this period is simply that no powerful interest demanded a continuous general operating control of the national government, and no serious attempt was made to implement that kind of demand in a situation in which the objectives of local and regional political organization were largely a matter of imposing a veto on the national government.

During the great period of Republican supremacy from 1860 to 1932, the Republican party was able to adapt the Jacksonian party structure and organization to its own uses. The Republican system after 1896 is one of the masterpieces of American politics, but it can be understood only in terms of its functions as interpreted by the dominant elements in the party at the time. The "strength" or the "efficiency" of the system is to be measured in terms of the purposes it was designed to accomplish. By the end of the 1890's the Republican party was a conservative movement closely identified with "big business," the most dynamic and

spectacularly successful minority in American society. What were the political goals of the business community?[5] Mainly, business leadership wanted to be let alone to exploit the economy without interference by the government. Aside from the protective tariff and the gold standard, *the Republican party had no important positive program of legislation.*[6] No one can read the newspapers, speeches, editorials, and party platforms of the period without sensing that the Republican party had become the political instrument of business. As a matter of fact, the Bryan-Populist-Democratic campaign of 1896, in which the system was attacked, served only to consolidate the connection between the Republican party and its business patrons. The whole agenda of American government during the period reflects the purpose of the dominant party to maintain its general policy of giving business what it wanted.[7]

5. Henry Adams wrote: "All one's friends, all one's best citizens, reformers, churches, colleges, educated classes, had joined to force submission to capitalism" (quoted in Matthew Josephson, *The President Makers* [New York, 1940], p. 8).
"Business dominated society" (Billington, Loewenberg, and Brockunier, *The United States: American Democracy in World Perspective* [New York, 1947], p. 315).
See statement on "Revival of Business" in the Republican platform in 1908 in Kirk Porter, *National Party Platforms* (New York, 1924), p. 300. The general point of view of this group is well described in R. G. McCloskey, *American Conservatism in the Age of Enterprise* (Cambridge, 1951); see p. 13, for example: "American life and thought were permeated with the gospel of wealth."

6. See, for example, the Republican platforms from 1896 to 1908.

7. "The main objective of capitalism in the postwar years was not to persuade the government to take action, but to prevent it from doing so" (McCloskey, *op. cit.*, p. 76). It hardly seems necessary to document the statement that the Republican party became the political instrument of the business community in the fourth quarter of the nineteenth

The achievement of the Republican party at the peak of its ascendancy cannot be understood in terms of the legislation enacted by Congress but in terms of *what was prevented*. The accomplishments of the Republican party might be measured more accurately, therefore, by the gap produced between the social legislation of western European countries and that of the United States before 1932. The American lag in social legislation suggests that the Republican party in terms of its own goals was a powerful and effective political organization.

II / REPUBLICAN CONCEPTS OF POLITICAL ORGANIZATION

What kind of political organization did the dominant interests of the Republican party require for the realization of their objectives? The objective was a small government, as inactive as possible. The chief instrument of the Republican party in the government was the presidency. The Republican party was therefore, first of all, a presidential party, a party organized for the election and control of presidents and working through the presidency for the minimization of the role of the national government in the economy. The powers of the president were well suited to the purposes of the party. He could veto legislation; he had the power to appoint and to remove law-enforcement officials, substantially a second veto, because, short of impeach-

ment, there is little that Congress can do to compel the president to enforce the statutes; he appointed the justices of the Supreme Court at a time when the court was developing the judicial veto of legislation to an unprecedented degree. From the Republican point of view, therefore, the presidency was the key to the government.

Moreover, Republican party discipline in the presidency was almost perfect. Of the eleven Republican presidents from Grant to Hoover, only one was ever suspected of any disloyalty whatever to the business alliance of the party. Republican concepts of the presidency at the turn of the century led James Bryce to write a famous chapter on the mediocrity of presidential candidates.[8] Obviously, the system did not call for great men as much as it required a succession of presidents who could be trusted to sustain the business-Republican coalition.[9]

Congress was a secondary instrument of the Republican party. When necessary, the party could take advantage of the labyrinthine congressional procedure, the seniority rule, the committee system, and the speakership to obstruct legislation; but, considering the objectives of the business-Republican alliance, it was not necessary for the party to mobilize a congressional majority for continuous general control of the government. Majorities are necessary to enact legislation but something less than a majority may be able to obstruct legislation, provided that they are well intrenched in the legis-

century. Thus Josephson refers to the Republican party after 1896 as "the party of big business, more firmly wedded to big business than ever before. Under Hanna the relationship of the Republican party with big business was more intimate and effective than ever before" (Josephson, *op. cit.*, pp. 4 and 5). "Hanna was genuinely convinced that the business interests should govern the country" (Morrison and Commager, *The Growth of the American Republic* [New York, 1937], II, 257).

8. "Why Great Men Are Not Chosen Presidents," *American Commonwealth*, Part I, chap. viii.

9. The fact that the presidency is now regarded as the chief instrument of a strong, active national policy proves that the role of the presidency in American politics depends on what people want to accomplish. There is nothing about the presidency itself that makes it a great or a little office apart from the political purposes of the nation.

lative apparatus. Apparently for this reason, the Republican party did not develop a serious national organization to elect Republican congresses and did relatively little to organize Republican members of Congress for action. The congressional and senatorial campaign committees were not used to influence congressional nominations or congressional careers or to place congressional candidates under a strong obligation to the national party leadership. In the twenty-four-year period from 1908 to 1932 the Republican party controlled the presidency and both houses of Congress (in the sense of being able to push through a party program) for only about six years, even though its general supremacy in the country was overwhelming most of the time. It seems reasonable to suppose, therefore, that party government in Congress was never perfected because the Republican party did not want it.

This is the point at which President Lowell formulated a classical interpretation of the American party system. In his famous study of party voting in the House of Representatives at the turn of the century, Lowell discovered that party voting in the House of Representatives was far less intensive than it was in the House of Commons. He concluded, therefore, that American parties were interested only in the *patronage and personnel* of government, not in its *policies*.[10]

It is easy to demonstrate, however, that the Republican party at the time Lowell wrote did have a well-defined and well-established policy—the policy of giving business a free hand to ex-

ploit the economy with a minimum of governmental interference. This indeed was a policy; it was general, and it was comprehensively and effectively imposed on the whole national government by a powerful party—but *it required very little legislation to implement it.* The meagerness and triviality of the legislative output are sufficient evidence of the power of the dominant party to execute its policy. The point is that President Lowell's statistics of congressional roll calls did not measure that kind of power. Lowell's miscalculation of the cohesion of the Republican party resulted from the fact that he measured its achievement in terms of aims and intentions which the party never contemplated. Lowell's evidence did not demonstrate the weakness of the Republican party but merely proved that he did not understand very well what it was trying to accomplish.

To say, as Lowell did, that American parties are interested only in "personalities" and not "issues" is to confuse the matter. Some kind of control of the government is essential to the aims of all parties, but control of the government is not an end in itself. People want to control the government to accomplish something or to prevent something. These objectives can best be defined in terms of policies, because governmental activities can be discussed most easily in terms of policies. In order to get control of the government, however, it is necessary to put party men into key places in the government. Control of government personnel is therefore a necessary means for getting control of the government, *but policy is what control is about.* In this sense the absence of policy is in itself a policy. Certainly, the great business tycoons of Lowell's day did not go into politics merely to get patronage.[11]

10. Lowell's words in *The Government of England* (1924 ed.), II, 95, are: "Parties in America are not, as a rule despotic on public questions, because they have little cohesion; but their influence or rather the influence of the machine, or of the individual politician, is freely exerted in things quite apart from those issues of public policy which form the only rational ground for party activity."

11. Lowell speaks of policy as the only rational objective of party activity. He could have thought that the Republican party acted

It is hard to exaggerate the effect of its functions on the structure and organization of the Republican party. Despite Bryce's criticism of presidential nominations at the turn of the century, it is obvious that the system served the dominant interests of the dominant party. Republican presidents and presidential candidates accepted the policy of the party so completely that no great intra-party issue was raised by contests for presidential nominations in which nearly all the candidates would have served the purposes of the party equally well.

The meaning of the generalization that presidential politics during this period concerned itself with personalities rather than issues is that agreement on policy in the upper levels of the party was so complete that the personality of the candidate was all that was left to consider. The candidates were not usually distinguished men, but it is difficult to see what the system could have done with a succession of strong presidents if there had been one. On the other hand, it would be a mistake to assume that anyone made a serious attempt to develop any other kind of system and failed.

The development of Congress during this period reflects the same general situation. The most important fact about Congress was not the lack of party votes, as President Lowell thought, but the insignificance of the legislative output. Congress became precisely the kind of institution most desired by people who wanted to insure the minimum possible use of the power of the government to check the supremacy of business in American society. The preoccupation of individual members of Congress with the details of public business, the inability of

Congress to define its role in the government, its disinclination to assume an over-all responsibility for the conduct of its business, its disorderly procedure, and the usurpation of powers by irresponsible committees and even by irresponsible individual members—all are characteristic of a *parliamentary body stripped of functions by a political decision*. On the other hand, it does not seem to be true that important and powerful interests and individuals in the country tried to create another kind of Congress and found it impossible to do so. The Republican party produced the kind of Congress it wanted, just as certainly as the British party system produced the kind of House of Commons it wanted, for there is very little about the American Constitution that determines what kind of institution Congress is to be.

Other political institutions of the time reflect the overriding purposes of the dominant party. The expansion of pressure politics was an aspect of the marriage of the Republican party and big business, a mark of the special consideration given to businessmen in a coalition in which business was the senior partner. The business pressure groups were, for all practical purposes, ancillary organizations of the Republican party. Thus the Republican party did not merely support a high protective tariff: *it invited industry to write its own rates*. To suppose that the Republican party was a reluctant partner in this arrangement (i.e., a "weak" party overcome by "strong" pressure groups) is to attribute to it intentions and purposes it does not seem to have had.

At every point the characteristic institutions and procedures of the period reflect the purposes of the dominant party. The political organization of the country was well adapted to exploit the political decision that put the Republican party in power. The simple

irrationally only because he did not understand what it was trying to do.

truth is that the people who won the election of 1896 accomplished what they wanted to accomplish. No party ever made better use of its political advantages to get what it wanted. If the "success" of the Republican party is measured in terms of its own objectives, there is little to show that it was frustrated by the separation of powers or by the federal system or by the special-interest groups. Considering the record of the period, it is appropriate to ask whether or not it is possible to produce a powerful political party in the United States. There is very little about the history of the Republican party from 1896 to 1932 to support the conclusion that Americans cannot create the kinds of parties they want.

III / IMPACT OF THE PARTY ALIGNMENT OF 1896

How was it possible for the conservative wing of the Republican party to gain the tremendous ascendancy described here? To understand what happened, it is necessary to take a look at the party alignment produced in the election of 1896, one of the decisive elections in American history. The 1896 alignment is important (1) because it was remarkably stable, maintaining itself almost without modification for thirty-six years and (2) because it determined the nature of American politics from 1896 to 1932. The party cleavage of 1896 resulted from the tremendous reaction of conservatives in both major parties to the Populist movement, a radical agrarian agitation that alarmed conservative interests all over the country. The Populist movement spread over wide areas west of the Mississippi in the late 1880's and swept into the South, where in 1890 it captured control of no less than eight state legislatures and threatened to overthrow the existing political order.[12] The southern Bourbons reacted to the Populist

menace so strongly that they were willing to revive the tensions and animosities of the Civil War and the Reconstruction in order to produce a noncompetitive one-party sectional southern political system in which nearly all Negroes and many poor whites were disfranchised.[13] One of the most important and least understood national consequences of the creation of the Solid South was that it severed permanently the connection between the western and the southern agrarian radicals.

The second stage of the conservative reaction to populism came in 1896, when William Jennings Bryan and his supporters took control of the Democratic National Convention, negotiated a Democratic-Populist fusion, and nominated Bryan for the presidency on a Populist platform.

The northern business community was so badly frightened by the Bryan candidacy that it adopted drastic measures to alarm the country against it. As a matter of fact, the conservative reaction to Bryanism in the North was almost as spectacular as the Bourbon reaction to populism in the South, as a glance at election statistics in 1896 and subsequent elections will show. The Democratic party in large areas of the Northeast and Middle West was wiped out, while the Republican party consolidated overwhelming support in all of the most populous areas of the country. The resulting alignment was one of the most sharply sectional political divisions in American history. The consequences were extremely impor-

12. See M. S. and S. W. Stedman, *Discontent at the Polls* (New York, 1950), p. 130.

13. "Intense agitation over Negro voting came as an aftermath of the Populist crisis" (V. O. Key, *Southern Politics* [New York, 1948], p. 8).

"While the upcountry man had no love for the Negro, he suspected, at times rightly, that the black belt was trying to disfranchise him as well as the black men" (*ibid.*).

tant; in effect, the new alignment turned the country over to two powerful sectional minorities: (1) the northern sectional business-Republican minority and (2) its southern Bourbon Democratic sectional counterpart. *The impact of the new cleavage on American politics was great because it was both overwhelming and stable.* It can be understood only when the interdependence of the two ruling sectional minorities is realized. The alignment became possible when the southern Bourbons decided that they were willing to abandon their ambitions to win power nationally in return for undisputed control of the Solid South. On the other hand, the influence of the Solid South on the status of the Republican party in American politics after 1896 can hardly be exaggerated.

As a matter of fact, the existence of the Solid South was a prerequisite for the supremacy of the business community in the Republican party and in the country. From the standpoint of national politics the principal function of the Solid South was to make impossible a combination of the southern and western agrarian radicals. The establishment of a one-party system in the South simplified tremendously the task of the conservative business Republicans in getting a strangle hold on the Republican party in the North, because *it isolated the western radicals.* Thereafter, the western Republican insurgents had no place to go; unable to make any combination able to win a national election, they were reduced to launching a succession of futile sectional minor parties. Much recent political history might have been better understood generally if more people had remembered the historical relation between the Solid South and the locus of power in the Republican party after 1896.

The ascendancy of the business wing of the Republican party was made pos-

sible, in the second place, by the extreme sectionalism of the party alignment. Sectionalism in the North was only superficially less intense than in the South. In large areas of both sections the opposition party was extinguished or became ineffective, and organized political alternatives disappeared substantially. Both sections became extremely conservative because one-party politics tends strongly to vest political power in the hands of people who already have economic power. So long as the parties compete for votes, people who have votes have power, even if they do not have money. But in one-party areas (areas of extreme sectionalism) votes decline in value. When sectionalism is pushed to an extreme, there is no way to keep a few people with economic power from taking over the government. It is a remarkable fact that the undemocratic character of sectionalism has rarely been recognized by American scholars.

The meaning of the 1896 alignment can be tested by asking: Who was excluded from power? Against whom was it directed? What emerges from this inquiry is the realization that there were two contradictory and inconsistent conflicts going on in American politics at the turn of the century. The Bryan-Democratic-Populist attack on business Republicanism cut squarely across the North-South alignment. The result was a conflict of conflicts in which the antagonists in one contest joined hands and exchanged partners in the other. Thus, in spite of the fact that the southern Bourbons and the northern Republican conservatives were able to organize politics about a sectional conflict that aligned one against the other, they shared a strong antagonism to the agrarian radicals everywhere. The relation between the two conservative minorities whose importance and power were based on the 1896 alignment was one of antagonistic interdependence in the face of a common enemy. The establishment of the sectional alignment of 1896 is the best example in American history of the successful substitution of one conflict for another. The radicals were defeated because the conflict they sought to exploit was subordinated to an inconsistent and overriding cleavage which split the radical movement, isolated the southern and western radicals from each other, and overwhelmed both wings of their movement in one-party sectional areas. On the other hand, the conservatives won power because they were able to impose on the country the conflict which divided the people as they wanted them to be divided.

TABLE 1

Year	Republican	Democratic
1876........	4,036,298	4,300,590
1880........	4,454,416	4,444,952
1884........	4,854,891	4,914,986
1888........	5,439,853	5,540,329

The impact of the alignment of 1896 on American politics was visible throughout the system. Before 1896 the two major parties were able to compete on remarkably equal terms throughout the country. Table 1 suggests the nature of the party equilibrium in the two decades before 1896 in the popular vote for president from 1876 to 1888.

Even in 1892, in spite of the Populist candidacy of General Weaver, the difference between the Democratic and Republican presidential vote was only 380,000 in a total of about 12,000,000.

The effect of the crisis of 1896 on the distribution of the popular support of the two major parties is shown by a comparison of the party vote in 1892 and 1896 in a number of states outside the Solid South (Table 2).

Thus the crisis of 1896 destroyed the balance of the party system. In 1892

there were thirty-six states in which a competitive party situation existed. By 1904 there remained only six states in which the parties were evenly matched, while there were twenty-nine states in which the parties were so unbalanced that the situation could no longer be described as competitive.

TABLE 2

State	1892	1896
Connecticut.....	D 82,395 R 77,025	D 56,740 R 110,285
Illinois..........	D 426,281 R 399,288	D 464,523 R 607,148
New Hampshire..	D 42,081 R 45,658	D 21,271 R 57,444
New Jersey......	D 171,042 R 156,068	D 133,675 R 221,367
New York.......	D 654,868 R 609,350	D 551,369 R 819,838
Pennsylvania....	D 452,264 R 516,011	D 427,125 R 728,300
Rhode Island....	D 24,335 R 26,972	D 14,459 R 37,437
Wisconsin.......	D 177,335 R 170,791	D 165,523 R 268,135

TABLE 3

State	1884	1904
South Carolina.....	21,733	2,570
Florida............	28,031	8,314
Alabama...........	59,591	22,472
Mississippi........	43,509	3,280
Louisiana..........	46,347	5,205

The decline of party competition was more marked in the South than it was elsewhere. Thus in 1884, before the Populist invasion, the Republican vote was less than half the Democratic vote in only three states—South Carolina, Texas, and Georgia. The extent to which the formation of the Solid South cut down the Republican vote in the southern states is shown in Table 3 comparing the Republican vote in 1884 and 1904.

Not only did the development of the sectional alignment after 1896 curtail party competition in large areas of the United States but it reduced interest and participation in elections sharply. In the South the decline of the total vote cast is shown by the comparison of the vote in 1884 and 1904 given in Table 4.

Sectionalism had a somewhat similar effect throughout the country. For example, there were fourteen states outside of the Solid South in which the total vote cast was less in 1904 than in 1896. It is profoundly symptomatic of the condition of politics after 1896 that

TABLE 4

State	1884	1904
Louisiana........	108,887	54,947
Mississippi.......	120,019	58,721
South Carolina...	91,623	55,670
Texas............	318,450	233,919
Virginia..........	324,853	130,842

the election of 1904 (1) produced the first popular landslide in American history and (2) did so in a declining total vote.

While the Republican monopoly of politics in the North was a little less obvious than the Democratic monopoly in the southern states, the results were much the same. The strength of the Republican party in the thirty-one states outside the South and the border states is demonstrated by the fact that (apart from the three-party election in 1912 and a few residues of the Populist fusion in 1896 and 1900) the Democrats won only nineteen state victories out of a total of two hundred and twenty-six states contests in eight presidential elections between 1896 and 1932. In other words, the Democratic party usually carried the Solid South, it carried the border states occasional-

ly, but, on the average, it carried only about two states per election among the thirty-one states in the North and West from 1896 to 1932.

The effect of the big Republican monopoly in the North and the little Democratic monopoly in the South on American democracy was devastating. Party competition was appreciable in the border states and was sometimes important in New York, Ohio, and Indiana; but the contests elsewhere in the United States were nearly always so one-sided that the voters had no significant alternative. In other words, the spread of one-party areas meant that in 1904 less than one-seventh of the population of the United States lived in states in which the parties contested the election on relatively equal terms, while in 1920 only about 12 million out of 105 million Americans lived in states in which they had a choice between two major parties both of which had some prospect of winning. Under these circumstances the Republican party had such good prospects of remaining in power permanently that there was no effective way to make it responsible either to the nation as a whole or to the rank and file of its own party membership.[14]

Other consequences of the 1896 alignment appeared throughout the party system. *Sectionalism tends strongly to depress party organization* because elections in a sectional alignment are won not by competing with a rival **party** but by eliminating it in certain areas. Thus after 1896 there were large areas

14. It is significant that the movement to establish the direct primary system began almost immediately after the election of 1896 as voters attempted to recapture some of the ground lost in that election. Needless to say, the direct primary never has been an adequate substitute for a competitive party system. The only effective remedy for the reduction of the area of political competition produced by the 1896 alignment was to break up the sectional system.

of the North in which the Democratic party virtually ceased to exist or was carried on as a paper organization which nominated few local candidates and kept alive only a microscopic party registration. In large areas of the North, Democratic representation in state legislatures diminished sharply or became nearly extinct. In other places weak local Democratic organizations were absorbed by powerful Republican machines, which took on a slightly bipartisan character as a double insurance against attack. All that has been said about the Democratic party in the North was doubly true of the Republican party in the South. On the other hand, the dominant party organizations, both North and South, became the administrators of the local and regional political monopolies. Thus the condition of party organization reflected the function of policties in a strongly marked sectional party alignment.

Why did the American people tolerate this political system? Only a major political upheaval could have disrupted the alignment, and the raw materials for a national (antisectional) combination to develop an alternative policy of strong national action did not exist. Edward Channing wrote in 1908 that the American people did not constitute a national community. No basis for a strong feeling of national unity existed either in a common national sense of danger from without or in any national domestic crisis from within. The Republican assumption that the economy was able to run itself indefinitely with only incidental and minimal interference by the national government was widely accepted by Democrats and Republicans alike. The truth is that the sectional party alignment was unfavorable to the development and exploitation of new alternatives in public affairs. How little basis was developed during the generation following 1896 for a strong national party opposition may be seen in the following summary of the state of public affairs:

1. The national domain. (Much of it had been given away; what was left did not excite the kind of interest needed to create a national party system, and must have seemed remote to the ordinary citizen.)

2. Foreign policy. (This was not the object of a continuing strong popular interest.)

3. Southern racial policy. (The Republican party tacitly accepted the idea that it was a local southern problem and was willing to abandon energetic federal measures to force the South to change its system. See President Taft's inaugural address of 1908.)

4. Protective tariff. (Industry and industrial labor as a whole accepted the policy; only the South was opposed.)

5. Currency and central banking. (This was not a great popular issue after 1896.)

6. Antagonism to Wall Street and big business. (Chiefly an agrarian issue that could not be exploited effectively because the opposition was unable to unite after 1896.)

7. Federal taxation. (Ordinary people were unconscious of federal taxes.)

8. People did not associate the federal government with welfare programs. (Unemployment compensation, price stabilization, social security, public housing, socialized medicine, etc., were unheard of.)

9. Labor and agriculture were largely unorganized.

A different kind of party system might have exploited the issues of American politics more successfully, but there was nothing much about the way in which public policy was allowed to develop that made necessary or even possible a major popular assault on the dominant sectional alignment.

The differences between British and

American parties noted by President Lowell in 1900 were probably related to the fact that the anxieties, hazards, and tensions involved in the management of the British Empire in an era of continuing diplomatic crisis were of an entirely different magnitude from the relatively unexciting matters to which the attention of the government of the United States was restricted.

The formal structures of the Republican and Democratic parties were roughly alike, but that is as far as the similarity goes. On the other hand, while the two historic major parties in the United States have long been profoundly different technically, it is impossible to understand one without the other. The Democratic party before 1932 was a loose combination of the Solid South and certain urban machines in the North and with some scattered Populist rural remnants in the West. A more incongruous and less promising political combination is hard to imagine. The Republican split in 1912 made it possible for the Democrats to come into power during an interlude in the long Republican tenure of power, but aside from this interval it can hardly be said that the Democratic party contemplated the prospect of coming into power nationally or that it had a well-developed conception of what it might do if it came into power. This is almost inevitably the condition of an opposition in a party alignment in which sectionalism is so accentuated that a regular alternation of the parties in power is impossible. The most substantial achievement of the Democratic party from 1896 to 1932 was that it kept itself alive as the only party to which the country could turn if it ever decided to overthrow the Republican party. Considering the circumstances and the consequences of the achievement, the long-sustained status of the Democratic party as *the* opposition proves something about the viability of the two-party system in the United States.

IV / The Revolution of 1932

This roughly was the status of the two major parties on the eve of the revolution of 1932. In 1932 the country, in the midst of a great depression, used the Democratic party to produce the greatest reversal of public policy in American history. This happened not because the Democratic party was an ideal vehicle for a revolution but because it was the only political instrument available. The election of 1932 was much more than the defeat of a political party; it was something very much like the overthrow of a ruling class, and the function of the Democratic party in the 1930's can be understood only as the somewhat reluctant and confused instrument of a revolution it did not plan and did not produce. It is hard to imagine a party less prepared for these responsibilities than the Democratic party was at the time of Franklin D. Roosevelt's first inaugural. The mere fact, however, that the country used the Democratic party to turn the Republican party out of power in the first real party turnover in more than a generation contributed greatly to the development of the idea of a *responsible* party system and was certain to give rise to a new concept of the uses of the system.

The Democratic party felt the full impact of the revolution in the functions of the political system because it came into power with the crisis. Even a casual comparison of the policy of the Democratic party before and after the election of Franklin D. Roosevelt will show how great the difference was between the old and the new functions of the party.

What was the policy of the Democratic party during the thirty-six-year period from 1896 to 1932? A glance at the Democratic party platform of 1912 on the eve of the eléction of Woodrow Wilson is sufficient to show what the party was thinking about. In 1912 Democrats talked about the preservation of the rights of the states and condemned as "usurpation" the efforts of the Republican party "to enlarge and magnify by indirection the powers of the Federal government." They argued that the protective tariff was unconstitutional. The general attitude of the party toward the function and scope of the national government is implied in their criticism of "the profligate waste of money wrung from the people by oppressive taxation through lavish appropriations which have kept taxes high and reduced the purchasing power of the people's toil." (Expenditures by the federal government in 1912 were about two-thirds of a billion dollars.)

Otherwise the Democratic party declared its support of the system of separation of powers and came out for the direct election of senators, for a presidential primary, and for a constitutional amendment limiting the president to one term. In other major areas of public policy the program may be summarized as follows:

1. *Labor.*—It wanted to restrict the use of injunctions, favored the creation of a Department of Labor, and advocated a federal employees' compensation act "as far as the federal jurisdiction extends."

2. *Agriculture.*—It sought an extension of rural credits, expansion of rural free delivery of mail, and opposed gambling in agricultural commodities.

3. *Business.*—The Democratic party wanted to reduce tariffs, tighten antitrust laws and the regulation of railroad rates, favored development of waterways and conservation of natural resources, and opposed the creation of a central bank dominated by the "money trust."

4. *Social services.*—Democrats wanted a parcel post system and favored establishment of a single national health agency, but socialized medicine was unheard of.

5. *Foreign policy.*—The Democratic party supported the Monroe Doctrine and urged a cautious expansion of the Navy.

It is true that the party supported the income tax amendment to the Constitution, but it is highly improbable that it foresaw the uses to which this new form of taxation would be put a generation later.

This summary of the platform is not made to show that the Democratic party has been inconsistent but to illustrate the thesis that there has been a profound and overwhelming change in the content and function of American politics. Furthermore, an examination of the platforms of 1912 shows how little difference there was between the Republican and the Democratic parties. The truth is that the Democratic party offered no comprehensive alternative to the broad outlines of the policies established by the dominant Republican-business coalition.

An analysis of the operations of American government before World War I shows that political discussion as illustrated in the party platforms of 1912 did not deviate greatly from the actual condition of public policy. In 1915 the government spent $760,000,-000, of which about one-third went to the armed forces and an almost equal amount to support the civil functions of the government, while another third was spent on veterans, refunds, interest, and debt retirement. Indeed, the government had not yet got around to adopting a budget system.

Less than 2,000 persons were sent to federal prisons in 1915 convicted of offenses such as counterfeiting and forgery, drug-act violations, immigration-act offenses, or violation of the interstate commerce act, liquor laws, the

Mann Act, and the postal laws. The new income tax hardly scratched the surface of the economy: 337,000 persons made returns and paid a total of $41,000,000. The armed forces in 1915 totaled 161,992 men.

Apart from the postal service and the management of the currency, the federal government touched directly only a few categories of people: its own employees, importers, interstate processors and dealers in certain foods and drugs, physicians and druggists who handled narcotics, the liquor business, the managers of interstate railroads, Indians, people engaged in navigation, people who handled excise taxes, certain contractors engaged in federal public works, immigrants, corporation lawyers and financiers interested in mergers and trusts, and a few counterfeiters and white slavers.

It is hardly necessary to document the proposition that the change in public policy that followed the 1932 election was the greatest in American history. The very power and scope of the Republican system made it certain that a major upheaval of policy would result from the overthrow of the party. Moreover, the New Deal itself was shortly swamped by an even greater revolution in foreign policy arising from World War II and its consequences. The cumulative effect of two revolutions has been to make over the whole agenda of government and to create a new base for public policy in the political alignments that have appeared since 1932. The number of people involved in public affairs has increased tremendously as a consequence of the policy revolution. What are likely to be the long-range political consequences of the fact that the social security system reaches 62,000,000, or that 13½ million young men are registered for selective service, or that 35½ million people pay income taxes, or that

the soil conservation system covers 5,000,000 farms?

The election of 1932 deserves to be called a "revolution" because it destroyed something very much like a permanent Republican lease of power; it was no ordinary election, and the overthrow of the Republican party was no ordinary alternation of the parties in power. The elections of the 1930's *substituted a national political alignment for an extreme sectional alignment everywhere in the country except in the South.* Graphically the nationalization of American politics can be seen in the flattening of the curve showing the percentage distribution of the major party vote outside the South. Statistically, the flattening of the curve can be expressed in terms of the percentage of the major party vote polled by the Democratic party in each of the states, taking into account the deviation from 50 per cent in each case. (Thus 44 and 55 per cent represent deviations of 6 and 5 per cent, respectively.) In the election of 1908 in twenty-nine states in the North and West (not counting Arizona and New Mexico, which did not vote) the Democratic percentage of the major party vote deviated a total of 283.8 points from 50 per cent. Twenty years later the total deviation was 312.1. By 1944, however, the figure had declined to 124 points. In other words, the 1944 curve was almost three times as flat as the 1928 curve. This is only another way of saying that there has been a sharp decline in the number of one-party states in the North and West. Thus in 1944, outside the South and the border, the Democratic party polled more than 60 per cent or less than 40 per cent of the major party vote in only two states, and a shift of 3 per cent of the major party vote would have changed the result in seventeen states.

The figures for the elections of the New Deal era suggest that these elections were dominated by factors working on a national scale. The result was a very great extension of the area of effective political competition.

Against this background, what did the election of 1952 do to the party alignment? It did nothing to reverse the nationalizing tendency of American politics and gave no indication whatever of a tendency to return to the old sectional pattern of politics. As a matter of fact, General Eisenhower's success in the South represents an extension of the nationalizing tendency. Whatever else may be said about the election, it was dominated by national influences. *The direction and the scope of the cleavage between the major parties have remained stable in spite of the party turnover. As a consequence, we are, for the first time in American history, within striking distance of a competitive two-party system in forty-eight states.*

V / THE NEW DEMOCRATIC PARTY

All that has happened to the structure and operations of the Democratic party since 1932 may be described as an effort of the party to adapt itself to its new role. The "purge" of 1938, coming on top of a series of Roosevelt landslides, resulted from the discovery that the program of the party required a kind of control of its congressional party never before attempted by an American party. The Democratic party was compelled by the nature of its new function to win the power required to push through the government a general program implicating the whole apparatus of government. The split between the northern and the southern wings of the party and the conflict between the President and Congress were aspects of the new status and function of the party. The familiar party institutions in Congress (the speakership, seniority,

the committee system, the filibuster) were unsuited to the needs of a party responsible for the formulation and execution of a program of governmental action as ambitious as the New Deal. For these purposes, success in presidential elections and a paper majority in Congress were not enough. The logic of the situation called for a functioning congressional majority co-operating closely with the executive as a top-level political team.

The repeal of the two-thirds rule for making presidential nominations and the "purge" of 1938 were merely the first fumbling gestures toward the making of a new kind of party system. The change in the character of the party became evident on all sides. From 1924 to 1936 the Democratic vote more than doubled. The position of the Solid South in the party was altered beyond recognition by the fact that in four successive elections Mr. Roosevelt proved that he did not need the support of the southern wing of the party to be elected; in each of these elections he would have won with one hundred electoral votes to spare if he had received no votes at all south of the Mason-Dixon line. Altogether, twenty years of Democratic government marked the emergence of the Democratic party as the political instrument of a new electorate committed to and supporting a revolution in a public policy. Not the least significant evidence of this transformation of the system has been the conversion of the labor movement to party politics.

Mr. Truman's successful campaign in 1948, waged almost wholly on the record of the Eightieth Congress, accomplished even more than the "purge" of 1938 in concentrating public attention on the problems of party organization and responsibility for the overall management of public policy. The emphasis in public discussion on the political role of Congress and the unprecedented efforts made by the parties in recent "off"-year congressional elections suggest that Congress is moving into the focus of politics, proving that the control of Congress has become crucial to party strategy. The agitation to abolish or reform the Electoral College, the attempt to reduce the powers of the House Committee on Rules, the continuing agitation to do away with the Senate filibuster, the expansion of the permanent staff of the National Committee, the proposal that the parties hold biennial national conventions, and the contest over the rules of the Democratic National Convention in 1952 indicate that the effort to create a new kind of national party organization continues.

The reorganization of the Republican party in recent years differs in some respects from that on the other side. Only when a full-fledged two-party system develops in the old Solid South will the Republican party deal with the problem of creating new organizations where mere paper organizations existed previously. On the other hand, the Republican party has felt the consequences of the decline of the local party bosses; it has been confronted with the pressures of national campaigning; it has been involved in intensified national campaigns for the control of Congress; and it has found it necessary to work closely with business interests now organized on a national basis. The impact on the Republican party of the nationalization of politics is illustrated by the fact that the Eisenhower-Taft contest for the presidential nomination in 1952 produced some kind of split in thirty-eight of the state delegations at the Republican National Convention. In this contest Mr. Eisenhower drew delegate support from forty states, and Mr. Taft was supported by delegates from forty-three states.

VI / The Nationalization of Politics

What is likely to be the effect of the nationalization of politics on the frequency with which the parties alternate in power? The question is important because the parties cannot be held responsible to the public if one of the parties is in power permanently while the other is permanently out of power. The development of a competitive two-party system in all parts of the United States makes it possible (and probably necessary) for the opposition party to develop an alternative national policy designed to appeal to a national constituency. It is probably impossible for the opposition to avoid this development, because the problems of the party in power are now so difficult that the demand for vigorous opposition is likely to be great. So long as the party alignment was sharply sectional, the opposition could do little more than intensify the sectional cleavage; but the more sharply the sectional alignment was drawn, the more deeply the party in power became intrenched. Thus sectionalism produced alignments which could rarely be overthrown by merely sectional attacks. Therefore, every sectional assault on the Republican party before 1932 served merely to increase the margin of superiority of the Republican party in the great populous regions in which it was supreme, while it tended at the same time to intensify Democratic supremacy in the South. In a political system in which one great bloc of states confronts another bloc of states no ordinary shift of opinion is likely to have any important political effect. A general shift of the vote has little effect, because the margin of superiority of each of the parties in its own sectional base is so great that no ordinary movement of voters can overturn the results. This is not true in a national party alignment, where a shift of a few per cent of the voters is likely to produce the greatest possible consequences. From 1896 to 1932 the sectional alignment was so one-sided that an alternation of the parties in power was substantially impossible. *One of the most significant consequences of the nationalization of politics in the last twenty years, therefore, has been the increased likelihood of a relatively frequent alternation of the parties in power.*

TABLE 5

DEMOCRATIC VOTE IN CERTAIN NORTHERN AND WESTERN STATES IN 1924 AND 1952

State	1924	1952
1. Connecticut	110,184	481,649
2. Pennsylvania	409,192	2,146,269
3. Michigan	152,359	1,230,657
4. Illinois	576,975	2,013,920
5. Wisconsin	68,115	622,175
6. Minnesota	55,913	608,458
7. California	105,514	2,197,548
8. Ohio	477,887	1,600,367
9. Massachusetts	280,831	1,083,525
10. New Jersey	279,743	1,015,092
11. North Dakota	13,858	76,694
12. Washington	42,842	492,845
Total	2,573,413	13,569,199

The consequences of an increase in the rate of party alternation in power may be important. First, the party in power must now realize that it can always be turned out on short notice. Party leaders have been slow to understand the implications of this situation. What the potentialities of the new alignment are is suggested by the sharp reaction of both political parties to Democratic gains in congressional and local elections in October and November, 1953, only a year after the Eisenhower landslide of 1952. It is inconceivable that the reaction of the parties to this development would have been so immediate and so intense if party leaders had not become aware of the fact that a relatively small shift of opinion is now able to produce a party

overturn. It is difficult to exaggerate the probable impact of this development on the programs, the organization, the responsibilities, and the reputation and importance of the major parties. The election of 1954 justified forecasts, based on the local 1953 elections, of the new sensitivity of the political system to changes in political trends. Meanwhile, the erosion of the old sectional alignment is shown by the redistribution of the vote seen in Tables 5 and 6.

The nationalization of politics, by increasing the likelihood of relatively frequent alternations of the parties in power, greatly enhances the importance of elections and of electioneering political organizations. It is therefore

TABLE 6

REPUBLICAN VOTE IN ELEVEN SOUTHERN STATES IN 1924 AND 1952

State	1924	1952
1. Virginia	73,328	306,925
2. North Carolina	190,754	558,107
3. South Carolina	1,123	168,082
4. Georgia	30,300	198,979
5. Florida	30,633	544,036
6. Tennessee	130,831	446,147
7. Alabama	42,823	149,231
8. Mississippi	8,494	112,966
9. Arkansas	40,583	177,155
10. Louisiana	24,670	306,925
11. Texas	130,194	1,102,878
Total	703,733	4,071,431

noteworthy that the presidential vote continued to rise from 29,000,000 to more than 61,000,000 between 1924 and 1952; for, if the one-party areas in a sectional alignment tend to discourage political participation, a great extension of the area of competition is likely to have the opposite effect.

The universality of political trends is a good index of the nationalization of the political system. Does the same trend appear throughout the country, or do conflicting trends appear in the various geographical areas of the country? In a sectional political alignment one might expect to find Democratic and Republican trends appearing simultaneously in the various sections of the country. Thus in 1904 the Republican party won by a popular landslide, but conflicting tendencies appeared in the vote. While the Republican party gained ground in twenty-six states, it lost ground in nineteen. In other words, the election of 1904 produced opposing trends in the South and the North.

We ought to suspect that something has happened to the political system when we observe that the Republican party gained ground in *every* state in 1952 and lost ground in forty-five states and gained in only two states in 1954. The trends appearing in these elections are remarkably national in scope. Moreover, the nationalization of politics does not seem to have been affected by the fact that there has been a double party overturn in these elections. An examination of the 1954 returns shows the extent to which American politics is now conducted within the limits of the 60–40 per cent party split. In this election the Democratic party polled less than 40 per cent of the vote in only two states and (outside the South) polled more than 60 per cent in none. It is no mere chance that observers gained the impression in November, 1954, that elections everywhere were won and lost by unprecedentedly narrow margins, because that is what a national alignment is apt to look like.

What is the impact of the nationalization of politics on party organization likely to be? It is not easy to describe a party system in transition. The reorganization of the American party system is largely a matter of developing new competing organizations in states that, until recently, were dominated by a one-party system. This process goes on at different rates throughout the country and at the various levels of government. Commentators have noted

that Republican gains in the South in the 1952 election did not produce a reorganization of politics at the local level, but party reorganization throughout the old one-party states in the North and West since 1932 has regularly developed first in presidential elections. The cutting edge of the transition has been at the national level.

Nor is formal organization the whole story. A demoralized local minority needs leadership, and it takes time to develop leadership. Often it has been necessary to destroy bipartisan local political organizations which had long held the minority party in captivity. In the case of these bipartisan local machines (they were almost as universal as the boss system itself) it has been necessary for the minority party to recapture its own organization before it could begin to contest the elections seriously. Above all, it takes time for submerged and depressed local party organizations to develop morale.

It is obvious that a nationalized political system calls for a very different kind of organization from that required in a sectional alignment. More precisely, a national alignment creates a demand for political organization throughout the country, whereas sectionalism depresses national organizations. What has therefore happened since 1932 has been a great extension of organization (especially by the minority party) into the newly developed two-party regions. In the case of the Democratic party this has meant the development of state and local organizations in wide areas of the United States where only paper organizations existed before 1932. To a great extent the stimulus has come from national sources, the Democratic National Committee, organized labor, and national citizens' movements.

The attack on the old local power monopolies (the earmark of sectionalism) is illustrated by the fact that the old lines of demarcation between the functions of the national, state, and local governments have been greatly blurred in recent years. To a great extent (in health, housing, education, highways, welfare, police, civil defense, race relations, etc.) American government at all levels now participates in the formation of public policy. As a consequence, political movements which are blocked at one level of government merely seek another level at which to push their programs. By this competition of the levels of government the old local power monopolies are likely to be greatly embarrassed. It is necessary only to observe the consequences of the development of a national race relations policy to see how important this process has become. The old strategy was to insist that the problem was exclusively local and could be attacked only on the chosen local battlefield, where the old local political monopolies were well intrenched. The obstacles to be overcome in bringing the *whole* government into the political system are formidable (rotten borough systems, rural overrepresentation in state legislatures, a chaotic governmental organization of metropolitan areas, the lack of state leadership in the development of local government policies, and the indoctrination of the public with ideas about nonpartisan local government). It can hardly be said that the concept of local government as an instrument of social policy even exists in the public mind today. Even the scholarly study of politics tends strongly to be one-dimensional, i.e., they treat national elections as if they were the sole dimension of politics. This whole discussion deals with the organization of politics in depth, at all levels of government, because the execution of modern policy involves the use of the whole government.

Moreover, in a nationalized political system, local party organization is never a purely local matter (to the extent that it can ever be safely neglected), because national interests may be defeated by weak local organizations anywhere in the country—a state may be lost because some small-town organizations did not mobilize their vote, and the country may be lost because a close state is lost. Moreover, we seem to be moving into a political alignment in which a little difference in any state is likely to have an important effect on the political control of the whole country.

One of the difficulties we have in understanding what is happening to the party system is that formal party organizations are not greatly affected by political change; a shift in the locus of power or a revision of party functions may leave the formal structure untouched, or new structures may arise without being recognized as parts of the party system. Thus pressure groups may become so partisan that they might properly be described as ancillary organizations of one or the other of the major parties.

Has the organization of American parties changed in fact? The Democratic party today is a new party, vastly different from the party that nominated John W. Davis in 1924. Since 1924 it has more than doubled in size. It has developed effective organizations, as measured by party registration, primary votes, etc., in large areas of the United States in which it had only a paper organization thirty years ago. The center of gravity of the party has moved from the Solid South to the great industrial states of the North. It has become involved in a great new party struggle for the control of Congress, tending strongly to draw congressional candidates into the national party conflict. This development is to affect the responsibility of these candidates to the party system. Finally, the labor movement has become involved in

Democratic party politics, in fact if not in theory. On the Republican side there has been so great a mobilization of economic groups and financial resources within the party that the formal committee structure reveals very little about that actual locus of power.

One of the discoveries made in a recent study of this question[15] is that "very few of the state political conventions of 1952 were within the grip of a recognized political boss." This conclusion is important because it is based on the first comprehensive national survey of American politics ever made. Evidence of the decline of the local party boss suggests that a profound change in the character of the party system has already taken place. It involves a shift in the locus of power within the party system; indeed, it involves a changed concept of power itself. Considering the central role played by the local boss in the literature of American politics it now seems likely that the whole body of traditional propositions descriptive of the political system must be revised.

The truth is that the old local party boss is inadequate to meet the demands made on the party system today. He is organized to do the wrong things, is incurably local, finds it impossible to organize on the scale now necessary, and is unable to utilize the new resources of the parties. Above all, he cannot endure competition.

The major parties are now the most highly competitive large-scale organizations in American society, more competitive than business (which usually competes marginally) or the churches or the labor unions. The area and scale of party competition have been expanded greatly by the extension of the two-party system and by the establish-

ment of the conditions for a much more rapid alternation of the parties in power.[16] Competition on this scale provides powerful incentives for organization. It tends strongly to draw all political organizations, i.e., the pressure groups, Congress, etc., into the vortex of party conflict.

Party organization today consists of the regular organizations, both legal and extralegal, plus ancillary organizations, which are theoretically neutral but often deeply involved in party conflict, and "citizen" or "volunteer" organizations designed to mobilize large bodies of partisans whom the regular organizations are unable to absorb. Thus labor political organizations such as CIO-PAC and Labor's League for Political Education engage in activities that parallel closely the functions of the regular Democratic organization in getting out the vote, raising money, and propaganda. The very existence of these ancillary political organizations has modified greatly the behavior of the regular party organizations.

The bad reputation of the parties in the United States has been an aspect of sectionalism, chiefly because sectionalism produced irresponsible parties. A whole family of antiparty ideas and devices has resulted from this condition. The glorification of the "independent" voter (i.e., a voter who rejects both parties), the concept of nonpartisanship, which was at the base of a great variety of proposals for reform, the direct primary (showing a lack of confidence in party leaders in one-party areas), and an almost endless series of attempts to divorce local and national politics—all illustrate this tendency. At every point parties and par-

15. Paul T. David, Malcolm Moose, and Ralph M. Goldman (eds.), *Presidential Nominating Politics, 1952* (Baltimore: Johns Hopkins Press, 1954).

16. Estimates of the expenditures of the major parties in the election of 1952 run as high as $200,000,000 (see Victoria Schuck, "The High Cost of Campaigning," *New Republic*, May 16, 1955). A lot of organizing can be done for $200,000,000!

tisanship have been treated as evils to be extirpated or repressed. To understand this attitude toward the party system, it is necessary to remember that it is a product of the sectional alignment following the election of 1896. The criticism of the system is formulated in language which seems to condemn all partisanship for all time but is, in fact, directed at a special form of partisan alignment which frustrated a generation of Americans. Conversely, the destruction of the old sectional alignment is likely to compel thoughtful people to revise their opinions of the party system and to produce a re-examination of the characteristic antiparty concepts and measures of the first third of the century.

At this point of radical transformations it would be mistaken and misleading prematurely to draw definite lines of demarcation for the newly evolving American party system; yet a careful check of this exciting development becomes a paramount task for the responsible student of public affairs in our time. No doubt the mounting material findings will confirm the rising significance of the political parties in this increasingly enlarged domain of American politics at home and abroad. The major parties have become the crucial and competing channels of policy formation in our national democracy. Whatever their changing organizational patterns and their pronounced policies may be, they are here to stay.

THE TOTALITARIAN COUNTERPART

The U.S.S.R.: Monolithic Controls at Home and Abroad

FREDERICK C. BARGHOORN
Yale University

I / STRUCTURE AND FUNCTIONS OF THE SOVIET PARTY-STATE

Stalin's death on March 5, 1953, removed a major element of the Soviet system and made the nature and study of Soviet politics even more complex and obscure. It is clear after two years, however, that the continuity with Stalinism and Leninism is far more important than the changes which have occurred thus far. A regime ended, a system survived. But Stalinism without Stalin may yet produce more profound changes than the dramatic developments of the last two years. Let us survey briefly these developments before discussing the system which produced them.

The post-Stalin period has already had its Beria, Malenkov, and Khrushchev stages. While Beria, Stalin's police chief since 1938, never became head of either party or state, he was until his arrest in June, 1953, perhaps the most dynamic of the leaders who replaced the ruthless dictator. Four men —Malenkov, Khrushchev, Molotov, and Beria—dominated the "collective leadership." The post-Stalin leadership instituted more flexible and sensible policies than those of the dread *Vozhd* ("fuehrer"). Some of the idiosyncrasies associated with Stalin's conspiratorial habits seemed to be on the way out. Indicative of this, for example, was the new business-like nine-to-six office day decreed on September 1, 1953, which ended Stalin's practice of calling his colleagues or foreign ambassadors to discuss business in the middle of the night.

But no significant changes occurred in the basic power structure and its system of controls. "Collective leadership" partially masked the raw struggle for power at the party pinnacle; hence informed foreigners and, we may be sure, Soviet citizens, whose future depended on guessing right, asked a number of questions: Would there be further purges? Of what scope and on what levels? To what new mixture of strengths and weaknesses was the post-Stalin group leading? How long could the Soviet system function without a single supreme arbiter-autocrat? The boldest guesses were made by Isaac Deutscher, who saw ahead, under certain conditions, an era of reform (in *Russia, What Next?*). In view of the record since November, 1917 (October, Old Style), most analysts were skeptical about early changes toward a less oppressive system.

A warning signal was the quiet ruthlessness in the elimination of Beria and his collaborators, largely fellow-Georgians, from their top posts in the political hierarchy. This had been preceded by the less spectacular, but highly significant, "voluntary" resignation of Malenkov from the post of first secretary of the party Central Committee on March 14, 1953. In September Khrushchev was confirmed as first secretary at a regular plenary session of the Central Committee, and following that the curious balance of power between party and state which characterized Soviet internal politics prevailed until Malenkov's public confession of incompetence and resignation as chairman of the Council of Ministers on February 8, 1955.

From the beginning, Soviet sources indicated impressively that the successor regime was dedicated to Stalinism. The capsule party history published on July 26, 1953, for example, was a thoroughly Stalinist document, although it shrewdly played down the name of Stalin, even lifting key passages from his *Problems of Leninism* without proper acknowledgment.[1] In the fall of 1953 appeared a new edition of the basic work, *The Communist Party in Resolutions*, in which, together with the textbook on political economy published in 1954 and the still venerated Stalinist "short course" on party history (1938), the integrity of Stalinist doctrine is intrenched.

On the other hand, the numerous developments, particularly the emphasis on increased productivity of consumers' goods, outlined in Malenkov's address to the Supreme Soviet on August 8, 1953, indicated that something new had been added to Stalinism, although observers wondered whether this was mere gesture or actual reform. Increased concern over popular welfare, together with the repudiation of the "doctors' plot" concocted by Stalin to stir up anti-Semitism to justify a new blood purge and the increased prominence of marshals like Zhukov, heralded portentous changes. All during 1954 there was evidence of strain in the new ruling groups. The crisis in Soviet agriculture brought increasing prominence

1. "Fifty Years of the Communist Party of the Soviet Union (1903–1953)." The dates are significant. Leninism and bolshevism date from the second party congress in 1903, although Lenin had laid many of the doctrinal foundations earlier, notably in his most important work, *What Is To Be Done* (1902).

to Khrushchev, and he began to overshadow Malenkov completely, analysts speculating as to whether the party secretariat was not still, as in the Stalin era, the real powerhouse of the Soviet system.

The events of February, 1955, furnished a temporary answer. At the initiative of Khrushchev, the "political" soldier, Bulganin, became head of the state, and a "real" soldier, Zhukov, became minister of defense. But age and instability still characterized the top ruling circle. The death of Stalin has set in motion forces which will almost certainly bring new surprises, but we can feel reasonably certain that the basic system will fiercely and successfully resist, in the foreseeable future, the pressures for change boiling and seething beneath the surface of enforced unity and harmony.

The only major rival of Stalinist totalitarianism, German National Socialism, never achieved the fusion into the unified, centralized, and remarkably homogeneous organization of all social initiative, skills, and power that was achieved some twenty years ago in the Soviet system. The inner sanctum of the party, the locus of arbitrary and absolute power, is "the Kremlin," a term which refers to the small group of self-chosen individuals who make party policy and who control the definition and distribution of values in the party and in the society which the party center dominates.

Another major meaning of the term "Communist party" is that of a vast, but elite and exclusive, organization of close to seven million persons, including all, or nearly all, members of Soviet society who possess any significant measure of power, privilege, or distinction. The major achievement of the Stalinist era was building and wielding this mass party as an instrument and source of cadres of the dictatorship.

The party has absorbed the state; the state now acts as its administrative arm in shaping and ruling society.

This situation was realized in its essentials by 1939. The eighteenth party congress in March, 1939, abolished discrimination against entry into the party of persons who were not of working-class or peasant origin. Rapid, state-directed industrialization during the five-year plans, under way since 1928, and the accompanying development of a vast state machinery and economic bureaucracy under Bolshevik control was the most important of the forces which created modern Soviet communism. The "Stalin constitution" of 1936 embodied this development. The great purges during 1936–38 represented a mopping-up operation against the Bolshevik idealist of the Bukharin type who could not adjust to this mixture of despotism and state monopoly capitalism.[2] The nineteenth party congress in October, 1952, carried still further the process of totalitarianization. The party statutes adopted at the nineteenth congress eliminated all reference to the leading role of the working class, and party members were described as "like-minded people, Communists" drawn from all segments of the "toiling" population, a change denoting the fusion into a unified and disciplined elite of party, state, and Soviet intelligentsia. Here are the "most advanced" and "best" members of society whom the Kremlin recruits, trains, utilizes, rewards, and punishes by standards alien to those of democracy or, to a lesser degree, of earlier forms of absolutism.

2. In view of the present importance of the nationality problem in Soviet Russia, it is pertinent to note that Bukharin, especially at the twelfth party congress in 1923, always stood up for the rights of non-Russians and in 1937 was excoriated for "slandering" the "Great Russian people."

The present Soviet system would perhaps shock Lenin; yet Stalin was his logical continuator, and their relationship was quite similar to that of Lenin's to Marx in its pattern of pragmatism in action and orthodoxy in belief. Both Lenin and Stalin were extremists and "radicals," both acted with extreme decisiveness and ruthlessness against the "class enemy"—on this basis they both might be considered to be among the most "sincere" of Marxists. But their very radicalism led them to take actions from which other more rational, humane, or sophisticated Bolsheviks shrank. This helps to explain why Lenin and Stalin could so vehemently accuse their opponents of "opportunism": their extreme pragmatism did not seem unscrupulous to them because they firmly believed that their ends justified any expedient means. Ruthless pursuit of ill-defined ends by dubious means led to the redefinition, the distortion, and, in effect, the repudiation of the values for which the Russian revolution was fought. The result is the triumph of political machinery over man's individuality. The administrator-politician-policeman becomes the dominant type in this new society.[3]

The structure and functioning of the political organization through which the holders of political power dominate Soviet society is the center about which the history of bolshevism revolves. The structure of Soviet society has changed kaleidoscopically and will no doubt continue to do so because of the rapid economic development which, despite its static continuity of political leadership and doctrine, makes it unusually dynamic.

3. In this connection it is interesting to note that a party political handbook published in 1950 included in its definition of Communism the mechanization and automatization of production.

II / History of the Communist Party of the Soviet Union

Early Days

Let us glance at the history of the Soviet Communist party. The formal organizational origin of the party dates from 1898, when a small band of Russian social democrats met in Minsk; then at the second congress, which had to flee from Brussels to London in the summer of 1903 because of pressure by the tsarist police on the Belgian government, the Bolshevik and the Menshevik factions emerged. The main difference between Lenin and his Menshevik opponents was that the latter were somewhat aware that Lenin's organization could be a trap from which no democratic or socialist exit would be possible. But Bolsheviks and Mensheviks co-operated, if fitfully, during the stormy 1905 revolution and its somber aftermath. In 1912 Lenin called a Bolshevik conference in Prague which arrogated unto itself leadership of the Russian Social Democratic Labor party to which both Bolsheviks and Mensheviks belonged. The Mensheviks refused to recognize the proceedings of this conference, and, from 1912 on, the two factions were really separate parties, each having its own "fraction" in the fourth Russian Duma (parliament), elected in 1912. Both "fractions," especially the Bolsheviks, were infiltrated by the tsarist secret police.

Lenin, although in exile during most of the entire period from 1900 to his return to St. Petersburg in April, 1917, dominated his party. Inside the Russian empire, underground Bolshevik leaders, such as Kamenev, Krassin, Sverdlov, Stalin, and Molotov, carried on what seemed at that time an unequal struggle against the tsarist secret police. The internal Bolshevik system of leadership was autocratic. Choice of members of the party's leading body, the Central Committee, was eventually by the co-option of Lenin and those who at any given time enjoyed his confidence. Lenin identified himself completely with the party; he was despotic, but he felt that he was acting for the benefit of the party and the working class. This temper and the requirements of conspiracy made a mockery of Lenin's professed belief in democracy, although this did not become fully significant until the Bolsheviks had become a ruling state party.

In time Lenin aroused the distrust not only of the Mensheviks but also of Trotsky and Rosa Luxemburg, the brilliant leader of the Polish Marxist Socialists, when both warned, even before 1905, that Lenin's scheme would lead to the dictatorship of the Central Committee over the party and of the party over the working class. Trotsky, however, shifted his position to support of Lenin in 1917; Lenin, despite previous differences, made Trotsky his right-hand man and, unlike Stalin, did not permit subsequent differences of opinion to sour their relations. In the struggle for Lenin's mantle between Trotsky and other top leaders, however, these differences gave his opponents a powerful weapon.

Lenin paved the way for Stalin's one-man rule in the party and set the pattern for suppressing rival parties. In his very first major decree he boasted of arresting the members of the provisional government; later he illegally dissolved the only truly democratic legislative organ in Russian history, the Constituent Assembly (January, 1918), in which the Bolsheviks were a minority, and subsequently outlawed even the Bolsheviks' only allies, the radical agrarian left SR's and the Mensheviks. Stalin, however, developed a new stage of Bolshevik internal leadership. Lenin dominated the party by his character, his knowledge, and his political wisdom; Stalin, while a more cunning politician and a better organizer than

Lenin, lacked Lenin's charismatic qualities of leadership. Lenin was a despot but derived little pleasure from personal power or its trappings; Stalin craved power and could not tolerate opposition, particularly from those who were his intellectual superiors, resorting to deception, cynical demagogy, intrigue, and eventually murder of most of the surviving members of the original revolutionary leadership in his ruthless struggle for supreme power.

It would be a serious error, however, to attribute the diminution of the values Marx thought socialism would produce solely to the personality and policies of Stalin. To realize this, one has only to imagine what Trotsky, his best-known Communist critic, would have done in his place. The man did contribute much to his times, even if he was the product of the prescientific and predemocratic Russian-Eurasian culture pattern and of the international anarchy of the twentieth-century state system. It is well to ponder all this, now that his successors attempt to carry on from where he left off.

The major factors which produced Stalin, his administrative apparatus, and the political system which he bequeathed intact to his successors were the Marxist-Leninist political sociology, especially Lenin's organizational concepts; the political, economic, cultural, and technological gap between the vast Russian empire and more advanced, but smaller, less populous states; and Soviet Russia's international isolation. Stalin succeeded because he learned to play the roles demanded in this situation. His concept of "socialism in one country" was shaped to enable his regime not only to survive but to become powerful; it faced the realities of international politics and yet appealed at home to the desire for a breathing spell after frightful wars, as well as to latent Russian nationalism. In 1918 Lenin brought about a

change in the name of the Russian Social Democratic Labor party to the Russian Communist party, to emphasize the new Soviet Russia's break with the "reformist," "rotten" Western Social Democrats. In 1925, after the formation of the Soviet Union in 1922 and the ratification of its constitution in 1924, the party's name was changed to All-Union Communist Party of Bolsheviks. The change of name in October, 1952, to Communist Party of the Soviet Union, removing the word "Bolshevik," marked another stage in the suppression of radical Marxist symbols within the Soviet Union, even while retaining them in foreign Communist efforts to subvert non-Soviet society.

The Bolsheviks took over in November, 1917, a war-wrecked country which was to experience four more years of civil war, intervention, famine, and revolution before Lenin's New Economic Policy, inaugurated in 1921, brought a measure of relief. From 1917 until he was stricken in 1922, thenceforth to be all but eliminated from operative leadership, Lenin was the active leader of the party and also, as chairman of the Council of Peoples' Commissars, of the state; thereafter he held nominal leadership until his death on January 21, 1924. Stalin meanwhile had already laid the foundations of his later predominance and was shrewdly beginning to exploit the minor post of general secretary of the party, which he assumed in April, 1922. This post was established when the death of Jacob Sverdlov, in 1919, deprived the party of its best organizer, and Stalin converted it from a technical into a political job—this his opponents realized too late. Before and during the fourteenth congress in December, 1925, they complained that Stalin's joint tenure of the general secretaryship and Politburo membership enabled him to dominate policy by controlling appointment of personnel, a criticism for which Sokolnikov, Kamenev, Zinoviev, and others eventually paid with their lives.[4]

Stages of Control

The political evolution of the regime after the civil war period (1918–21) falls into three parts. During the "breathing spell" from 1921 to 1929 Stalin gradually acquired predominance; at first he co-operated with Kamenev and Zinoviev against Trotsky, then with the "right" of Bukharin, Rykov, and Tomsky and the party center against erstwhile partners now joined by Trotsky. Finally, in 1929–30, he ousted Bukharin, Rykov, Tomsky, and the other "right" oppositionists from the power centers of the increasingly bureaucratized party apparatus. Stalin's weapons were his powerful will, his spy system, his capacity for deception and combination, and, above all, his understanding of the outlook of the party functionaries. Unlike most of his opponents, he was not only a revolutionary but, more important, also a practical and ruthless politician.

Stalin already had full control of the party by 1930, but Stalinism did not take shape until 1932 or 1933 at the earliest. Perhaps the year 1935, when the society of "old Bolsheviks" was dissolved, would be a more pertinent date to signify the triumph of Stalin's peculiar kind of "Thermidorian reaction," although it did not culminate in a "restoration" such as that which followed the great French Revolution. The

4. Hugo Dewar in *Problems of Communism* (No. 2 [1954], p. 19) suggests that the post-Stalin rulers want to avoid the rise of a new Stalin who would threaten their lives. Malenkov's "voluntary" renunciation of the general secretary's post shortly after Stalin's death was one of many facts indicating that this is true. The failure of Khrushchev, after the ouster of Malenkov as chairman of the Council of Ministers, to assume a state post may fit into this pattern, as may also the leniency shown Malenkov. It would be conservative, however, to say that Malenkov's prospects are poor.

purges of 1936–38 installed the Stalin generation of young cadres in all but the top levels of power and eliminated the anti-Stalin "old Bolsheviks" from the top and middle levels of command —but this process did not end with the great purges. In the ten-man Presidium set up after Stalin's death, two men— Pervukhin and Saburov—were particularly representative of the now middle-aged "Stalin generation," while Malenkov and Beria represented connecting links between this generation and the surviving "old Bolsheviks"— Molotov, Voroshilov, and Kaganovich. Khrushchev, who achieved Politburo membership in 1939 and was sixty years old in 1954, might also be included in the latter category.

The Stalin totalitarian revolution broadened vastly the scope of power of the new party-state. All of life was increasingly organized, co-ordinated, and politicized. It was during this period that what Jay H. Cerf calls the "membership state" developed, in which an individual counts for nothing if he is not certified and documented as a member of one or more of a hierarchy of centrally managed pyramidal organizations; "natural law," "natural rights," and the "rule of law" disappear; and society becomes one big factory specializing in the production of military goods or one vast armed camp. It is no wonder, then, that the Bolsheviks are so fond of such mechanistic and military imagery as in the Soviet dictum that writers are "engineers of human souls" and in such expressions as "the cultural front."

It would be unrealistic not to recognize that some of the impetus to Soviet totalitarianism was fear of the rising power of Nazi Germany, even though the five-year plans and their accompanying organizational and ideological features were well under way before Hitler came to power. In February, 1931, Stalin made a famous speech in which he revealed much of the motivation of Soviet policy. Speaking to Soviet industrial executives, he defended the grinding tempo of the first five-year plan; the history of old Russia, he said, had been one of defeats by the Mongols, the Swedes, the Germans, the French, etc., which revealed the fatal effects of economic and technical backwardness; Soviet Russia, he warned, must catch up with the more advanced nations within ten or fifteen years or be crushed. Beginning as early as December, 1925, when the party took a decision looking to transforming Russia into a great industrial power, fear was expressed that the capitalists would attempt to crush the Soviet state because its example would lead to revolutions in capitalist countries—this became the leitmotiv of Soviet propaganda.

With the rise of Hitler, "Soviet patriotism," of which Russian nationalism is an important element, was added to the body of Stalinist thought. It, and especially its Great Russian component,[5] is probably the most popular element and a major unifying force in current Soviet ideology. Despite its growing economic-military potential, however, Stalinism remained on the defensive until the last phase of World War II, when the imperialist and expansionist phase of Soviet totalitarianism began.

Leadership of the Party

Let us now examine the top level of the party machine which was shaped by the pressures of Soviet industrialization under Bolshevik dictatorship. From 1919 until October, 1952, power was concentrated in the Central Committee's nominally subordinate organs: the Organization Bureau, the Secretariat, and the Politburo. Under this central leadership, "unity of will" and pro-

5. The term "Great Russian" is often used to distinguish the predominant Slavic nation from all other peoples of the Soviet Union.

hibition of "factions" in it and throughout the party were principles laid down by Lenin and ruthlessly applied by Stalin. Party morality and discipline were maintained by a Party Control Commission which, until 1934, had a measure of independence but thereafter acted as Stalin's superintelligence agency, administratively controlled by the Central Committee. In the nonparty sphere the work of the Party Control Commission was supplemented by that of the Workers' and Peasants' Inspection, abolished in 1934. Increasingly, surveillance and physical removal of "unreliable" elements were exercised by the secret police.

Important developments in the top party command occurred after October, 1952. The October congress replaced the Politburo by the Presidium; the Orgbureau was eliminated; the Secretariat was enlarged to ten members, presumably to take over the Orgbureau's organizational and personnel control function. The Party Control Commission was replaced by the Committee of Party Control, with somewhat reduced power, which continued to report directly to the Central Committee in Moscow, whose local agents throughout the country, like those of the secret police, are independent of the local party organizations. The new structure, like the old one, has a Central Auditing Commission responsible for the administration of the party finances.

One plausible explanation for the October enlargement of the supreme party body through transformation of the eleven-man Politburo into the October Presidium is that it was an attempt simultaneously to make the party center more representative by adding other competent and favored persons and, at the same time, to pave the way for demoting others and eliminating the old Politburo, which as early as World War II was deemed no longer useful and, in fact, obsolete. For the Politburo was a survival of an early period in which, at least in the higher party circles, there had been some genuinely deliberative political life. More and more, with the increasing growth of dictatorship methods, this body hardened into a solid aggregation of powerful administrators, some of whom had been powerful for years either as state administrators or as directors of the party machinery, while others, such as Voroshilov, had little power but were retained probably because of their previous services and long association with Stalin.

The Soviet empire was ruled by the dictator assisted by a small inner circle, which, in turn, directed a number of crucial committees at the disposal of which were appropriate sections of the party Central Committee with its expert staff. The Presidium was in part intended to furnish a decorative façade behind which this committee system would function and at the same time eliminate any potential danger to the power of the smaller inner core which could conceivably arise from evocation of the tradition of the Politburo as a body of equals—a fact perhaps explanatory of the crucial situation between October, 1952, and the death of Stalin on March 5, 1953, which, occurring perhaps considerably before it was expected, created something of a crisis.[6]

Almost immediately after Stalin's death the Presidium was reduced from twenty-five members and eleven alternates to ten members and four alternates. Thus the old Politburo returned under a new name, but with changes in membership. The essence of the new structure adopted was that of a five-man ruling committee consisting of Malenkov as chairman and Beria, Molotov, Bulganin, and Kaganovich, all of them members of the now smaller party Presidium which was, in effect, a return to the old Politburo. But at the same time—and this constituted a change from the setup adopted in October—each held an important government position: Malenkov was chairman of the Council of Ministers, replacing Stalin in this post; Beria was minister of internal affairs; and Molotov returned to the job of minister of foreign affairs which he had relinquished to Vyshinsky in 1949. Now this structure closely resembled that of the Soviet administration during World War II. In June, 1941, a State Defense Committee had been set up with Stalin as chairman and Molotov as deputy chairman.

This committee had "complete state power" until its dissolution in September, 1945, and was dominated by four men: Stalin, Molotov, Beria, and Malenkov. In 1943 Molotov, Beria, and Malenkov were given extensive publicity when each was named "Hero of Socialist Labor" for directing the production of tanks, fuel, and airplanes, respectively; and these three, but in reverse order, delivered the funeral orations for Stalin. Thus there was much continuity between the war leadership and the supreme power after the death of Stalin, and, by and large, the same small group which had held the levers of power during the war held them after Stalin's death. The crucial question that confronted them was whether they could hold their power against challenges from outside their little circle and maintain a unity which would prevent them from destroying one another.

The purge, particularly at the top personnel level, continues to be a characteristic of the Soviet system.[7] On the other hand, the post–1939 period fur-

6. It is, of course, conceivable that the post-Stalin "inner core" did away with the dictator in self-defense. The "doctors' plot" may have been preparation by Stalin for a purge of most of his colleagues—B. Nikolaevski has hinted this in some of his *New Leader* articles.

7. Further evidence of the continued importance of the purge mechanism is furnished by the extensive changes in party leadership in Beria's native Georgia subsequent to his execution in December, 1953.

nished impressive evidence of the existence of a process of systematic orderly promotion on the basis of merit, and it is important to keep this in mind as a check against wishful thinking about Communist party disintegration, for one must strike a balance between integrating and disintegrating tendencies. Among the integrating tendencies must be mentioned intense indoctrination, the enjoyment of power and privilege which would be menaced by disunity among the ruling group, and perhaps the *esprit de corps* based upon a long period of common service and association, while one of the strongest disintegrative tendencies is the fact that each one of the few top leaders, as he rose, brought with him his own trusted associates. Thus the top leadership consists of clusters of powerful individuals rather than a homogeneous inner core; and, judging from the earlier political struggles within the system, apparently power groups at the top levels usually cut across functional lines, for powerful party leaders have friendships and alliances not only within the party organization in the narrow sense but also within the economic bureaucracy, the armed forces, and the secret police. The ruling center, however, through vigorous organizational measures, sharp vigilance, and ruthless terror, has always been able to break up tendencies of these various chains of command to act as units against the party center; but this problem has never been finally and completely solved, and Stalin's successors must have had to face it when they took the power into their own hands.[8]

The Stalin breed of the type of Khrushchev and Malenkov rules the Soviet Union today, and, barring a disastrous war, this type of superbureaucrat seems likely to continue to rule Russia for the foreseeable future. In 1946 the historian, G. Fedotov, described this type: "Robust physically and mentally, he lives according to rules, dislikes thought and doubt and appreciates practical knowledge." Fedotov's observation seems to be applicable to the upper levels of the whole Soviet elite, although a more hopeful view is taken by the Soviet refugee scholar, Herman Achminow, who argues in his book *Die Macht im Hintergrund* that there is a sharp cleavage of interest and outlook between the party functionaries and the "technical intelligentsia." Mosely writes that "real power continues to be exercised in the main by the managerial elite concerned with the manipulation of large units of power," and he sees indications that party functionaries are often chary of challenging the power of industrial and political "magnates." Only the future can disclose whether there are serious conflicts among the components of the leadership class and whether these conflicts could be reflected in political divisions at the highest levels. We hope that careful study of such biographical data as are available may shed some light on this problem and even enable us in the future to make modest short-term predictions.

Soviet claims for "democratic centralism" are discussed below; however, even if this principle of party organization were faithfully applied, it would provide a design for dictatorship. But under Lenin and to a far greater degree under Stalin and his associates, this formal principle was adhered to only in so far as it served the interests of the dictatorship; often it was invoked, usually in a highly disingenuous fashion, against opponents or scape-

8. Beria's fall illustrates several points: he was Malenkov's and Khrushchev's most dangerous rival, and the East Berlin rising of June 16–17, 1953, furnished at least a pretext for removing him (arrest announced July 10); there may be a "nationality" angle, too, in his case, for he and his henchmen were Georgians, like Stalin, and Russians had long been irked by the power of the Georgians.

goats who were slated for demotion or liquidation.

III / COMMUNIST PARTY STRUCTURE

Central and Local Organizations

Most of the remainder of this chapter consists of a development of the thesis suggested by the foregoing paragraphs. Now let us start at the level of the party Central Committee and work down. According to the party statutes, the Central Committee is the supreme executive organ of the party, elected by the party congress. The 1952 statutes, it should be noted, stipulated that the party congress was to meet once every four years, but just how seriously even this formality will be taken is impossible to predict. According to the old statutes, the congress was supposed to meet every three years; yet there was no congress from 1939 until 1952. The new statutes abolished the party conference, which, according to the old statutes, was supposed to meet every eighteen months.

The Central Committee chosen at the October congress of 1952 was much larger than its predecessor. The new Central Committee had 125 full members and 111 alternates or candidates, whereas the Central Committee chosen in March, 1939, had 71 members and 68 alternates. It is obvious that bodies as large as these could not be deliberative. But there was a time, even under the Stalin regime, when the Central Committee witnessed lively and often bitter debates; and its much greater freedom during Lenin's lifetime was evident in the dispute over policy between Lenin, Trotsky, Bukharin, and others in connection with the peace of Brest-Litovsk with the Central Powers in 1918, and in still other clashes of opinion at this level. And even after the establishment of the Politburo as a permanent organization in March, 1919, the Central Committee continued for some time to be a truly policy-making organ. For many years, however, the Central Committee has been, to use the words of Louis Nemzer, the Kremlin's "professional staff," and as such it has long assisted the top policy-makers in the preparation of background material for drafting decisions. But the committee is also an assembly of Soviet notables, for every important element in the Soviet bureaucracy is represented in the Central Committee. According to Boris Meissner's careful tabulations, the dominant element in the new Central Committee, as in the old one, is the group of paid party functionaries, followed by government and economic executives, including 27 heads of production ministries;[9] two other groups represented on the Central Committee are the military and the professional political police officials. These four groups are undoubtedly the most important and most powerful in Soviet society.

But there are also representatives of the trade-union bureaucracy and of artists, scientists, and scholars. For example: Yuri Zhdanov, who holds a doctorate in chemistry, heads the Central Committee science section; Alexander Fadeev, until recently the head of the Union of Soviet Writers, an organization which completely controls Soviet literature, has been a member of the committee since 1939. Study of Central Committee membership since 1939 indicates markedly both continuity and change. Of 71 full members of the 1939 Central Committee, 34 were elected full members in 1952; however, only 10 of the 1939 alternates achieved the same rank in 1952. Death by natural causes and demotion due to dis-

9. These data refer to the period before Stalin's death. Failure of 180 members of the Central Committee, elected at the nineteenth congress, to be elected in March, 1954, to the present Supreme Soviet indicates that they had either died or been purged in the post-Stalin reshuffle.

favor or demerit, including the apparent purge of the Zhdanovites, and finally a conscious systematic effort to bring new blood into the top ranks account for the turnover. Out of the total of 236 Central Committee members and alternates as of October, 1952, 179 had not been in the 1939 Central Committee. It should be remembered, however, that the average age of these men was already fairly high in 1939.

It should also be noted that a vastly greater turnover occurred in the cataclysmic years between the seventeenth (1934) and the eighteenth (1939) party congresses. There can be few more startling experiences than to compare the lists of Central Committee members as of June, 1934, and March, 1939.

Thus far we have been concerned with the composition, stability, and structure of the central party organization. We must now sketch the pattern of intermediate and lower party organization, for upon its effective functioning ultimately depend the power and survival of the regime. Below the top all-union party organs which we have discussed rank the fifteen party organizations of the constituent Soviet "republics"; the Russian Federative Soviet Socialist Republic (RSFSR) has no "national" party organization. Within each republic there are a number of *oblasts*, variously translated into English as "region," "area," or "province"; oblasts are divided into *rayons*, which in the countryside correspond to American counties and in the cities to wards or boroughs. The oblast-rayon system of territorial-administrative divisions was established in 1929, replacing the *gubernias* or provinces carried over from the Russian empire. In addition to oblasts and rayons, there are also large, sparsely populated *krays* and *okrugs*, the latter units established to take into account the existence of minority nationality enclaves within the territories of larger nationalities.

Oblast party organizations within the RSFSR rank roughly on a level with the fifteen non-Russian republic party organizations and are likewise directly subordinated to the Central Committee; but oblast party units of the non-Russian republics are indirectly controlled by Moscow through the central committees of their republic party organizations. In conformity with their streamlining tendency, the new party statutes provided for the setting-up of secretariats to handle current work in republic party central committees and in oblast and kray party bureaus having not less than eleven members, which correspond on the local level to the all-union central committee. This development indicates that the network of secretariats heading up in the Moscow Central Committee Secretariat is the operating chain of command.

Rayon party bureaus have, according to the new statutes, seven to nine members, and as of the nineteenth congress there were 4,886 rayon party organizations. The executive committees of rayon, oblast, and republic party organizations have three secretaries; additional special secretaries for economic, technological, or other special fields are sometimes appointed. Presumably, as in the past, one of the three secretaries in each party organization specializes in and directs all agitation and propaganda in his territory, and each party organization publishes a party newspaper, the main one in its area. At the center, of course, is *Pravda*, newspaper of the Central Committee of the Communist Party of the Soviet Union. Provincial newspapers often reprint *Pravda* editorials and are replicas of *Pravda*, with a slight local flavor, even though their language may be Kirghiz, Georgian, etc.

The lowest rung of the party ladder is the primary party organization, which until 1934 was called "cell" (*yacheika*). The new party statutes, like the old, state that the primary organizations "link up the masses of the workers, peasants and intelligentsia with the leading organs of the Party." Primary organizations must have at least three members, and provision is also made for "candidates' groups" composed of one or two persons directly supervised by the rayon committee. Primary organizations are tightly controlled and vigilantly supervised by the rayon committees, although there are occasional complaints in party publications against the rayon committees' "lack of vigilance" in their direction and control— a reflection of the malfunctioning which is one of the curses of bureaucracy. Also frequent are accusations against rayon secretaries of a "bureaucratic" approach to primary organizations, of failure to go out into the field and get acquainted with their members, etc. Occasionally these reports are couched in terms indicating extreme stagnation and bureaucratic rot.

Full-time party workers, beginning at the level of the larger primary organizations, are paid. While pay and perquisites are substantial at the higher levels, power is the main incentive for a party career. For the party seeks to assure the loyalty of writers, artists, and scientists by financial rewards much greater than those available to party functionaries.

The elaborate controls in primary organizations are designed to facilitate mobilization for Moscow's purposes and to prevent penetration of the party by "careerists" or "hostile elements." Thus very large organizations—the new statutes use the ambiguous expression "over 300"—and those in the smaller agencies such as government ministries are controlled directly by the Central Committee in Moscow. Particular emphasis is placed on safeguarding party and state secrets; according to Soviet refugees, there is a special secret courier service, special safes, etc., for this purpose.

Many of these principles and regulations were set forth in a collection of articles entitled "Party Housekeeping" (*Partiinoe Khozyaistvo*) published by the Moscow party organ *Moscow Bolshevik* in 1945. There is no reason to doubt that the system of regulations it describes is still in force. It stipulates further that precise data on social origin, employment, and other biographical details on party candidates and their parents must be forwarded to Moscow and that rayon party organization secretaries are held personally responsible for the authenticity of documents submitted by applicants for membership or candidacy in the party. A melodramatic touch is provided by the requirement that specified categories of party documents and records be filled out in special "Central Committee" ink.

To join the party, an individual must be recommended by three party members who have themselves been members for three years. If, as is usually the case, the applicant belongs to the Komsomol (the Young Communist organization) and is recommended by his Komsomol unit, he needs only two party sponsors; then he must go through a "candidate" or probationary period of one year. His primary organization elects him to candidacy or membership by unanimous vote, although he is not considered a party member until his election has been confirmed by a first or second secretary of a rayon committee at a solemn ceremony attended by the secretary and himself. Vera Inber, prominent Soviet poet, describes in her *Leningrad Diary* the ceremony and the reaction of the newly elect, stating that she was quizzed severely for a few minutes and then, the ceremony completed, she felt that petty private concerns were no longer important to her and that henceforth her whole being belonged to the party.

We have dwelt on control of party primary organizations by the rayon committees because it is at this low level that the gulf between the rank and file and the party apparatus begins. Broad at this level, it widens to infinity if one compares an ordinary member of a primary organization with an important oblast secretary or a member of the Central Committee. Before ascending the pyramid to survey the controls of the center over the periphery, we must emphasize several points: It is fundamental that the relation of the primary organization to its superior organizations, and of the individual member to it, has not been basically altered since Lenin presented his centralist demands which lost him the support of his former colleague, Martov, at the 1903 Congress. He demanded that a member not only accept party doctrine and exemplify and disseminate party principles but work continuously under orders from above in one of the organizations of the party and carry out all its decisions. As later interpreted with increasing severity, this principle makes the rank-and-file communists mere privates in a political army.

Control from the center has been vastly intensified—in fact, rendered a matter of life and death—by the steadily increasing power of state organs and especially the police over party members. Long gone are the days when party members were immune from arrest and execution. In abolition of this principle lay much of the significance of Stalin's totalitarian revolution of 1936–38. The 1952 statutes carry central control a step farther in stipulating that when a party member commits a legally punishable act, he is expelled, reduced to being, in Orwellian terms, an "unmember" of the "member-ship society"—a provision greatly facilitating the conversion of the party mass into one of the Kremlin's instruments of power and intrenching the state's supremacy over all but the top echelons of the party.

It should also be noted that articles 11 and 12 of the 1952 statutes further strengthened the hand of party "officers" by special rules safeguarding them in matters of expulsion from the party from the influence of the "privates." On the other hand, the statutes enjoin all members to report all shortcomings of party members, regardless of rank, to superior organs, including the Central Committee, a caveat which, together with such facts as Malenkov's castigation of economic officials for "stifling criticism," lends weight to Mosely's opinion (see above) that apparently the party felt constrained to strengthen its authority against powerful top-flight industrial managers.

Perhaps the regime can satisfy the managers, by giving them greater freedom in their special field, and also the lesser party functionaries, by stressing the party's power of control. The main lines, however, were laid down in the 1930's, when a loyal Stalinist technical intelligentsia and industrial management group was installed in power and labor was regimented by the reintroduction of internal passports and other formerly despised "reactionary" tsarist control methods. It is revealing to compare early Soviet denunciations of the "passport system" with the later espousal of such controls in Soviet legal and reference texts.

The Kremlin, through the Central Committee and other top organs, holds as firm a grip on the party apparatus as the latter has on the thousands of primary organizations, and the whole network is held together on the "production-territorial" principle. The party organization of any territorial unit is supreme over all party units within the given territory.

Organizational Principles

The system combines monopoly and monolithic form, mobilizing and penetrating capacities, with compartmentalization. Units and agencies are sealed off both vertically and horizontally from relationships and information which the party command considers unnecessary or harmful to their function. Command, surveillance, and pressure, ceaseless and insistent, flow down; obedience, sometimes adulterated by evasion or collusion, flows up. Only the integrating system of party and police organs disposes of the personnel, information, symbols, and facilities of power. The Bolsheviks have always been exceptionally intelligence-minded in both domestic and foreign operations. Their attitude is indicated by an article in the old Central Committee journal *Partiinoe Stroitelstvo* ("Party Construction") (Nos. 11–12 [1944]), which states that "party information has the same significance as intelligence has for the successful combat operations of armed forces" and stresses the duty of party leaders to supply their superiors with a steady flow of complete and objective information. Such a system creates a virtual monopoly of information at the center and leads to ignorance, isolation, and helplessness at all but the highest levels.

An impressive array of organizational forms and devices is used to implement directives drafted at the center. The Central Committee has sections for propaganda and agitation, schools, and science and culture; for party, Komsomol and trade-union affairs; for agriculture, heavy industry and other economic matters; and a main political administration which controls the party organizations in the armed services. Even the names of many of these sections are at any given time not known

to us. In addition, there are numerous special institutions attached to the Central Committee, including the Marx-Engels-Lenin-Stalin Institute, custodian of doctrinal texts, manuscripts, and their publication and supplier of reading matter to "party cabinets" in local party organizations; the Central newspaper courses under the Central Committee, the Higher Party School, the Academy of Social Sciences, etc. The latter two, reopened with pomp in 1946 after wartime inactivity, are the supreme bodies for the training of higher party officials and propagandists.

The Central Committee apparatus operates mainly through the party network described earlier. For example, the section for propaganda and agitation has at its disposal the party secretaries at oblast and rayon levels who specialize in this field. Thus arises the duplication, or "dual subordination," characteristic of both party and government administration. The local party secretary for propaganda, for example, is subordinate to his superiors in both territorial and functional commands, while the local office of a central government department is subordinate in various and not clearly defined ways to both the local government and the local party organization.

The Central Committee's agencies possess further special controls. Whenever a field operation is considered unusually vital or sensitive, it is placed under control by special agents of the center; thus there are permanent Central Committee liaison officers attached to republic central committees, and Central Committee "partorgs" direct party work in important industrial enterprises.

Similarly, oblast party organizations send "instructors" into rayon organizations to check up on or improve their operations, while rayon "instructors," sometimes trained in oblast committee "seminars," perform similar functions, if necessary, in primary organizations. These "instructors" devote two-thirds of their time to on-the-spot work and refrain from spending too much time in paper-work at headquarters—an interesting phenomenon, in that the Bolshevik party has always had to fight the Russian tendency, inherited from the past, to prefer deskwork to manual or field work.

There is an important party intelligence corps in the roving correspondents of central party publications. Dread of the consequences of campaigns against local abuses in the columns of *Pravda, Bolshevik, Trud,* or other publications helps to discourage the formation of local groupings based on "friendly relations" which are so feared by the center.

When conditions in a local organization get too far out of hand, the center dispatches emissaries to straighten things out; the Soviet press was particularly rich in disclosures of such actions in 1946, when the party was being restored to prewar efficiency and tuned up for new tasks. Kaganovich, veteran Politburo trouble shooter, was sent to the Ukraine to prune the deadwood in their party organizations; Central Committee inspectors helped purge party organizations in the Crimea (whose Tatar population had been exiled to central Asia for wartime "disloyalty") and in other areas.

Only occasionally does the press describe the results of such investigations in vivid detail somewhat reminiscent of Gogol's classic *The Inspector General.* On July 4, 1946, *Pravda* reported on the mission of Central Committee inspector Zadionchenko to the Astrakhan oblast; in the presence of the powerful Moscow representative, members of the Astrakhan party organization turned on the first secretary of their organization and denounced the corrupt practices and "suppression of criticism" he had hitherto succeeded in keeping quiet.

Personnel Policy

Questions that often occur to students of party organization are: How is the apparatus staffed? How is personnel drawn into the machinery, trained, assigned, advanced? An initial stage seems to be that of co-operation of the local party organizations with the Komsomol organizations in bringing forward promising young people, first into executive work in the Komsomol and later into junior party leadership assignments. The Komsomol now has 20,000,-000 members and is the main recruiting ground for the party. Both the party and the Komsomol statutes make quite explicit the subordination of the youth league to the senior organization. Recruits brought in through youthful enthusiasm, social pressure, or other factors are carefully studied.

The source of official personnel is the *aktiv* ("active group") of the Komsomol, the party, and the "mass organizations." Exploitation of the "activist" personality is highly developed in the Soviet system and the *aktiv* consists largely of the zealous and the ambitious who voluntarily assist the paid party functionaries in performing their duties. All members of Soviet "voluntary" organizations must perform a certain amount of unpaid labor, known as the "social assignment" (*obshchestvennaya nagruzka*); but the activist usually does extra work, displays overenthusiasm. According to Soviet refugees, these extra assignments often involve unpaid work as police informers. The *aktiv* enjoys a formal status at the lower levels, honorifically defined in the party statutes and regularly mentioned in the press; from its ranks some are advanced to paid, professional party, Komsomol, trade-union, or police work.

Much of the information which a Western student of public administration would consider essential regarding personnel policy is simply not available in Soviet sources. Scattered press data and refugee accounts, however, help fill in the broad background given here. An important feature of personnel management is the system of "nomenclatures" (*nomenklatury*) maintained in the Moscow Central Committee, republic central committees, and lower party units and probably also in the party agencies responsible for assignment and surveillance of police and army personnel. At each specified level a list is maintained of personnel whose rank and qualifications make them subject to the jurisdiction of the given party unit and who may be appointed to leading posts within the given area—truly a "government by card index." Although a cumbersome system, it enables the Kremlin to focus on tasks which it considers vital.

Party apparatus personnel constitutes a remarkably homogeneous, freely disposable pool. While they are subject to assignment and transfer without notice and without regard to previous residence or work, every attempt is made to equip them with all necessary professional, technical, and political skills. The body in Western countries which they most closely resemble is the officer corps of an army, although even more than that group it is one of long-term, planned training, directed allocation, and constant supervision of cadres. This does not, however, assure stability of careers because of the prevalent Soviet atmosphere of political suspicion.

Party assignments, especially at lower levels, seem to be peculiarly short, and turnover is disturbingly rapid. This was particularly true during 1945 and 1946, when, for example, in the Belorussian party organization 90 per cent of all secretaries of rayon party organizations were replaced and when in Kazakhstan during two years 67.3 per cent of "basic leading workers" were replaced. These and similar data were published by the now defunct Central

Committee magazine "Party Life," also a casualty of reorganization.

Refugees' testimony that the rayon and city party organizations assist members in good standing in finding employment sheds further light on the personnel system, as do numerous postwar press reports that demobilized party members were in many cases made chairmen of collective farms. In addition to these party channels, employment placement is handled through cadre departments of government agencies. Tables of organization and salaries of government jobs are fixed by the State Personnel Commission (*Gosudarstvennaya Shtatnaya Kommissya*), established in 1941. Persons with higher education get their first jobs on recommendation of their educational institutions and must serve for a specified period in the assigned post or be prosecuted. All this is subject to the approval of party organizations, which are especially well developed in higher educational institutions.

"Democratic Centralism," "Federalism," and the Nationality Problem

We have been concerned thus far with the very highest-level party and state leadership, and our discussion strongly indicates that we cannot take seriously the Soviet claims that the basic principle of formal party organization, "democratic centralism," is really applied. But since this principle is incorporated into the latest version of the party statutes published in *Pravda* for October, 1952, we should at least examine it as it is formulated in these statutes. It calls for "popular" election of all "leading organs" from top to bottom, periodic accounting by these organs to their party organizations, strict party discipline and subordination of the minority to the majority, and unconditional fulfilment by the lower organs of the decisions of the higher organs; but it subordinates "legislative" organs such as the party congress, which since the mid-1920's has met only briefly and infrequently, to the permanent, appointed executive organs. The pattern of executive domination contained in this formula has been projected from the party structure into the structure of all Soviet state and public organizations. In the case of the latter, which Lenin and Stalin aptly described as "gears" and "transmission belts," the domination of the rank-and-file membership by a tiny ruling group is still further intensified by the fact that all these organizations are controlled by the ruling Communist party.

The more one studies party structure, the more illusory is the concept of "democratic centralism." Even the basic terms used in discussing it—"internal party democracy," "mass participation," "criticism and self-criticism"—are merely empty symbols for deceiving the non-Communist world and for creating among the party masses an imaginative identification with their superiors. Summarily we might say that the so-called "party democracy" is hardly more than a set of procedures used by top party authorities to divert the resentments and frustrations arising among the masses away from the "middle-rank" functionaries, with accompanying scapegoat sacrifices as the domestic equivalent of the diversion of aggression against the capitalist enemy.

Formally, the party system of "election and accountability" is impressive. At all levels, from the primary on up to the all-union party organization, there are elections, and elaborate rules prescribe the representation system as one moves up the scale from the lower to the higher bodies. Nominally these elections determine the choice of party executive bodies at each level, and, once elected, each such body is directly responsible to the appropriate "legisla-tive" organ and renders an accounting of its stewardship at stipulated intervals. In primary organizations the term of office is one year, and the "elections-accounting meeting" is annual. The statutes provide for "free, business-like" discussion at meetings and contain elaborate and seemingly superfluous rules to permit, as well as to keep from getting out of hand, discussion of major party policy; these rules have been largely meaningless, however, at least since 1934, when Stalin in his "report" to the seventeenth congress declared that the danger of a "split" had passed. But perhaps they may one day be invoked if the new Soviet intelligentsia gradually generates a more active political life. And it may be that they have more real significance on higher than on lower levels.

Apparently, the last publicly reported plenary session of the Central Committee prior to that which announced preparation for the October, 1952, congress occurred in February, 1947.[10] We might expect that a regime whose supreme leaders dispense so consistently with even the most perfunctory gestures of "democracy" at the highest level would find it necessary to criticize and punish lower echelons for imitating their superiors' style of work. And such is the case.

The Soviet press for years has disseminated Moscow criticism of the prevalent "suppression of self-criticism," a theme perpetuated in a steady stream of accusatory articles on party life published in all the party organs. The real

10. A plenary session was held shortly after Stalin's death to legitimize the new party command; others occurred in September, 1953, February–March, 1954, and January, 1955. The ouster of Malenkov undoubtedly occurred at this last, decisive plenum which also resulted in important new agricultural policies. The world, however, learned of the most dramatic developments of this plenum only at the Supreme Soviet session on February 8, 1955.

significance of this was revealed in its systematic application to the arts and sciences during the postwar period, when Zhdanov (in 1946 and 1947) precipitated a vast and energetic ideological "housecleaning" with a series of addresses on literature (Leningrad, August, 1946), music, and philosophy. In these he chided the "professionals" for restricting the "freedom" of creative activity; thereupon followed demotion, disgrace, or dismissal of the cultural "dictators" in question. He accused the satirist Zoshchenko, for example, of being the "literary dictator" of Leningrad and deplored his popularity. Then, too, Stalin attacked (June, 1950) the "Arakcheev regime"[11] in linguistics, declaring that scholarship could not flourish without freedom; and there followed a grand reshuffling of top personnel in this field. And Malenkov warned (October, 1952) that there were still fields of research in which the upward path of promising scholars was being dictatorially blocked. We can expect future vigorous application of "self-criticism" and "democracy" in Soviet intellectual life,[12] the forcing of savants under pressure by the party committees of their institutions to do "useful" work. Of course, it is possible that the party leaders were right from their point of

11. Arakcheev was in charge of the notorious "military colonies" in the 1820's, and his name is synonymous with brutal reaction. Zhdanov's speeches accompanied an important series of Central Committee decrees in 1946–48 on literature, drama, music, philosophy, biology, etc. That the basic doctrine of regimentation of intellectual life has not changed is indicated by inclusion of the key ideological decrees in a new two-volume book of Central Committee decrees and resolutions covering the period 1898–1953.

12. After Stalin's death, Ehrenburg in literature and Khachaturian in music have been allowed to criticize excessive severity of political controls. This was a hopeful symptom, but the line taken at the Second Congress of Soviet Writers in December, 1954 (first held in 1934), signaled a relapse.

view in accusing various groups of intellectuals of establishing rule by clique, for they set in motion the machinery of "democracy" via the competent party organs in order to introduce greater efficiency of function, in this case intellectual production. But can this be done?

The situation in the sphere of party political functions is similar. Zhdanov at a Central Committee plenary session in 1937 presented shocking figures indicating widespread failure to hold elections in primary, rayon, and even higher party organizations. Co-opting of party officials was rife. Perhaps Zhdanov was in part acting in his role of prime exponent of the formal aspect of Leninist traditions of "party democracy," but he was also, as a key member of the Stalinist group then purging the party, utilizing the slogans of democracy as a weapon of the purge. Is it accidental that this renewed emphasis on party democracy together with the granting of the "most democratic constitution in the world" was accompanied by bloody purges? Such parallelisms, quite frequent in party history, would suggest that the Kremlin has a well-developed technique of alternating and combining deprivations and indulgences, cuffs and caresses, or, in Vyshinsky's terms, compulsions and persuasion!

It is generally agreed in the West that popular sovereignty in the Soviet party and state system exists only on paper, although one aspect of "democracy" in a broad sense—namely, the "federative" and "nationality" principles of the system—still command some measure of respect. Even these principles, however, upon examination prove to be only a façade for party dictatorship operation.

The Soviet state, including both its administrative core and its legislative façade, is penetrated and controlled by the Kremlin's agents; at the highest levels party and state are usually the same persons wearing different hats. Thus three[13] former Politburo members now on the Presidium of the party were (1953–54) deputies to Malenkov as chairman of the Council of Ministers (roughly equivalent to a prime minister). Moving down a bit, there are the party secretaries, the local head of the MVD (formerly MGB), the political police organization, and several other top local officials sitting together in the bureau of the oblast or city party organization. While locally "elected" in their capacity as party officials, all these executives must be "confirmed" by the Central Committee.

True federalism is indeed impossible under these conditions. But, to make doubly sure that the constituent republics and other "national" or local units do not develop corresponding national party organizations that might interfere in any significant way with control from the center, the party statutes and their recurrent interpretations insist that the party, unlike the constitutional government, is a "single, unified organization." It is true, as described here, that its personnel is a unified national pool. Then, too, the language of party meetings, except for some local primary units, and of correspondence and records seems to be Russian. In recent years the regime has increasingly utilized Russian language, traditions, and culture as unifying forces. Striking was the replacement of the "Internationale" in 1943 as the Soviet national anthem by a new "hymn" which hails "Rus" (a traditional native word for Russia) as the liberator and unifier of the Soviet "family" of peoples. Equally interesting, however, is the retention of the revolutionary "Internationale" as the party anthem, and

13. Before Beria's liquidation, he was a fourth.

it was sung at the October, 1952, congress, although subsequently frequent mention was made of a new party song, "The Party, Our Helmsman."

A distinctly centralist, "antilocalist" policy seems to be followed in assignment of high party and police personnel; this has been particularly true in respect to the Ukraine. All except the present head of the Ukrainian republic party organizations, Kirichenko, were Russians like Khrushchev or members of other non-Ukrainian ethnic groups like Kaganovich; "Nationalist" Ukrainian party leaders like Skrypnik committed suicide or were purged. In Central Asia and the Baltic units the prevalent non-local nationality of the top leadership is usually masked by having a native first secretary or chief and a Russian or other non-native deputy. A series of national groups has been favored in high posts in the MGB, depending on the nationality of its current chief. In early years Latvians, Poles, and Jews were prominent; after Beria's elevation in 1938 Georgians held a disproportionate number of top posts. Some of the present top police personnel are apparently Great Russians.

The non-Russian republic in which top party and police personnel were long least infiltrated by outsiders was Stalin's and Beria's native Georgia, although it has not been completely immune to shakeups directed by Moscow. An uprising in Georgia in 1924 was brutally crushed; Beria acted as Stalin's agent in vicious purgings of the Georgians in 1936–38, settling old scores dating back to the 1920's. Again in 1948 about 25 per cent of Georgian party membership apparently was purged. In the fall of 1951 Charkviani, head of the party and a close associate of Beria, was removed from office at a republic congress attended by Beria. For years Beria was Stalin's viceroy for the Caucasus, a fact vividly impressed upon this writer by conspicuous poster and portrait displays during his visit in 1946; and the Frenchman, Michel Gordey, found the same thing on his visit there in 1950.

We can only speculate as to the possibly preferential treatment of Georgia, but one suggestion made to the writer by Georgian and Armenian acquaintances in Moscow may be pertinent. This was that, unlike the Russians, these people display intense, clannish local loyalty and are less likely to inform on one another to the police than are the Russians. This trait renders them somewhat less susceptible to police penetration and manipulation. The writer had the impression that the Georgian Communists were somewhat favored by the regime.

We cannot deal at length with the big problem of national minority discontent as a possible disintegrating force in Soviet society, for our present information about it is very inadequate. We can be sure, however, from what has been mentioned earlier, from the brutal liquidation of six Soviet national groups—Volga German, Crimean Tatar, Chechen-Ingush, Balkar, Karachai, and Kalmyck—and from much other evidence that apparently there is deep resentment among non-Russians, especially the Soviet Moslems, against Soviet administrative centralism. It is directed particularly against the Russians as Moscow's main agents, a feeling intensified during the war partly because of Nazi propaganda and partly as a reaction against "Great Russian" chauvinism. Stalin's successors, without altering his long-term "Russification" policy, have made important gestures toward psychological mollification of the non-Russians, including a loud celebration in 1954 of the three hundredth anniversary of the "reunion" of Russia and the Ukraine. But, on the other hand, non-Russians have been "urged" to join in the compulsory migration to settle "virgin soil" in the East.

IV / SOCIOLOGY AND PSYCHOLOGY OF THE PARTY

Elite Privileges and Controls

The vast party-state structure which we have surveyed directs, mobilizes, and controls both the material and the spiritual resources of Soviet society, a role stressed by Stalin in his pronouncements on linguistics, nations, and states in the summer of 1950. In his *Economic Problems of Socialism in the U.S.S.R.*,[14] however, whose doctrinal authority has in turn been re-emphasized by his successors, Stalin declared that even the Soviet state is not all powerful, as he implied some Communists thought, but is subject to the laws of socialist society. He then goes on to explain that the chief difference between the capitalist and the socialist order is that development in the socialist system proceeds smoothly and gradually, while in the capitalist society change can be effected only through revolution, which must be inevitable. These dicta, seemingly contradictory to each other, actually represent two sides of the same coin and sum up the practice of mature Soviet totalitarianism.

In this system language, science, and literature are as much instruments of government as economics, law, and administration. It is important to note that as the internal homogeneity of the elite strata has increased, the differences between Soviet and "capitalist" society have been emphasized more and more in official doctrine, despite surface gestures to the contrary, particularly in the field of cultural relations. In part, at least, the accentuation of these differences may reflect the Krem-

14. Released on October 3, 1952, this work furnished the ideological framework for the nineteenth party congress.

lin's fear that the claims and promises of Soviet ideology will lose their power unless bolstered by a synthetic nationalism revolving around the concept of the struggle between capitalist and socialist nations.

Barrington Moore describes in his *Soviet Politics* the development in the U.S.S.R. of the "bureaucratic state." Such a state, with its graduated hierarchy of officials, ranks, salary scales and perquisites, and the dangers attendant on its creation of special-interest groups, was certainly not envisaged by Marx or Lenin. Stalin sought to bring new elements into the party but at the same time retain an exclusive inner party equipped with a special *esprit de corps* and organizational devices by which it could control the enlarged "outer" party. A vital part of this process was swelling the ranks of the secret political police, that portion of the society which, siphoned off by early selective recruiting, isolation, privilege, and special training, acts as the rulers' watchdogs over the rest. But even this caste is controlled with frightful severity—the elimination of the Beria clique indicates that. Details of the control process are naturally hard to come by, but under Stalin a supersecret party agency, the special sector of the Central Committee, together with Stalin's personal secretariat, played the key roles. Also the party apparatus as a whole, particularly the Committee of Party Control and the regular armed forces, acts as checks on the power of the police. Thus far these checks have apparently been effective: the last four police heads have met destruction at their hands.

Control of the army and navy officers' corps which, together with the police, constitute the most highly organized element in the bureaucracy, presents perhaps even more difficult problems than control of the police; for the armed forces, being much larger, are more representative of the society as a whole and do not so easily tend to identify with the party and its leadership. The 1937 purge not only of the top army commander, Tukhachevski, and most of his military colleagues but also of Gamarnik, the head of the army political administration, indicates how the mechanism of control can get out of hand.

The Kremlin's methods of controlling these bodies of armed men include privilege, intimidation, and conditioning. Their privileges in a society most of whose members live shabbily or, at best, by American standards, very plainly, consist of superior food, housing and clothing, cultural advantages for themselves and their children, and prestige. Prestige, according to Soviet refugees, is associated with the ability to inspire fear.

Conditioning is achieved by formal discipline and intensive training in the group life of the officers' academies, clubs, and special apartment houses, as well as in isolation not only from the forbidden outside world but also from other groups in Soviet society. In this abnormal communications pattern, as we can imagine, rumors naturally flourish.

Despite their privileges, even the elite members of Soviet society seem to lead a prison-like existence as judged by our standards, although they probably resent it less than would Americans, Britons, or Frenchmen. Under conditions of foreign service, as in the Soviet zones of Germany and Austria, resentment can become intense. Soviet enlisted men on occupation duty are almost never out of formation—they even march to the movies. They are subjected to daily propaganda lectures; leaves are almost never granted, even in cases of a parent's death. Officers, despite privileges which inspire envy among enlisted men, are not much better off in respect to freedom: they must obtain permission from superiors, even as high as divisional commanders, for simple requests such as a pass to visit a near-by town. Fraternization is strictly forbidden and severely punished, although occasionally, especially in 1946–48 before the regulations became so severe, Soviet personnel did mix with the Germans, and some of them had to flee to British- or American-controlled territory after their offenses had been discovered. Gregory Klimov, a former Soviet officer, has given us a vivid account of this regime in his book *The Terror Machine*.

Political control and surveillance are especially powerful in the armed services, exercised by commanding officers, by a network of "deputy commanders for political affairs" (*zampolits*), and by "secret sections" headed by counterintelligence officers. The zampolits direct the work of party organizations in the services; every unit down to the battalion level apparently has a zampolit. The zampolits are successors to the political commissars, so often "abolished" and reinstated, now functioning in this new guise. They have a special chain of command heading up in the chief political administration of the army and navy; they have their own special secret channels of communication. Besides controlling the army and party organizations as indirectly and as tactfully as possible, zampolits prepare monthly detailed reports on the political and moral complexion of their colleagues and subordinates and exercise numerous important propaganda, indoctrination, and welfare functions.

The history of the Soviet army (called the "Red Army" until 1946) might be written in terms of the balancing of political and technical demands. Since Timoshenko's reforms in 1940 following the disastrous experience of the Finnish war, the trend has been to fuse politics and techniques, though never eliminating a special political service. A speaker at the nineteenth congress declared that zampolits must now possess all the military knowledge and training appropriate for their command, in addition to their political assets.

This development indicates that the Kremlin is shrewdly aware of the friction which can develop when politicians meddle in the affairs of experts, and refugee accounts offer striking evidence that political officers are sometimes hated and feared but more often merely tolerated or even patronized. On the other hand, apparently some of them live up to the official ideal. *Pravda* (September 14, 1939) described the political officer's role as that of the "father and soul" of his unit. But a sterner image was supplied in a story, "The Party Investigator," which appeared in *Red Star* (September 25, 1946). In this story a colonel, holder of many decorations, reacts with abject fear to an investigator's unfavorable analysis of his work and even bursts into tears.

Police control in the army is more feared than party-political control. It is exercised by the counterintelligence administration functioning through "special departments" (*osobye otdely*). Besides this network of departments throughout the forces, there are special units for personnel of the service ministries and for army and navy academies which are responsible directly to counterintelligence headquarters in Moscow. The counterintelligence network extends from top to bottom of the services, although the formal structure stops at the divisional level. From this level down, it functions through plenipotentiaries, each responsible for a separate net of secret informers who are unknown even to their comrades. And there are informers even in tanks and planes, according to some refugee accounts.

Like the zampolits, the counterintelligence officers have their own secret channels of communication; unlike them, however, they have the power to arrest. Normally the two special services seem to function co-operatively, the former exercising a "positive" and the latter a "negative" check.[15]

The control system sketched here extends throughout the entire society. As the military and civilian bureaucracy and industry and agriculture have expanded, so have the control and checking mechanisms. This is a major reason for the growth of the party, which we shall presently examine statistically. The lower echelons of the party serve as auxiliaries and agents of the higher party command in the exercise of controls. In factories and other economic enterprises, party organizations possess a right of control over production. This right of control is not granted to the party groups in governmental organizations such as all-union ministries, but it is not necessary, since it is exercised by the Central Committee directly over the ministers. The central committees of party organizations of republics control the two lower ministries —the quasi-local counterpart or union republic ministries and the completely local republic ministries.

Economic Controls

Let us examine the controls found in industry. Apparently, reconciliation of political and economic objectives has always been quite difficult, for while the aim is maximum success in both spheres, economics is usually subordi-

nated to politics when a choice has to be made. Often this involves extreme forms of social pressure, police methods, or, as in the case of the collectivization of agriculture, large-scale violence, to force co-operation from the social groups whose regimentation was necessary for the achievement of the Kremlin's objectives.

As the party and state machine has been expanded and perfected, coercion of the economically productive elements apparently has diminished and has been partially replaced by the function of over-all direction and co-ordination of the economy—but this statement is subject to major qualifications. For there is a striking tendency for the party to usurp the functions of the economic administrators in crucial times or at any time in sectors which may require special attention.

The principle has been established that the party is dominant in leadership (*rukovodstvo*), while the state is dominant in administration (*upravlenie*); this means that the over-all policy is made by the party but that implementation is normally in the hands of the economic ministries and enterprises under their control. The party impinges at many points upon the sphere of the economic administrator, for at every territorial level it exercises supervisory and intelligence functions in each and every economic enterprise operation within the particular territorial division. This supervision is exercised by the oblast and rayon party organizations.

Besides this intermediate level of supervision, there is also the right of control of party organizations in individual enterprises. This right of control does not, in theory at least, give the primary party organizations the right to interfere in day-to-day plant operations; rather it simply involves calling the attention of factory directors—al-

15. According to articles by Boris Nicolaevski, published in the *Sotsialisticheski Vestnik* and *The New Leader* in 1954, there is also a special military police, in which party leaders like Bulganin have the decisive influence.

most all of whom, like any officers, diplomats, school directors, and executives generally, are party members—to defects in the work of the enterprises and assisting in their correction. But if the economic officials resist or, as is more often the case, evade the primary organizations' suggestions, the party organizations may then carry the matter to higher party levels, which in turn may bring about the issuance of instructions through appropriate government channels to offending or incompetent officials. In emergencies factory primary party organizations often take over direction even of current operations.

In extreme cases the "signaling" of defects may involve dismissal or more severe punishment of state officials. As already indicated, the right of control applies only to economic enterprises, which the Soviets call "cost-accountable" institutions; it does not apply to ministries and other state institutions whose personnel is paid directly out of the state budget. These "state" and "Soviet" agencies have party organizations, of course, but the latter have the right only to pass on to the responsible state officials, as well as to their party and state superiors, information on matters which in their opinion require special treatment.

But the intermediate and primary party organizations also perform other important economic functions, for which they are equipped with specialized organizations and personnel. At the lowest level, that of the primary party organizations, the major single task appears to be that of instigating political and economic agitation intended to increase productivity per man, and one of the major tasks of secretaries of primary party organizations is to deploy party resources most effectively into the agitation program. An important job of the first secretary of a large primary organization is to direct the work of the "agitation collective," which recruits party and nonparty "volunteers." At the rayon and oblast level the responsible secretaries perform a myriad of economic functions. Most of the content of the party press is devoted to describing ways in which this back-stopping of the economic administration is carried out; summarily it is the adoption of any measures necessary to assure the fulfilment of the production quotas assigned to enterprises by the economic plan.

This system of party-checking is the Soviet substitute for competition and the price system in a free-market economy and also for a free press. The organizational mechanisms necessary for the performance of these functions involve a good deal of duplication, and this has clearly been a sore point with the Kremlin, judging from exhortations in the press and the twists and turns in the development of the party structure. Only a few highlights in this development can be noted here. At the seventeenth party congress in 1934 it was decided to set up economic units in the intermediate party organizations. This practice was abandoned for a short period following the eighteenth party congress in 1939 as an interference with "one-man control" by economic officials. But in 1941 Malenkov, then Politburo alternate, in his very important speech at the party conference (February, 1941) discussed how necessary it was to establish several industrial party secretaries in cities, oblasts, and republics with highly developed industry. He said that party organizations must assist the ministries in controlling the work of enterprises and must realize that the latter were not capable of exercising this control unaided. In the course of the large-scale reorganization of the party apparatus of late 1948 a full panoply of economic sections was reestablished in the republic and oblast party organizations, thus continuing the trend inaugurated by Malenkov in 1941. But this picture is confusing, in that postwar commentary on these problems has also insisted that the sharp line of demarcation between party and economic administrations so blurred during the war be re-established.

Formal Political Structure

The salient features of party control of the Soviet legislative, or constitutional, organs should now be mentioned. Constitutionally the whole Soviet system heads up in the U.S.S.R. Supreme Soviet. "Soviet democracy" propaganda, disseminated with an especially deafening roar during elections, is built around the thesis that only "socialism" can assure its citizens the popular sovereignty and genuine rights eschewed in the sham, "formal," and "bourgeois" democracies of the West.

The propaganda promulgated in the Supreme Soviet elections of 1946, 1950, and 1954 emphasized, as it had done before the war, that a vote for the candidate of the bloc of Communist and nonparty people was a vote for Bolshevik party policy. And the party proclaimed that the elections constituted a popular vote of confidence in itself. Now agitators are, among other things, instructed to mobilize professors, engineers, and other "brain" workers for propaganda work. As an example, a former Soviet citizen, an engineer, told the writer how he was once ordered to deliver an election speech—with an agent of the political police standing right behind him!

Despite skepticism among Soviet intellectuals and even among the masses about the party-directed "elections," in which there is never more than one candidate and in which the "campaign" is a farce by Western standards, it would be a mistake to consider that the Soviet people are indignant about them or would easily understand the Western system of political competition. A Soviet refugee explained to the writer that the masses are indifferent to the elections; they even regard them as a kind of holiday. Every effort is made to turn the elections into a gala occasion; the goal is a 100 per cent vote. Skeptical Soviet intellectuals are afraid to express their opinions regarding them. On the other hand, Soviet refugees do not need to be outside the U.S.S.R. long to become aware that this system of elections is a "comedy," as they sometimes describe it to Westerners.

The way in which the party mobilizes nonparty persons during election campaigns is but one illustration of its all-pervasive "social service," whose demands turn the Komsomol, the trade-unions, and the soviets into devices for obtaining unpaid labor from the population. Not the least important aspect of this system is that it keeps people so busy, tired, and politically exhausted that they cannot even think effectively about political resistance, much less organize to pursue nonparty objectives. And political apathy, which the party fears, is perhaps the most significant negative response of the masses.

Party Strength

The party today is probably more than one hundred times as large numerically as it was at the time of the "February"[16] revolution of 1917. In April, 1917, at the time of the sixth congress, the party had, according to the *Small Soviet Encyclopedia,* 80,000 "organized members." By March, 1918, it had grown to 270,000. During the civil war its growth was rapid, though not healthy from the point of view of then prevalent standards, for the proportion of peasants to workers was too large.

16. The "February" and "October" revolutions are still so referred to in deference to revolutionary tradition, although by the Western calendar adopted by the new regime they occurred in March and November.

Also many careerists, opportunists, and "disguised Mensheviks" gained entrance. By March, 1921, at the tenth congress, which introduced the policy of temporary concessions embodied in the "New Economic Policy," the party had 732,000 members.

Then came a series of purges, the first of which (1921) reduced membership by 25 per cent. Continued weeding out brought membership down to 386,000 by April, 1923. The purges indicate that the policy of concessions was not applied in this basic organ of Bolshevik power; on the contrary, despite the weakened condition of the country in the postwar period, increased militancy reigned. But by 1924 it was felt that the party had become too small for effective performance of its tasks. The "Lenin enrolment" was proclaimed; a vigorous effort was made to recruit factory workers; and by 1928, on the eve of the "Iron Age" of Soviet industrialization, the party had 1,304,-047 members and candidates. Even during this period of growth there were checkups of party documents and records of the production cells in industry, one reason for which was that Trotsky, then being rapidly stripped of his influence by the Stalin majority faction in the Central Committee, was still popular among the workers, especially in Leningrad. There were also purges among students and clerical workers, for this was a period when there was still sharp suspicion of penetration into the party by "petty bourgeois" elements.

There was another big purge in 1929, following which, under the spur of the first five-year plan, the party grew rapidly; it had over 3,000,000 members by early 1933.[17] In that year another major purge occurred, as a result of

17. A vivid illustration of the comparative lack of secretiveness of the Soviet regime twenty-three years ago is the publication of detailed statistical analyses of the 1929 purge.

which about 25 per cent of the party members were stricken from the rolls. During 1935 and 1936 "verification" of party documents occurred; from 1933 to 1936 no new members were admitted, and more than 200,000 were expelled. In 1936–38 came the terrible purges, during which the Commission of Party Control and the NKVD (now MVD) expelled and arrested thousands. A period had arrived when a party member stood in far greater danger of arrest than did a nonmember. This marked the first use of police methods of party control on a large scale and the party's rolls shrank to less then 2,000,000. This period was known as the *Ezhovshchina,* from Ezhov, who replaced Yagoda as head of the NKVD after his arrest and execution in 1937; then he too was purged and replaced by Beria late in 1938. A purge of the purgers followed, during which many "purgees" were released from prison and restored to all or part of their former status. Nevertheless, Soviet people who lived through these events refer to them with a shudder. One reason for some of the gestures of Stalin's successors is that they wish to assure the population that there will not be a new Ezhovshchina.

Perhaps fearing that Ezhov, who seems to have suffered from a persecution complex, in consequence had carried the purge to the point where it threatened social disintegration, the party inaugurated a new policy of expansion. By March, 1939, there were 1,588,852 members and 868,886 candidates. In one of the major speeches at the 1939 congress Zhdanov declared that mass purges were a thing of the past; by 1941, on the eve of the German onslaught, the party had 3,800,000 members and candidates.

World War II was a period of exceptionally rapid growth, despite very heavy losses at the front. As in 1918–21, the Kremlin, after initial reverses, showed its ability to exploit traditional Russian resistance to foreign invaders. Party membership, with Kremlin approval, became identified with superior patriotism. Those were the days when "Papa" Kalinin, the aged Soviet "president" and one of the few genuinely popular figures in the Politburo, suggested that party propagandists disseminate the idea that to be a good party member it was sufficient to be a good fighter or a good producer.[18] On the mastheads of all but strictly party publications the slogan "Everything for the Front" replaced the old slogan "Proletarians of all countries, unite!"

The majority of those who entered the party during the war were military service personnel, most of them farm boys, peasants being then, as today, the numerically preponderant element of the army. By March, 1944, party strength was 5,000,000; by January, 1945, it was 5,700,000; in April, 5,800,000; in October, 6,000,000; and by January, 1946, it had dropped back to 5,800,000.

Apparently there were numerous exclusions in late 1945 and early 1946. During the later months of 1944 and early in 1945 the press indicated that the Kremlin was moving to restore traditional ideological requirements; the full return to orthodoxy took place in 1946. One landmark was Stalin's reassertion of the gloomy tenets of Lenin regarding relations with the non-Soviet world in his crucial February 9, 1946, election speech as a candidate from Moscow (Stalin's district).

The Central Committee on July 26, 1946, issued a decree entitled "On the Growth of the Party and on Measures for Intensified Party Organizational and Party Political Work among Those Who Have Recently Entered the Communist party." Although this decree was not published, numerous editorial commentaries made it clear that it laid down a policy of checking party growth and inaugurated a vigorous campaign for the political indoctrination of new members. It was followed on August 2, 1946, by a very important decree on the training and retraining of leading party and soviet cadres.

The size of the party was stabilized at a level considered adequate, and subsequent data indicate no basic change in this policy. In December, 1947, the press published a membership and candidate figure of 6,300,000, given by Malenkov in his September speech at the founding of the Cominform, while in his nineteenth congress address Malenkov indicated that on October 1, 1952, the party numbered 6,013,259 members and 868,886 candidates—the party had gained 1,600,000 members and candidates during the early part of the war. He expressed satisfaction with the results of the postwar indoctrination program but warned that the task of narrowing the lag between political quality and quantitative growth was not finished. A strict admissions policy must be continued, he urged, and called for "vigilance."

Only time will tell whether the Kremlin's admission of more than four million new members between congresses strengthened or weakened the party, but the record thus far indicates that the operation was a success. While the millions of new members constitute no threat to the absolute power of the small inner core, absorption of such a vast mass may eventually weaken the party or at least significantly affect its character. And certainly it will tend to lower its intellectual and ideological level, thus carrying further a process

18. The exploitation of Kalinin as a father-image was clever. Typical is the reference to him as "All-Union village chief" in F. Gavrilova, "Notes of a Rank-and-File Party Worker" (Moscow, 1940; in Russian), p. 133. The post-Stalin regime gave the post of president of the Presidium of the Supreme Soviet to the old, militarily unsuccessful, but shrewd and not unpopular Voroshilov.

dating from Stalin's totalitarian revolution of the 1930's. As the differences between party and nonparty people grow less and as the obligations of membership exceed the privileges more and more, it is not unreasonable to suppose that the party as a whole will become a less reliable instrument of the dictatorship. One indication, though an inconclusive one, of this trend is the fact that among Soviet defectors of recent years party members have constituted a proportion far exceeding their percentage of the Soviet population.

Carriers of ideological infection are removed from the party before they can contaminate their fellows. In this connection it is interesting to note that, according to refugee sources, the MVD has a section for "purification" of the party. Such are the methods which a totalitarian regime, and it alone, can practice without shattering internal unity. But a mass organization controlled by police methods degenerates morally. We examine some aspects of party morale in the final pages of this chapter.

Social Composition

Changes in the social composition of the party have been as striking but less unstable than fluctuations in its numerical growth. Though statistical information since 1930 has been extremely scanty, some general outlines are clear. The two major stages in the social development of the party correspond roughly to those of Soviet economic development: before and after the five-year plans. Prior to the Stalin era of industrialization, the ideal image of the party member was that of the superior, fully class-conscious proletarian. In reality, as in the underground and exile party of Lenin, even this class was dominated by, or at least shared leadership with, the "professional revolution-ary" of middle-class origin; and Lenin, Trotsky, Bukharin, Radek, Yaroslavsky, Pokrovsky, and many others belonged to this bourgeois "vanguard" group.

In the 1920's the proletarian kernel of the party continued to grow. The official publication, *The All-Union Communist Party (of Bolsheviks) in Resolutions,* for 1933 stated that, when Lenin died, the proletarian component was 44 per cent. It was 57 per cent in December, 1925; on July 1, 1928, it was 62 per cent. As late as April, 1929, the sixteenth party conference complained that the percentage of workers in the party was insufficient to carry out the tasks of "socialist reconstruction" of the economy. The working-class kernel was 68 per cent in 1930, but only 60 per cent in 1934. No figures on this point were published subsequently, but David Dallin estimates that 90 per cent of party members today (1954) are "Philistines" of a "petty bourgeois" type.

Even during the early 1930's the percentage of party members belonging to the working-class kernel who were actually engaged in production was falling pretty rapidly: the party, and thus the Soviet elite, were already on their way to becoming a ruling caste of former proletarians and their children.

Before World War II the party network was relatively thin in the rural areas. As Andreev pointed out at the eighteenth congress, in the country's 243,000 collective farms there were only 12,000 primary organizations, with 153,000 members and candidates, a startlingly small fraction of the party's total membership. In more than 100,000 collective farms there were not even any Komsomol organizations. The early Komsomol had only about 5,000,000 members, mostly in the cities; in 1949 it had 9,000,000; and it was revealed at the nineteenth congress in 1952 that this figure had risen to 16,000,000.

Pegov declared at the nineteenth

congress (1941) that there were more than six times as many collective farm primary units as in 1939. The rate of increase in their number was about twice as great as the increase in the growth of primary organizations throughout the party. Together with the growth of the Komsomol and the reduction, by consolidation, of collective farms from 254,000 to 97,000 between January and October, 1950, the denser party network tightens the Kremlin's grip on the peasantry, backbone of the armed forces and politically less organized than the urban population.

In reality, as we have already indicated, carrying out the tasks of industrialization required development of the so-called "new Soviet intelligentsia"; hence the percentage of "workers in production" fell rapidly as industrialization progressed. But no over-all statistics reflecting this change have been published, a reticence due no doubt in part to an intentional concealment of the development of the new ruling caste —an indication of the increasing suppression of political, social, and economic information as Soviet totalitarianism develops. This practice reached a peak during the great purges, when almost any information became a military secret, and still continues today.

The shift from revolutionary workers to intellectuals as the predominant party type was reflected in the top levels by the replacement of the Lenin-Trotsky type of leader by the Stalinist. Then the next shift seemed for awhile to be toward the Malenkov production-man type, and one of the most striking aspects of this process was the elimination of "internationalists" by the 1936–38 purges. Men like Trotsky, who had spent years abroad, spoke foreign languages, and were more cosmopolitan in their outlook, were eliminated from top and intermediate levels during the 1920's and 1930's. One of the last strong-

holds of their influence, the Commissariat (now Ministry) of Foreign Affairs, was drastically reshuffled when Molotov replaced Litvinov as its head in 1939; its Jewish element, in particular, had already been decimated in the big purge. What remained was almost entirely eliminated after World War II, when some of its survivors, such as Litvinov and Maisky, were taken off the shelf to influence Western opinion during the period of the anti-Nazi coalition. The cosmopolitan Jew, however, still played a prominent role in the arts and professions, although the postwar period has witnessed a mopping-up operation in which the anticosmopolitanism campaign of 1949 and after was apparently designed to reduce or eliminate altogether their role in these fields too.

The ascendancy of the socialist administrator, often with engineering training, has been accompanied by the development of a new, chauvinistic, and suspicious Soviet patriotism. This new nationalism is certainly not a direct continuation of tsarist policy but is undoubtedly a reflection of the chauvinistic attitudes of a new managerial and administrative elite, at the same time substituting for the values promised, but not realized, by the revolution. Its ugliest aspects, such as its anti-Semitism, reveal that sovietism is following in the footsteps of other tyrannies in their elevation of a tribal xenophobia over individual human rights and dignity. Yet the Kremlin is too shrewd to abandon completely proletarian internationalism, for it, like love of the fatherland, is required of all members by the new party statutes. Its content, however, has been debased beyond the recognition of a Lenin, who inveighed against all forms of national chauvinism and regarded Russia as a backward, though potentially great, country, its revolution in large part on the basis of the unusually rich foreign contacts of **Russian revolutionists.** Stalin's proletarian internationalism, in contrast, is only a slogan for export to the unwary and the ignorant.

Education, Age, and Sex

Party members and leaders have a good, if narrow, education, one both vocationally utilitarian and politically orthodox, for the main objective of Soviet education is to train efficient technicians and administrators and to inculcate political loyalty. Since the 1930's and especially since the publication in 1938 of the *History of the Communist Party,* often called the "short course," loyalty to Stalin and the party rather than mastery of Marxism has been the primary political criterion for party membership.

The essence of Stalinism was for years contained in the militant and crude *Short Course,* for which a special set of detailed directions for dissemination and use was issued by the Central Committee. There has been no indication that this *Course* has been superseded by any other since Stalin's death, although it has been supplemented with the materials of the nineteenth congress, Khrushchev's main speeches, post-Stalin Central Committee resolutions, and other political and doctrinal material.

As was pointed out in an instructive pamphlet published in 1944 entitled *The Primary Party Organization in a Soviet Institution,* political work among Soviet employees must be conducted "differentially," a term suggestive of the approach used in the political indoctrination of party and nonparty Soviet citizens and, indeed, in the entire area of control of the public mind by the Kremlin since the late 1930's. The basic ideology is set forth in the party statutes, in the Soviet constitution, the *Short Course,* and in such materials as the brief "history" published in Soviet newspapers on July 26, 1953. These are required reading and study for everybody, but those who wish to rise to high positions in the party or in the state must work strenuously to "master bolshevism." This does not mean that they are to become critical philosophers; for, as Stalin and other top party leaders pointed out in connection with the adoption of the present approach to Marxism-Leninism in the late 1930's, a party of intellectuals is not desired.

Prolonged study of a range of difficult subjects, including dialectical and historical materialism, party history, political economy, and—since 1946, at Stalin's order—formal logic, is required before the party member can consider himself fully qualified for the highest positions. A wide range of media and educational institutions has been set up to train party members, at the summit of which are the Higher Party School, with its dual party and Soviet faculties, and the Academy of Social Sciences—both directly responsible to the Central Committee. These institutions train and retrain party and government leaders, newspaper editors, and professors of "Marxism-Leninism."

Despite rejection of the liberal education objectives found in Western schools, the massive new Russian secondary and higher educational systems do provide the party with an abundance of trained personnel. Formal education is highly valued, perhaps even more so than in the United States, and a youth's scholastic record is a springboard to career opportunities. Apparently, higher education is increasingly becoming a prerequisite for access to the highest party posts; thus Pegov pointed out at the nineteenth congress that, of the 1,192 voting delegates to the congress, 709 had a higher education (282 of whom were engineers), 84 had an incomplete higher education, and 223 had a secondary education (tenth grade), while 65 delegates had academic degrees or titles. In 1939, out of 1,569 voting delegates, only 418 had had a higher education, 78 some higher training, and 352 a complete secondary education. Pegov also said that the number of primary party organizations in educational institutions had increased sevenfold since the 1939 congress; this, together with the great growth of the Komsomol, indicates much wider coverage of the Soviet student youth by the party. These trends lend interest to the assertion made by a Soviet refugee, himself scientifically trained, that the regime was rearing a generation of "Communist scientists."

In view of the foregoing, it is not surprising that the vast majority of the nineteenth congress delegates were persons who joined the party after the revolution and that over half had joined since 1931. Among congress delegates, almost the only "old Bolsheviks" who joined before 1917 were early adherents of Stalin, 16 per cent joining between 1941 and 1945 and only 4 per cent since 1945.

In terms of age, 61 per cent of the voting delegates were between forty-one and fifty, and 15 per cent were over fifty. These seniority and age figures contrast with those of the 1920's and 1930's, when a much higher percentage of members were of prerevolutionary vintage but when the average age of party leaders as a group was much lower. The figures also indicate that while the party retains its willingness to open the ranks of leadership to aggressive and ambitious youth, it is far less a young men's party than it was fifteen years ago. For only 15 per cent of the voting delegates at the 1939 congress were between forty and fifty years of age, and only 3 per cent were over fifty. The Stalinist veterans are still dominant but no longer young. One is tempted to speculate on disruptive forces which may be developing among what some refugee writers call the

"second soviet generation" and on a possibly even more interesting "generations problem" looming ahead.

It is possible that one reason for the new statutes' provisions excepting party officials from the rules governing expulsion of rank-and-file members is to prevent expression of the will of the mass of relatively undisciplined younger members. Along the same line, the age of election of deputies to the Supreme Soviet was raised from eighteen to twenty-three in October, 1945.

There were 147 women, or 12 per cent of the total, among the voting delegates at the nineteenth congress; at the eighteenth congress they had represented only 9 per cent. And *Bolshevik* and other party organs reflect an effort to increase the percentage of women in the party: *Bolshevik* (No. 1, [January, 1951]) reported that, as of July 1, 1950, 20 per cent of the party members were women and contrasted this proportion with the previous lower percentages. A Central Committee section for women's affairs was set up in 1948, which has counterparts in some of the republic party organizations such as those in Central Asia, where current rapid industrialization of a backward area requires special efforts to bring women into the factory and office labor force. The increasing percentage of women in the party probably also reflects the shortage of male labor power from which the U.S.S.R. suffers.

Women do occupy some important positions in the party. Pegov announced that, of the women delegates at the nineteenth congress, six were secretaries of oblast or republic committees. And the first secretary of the important Moscow City Committee is a woman, Furtseva. These data, however, reveal how far women are from anything remotely approaching equality of rank with men. For example, there never has been a woman Politburo member. In January, 1947, death removed the last woman member of the old Central Committee, the "old Bolshevik" Rosalia Zemlyachka, a member of the Commission of Party Control. There are two women on the new Central Committee, and six alternates. The status of women, inside and outside the party, must be appraised in light of the fact that even more than men they suffer from the burdens of an "equality" which often imposes requirements ruinous to health and normal living. It was the writer's impression during his residence in Soviet Russia that discontent was greater among women than among men because to them the glaring difference between revolutionary ideals and Soviet reality was exceptionally clear. This is probably far less true in areas such as Central Asia, where the status of women was so unusually low before the revolution. It may also be balanced by the fact that women bulk so large in many Soviet professions, particularly medicine.[19]

Morale and Attitudes

We conclude this analysis of the totalitarian party with a sketch of the attitude patterns of its members. What sort of people are these "new Soviet men"? How loyal are they to the party and to the Kremlin? Do they love or hate the regime, or are they passive and indifferent? These are the most difficult questions one can ask about this system, and among the most important.

It is not too difficult, with careful use of the published sources, to define the official Soviet image of authority and command-subordination relationships. It is set forth in the *Short Course*, in the approved editions of Lenin's and Stalin's works, and in the official biographies of Lenin and Stalin.

19. By the end of 1952, according to Nicholas De Witt, 50 per cent of Soviet professionals were women (see *Science,* July 2, 1954, p. 2).

The official ideal is still that of the fearless soldier of the revolution, boundlessly devoted to the cause of "progressive" humanity. Since the society is considered to be in a state of war with a decaying but malevolent and still powerful "capitalist" enemy, the utmost "vigilance" is demanded, to prevent being "disarmed" by the external enemy and its "concealed" agents. This motif was very prominent in proclamations issued during the weeks after Stalin's death, especially in the announcement by Beria's Ministry of Internal Affairs regarding the "political blindness" of former Minister Ignatiev. By a sort of moral double bookkeeping, the Communist justifies the use of all available means against the enemy but displays intense moral indignation for allegedly being treated as he treats or wants to treat his opponent. The tactics required in the struggle have been called (by Nathan Leites, for example), the Bolshevik "operational code." Students of history may feel that these principles are far older than Machiavelli's but the modern world had forgotten that "practical" politicians could live by such a creed, combining as it does fanatical self-righteousness with uninhibited expediency.

As Raymond Bauer in his *The New Man in Soviet Psychology* shows, Soviet people are expected to live by a morality which might be called one of planned free will. Individual responsibility and guilt are emphasized despite the fact that policy determination and doctrinal interpretation are imposed from above.

We may sketch broadly the outlines of the real Soviet political mentality in the revealing bits of information in some of the published sources and in often impressionistic and individualistic but trenchant testimony of Soviet escapees. Again it must be emphasized, especially to Americans, that while Soviet life seems intolerable to us, it is not nearly so difficult for Soviet people to adjust to as it would be for Westerners, for the peoples of the U.S.S.R., because of their very different history, have a conception of authority widely variant from ours. For while these peoples have been brought somewhat closer to Western standards of judgment and action through their Soviet experience, especially in their industrial mores, in many ways cultural differences between them and us have widened. They are certainly more punctual, energetic, and efficient than they were in 1917. Much of their new knowledge is superficial, however, and behavior is often ritualistic.

The Russian experience suggests, however, that new production techniques are much easier to acquire than are new political habits and attitudes. It often seems to the student of Soviet Russia that the past has taken revenge in the political sphere for the defeats suffered in those of science and industry. In its political morality Russia today seems in many ways to resemble the Russia of Ivan the Terrible. Contrary to its avowed purposes, the revolution swept out the rudiments of government by consent borrowed from the West but understood by only a fraction of the Russian middle and upper classes. Then, too, the nondemocratic political framework of industrialization and the Bolshevik image of politics as a form of warfare added a new totalitarian dimension in the transformation of the empire into the Soviet Union. The result was the total state, in which the power is seized by the most ruthless personalities and the scope and character of which are restrained by neither law nor custom. This is, of course, much more true in the higher echelons than in the lower and applies especially to the attitude of the MVD toward its work. A kind of crystallization of political functions and vices occurs; concentrated as a special caste,

it seems to be distilled out of the population, the "left-overs" becoming very "unpolitical." This is one reason why "ordinary" Soviet citizens profess to know so little about politics and display so little interest in it. For political authority becomes an evil, something one has to put up with, like the wild and elemental forces of nature. But at the same time it loses some of its moral authority: the individual conforms to it outwardly but inwardly does not identify with it or its representatives. The result is a conflict between official and personal morality which can be very painful. Perhaps this helps explain why a Soviet émigré can say: "I am a very frank, but a very cunning person." By "frank" he probably meant open and simple in his personal relations, at least whenever possible; by "cunning" he was probably describing his dealings with the authorities and situations where cunning and ruthlessness were required.

Soviet people, both party and nonparty, seem to think of holders of power as inevitably hard and cunning. They have a certain contempt for the naïveté of American political leaders, and bluff, deception, and camouflage seem to bulk unusually large in their conception of normal political behavior. It is significant that even refugees who expressed hatred for Stalin also admired his slyness.

In their political ideas the Soviet people still bear much of the cultural heritage of the past. The ideal ruler seems to be thought of as the stern but just and human patriarch; similarly, an army officer is liked and respected if he is capable, though not a grindstone, and willing to wink at occasional lapses. Russians are similar to Americans in liking a "good guy," and their conception thereof does not differ in essence from ours. A widespread reverence for Lenin even among refugees who are hostile to Stalin illustrates this aspect of the popular ideology, and even those who served in the U.S.S.R. were aware of it. The writer encountered no open enthusiasm for Stalin, although people he knew had respect and even awe of him, while spontaneous expressions of affection for Lenin were common. It is probable that a very small percentage of Russians suspect that Lenin's program led them to their present situation, for to the Soviet people Lenin was the image of a good ruler—wise, stern, but kind—while Stalin's figure was identified with the unnatural coldness, harshness, and impersonality of the regime.

In view of the foregoing, it is easy to see why Soviet political attitudes differ from ours and how unfair it is to expect these people easily to understand our concepts. This point can be illustrated briefly in two very fundamental areas: (a) One must always bear in mind the Russians' highly personal view of government and their indifference to abstract ideas of law and government. Political issues, to become meaningful to them, must be personified, which is also true of Americans but to a lesser degree. And Stalin shrewdly realized this aspect of the Soviet mentality. (b) Intrinsically the Russians are socialists, though most Russian refugees angrily reject this word and even the whole terminology of Marxism. But very few of them, even after they have been out of the country for a long time, can conceive of a Soviet state in which heavy industry and the railroads, for example, are privately owned.

Even if the aspirations and values of Soviet people differ from ours, they do not necessarily conflict with ours. Soviet people certainly highly value human dignity, a concept for which they evince deep respect; then, too, party and nonparty members alike hate the political police and have little respect for the ordinary police, or militia, which has little power; and, above all, they desire peace and more enjoyment of a private personal life. They may not be the noblest ideals, but they are certainly human and understandable.

It is difficult to distinguish between party and nonparty Soviet citizens' "official" and "unofficial," or informal, thinking. There is probably a far wider chasm to be found between the high- and the low-ranking than between the party and the nonparty elements, for the higher placed a person is in any of the pyramids of the Soviet hierarchy, the more he seems to identify his values and purposes with those of the regime: both the "natural selection" which brings him to the top and his disproportionate share of the available material values lead in that direction.

Soviet refugees in their various interviews and writings usually divide party members into three main categories, which we, if cautious of the pitfalls of classification, can use as a handy rough guide. This grouping tallies fairly well with that of the writer after four years' observation in Moscow.

1. The first group consists of the idealists, those who take seriously the utopian values of Marxism. This group is probably smaller than ever today in Russia, although many Asian Communists may belong to it. Even in the U.S.S.R. today many young people still go through a phase of Communist idealism. Disillusionment comes with experience and can be a slow, painful process, as Mikhail Soloviev reveals in his recent autobiographical novel, *When the Gods Are Silent.*

2. Then there are the ambitious "activists," those who forge to the top, who as as they rise become more and more alienated from the mass of their fellow party members. They learn all the arts of party intrigue and double-talk. And they, together with that very special

element, the political police, whom the party recruits from among them, are hated and despised, though often respected, by the rank and file. These represent the new elite of manipulators and conspirators, and their mentality is closely modeled after the Bolshevik "operational code."

3. Finally, there is the group largest and closest to the nonparty pattern in its outlook, called *shkurniki* (from *shkura*, "skin") or "bread" Communists and other uncomplimentary names. Most refugees who have been party members are of this type. As one refugee says, such people join the party "to get a little warmer place on the stove." Many Soviet party-member intellectuals also belong to this group and often, especially if they have been affected by experience with foreigners, constitute one of the most unstable elements of the Soviet population. This is one reason why the Kremlin devotes so much attention to the political indoctrination of intellectuals, most of whose younger contingent belong to the party or have been Komsomols. For the intellectuals have strongly ambivalent attitudes: as party members and as beneficiaries of privilege they identify with the regime, while as functioning intellectuals they are irked by its interference and sometimes shocked by its harshness. This is particularly true of the more creative intellectuals rather than of the large mass of intellectual technicians. The intellectuals, however, more than any other significant group, can achieve status and material preference without rising high in the party hierarchy and indeed, to a somewhat surprising but probably diminishing degree, without even joining it.

These groups are loyal to the Kremlin partly because of fear and inertia. But they also are bound to the regime by more positive sentiments, such as love of native hearth and haunts, which can be manipulated by the political authorities with real effect.

Fear of punishment for infractions of regulations becomes more powerful than these determinants of action, but defections do occur. There seem to be extremely few ideological defectors, but then there are few real idealists or heroes anywhere today. World War II offered the greatest chance for escape from the system: when Germany's victory seemed likely, some Russian prisoners of the Germans did don German uniforms, though mostly through hunger.

For obvious geographic reasons, it is difficult to see how the Western nations can have such an opportunity directly to influence millions of Soviet people as the Nazis had and so badly misused. Despite the Kremlin's hate propaganda, the West, and especially the United States, have psychological assets of great potential value in the attitudes of Soviet people. For years Stalin had urged the Russians on to "overtake and surpass" the industrial achievements of the United States, and today Khrushchev revives this slogan by ordering introduction of "the corn-hog" agricultural balance. These exhortations, plus the profound knowledge of American strength gained by visits to America and by study, have created a respect for that power which has real force to deter rash adventures.

Respect, together with the considerable moral capital left over from happier periods of American-Russian relations, gives a basis upon which to build. It would be rash to predict that these assets will enable us to gain allies among the Soviet peoples, but, whether in long and frustrating "cold war" or in ultimate peace, they are intangibles that neither the Kremlin nor we can afford to ignore.

V / Techniques of Subversion: Comintern and Cominform

Russian Background

The Soviet Communist party, whose structure and internal life we have just surveyed, operates outside the Soviet state through its international Communist movement and a network of Soviet front organizations. Traditional, conventional forms are also used which have proliferated as the Soviet state has increased in power and restored many of the once-despised tsarist tactics. Since the November revolution, men's lives everywhere have been affected by the Soviet high command's attempts to expand the area under Soviet control, an endeavor obscured by recessions of Soviet expansionism but fostered by internal conflict in the non-Soviet world. In this section we shall analyze interaction of these two worlds as they are sometimes in open conflict, sometimes in uneasy equilibrium. Let us recall some of the major trends against which background this process stands out. The Bolsheviks in Russia and Communist parties everywhere are in large part the offspring of the wars, the depressions, and the social dislocations of our era: children of catastrophes themselves, they are skilled in exploiting crises in other societies. Sometimes, particularly since the end of World War II, they seem to have deliberately created or aggravated international crises with a view to their exploitation. And Soviet foreign policy reflects the compulsions of a domestic order which fears freedom and seeks to impose rigid controls on society.

After Stalin's death the Kremlin somewhat eased its outward pressure, partly to create a climate favorable to profitable negotiation, but perhaps more to reap the psychological benefits of appearing to do so. Knowledge of the theory and techniques employed by the Bolsheviks to disintegrate, re-organize, and eventually digest segments torn from the body of the non-Communist world is of the utmost importance. It is equally essential, however, to understand that the situations to which this process can be applied would not exist, were it not for the defects and instabilities of the non-Communist world. Finally, we must emphasize that will, as well as skill, has made Moscow powerful.

A glance at the Russian background of Soviet foreign policy is necessary to the understanding of the ends and means, doctrines, organizational weapons, strategies, and tactics employed by international communism.

Soviet communism reflects the results of rapid and violent implementation of revolutionary Western social doctrine by men sprung largely from a prescientific culture pattern, among a people gifted and vigorous but unprepared for modern industrial life and the tasks of organization and self-discipline which it imposes. Too much was done too quickly and too crudely: herein lies the significance of the Russian component of bolshevism. This does not mean that bolshevism was the only possible path of development for Russia or that it was consciously or freely chosen by the peoples whom it engulfed; on the contrary, it was their misfortune to be its first and major victims.

As indicated, Russia's political tradition rendered her more susceptible to the appeals of Marxism than were the economically developed and politically more sophisticated Western nations for which Marx and Engels designed their program. As applied to still partly medieval societies, this program tends to inject a new content of forced-draft industrialization into older patterns of culture; but new techniques and old attitudes combine into a potent, world-shaking force. As the Russian revolution recedes into the past, it seems in many ways as if old Muscovy, with its intolerance and messianism enhanced, has revived in the form of bolshevism. For even Lenin was only partially a "Westerner." The real socialist "internationalists" were, by and large, the Mensheviks, who, despite their hatred of the Russian and European bourgeoisie, were cultivated and cosmopolitan intellectuals; these carried on the traditional role of Russian Westernizing intellectuals, acting as a bridge between the West and Russia.

Lenin's political philosophy was abhorrent to most Western socialists, for it was in many ways an inversion of Russian autocracy and led to a system of permanent purge and martial law. But, of course, the world into which bolshevism was born often acted as if Lenin had been right in regarding politics as a form of warfare. The Bolsheviks claimed to be the only real Marxists in Russia; later they extended this claim, in a frighteningly intolerant and ruthless spirit, to the whole world and proclaimed their right to the leadership of all mankind. Then victory in World War II strengthened the Kremlin's belief in this mission.[20]

World Marxist leadership was, by the Bolshevik victory, transferred to a country which Marx and Engels feared and abhorred as the embodiment of backwardness. Although at times they looked with hope to a Russia then seething with unrest, they did not regard it as a major factor in international socialism—to them Russia was "Asiatic," semibarbarous. Soviet propa-

ganda, of course, conceals this aspect of Marxism.

Most of the leaders of western European socialism and, of course, the vast majority of non-Marxist leaders in the West continued to view Russia in its Leninist phase with suspicious hostility and ignorance. But a few Western radical socialist leaders, together with large segments of youth, some intellectuals, and part of the European working class, hailed "socialist" Russia with flaming enthusiasm. To these groups was added another destined to be still more significant and now one of the main breeding grounds of world communism: the radical intelligentsia of the "underdeveloped" countries attracted by the Soviet ideal. Moreover, socialists in the West, though repelled by Soviet fanaticism and constantly attacked by Moscow, found it difficult completely to repudiate their Marxist brothers; their situation was rendered difficult by the rise of fascism and the blind hostility of European conservatives.

The fateful consequences of these developments have not yet fully unfolded; in truth, they are not as yet fully understood. Even the Soviet leaders took time to adjust to them. One of the major results of this process was the degeneration of Russian Marxism: Stalinism became in large part the Russian form of totalitarianism masquerading in Marxist formulas. The other major result of the Bolshevization of Marxism has been a movement with considerable appeal to underdeveloped areas but which can capture advanced nations only by force. The Russians never developed the more offensive types of racism and national snobbery prevalent in Western imperialism; culturally more akin to Asiatic peoples than were the great Western nations, they also shared to a certain extent the Asiatic's resentful envy of the West. And the Kremlin took full advantage

20. Enhanced messianism was reflected in postwar rewriting of history. It is interesting to compare the 1940 and 1949 editions of M. Nechkina's *Istoriya SSR*, the standard college text in Russian history. The 1940 version says almost nothing about the "world mission" of Russia, which is prominent in the 1949 edition. Considerable light is shed on some of the ideological roots of bolshevism in the writings of Nicholas Berdyaev, particularly in his *The Origin of Russian Communism*.

of the opportunities offered by this pattern.

One of the main charges brought by the Third International against the Second International was that it had neglected the non-European world. Lenin's *Imperialism, the Highest Stage of Capitalism* (1916) argued that European and American capitalism owed much to the "superprofits" extracted from "colonial" areas. One of the most effective early Soviet propaganda enterprises was the Congress of Peoples of the East held in Baku in September, 1920. The Soviet appeal to the youthful nationalism of the colonial areas was potent because conditions in these societies were more similar to those of Russia before 1917 than to those in advanced industrial countries and because the Bolsheviks' ideology and organization were adapted to exploiting these conditions, whereas the West, by exporting capital and techniques, had helped to disintegrate patriarchal societies. Now a class of discontented intellectuals arose. Moscow promised national rebirth to disintegrating societies, many of whose intellectuals both hated and envied the West.

Lenin laid the foundations for Bolshevik strategy and tactics in the underdeveloped areas, and Stalin perfected them. Among Lenin's main contributions, besides his doctrine of imperialism, was his emphasis, after the Russian revolution of 1905 and later, on the role of impoverished peasantries as "reserves" of the proletarian revolution. His doctrine of the tightly organized party of professional revolutionaries has had great appeal for ambitious intellectuals of societies in which the elite groups were unable or unwilling to absorb the new intellectual proletariat created by industry or to offer a meaningful life to the scions of aristocratic families in revolt against the authority and mores of their elders. This appeal was heightened by the naïve Bolshevik emphasis on technology and science, a heritage of Russian pre-Marxian radicalism. This kind of optimistic "scientism" generally appeals to peoples whose situation makes them impatient for radical change. Finally, Lenin's and Stalin's nationality doctrine stressing "self-determination" found support not only among the non-Russian peoples of the tsarist empire but among other peoples, especially in the East, who resented Western condescension and "imperialist" exploitation. To the "oppressed billions," the Bolsheviks offered a seemingly easy path to restoration of group self-respect.

Yet, at first, even Lenin and Stalin looked to the western European workers as the main allies of Bolshevik Russia and were confident that Germany, Austria-Hungary, and other Continental European countries would soon follow Russia's example. Despite his anger at the "treason" of European socialists, Lenin always regarded western Europe as more advanced, more cultured, than Russia; and Trotsky had even greater respect for European culture, as did Bukharin, Radek, and other "cosmopolitan" Bolsheviks.

Liquidation of the cosmopolitan aspects of bolshevism was the contribution of xenophobic Stalinists, who regarded—and probably still do—foreign Communists as expendable agents. But it was only after disastrous defeats in China and other oriental countries that even Stalin, prodded by the experience of Mao Tse-tung's unorthodox Chinese peasant "soviets," emphasized the peasantry's role in the "socialist" revolution.

Thus Soviet ideology has laggingly admitted what history and Soviet practice have demonstrated—namely, that bolshevism's greatest appeal is to societies seeking an alternative to traditional authoritarian patterns undermined by modern social forces. This is particularly true where parliamentary institutions and a strong, native middle class with devotion to legal procedure have not been firmly established. In view of this, perhaps India's period of tutelage under Britain may have been a blessing in disguise.

The Bolshevik revolution failed to capture Europe despite temporary success in 1918–19 in Hungary, Bavaria, Finland, and the Baltic states. In these areas Communist regimes were in power for a few months. In France, while there was no revolution, prospects looked bright at times, at least from Moscow; a large section of the French Socialist party broke away from the Second International and joined the Communist International in the summer of 1920. In the Near East there was a short-lived Moscow-oriented regime in northern Iran. But Lenin's and Trotsky's hopes were dashed, except in Russia. Even there bolshevism survived by the skin of its teeth and with the loss of the Baltic states, Finland, the Caucasus, and the Ukraine; the last two, however, were recaptured by a combination of internal subversion and Red Army invasion in 1919–21. The only significant areas outside Russia in which "capitalism" was overthrown and replaced by the new social order were outer Mongolia and Tannu Tuva, prototypes of the Moscow-dominated captive states of today. The techniques of their seizure and control were also applied in the Sovietization of the Ukraine and Central Asia. The basic principle of Sovietization is concentration on the elimination of one or more hostile social groups while allying with other groups, some of which are to be liquidated in the future. This has been called the "salami" technique, an expression actually used by the Hungarian Communist leader Rakosi in a speech in 1949.

Throughout the first *Sturm und Drang* era of bolshevism, especially 1917–19, Kremlin foreign policy relied mainly on direct propaganda appeals to "peoples" over the heads of their governments and on the subversive activity, strikes, and violence instigated by the Communist parties.[21] Moreover, the Red Army played a decisive role, repeated on a far grander scale during and after World War II. Traditional diplomacy and the normal methods of international intercourse were relatively unimportant during the civil war and the intervention periods.

Establishment of diplomatic relations—first with the Baltic states, Persia, Turkey, and Afghanistan in 1920–21; and with Britain and other major European nations in 1924—began the second of the three main periods of Soviet foreign relations. There have been four quite distinct periods, two of which (1917–21 and 1939–49) were periods of advance and expansion.[22] The longest period, 1921–39, was one of "breathing spell," "temporary stabilization," and "united front"—all key Soviet terms. This was the period of consolidation of Soviet power; of relative passivity in Europe at least (in Asia, Soviet pressure for revolution seems never to have stopped); and of perfection of political techniques, most of which were first tried out in the early years by the new state and retained in the arsenal of bolshevism. Since 1949 there has been something of a stalemate between the two camps.

The second period seems, in retro-

21. Soviet Foreign Commissar Chicherin openly admitted this tactic. For examples see *Soviet Documents on Foreign Policy*, ed. Jane Degras, I (1951), 83–85, 91–93, and *passim*.

22. Possibly we are living in a fifth period, that of post-Stalin "coexistence," today. If so, it differs from the second period in being based on much greater Soviet power and a significantly different phase of Soviet internal develpoment. This phase has been highlighted by a skilful Soviet campaign for expansion of cultural exchange designed apparently to demonstrate that the United States, not Moscow, fears "cultural relations."

spect, to have been one of strengthening of the domestic base for foreign expansion. Many in the West thought that bolshevism had mellowed. Stalin never repudiated, but merely postponed, Lenin's aims of expansion of Soviet power and continued to use physical force when feasible.

Behind this screen a very important development occurred: a mighty one-party totalitarian state controlled by Stalin and his lieutenants loomed ever larger among the instruments of Soviet power. The aims of the Kremlin were hidden from the world as the U.S.S.R. mastered the arts of statecraft. The gradual adoption in recent years of conventional political terminology (use of such terms as "minister" and "presidium") culminates in today's practices: the Soviet ambassador rides to Buckingham Palace in a gilded coach. Techniques have been perfected; and while hopes of realizing revolutionary values and ideals have faded, power continues to expand. When as a result of World War II the Soviets resumed their revolutionary advance, they had a much more potent instrument with which to exploit a far more favorable situation.

Against this background let us examine some of the typical means used by the Kremlin to extend Soviet influence.

Export of Leadership and Ideology

The core of the Sovietization process lies in the selection, training, disciplining, and eventual installation in power of Soviet cadres, all directed by Moscow and dedicated to the destruction of the social order in their native countries and its replacement by the Soviet model. To this end, interpretation of doctrine, manipulation of symbols, organizational weapons, and Soviet foreign policy all contribute. The word "cadres" is used here to denote personnel trained to take over the political, economic, and spiritual life of any

country whenever the opportunity presents itself. One of Stalin's favorite pronouncements was "cadres decide everything." In this operation the leadership is totalitarian and involves the political organization of all aspects of life and, barring revolution or collapse, the permanent exclusion of competition for power, once communism has gained control of an area—a fact which helps explain the impossibility of genuine or long-lasting coalition governments in which Communist parties participate, for, unless the non-Communists are stronger than the Communists, they are in grave danger.

The struggle for the installation of Moscow-oriented elites has been proceeding continuously since Lenin first seized state power in Russia in 1917. Despite the urgency of the problem, it is impossible at the present time to deal adequately with this question of Communist elite formation, one reason being the secrecy of Soviet leadership. For another thing, there is the serious language problem, since we are confronted with a pattern of action adapted to the conditions and culture of countries speaking various languages. It should also be emphasized that cadre building is continuous and involves relatively innocuous activities, as well as more sinister types of testing and training.[23]

There are three interrelated means which the Kremlin uses to put its agents in power: the first is through the influence over men's minds exerted by Marxist-Leninist doctrine, which is reinforced by propaganda; the second is

23. In the first stages, so far as we know from such cases as the recruiting of Poles on Soviet-occupied territory in 1940, the approach is cultural. As organization tightens, screening proceeds, and indoctrination is intensified. Threats and blackmail are also used; agents are produced. Former liberals or socialists such as the Polish writer Wanda Wasilewska, now a leading Soviet citizen, have played major roles in this process.

the techniques of penetration and control used by what Philip Selznick in his study *The Organizational Weapon* called the "combat party"; the third is the use of the Soviet state and, in particular, its mighty army, secret police, and diplomatic service to exploit "contradictions" in the non-Soviet world in order to create favorable conditions for the seizure of power by the Kremlin's agents.

Despite the failure of the U.S.S.R. to realize the utopian and humanitarian values for which the socialists had been fighting, ideology still remains an important source of strength for the Kremlin, particularly in the poorer and more disorganized communities of the world. Although the Leninist ideology has lost some of its appeal, the political mythology of sovietism has been powerfully reinforced by new elements derived in the main from the success of Soviet Russia as a great power; for Soviet vitality and power have fascinated many in a world weary of war and baffled by its problems.

While respect for Soviet power is primarily a result of World War II, it was already a potent force before 1939 and is in part a reflection of the Soviet Union's apparent success in solving problems which appeared to be insoluble. As many former Communists have pointed out, however, the Soviets did not really solve the problems they claimed to solve, but their apparent success impressed some people.

Why has Leninist-Stalinist doctrine remained a potent political force? Many of its victories have been won largely by default: Western division and disillusionment, lack of a real counterpersuasion program, and the wars and depressions of our times have greatly assisted the Soviet propagandists. But this, of course, is not the whole story. Soviet tactics and institutions—particularly the "Iron Curtain," which hides the truth about the Soviet world and at the same time shields its population from external influence—and the plausibility of the Leninist-Stalinist system of half-truths and distortions also play essential roles. While this applies to persons whom the Communists wish to recruit into their movement and to party members, it applies probably more to the former than to the latter. While propaganda is most important in recruiting, organization is most strategic in controlling members of Communist parties.

The Communist propaganda most important in attracting members and sympathizers is that encouraging the discontented to look to the Soviet Union for realization of their own aspirations. The maladjustments of a complex and rapidly changing society and Soviet promises open up a wide range of possibilities. In some ways Communist doctrine is a sociology of disintegration; its claim that the society of the future has already been created in the U.S.S.R. appeals to all who are dissatisfied with the established order. Its identification of the capitalist status quo with decadence and of the Soviet order with the wave of the future furnishes a powerful appeal to the discontented.

Communism's most general appeal is that of a "political religion"; yet at the same time it also appeals to the self-interest of various social strata. Thus the Communists appeal to labor against capital, to farm laborers against landowners, to farmers (especially peasants) against bankers and moneylenders, to Negroes against whites, and to "colonial" peoples against their "imperialist" oppressors. This aspect of communism can be potent in societies in which conditions seem to resemble the picture painted by Communist propaganda. The most important areas are the underdeveloped countries in the harsh early stages of industrialization, usually complicated by a background of colonial dependence on advanced capitalist countries, and the advanced countries whose social structure has been undermined as the result of wars and economic crises:[24] under these conditions the Communists win support by exploiting grievances. At the same time they link up everyday grievances and problems with the basic propositions of their doctrine and gradually convert individuals who in the initial stage of their involvement had not intended becoming Communists.

Joining a Communist party is the most important step in a long process. Even a rank-and-file party member is to a certain extent a conspirator, particularly where Communist parties are semilegal or illegal and hence persecuted minorities. A long road lies between joining a Communist party and becoming a member of its "apparatus." As individuals rise in the party, their emotional isolation from non-Communists and also from rank-and-file party members becomes greater; absorption in party activities and the satisfaction of wielding power grow deeper. Certain aspects of Soviet ideology still continue to play an important role, and members of the "apparatus," especially the tiny group of leaders of foreign Communist parties, identify themselves with the Kremlin. Like the Soviet elite, they tend to view human relations as a struggle of "us" against "them" in which any and all means are justified so long as they contribute to success.

Communist Fronts in War and Peace

Something should be said about the concept of the "party line" and "fronts" in communism. The party line is the

24. A major feature of Soviet propaganda since the nineteenth party congress has been intensified appeal to "colonial" peoples. As recently as October 20, 1953, *Pravda* stated editorially that 70 per cent of the population of the "capitalist world" were living in "colonial slavery."

stream of communications which apply Soviet doctrine and policies to changing conditions. It need not be set forth in secret instructions; a common form is probably the pronouncements of Soviet leaders or foreign Communists. In April, 1945, Jacques Duclos contributed an article to the French party journal, *Cahiers du communisme*, which dealt a death blow to "Browderism" in the American party and inaugurated a world-wide open Communist offensive against the United States. The better indoctrinated a Communist is, the more fully he understands the party line, although it is probably true that only a very high-ranking Communist fully understands it at any given time. The line is deliberately vague, though very carefully drafted, and is designed to furnish guidance to party leaders as well as to hold together the rank and file in a bond of plausible slogans. The relationship between basic doctrine and the party line resembles that between the invisible and the visible portions of an iceberg.

Fronts are of two main kinds: one is the type of organization in which a hard core of highly conscious, highly organized Communists is surrounded by an amorphous, manipulable mass. Communist youth, women's, "peace," and similar organizations belong to this category. Such organizations exploit the ignorance, idealism, and gullibility of their members; they are designed to manipulate, neutralize, or use for recruiting purposes masses who do not realize what is being done to them.

The other main type of front organization is the "united front" in which the Communists "co-operate" with rival parties or groups which they seek to utilize and eventually to destroy. The united front may be "from above," on the leadership level as during the 1930's, or "from below," on the level of mass agitation, as in the early 1920's.

The former, proclaimed by Georgi Dimitrov at the seventh Comintern congress in 1935, enjoyed its greatest success when the Soviet Union appeared to many to be the only powerful European opponent of fascism; the latter has been employed when Moscow felt that it was inexpedient to collaborate with its competitors, such as with the socialists, for mass influence. Usually the use of these tactics has reflected the Communists' distance from the rank and file of the workers, and recognition of this has influenced Soviet strategy in the years following the failure of the Communist strikes in western Europe in 1947–48.

The policy set forth by Stalin at the nineteenth congress in October, 1952, combines the united front "from below," directed against the socialist and liberal parties, with the vigorous use of mass nonpolitical organizations designed to exploit fear of war and to inflame national passions everywhere against the United States. These are complex tactics whose appeal is more to irrational feelings, especially jealousy and resentment, against the United States than to class interests.

Bolshevism owes its rise to power and its independence from non-Bolshevik socialism to World War II. The most important single Bolshevik doctrine is that war is the inevitable product of capitalism; the Bolsheviks have been the principal beneficiaries of the wars of our age.

Believing that war was inevitable, Communists have done everything to exploit its results; at the same time, they proclaim their bitter opposition to it. They despise pacifism; they speak constantly of "the struggle for peace," an expression which correctly describes their attitude or would if it were altered to "the armed struggle for peace on Soviet terms." For apparently it is still a tenet of Soviet doctrine that only the dominance of Soviet power can bring lasting peace. But Bolshevik propaganda has always displayed great flexibility in its effort to convince the masses that it is only the capitalist governments and not the Communists who regard war as inevitable and even desirable.

With this background in mind, it is not surprising that the main theme of Soviet communism has been the exploitation of war and peace. For example, in 1922, during the "united front from below," when Communists sought "unity" with socialists in order to "unmask" them, representatives of the Comintern participated in the Hague peace conference. According to an article in the *Small Soviet Encyclopedia* (Vol. I, published 1937), when the Soviet united front, with socialists and liberals, this time "from above," was being pushed by all available propaganda facilities, the Comintern representatives met (in 1922) to fight the "dangers of new imperialist wars and pacifist illusions."

From 1924 until 1934 the Communists waged a bitter campaign against socialists, liberals, and pacifists as alleged allies of the bourgeoisie. During these years Litvinov at Geneva advanced disarmament proposals which it was safe to proclaim, since their character rendered their acceptance impossible. One of the main tasks of Communist parties during this period was propagandizing Litvinov's proposals. In 1932 at Amsterdam the Communists organized an international antiwar movement. In 1935 at the seventh Comintern congress Dimitrov, Togliatti (using his party name, Ercoli), and other Comintern leaders held out the olive branch to socialists, democrats, and liberals and called for the creation of a united front against fascism and war. These speeches signaled the creation of front organizations throughout the world. In the United States there was organized the American League against War and Fascism.[25] It is one of the tragedies of our times that many who joined these Communist-created antiwar movements were completely ignorant of the true meaning behind them. Communist texts, even during the 1935–39 period, would, if carefully studied, have revealed the expectations and motives of the Kremlin.

Togliatti, for example, in his speech to the seventh Comintern congress linked up the struggle for peace with the familiar Leninist concept of transforming the "imperialist" war into "civil war against the *bourgeoisie*." During the period of the Soviet-German pact (August, 1939–June, 1941) Communists and their fellow-travelers, addressing national and international peace congresses, denounced England and France as the aggressors against Germany, only to turn against the Nazis after Hitler attacked the Soviet Union.

Prosecution of the anti-Nazi war and in particular the organization of resistance movements in German-occupied territory and their conversion into instruments of Communist power became the main activity of Communists. These wartime resistance movements were really continuations of the prewar peace movements, and so were largely the postwar Soviet activities aimed at the "moral and political" liquidation of fascism. When the Soviet leaders felt that the time had come to transfer to the United States the symbols of hostility and aggression formerly directed against Germany, the "peace" movement was revived on a new, grand scale.

Their attack was now directed against America. The accusation that America wishes to make war to destroy the Soviet Union and the "peoples' democracies," to establish world domination, and to liquidate all progressive movements and forces everywhere has been the basic theme of Soviet propaganda since the "cold war" broke into the open in 1947. One of the major vehicles for this propaganda has been a series of "peace" congresses beginning in Poland in August, 1948; major events in the "peace mobilization" were the first and second world congresses of partisans of peace in Paris and Warsaw (1949 and 1950) and the Far Eastern peace congress in Peiping (October, 1952). The 1950 congress established the World Peace Council, which held its first meeting in Soviet-controlled East Berlin in February, 1951; this council claims to be a more representative organization than the United Nations. It held an "extraordinary session" in July, 1952, which demanded a "peaceful solution" of the German and Japanese problems, an end to the war in Korea, and a "congress of the peoples of the world in defense of peace."[26] Its major purpose thus far appears to be to capitalize on the world-wide fear of war. Through this international "peace" movement the Kremlin disseminates and seeks to give respectability and plausibility to such major propaganda lines as the demand for abolition of atomic weapons, though without any indication that it will accept the necessary control and inspection, and its denunciation of the United States for allegedly engaging in germ warfare and crop destruction against the peoples of China, North Korea, and eastern Europe. Some of the activities of this movement, particularly its campaign for signatures for the "Stockholm peti-

25. It is interesting to recall that in those days Earl Browder, then chairman of the American Communist party, operated under the slogan "Communism is twentieth-century Americanism!"

26. The Budapest session of the World Peace Council in June, 1953, played a prominent role in launching the Soviet campaign for "relaxation of international tension."

tion" in 1950, appear to be at least in part designed as weapons of mass intimidation. But at the same time such campaigns are massive demonstrations of the Soviet "propaganda of the deed," and in the "international arena" they resemble somewhat the "demonstration trials" used domestically by Communist governments for "education" of the masses.

The "peace" movement is, of course, only one, though perhaps the most important, of the Communist fronts. Another important organization is the World Federation of Trade Unions founded at London in 1945.[27] Its president is an Italian, Di Vittorio, and its general secretary a Frenchman, Saillant. During 1945 and 1946 the WFTU was the main international instrument of the Kremlin. It is still powerful, although its influence has declined somewhat partly because of the economic recovery in western Europe following adoption of the Marshall Plan and partly because of the countermeasures of European anti-Communist trade-unionists assisted by such American labor leaders as Irving Brown of the American Federation of Labor. But neither the WFTU nor the local Communist parties were able to carry out successfully sabotage of the defense program of the western European governments or delivery of American aid. Fear of a rapidly reviving West Germany, the post-Korean letdown, and possibly uncertainty about the long-term stability of American commitments, however, have given new hope for Kremlin manipulation of western European public opinion since 1952.

There is a broad gamut of fronts. Their activities are utilized sometimes to advertise, at other times to conceal, Communist purposes. Most of the

27. The WFTU held its third World Congress in Vienna in October, 1953, allegedly representing 88,600,000 members from seventy-nine countries.

propaganda of all these fronts since 1945 has been subordinated to the "peace" campaign, an interesting example of which was the visit to Korea in May, 1951, of a "commission" of the International Democratic Federation of Women (founded in 1945), which sent a message to the World Peace Council in Berlin accusing the United States of violating the "laws of war."

Fronts are instruments of high policy of the international Communist movement. They provide activity designed to keep a Communist party and its membership active and militant; they also have "educational" value, calculated to bring new recruits into Communist parties, to give them exciting work to do, and to test their loyalty and willingness to reject "bourgeois morality" in favor of underground conspiracy.

Organizational and Cultural Weapons

The international Communist movement was equipped with a pattern of organizational structures and weapons which enabled it to exploit the opportunities presented by the rise and decline of German and Japanese power and the crises attendant thereon in the 1930's and 1940's. The most essential feature of this pattern was its projection of Soviet control and methods into the organization of foreign Communist parties, an operation effected partially through direct intervention of the Soviet state and partly through the activities of the Comintern and the Cominform, the creations and instruments of the Soviet state. Consequently, we shall deal here at some length with the development of the Comintern and of some of its member Communist parties. We shall have also to deal with Moscow control subsequent to the maneuver of Comintern dissolution, ordered by the Kremlin in the spring of 1943 and unanimously ratified by the member parties. But before turning to this main theme, let us discuss certain subsidiary, but extremely important, Soviet methods of training and organizing Communists.

Perhaps the most important of the training institutions is the system of schools for Communists operated in the Soviet Union since the early 1920's. This is a very large subject, about which unfortunately only scattered material is available in English, but some indication of its scope and significance is suggested by the fact that Stalin himself delivered a long speech (May 18, 1925) to the students of the Communist University of the Toilers of the East. He noted that this was the fourth anniversary of the existence of the university and that in its student body there were represented no less than fifty nations and national groups from among the Eastern peoples. Stalin spoke of the Communist struggle for power in colonial countries and defined as the mission of the university the training of foreign Communists. Continual stress on "colonial" peoples, but without hints on schools for training Communists from among them, was contained in the *Pravda* coverage of the WFTU congress in October, 1953.

The Lenin Institute under the direction of the Comintern played a big role and figures in many accounts of international Communist activities. Sam Carr, one of the Soviet agents investigated by the Royal Commission in Canada in 1946, received his training there. Other foreign Communists were trained at Soviet military institutions: the Spanish former Communist, El Campesino, for example, in his *La Vie et la mort en l'USSR* tells of his studies at the Frunze Military Academy in Moscow. Mention should also be made of the scientific institutes in Moscow and Leningrad for the study of foreign languages and culture which prepare Soviet cadres for work with foreign

peoples. The peculiar Soviet version of what we in America call "foreign-area study" has long been very highly developed. The major party theoretical journal, *Kommunist,* furnished guarded but interesting indications of the importance of area research in October, 1953.[28] To help woo Near Eastern Christians, Byzantine studies were revived. Cultural relations, in which censorship, political criteria of ingress and egress of persons to and from Soviet-controlled territory, and skilful manipulation of such symbols as "cultural freedom" are some of the ingredients, has always been an important Soviet foreign policy instrument and one which has been intensified by Stalin's successors. *Voks* (All Union Society for Cultural Relations with Foreign Countries) and *Intourist,* which has charge of foreign tourists, play important roles in this field.

The training and indoctrination of prisoners of war, many of whom subsequently became important Communist agents or even leaders, began during the first months of the Soviet regime. Among the former war prisoners who became Communist leaders, the most prominent is probably Tito. The use of war prisoners to conduct defeatist propaganda to break down enemy morale was begun by the Bolsheviks at this period. Austrian and German soldiers played an important part in crushing the anti-Soviet revolt in Central Asia in the early 1920's. During World War II special anti-Fascist schools were set up on a far larger scale than similar enterprises during World War I; they classified German prisoners of war by rank, Nazi party membership, etc., and engaged in appropriately differentiated

28. Review of *International Relations in the Far East,* a collective study (in *Kommunist,* No. 15, pp. 122–28). The authors were praised for bringing out American "expansionist policy," "correcting" overemphasis on tsarist aggressiveness, etc.

indoctrination. In 1943 the Union of German Officers and the "Free Germany" national committee were set up. Members of these organizations were subsequently used in the establishment of Soviet control in Eastern Germany. Alumni of the anti-Fascist schools are also active as Soviet agents in Western Germany today. Similar methods were used on Japanese war prisoners.

In concluding this list of some of the techniques by which foreigners were influenced and Communists were recruited, to be subsequently trained in the Soviet Union, mention should be made of the various colonies of foreign Communists in Moscow and elsewhere, particularly the Comintern personnel housed in the famous Hotel Lux in Moscow mentioned in the memoirs of former Communists, such as Freda Utley and Anton Ciliga. The inhabitants of these colonies lived a strange, isolated life.[29] Many of them, including most of the leaders of the Yugoslav Communists, fell victim to the great purges of 1936–38. But from their ranks came many of the most powerful leaders of the Soviet-controlled regimes which today rule eastern Europe and China and of Communist parties which were suppressed before 1945 but which are now powerful political movements, particularly in the Far East—Ho Chi Minh of Indo-China and Nosaka of Japan are two such leaders that come to mind.

The Comintern

The Communist International (Comintern) was founded in March, 1919, in Moscow. Subsequent Comintern congresses were held in 1920, 1921, 1922,

1924, 1928, and 1935, all of them in Moscow. The most important congresses were those of 1920, 1928, and 1935. The special importance of the second congress (1920) was that it established the domination of the Soviet Russian party over the other Communist parties both in doctrine and in organization. All member Communist parties were required to accept twenty-one "conditions" prescribed by Lenin. Taken together, these "conditions" defined the character of the Comintern as a single, world revolutionary organization composed of national sections, each one of which was dedicated to the overthrow of the established government of its own country. According to the Soviet newspaper *Izvestia* (July 16, 1920), the purpose of the Comintern was "the introduction of complete unity of tactics into the international movement of the proletariat and the creation of a strong international headquarters for a proletarian uprising against world imperialism." One of the most important of the twenty-one conditions was that providing for periodic party purges.[30] Lenin dominated the first three Comintern congresses and delivered the main political reports to them. He sought to prevent the entry into Communist parties of individuals under the influence of socialist or other rival ideologies. Thus, from the start, the Comintern bore the stamp of Kremlin monolithism, which was to be deepened with the passing years. One reason Lenin demanded such rigid conditions for admission to the Comintern was that he blamed the failure of the Hungarian Bolshevik regime of 1919 on a Communist alliance with the Socialists and consequent lack of central con-

29. The author was told by a German former Communist who worked for years for the Comintern that Wilhelm Pieck, head of the German party and at the time of writing still the "grand old man" of German communism, had to sign in and out of the Hotel Lux—his movements were so strictly controlled by the political police.

30. This is a particularly striking example of the way in which international communism seeks to project to the whole world Lenin's political mentality. Lenin began his *What Is To Be Done?* with a quotation from the pioneer German socialist Lassalle on the salutary effects of purges on parties.

trol of organization and strategy, a fact interesting because it marked the introduction into Comintern politics of the Russian practice of blaming political defeats on mistakes of individual subordinate leaders. Moscow's infallibility became a sacred tenet; and, as Whittaker Chambers brings out in *Witness*, even American Communists stood in awe of the Russians.

The first two Comintern congresses took place when foreign intervention and civil war were rife in Russia. This was a period when revolutionary hopes ran high in Moscow and when the popularity of communism among the western European masses was at a peak, which it soon lost and regained, if ever, only in 1944–46. But by the time of the third and fourth congresses in 1921 and 1922, Lenin considered it necessary for the Soviet state to pursue a cautious policy of recovery from war and chaos. At these two congresses and also at the fifth in 1924 attention was focused on the problem of winning the now largely indifferent masses of workers for the Communist parties. Outside Russia these were years of defeat and failure for the Communist parties, marked by events such as Mussolini's seizure of power in Italy in 1922. After ups and downs, hopes for revolution in Germany failed; the objective of eliminating the socialist parties as powerful competitors for the allegiance of many workers and members of the middle classes failed to be realized. In the Far East the Communists were more successful than in Europe until Chiang Kai-shek administered a crushing defeat in 1927; similarly a Communist uprising in Java was crushed in 1925.

Against the background of these events a bewildering pattern of Comintern strategy and tactics and of zigzags on the propaganda and organizational fronts developed. However, the concepts of the U.S.S.R. as the base of world revolution and of foreign Com-

munist parties as its dependent allies remained constant. Equally important was the fact that the main hatred and hostility of the Communist parties was directed not against the "capitalist" parties but against the rival socialists, who were denounced as "social Fascists" and "social patriots." All the main trends of Comintern policy for the period 1924–35 were summed up and stated succinctly at the sixth Comintern congress held in 1928. Among other things, this sixth congress systematized and revised the propositions adopted at earlier congresses and drafted the Comintern program which remained in force throughout the subsequent history of the Communist International.

The seventh and last congress of the Comintern, held in 1935, adopted a tactical line radically different from that of all preceding congresses—the well-known "Trojan horse" or "united front," this time revived on a new, grand scale. While this congress, like all the preceding ones, was dominated by the leaders of the Soviet Communist parties and the Soviet state, it introduced an important innovation, henceforth utilized in Communist fronts of all sorts—they elected a non-Russian, the Bulgarian Georgi Dimitrov, head of the Comintern executive committee. Dimitrov, who had become a hero in world Communist and to a considerable extent democratic opinion by his defiant and skilful conduct at the Reichstag fire trial in Leipzig, Germany, also made the principal speech at the seventh congress. It should be noted that the decreasing frequency of Comintern congresses paralleled the similar phenomena in the Soviet party, marking its increasing bureaucratization.

The first Comintern congress was preceded by a number of direct and open appeals by the Bolshevik leaders for international revolution. It was held as the result of a proclamation signed by Lenin and Trotsky and broadcast to the world by the Commissariat for Foreign Affairs of Soviet Russia. Until 1921 the Soviet leaders made no attempt to hide the connection between the Soviet state and the Comintern; subsequently they sought to conceal or disguise this connection in statements intended for foreign consumption, while admitting or emphasizing it from time to time in statements for domestic consumption or intended for foreign Communists. The major documents both of the Comintern and of the Soviet government made it clear that Soviet Russia regarded itself as the fatherland of the international proletariat and as the base of world revolution and that acceptance of these claims of Moscow was obligatory for Communist parties and their members. The main instrument of Kremlin control of the Comintern was the same as that used within the Communist party of the Soviet Union, namely, life or death control over personnel. The leading role of Lenin in the Comintern was assumed after his death by Stalin. Even a cursory examination of the collected works of Stalin published in the U.S.S.R. beginning in 1946 makes this point clear. Among other things, Stalin played the decisive role in the commission which drafted the program of the Comintern in 1928. Lenin, Stalin, Rykov, Molotov, Trotsky, Chicherin, and Litvinov played important roles in the Comintern. Zinoviev and Bukharin, the two first and most active presidents of the Comintern executive committee, were important leading members of the Bolshevik party until purged by Stalin.

In order to understand how the top personnel of the Soviet Communist parties and the government dominated the Comintern, it is necessary to examine briefly the Comintern organizational structure. Nominally the supreme organ of the Comintern was its world congress, which was supposed to meet once a year according to the statutes of 1920 and once every two years according to those adopted in 1928. Between congresses the "leading organ" was the executive committee elected by the congress. Through a provision of the Comintern's statutes which gave substantial control of the executive committee to the Communist party of the country in which its seat was located, Soviet Russian organizational control was written into its formal constitutional foundation.

The powers of the executive committee were very great. It could exclude national organizations ("sections") from the Comintern and even purge individual members of national parties; rules requiring "iron discipline" and prohibiting "fractions" further strengthened its centralist principles. After Stalin established his full dictatorship in Soviet Russia, additional methods of controlling foreign Communists, including prison and execution, became routine.[31]

The executive committee elected a Presidium, responsible to it, to conduct its work in the intervals between its meetings. This body in turn elected a political secretariat with power to make decisions and to act as the executive body of both the executive committee and the Presidium. The process by which centralism was established in the central organization of the Comintern was known as "Bolshevization." The result, according to Franz Borkenau, perhaps the leading Western authority on the history of the Comintern, was that "between 1929 and 1934 the Communist parties finally and definitely transformed themselves into quasi-military organizations ready to obey anything."

Even "Bolshevization" of the Comin-

31. Ciliga arrived as a "left" Communist from Yugoslavia in 1928; a year later he was in prison.

tern does not convey the full sense of Soviet domination over international communism. Despotic as it was, the Comintern carried over from the early days of the Bolshevik revolution certain residues of "proletarian democracy"; in form at least it was an organization of political parties with a measure of independence. As the Soviet Union grew more powerful, there took shape what the writer Ypsilon (the pseudonym of two veteran former Communists) called the "Stalintern." The modes of action and the atmosphere of this era were established during the great purges of 1936–38 and have persisted to the present. They are characterized by increasingly close control of foreign Communist parties directly but at the same time, so far as the outside world is concerned, clandestinely by the secret police and other instrumentalities of the Kremlin.

Increased dependence of foreign Communist parties on the Kremlin has been accompanied by the development of a wide variety of tactics of camouflage and deception which permitted the Kremlin to create the illusion that Moscow had given up hope of expansion. However, such illusions should be finally dissipated by Stalin's emphasis on the leadership of foreign Communists by the Soviet Union at the nineteenth party congress. As reported in *Pravda* (October 15, 1952), Stalin described the Soviet party as the "shock brigade of the world revolutionary and labor movement."

Deviations and factionalism and the resulting purges have been inherent in communism, springing from the attempt to force foreign Communist parties to apply tactics made in Moscow to problems which some local Communists have sometimes thought they understood better than the Kremlin or the Comintern. Such Communists, if they aired their views, have been attacked as "deviationists" and

discredited, expelled, or even liquidated.[32]

Factionalism has been a main weakness in international communism, although it lost much of its significance with the great increase in the power of the Soviet state as a result of World War II. Titoism, however, is in a sense factionalism on a state level. And as Adam Ulam points out in his *Titoism and the Cominform*, Titoism is an endemic, though perhaps indefinitely controllable, disease. Langer and Swearingen in their *Red Flag in Japan* show the considerable significance of factionalism in Japanese communism. It is probably especially important in countries like Japan with a markedly "feudal" political tradition.

The purges in Russia and the struggles which underlie them were, of course, reflected in foreign Communist parties. "Left" and "right" deviationists had to be exposed and eradicated wherever they were detected. In these matters Stalin himself intervened often, as when in 1929 he personally directed the purging of Lovestone and other American Communist leaders.

Both the dissolution of the Comintern in 1943 and the establishment of the Cominform in Poland in September, 1947, belong, in different ways, to the tactics of deception. At the same time, these developments furnish impressive evidence of the purely instrumental attitude taken by the Kremlin toward foreign Communist parties. One major aspect of the dissolution of the Comintern was its favorable reception in the United States and Great Britain: Soviet propaganda had cleverly presented it as strengthening the unity of the anti-Nazi coalition. But this step had an-

32. However, some top-flight Communists, such as Mao Tse-tung, survived Kremlin displeasure and rose to supreme power. Mao, of course, never disputed the Kremlin's leadership, although in the 1920's and early 1930's he differed with it on tactics for China.

other quite contrary meaning: the resolution proposing dissolution stated that the Comintern had become a hindrance to the further strengthening of the "national working-class parties." Subsequent Communist tactics and the fact that so many of the eighteen signers of the resolution were soon to wield supreme power in the "liberated" countries of eastern Europe spelled out the significance of this statement. In this instance, as so often, the Kremlin adapted formal organization to the requirements of propaganda. In a broad sense this tactic was a part of the very important Soviet practice of manipulating the symbols of nationality for its own ultimate aggrandizement.

The Cominform

The Cominform (Communist Information Bureau) was devised to enable the Kremlin to co-ordinate more effectively the policies of its eight (nine including the Soviet party) member Communist parties but at the same time foster the impression that these parties enjoyed a measure of autonomy "the latter result, it was apparently hoped, being achieved by establishing and locating the new organization outside the Soviet Union. Founded in Poland in September, 1947, the Cominform was first located in Belgrade, where it also published its organ *For a Lasting Peace, for a People's Democracy!* Central offices and publication headquarters were moved to Bucharest after the Tito-Stalin break in June, 1948.

The Cominform was founded by representatives of the Communist parties of the Soviet Union, Yugoslavia, Poland, Hungary, Rumania, Bulgaria, Czechoslovakia, Italy, and France. The keynote of this meeting was sounded by Andrei Zhdanov in his address "On the International Situation," a speech which ranks in importance with Stalin's election speech (February 9, 1946)

and his article "Economic Problems of Socialism in the USSR" and with Malenkov's speech of August 8, 1953, to the Supreme Soviet. Summarily, Zhdanov's address signaled a "counteroffensive" of international and particularly European communism against American efforts to aid the economic recovery of Europe; it and the early phase of Cominform activities are associated with Communist efforts to sabotage the Marshall Plan by violent strikes and other revolutionary methods. The Cominform also represented a defense against a possible weakening of Soviet control in eastern Europe.

The other main Soviet representative at the founding of the Cominform was Georgi Malenkov. According to the testimony of Igor Gouzenko in the Canadian Royal Commission's report, Malenkov was the head of the foreign section of the Soviet Communist party. Then possibly due to Gouzenko's defection with all its implications, Malenkov fell into temporary eclipse, and Soviet policies in 1947 and for a while in 1948 were apparently dominated by Zhdanov's revolutionary "Western" line.[33] The failure of this line, in which the Tito affair and the failure of the Soviet-Berlin blockade so largely figure, may have had something to do with a shift to emphasis on a more cautious line in Europe and a more aggressive one in the Far East. At this point, however, it is well to point out that international Communist policy is one of exploiting opportunities as they arise, and it is spurious to see in Soviet policy any long-term choice between "East-

33. For an interpretation which develops brilliantly but to extremes the conception that Malenkov-Zhdanov rivalry in the U.S.S.R. rent the international Communist fabric see Franz Borkenau, *European Communism* (New York, 1953), pp. 519, 539. Borkenau has more recently contributed a number of provocative articles to *Commentary*, further developing his thesis of international rivalries among highly placed Communist factions.

ern" or "Western" orientations; this also applies to the choice between "legal" and "illegal" tactics. For whatever will contribute to Soviet power will be utilized, and tactics will be shifted immediately and drastically to exploit developing opportunities or deal with threats.

Titoism made the Cominform relatively meaningless, even as a façade. The Czechoslovak coup (February, 1948), the purges in eastern European parties which began on a grand scale in 1949, and many other developments furnished evidence of ruthless intervention by the Kremlin in the internal affairs of the "sovereign" and "equal" parties and governments of the Cominform bloc. And, as usual, the machinery of communication and control operated very secretly. Occasionally bits of interesting but not very revealing information about the channels of control become available, as when Malenkov and Suslov—presumably in their capacity as secretaries of the Central Committee of the Soviet Communist party—attended the ninth congress of the Communist party of Czechoslovakia held in Prague in May, 1949.[34]

Enough has been said in the foregoing to indicate the character of Soviet control of the Comintern and Cominform. Let us now examine briefly the political behavior of foreign Communist parties and some of the major tasks which they have performed, and continue to perform, on behalf of their ultimate leaders in the Kremlin. At this point, another word of caution is in order. The literature on international communism, despite brilliant individual books and articles, is still inadequate to furnish the basis for a systematic account of the sociology and politics of communism. This is true of all areas of the world but particularly of

34. Since Stalin's death Khrushchev has participated in Polish, and Mikoyan in East German, party meetings.

Asia, Africa, and Latin America. Selznick in *The Organizational Weapon* has shed a good deal of light on some general characteristics of Communist parties in the following remarks: "The special problem of leadership posed to Leninism is that of joining a revolutionary elite to the social force which it hopes will carry it to power. This relationship must (1) hold the leadership group together and (2) bind it firmly to the mass." Holding the leadership group together means building and maintaining Communist parties; the use of doctrine and propaganda as devices for achieving these results has been discussed. Isolating and insulating Communists from "subversive" or "alien" influences, particularly in Communist-controlled countries but to a large extent in other countries too, is also a major means of achieving this end. Involvement of Communists in party activities which absorb their attention and heighten their emotional involvement in the cause is very important. These devices achieve "total control of the individual."

Revolutionary Doctrine

Stalinist political strategy has defined the social targets at which the organizational weapon is aimed. The elements of this strategy have been well formulated by "Historicus" in his article "Stalin on Revolution" (*Foreign Affairs,* January, 1949). The main force of the revolution is the proletarian and peasant masses in the advanced countries and the "liberation movement" of colonial countries. In his "Economic Problems of Socialism in the U.S.S.R." Stalin declared that it was necessary to find a social force capable of overcoming the resistance of the "dying" social forces. This force, he maintained, had been found only in Soviet Russia in "the union of the working class and the peasants." To these groups there should, of course, be added members of the intelligentsia who identify with the masses and often become their Communist party leaders. While it is not difficult to define in general terms the social targets of Communist activity, it is much more difficult to solve the problem of how Communists develop organizations which capture and direct these social forces.

The fundamental and most basic technique is the establishment of Communist nuclei or "cells" in non-Communist organizations, although the organization, training, and employment of this personnel constitute the main work of Communist parties. Traditionally, mass organizations such as labor unions have been the main targets of Communist penetration. The Chinese Communists, building on certain ideas of Lenin first suggested in his *Two Tactics of Social Democracy in the Bourgeois Revolution* (1905), added an important dimension to Communist strategy and tactics by perfecting methods of organizing mass peasant movements. Much of the work of Communist penetration has been secret, illegal, and conspiratorial. Among the requirements laid down to the Communist parties by the Comintern was that they have in readiness illegal as well as legal organizations, so that they could function covertly,[35] if necessary.

One of the main reasons for the Communists' success has been hard, grinding work, and they have often been successful far out of proportion to their numbers because they were able to create the impression among the members of mass organizations that they and they alone knew how to defend and advance the interests of the rank-and-file members. Thus they bound the masses to themselves by heeding Stalin's oft repeated warning that the

party would remain strong so long as its roots were intact.

Espionage Rings

An especially important aspect of Communist penetration of non-Communist institutions is the formation of espionage rings capable of penetrating sensitive government agencies. On this subject we now have considerable evidence, the most substantial of which is that contained in the report of the Royal Commission published at Ottawa, Canada, in 1946. The Royal Commission's investigation led to the conclusion that several rings of Communist agents were operating under direction of Soviet supervisors. As to the motivation of these persons, the commission concluded that "motivation was a product of their political ideology and of the psychological conditioning received in the study groups." As the Report brings out with documentation which all anxious to understand communism should study, these groups made conspirators and traitors out of selected party members; thus the Kremlin received the free services of loyal agents. Here is the foreign-policy application of the principle of the "social obligation" mentioned earlier.

Sometimes foreign Communist espionage agents are used in their home countries, as in the case of Elizabeth Bentley; sometimes, as in the case of Richard Sorge in Japan and Klaus Fuchs and Bruno Pontecorvo in the United States and Great Britain, they function abroad. In the particularly sensational Sorge and Fuchs cases, the agents avoided contact with local Communists and functioned in effective cover positions, using secret communications channels to the MGB. These cases indicate that services of decisive historical influence were rendered by these expendable Kremlin dupes. Non-Soviet states can scarcely expect to enjoy equivalent facilities because of

35. Selznick's analysis and the personal-experience accounts of Whittaker Chambers and Herbert Philbrick shed much light on these matters.

the well-known Soviet devices for insulating Soviet and Communist personnel from "alien" influences. Thus in fields ranging from espionage to cultural relations the Kremlin exploits ruthlessly the advantages of its militarized polity.

We have already discussed Communist fronts as agencies of propaganda. Now a word should be said about the organizational implications of the "united-front" tactics set forth by Dimitrov at the seventh Comintern congress in 1935. As Selznick points out: "Bolshevism was now to wrap itself in any ideological mantle, or to infest as a parasite any expedient host, which would yield increments of power to the party, even though this power could not be exercised in its own name." Eugene Lyons in *The Red Decade* has presented massive evidence of the success of this policy during the prewar years in the United States, and its continuation in the postwar years was extremely successful among demoralized and impoverished intellectuals in western Europe. During what seems to be a tactical retreat of communism in the West begun in 1951, a new version of the united front has been introduced. This new united-front policy was manifested in France, for example, with the demotion and expulsion of Marty and Tillon, two of the "left-wing" militants of the French Communist leadership. Malenkov added a new integrating slogan for use by the world Communist movement in its efforts simultaneously to extend mass influence and atomize opposition with his campaign for the "relaxation of international tension," set forth in his August 8, 1953, speech. Various gestures by Khrushchev, such as his reception of William Randolph Hearst, Jr., may fit into this pattern.

A major result of Soviet and Comintern activity is the incalculable harm which it has done to the general cause of social progress, harmony, and international peace. Take the case of Germany: A number of powerful European Communist parties were built up, among which the German party of the 1920's and early 1930's stood out. This party's activities contributed considerably to the rise of Hitlerism by splitting the labor and the liberal forces of Germany. Western European communism experienced an upsurge of membership in the middle and late thirties. This was particularly true in France, where the alliance with Russia against the traditional enemy Germany was a major political factor. But the Stalin-Hitler pact struck a blow at the Communist movements in Europe and the Americas; not much was left except the hard core, but, of course, this has always been the most important ingredient of the Communist movement. It was during the pact period that some of the most grotesque features of Communist propaganda and organization flourished. According to the evidence which Rossi, the Italian expert on international communism, has set forth in his book *Les Cahiers du bolchevisme pendant la campagne 1939–40*, French Communists distributed underground literature printed for them in Germany. In 1940 the American party received permission to withdraw from the Comintern. It is interesting that, following the nineteenth party congress in Moscow, French and German Communists issued joint denunciations of the European army plan; at the same time, on the diplomatic level, Moscow worked to split France and the Anglo-Americans by manipulating the bogy of German militarism.

Chinese Communism

The only Communist party outside France that grew steadily and significantly in numbers and power during the middle and late 1930's was China's, and this was also the only Communist party outside the Soviet Union that wielded a measure of state power. When World War II began, the Chinese Communists ruled a large territory with millions of people and had their own government apparatus and army. The Chinese Communist movement after Mao Tse-tung got control of it in the early 1930's remained loyal to the Kremlin, despite the fact that the Soviet Union during the Sino-Japanese war, which began in 1937, rendered extensive material aid to its enemies, the Nationalist government. This pattern of loyalty to Moscow, despite what to the outsider would appear to be brutal treatment by the Soviet Union, persisted in the postwar period. On the other hand, the Chinese Communists freed themselves to an important degree from Soviet interference in day-to-day operations. As Ypsilon says of Mao: "His power grew not at the court of the high command, but in China itself. For that reason it became real power."

There is disagreement as to whether or not Mao ever went to Moscow, but he did seem to keep clear of Comintern politics. Loyally though cautiously and with a measure of independence, he broke away from reliance on the industrial proletariat as the main revolutionary force and succeeded in organizing peasant Soviets and a Chinese peasant army: on this base he built his power. Of course, he was mightily assisted by the war between Japan and the legal Chinese government, which sapped the forces of the latter. He was also to be assisted in the postwar period by the legend assiduously disseminated in the 1930's by Soviet propaganda that the Chinese Communists were mere "agrarian reformers" and not Communists in the strict sense of the term. Finally it should be remembered that Moscow-trained Chinese Communists and Soviet generals and officers working with the Chinese Communists played impor-

tant roles in the growth of Chinese communism. As of 1945, according to Robert C. North, 57 per cent of the membership of the Chinese Communist Central Committee were Moscow-trained.

On the whole, the balance sheet of international communism did not present a very favorable picture on the eve of World War II. For this reason Borkenau concluded, in his major study published at that time, that the Comintern had been a failure. Today such a judgment seems premature indeed, although in a sense it was correct. For, as we shall point out later, the strength of international communism in our period is more an extension of the power of the Soviet state than an expression of local movements for social change. In other words, communism is not international but imperialist; it is the reflection and extension of Soviet nationalism, the nationalism of a supra-national state. This supra-national state could be expanded until it became a Soviet world state. As an official Soviet source has stated it, a "single, world socialist culture" can develop after victory everywhere of the "socialist" revolution.

VI / COMMUNIST IMPERIALISM

The Extension of Soviet Power

A major factor in the extension of Communist power has been the development of specifically Soviet methods of using military power, including the proximity of force for political purposes. Until the Communist conquest of China, both material power and political direction had been supplied by the Soviet Union. In all cases of Communist expansion, including that of China, an indispensable factor has been Soviet power. Since their victory in 1949 the Chinese Communists have become a second major military base of Communist power. For Communist

China, perhaps even more than the Soviet Union, is militarist and expansionist, as indicated by its seizure of Tibet, its role in the Korean and Indo-Chinese wars, and the pressure which it exerts partly through its attempt to utilize Chinese minorities in neighboring countries upon the whole of Southeast Asia. Since they are in an earlier stage of revolutionary development, the Chinese Communists can be more radical. There are indications that Moscow has accorded Mao a measure of doctrinal autonomy and is using China as its major instrument for expansion in Asia. But it is also probably true that Moscow fears too great an increase in Red China's power.

The decisive role of Soviet armed force was emphasized in 1948 by a supremely authoritative source, the Central Committee of the Communist party of the Soviet Union. In its letter of May 4, 1948, to the Central Committee of the Communist party of Yugoslavia, the Soviet Central Committee stated that the Soviet army "created the conditions which were necessary for the Communist party of Yugoslavia to achieve power."[36] The Soviet Central Committee added that "unfortunately the Soviet army did not and could not render such assistance to the French and Italian Communist parties." From this letter and other Soviet sources we can conclude that recognition of the indispensable role of Soviet military force for the establishment of communism in power outside the Soviet Union has become a major tenet of Soviet political doctrine. The doctrine reflects practice: the cornerstone of the Soviet theory of international relations is that the Soviet Union is the "base" and "shock brigade" of world revolution, though this doctrine as set forth in the Kremlin's dispute with Tito does not apply quite so clearly to Asia as it does to Europe.

In Asia, Africa, and Latin America the Kremlin relies very heavily on the strategy of mobilizing the "colonial reserves" of the revolution in the "struggle for national liberation." The death of Stalin, despite surface changes of line, did not lead to any real alteration in the doctrinal basis of this policy.[37] Lenin and especially Stalin regarded the "reserves" in underdeveloped countries as the main basis of the power of "imperialism"; if captured, the Communists would mortally wound the advanced capitalist countries. And at the same time control of these resources would add tremendously to the power of communism. In China the local Communists, if one overlooks certain important facts, seem to have taken power without outside aid; but close examination of the development of the Chinese revolution indicates that it, too, was successful partly because of Soviet actions. In 1945 the Soviet armies illegally turned over to the Chinese Communists huge quantities of Japanese arms and equipment, which contributed greatly to the strength of the Communists; and the Soviet army and political administration in Manchuria furnished very important aid to the Chinese Communists. By a combination of direct assistance and interference with the efforts of the legitimate Nationalist government to establish its administration in this decisive area, the Soviets helped to create conditions that tipped the balance in favor of the local Communists. Even the Soviet dismantling of Manchurian industry, though deeply harmful to the interests

36. See the important source materials in *The Soviet-Yugoslav Dispute* (London, 1948), p. 51. The Soviet party here also referred to its tactics of "combined operation" of regular military force, partisans, and local insurrection.

37. *Pravda's* editorial for June 24, 1953, discussing the "world campaign for negotiations" inaugurated after Stalin's death by the World Peace Council, warned that "use of force" against any "national-liberation movement" might lead to "a new center of war."

of the Chinese people, indirectly helped the Communists by weakening the economy.

We do not wish to suggest, however, that Soviet policy and power were solely responsible for the Chinese catastrophe. Other factors, including an incorrect appraisal by American public opinion of the situation in China, unwillingness to devote sufficient resources to what seemed a very remote area, as well as terrible internal problems such as inflation on a grand scale and widespread corruption, played very important roles. It remains to be seen whether other countries, such as India, facing similar internal problems can solve them, compounded as they are by Communist pressure, propaganda, and subversion. It may be hoped, however, that India, Burma, and some other Asian countries will have a better chance, partly because of their long association with Great Britain, to build a viable democracy.

We do not believe that the interests of Soviet and Chinese communism always were, are today, or will be identical. There is, for example, evidence that Stalin and Mao differed sharply on policy in 1945 and after. The crucial question for the future is whether Sino-Soviet relations will be mutually satisfactory.

Recognition of the role of force in Communist expansion is not so important as understanding the political character of Communist violence. Revolution, war, and military occupation are only the last, decisive stages of a series of steps; the most important aspects of Soviet military operations have always been the political activities which have preceded, accompanied, and followed them. The Soviet leaders are more conscious of the close and complex relationship between war and politics than are other statesmen. To them peace means the conduct of war by nonviolent means, an attitude which

flows logically from their conviction that the capitalist system is disintegrating but that, unless channeled in accordance with Soviet influence, it will not lead to the desired end.

Weapons of Expansion

Let us now briefly analyze the process by which Moscow exploited the opportunities created by World War II. Soviet diplomacy, military occupation, and military government policy and the activities of the local Communists directed by Moscow—all played important parts in this process. Diplomacy and the propaganda which was utilized in support of diplomacy served to conceal Soviet aims, to confuse and deceive the governments and public opinion of both the Soviet Union's wartime allies and the victims of Soviet expansion. Soviet diplomacy and propaganda were surprisingly successful in creating the impression that the U.S.S.R. was fighting a "national war of liberation," and Communists everywhere achieved recognition as ardent national patriots. But great care was taken to avoid arousing the fear that Moscow wanted to instal Communist regimes outside the borders of the U.S.S.R.

This was a continuation of the tactics developed in the united front after 1935; since then a synthetic nationalism has been one of communism's most potent weapons.[38] One of the greatest successes of Soviet diplomacy was

38. Exploitation of nationalism, however, is as old as Leninism; this is clear to any careful reader of Lenin's 1914 study, *On the Right of Nations to Self-determination*. And in the debates on the national questions at the twelfth party congress in 1923, still the best source for Soviet theory on this question, Stalin urged drafting the Soviet constitution in such a way as to make a favorable impression on the peoples of China and India! Since the nineteenth congress and particularly since Stalin's death, European Communist parties, especially in France, have made exceptionally effective use of a combination of Soviet-determined goals and local symbols.

the treaty between the Soviet Union and Czechoslovakia (December, 1943), signed by the Czechoslovakian premier, Dr. Beneš, which was opposed by the British and the American governments. An important feature of this treaty was the solemn assurances given by the Soviet government that it would not in any way interfere in the internal affairs of Czechoslovakia. A similarly reassuring statement was made by Molotov (then Soviet foreign minister) in April, 1944, when Soviet troops crossed the border into Rumania; he declared that the Soviet troops were in Rumania solely for the purpose of conducting military operations against the German enemy and that they would not be used to bring about social and political changes. It is difficult to believe it now, but such Soviet statements, coming after the dissolution of the Comintern, had a great effect on world public opinion; they helped people believe what they then wished to believe: that Soviet Russia was a "normal" national state with limited objectives.

During this period of the "Anglo-Soviet-American coalition" the Kremlin succeeded in building up in Western upper- and middle-class public opinion and even in the minds of some of the most responsible political and military leaders of the West, particularly in the United States, a new and favorable image of Soviet Russia. In so doing they were continuing the practice of fashioning a climate of opinion and sentiment to facilitate the achievement of military and political objectives.

Soviet foreign policy is based explicitly on the exploitation of the contradictions within and among capitalist countries and between the "socialist" Soviet Union and the capitalist world. In a broad sense the whole Soviet policy toward both sides in World War II was an application of this doctrine.

As David Dallin emphasizes, Soviet policy is that of a "third power." The Kremlin hopes that its enemies will destroy one another: the coalition propaganda was intended to conceal this fact from temporary allies. If one understands this Soviet doctrine, the tone and style of Soviet diplomacy will seem less peculiar. For "correct" and even momentarily jovial though it appears, this is a diplomacy of conflict, not consensus, and negotiation is a formidable weapon. Many peculiarities of Soviet diplomacy, however, are a natural response to years of existence as a pariah power always in the minority in international negotiations and organizations.

While Soviet diplomacy was doing its best during the war to deceive and disarm opponents who considered themselves allies, other agencies of the Soviet Communist party and state were fashioning instruments to be used in Sovietizing neighboring countries. These instruments were wielded in the military occupation of Yugoslavia, Bulgaria, Rumania, Poland, Czechoslovakia, Hungary, Albania, and North Korea. From late 1945 until late 1946 the northern Azerbaijanian-speaking part of Iran lived under a Soviet system, and, of course, that country—and, indeed, most of the Middle East—are today in the shadow of Soviet power.

To say that new political instruments were being forged in Moscow during the war is something of an overstatement, for most of these developments involved new applications of an old method. "Sovietization" is as old as the Bolshevik revolution and simply means the reorganization of a society and its culture at the will of the Kremlin under local Communist leadership. It results, among other things, in the creation of what are sometimes called "Soviet satellites," the earliest of which, as noted previously, were Outer Mongolia and Tannu Tuva. Tannu Tuva also enjoys the distinction of having been the first satellite "state" to become a part of the Soviet Union. The manner of its incorporation is significant: it happened secretly. According to Soviet newspaper accounts published on August 16, 1946, a "popular movement" had arisen in Tannu Tuva during the war, and in response to it the country became an "autonomous" oblast of the RSFSR. Foreign diplomats in Moscow did not become aware of this development until 1945, and the world at large first learned of it in 1946. Outer Mongolia, or the Mongolian Peoples Republic as it is officially known, is still treated by the Soviet Union as a nominally independent country. And to a certain extent it may be a weapon held in reserve against Communist China.

Some of the present constituent republics of the U.S.S.R. at one time enjoyed a status rather similar to that of the present-day satellite states. Manipulation of the symbols of sovereignty is important, particularly in the "colonial" world with its legacy of resentment against Western "imperialism," in Moscow's effort to enhance its appeal to susceptible elements, especially among intellectuals. The Soviets regard Latin America as a "colonial" region. The ministries of foreign affairs which were set up in some of the Soviet Central Asian republics in accordance with a constitutional amendment of February, 1944, fit neatly into this pattern. In connection with this amendment Molotov proclaimed that it would appeal to the "peoples of East and West," a phrase that must have reminded his party-trained audience of numerous statements by Lenin and Stalin about the "reserves" of the world revolution.

Thus Moscow had acquired a wealth of experience long before World War II in the practice, and also in the propaganda presentation, and, when necessary, even concealment from the world, of the facts of Sovietization, for it is carefully planned and proceeds through definite stages. During the preparatory stage the instruments of power are created;[39] second, there is the stage of actually installing the new regime in power, characterized by the existence of a front of political parties and a coalition government which might be called one of partial Sovietization; the third stage is that in which agriculture is collectivized, Soviet-type industrialization is well advanced, and a totalitarian political regime is established. It remains to be seen whether this pattern must lead to formal incorporation in the U.S.S.R., which Soviet cultural and especially linguistic theory indicates is the logical end result.[40] This final stage, however, may be indefinitely postponed in the interests of propaganda against the Western powers.

"Peoples' Democracy"

The beginning of the third stage may be heralded by violence, as it was in Czechoslovakia in the coup of February, 1948. The Soviet satellites of eastern Europe and also Communist Korea entered this third stage in 1948. This is the stage which is characterized in Soviet doctrine as "peoples' democracy." It is not considered "socialism" such as the Soviet Union itself enjoys and from which, it is maintained, it is making the "transition" to communism. "Peoples' democracy" is, however, admittedly a form of "proletarian dictatorship."

Soviet doctrine maintains that China is also living under a regime of "peo-

39. It is important to understand that much of the activity of this stage consists of "making friends" by establishing false but appealing identities between non-Communist aspirations and disguised Communist goals.

40. Soviet doctrine envisages the development first of "zonal" international languages and ultimately of a "single world language."

ples' democracy" but that there are differences between the Chinese and eastern European types of peoples' democracy, the most important of which center around the problems of "feudal survivals" in China and the predominant importance of the peasant question.

The countries of eastern Europe, although they were not aware of it, were in the first of these stages in the last year of World War II. And it is doubtful that even eastern European Communists fully realized what was afoot. The higher-ranking ones, however, probably had a pretty good idea of what was being prepared. In this connection it is interesting to recall that Kopecky, a high-ranking Czechoslovakian Communist, gave a public lecture in Moscow in late 1943 in which he outlined in all essentials the future of Czechoslovakia and its relationship with the Soviet Union; this was one of the very few of the numerous public lectures delivered in Moscow known to the writer which shed some light on real Soviet strategy as distinguished from ritualistic enunciation of doctrine.

Some of the organizational forms set up in the Soviet Union during the war and carried into other countries as part of the political baggage of the Soviet army have already been mentioned. A wide variety of committees, special military formations, publications, and other activities were set up. In Poland, for example, there was the "Union of Polish Patriots" and the "Polish army,"[41] whose personnel were mostly Soviet Poles. In 1943 the Soviet Union broke off diplomatic relations with Poland after the Polish government requested an International Red Cross investigation of the Katyn massacre, in which, as now appears clear, the Soviet au-

thorities killed some nine thousand Polish army officers who had fallen into their hands after the Soviet invasion of eastern Poland in 1939. The stage was thus set for the creation of an organization which entered Poland with the Soviet army and which was to furnish an important element of the cadres of the Communist government of Poland—the "National Council of Poland" headed by Boleslaw Bierut, a veteran Comintern man. Bierut, Jacob Berman, and other Comintern agents were among the most important Polish Communists involved in setting up all this machinery, and they are also among the top leaders of Communist-controlled Poland today.

Not all the leaders were Comintern veterans; some were members of Soviet underground and partisan movements who had never been in the Soviet Union and who had fought or conspired against the Nazis during the war—Laszlo Rajk, the Hungarian police head purged in 1949, was such a one. Conflict between these two types of Communist leaders may help somewhat to explain ferocious purges in satellite Communist parties. Both types of leader and both types of organization played an important part in setting the stage for Sovietization of these countries, although the details of the process varied considerably. Thus, for example, in the case of Czechoslovakia, whose government did everything it could to achieve friendly relations with the Kremlin, no political organization of the type of the "National Council of Poland" was created; but a Czechoslovak military formation was set up in Moscow during the war. Incidentally, there was also a French air unit, the "Normandie" squadron.[42] The degree of

41. In 1943 the "Union" began to publish *Wolna Polska* ("Free Poland"), which took a nationalist, anti-German, but not Communist, line.

42. This and other features of Soviet policy indicate that only geographic and power considerations restrained the Kremlin from attempting even greater extension of its orbit than was actually achieved.

secrecy or openness of these various activities also varied; thus, so far as this writer knows, no indication was given until after the war, and even then not in Soviet-published sources, that the cadres of a Korean army were being trained in the Soviet Union.

We have already mentioned the part played in Soviet tactics during World War II by participation in the resistance movement; this was perhaps the most important of all the ways in which Communist cadres grew during the war. It was also a very important political weapon which the Soviet Union and foreign Communists used to discredit and weaken not only enemy governments but also governments such as those of Czechoslovakia whose leaders had emigrated to London or elsewhere. This statement applies also to western European countries, such as France, where the Communist element in the resistance movement would have taken over the country under supervision of Comintern Communists if Soviet and not Western allied troops had defeated the Germans.[43]

A word should be said here about the very special role of the Soviet armed forces and particularly their political officers in the installation of Communist regimes in the satellite states. The MGB, the Soviet political police, also played a vital role in the process. A top-flight political figure was assigned to direct the process in each country; in Poland it was apparently the political "general" Bulganin, who was later to become a member of the Politburo and chairman of the Council of Ministers of the U.S.S.R.

The role of the MGB is indicated by the fact that an MGB officer, G. S. Zhukov, was photographed with Stalin in the Soviet press (July 27, 1944)

when Stalin signed an agreement with the Polish Committee of National Liberation on relations between the Soviet commander-in-chief and the Polish administration, to go into effect in Soviet-occupied Polish territory. Agreements such as this provided a façade of legality for the actions of the Soviet occupation forces. According to the former Czechoslovak political leader, Dr. Ivo Duchacek, the application of a similar agreement for that country "by the political service of the high command of the Ukrainian front under General Mechlis is a classic example of how a legal text can be not only emptied of its contents, but changed into an instrument which defeats its intended purpose." The Soviet military and police forces in the occupied countries performed numerous valuable services for the Communists in their contest for power against non-Communists, and, of course, they also kept the local Communists under control.

It is significant that Yugoslavia is the only European Communist state except Albania which did not experience complete or long Soviet military occupation. Soviet forces gave confidence to local Communists and intimidated their opponents; they also provided important logistic support to the Communists by furnishing them with scarce items such as paper or typewriters, which, as Duchacek points out, were of crucial importance in the early unsettled postwar period. In some cases the Soviet forces took drastic action against anti-Communists, a striking example of which was the arrest by the Soviet secret police (May, 1945) of sixteen Polish democratic leaders and their subsequent trial in Moscow on sham charges that they had been conspiring against the Soviet armed forces.

Although effective power was in the hands of Soviet agents in the satellites from the very beginning, it is important to remember that the governments of

---

43. In some ways the resistance movements in non-Soviet countries represented an extension of methods used in the Soviet Union in the partisan warfare against the Nazi invader.

these countries were "coalition" governments. This was true in Czechoslovakia until February, 1948. The Communists went slowly at first, seeking as much non-Communist support as they could use without sacrificing anything essential. By this time it is probably forgotten that in Rumania, for example, there was a kind of collaboration between the Communists and the young King Michael. It must be remembered that this was a period during which Moscow was still somewhat concerned about Western public opinion. However, even in this second stage of Sovietization, more or less free and "normal" elections were permitted only twice. The two cases are those of Hungary in December, 1945, and Czechoslovakia in May, 1946. The 38 per cent of the votes which the Communists received in Czechoslovakia was the best score they ever made anywhere in a "free" election—and, of course, even these two elections were not genuinely free. They could not be, for in these countries the Communists controlled the police and other key sectors of the administration; above all, it was known that local Communists were backed by the Soviet secret police.[44]

The outstanding characteristic of the second stage of Sovietization was that, while the Communists could not fully control the government, they had penetrated those branches of the administration which gave them control of organized violence and, to a predominant degree, of communications. This and the presence or proximity of the Soviet army put them in a position where they could seize full power and inaugurate a totalitarian regime at will. This was the situation known in Leninist political science. as "dual

power." It corresponded to the months in 1917 during which the Bolsheviks were widening their wedge among the Soviets.

The general pattern, which Duchacek has documented for Czechoslovakia and Kertesz for Hungary, was one of "active interest and impressive display of Soviet power in contrast to the West's hesitant policy." Duchacek adds that "careful, professional infiltration of democratic institutions and the wishful thinking of the democrats did the rest." Elements of this pattern were present in western as well as in eastern Europe until the spring of 1947. It is startling to recall that from the summer of 1944 until the spring of 1947 Comintern agents, including Togliatti and Thorez, were members of cabinets in Italy, France, and Belgium.

By now the eastern European countries are far into the second or even the third phase of Sovietization. In these countries the stage roughly corresponding to Stalin's destruction of the Russian old Bolsheviks in 1936–38 has already occurred; revolutionary cannibalism occurred earlier here than in Russia.

Expansion in Asia

Let us now survey Communist "combined operations" in Asia. In 1949 the Pacific Ocean Institute of the Academy of Sciences of the U.S.S.R. published *The Crisis of the Colonial System*, with chapters on China, India, Ceylon, Indonesia, Indo-China, Malaya, the Philippines, and Korea. It follows the postwar Soviet line, the first all-out militant expression of which was given in Zhdanov's Cominform speech in September, 1947, in which he revived the early emphasis of Lenin and Stalin on revolutions in the "colonial world." Among other things it describes the Communist-led uprisings in postwar India. While the work deals mainly with eastern Asia, its introduction also reflects Soviet postwar activity in Af-

44. In the light of the foregoing the achievement of the Finns in retaining at least a large measure of internal independence is heroic. Perhaps Beneš might have resisted successfully too.

rica, for it expresses satisfaction with armed uprisings and strikes in Madagascar, Nigeria, Uganda, and other areas. This is an indication of the breadth of the Soviet power horizon. A similar indication is the statement in a 1951 Soviet book, *The Struggle of the Peoples of the World for Peace,* that African natives had walked 30 kilometers through the jungle to sign the Stockholm peace petition.

Soviet sources claim that the main factors in the postwar disturbances in the colonial world are the increased power and prestige of the Soviet Union, the social dislocation resulting from the war in the Pacific, and the growth in the years before the war of the native industrial working class. Since the establishment of the Cominform, they have openly admitted and often boasted of the role of Communists in the leadership of Asiatic revolutionary movements. They also emphasize, particularly with respect to China and Korea, the contribution of the Soviet army to the struggle for "liberation." Let us look at the case of Korea as a particularly important testing ground for Soviet Communist "colonial" techniques.

North Korea is in some ways the counterpart to East Germany—or, even more grimly, one can say that East Germany possesses some of the geopolitical attributes of North Korea. Like Germany, Korea is a strategically vital country partitioned into Soviet and non-Soviet spheres of control. In both cases the territorial divisions were not, on the allied side, intended to be permanent, and there was no intention that the Iron Curtain should be drawn across the middle of a country. But in both cases Soviet policy has established a satellite state in the Soviet-controlled part of the country and has used the puppet state as a base of operations to gain control of the rest of the country. This process has, of course, involved a political and cultural competition be-

tween "peoples' democracy" and "imperialism." Finally, while realizing the limitations of the comparison, we may note that if Germany is the main key to Europe, Korea is a key to control of Japan. It is also, of course, important to the defense of China.

With the entry of Soviet forces into Korea in August, 1945, came the revival of the Korean Communist party. This party had been underground for years, and, as in the case of most of the Communist parties of eastern Europe, many of its leaders were in prison or in exile.[45] According to Soviet sources, the Communist party immediately became the "fighting center of all the democratic progressive forces of the country." It organized trade-unions, a Communist youth league, a women's group, and other mass organizations, and, as in other backward areas, a great play was made of the "emancipation" of women. The most important of the agencies by which the Communists established control over northern Korea were the "peoples' committees," which corresponded to the soviets of Russia or to the "national committees" used by the Czechoslovak Communists as a means of infiltration and penetrating in the first years after the war. Representatives of the peoples' committees in a Soviet-type election chose a "Peoples' Assembly" of North Korea in February, 1947. The Soviet authorities never permitted the United Nations to carry out plans for a genuinely free election for an all-Korean government. In the fall of 1948 a second Soviet-type election was held in North Korea. Since September 10, 1948, the deputies elected in this second election have been referred to in North Korean and Soviet communications media as the "central government of Korea." This regime has echoed Soviet

45. Some of them were with Communist Chinese units in China during the Sino-Japanese War, 1937–45.

demands for the unification of Korea. The Soviet Union established diplomatic relations with it in October, 1948; in March, 1949, an agreement on "economic and cultural co-operation" was signed between the Soviet Union and the "Korean Peoples' Democratic Republic," the Soviets proclaiming this the first "equal" treaty in the history of the Korean people, a boast designed to capitalize on memories of foreign imperialist rule.

This North Korean regime, with all the characteristic features of a Soviet satellite state and with an even thinner veneer of "united front" hiding its Soviet control than in the eastern European satellites, was exploited in Soviet propaganda as an example of democracy in action. At the same time the Soviets concealed their own aggressive aims in Korea by attacking "reactionaries" in South Korea and, above all, by accusing the United States of inciting its "puppets" to civil war. In the meantime the Soviets organized a partisan movement in South Korea and in other ways pressed for unification of the country by force under Soviet control. As in Europe, they pressed their demand for the withdrawal of American armed forces and gave plausibility to this demand by withdrawing their own army in the fall of 1948. They did not do this, however, until they had built up a powerful Korean army officered largely by Koreans brought in from the Soviet Union. When the United States withdrew its troops from South Korea, Soviet propaganda claimed that this was a maneuver designed to conceal "the strengthening of the occupation system." With this background in mind, it becomes a little easier to understand the tactics involved in the Soviet accusation that the Korean War was started by the United States. Soviet preparation of the Korean War and the propaganda preceding and following the outbreak of the war glaringly illustrate the Soviet technique of preparing for an act of aggression by first accusing the enemy, or the victim of the action, of intending to commit it.

Soviet policy in Korea was particularly important, in that it was the first case in which a Communist-controlled military force attacked Americans. Thus it aroused fear that the Korean aggression might be the beginning of World War III. It now appears that the Kremlin blundered into this war in the conviction that no effective opposition would be offered; it may have occupied in Kremlin strategy a position somewhat similar to that of the other Far Eastern "liberation struggles" led by the Communists. Thus Korea fits into a Soviet-planned strategy of piecemeal conquest of the world. In the long run this strategy may be the most menacing that the Kremlin could adopt but in the foreseeable future it does not call for an all-out Soviet–United States war.

The main elements of this strategy would be the following: first, internal consolidation and military buildup of the Soviet empire; second, support by propaganda and other expedient means of revolutionary movements in colonial and semicolonial countries. Even if it does not result in increasing the resources directly under Soviet control, this policy—now being applied in Indo-China, Burma, Malaya, the Philippines, and other areas—dissipates the resources of the free world and creates sharp tensions between the United States and its western European allies. The effect of the Indo-Chinese and the North African problems of France upon the economic and military strength of France and upon Franco-American relations is an obvious case in point. The third major element in Soviet strategy is to utilize the "contradictions" among the Western powers and particularly fear of Germany and Japan to keep them divided and render them incapable of matching the Soviet drive for power based on unity within the area under Moscow's control.

This Soviet grand strategy, one of piecemeal accumulation of power, represents the most insidious but not the only possible Soviet threat to the existence of human freedom and the culture which requires freedom and spontaneity to live. In this atomic age decision by obliteration is also a possibility for both power centers. Malenkov's statement in his remark to the Supreme Soviet (August 8, 1953) that the United States was "no longer a monopolist of the hydrogen bomb" gives pause.

Whether the trend is toward the One World hoped for by Wendell Willkie or the anti-Utopia feared by George Orwell or even toward no world will depend largely upon unforeseeable developments, including the ability of the non-Soviet world to cope with Soviet strategy without sacrificing democratic principles. In the long run it will be necessary to discover and apply better ways of utilizing scientific capabilities for human welfare. The peculiar experience of the Soviet regime gave it a head start on the non-Soviet world in the techniques of organizing men to maximize the power of the political control group. The future will depend on whether the balance will be redressed by the West's ability to realize on its superior capital of free brain power and on the rigidities in the Soviet structure which correspond to its superior powers of mobilization and its monolithism. We must be alert to perceive and, if possible, encourage development of the forces in Soviet society with which we have common interests. In the meantime two of the main keys to world equilibrium remain: the sober use of power and a sensitivity to the legitimate aspirations of all peoples, particularly those of underdeveloped countries.

Satellite Parties in Eastern Europe

ANDREW GYORGY
Boston University

I / Prewar and Wartime Characteristics of Political Parties in Eastern Europe[*]

The seven nations and approximately ninety million people of eastern Europe engaged in World War II fought not only against the oppressive control of Nazi Germany but also against the detested *ancien régime* of corruption and dictatorship; for the people of eastern Europe had long yearned for a complete break with the distressing interwar era of authoritarianism and they eagerly anticipated a "New Deal" based on social justice and mass participation in governmental affairs. And it was because of this that the Communist-engineered and Soviet-guided revolutions of the postwar period were at first able to capitalize on the spontaneous movement of millions of people in Danubia and the Balkans.

The real tragedy of this turbulent area in world politics was that the popular enthusiasm of the postliberation period was ruthlessly abused by the Soviet Union, for the makers of Russian foreign policy cynically subverted the energies of native leaders and the well-intentioned efforts of indigenous political parties in order to consolidate Soviet control over eastern Europe. Because of their potential postwar function, the Danube Valley and the Balkans, comprising over 300,000 square miles, were of great strategic and political importance. While hastily drawn boundaries had broken up the fundamental unity of the region, the seven states still shared a common historic tradition and similar economic problems. All these states had once formed part of the old Turkish and Hapsburg empires. Poland is the largest, with a population of about twenty-five million; Czechoslovakia, westernmost and most industrialized of them all, has about fourteen million people; Hungary, occupying a particularly strategic area in the heart of the Danube Valley, has a population of almost nine million; Yugoslavia, possessing a precious outlet to the Adriatic Sea, has a population of about sixteen million; Bulgaria, located at the lower end of the Danube and precariously facing the Soviet Union, has a population equal to Hungary's; Rumania, another Black Sea country and probably the most obedient postwar satellite of Russia, has an estimated population of sixteen million; and Albania, wedged into a small corner of the Balkan Peninsula neighboring on hostile Yugoslavia and Greece, is an insignificant and politically drab country of about a million people.

The authoritarian regimes characteristic of the pre–World War II scene first established their power position in the early 1930's, when the progress of political parties in eastern Europe was blocked by the appearance of artificial, uneasy government coalitions and the polarization of political extremes. At one end was the aggressively Fascist nucleus of a nationalist right wing, while at the other were the left-wing

[*] A table of the major political organizations in eastern Europe since 1919, with principal leaders and their dates of tenure in office, appears on p. 302.

Socialists and the clandestine, illegal Communist parties. A promising "third force," such as peasant party groups and moderate Socialists, was gradually squeezed in the vise of government-imposed restrictions which sharply curtailed or completely outlawed the activities of independent leaders and vigorous opposition movements. The thinly disguised military dictatorships were strongly upheld by an elite of small, politically active yet socially indifferent groups of sycophants in parliament.

In this atmosphere political parties were distorted and eventually reduced to mere mechanical devices for deciding conflicts within the gentry and bourgeoisie, and new and rigid party alignments were created around the carefully selected representatives of these two social groups. At the same time the masses of industrial and agricultural workers were unscrupulously disfranchised and largely excluded from the spectrum of political representation. Such blatantly unfair legislation as the Hungarian electoral law of the 1930's, providing for secret ballot in the towns but open voting in the countryside, was designed to swell the government's inevitable majority and openly sanctioned the mass exclusion of all "politically undesirable" elements. Throughout the interwar period, observes Isaac Deutscher, the life of eastern European peoples "had been bogged down in savage poverty and darkness; their politics had been dominated by archaic cliques who had not minded the material and cultural retrogression of their subjects as long as their own privileges had been safe."[1]

Political life in prewar eastern Europe revolved around three major groups: the Right, the Center, and the Left. The Right was favorably inclined toward Fascist-militarist political goals

and imitated the then fashionable pattern of Mussolini's or Hitler's regime. The membership of rightist parties consisted usually of army officers, the upper crust of civil servants, church leaders, and occasionally owners of landed estates. Their political models were Konrad Henlein's Sudeten German party in Czechoslovakia; the Arrow Cross movement of Hungary; the National Christians and the Iron Guard of Rumania; the Yugoslav People's party, the semi-Nazi Zbor, and the Yugoslav Nationalists; and the Military League and the so-called National and Social Movement in Bulgaria. The Left embraced the traditional opposition groups of Social Democrats, National Peasants, and some of the more prominent public figures with Western sympathies, like Jan Masaryk of Czechoslovakia, Nikola Petkov of Bulgaria, and Stanislaw Mikolajczyk of Poland. The multicolored membership of various social-democratic, agrarian, liberal, and radical-socialist parties included both the agricultural worker and the urban proletariat, the lower middle class, university students, and scattered intellectuals of both town and country.

Among the courageous but highly ineffective Socialist groups, the Czech, Polish, and Hungarian Social Democrats were the most prominent and articulate in insisting on more progressive patterns of national administration. Undaunted by the overwhelming political odds against them, they frequently challenged official government parties in parliament and in towns and among agricultural and industrial workers; and although disfranchised en masse, for some twenty-five years they fought hopeless and embittered campaigns against the government and the militarist cliques representing official coalition forces.

In the overwhelmingly agrarian countries of eastern Europe the peasant population succeeded in forming a few

1. *Stalin: A Political Biography* (New York, 1949), p. 535.

carefully integrated and soundly organized political parties. The most vigorous ones appeared in Rumania, Bulgaria, and Yugoslavia, each systematically struggling for social reforms, political democracy, and essential economic measures. When Rumania's constitution of 1923 granted the franchise to peasants, the new voters overthrew the powerful Liberal party that had dominated Rumanian politics since the establishment of national independence. In the 1928 elections the National Peasant party won a striking victory, and its leader, Juliu Maniu, became prime minister. Under Maniu taxes were sharply reduced, agricultural education fostered, co-operatives encouraged, rural savings banks established, and rural credit enlarged; for the peasant leaders insisted, as Schevill said, that "the first business of the government is to place agriculture on a sound basis."

In Bulgaria in Alexander Stambolisky's revolution of 1920 the scepter of political power passed to a major peasant party; and the marked antibourgeois and anticapitalistic bias of the new peasant leadership caused a veritable upheaval in the domestic affairs of Bulgaria, where politics had always been the prerogative of a comparatively small group of intellectuals. In Yugoslavia the Croatian Peasant party, led by the eminent Stephen Raditch, played a significant political role throughout the 1920's; serving as a determined front of opposition to the Serb policy of centralization, it was able for many years to dictate national policy in both domestic and foreign relations of the new Serb-Croat-Slovene state. On the whole, such organizations as the Rumanian National Peasants, the Bulgarian Agrarians, and the Croat Peasants achieved a number of social reforms which steadily influenced their country's party system and political development.

The Center parties usually found their way into government coalitions characteristic of the interwar era. Heading these coalition-forming groups were typically middle-of-the-road politicians, selected on personal grounds of proved loyalty and enduring usefulness to the national cabinet. Surrounded by a few mediocre splinter parties but seldom hampered by recalcitrant dissidents, the coalition represented a solid block of 150–200 votes in the lower house (Chamber of Deputies) of the typical Danubian or Balkan parliament. Most of the government coalitions pursued policies advocating violent opposition to the gathering forces of liberalism, a frantic support of crumbling monarchies and often corrupt royal families, and an aggressive militarism that encouraged the gradual emergence of regular army officers in leading positions. The evolution of Rumanian and Yugoslav domestic politics throughout the 1930's aptly illustrates the corrosive influence of these policies.

In 1937 and early 1938 a cabinet of National Union held together the strange multicolored assortment of Rumanian parties. Carol's ubiquitous personal dictatorship shed its thin disguise when a decree of April 14, 1938, dissolved all existing political parties, which were replaced by a Front of National Rebirth intrusted with the task of preparing a program of "national regeneration." Artificially created as a single party, the Front centered around an assortment of discredited pro-monarchist leaders, who strengthened their hold over the country by equipping themselves with a paramilitary organization known as the National Guard. The political program of the Front reflected the prevailing indifference toward agrarian and social reform programs and was concerned primarily with anti-Semitic legislation and persecution of Rumania's sizable minorities. Condoning waves of unmitigated terror, the Front quickly lost the loyalty of the masses; splinter parties were formed, and large groups of Hungarians, Ukrainians, and Bulgarians gradually seceded from the government and joined the opposition. These breaks in the screen of artificially enforced unity contributed in turn to the rise and consolidation of native military dictators and enthusiastic Nazi supporters, who paved the way for a full-fledged German occupation of Rumania.

In Yugoslavia a government coalition was first imposed by the constitution of 1931, which forced political parties into one group and excluded a majority of the electorate from effective influence. Between 1931 and 1936 most of the government officials and cabinet ministers were drawn from the newly formed Yugoslav National party, which favored the policies and general orientation of the regime. After 1936, even the scattered forces of the opposition embraced the coalition principle and under the aggressive leadership of Dr. Maček formed a new United Opposition party. Thus a series of *mariages de convenance* were formed, forcefully aligning the government Front against the "superparty" of the opposition.

This picture of partisan bipolarity strikingly characterized a number of Danubian and Balkan countries. Their outlawed Communist parties usually withdrew behind the façade of seemingly unified opposition groups and either infiltrated the ranks of the Social Democrats or engaged in widespread underground activities.[2] Although weak and unpublicized, the Communists swiftly came to represent an organized chal-

lenge from the extreme Left, while in their violent struggle against the Right they neglected the basic social and economic problems of their countries fully as much as did the members of the government coalition. The major qualitative difference appeared in the field of foreign relations: government parties were persistently and implacably anti-Soviet, while the Communists were violently anti-German except in the short-lived Nazi-Russian "honeymoon" period of 1939–41.

The war years sharpened the conflicts inherent in the basic social and political structure of prewar eastern Europe. Under the onslaught of German and Russian conquering armies, the familiar framework of domestic politics collapsed, the artificially transplanted Western democratic institutions swiftly died, the aura of medieval feudalism disappeared, and even the spirit of aggressive irredentism was temporarily silenced. Only two tangible facts emerged from the terrible bloodletting of World War II, one military and the other political. In the military constellation of postwar eastern Europe three major countries—Czechoslovakia, Poland, and Yugoslavia—aligned themselves with the victorious side as constructive members of the wartime United Nations, while Hungary, Rumania, and Bulgaria, more or less faithful satellites of the Axis, joined the ranks of the defeated. In terms of postwar reconstruction, this division is probably of less immediate significance than the emergence of the Soviet Communist party as a new political factor. Following in the footsteps of the Red army, the Bolshevik party appeared both as a revolutionary instrument and as a weapon for the conquest of power, a dual function in which it not only unfurled the banner of ideology but also obediently supported the principal objectives of Soviet foreign policy. It

2. The Communist party was not outlawed in Czechoslovakia, where it had a steady parliamentary representation throughout the interwar period. Klement Gottwald was the leader and vocal champion of the party in sessions of the Czech parliament.

characterized in a striking manner the new Soviet state, defined recently as a marriage between the territorial or ethnic power-complex and an ideology.[3] The postwar development of eastern European politics is inextricably interwoven with the principal strategies and globe-girdling activities of the Soviet Communist party.

II / POSTWAR DEVELOPMENT OF POLITICAL PARTIES

First Phase: Liberation Fronts, Coalition Governments, and National Elections

One of the significant instruments of Soviet policy has been the control exercised by individual national Communist parties in the postwar liberation fronts. The first phase in the recent development of eastern European political parties was characterized largely by a minority participation of Communists in the newly established united-front governments. These governments had a broad base of popular support and found a generally suitable expression in democratic coalitions which united liberal remnants of the prewar "historic" parties,[4] the more permanently organized elements of wartime resistance movements, and other influential independents. The political left was represented by a fairly vigorous Social Democratic party and a small, seeming-

ly mild-mannered Communist nucleus tactically still on the defensive. One of Hungary's Muscovite Communists, Ernő Gerő, expressed the immediate wartime orientation of the party most clearly when at the first session of the National Assembly in December, 1944, he emphasized that the Hungarian Communist party intended to pursue a Hungarian, democratic and national policy.

The large number of independent parties guaranteed a democratically inclined initial phase in postwar reconstruction. The Fatherland Front in Bulgaria and the National Independence Front in Hungary were directly responsible for achieving such crucial and long-delayed social reform measures as the nationalization of basic industries and the redistribution of the land. The term "new democracy" had an acceptably Western connotation so long as the colorful multiplicity of political parties prevailed, the army and police were largely non-Communist, and the liberal (bourgeois) political leaders were able to retain important positions in the government.[5] The Bulgarian Fatherland Front was particularly effective so long as it united such ideolog-

3. Max Beloff, *The Foreign Policy of Soviet Russia* (London, 1949), II (1936–41), 390–91.

4. The term "historic" applies to parties which, founded in the nineteenth century, had an uninterrupted political career of several decades. They often helped to allay serious governmental crises and to combat the dangers of a constitutional vacuum by maintaining a sense of long-range historic unity in the nation. In eastern Europe the Rumanian National Peasant party and the Liberals, the Hungarian Smallholders, the Czech Catholic People's party and the Agrarians, and the Croat Peasant party were generally characterized as historic parties.

5. The Soviet interpretation of the initial period in the life-cycle of "new democracies" was vastly different from any Western analysis. Leading theoreticians of the U.S.S.R. expressed contempt for a concept of democracy which insisted on the free existence and sound competition of several political parties. According to G. F. Aleksandrov, the noted Russian student of philosophy, the question of whether democracy is compatible with a one-party system can be answered by the Soviet people in a clearly and unequivocally affirmative manner: the existence of several parties in society is *not* the sign of true democracy in the Soviet sense of the term. "The democratic nature of public life," adds Aleksandrov, "is determined not by the number of parties but [by] whether this policy is carried out in the interests of the people and in the interests of its overwhelming majority" (see *O sovetskoy demokratii* [Moscow, 1947], a speech delivered at the Academy of Sciences of the U.S.S.R. on December 4, 1946).

ically differentiated groups as the Republican, Agrarian, Communist, and Social Democratic parties and the other minor groups. Its aggressive vigor was greatly upset when Petkov's Agrarians were forced out by the Communist party in the summer of 1945 and the Republicans eliminated in the army's wholesale purges. The national elections of October, 1946, held under conditions of intensified police terror, gave the Communists an over-all majority of 60 per cent. It is a tribute to the initial democratic momentum of the Front that, in spite of Communist intimidation and fraudulent practices, the opposition received over 1,300,000 votes, a third of the electorate and certainly one of the highest opposition votes recorded in eastern Europe after the war. The surprising strength of a liberal-minded opposition and the prestige setback suffered by the Communist party soon provoked a Moscow-guided campaign of forced consolidation. George Dimitrov, former secretary-general of the Comintern, became prime minister in November, 1946, and succeeded in establishing a people's republic without competing political parties, opposition groups, or an independent-minded, and thus obstructionist, liberation front.

The development of Hungary's Independence Front clearly illustrates the strategic orientation in this phase of postwar politics. The emergence of a broadly representative National Assembly marked a new era of high expectations and moral renaissance for the shattered Axis satellite. There was both traditional safety and real promise in the number of organized groups which set out to assert themselves in the political arena. In 1945 the assembly was composed of large representations of the Social Democrats, the Smallholders, the National Peasant party, the Communist party, and the Democratic Citizens party; in addition there were nonparty members and trade-union representatives.[6] Most of these groups presented significant obstacles to a direct Communist seizure of power and simultaneously exerted an impressive influence in counterbalancing rightist nationalist forces. This massive grouping around the center guaranteed that the progress of national reconstruction would not be threatened by extremists or sources of ideological infection inherent in the eastern European political scene.

In spite of scattered warning signals and early fissures in some of the post-liberation governments, the years 1945 and 1946 held great promise for both the future of political democracy and the continued economic progress of the eastern European countries. The coalition principle was in effective operation; democracy, Western style, was at least praised, if not practiced; harmonious co-operation characterized the relations of state and church; and the new governments laid ambitious plans for the careful administration of their nations' first postwar elections.[7] In his recent work on communism Franz Borkenau aptly appraised this meaningful period as one of "a definite coherent attempt to return to normality . . . social normal-

6. Even the numerical distribution of assembly seats reflected the spirit of this vigorous multiple competition: In early 1945 the National Assembly was composed of 94 Social Democrats, 127 Communists, 123 Smallholders, 39 National Peasants, 22 members of the Citizens party, 30 nonpartisans, and 63 trade-union members (see István Száva, *New Hungarian Domestic Policy* [Budapest, 1946; in English], chapter entitled "Democratic Hungary," pp. 24 ff.).

7. Throughout the 1945–46 period it was the firm hope of Soviet foreign policy-makers that not only in the prospective people's democracies but also in France, Italy, and Finland, Communists would be able to retain the leadership of wartime anti-Fascist resistance movements, thus extending their position in the government and finally winning state power in a climactic struggle with the bourgeoisie.

ity, in so far as the progress of expro-
priation was stopped, and political normality in so far as . . . a show of democracy was put into operation."⁸ A transitional period of fresh zeal and optimistic expectations opened up; people
were urged to try out new methods of
communal work and social organization.
On the whole, broad vistas of reform
and advancement characterized this
short-lived era of hope for the future.

Still wedded to the minority participation stage of their strategy, Communist leaders pursued a cautious and
slow-paced policy during this era of *lu-
cidum intervallum.*⁹ Communists mas-
queraded as nationalistic and strongly
anti-Fascist groups anxious to form alliances with other anti-Fascist political
parties. The reforms they demanded
were surprisingly mild and were generally harnessed into the service of progressive movements operating on a
seemingly nation-wide basis. To the
leaders of eastern European Communist parties this strategy implied a hesitant beginning on the road of long-
range "socialist transformation." In the
course of their prerevolutionary agitation, members of the Communist hierarchy admittedly confined their struggle "*only* to a steadfast achievement of
bourgeois-democratic tasks."¹⁰ This initial stage was earmarked by a systematic infiltration of liberal parties and an
insistence on such economic measures
as land reforms that proved useful in
breaking up the class of landowners,

the aristocracy of the latifundia. Communist leaders felt compelled to advocate a coalition government and to
preach the necessity of collaboration
with the church. These flexible principles proved particularly useful to the
Communists, who freely reinterpreted
and systematically subverted the results
of the first wave of postwar elections,
which were generally unfavorable to
their cause.

Throughout these national elections
the governments of the United States
and Great Britain insisted on an observance of the Yalta formula. Applied to
eastern Europe, the Western conception of "free and unfettered" elections
claimed that all democratic and anti-
Nazi parties be allowed to conduct
election campaigns freely, "without
arrest or threat of arrest." The pre-
election phase also postulated that the
broadened coalition governments definitely include representative members
of the opposition on a mutually acceptable basis. Both the Bulgarian and the
Rumanian governments were urged to
bring into their coalition two opposition members as cabinet ministers to
serve as guardians of the rights of non-
government parties.¹¹

The coalition-forming center parties
frequently displayed symptoms of innate weakness and yielded to the impact of strong Russian diplomatic pressure or to the presence of Soviet troops.

8. Franz Borkenau, *European Communism*
(New York, 1953), p. 502.

9. It must be remembered that Yugoslavia
was fully under Tito's rule by 1945 and therefore loomed as the major exception in this
popular-front period of eastern Europe's post–
World War II development.

10. József Révai, "On the Character of
Our People's Democracy," *Társadalmi Szemle*
(Budapest), March–April, 1949, republished
in *Foreign Affairs*, October, 1949, pp. 143–
52; see also Andrei Zhdanov, *On the International Situation* (Moscow, 1947).

11. See the United States note of February 22, 1946, to the Bulgarian representative
in Washington, stating in part: "It was and
is the earnest hope of the United States government that, meeting in a spirit of conciliation, representatives of the Bulgarian government and of the opposition could and would
agree to work together on a . . . basis which
would enable two truly representative members of the opposition parties to participate
in the Government" (*State Department Bulletin*, March 17, 1946, p. 447). Similar requests were outlined in the United States note
to the Polish Foreign Office, submitted on August 19, 1946, and discussed by Arthur B.
Lane in *I Saw Poland Betrayed* (Indianapolis, 1948), p. 322.

This fundamental feebleness in personnel and political convictions helped to undermine the resistance of anti-Communist elements in both Polish and Yugoslav liberation movements, thus accelerating the process of Communist *Gleichschaltung*, which was accomplished by winning the co-operation of some political parties and causing the destruction of others. Groups like Hungary's Smallholder party engaged in a self-liquidating appeasement policy toward the Communists in a shortsighted attitude of calculated weakness, where the Communists did the calculation and the moderate parties furnished the element of weakness. Acceding to one Communist demand after another, some of these parties lost their ablest leaders (Kovács, Petkov, Peyer) at an early stage and were subsequently relegated to the background of national politics. By making full use of the blind appeasement gestures of middle-class parties, the Communists eliminated vigorous and competitive aspirants to leadership and forced even the most skilled non-Communist politicians into endless tactical retreats. These defeatist moves were accelerated by secret pre-election agreements invariably allowing the Communists a larger share of the cabinet positions than their popular vote warranted.

Communist leaders frequently issued calls for single-list elections, which created a glittering illusion of an all-embracing unity among the major political parties. Single lists served as a particularly valuable inducement to combine on one ballot most of the political parties not in opposition. But in exceptional cases even parties in open opposition were approached with a request to join the government bloc, of which the most flagrant illustration occurred when the Polish Communists insisted that the major opposition parties, and principally the nationally popular Peasant party, join the government in a single electoral list. This request to capitulate was cleverly camouflaged by the Communist Polish Workers party's generous promise to allot 20 per cent of the parliamentary seats and government ministries to the Peasant party. Stanislaw Mikolajczyk, leader of the Peasant party, refused to accept the double bait of single list *plus* a fixed percentage of the political spoils, denouncing it as an obvious ruse to entice opposition parties into gradual and conditional surrender. Sensing the political significance of the issue, the United States government vigorously protested the unwarranted restriction in the number and effective operation of the major parties of Poland as contrary to the letter and spirit of the Yalta declaration. When it appeared that the Communist party could not risk an early election, its chief protagonists adopted a strategy of delay and, as an obvious subterfuge, demanded a national referendum on a few hastily contrived and irrelevant constitutional issues.

In other satellite countries Communist leadership resorted to fraudulent balloting and the "unofficial" capture of key administrative posts. Such governments as the official Smallholder cabinet of Ferenc Nagy in Hungary and the coalition-type Fatherland Front in Bulgaria progressed through a Communist-engineered process of self-liquidation. In comparing the fate of his coalition government with those of Poland and Bulgaria, where men like Mikolajczyk and Petkov "abandoned their rightful place in their country's history as early as 1946," Nagy asserts that he was able to keep a "citizens'" democracy alive in Hungary as late as May, 1947. He poses the dilemma of the non-Communist Danubian or Balkan party leader with curious simplicity and eagerly rationalized crudeness: "We too could have failed a year earlier if instead of playing politics we had been virtuous. Being virtuous would have been more popular; but being political was more profitable to the nation."[12] Unhappily, the political tactics of Hungary's Small-holders and Bulgaria's Agrarians proved totally ineffective in delaying the "pene-tration timetable" of the Soviet Union and in preventing the ultimate ideo-logical destruction of the two countries.

Communist leadership was principal-ly interested in infiltrating the coalition governments. The new arrivals from Moscow—Rákosi, Gottwald, Dimitrov, and Ana Pauker—insisted on determin-ing the composition of postliberation governments and on acquiring key posi-tions for themselves. They instigated public name-calling and private de-nunciation, wildly brandishing such double-edged clichés as "reactionary" and "conspirator" to intimidate mem-bers of opposing parties. An ever ex-panding wave of "reaction" closed in around such parties as the Social Demo-crats of Czechoslovakia and Hungary, the Polish Peasant party, the Hungarian Smallholders, the Rumanian Peasants, and the Bulgarian Agrarians.[13] For "re-actionaries" were really those who hin-dered the Soviet-dictated political and social progress of the people, and in

12. F. Nagy, *The Struggle behind the Iron Curtain* (New York, 1948), pp. 372–73.

13. The intensity of Communist-guided cam-paigns against "reactionary conspirators" was considerably slowed down by the resistance of opposition parties, which frequently com-manded overwhelming popular support. In October, 1946, foreign observers in Rumania reported that Juliu Maniu, veteran leader of the National Peasant party, was more popu-lar than ever in his long career. "His past mistakes and weaknesses are forgotten. He stands now not for any program or ideology but for the idea of national independence. His is the symbol of the Rumanian nation. . . . Maniu is a brave man. He has no illusions about the methods his opponents will use. But he feels that today he cannot compro-mise and that if he goes down in the struggle it will have been worthwhile" (see "Dictator-ship in Rumania," London *Times,* October 18, 1946).

actual practice anyone who, as a simple citizen, had attended to his office dur-ing the former regime was now charac-terized as a hopeless reactionary. The charges usually involved flexible varia-tions on the theme of serving an anti-democratic reaction. "We are not ene-mies of the army," stated leaders of the Greek Communist party (K.K.E.) in a 1944 resolution, "but we demand that it be purged of Fascist antipopular ele-ments, so that only children of the peo-ple remain." A purge of reactionary military officials, they wrote, could pave the way toward a "real and substantial satisfaction" of the "national fighters" of Greece.

The Soviet-inspired pattern of strug-gle against reaction became an early hallmark of satellite political life. In Hungary, Czechoslovakia, and Poland new categories of "reaction" were es-tablished daily. The nonpartisan official who refused to join the Communist party and whose conception of democ-racy differed from the Muscovites' was as much to be branded as those who protested against the crimes of the Communist police. Partisans of "reac-tion," particularly members of oppos-ing political parties, were invariably arrested for "antidemocratic utterances." They were then convicted for violations of the "Defense of the Republic" act, which defined as criminal any incite-ment against the republican form of government and could be conveniently cited against the non-Communist ene-mies of Stalinist "progressivism."[14]

14. The two most frequently invoked acts were the Law for Defense of the People's Power (1945) in Bulgaria and the Defense of Hungarian Democracy Act (1946; VII). Every one of the Soviet satellites passed simi-lar legislation in the 1945–47 period (see *The Strategy and Tactics of World Communism* [Washington, 1948], Appendix, pp. 30–31). According to Nagy, then prime minister of Hungary, the worst reactionary sin during the coalition period was to criticize the be-havior of the Soviet army of occupation.

Second Phase: Communist Access to Power; Emergence of Peoples' Fronts; the Socialist Dilemma

In characteristic Communist terminology, the second phase of postwar evolution was the era of ideological and political consolidation in the peoples' republics of eastern Europe. This brief two-year phase included the systematic undermining of other political parties and the use of coercion to obtain Communist control of the police and the army. In Yugoslavia and Bulgaria the battle-experienced wartime guerrilla movements played an important role in this process, while in Hungary, Poland, and Rumania the local Communist party nucleus relied on the presence of Soviet troops and occupation officials. According to the succinct explanation of József Révai, master-mind of Hungary's Moscow-inspired Politburo: "We were a minority in the Parliament, and in the government, but at the same time we represented the leading force. . . . *Our force, the force of the party and the working class, was multiplied by the fact that the Soviet Union and the Soviet Army were always there to support us with their assistance.*"[15] In Czechoslovakia, Soviet assistance was diplomatic rather than military. Through the formation of conspiratorial "action" committees the Communists succeeded in creating their own militia, which eventually turned against the friendly coalition government. Only in Greece and Finland have they failed to establish control over the police and the army, and without these necessary instruments of power they were unable to destroy opposing political parties and carry out the familiar blueprint of total Sovietization.

This phase of political development witnessed the emergence of peoples' fronts in most of eastern Europe. Unlike the moderate, ideologically well-balanced coalition governments of the previous era, the fronts were clearly dominated by national Communist parties. Other political groups were ordered to fall in line, to assume a "positive attitude" toward the Communist party, which became the leading force in the country's rapid "progress toward socialism." Education, claimed belligerent defenders of the new creed, must now "go forward to the conception of Marx, Engels, Lenin, and Stalin: from the idealistic viewpoint to the progressive conception of dialectical materialism."[16] In an effort to consolidate the power of the new peoples' fronts, the Communist hierarchy engaged in two carefully synchronized lines of strategy. One implied the destruction of all remaining independent political parties, whether or not they were participants in the peoples' fronts. Previously independent and aggressively minded parties were now reduced to silent partnership in the new front-coalitions; the Smallholders and Peasant parties of Hungary, the Catholic People's party of Czechoslovakia, and the Agrarians of Bulgaria were examples of such political groups forced into complete surrender. The other strategy called for a dissolution of the Social Democratic parties in eastern Europe and for the involuntary incorporation of their members into the Communist parties.

Under the impact of revolutionary Communist tactics, the thinning party ranks of the Social Democrats were decisively split between Left and Right. Socialist groups found it generally impossible to develop an effective international policy encompassing the divergent objectives of their numerous and loosely related splinter factions.

---

15. See Révai, *op. cit.* (italics mine).

16. These quotations are from a speech given by Vaclav Kopecky, Czech minister of information, at a teachers' conference in Prague in August, 1948 (reported in *Rude Pravo* [Prague] in August, 1948).

Their political faith was founded on concepts too indefinite to permit the co-ordination of political strategy among the various Socialist parties facing problems in widely diverse social and ideological contexts. Although they had an infinitely stronger appeal to the working classes of their countries than the Communists, they were unable to match the experience and ruthlessness with which the latter attacked the peculiar postwar problems of economic and political reconstruction. Socialists were called upon to make a choice between working-class solidarity with the Communists or democratic solidarity with other parties representing the old prewar order. Hungary's Social Democratic party relied both on a close co-operation with the Communists and on the strengthening of ties with the West. And those who collaborated with Communist leaders were often rewarded with high office. Their left-wing views symbolize a new trend toward extremism in the European socialist movement: a liquidation of the non-Communist Left and the advocacy of unconditional surrender to the Communists. Driven by political opportunism rather than by ideological convictions, politicians of this complexion usually underwrote Communist decisions and lost their political identity as Social Democrats.[17]

The right-wing movement relied on Socialists who have resisted co-operation with the Communists and maintained a friendly disposition toward the democratic socialism of western Europe. Their guiding slogan could well be based on Alexander Hertzen's prophetic remark: "We socialists above all are profoundly convinced that social progress is not possible without full republican liberty, without full democratic equality. . . . A socialism which could dispense with political freedom and equal rights would swiftly degenerate into an authoritarian Communism."[18] In the early phases of postwar political development, Hungarian, Rumanian, and Bulgarian right-wing Socialists succeeded in maintaining a core of open opposition under such liberal standard bearers as Charles Peyer, Titel Petrescu, and Kosta Lulchev. Those who chose to fight for democracy were dealt with swiftly and inexorably; they were tried for treason and either sentenced to death or exiled.[19] The obvious reluctance of right-wing Socialist leaders to follow the dictates of Stalinism infuriated the new regimes, which were carefully laying the groundwork for a formal merger of Socialist and Communist parties.

Yugoslavia was the first eastern European country to succeed in the elimination of "resistance" Socialists from political life. The ruthless liquidation of prewar Socialists, completed as early as 1945, prompted Milovan Djilas, then

17. One noteworthy exception was offered by the political attitude and behavior pattern of the left-wing Socialists in Poland: their movement represented a genuine effort to create and maintain a vigorous non-Communist party of the Left, inspired by imaginative leadership. The reply of the leftist Socialist leaders to the Communists' first overture for an alliance was characteristic: *"You, the Workers' Party, are agents of Moscow, while we have grown upon Polish soil"* (see *Nowe Drogi*, September–October, 1948, p. 65; italics mine).

18. Alexander Hertzen, *Complete Collection of Works and Letters* (Moscow, 1923), XX, 132.

19. Denis W. Healey, "The International Socialist Conference, 1946–1950," *International Affairs*, July, 1950, pp. 363–73. From the perspective of a militant eastern European Communist, the *Gleichschaltung* of Socialist leaders is analyzed in detail by Vulko Chervenkov in a significant speech to the National Congress of the Bulgarian Communist party on June 8, 1950. Chervenkov views the elimination of Socialist political groups as the success of a struggle against "unhealthy tendencies" in domestic politics. Right-wing Socialists are thus fully as dangerous as the political deviationists and should be punished like Titoists, Kostovists, and other determined party enemies.

spokesman of the Tito regime, to re-mark: "Reactionary social democrats here, as they were throughout the whole world, were the bearers of the policy of stifling the revolutionary strug-gle of the working class and breaking up its unity." According to the boast-ful report of the Yugoslav Communist party, reactionary Socialists, believers in the theory and practice of a ludicrous "civil peace," remained isolated from other political groups, had no support among the working class, and eventual-ly "were completely unmasked."[20]

The center groups among eastern European Socialists were anxious to pursue independent policies, firmly re-sisting Communist pressure for party fusion. Despite their fundamental be-lief in working-class unity, they opposed the merger of the two left-wing par-ties, fully realizing that it would in-volve an immediate conquest of their party machine by Communist power cliques. Members of the center were temporarily in control of the Czech and Hungarian Socialist parties, some were to be found in the official Ru-manian party, while a few were still alive in Yugoslavia and Bulgaria. Com-mitting a serious tactical error, the leaders of these independent-minded Socialist groups nourished the secret hope that labor would sooner or later be disappointed by the aggressive meth-ods of the Communists and, "looking toward theoretical Marxism," turn to the Social Democrats. This view rested on the optimistic assumption that the industrial and agricultural workers of a Communist-dominated state were to be given freedom of political choice and offered the chance of embracing theo-retical forms of Marxism. The tragic misreading of the impact of commu-nism contributed to the liquidation of

liberal Socialists, while their more pli-able brethren were gradually forced into the straitjackets of newly created United Workers' parties.

Third Phase: The Party Omnipotent; Principal Methods of Communist Control

The third phase in the development of eastern European politics is marked by the growth of artificially unified workers' parties based on the merger of Communists and Social Democrats. Rumania was the first country in which a United Workers' party was formed in February, 1948; Hungary and Czecho-slovakia followed in June, and Bulgaria in August of the same year. By early 1949 the last representatives of inde-pendent socialism were driven into the Communist camp, thus ending any hope that Western-oriented political groups would survive as captive nuclei of liberalism within the Communist-dominated Left. Appearance of the new workers' parties marked the end of the united front and the beginning of an era dedicated to the construction of "peoples' democracies."

The principal objective of this de-velopmental phase was to legalize the *de facto* political monopoly of the Stalinist hierarchy. "The working class does not share power with other classes," proclaimed József Révai, Hun-gary's "Minister of Popular Enlighten-ment." "The leader of the dictatorship of the proletariat is but one party, the Communist Party, which does not and cannot share leadership with any other parties." In fact, therefore, the Commu-nists set out to achieve a new degree of forced ideological unity at the expense of other political groups. And satellite theorists, whose function was to inter-pret and apply party theory to their respective "peoples' democracies," pub-licly defined the role of the "Party Omnipotent" in their nations. These ex cathedra pronouncements, proudly

20. See Milovan Djilas, *Report on Agita-tion-Propaganda Work of the Central Com-mittee of the Communist Party of Yugoslavia* (Belgrade, 1949), pp. 15–16.

affirming the inviolability of the Communist (Workers') party, included the following directives to the rank-and-file membership of the party:

1. The party represents the real will of the people, and in turn the workers can place absolute reliance on the party.

2. The party must discipline its members and exert self-criticism as effectively as possible.

3. Through its operations the party reaches into the most remote villages and guides domestic affairs on every level of government.

4. The party acts as final authority in appraising and acting upon the complex issues of international affairs.

5. The party stands unchallenged, and its members have pledged total allegiance to it. The party must not tolerate any criticism. There can be no mercy for deviationist views, since the Communist party is called upon to mold the fate of all the people.[21]

An important corollary of these vigorous party activities was a relentless, country-wide drive for membership. In obvious contradiction to the traditional Soviet policy of admitting only selected persons to the ranks, the motto "Everyone join the party!" prevailed, a battle cry implying that the Communist leadership was anxious to bring the masses of recalcitrant citizens in line by exposing them to the strict party discipline of Moscow-trained Stalinists. It also stressed that those not joining the Communist party were not true democrats but, instead, followers of patently antidemocratic movements. Particularly vigorous pressure was exerted on members of the police force and government employees, and the naïve or indifferent fringes of these two groups were attracted by promises of

21. This summary of Communist party doctrines is based on some of the more significant policy-making speeches of such satellite leaders as Mátyás Rákosi, Ana Pauker, Vulko Chervenkov, Klement Gottwald, and Boleslaw Bierut, delivered in the 1950–52 period and reported by official Communist dailies.

economic security and political promotion. Their temporary allegiance was an essential prerequisite of success, for the destruction of non-Communist political parties could not be carried out systematically without a reliable police force and a submissive corps of civil servants.

The membership drive itself was supposed to resolve the continuous "crisis of cadres" which gripped several Communist parties in eastern Europe. The loyal membership of these parties was only a paltry few hundred, which, in addition to a hard core of permanent revolutionaries, usually included "professional joiners" attracted by material inducements or intimidated by threats. Former Fascists and Nazi-minded officials joined, partly because they liked extremism and violence and partly because, if they refused, they might be accused as war criminals; members of national minorities joined because they hoped to obtain government protection; Jews joined because they saw an opportunity to avenge their persecution of past years. The unusual composition and limited political reliability of these groups compelled the Communist leadership to strengthen the framework of its party cadres and seek the practical support of the Socialist parties.

The Communists of eastern Europe formulated three main lines of strategy, using both intimidation and cajolery in their final drive for party unification. For several crucial months they sedulously fostered the belief among Socialists that the only alternatives before them were acceptance of a dictatorial working-class party regime, complete with secret police and political terror, or a return to the repressive reaction of the prewar days. The Communists were also quick to point out that, should "reactionary" governments be elected, the Soviet Union might send troops and occupy the country. This strategy was merely the groundwork preliminary to the use of more direct and aggressive instruments.[22] As a second important tactical move, the Kremlin was frequently called upon to interfere in the struggle of Communists and Socialists, and when differences arose between the two parties their representatives were sent to Moscow. Thus the personal influence of Russian leaders was used to further the aims of Communist-dominated workers' parties and to press upon the Socialists those very policies which were designed to destroy them.

A third line of Communist strategy was frequent use of the political police; these officials exploited the charges of espionage and antistate activities so ingeniously and in such a deliberately threatening manner as to warn leaders of opposing political parties that their failure to co-operate with the Communists would be tantamount to treason. The warning had the desired effect in undermining the morale of the Socialists, psychologically compelling them to accept the idea of a unification of leftist parties. Thus the complete servility of present eastern European regimes to the U.S.S.R. has been made possible by the gradual concentration of all administrative and police powers in the hands of the United Workers' parties.

Controlled by Moscow-trained Communists, these parties express the political will of a new state—the one-class state of the proletariat, which developed on the ruins of "decadent bourgeois nations."[23] The flexible social

stratification of this state centers around the working class, which draws its members from industrial workers, "poor" and "middle" peasants, and intellectuals "attached to the people." In order to perfect this social structure, class warfare has to be waged against such remnants of the exploiting classes as the kulaks, the urban profiteers, and the nonworking intelligentsia. Only by means of a relentless struggle against surviving "class aliens" and "class enemies" can the Leninist ideal of a uniform class-state be established. Within this administrative framework the sharp dividing lines between industrial workers, the peasantry, and the intelligentsia will gradually be obliterated and the old "class exclusiveness" be forced to disappear while the socialist state eventually emerges.

The contemporary satellite-state form of dictatorship of the proletariat is itself a transitional stage. The objective is to lay the groundwork for the transformation of eastern European peoples' republics into the more definitive state structures of Soviet republics; leaders of contemporary United Workers' parties therefore reject the doctrine of the "withering away of the state." Instead, all reliable party members are now called upon to strengthen the proletariat, broadening its foundations and preparing it for the politically more "advanced" way of life carefully prefabricated by the Soviet Union. Recent constitutional documents of eastern Europe strongly emphasize the building of this socialist society and (indirectly) assure the Workers' parties of a special status. In actual practice political control resides with the hundreds of local peoples' committees, the deputies elected to parliament, and members of the Presidium and the national cabinet. In recent years only reliable members of the United Workers' parties qualified for these committees, offices, or appointments, thus strengthening the

22. A characteristic remark, imputed to President Bierut of Poland, clearly describes this phase of political development: "I can assure you there is no intention of liquidating opposition parties or arresting their leaders. *There is no need. They are compromising themselves*" (United Press report form Warsaw, September, 1947; italics mine).

23. János Beér, "Népünk első alaptörvénye," *Állam és Közigazgatás* ("State and Public Administration"), Nos. 3–4 (July–August, 1949), p. 181.

role of the Communist hierarchy in "directing the implementation of all economic, social, and cultural undertakings" of national significance.

The political program of the new monolithic parties is carefully camouflaged by the use of glib clichés and the ambiguous terminology so characteristic of Soviet communism and its creation, the Communist Information Bureau. Official party platforms are longwinded, purposefully repetitious, and rich in appealing ideological slogans. In December, 1948, shortly after its creation, the United Workers' party of Poland proudly defined its basic domestic policies as "reconstruction" and the long march toward socialism. In foreign relations it emphasized the struggle for peace as "the criterion determining the new relationship of international forces."[24]

Occasionally, party blueprints contain such broadly defined guaranties of civil liberties as freedom of expression and the inviolability of person and domicile, but the majority of platforms have stipulations drastically limiting the use of even the most fundamental human rights. As a final arbiter, the Communist leadership determines the scope of human rights and the meaning of personal freedom. The characteristic relationship of individual subservience to an all-powerful police state was strikingly summarized by the late George Dimitrov, leader of the Bulgarian Communist party: "It is obvious that in a people's democracy . . . there is not and cannot be a place for such freedom as harms the interests of the Bulgarian people and might serve its enemies."[25]

Along with this de-emphasis on the individual, eastern European Communist parties have increasingly relied on the use of such mass organizations, political and nonpolitical, as peasant unions, youth groups, students' associations, intellectual groups, and professional associations. Communists were willing to expend an almost endless supply of "infiltrators," funds, and energy on the ideological penetration of these mass organizations. It was part of their strategy to capture or neutralize the labor unions, which had traditionally been loyal to the Socialist party. After a period of preliminary infiltration on the local levels, the new Workers' parties moved in to capture the national leadership of these groups, turning them into obedient organs of the Communist state. Once the trade-unions and co-operatives were subverted by variations of this technique, the Socialists were deprived of the most stable source of their ideological and electoral strength.

In Czechoslovakia the Communist party made good use of the old tradeunionist tradition of unifying all labor unions and keeping them free from any connection with political parties. "The slogans of labor unity and national unity were identified as closely as possible," observes Ivo Duchacek.[26] After the war the Nazi labor front was taken over almost without change by the Communist labor leaders and became the only unified Central Labor Union (U.R.O.). Former Nazi labor leaders were promised immunity by the Communist Ministry of the Interior if they agreed to co-operate with the party.

24. Boleslaw Bierut, "Two Worlds, Two Paths," *For a Lasting Peace, for a People's Democracy*, May 1, 1949, p. 2.

25. *Otechestven Front*, February 3, 1948. Several recent eastern European constitutions contain similar clauses of a strikingly restrictive character (see Art. 34 of the Albanian Constitution and Sec. 37 [1] of the Czech Constitution of 1948).

26. *The Strategy of Communist Infiltration: The Case of Czechoslovakia* (New Haven: Yale Institute of International Studies, 1949), p. 19. The Communists' unification and centralization of mass organizations, which attempted to divide the country into professional categories on a supposedly nonpolitical basis, reminds Duchacek more of the Fascist corporative pattern than of a democratic structure.

Labor was thus forced into assuming a common "national" (Communist) ideology, which further accentuated its usefulness to the present masters of the country.

Among other mass organizations gradually raised to a significant, new political level, youth groups have played a noteworthy role. The success of Stalinist ideological penetration made it strikingly clear that the lower the age group, the greater its devotion to the tenets of communism. Probably the most ardent supporters of eastern European regimes are the Pioneer organizations, youth movements for boys and girls between the ages of six and twelve. The Pioneers are members of their respective national youth associations, which in turn are affiliated with the Communist-controlled World Federation of Democratic Youth (W.F.D.Y.). All these groups have become strict adherents of the Soviet-imposed Communist party line.

III / THE TITOIST CHALLENGE TO INTERNATIONAL COMMUNISM

The break between Tito and Stalin, officially announced to a startled world on June 28, 1948, opened the most significant fissure in the armor of eastern European political movements. Titoism, described by Soviet writers as a combination of "disloyal thoughts and incorrect historical analysis," presented a determined and successful challenge to international communism and its obedient eastern European mouthpiece, the Cominform.

Organized in September, 1947, and originally composed of the Communist parties of the Soviet Union, Poland, Yugoslavia, Hungary, Bulgaria, Rumania, Czechoslovakia, France, and Italy, the Communist Information Bureau planned to use every instrument of pressure to bring about a Communist-directed reconstruction of Europe and to combat the "imperialism" of the United States. Its official inaugural statement outlined the activities of Communist parties in their forthcoming struggle against the exponents of a Western way of life. The founding fathers of the Cominform set for themselves two major goals: in domestic politics, the special task of "defending the national independence and sovereignty" of their countries; and in foreign affairs, the duty of displaying firmness and solidarity so that the plans of aggressors would "suffer complete collapse." These Cominform objectives tacitly implied an appeasement of the nationalist ambitions of individual Communist parties in eastern Europe by creating an impression of equality with the Soviet party.

In reality, the Cominform failed to achieve the stature of the prewar Comintern organization. It exercised primarily the functions of a clearinghouse, of a nondescript propaganda-co-ordinating agency rather than those of an independent policy-making organ of considerable ideological significance. Its weakly newspaper, *For a Lasting Peace, for a People's Democracy,* published in Bucharest, appeared to be a monotonous record of lengthy addresses delivered by the Kremlin's chosen few from the elite of eastern European Communists. The infrequent meetings of its international strategy board were held surreptitiously and resulted in renewed denunciations of deviationists and in a further tightening of the economic and social discipline of the peoples' democracies. Most of the satellite leaders clearly realized that they were sailing between the Scylla and the Charybdis of two dynamic forces—nationalism and communism. The endless conflicts and disturbing contradictions of these two political currents immeasurably complicated the life of Communist politicians, who were caught in the cross-fire of a Russian-dictated internationalism and the nationalistic aspirations of their own parties.

By presuming to decide for himself how to apply the Marxist-Leninist dogma to the Yugoslav situation, Tito successfully challenged the hierarchy of Soviet communism and committed an unpardonable heresy. The schism between Tito and the Cominform, so far-reaching in effect, was essentially the result of a qualitative difference between the powerful Yugoslav Communist party and several relatively weak and dependent Communist parties in Danubian Europe. Tito's strong army and secret service, his continued resistance to Soviet infiltration, and his country's proud spirit of nationalism were destined to precipitate an open break either with competing Communist leaders in eastern Europe or with the absolutist authority of the Kremlin. His deviation, therefore, combined two principal political elements: an *ideological* challenge of the Soviet-imposed political party system in eastern Europe and a *nationalist* assertion of traditional Yugoslav freedom and independence.

Within the general framework of Titoism there are several major types of deviation from Stalinism. A fundamental type is the one challenging the role of the Soviet Union as the permanent base of a Communist-organized world revolution. Being the base for world revolution, the Soviet Union is allegedly superior in status to the non-Soviet Communist world; its needs are given the highest possible political priority in the satellite world of eastern Europe. To deny this is the most serious type of deviation, since it challenges the world-revolutionary role of the Soviet Union and the present structure of Soviet society, denying its importance in setting the course for future action by the new "peoples' democracies."

The following cases of dissidence represent variations of this basic theme: (1) the refusal to express unswerving and blind allegiance to the Soviet Union; (2) a rejection of the necessity of accepting Soviet military control and political guidance; and (3) a refusal to recognize the preponderant role that the "leading socialist nation" or the "largest socialist state" (the U.S.S.R.) was to play in the consolidation and economic integration of the entire socialist world.

These are some of the basic stipulations formulated by present-day Soviet theory. Even a minimum repudiation of any one of these tenets is considered a direct and total attack on the Soviet Union. Such dissidence therefore implies "crimes" against Stalinism on a broad and dangerous front; it obviously covers everything that displeases Moscow in any way, however slight. Of the several types of dissidence, Titoism undeniably presents one of the most outspoken challenges to the Soviet Union and to the countries of eastern Europe. Tito's deviation is based on the power struggle of two political systems conspicuously similar in detail and orientation and yet incapable of coexistence or even minimum agreement. Tito's movement threatens the ideological and organizational front of Soviet power and demonstrates with unprecedented urgency that, as a prototype of national deviation, it is not confined to Yugoslavia alone but can cause secondary and tertiary infections throughout the Communist body of satellite nations.

In general, it is fairly evident that three types of purges are of immediate significance in the life of eastern European Communist parties. One type, aimed at the elimination of certain top-level leaders, succeeds in dislodging such public figures as the Czechs Clementis and Slansky, the Hungarian Rajk, and the Bulgarian Kostov. A second category can well be described as group purges: here the personal friends and political allies, subalterns of the recently silenced or liquidated leaders, are subjected to purges by the party. In the case of men like the Czech Rudolf Slansky, the group purge usually reaches deep down into the party membership and covers a wide area of people who either agreed with Slansky's views or received their jobs through his personal intervention. For example, along with Slansky, his personal secretary was promptly arrested; following her arrest, her relatives, friends, and colleagues were jailed, and the purge of the Slansky group was on its way. Simultaneously intricate and thorough group purges were directed against other prominent "national deviationists" whose arrests implicated hundreds of people around them.

The third form of purge consists of a mass liquidation of the party membership. These purges steadily weaken the party and tear into its social and political fabric; yet, so long as the possibility of an organized opposition is largely destroyed, Soviet foreign policymakers seem to be willing to pay the price. Party members are frightened and seriously intimidated. The spectacle of Communist leaders denouncing as traitors and "Titoists" fellow-members whom they have known for many years, only to be denounced themselves at the next swing of the pendulum, conjures up recollections of the French Revolution. While vicious attacks are leveled against their superiors, party members themselves get used to the idea of being purged some day. By the time their own turn for liquidation comes, their will to resist is often completely sapped, and they willingly accept their own inevitable destruction.

On the whole, the nonparty masses are not directly affected by the frantic purge campaigns and severe convulsions gripping the Communist parties of eastern Europe and their rank-and-file membership. For once, the majority of ordinary people, who have never had the privilege of knowing the secrets of party affairs, receive the news of party purges with a feeling of ill-concealed but frank satisfaction. This feeling is not difficult to analyze. It is a compound mixture of an "it-serves-them-right" mentality combined with the realization that some sort of justice is done, though in a haphazard and crude way. Then the notion of a "liquidation of the liquidators" enters the picture and becomes a dominant theme in the political life of the "peoples' democracies."

TABLE 1

MAJOR POLITICAL ORGANIZATIONS IN EASTERN EUROPE SINCE 1919 (WITH PRINCIPAL LEADERS AND DATES OF TENURE OF OFFICE)*

Country	Liberal	Socialist	Agrarian	Communist	Authoritarian
Albania	Conservative party (Zogu, Vrioni, Ypi), 1920–4 Democratic party (Noli, Delvino, Kruja), 1920–1, 1924		Agrarian Democratic party (Dosti)	Communist party (Hoxha, Xoxe, Maleshova), 1944—	Republican dictatorship (Zogu, Kryeziu, Dibra), 1925–8 Royal dictatorship (King Zog, Kotta, Evangheli), 1928–39
Bulgaria	Democratic Entente coalition (Lyapchev, Burov), 1926–31 Democratic party (Malinov, Mushanov), 1931–4 Radical party (Kosturkov)	Social Democratic party (Sakazov, Pastukhov, Lulchev)	National Agrarian Union (Stamboliski, Gichev, Muraviev, Petkov, G. M. Dimitrov), 1919–23, 1931–4	Workers' [Communist] party (Blagov, Georgi Dimitrov, Kostov, Chervenkov), 1944—	Coalition dictatorship (Tsankov), 1923–6 Zveno National Union (Georgiev, Velchev), 1934–5 Royal dictatorship (King Boris III, Kiosseivanov, Filov), 1935–44 Internal Macedonian Revolutionary Organization (Alexandrov, Protogerov, Mihailov)
Czechoslovakia	People's [or National] Socialist party (Beneš, Zenkl), 1920–1, 1922–38 National Democratic party (Kramář), 1921–38 People's Catholic party (Šrámek)	Social Democratic party (Tusar, Hampl), 1919–20	Agrarian Republican party (Švehla, Malypetr, Hodza), 1922–38	Communist party (Gottwald, Nosek, Slánský, Zápotocký), 1945—	Slovak Autonomist party (Hlinka, Tiso) Sudeten German party (Henlein)
Finland	National Progressive party (Cajander, Stahlberg, Ryti), 1919–23, 1927–46 National Coalition party (Pennanen, Paasikivi), 1924–6, 1930–7, 1939–46 Swedish People's party (Rettig, Born, Törngren), 1919–22, 1927–36, 1939–46, 1951—	Social Democratic party (Tanner, Fagerholm, Skog), 1922–3, 1926–7, 1937—	Agrarian party (Kallio, Relander, Kekkonen), 1919–26, 1927	Communist party (C. & H. Kuusinen, Pessi, Aaltonen, Leino), 1945–8	White Guard (Mannerheim) Patriotic National [Lapua] movement (Wallenius)
Hungary	National Democratic [Liberal] party (Rassay) Christian Social party (Wolff, Zichy)	Social Democratic party (Károlyi, Peyer), 1918–9, 1945–7	Smallholders party (Nagyatády-Szabó) Independent Smallholders party (Szijj, Tildy, Nagy, Varga), 1945–7	Communist party (Kun, Rákosi, Rajk, Gerő), 1919, 1945—	National Union party (Bethlen, Gömbös, Teleki, Kállay), 1920–44 Arrow Cross party (Szálasi), 1944–5
Poland	National People's party (Glabinski, Grabski, Dmowski), 1919–26 Christian Democratic party (Ponikowski, Korfanty)	Social Democratic party (Daszynski, Arciszewski)	Peasant party (Witos, Mikolajczyk), 1926 Liberation party (Rog, Thugutt)	Workers' party [United Workers' party, after 1948] (Gomulka, Bierut, Nowak), 1945—	Nonparty Union [National Unity Movement after 1937] (Pilsudski, Smigly-Rydz, Koc, Beck), 1926–39
Rumania	National Liberal party (C. I., & V. Brătiánu, Duca, Titulescu, Tătárescu), 1922–8, 1933–7, 1944–5 Young Liberal party (G. Brătiánu) People's party (Averescu), 1926–7 National Democratic party (Iorga), 1931–2	Social Democratic party (C. Dobrogeanu-Gherea, Bujor, Petrescu), 1944–5	National Peasant party (Maniu, Mihalache), 1929–31, 1932–3, 1944–5 Plowmen's Front (Groza)	Communist party (A. Dobrogeanu-Gherea, Pătrăscanu, Pauker, Gheorghiu-Dej), 1945—	Iron Guards (Codreanu, Sima) Front of National Rebirth (King Carol II, Calinescu), 1938–40 Nonparty regime (Antonescu), 1940–4
Yugoslavia	Serbian Radical party (Pašić, Ninčić, L. Marković), 1919–29 Democratic party (Davidović, Grol), 1920–3 Independent Democratic party (Pribičević, Kosanović), 1939–41 Slovene Clerical party (Korošec, Krek) Bosnian Moslem party (Spaho)	Social Democratic party (Korać)	Croatian Peasant party (A. & S. Radić, Maček, Šubašić), 1939–41 Serbian Peasant party (J. Jovanović, Gavrilović, D. Jovanović), 1939–41	Communist party (S. Marković, Djaković, Gorkić, Tito, Ranković), 1945—	National party (King Alexander, Živković, Jevtić), 1929–35 Yugoslav Radical Union (Stojadinović, Cvetković), 1935–41 Croatian Ustaši party (Pavelić)

* Reprinted from *European Political Systems*, ed. Taylor Cole. The table was prepared by C. E. Black. Used by permission of Alfred A. Knopf, Inc., copyright 1953 by Alfred A. Knopf, Inc.

PARTIES IN TRANSITION

Japan: Between Traditionalism and Democracy

ROBERT A. SCALAPINO
University of California

Thus far, western Europe and the United States have furnished most of the empirical data upon which the generalizations about modern political parties have been based. Few materials have been drawn from such "late-developing" areas as Asia. But the chief reason for this is backwardness of research on these areas, not their inapplicability to the central problems posed. It is true, of course, that only in the West can contemporary parties be studied in their "native habitat"; in Asia, for instance, they are essentially transplantations. But in formulating any general theory of parties it is instructive to observe how these transplantations have interacted with their new environment and how they have responded to various institutional and social conditions.

Perhaps Japan offers some advantages for such observations; for the Japanese parties can be viewed against a background of major changes in formal political institutions, as well as in the socioeconomic structure of their society. Moreover, Japanese party history is more than a fleeting episode. Among the nations of eastern Asia, Japan has had the longest experience with political parties modeled in general after those of the recent Western pattern. The direct antecedents of the present Japanese party system go back more than eighty years to the period immediately following the Meiji restoration of 1867. By 1881 the first full-fledged party movement had been launched in Japan, and from that time until the present, except for occasional inter-ludes, political parties have been an important component of the Japanese political scene. Indeed, this rather lengthy background must be explored, if only briefly; for even if the pre-1945 legacy was largely one of failure, it is nevertheless important to an understanding of the basic nature of Japanese parties today. The theory of the death of the old Japan and the birth of the new in the events after 1945 can be accepted perhaps by those who believe that transmigration is applicable to the body politic but by few others. The American new deal for Japan did, to be sure, initiate certain new trends promising major change and stimulate certain old ones. But the element of continuity linking pre- and postwar Japan comes into focus more clearly as the occupation era fades away. It is a rather substantial element and one requiring a search into earlier periods.

I / THE ORIGINS OF THE JAPANESE PARTIES

The early emergence of Western-derived political parties in Japan may seem quite remarkable in view of the background of that society, although the conception of that background has been altered in recent years. Earlier, to most Westerners, Perry's Japan had represented the very extremity of oriental medievalism when left untouched by Western currents. Modern research on Japan has corrected—in some cases perhaps overcorrected—that earlier impression. It is now well known that the Meiji restoration had many of its roots in socioeconomic events that long pre-dated Perry. Thus while the first self-styled "political party" emerged in Japan in 1874, just seven years after the restoration and only two decades after the initial abandonment of isola-tion, still this development was but one evidence among many of the spirit of the times.

The development of commerce after the middle of the seventeenth century ultimately had far-reaching repercus-sions on nearly every aspect of Japa-nese society. The rising merchant-entre-preneur groups did not challenge the political system directly and, indeed, in various ways were closely tied to the old order. Nevertheless, the pressures of an expanding commercial-monetary economy were felt with particular force by the military (now essentially civil administrators) and the purely agrarian elements. The intrusion of the West, at first sporadic and then sustained, added further complexities and accelerated the crisis.

Thus the decade between 1857 and 1867 produced a series of threats to the 250-year rule of the Tokugawa family. Finally, the Tokugawa government was overturned by an alliance headed by a few southwestern provincial leaders from the military class and a group of imperial court officials in Kyoto. As in all revolutionary eras, the cross-currents were many and complex, but two burn-ing issues provided purpose and in-creasing strength to the dissidents: (1) the plight of the old quasi-feudal sys-tem that had sustained the military class and placed a premium upon agri-culture in terms of both production and values and (2) the threat of Western imperialism. The anti-Tokugawa forces, dominated by military-agrarian ele-ments, had the initial advantages of the "outs." They could play upon mounting grievances and major problems without assuming any responsibility for national policy formation and hence did not have to face squarely the thorny ques-tion of realistic solutions. The chief slogans of the rebels were "Revere the Emperor" and "Oust the Barbarians." Behind these slogans lay a developing Japanese nationalist movement, deeply rooted in agrarianism and dedicated to a romanticized *ancien régime*. The orig-inal appeal was largely directed toward restoring the emperor to a position of power wherein he could exclude the West and re-establish the old order.

But this was impossible, and the Meiji restoration ultimately came to symbolize the modernization of Japan. Using the emperor as their shield, a small oligarchy of able and aggressive young samurai, together with a few court nobles, discarded feudalism and isolation as logical remedies for the major problems. Faced now with re-sponsibility, they embarked instead upon a program of "Europeanization," which, at first indiscriminate, eventual-ly became with experience more selec-tive and attuned to deeply rooted con-cepts and goals. This program focused on building a strong, centralized state, using industrialization as a weapon for national defense and economic health. Naturally, such a program evoked op-position both inside and outside the government, for it diverged consider-ably from the dreams cherished by many of the military-agrarian groups, who wanted not a revolution, but a restoration; not capitalism, but feudal-ism refurbished; not intercourse with the West, but a militant policy of ex-clusion. It has been said that one basic political problem of modern France lies in the fact that the French Revolution has never been fully accepted. In a somewhat different sense, but with at least equally important implications, it might be said that the Meiji restora-tion has never been universally ac-cepted in modern Japan. And in the

Japanese setting it has been possible to argue that the original purpose of the restoration was betrayed.

Building upon this brief summary, we should be able to explain the early development of Japanese political parties and give some analysis of their structure and function. In the first place, these parties could emerge because in the early Meiji period political leadership was consciously dedicated to exploration and experimentation. Furthermore, since no element within the oligarchy dared push its uncertain powers too far, this was also a time of considerable political freedom. New ideas and institutions were allowed to compete or merge with traditional ones. For a time a precarious balance between suppression and anarchy was maintained, with the resultant flowering of political concepts that could have some national scope. Now aroused, young intellectuals from the samurai class plunged into the study of Westernism; and, though often mystified and confused, they embarked upon their great intellectual adventure with earnestness and seriousness. Translations of Bluntschli, Mill, Locke, Rousseau, and many others were undertaken. The political understanding and the political vocabulary of at least the articulate Japanese were expanded, and new phrases like "constitutional government," "parliament," and "popular rights" were coined by using new combinations of Japanese characters. Around 1871 the term *seito* made its appearance as the word for "political party"; this term was identified with Western systems of representative government and distinguished from *toha*, or "factions," which Japanese had long been expected to shun and hate, although it cannot be doubted that there was some carry-over from the older connotation. Still the stage was being set for political movements flying new banners and operating under new methods.

But if this explains why the political parties of the early Meiji period could emerge, it does not go far enough in explaining why they did emerge. To approach a fuller answer to this question, one must interrelate three factors: (1) the rivalry for power within the new Meiji oligarchy, (2) the economic and social unrest incident to a period of great transition, and (3) the initial contacts between disaffected elements and Western ideas. The first factor obviously played an important role. The most immediate causes for the establishment of the early Japanese parties were a series of splits in the ruling oligarchy, largely the result of personal rivalries and a sectional struggle for power. The problem of personal rivalries in Japanese politics is significant enough to receive special treatment later. The problem of sectionalism, however, might be emphasized at this point. During the Tokugawa era Japan had been divided into nearly three hundred *han*, or "fiefs," varying greatly in size and importance. The policy of the central government was to discourage political contacts among the *hans*, because hostile alliances had to be avoided. With political regulations added to such natural communications barriers as existed, *han* boundaries in the Tokugawa period were important in fixing the general perimeter of the average person's world. Even in this era of so-called "centralized feudalism," *han* autonomy was very great, especially in those fiefs far separated from the central military administration or *bakufu*, located in Edo (modern Tokyo). Hence provincial patriotism flourished. One's country or native land was one's *han*; indeed, the term *kuni*, now translated as "country," was used in this manner. And primary allegiance went to the *han* lord; he was the true ruler and father in a period when the emperor was a shadowy and little-known figure to the common man. Primary loyalties were clearly at the *han* levels, and they were often intense.

It is true that this heritage gave Japan some distinct advantages over China in launching a successful nationalist movement. China had a tradition of intensive competition and conflict between family and state. The Chinese family, when compared with its Japanese counterpart, maintained a more separate and aloof identity from the larger community, retained more civic-social functions for itself, and exacted a clearer priority of loyalty from the individual. Japan, on the other hand, presented a tradition of integration of family and state beginning at the village level. Both functions and responsibilities were strongly communalized within a rigid hierarchical structure: thus a sense of both class and community was inculcated. Communal consciousness and a hierarchical society, with its established pattern of loyalty to superiors and benevolence to inferiors, laid the foundations for the state priorities of modern nationalism. Thus in the case of Japan it remained only to transfer and expand loyalty from the *han* and the *han* lord to the nation and the emperor. But if this task was less difficult than that confronting modern China, it was not accomplished so easily and so thoroughly as many have assumed. Generally the persistence and importance of sectionalism to modern Japanese politics have been underestimated. We have been too dazzled by the glitter of recent Japanese nationalism to see adequately this other aspect of Japanese society. In its very potency the nationalist movement has paid an involuntary tribute to that sectionalism which was so deeply intrenched in the early Meiji era and which still exists in some force. A stubborn opponent requires vigorous countermeasures. In Japan as elsewhere, of course, there has been that curious alliance between provincialism and "ultra-nationalism" in some areas whereby regional values are identified with national values and in such combination not only protected against foreign infiltration but also propagated to the usually unwilling world. From the Kyushu area have come most evidences of this kind of interaction.

Sectionalism figured prominently in the Japanese party movement. Even before the final overthrow of the Tokugawa there had been concern over the possibility of some new coterie seizing absolute power in the name of the emperor. From some smaller *han* like Tosa had already come the suggestion of power through a *han* assembly. Thus when four of the southwestern *han* finally assumed leadership of the restoration movement, it is not surprising that the coalition was always unsteady, especially since men from two of these *han*, Choshu and Satsuma, took most of the major positions, relegating the men of Tosa and Hizen to a minority status. It was men from these latter two *han* who first formed parties in opposition to the government. The Jiyuto, or Liberal party, was established in 1880 by Taisuke Itagaki of Tosa, and its initial membership was almost exclusively composed of Tosa men. The other anti-government group, the Progressive party, was formed in 1881 by Shigenobu Okuma of Hizen, and it included a number of his compatriots. Both Itagaki and Okuma had been members of the original oligarchy, and it is revealing that, despite their mutual opposition to Sat-Cho (Satsuma-Choshu) power, they found the greatest difficulty in cooperating with each other or in attracting men from other regions into their organizations in the formative period. There can be no doubt that the early Japanese parties were in part sectional struggles for power, with democratic theories serving as a convenient weapon of attack.

It is insufficient, however, to explain the early parties solely in these terms. While personal and sectional rivalries were and still are important factors in the Japanese parties, they cannot serve as exclusive explanations. The Meiji parties also represented a broader protest movement against the new government encompassing a wide range of grievances, economic as well as political, and their appeals soon went beyond Tosa-Hizen and the former samurai class. Moreover, many of their able spokesmen acquired a sincere ideological conviction from their study of Western ideas and institutions. To illustrate these facts, some exploration of trends in Japanese society after 1867 is required. The most important task of the new government was to complete the removal of antiquated economic-political institutions that were serious barriers to the new goals of "progress" —that is, nationalism, centralism, and economic diversification. To accomplish this task the government used both coercion and persuasion; to edicts it added pensions and various other emoluments for an ex-military class who were being asked to accept severe changes in their socioeconomic position and their general way of life. The government was willing to pay rather heavily for the abandonment of feudalism in its late Japanese forms. Not only were they interested in easing the pangs of transition for members of their own class, but they also recognized the dangers of unrest among the most important pressure group of the period.

Notwithstanding government efforts, tensions and hardships were the lot of many of the old military class. Some made a successful transition into the new government or business, and even more were reasonably successful in agriculture, but most were reduced to lowly jobs after having failed to make a satisfactory adjustment. The dislocation of the military class which had begun in the middle Tokugawa era was now reaching a climax. Particularly difficult was the plight of many lower-class samurai or warriors deprived of their function in society, stripped of their class privileges, and usually given very little capital with which to start a new career. It is little wonder that various types of protests and opposition movements were spearheaded by this group. Some of these protests took the form of a call to arms. The early Meiji government was confronted with the ever present danger of assassination and civil war. The first decade of the Meiji period was filled with incidents, leading up to the great Satsuma rebellion of 1877. It was partly because of this more or less constant threat that the government moved so rapidly to bolster its defenses with a modernized, conscripted army. And the wisdom of this move seemed clear with the events of 1877, in which the peasant conscriptees defeated the Satsuma samurai and thereby established as an indisputable fact the power of the national government. The failure of the Satsuma rebellion marked the end of large-scale attempts to overthrow the government by direct action, at least until the 1930's. But there remained another method—the party movement.

The first political association established after the restoration, the "Public Party of Patriots," was set up in 1874 by a small number of ex-samurai headed by men like Taisuke Itagaki, who had just broken with the government over Korean policy issues. The dissenters had favored a "strong" policy and had resigned after a majority within the oligarchy supported a more cautious policy of peace with Korea while Japan developed greater strength and economic stability. In this first political association it is interesting to note that fusion of military expansionism and elements of internal reform so characteristic of many later Japanese protest movements.

The Itagaki group borrowed their ideas of political party and political liberalism from the West; they had read John Stuart Mill thoroughly and quoted him lengthily in their manifesto. The heart of their argument was that for Japan to compete successfully in power and influence with the advanced nations of the West, she would have to develop institutions that encouraged the education and participation of the people in civic affairs. They insisted that only through an alert, educated people, working with a sense of purpose and unity, could a nation become great.

The tiny flickering spark that was the Public Party of Patriots soon disappeared, however, and only with 1880 does the Japanese party movement begin in earnest. In the years 1880–81 three "national" parties were established, two of which have existed, with a few interruptions and certain changes, down to the present time. The first party to emerge was the Jiyuto, or Liberal (Liberty) party, whose antecedents were the association of 1874 and the various district associations set up later, especially the "Self-help Society," a group of Tosa ex-samurai. Its leader was again Itagaki, and its main intellectual lights were Emori Ueki and Chomin Nakae. Ex-samurai from Tosa still constituted a very important element of the party, especially at the leadership levels; but party branches soon existed in various parts of Japan, particularly in the agrarian heartlands of Kinki (the district around Osaka), southwest Honshu, and Kyushu. In addition to its ex-samurai recruits, the party attracted diverse elements from the agrarian classes. It has frequently been noted that this important branch of the Japanese party movement, though it flew the banners of liberalism, was largely an agrarian rather than an urban middle-class movement. The Jiyuto and its successor, the Seiyukai, were generally known as agrarian parties (the latter as the landowners' party), despite the fact that a powerful urban-business wing was subsequently developed. Indeed, the most important reason for the general dominance of the Jiyuto-Seiyukai in prewar Japanese politics was their supremacy in the rural areas.

The grievances of Japanese agrarian groups in the early Meiji period fall into several categories. For the more affluent landowners and rural entrepreneurs the main complaint was the taxes paid for the development of urban industries, defense expenditures, and other activities of dubious benefit to the farmers. Actually, taxes in kind during the latter part of the Tokugawa period were generally higher than the early Meiji taxes levied in money upon the farmer, especially during the inflationary period when the value of money was reduced. Still the farmer had to pay most of the cost of the industrial revolution in Japan, and he did not particularly like it. Nor did he like the steady inroads made into local autonomy. It must not be thought, of course, that all landowner-rural entrepreneurs were antigovernment, and it would be especially misleading to believe that all those with grievances were politically active. Actually, the membership of the Jiyuto was quite small. Still, among its leading supporters this group was important and for the reasons just mentioned. In addition, however, the Jiyuto also acquired some follownig among the poorer peasantry. In the early 1880's economic conditions for the lower-class farmer were very bad. Deflation hit the part-owner/part-tenant and pure-tenant groups very hard; thousands lost all of their land because of nonpayment of taxes, and tenants frequently found the pressures passed along to them by the landowners. The emergence of the Jiyuto coincided with a time of trouble in the rural areas. A few radical ex-samurai leaders sought to appeal to the restive peasants with liberal slogans and promises, and many a banner was emblazoned with exhortations for "Popular Rights" and "Farmer Relief." In the years between 1881 and 1885 violence spilled forth over the countryside; peasant riots occurred in which land deeds were burned, property destroyed, and government offices assaulted. In all of this there is a kind of parallelism with the later Communist movement in some Asian areas. But at no point did large numbers of peasants actually affiliate themselves with the early Meiji party movement, and those with any thorough understanding of Jiyuto ideology must have been no more than a handful.

It is not surprising, then, that both the government and the conservative elements within the party viewed these happenings with great alarm. To the government there seemed ample proof of the subversive nature of the Jiyuto: its leaders had been very close to the Satsuma rebellion group, and during those fateful months of a few years previous the government had watched with anxious eyes the actions of the Meiji "liberals." And if these men had trafficked or threatened to do so with rebellious ex-samurai in 1877, now some of them were agitating the simple peasant to riot and bloodshed. Could anything be more subversive than this? Consequently, the government stepped up its program of control and pressures. Actually, until about 1875 Meiji Japan had experienced an extraordinary period of political freedom, but thereafter the government felt obliged to retreat via a series of edicts on press, assemblage, and general political activities. Although these authoritarian moves were rather moderate when compared with actions in modern totalitarian states, they hampered political activities and shaped them to some degree.

The interaction of terrorism and suppression in the early Meiji period continued to play some part during the whole course of modern Japanese history—any analysis of the Japanese parties must take account of this fact. The early Meiji parties and particularly the Jiyuto did not draw any absolute line against violence and revolt, although many Jiyuto leaders did deplore such tactics as futile. As soon as such early parties as the Jiyuto became more conservative, new radical parties, uncommitted to any belief in peaceful change, began to emerge in Japanese politics. Thus while government power in Japan maintained a constant rationale, the competitive party system operated under greater limitations than it did in the democratic societies of the West. The extent to which these limitations were justified under some theory of "self-preservation" or the broader issue of cause and effect as it relates to suppression and extremism need not concern us here. It need only be noted that the Japanese parties—and especially those on the "left"—operated under certain restrictions throughout the whole of the pre-1945 period, even though there was considerable relaxation in the decade of the 1920's.

But if government opposition contributed to the temporary decline of the Jiyuto after 1884, another important reason was the split within the party. The conservative ex-samurai and landowner elements were antagonized by the activities of the party "left wing," and many of them withdrew their support. While they were willing to support the general political principles of the party—the establishment and implementation of constitutional government—they wanted none of economic or political radicalism. Moreover, the government as early as 1880 had made a firm promise of constitutionalism by the end of nine years and was working steadily toward this goal. Thus the Sat-Cho oligarchy had already stolen the thunder of the popular rights movement by conceding the issues of constitutionalism and a representative assembly just before the liberal parties got organized and was working on these matters in the greatest secrecy, removed from even party scrutiny, until the final unveiling in 1889. During their early existence between 1881 and 1885, therefore, the opposition parties were in a curious position. Their major demand was going to be granted in some form, and meanwhile they had no real function at the national level; only in the prefectural assemblies could they play some official role. In view of this, it is not surprising that the parties temporarily disbanded in 1885, to await the advent of constitutional government.

The second opposition party of this period was the Kaishinto, or Progressive party. The fortunes of the Progressives were closely tied to the career of Shigenobu Okuma, sometime member of the early Meiji oligarchy, a keen student of British institutions, and foremost example of the Meiji liberal-nationalist. Around Okuma's leadership clustered a small but dedicated group of young officials, journalists, and students which formed the nucleus of the party—an enlightened and urbanized intelligentsia with a sprinkling of business support. The great benefactor of the party was Iwasaki, head of the Mitsubishi interests and a close personal friend of Okuma. The actual party membership of the Progressives, like that of the Liberals, was very small, certainly not exceeding three or four thousand over the whole nation. This is no real measure of its influence, however, for through a number of magazines and newspapers it reached a large percentage of the articulate Japanese and had considerable intellectual support, especially in such important private universities as Keio and Waseda, the former founded by Yukichi Fukuzawa, himself an important leader in the popular rights movement,

and the latter founded by Okuma. Considering the nature of Japanese society at this time, it is not surprising that membership in the popular rights parties was limited; it is significant, however, that the emerging commercial-industrial groups, with few exceptions, stayed aloof—but we shall have more to say about this later on.

Despite the problems of membership, the two popular rights parties did have some appeal, especially to the younger intellectuals. It is significant, therefore, to examine the ideological positions that they took and the sources of their thought. At the outset it might be remarked that nothing is more problematic than the nature of foreign inspiration, especially in its initial stages. Mediocrities march alongside of great names in the parade of foreign authorities. To a considerable extent, chance governs the timing of introduction; there is no way to forecast whose works will be translated early and whose late or not at all. It is likely, of course, that the main streams of world thought will come to be represented, and with some relation to the current trends. One can also predict that sooner or later the universal saints of political theory will be discovered or rediscovered by every society in ferment. Still, the elements of chance and accident remain to season and make intriguing the study of ideological adaptation. The Japanese liberal movement early discovered several Western "saints," in addition to a large number of minor figures and secondary sources. John Stuart Mill was the first major source of Japanese liberal concepts, and his *On Liberty* was used extensively in the manifesto of the Public Party of Patriots in 1874. He remained a great favorite of the Progressives, along with other British writers; the Itagaki group, by the time of the Liberal party, had turned increasingly to the French political theorists and particularly to Rousseau. Perhaps the great attraction of Rousseau to Jiyuto writers lay in that very ambivalence of his so frequently noted in the West. If Rousseau spoke for liberty and freedom, he also spoke for the greater unity, "the general will," and the public interest. Clearly, one face was turned toward the individual and another face toward the corporate body, the state—an ambiguity that posed a problem for the early Japanese Liberals, as we shall soon see. It should be stated, however, that the Progressives more than the Liberals used Anglo-Saxon nineteenth-century thought, that of the British utilitarians in particular, to bolster their philosophic position. And if they were somewhat more moderate than the early Liberals, they were also somewhat more consistent philosophically.

Nevertheless, all of the early Meiji political parties had major ideological problems. This is not surprising, in view of the background and prevalent dictates of Japanese society. The early Meiji period placed a premium upon a strong state and a maximum degree of public support for state policy. If Japanese society was to make a rapid and successful transition from backwardness and thereby create a powerful defense against foreign imperialism and domestic chaos, how much disunity could be permitted—how much liberalism could be afforded? To put the question in this manner, however, is to emphasize too greatly the element of state decision on this matter and to minimize the crucial factor of private "decision" —or, more specifically, the interests of the main pressure groups in modern Japanese society. Was Western-style liberalism either possible or desirable for such groups?

It is clear that Mill, Rousseau, Locke, Spencer, and a host of other Western writers made a deep impression on party leaders, as did their trips abroad to observe the workings of constitu-tional government. Some inspired writings on natural rights, constitutionalism, and party government were produced. But on certain vital issues popular party spokesmen equivocated. For example, there was little acceptance of the individual as an end in himself. The tendency was, especially in the Liberal party, to conceive of the enlightened individual as only the means toward a strong state and liberalism as merely a tool for the prestige and glory of the nation. The emphasis was on the *unity* with which an educated, aroused people would act and the manner in which this would add to the power of the state. But by this process of reasoning, such important liberal concomitants as minority rights and power limitations were frequently minimized or ignored. To the concept of a nation-people and to the support of greater egalitarianism, the early Japanese liberals contributed much that was derived from Mill and others, but the intensity and timing of the nationalist emphasis, together with the Japanese heritage and goals that fed it, prevented them from placing the same emphasis upon other vital aspects of the Western liberal creed.

Related to the foregoing problem was the matter of the emperor and the imperial prerogatives. Few, if any, of the popular party writers could face this problem squarely. There was no tradition of monarchical absolutism in Japan to attack. Moreover, the throne, protected in a very real sense by its innocuous past, had been fashioned into the symbol of the entire nationalist movement. It could not easily be challenged, and there were few who wanted to do so. Thus the popular parties not only shunned republicanism but also confused the relationship between popular rights and the emperor by constantly proclaiming their great solicitude for imperial happiness and an undying loyalty to the throne—a position from which they were forced to watch with increasing helplessness the manipulations of imperial prerogatives directed against them by exceedingly dexterous hands. These facts help to explain the persistent connection between the early "liberals" and a militant program in foreign policy. Indeed, there were close ties between Jiyuto men and such societies as the Genyosha, the "Black Current Society," a group dedicated to a forceful continental policy and forerunner of such ultra-nationalist societies as the Kokuryukai, the "Amur River Society." The dual goal of internal reform and external expansion was characteristic of many protest movements in prewar Japan, and the early Meiji "popular parties" were a part of this stream, with its widely divergent philosophic currents. The protest against Western privilege in Japan, the identification of the Japanese mission with the freeing of Asia from Western imperialism, and even the opposition to excessive "Europeanization" of Japanese society were forceful aspects of the early popular rights movement in Japan and found expression in party organs. That there was a legitimate relation between these goals and a liberal creed is easy to see, although subsequent developments were to emphasize the cleavages. In any case, the early party movement in Meiji Japan was a part of—not apart from—the nationalist tides, and its leaders were fervent nationalists dedicated to the cause of a greater Japan.

The popular parties, however, came under vigorous attack not only because they were accused of promoting violence and revolution but also because they were charged with inciting factionalism and thereby threatening to destroy the unity so necessary to Japan's successful competition with the Western world. The idea of parties was no more readily accepted by Meiji statesmen than it was by some of the

early Western leaders like George Washington. The goal of the new government was loyalty to the throne alone and "representative of all the people," rejecting any idea of specialized political affiliation. But this ideal could not be maintained, and the emergence of the two popular parties, as has been noted, was the result of factional splits within the government. Thus the government was plagued by a dilemma: its main objective was a government transcending all parties—a complete rejection of parties and party men; yet, if government men were to shun completely the party movement, how could they compete for popular support? Even before the advent of the Meiji Constitution and the Diet, this problem bothered the more discerning of government spokesmen. Gradually and with varying degrees of reluctance, some of them came to accept political parties as a necessary, if probably evil, part of modern government; indeed, from behind the scenes a few government men even encouraged the establishment of the Teiseito, the Imperial party, in 1882, to challenge the Liberals and Progressives. This party, composed of a small group of newspapermen, officials, and some Shinto priests, stood on a staunchly conservative program of awaiting the imperial word on constitutionalism and supporting imperial sovereignty. With no substantial popular following, the party was largely impotent and quickly dissolved in 1885, when its two opponents also left the political arena temporarily. Its significance lies largely in the fact that at least some members of the oligarchy early realized the futility of using coercion alone against their political opponents. Thus the Imperial party presaged the partial acceptance of a competitive party system in modern Japan.

The early parties all dissolved more or less voluntarily in 1885, and while there were some continuing party activities and a brief flurry in 1888–89 when popular party elements joined in a coalition party led by Shojiro Goto to oppose a "soft" foreign policy, national party development now awaited the establishment of the constitution and the first general election of July 1, 1890. The first period of party development in Japan was over. In certain respects the achievements won were substantial. The idea of a competitive party system, introduced from the West, had, within two decades, spread throughout Japan, finding widespread support from many of the articulate elements of Japanese society, such as the intellectuals and students, and a rather begrudging recognition from even some high officials. And the popular parties, despite their problems of principle and limited membership, had played a part in speeding up the timetable of constitutionalism. After 1890 they were to play an active role in Japanese government. In briefly analyzing party development between 1890 and 1940, it will probably be most effective if certain topical divisions are established.

II / The Prewar System: An Organic State

The Institutional Structure

Modern Japan's political institutions have been the subject of a great body of literature written by both Japanese and foreign scholars. Detailed legal analysis and formal constitutional theory were especially favored topics among those prewar Japanese scholars whose training came from German sources, though such studies were not confined to this group alone. The variety of interpretations, too, was constantly growing as the weight of new scholars and disciplines was added to the field. How should we judge the influence of the Meiji Constitution of 1889 upon the Japanese political parties—or, put more broadly, how should

we weigh the impact of Japanese constitutionalism, in both its written and its unwritten aspects, upon the party movement? To consider the two forms of this question together is entirely legitimate, for modern Japan is another convincing illustration of the fact that fundamental law cannot be completely encompassed within the written words of a single document.

If for the moment, however, we consider the Meiji Constitution itself, two initial generalizations may be ventured. On the one hand, the constitution, when promulgated, was a reasonable representation of the nature of Japanese society or at least of its then current trends; at the same time, however, it "fixed" in permanent form the dominant institutions and ideas of a society then still in flux. For this reason, the Meiji Constitution played a creative role and had greater significance than that of a mere reflection. There is ample evidence to support both these points. The Meiji Constitution was, of course, heavily indebted to the Prussian constitution and to certain individual Germans who contributed to its drafting; these facts reflected important similarities in timing and goals shared by the two societies. But if this document was basically attuned to its society, it also passed "final verdict" on various crucial controversies not yet conceded. One of its prominent features was the degree of political centralization it imposed. In some respects this had been the central issue in the early modern period, although trends were consistently opposed to the supporters of strong local autonomy. The constitution added a very heavy blow to their cause, even though rear-guard actions continued to be fought over the issue throughout the Meiji era.

The question of sovereignty and imperial prerogatives presents a somewhat similar picture. As noted earlier, these matters had been subject to discussion and debate since the restoration, despite the handicaps which beset the "liberals." Again, both the content of the constitution and the method of its adoption provided important strength for the conservative position. The constitution was carefully labeled as a "gift" from the emperor, not a contract between him and the people. One widely publicized constitutional debate subsequently became whether the emperor was completely above and separate from the state or whether he must be considered a part of the state organism. The very fact that the issue should be framed in this manner, however, and its distance from some of the more forthright discussions of the earlier period is significant. That the words of the constitution resolved supreme power in favor of the emperor, of course, could not be denied.

Even when this has been said, however, it is doubtful that the most important aspect of the Meiji Constitution or of modern Japanese constitutionalism was the homage paid to imperial absolutism. There was a more meaningful and complex aspect than this. It has been said that the genius of Japan lay in oligarchy; constitutional developments of the modern period underwrote that genius in a variety of ways. The most important premise of Japanese constitutionalism was an organic theory of state, however much that concept might be debated. For the successful operation of the prewar Japanese state, the premium was upon a very high degree of harmonious integration of its disparate parts. This had to be the case because the principle implicit in the constitution was not that of separation of powers and hence not that of checks and balances in its specifically related sense; it was rather that of a mixture of powers. The National Diet had the weakest powers, but its assent was necessary to pass legislation (although there was the oft-mentioned

proviso that in the case of financial bills the budget of the previous year would go into effect if the Diet failed to approve new measures). The cabinet could dissolve the Diet at will, but events were to show the impracticality of this, and in any case it did not have a firm control over the military branches of government. But if the military did have direct access to the emperor and certain independent powers, it was still necessary for them to work with the civilian branches if they were not to disrupt the state. With this general mixture of powers, it is true, an overall supremacy was assigned to the throne, but this was not accompanied by an applied doctrine of personal absolutism. Here was the most vital part of Japanese constitutionalism. Personal absolutism was the rationalization of the power structure but not its embodiment. That embodiment was to be found in a series of "extra-constitutional" groups whose function was to provide co-ordination or liaison, performing the necessary tasks in the name of the emperor.

The most successful of these groups was undoubtedly the original one, the Genro, or Council of Elder Statesmen. The Genro developed naturally out of the early Meiji oligarchy and contained within itself the sources of power that gave to Japanese constitutionalism much of its meaning and workability, even though there was no mention of this group in the constitution. When the decline of the Genro began because of the death and old age of its members, in the period around World War I, the problems of Japanese constitutionalism became more complex. Neither a completely adequate substitute nor a satisfactory replacement for that body could be found, although various devices were attempted. It even looked for a brief time in the mid-twenties as if Japanese constitutional procedure might evolve toward a modified parliamentary system, but trends both in Japan and in the world quickly became more adverse. Heavy reliance upon co-ordinating and liaison agencies continued, but now real power, in addition to being more diffuse, was also more fluid. A period of mounting confusion ensued, with the various branches of government wavering between conflict and compromise. In the quest for leadership and direction Japanese society gradually accepted or acquiesced in the rather uncertain hegemony established by the military elements. It might be said in summary that, while the evolution of Japanese society was to some extent away from the premises of Meiji constitutionalism, this trend was not sufficient to permit the successful development of new premises or even an orderly modification of the old ones.

Certain long-established techniques, to be sure, were available to facilitate co-ordinated government. Out of family and group life in Japan there had evolved a complex set of rules and procedures for social intercourse. Here also the emphasis was upon harmonious organic life, with the great opponent being conflict, that indispensable price of a democratic society. In such traditional institutions and procedures as the go-between, the senior councilors, and the group consensus, one can glimpse certain aspects of historic private government in Japan. That these aspects would accompany the stylized familial pattern of paternal absolutism as essential elements of modern Japanese constitutionalism was inherent in the nature of the Meiji Constitution and its society. And among the traditional modes of political procedure sustained, several were of particular significance. The system of indirect government was fortified. Position did not necessarily represent power. And, by the same token, as viewed by Western standards, responsibility could never be clearly fixed. Decisions issued forth

from anonymous groups, the product of many secret conferences and compromises between those with office and those with power. These, the unwritten elements of Japanese constitutionalism, were as vital as any of the printed articles.

It is easy to see that the Japanese political parties would be greatly affected by these various institutions. Perhaps that effect can be summarized by emphasizing three interrelated trends. In the first place, since the strength of the Diet was very limited and the short cut to power lay in cultivating those who manipulated imperial prerogatives, there was a constant pressure on the parties to compromise and to submit. And, indeed, the history of the prewar party movement in Japan is marked by a series of such steps. After a brief initial struggle, which served to test and ascertain the power implications of the new constitution, the popular parties came generally to accept the necessity of coalition with some part of the elder-statesmen group whose power had a more permanent base. This move was facilitated by the fact that most of the Meiji oligarchy had accepted such coalitions as necessary, although there was some inclination to buy Diet votes rather than to bargain for them on the basis of political concessions. When the coalitions proved unstable, it was another relatively short step to a type of union whereby the parties accepted the leadership of top Meiji statesmen or their protégés. This began in 1900, when the Liberal party was reorganized as the Seiyukai, or Association of the Friends of Constitutional Government, with the famous Hirobumi Ito, chief drafter of the Meiji Constitution, as its head. Ito brought to the party a conservative constitutional theory, a number of new members from the bureaucracy, and, not least of all, a measure of power. The old Okuma party, then undergoing a series of name changes, relied for some time upon coalition rather than amalgamation, trusting in its leader, Shigenobu Okuma, who had been given distinguished governmental positions and was on intimate terms with the Genro (although not trusted or liked by some). This party, however, remained essentially in a minority status until it was reorganized in the period between 1913 and 1915, ultimately becoming the Kenseikai, or Constitutional Association, under Takaakira Kato, a diplomat and a student of British government, who had married into the Iwasaki family (Mitsubishi). Large numbers of officials entered the party at this time, although Kato himself was in some respects the finest example of a conservative liberal and champion of party government in prewar Japan.

Thus it can be said that when the political parties of Japan finally acquired a kind of quasi-supremacy in Japanese politics, beginning with the Hara cabinet in September, 1918, it was partly because the parties had undergone a long process of amalgamation with key elements of the military and civilian bureaucracy. Professional officials had become very important elements at the leadership level; to some extent this had always been true, but events after 1890 gave it added impetus. Naturally, this development had an effect upon party principles, programs, and organizational structure. In a broad sense it can be said that the Japanese party movement was turned inward to the bureaucracy rather than outward toward the Japanese people, and the institutional structure certainly facilitated this.

Another characteristic of the parties was a factionalism based much more on personal and sectional rivalries than upon differences of principle. This was not peculiar to Japan, of course, although its proportions in Japanese politics were perhaps greater than elsewhere. The problem of this type of fac-

tionalism was deeply rooted and derived from many sources, as the postwar period has indicated. Again, however, it should be noted that the former institutional structure contributed its share. The unity of those parties with similar principles was largely meaningless, in that they lacked the capacity, even when united, to control the government. That capacity lay rather in a coalition between parties and bureaucracy, and this, as has been noted, was the general pattern of prewar politics.

It remains to examine briefly the effect of certain more technical aspects of the prewar Japanese institutions upon the parties, particularly the regulations governing suffrage and elections. There were three general changes in national suffrage regulations during the prewar period. The initial act of 1889 gave voting privileges for the lower house of the Diet to males twenty-five years of age or over who paid a direct national tax of 15 yen or more. A few categories, such as active-service military men, were excluded. The first national electorate numbered only four hundred and fifty thousand persons out of a total population of forty million. The tax qualification for national elections was first reduced in 1900 to 10 yen, with the electorate increased to just under one million, with the total population now forty-four million. Again in 1919 another reduction was made to 3 yen, with the electorate becoming some three million out of a total population of fifty-five million. Finally, in 1925, the tax qualification was abolished by the so-called "Universal Manhood Suffrage Act" of that year. This act first went into effect in the general elections of 1928. There continued to be some minor restrictions upon male suffrage, particularly the exclusion of those on public or private relief. And women were not granted suffrage in the pre–World War II period.

Under almost any kind of suffrage

regulations the Japanese electorate in the earlier period would have been predominantly from the rural districts with essentially agrarian interests. Despite the existence of great cities like Tokyo and Osaka, Japan at the time of the restoration had about 80 per cent of her population engaged mainly in agriculture. This percentage steadily declined, and by the time of World War II it had dipped slightly below 50 per cent, although the farmer remained, by a wide margin, the largest single occupational group in Japan. At first, suffrage restrictions tended to emphasize the importance of the more affluent rural elements, because land taxes were the most important part of the national taxation structure. In the early diets the agrarian representation in the lower house was very heavy, and the Seiyukai, often known as the landowners' party, usually had a dominant majority. Gradually urban and other nonagrarian forces made their power felt in a variety of ways, but the rural areas continued to be a key factor in political success. Needless to say, the lower economic classes did not participate in national elections until 1928 and after. The well-established major parties represented mainly the interests of the landowner and the commercial-industrial classes of Japanese society.

The government did a considerable amount of experimentation with the size of election districts. With a few minor exceptions, the original law of 1889 established single-member districts. This was changed in 1900, with the so-called "large-district system" going into effect. Under this system each district corresponded in size to the prefectures and metropolitan cities, with the number of candidates to be elected ranging up to twelve from a single district. In 1919 a return was made to the single-member district. The law of 1925 provided for a compromise with the so-called "medium-district system." Under the 1925 act the number of candidates to be elected from each district varied from three to five, with each voter having one vote.

In the case of prewar Japan it is impossible to maintain that these changes made any substantial difference in the general party system. That system was characterized by the continuous dominance of two parties, both conservative, and a great variety of short-lived minor parties, most of them having negligible strength in the Diet even during their period of peak activity. Furthermore, each election witnessed the choice of a fairly substantial number of independent candidates, a majority of whom usually joined one of the major parties in the aftermath of the election, although frequently there were also clubs or groupings of independents in the Diet. Sometimes the independents were in a very strategic position and the bids for their votes or affiliation extremely high. The major parties were the Seiyukai, strongly conservative and usually dominant because of its extensive hold on the rural areas, and that party which was finally known as the Minseito, successor to the old Okuma party, generally stronger in the urban areas and considered somewhat more progressive than its rival. Prior to the advent of the labor parties, there were some small, ephemeral groups and a few rugged individuals who represented the liberal Left. The labor parties began to emerge in 1926, but they cannot be considered a major factor in the prewar political scene, despite the seeming advantages of the middle-district system. Many factors entered into this: the limited political consciousness of the lower economic classes, the serious ideological cleavages and personal factionalism which promoted disunity in the socialist movement, and the very adverse trends of the 1930's. Generally there were at least three labor-farmer parties in the election field, with a fourth in the illegal Communist party which worked through the legal far Left. With the establishment of the Shakai Taishuto, or Social Mass party, in 1932, the Left managed to attain some degree of unity; and in the last free elections in prewar Japan, those of 1937, this party obtained 36 seats in the 466-member House. This was double the number of seats it had obtained in the 1936 general elections and possibly foreshadowed the trends of the post-1945 period. Nevertheless, it cannot be said that the two conservative parties were seriously challenged in the prewar era, for even in the 1937 elections they polled together approximately 85 per cent of the vote.

Neither changes in the district system nor enlargement of the electorate had in themselves any great effect upon the Japanese party system during the rather limited period in which they were operative. It is true that universal manhood suffrage stimulated the organization of labor-farmer parties, and these made very modest and uncertain progress against great odds. The odds, however, proved more important than the progress until the debacle of war ended the militarist era. In a more general sense, however, the prewar institutional structure did have an influence on the Japanese parties in ways we have indicated earlier. It has become fashionable recently to argue that the Meiji Constitution could have evolved so as to have served the cause of parliamentarism, with the implication that, in creating a new constitution, the occupation forces acted in an unwise manner. This is a complex matter, but, on balance, the thesis is, in my opinion, more false than true. With reference to the prewar period, constitutionalism could have developed in such a fashion as to give strong support to parliamentarism and a competitive party system only if the evolution of Japanese society itself had thoroughly supported this trend. But it did not, and, as a result, by the close of

the war Japanese constitutionalism, whether in practice, theory, or symbolism, was in profound contrast to the concepts of democracy. And so long as this structure was kept more or less intact, there was another heritage with which to cope: that of the prewar "progressive" opposition. Had there been a significant record of forceful, democratic interpretations of modern Japanese constitutionalism, there would have been greater reason to support the tactic of "reinterpretation" after 1945. But these necessary preconditions did not exist in sufficient degree to make this a legitimate risk. The field of battle had been so constructed as to force the progressives into a lengthy series of crucial compromise and concessions. This record would continue to be important unless there could be some truly radical changes made and arguments take place in a new context. It would be foolish, of course, to assert that such a step could insure democratic success or even that it would create no additional problems. Nor is one forced to defend the precise tactics and form of changes made. That the basic issue lies in the broad trends governing Japan and the world is readily admitted. That there are likely to be —and perhaps should be—some important changes made in the new structure is also granted. It is not yet clear how far these changes will go. But changes would have been probable in any case in the aftermath of an occupation; now at least there is a relatively favorable framework within which to debate them. And the pendulum theory—that the stronger the shift, the more extreme the reaction—can be very misleading in the field of government and politics if applied too mechanically. One thing is clear: constitutionalism in prewar Japan was not favorable to party government and hence to the healthy development of the Japanese political parties.

Party Affiliation and Social Classes

If the prewar parties were generally regarded as exclusive clubs, it was partly due to the limited nature of membership and participation. There was no primary system in Japan requiring registration by party label. All the parties had formal membership provisions that generally included sponsorship, initiation, and dues. Under these conditions it is hardly surprising that even the major parties had a membership that was only a tiny fraction of the electorate. After the emergence of the labor parties their formal membership was sometimes greater than that of their massive rivals. Generally speaking, the large percentage of members of the conservative parties were district leaders and professional politicians, with a few influential families and political aspirants represented. To ask the political affiliation of an average Japanese citizen was to elicit a response of surprise and even shock that anyone should think he had one. Nevertheless, that citizen did vote in the general elections if he was eligible. Actually, the percentage of votes in terms of those eligible was rather high except in the metropolitan centers toward the close of the prewar period. The key to party power lay in the vote rather than in the number of names on party registers. In assessing this vote some attention should be given to the political tendencies of the main socioeconomic groupings in Japan, bearing in mind that only very general measurements can be applied.

The rural vote was always the heart of conservative party strength. The Japanese farmer, whatever his category, tended to vote conservative in the prewar period, and in most rural districts the Seiyukai was the leading party. This might seem strange in the light of rural conditions. The overwhelming number of Japanese farmers were small-scale landowners, part-owner and part-tenants, or pure tenants whose economic position was usually precarious. In general, the small farmer or peasant gained least from developments after the restoration and suffered most. If he owned his small plot, there were problems of taxes and his increasing dependence upon the urban, commercial market—upon the middlemen and various agencies of credit. If a tenant, he had to compete for available land in a period in which many of his traditional rights, such as the right of perpetual tillage, had been forfeited, while some of his traditional duties, such as the payment of taxes in kind, remained. Community or village lands rapidly disappeared; the shift to commercial crops became necessary; cottage industry tended to decline in those fields where it was challenged by more modern production methods; farm girls were recruited for factory work; and younger sons also migrated in search of a livelihood. These developments could be recognized as rather commonplace tendencies in the course of an industrial revolution; but the fact that they were not unusual occurrences made their impact upon rural life in Japan no less severe. Together they represented multiple tensions caused by a growing cultural conflict between a materialist, urban world and a world of traditional agrarian patterns and values. And this conflict was reflected in each village, in each individual. This is the stuff from which radicalism is made—and, indeed, there was some fear of agrarian radicalism. The government had been quick to sense the danger of the early Jiyuto movement and was now alarmed by the rise of tenant associations and the sizable number of agrarian disputes after World War I. And it viewed with great and justifiable apprehension the rise after 1925 of the so-called "radical" right-wing, agrarian-centered movements dedicated to an assault upon urban capitalism and the rebirth of a peasant-soldier alliance.

But there is another side to this picture. Hierarchy and paternalism were deeply rooted in the Japanese countryside and operated with great force on behalf of stability. The smallest unit of Japanese rural society is the *buraku*, or hamlet, a cluster of thatched houses, frequently no more than two dozen or so, which adjoin the paddy fields and dot the landscape. Above this is the *mura*, or village, which may comprise a number of *buraku*. The nature of power at these local levels of rural society has never been uniform, but, in general, it has been characterized by the dominance of prominent families through the offices of headman, village chief, and district leader. This dominance has been not merely political but also social in the broadest sense. And along with it has gone the ideal of paternal benevolence, derived from a sense of elitist responsibility for the group and a deeply ingrained acceptance of its status by the group. The strains upon this structure after the late nineteenth century were many, as has been noted, especially in those areas close to urban centers, and rarely was the traditional structure left wholly intact. Yet, its tenacity was indeed surprising, especially in the realm of voting behavior. Professor Tadashi Fukutake has remarked that for the Japanese farmer elections do not represent a choice based upon party, principle, or even personality as much as they represent the confirmation of a power already existing in the area. Thus the scions of prominent rural families were more or less automatically elected in many districts when they chose to run. The position of a party depended upon its affiliation with such families, and it was because the Seiyukai had the largest number of these affiliations that its rural position was good. In return for prominent rural support the Seiyukai

generally protected landowner interests, especially against protenant legislation, although it did have some difficulty in matching the interests of the leading rural and urban pressure groups whom it served.

Another factor which played some part in determining the rural vote was the practice of vote-buying. Although less important than the factors mentioned previously, still the purchase of votes was widespread. There was even an occupation of vote broker, who contracted with the various local officials for blocs of votes and then contacted candidates with sufficient funds to make the transaction. The practice of vote-buying was not confined to the period of universal manhood suffrage; there are numerous references to it during the period prior to World War I, when only the higher taxpaying landowners could vote. But at whatever period, vote-buying was essentially a conservative tactic, in that only the major conservative parties had access to the large funds necessary.

It would be a mistake to leave the impression that voting in the rural areas was uniform or that its patterns were to be explained solely in the foregoing terms. While the Seiyukai ordinarily showed the greatest strength, there were some traditional strongholds of the Minseito, a certain number of closely divided areas, and a few other districts where independent or minor party candidates did well. Moreover, party programs usually attempted to give some weight to various rural interests. In the early period of Diet politics there was strong resistance by the Jiyuto to increased land taxes, even when the military budget was at stake. The later Seiyukai took the initiative with various forms of agrarian aid in the troubled 1920's, and strong elements within this party also supported certain aspects of the agrarian-based nationalism with which the rural areas were associated. Many additional details could be added, but they would not substantially change the picture of dominant tendencies in the prewar voting pattern of the Japanese agrarian classes. It might also be noted that these tendencies were not greatly affected by the change in suffrage regulations which added the tenant class to the voting lists.

The political actions and attitudes of the commercial-industrial groups were in some respects even more significant for the trends of the time. While it is not possible here to discuss developments in the Japanese industrial revolution, a few pertinent remarks are essential. The structure of Japanese industry was pyramidal, with a great mass of small units at the base and tapering off to middle-sized units in the center and a few large combines at the apex. The interrelations among these three types of units is one of the fascinating aspects of modern Japan. The survival of small industry in Japan was partly the result of the speed of industrialization and the limits upon private capital and state support, partly of its utility to large-scale industry through such techniques as subcontracting, and partly attributable to other factors. At this lower level the distinction between management and labor was frequently unclear, the element of dependency usually very strong, and the struggle for a livelihood often intense. This was scarcely a prototype of the Western middle class in its classical liberal form. Even the upper echelons of the commercial-industrial group began the modern period with a heavy dependence upon government and moved toward interdependence with it as the industrial revolution progressed. The early Meiji leaders were not opposed to private capitalism; indeed, they encouraged it in a great variety of ways. It was necessary to follow a neo-mercantilist policy, however, to supplement

the obvious deficiencies of Japanese society, if progress were to be made rapidly. Later the government withdrew from many aspects of direct participation in and control over Japanese industry, but its general support was always of crucial importance to the big-business interests. It must not be forgotten that these interests not only faced the competition from the advanced West but also formidable opposition from both the Right and the Left within their own society; nor did economic conditions within modern Japan permit of any maximum feeling of security on the part of the general business class.

These factors helped to sustain certain traditional values which prevented the industrial revolution from being the harbinger of liberalism in prewar Japan. Essentially, the philosophy of the bulk of the commercial-industrial group was that of the organic theory of the state. Acting with considerable rationality, they placed the emphasis not on the need to limit the power of government but rather upon the desirability of unifying and using that power. There were some complaints against the officiousness of the bureaucracy and opposition to such legislation as might strengthen organized labor. In these respects one can see a certain parallel with the West, but in the total picture the differences are far more significant. An industrial revolution is capable of producing more than one form of political expression, depending upon the timing and nature of its development; the role of the modern Japanese business class is proof of that fact.

In the early stages of party development the rising business class played a very limited part. There were a few exceptions, notably Yataro Iwasaki, founder of Mitsubishi, who strongly supported his friend Okuma and the Kaishinto. Generally speaking, however, the businessman was too busy and too inexperienced in political affairs to take any active role; moreover, considering his heavy dependence upon government, party activity could be dangerous. Even Iwasaki got into serious difficulties, with the government attempting reprisals. Rather quickly, however, certain businessmen, especially the type known as "political merchants," served in the important capacity of facilitating negotiations and compromises between the oligarchy and party leaders. Sometimes this was on their own initiative; sometimes at the request of others. But in any case, having cultivated important friendships on all sides, it was obviously to their interest to help in fashioning a workable coalition on their behalf. Thus the Iwasaki family aided in bringing Okuma and Matsukata together, and such business groups as Furukawa and Mitsui helped in events preceding and following the establishment of the Seiyukai under Ito.

But most of these activities were behind the scenes. Both oligarchy and parties were troubled by the general reluctance of business interests to enter politics directly, in the sense of running for office or joining openly in partisan politics. It must not be forgotten that the position of the business community was still subordinate to officialdom in a variety of ways. Moreover, this community was a small minority of the electorate as compared with landowners and hence could not safeguard its position by its numbers at the polls. In addition to its connections, however, it also had funds, which were made increasingly available. Usually these were requested, sometimes demanded, and not infrequently proffered voluntarily in an effort to influence legislation, votes, and trends. The question of political corruption in Japan, as in most societies, is a complex one. The historic role of the merchant has always been that of supplicant to power: there was a moral as well as a practical obligation

to repay favors granted. Along with this went the fact that commercialism was not without its social stigma, and the merchant had traditionally accepted his inferior status before the lofty official, giving evidence in a variety of ways. The necessities of government paternalism running into the modern period buttressed many of these traditions, although one must not ignore the changes that have taken place. Certainly by the turn of the twentieth century, the top business class was beginning to have considerable political influence, while still complaining about the condescending attitude of many officials. Business reaction to governmental policies sometimes determined their success or failure. Individual officials and party leaders were often indebted to business elements for personal favors. Large sums of money were being channeled into political circles. Not all this money was going to party men; the bureaucracy, even the subordinate administrative bureaucracy, were sometimes recipients. But the election and upkeep of Diet members were increasingly expensive, and the parties quite naturally turned to these sources of support. Frequently the funds were handled through intermediaries, with party leaders playing key roles and often being chosen because of their access to funds. Much of this was not illegal or even immoral as measured against Western democratic standards; in addition, however, there was a large amount of plain and simple bribery, and the line was sometimes very difficult to draw, as might be expected.

After World War I, Japanese business elements played a more active part in politics at every level. Their representatives occupied positions in nearly every segment of the Japanese government and were important in both the parties and the bureaucracy. Indeed, to the popular mind the major conservative parties were sometimes equated with big-business interests. Mitsubishi was closely identified with the Kensei-kai-Minseito and had many strategic connections with important individuals in the party. Baron Kato, whose personal power derived from his connection with the Iwasaki family, led the party until his death in 1926. The Mitsubishi company usually supplied millions of yen for election expenses. Similarly, the Seiyukai had connections with Mitsui, Sumitomo, and Yasuda. It would be an oversimplification to say that there was a complete identity between the *zaibatsu*, or financial cliques, and the major parties; that the relationship was extremely important, however, cannot be denied. And as Japanese capitalism came under increasing assault in the late 1920's, the major parties shared the attack; for it was easier to highlight the shortcomings of capitalism than to defend its strengths. The rising productivity of Japan was accompanied by heavy populational increases, tending to prevent dramatic improvements in living standards for the masses. Cyclical economic trends often found slump or crisis conditions coexisting with a steadier, rising curve of demands and expectations. And, ironically, capitalism in Japan produced only a quasi-liberalism at best, one seriously hampered by the grave philosophic and practical limitations previously set forth. The quest for unity, the support for an agrarian-military-based nationalist ideology with few radical amendments, and the slight attention paid to individualism and its political credo were clearly aspects of this general problem. It would be difficult to overestimate the importance of this upon trends within the prewar political parties and Japanese society as a whole.

The urban labor class could play only a negligible part in the prewar parties. The worker was unorganized and a recent immigrant from some rural area, with his agrarian ties and attitudes still largely intact. At the height of their success the prewar labor unions had enrolled only about 7 per cent of the Japanese working class. The first significant organizational activities on a national scale began just before World War I, reaching their climax at the close of the hectic 1920's. Both the internal and the external events of this period contributed to deep ideological cleavages in the labor movement. In its earliest stages the struggle had been mainly between democratic socialism and anarcho-syndicalism, but with the Russian revolution the anarchists gradually gave way to the Communists as chief contestants with the socialists for union control. The struggles within the labor movement were mirrored in the proletarian party divisions. The Japanese labor movement was basically a political movement, but its organizational efforts were largely unsuccessful, and even within the organized fragment political divisions precluded any unified influence. Labor leadership was divided between a few worker-leaders and a handful of intellectuals, who wielded considerable influence on overall trends. The tasks of organization were discouraging. The worker was tied to a paternalistic management and his own agrarian past. Small and medium enterprise, so important in the Japanese industrial scene, made its unique contributions to labor psychology and conditions. In some key fields the percentage of temporary women and child workers was very high and provided additional problems. Governmental legislation gave no assistance; most of the laws pertaining to the worker were restrictive in nature and intent, and never were the unions given any positive legal protection in the period before 1945. Thus even after 1925, when the male worker was first privileged to vote in national election, he took little active interest in politics and generally voted for one of the conservative candidates, as election figures show.

Among other groups in Japanese society the intellectuals merit some attention. The term "intellectual" in its Japanese context refers roughly to the academicians, journalists, students, and assorted literary-artistic elements. Perhaps, when compared with China, Japan had an anti-intellectual heritage, notwithstanding the efforts devoted to the education of the military class during the Tokugawa period. Yet with the challenge provided by the West and the goal of modernization held high, a new premium was placed upon ideas, concepts, and actions based upon these. It was the tragedy of the modern Japanese intellectual, however, that he could play a truly positive role in his society only if he accepted the fundamental values of the ruling bureaucracy. And these values, with their emphasis upon familial-type ethics, unqualified support for the throne, and complete social integration, were in sharp contrast to the stimuli which the intellectual was currently receiving from the West—to the new mental horizons that were opening up before him. Consequently, an important portion of this class took up a function essentially negative: they became the trenchant social critics of their society. And within this group it was perhaps inevitable that a sizable majority would find Marxism an excellent tool of social criticism, a practical methodology, and a source of personal solace.

Marxism appealed because, while basically it was a simple philosophy, there was also an aura of high intellectual respectability about it. With Leninist modifications, it was tailored to late-developing societies, providing symbols for the domestic and foreign scenes that were interchangeable. It offered both realism and idealism: the former at the level of tactics and in certain reaches of analysis; the latter at the level of ulti-

mate goals. It also gave the Japanese intellectual a sense of belonging to the whole world—past, present, and future; it relieved his sense of physical and mental isolation from the main stream of history. Ultimately, many of the intellectuals active in politics thus came to be powerfully influenced by Marxist doctrine, as did a number of their colleagues, who confined themselves to writing and research. But very few became Communists, either in the sense of party membership or complete affiliation to prevailing Communist doctrines. The great majority became social democrats of one type or another, engrossed in heated polemics and developing rival schools of interpretation. Almost every branch of Western socialism was injected into the scene—the Fabians, Bebel, Bernstein, Plekhanov, and many more. Considering these facts and the conditions of Japanese society, it is not surprising that the left-wing and largely intellectual-led movement suffered from great disunity. Perhaps the most consistent, concrete source of division among the non-Communists was the issue of the popular front with the Communists or fellow-travelers. Time and time again this split the social democratic group. But actually, of course, this was only one manifestation of a wide range of differences in foreign inspiration and ideological position.

Thus the active role of the Japanese intellectuals in politics could not be considered very successful, for, despite their efforts, they remained isolated from the masses. Their critics used the familiar charge that the intellectuals would not like the common man if they really became acquainted. And within the activist group itself there was the constant lament that the majority of intellectuals appeared indifferent to active politics and autocratic in personal demeanor, however radical in theory.

There was a considerable element of truth in these statements. In any case, the intellectual-labor protest movement never equaled in scope or significance the more broadly based agrarian-military protest movement; nor was there any fusion, although certain strands of influence and connection can be found. The intellectuals did give some support to agrarian radicalism when they attacked capitalism, oligarchic absolutism, and the plight of the farmer. They helped to cultivate the socialist idealism that affected certain younger elements in the so-called "radical right," and a few—a very few—joined with these elements. But this type of combination was strongest in the early Meiji period, when some of the most basic issues were confused and the evolutionary process that would tend to disperse such groupings was just beginning. As time passed, the urban intellectual was drawn increasingly toward individualism, internationalism, and modernism in general (those who espoused Marxism had generally passed through this phase). The true prototype of the agrarian-military radical, on the other hand, even when he preached "socialism," was steeped in traditional and primitive theories; in many cases he was not only anticapitalist but antiurban and antimodern as well. The means of theoretical communication between these two groups was not completely destroyed, especially since elements of paradox and confusion persisted, but, in general, the lines were more sharply drawn by the beginning of the Showa era (1925). And as the militarist-led protest movement of this period became more activist, its basically anti-intellectual qualities became clear. After 1930 every Japanese intellectual had to cope in some fashion with the surging nationalist tides.

Perhaps a few final words should be said about Japanese officialdom as a class and about its relationship to the parties. In this connection there are two significant trends: (1) A small but important number of top officials joined the conservative parties and soon assumed leadership roles within them, as we have already described. This led to many conflicts between the bureaucratic- and the professional-type politician groups in the major parties and particularly in the Seiyukai. It also led to changes in party programs and principles; and while joining a party might be politically desirable or necessary, a person was not required to commit himself to the party's current or even previous principles. (2) If some officials did join parties under such circumstances, the greater part of the bureaucracy remained aloof, always critical of and competitive with party men. This phenomenon exists in almost all modern societies and hence requires little discussion. We should note, however, that the Japanese official could rarely be called a civil servant in the democratic sense. There were some remarkably progressive officials in certain of the ministries in their attitudes toward legislation and reform—indeed, much too progressive on occasion for their superiors or the conservative parties. But a democratic concept of public administration was truly rare. The traditional approach has been summed up in the Japanese phrase *kanson mimpi*, "officials honored, people despised," which, though somewhat harsh for the modern period, was nevertheless valid. And the official, after all, could draw conclusions only from the context of his education and his society; there was little in these sources to support the thesis that he should be governed by the popular vote as it reflected itself in party majorities. On the contrary, he found considerable reason to question the legal right of the parties to be considered supreme and their moral right to be considered representative.

Party Structure

The Japanese political parties were influenced by Western parties in their formal organization as well as in their philosophy. From the start, party by-laws reflected the experiences of the European parties and contained many of their institutional provisions. At the same time, it was inevitable that, in actual operation, Japanese party leadership and organization would reflect even more basically the traditional, though changing, nature of Japanese interpersonal relations. In this respect there were important similarities between the parties and all other private associations in Japan—family, business corporation, and labor union. Indeed, Japanese parties should be studied as a part of, not apart from, the whole nature of social organization in that society. Here we can only suggest some very limited aspects of this matter in terms of a few basic features of the parties themselves.

The heart of the parties was contained in the *kambu,* or headquarters organization. For the major parties this organization included the party president, the senior advisers or party elders, a chief secretary or secretary-general at the head of a small secretariat, the party Diet members or representatives of that body, and a few necessary sections for party work, each with its head. Ordinarily, the sections included those of party affairs, elections, information or propaganda, and party policy. Basic party policy and party officials had to be ratified by a general party convention composed of delegates from the branch organizations throughout the country. Usually at election time the elections section was enlarged, or a special *ad hoc* election committee was established to select official party candidates, raise funds, and determine cam-

paign strategy. This committee was dominated by headquarters personnel.

The issue of leadership was always a troublesome one. In the Seiyukai particularly, the party president frequently exercised or sought to exercise strong powers. Hirobumi Ito and Takashi Hara might be cited as examples of presidents who held the reins firmly and received heavy criticism for the indifference or the officiousness with which they treated the rank and file. Yet, as has been noted, groupism or oligarchy and indirection were two predominant characteristics of Japanese political leadership. Even where one man stood forth as party spokesman, major decisions were usually the result of negotiations among party elder statesmen, factional leaders, and political figures outside the confines of the party itself. Although Japanese society has not yet produced either a demagogue or a Führer (not even Tojo fitted these categories), it also has not produced a political leader or a pattern of leadership symbolizing the Western democratic creed. Japanese leaders have never been accepted on the basis of their ability to sway the minds and hearts of the masses; rather, public speech-making and oratory have been classified as vulgar by a large proportion of the political elite. Neither has independent thought and action achieved acclaim. The leader prototype has been a man distinguished by age, culture, and character—an individual with many "connections" and a capacity for intricate behind-the-scenes negotiations. The party leader has been but one branch on a tree whose roots have extended into the homes of retired statesmen and prominent industrial and military leaders. Thus policy-making has had an air of anonymity, and the fixing of responsibility has been extremely difficult because of the devious course of its channels.

To this picture must be added the

pattern of leader-follower relations. Actually, instead of being characterized by a single leader, the Japanese parties have generally contained a series of leader-follower groupings, each vying for power. Loyalty to superiors, so basic in the traditional period, has remained an important factor in modern Japanese politics. Leaders have attracted support on the basis of sectional loyalties, personal favors, or for other reasons mentioned previously, in addition to, or even to the exclusion of, agreement on policies. The deep-seated sense of obligation connected with this support, often combined with the hope for mutual gain, has produced rather tightly knit unions, although examples of "treachery," as in the feudal period, have not been infrequent. Still, leaders have often been able to engage in major political deviations or compromises and yet retain the solid core of their support. But if this contributed to strange alliances, it also produced strange divisions. Factionalism based purely upon personal differences, questions of prestige, or power rivalry—with no basic policy differences involved—has always been present in the Japanese party movement as in other private associations in Japan. Partly for this reason the Japanese parties have consistently been under heavy attack as having no real political principles and hence of not being "true political parties" but representing rather the type of private coterie or faction that pushes the opportunism inevitable in politics to its extreme. The weak links between the parties and the Japanese citizen at all levels, of course, added fuel to this kind of attack. It is not correct to say that the Japanese parties have had no political principles of significance, especially if these are viewed in a fairly broad sense; evidence against this view can be found in terms of the economic groups which tended to support consistently one party or one group of parties as opposed to others.

It is probably correct, however, to assert that in the context of Japanese society certain ingrained principles of social or group relationship vied with "pure ideological or political principles" in such a fashion as to extend the range of political compromise or fluidity beyond that degree considered legitimate in most modern political societies. Even the social democratic parties of the prewar period did not escape from these problems, although their divisions were undoubtedly due in somewhat greater measure to the ideological cleavages mentioned previously.

The Demise of the Prewar Parties

The political parties achieved their greatest power in the Japanese government during the period from 1918 to 1932, and this era was followed by the "militarist period." The transition, however, was somewhat more gradual and the balance of power more complex than this term indicates. Yet after 1932 the power and importance of the parties declined, except for a few, sporadic upsurges with no long-range significance. The old parties were heavily dependent for their survival during the next eight years upon the highest echelons of the bureaucracy, the court officials and advisers, who for the most part were anxious to check extremist elements in Japanese society with whatever instruments lay at hand. After 1936, however, the more conservative faction of the military group attained its own quasi-supremacy over Japanese institutions. While this faction vigorously opposed the social and economic radicalism implicit in the policies and actions of the "right-wing extremists," it was quite willing to push the theory of organic unity to its logical conclusions. The role that world developments were playing in this scene need not be elaborated here. The formal surrender of the parties occurred in July and August, 1940, when each of them "voluntarily" disbanded. In their places was set up the Taisei Yokusan Kai or "Imperial Rule Assistance Association." As its title suggests, the new organization was dedicated to developing national unity, "assisting the emperor" by formulating public opinion, and serving the general purposes of an authoritarian state. It was widely heralded as an instrument for achieving the true purposes of the Meiji Constitution, and this claim was not without some justification, as we suggested earlier. Actually, neither this group nor its wartime successor, the Political Association of Greater Japan, was able to accomplish these objectives to the degree desired. Public apathy in politics continued to be strong; factions representative of the old parties and rival groupings also remained prominent features of the World War II diets. The competitive party system and the old parties were gone, however, having left a record of failure behind them.

This record was not forgotten by the Japanese people. When the parties were re-established in 1945, one frequently heard such comments as "How many yen will a vote bring this time?" or "Parties are only mutual benefit associations of a few corrupt politicians. No one joins a party unless he aims to get rich in politics." However unconscious of those basic causes for party failure that lay in the whole structure of their society, many Japanese were acutely aware of the results. The return of the parties was not marked by any spontaneous enthusiasm on their part; apathy, indifference, or hostility were more prominent expressions; and interest and enthusiasm remained to be cultivated.

III / Toward a Democratic Party System?

Democratization from the Outside

For six years after August, 1945, Japan was a society under tutelage, with foreign tutors establishing far-reaching new objectives and formulating in large measure the methods to be used in attaining them. The stipulated purpose of the occupation was to destroy the roots of militarism and authoritarianism in Japan and to guide the reorganization of that society so as to strengthen "democratic tendencies" in all institutions. This assignment, admittedly ambitious, was regarded as both a practical necessity and a moral imperative. It was conceived during one of those brief intervals of general Western optimism concerning the world future which have become so rare in the twentieth century. The democratization experiment was naturally a reflection of American society in most of its general goals and methods; in certain respects it also shed light upon what the New Deal was— and what it was not. For, despite the fact that the new Shogun in Tokyo, General MacArthur, was scarcely its self-proclaimed champion, the New Deal was expressed in an infinite variety of ways during the initial stages of the occupation. In this vast experiment, what is to be emphasized? Some scholars would seize upon the human factor, seeking to portray those elements of skill and incompetence, certainty and confusion, sophistication and naïveté, and power and ideological rivalry that figure in any massive political operation. Others will dwell more heavily upon the impersonal components, seeking to encompass the nature and proclivities of both American and Japanese societies as well as this particular juncture of world history. Meanwhile, the results of the democratization attempt will be continuously re-evaluated as the time perspective lengthens. At this stage it is possible only to hold a few hypotheses, and some of my own will be set forth in the succeeding pages.

Among the political changes, the

constitution of 1946 still stands as a monument to democratic objectives. It underwrites all the premises of a limited and responsible government. According to its provisions, supreme political power is vested in the people, with a two-house Diet elected by them constituting the highest organ of state. The emperor has been relegated in legal power to matters of ceremony, and the militarist-bureaucratic elements which formerly wielded his power either abolished or subordinated to the parliamentary system. As a protector of civil rights the new constitution represents one of the most liberal documents now existing in the world, and, though its wisdom has been questioned, a system of judicial review patterned after the American model has been instituted to guarantee observation of constitutional provisions. The old constitutional structure established by the Meiji Constitution has been replaced by a framework for Western-style democracy. This was not accomplished without opposition, and, now that Japan is independent, constitutional revision is likely to be a central issue for the indefinite future. It has already figured strongly in recent elections, particularly with respect to the famous section on "renunciation of war" and permanent demilitarization. At present any revisions would be those supported by the conservatives, dedicated to "closer adaptation to the nature of Japanese society and the world." Changes in this direction, however, will not be easy so long as the parties of the Left hold more than one-third of the Diet seats. It seems likely that the constitution will remain basically unaltered for at least the near future, except possibly for the antiwar section, and even here revision is not certain.

Immediately after the surrender, occupation authorities and Japanese leadership were given the joint responsibility for making this kind of funda-mental law operative; their initial task was to execute a program of broad reforms extending into every facet of Japanese society. And when the conservative Japanese leaders procrastinated or took what were considered half-hearted measures, SCAP[1] moved ahead on its own. There is no need here to describe in detail the wide range of changes undertaken, but it would be desirable to mention the major attempts, since these, too, served as a part of the framework within which the postwar parties emerged and have operated. The first issues attacked were those of an essentially political nature. Complete demilitarization was carried out, and a program of political purges was inaugurated for the purpose of removing from future leadership those who had contributed to the ultra-nationalist, militarist era through their positions or activities. A very large number of military men, together with some of the most influential bureaucratic and old party leaders and a small group of business and educational representatives, were purged.[2] Simultaneously, emergency decrees were issued and laws enacted to remove the heavy restrictions against political parties, labor unions, the press, and the other instruments of a free society. Legal reforms were gradually extended to every level and every branch of government; new electoral laws and regulations for parties were established; the recodification of Japanese statutes begun; and belatedly even the thorny problem of the administrative bureaucracy received some attention.

Economic and social reforms were also inaugurated. Heading the list was

1. SCAP stands for Supreme Commander of the Allied Powers, although it is frequently used to stand for the occupation as a whole; but the context should make the meaning clear.

2. After 1950 almost all purgees were readmitted to Japanese political life.

the famous land-reform program for the complete overhauling of land distribution and ownership which still stands as one of the most radical programs ever executed in modern Asia. Another radical, if less realistic, program of segmenting the great financial cliques and decentralizing economic power in general was worked out and was intended to insure a reformed Japanese capitalism shorn of the political and economic abuses that had previously characterized it. These were but the most spectacular of a host of economic experiments, either temporary or permanent, that marked the initial postwar period. In addition, an assault was launched against the Japanese family system. Women were legally emancipated, and their emancipation was incorporated into laws on marriage and divorce, property rights, and suffrage; primogeniture was also abolished; and an alteration of education was set in motion with a new administrative structure, revised curriculum, and new texts reflecting the new democratic currents.

While various trends can be recorded covering the decade or so that has now passed since these reforms were enacted into law, the long-range results of the Japanese democratization experiment remain in much doubt. The ultimate course of Japanese society will be governed by the direction of both world trends and broad internal developments. Such questions as war or peace for the world, future Western policy toward an independent Japan, and the operative results of Asian communism, together with internal questions relating to the structure of the Japanese economy and its potentialities for improving living standards, the policies and attitudes of Japanese leadership, and a host of similar questions will spell out the answer. From the democratic viewpoint there have been some encouraging signs among the internal trends. First, although the central ideological

issues of our times have been by no means solved in Japan, the framework of reference and disputation has been altered to the general advantage of the liberals (using this term to cover all those who accept the dignity of the individual as an ultimate goal and competitive political institutions as the best means). In the light of Japanese history the importance of this would be difficult to overestimate. Furthermore, the occupation set in motion certain changes in the class structure of Japan and speeded up others already under way. The decline of some pressure groups and the rise of others are both significant and of potential value to the democratic goal. The professional military class, so strongly intrenched in prewar Japan and so profoundly antidemocratic, has been largely submerged up to the present at least, although the effect of the developing rearmament program cannot yet be determined. The disappearance of the tenant-farmer class as a numerous group and its replacement by a landowning and operating peasantry may be important, if permanent. Perhaps of greatest significance is the phenomenal rise of organized labor, at least in terms of organizations and membership. While still extremely weak in many respects, the labor movement may prove capable of redressing some of the past inequities and supporting the kind of balance of conflicting economic interests upon which the welfare of a democratic state depends. On the other hand, the real position of the Japanese farmer may not be sufficiently changed to realize the premises of the new political structure, and labor in its discouragement may succumb to antidemocratic theories and actions. Both of these latter dangers are now very apparent.

There are additional factors that warrant concern. The attempt to impose democracy from the outside obviously creates problems. The relationship between force and democracy in the context of a foreign occupation is a difficult one for liberals to resolve. For six years Japan had a "democratic government" at one level and a "military dictatorship" at another, higher, level. SCAP decisions represented final power, despite all constitutional guaranties and provisions. It was impossible under these conditions to move away from indirect government and the confusion of responsibility, two primary problems of the prewar period. Party platforms, for instance, could be meaningful only to the extent that they accorded with SCAP policy, at least in the range of critical decisions. Even sophisticated electorates would have been baffled under conditions in which radical land-reform and industrial deconcentration measures were enacted under conservative leadership and a shift toward restrictions on labor unions was carried out while the socialists were in nominal power. Out of any situation involving foreign control, moreover, the issue of national independence will inevitably arise to complicate further the problem of induced democracy. This issue affects both indigenous leadership and the people at large. Leaders within an occupied country, irrespective of their political creeds, will usually be quick to note the deficiencies of foreign supervisors and anxious to assume their own control; and this urge will be less susceptible to control under democratic than under totalitarian conditions. And when the issue of national independence can be more or less freely used in the public arena, it may well wreak some damage upon all institutions that are coupled with foreign control in the public mind. The rise of Japanese nationalism in the last few years has been a natural development, and it has also been one of great power. At first, it found its most forceful expressions on the Left, especially the extreme Left, contrary to the prewar pattern, and as

an expression of ideological opposition to the United States. At present, however, every political group in Japan is seeking to use a nationalist appeal, and conservative nationalism appears to be increasing in effectiveness.

If these are problems related in some measure to the occupation, there are others of an even broader nature. Assuming that some form of democracy was and is possible in Japanese society, did SCAP show sufficient wisdom and understanding of Japan to lay the most successful foundations? To put it more succinctly: Has American society shown itself capable of playing a successful revolutionary role in Japan on behalf of democratic fundamentals? Upon this question and the premises underlying it there will always be debate. But one thing is clear: there was a natural tendency for American authorities in Japan to set up by action and inaction a democratic framework patterned after the American model. The degree to which this framework can fit the needs and nature of Japan is now being tested. There is no doubt that American policy toward Japan has gone through a series of changes, and three phases have commonly been recognized: (1) the era of punishment and reform; (2) the period of emphasis upon recovery and revision to reflect American concern over radicalism in Japan and the world; and (3) the recent stage of proffered alliance. These changing emphases naturally produced shifts in policy, marked in general by an increasing American conservatism which was quickly reflected in the Japanese scene in a variety of ways.

Apart from the issues raised by the American occupation, there are still other factors to be weighed. It is generally agreed that what may be termed "political consciousness" needs a great deal more development within the average Japanese citizen if popular government is to be meaningful. Democracy has not yet found a technique whereby rapid progress can be made in this area. Thus Japanese representative government continues to be plagued by corruption, bureaucratic officiousness, and the manipulation of large portions of the electorate by leaders who cannot be said to reflect their constituents' interests. The fact that the Japanese "common man" is an eyewitness to some of its current weaknesses jeopardizes his successful education in the democratic way. Whenever authoritarian alternatives present themselves, his free ballot is no positive safeguard for democracy. Trends in the Japanese economy are closely related to this problem. Japanese society today is struggling to survive, and for the average citizen this struggle takes precedence over everything else. Eighty-seven million people are trying to live on four small islands, and their numbers are still increasing. War and its aftermath have produced enormous problems. While a considerable amount of reconstruction and economic stabilization has now been effected, there has been no basic solution to such problems as overpopulation, foreign markets, and many other matters related to production and the standard of living. In the long run, the Japanese people are likely to gravitate toward whatever political group or system seems to offer the best solution to these problems.

The Formation of the Postwar Parties

It is within this context of change and continuity, of democratization and its problems, that the postwar Japanese parties have emerged and developed. Within four months after the surrender, five major parties and literally hundreds of minor parties had been established. One important factor became apparent at the earliest date, namely, the large measure of continuity from the prewar

period in terms of party divisions and leadership. The very month of surrender, August, 1945, witnessed the beginnings of negotiations among certain well-known politicians and officials for the formation of new parties. It was clear that the new era would wipe out the Political Association of Greater Japan, successor to the Imperial Rule Assistance Association and establish competitive party politics again. There was frenzied activity to become affiliated with "democratic" parties as quickly as possible. Professional politicians almost trampled one another in the rush to join parties with new names and new programs. Two conservative parties, the Liberal party (Jiyuto) and the Progressive party (Shimpoto) were quickly established, absorbing most of the current and past political leaders. Even in name these parties harked back to earlier eras of Japanese politics. The Liberal party stemmed from initial discussions led by Ichiro Hatoyama, a veteran Seiyukai leader, and comprised chiefly elements from that party, especially the so-called "Hatoyama faction." On October 7, 1945, a caucus of fifteen leaders met to discuss policy, and on November 9 a general conference of some hundred and fifty delegates was held to inaugurate the party formally. It was hoped that the Liberal party could rally all conservative forces. But factional rivalries prevented this, and the Progressive party was quickly established. Its formation was directed by a group of elders from the old Minseito, especially the Machida faction, and also the group within the Seiyukai formerly led by Chikuhei Nakajima. More than two hundred and seventy members of the wartime Diet rapidly joined its ranks, making it by far the largest party in the Diet. Many of these affiliations were undoubtedly due to the hope that the Progressive party was the inheritor of a more liberal tradition and hence would be more favored by American authorities. In mid-December, 1945, the party elected Chuji Machida, political veteran and former Minseito president, as its leader.

The forces of the Left, however, were not slow in forming or re-forming political organizations. By the middle of September a committee had been created for the establishment of a Socialist party. Every effort was made to create a united party encompassing all the fragmented prewar proletarian parties except the Communists. These efforts were at first successful, and on November 2 the Shakaito, or Social Democratic party, was formed. Nearly all the prewar labor and socialist leaders were active in its organization. The Communists were also busily engaged. The abolition of the Peace Preservation Laws on September 29, 1945, and the release of all political prisoners still held on October 4 opened the way for the first legal formation of the Japanese Communist party. Out of many years of imprisonment came a small band of die-hard Communists led by Kyuichi Tokuda and they immediately proceeded to stump the the major urban centers for party support. A shrewd leader was added in January, 1946, when Sanzo Nozaka returned from Communist China.

The Co-operative party was a fifth party of some national importance to make its appearance in the early postwar period. A small group of Diet members with rural and middle-class connections, aided by certain outsiders with an interest in the co-operative movement, established the party in December, 1945, and set up its principles in a meeting of February 28, 1946. In addition to these five major parties, the months after surrender saw Japan flooded with hundreds of minor, sectional parties. In many cases these "parties" consisted of no more than an ambitious political aspirant and his handful of followers, and even the stronger ones were generally confined to but a single prefecture.

Trends in Postwar Party Politics

The period since the first establishment of the postwar parties has witnessed several important party reorganizations and some turns in political fortune. The same basic party divisions have thus far remained, however, and, despite the fluid nature of postwar Japanese politics, several consistent factors can be noted. Some of these may prove ephemeral, but no analysis of the present Japanese parties would be complete without a recognition of the broad trends characterizing postwar party politics up to date. The most concise account of party fortunes is, of course, contained in the statistics of the six general elections for the lower house held between 1946 and 1955 (see Table 1). The first postwar general election of April 10, 1946, resulted in a fairly decisive victory for the conservative parties and was followed by the establishment of a coalition Liberal-Progressive cabinet headed by Liberal party president Shigeru Yoshida. The second general election of April, 1947, provided the Social Democrats with a sizable gain, and, by a narrow margin, they became the first party in the House of Representatives. Their popular vote, however, was slightly less than that of the Liberals and amounted to only about one-quarter of the total vote, as against some 52 per cent for the two leading conservative parties. The two coalition cabinets of Tetsu Katayama (Social Democrat) and Hitoshi Ashida (Democrat, formerly Progressive) that followed this election were shaky and largely unsuccessful attempts to weld together a three-party coalition of Social Democrats, Democrats, and Co-operatives. The fall of the Ashida-

TABLE 1

Parties	Election of April, 1946* Total Vote	Per Cent	Diet Seats	Election of April, 1947 Total Vote	Per Cent	Diet Seats	Election of January, 1949 Total Vote	Per Cent	Diet Seats	Election of October, 1952 Total Vote	Per Cent	Diet Seats	Election of April, 1953† Total Vote	Per Cent	Diet Seats	Election of February, 1955 Total Vote	Per Cent	Diet Seats
Liberal (Dem.-Lib.)	12,659,877	24	142	7,260,377	26	132	13,480,504	44	264	16,983,515	48	240	13,474,591 3,088,297	39 9	199 35	9,781,456	27	113
Democrat (Progressive)	10,015,470	19	...	7,097,208	26	126	4,699,707	15	69	6,422,874	18	85	6,151,138	18	76	13,483,319	37	185
Co-operative	1,874,616	4	...	1,940,105	7	31	1,012,678	3	14	394,078	1	2	...	...	...	...	...	...
Social Democratic	8,987,909	17	...	7,170,484	26	143	4,163,130	14	48	(Split)								
Right wing										3,970,315	11	57	4,622,123	13	66	5,091,712	14	66
Left wing										3,461,274	10	54	4,577,479	13	72	5,633,589	15	89
Labor-Farmer							606,840	2	4	261,190	7	4	358,773	1	5	347,534	1	4
Communist	1,929,726	4	5	996,507	4	4	2,984,464	10	35	891,695	3	0	652,717	2	1	726,311	2	2

* A plural voting system at the time of the 1946 elections accounts for the higher total votes.

† In the 1953 elections, the Liberal party was split into the Yoshida and Hatoyama factions, running separate candidates; the first statistics in the Liberal column refer to the Yoshida group, the second to the Hatoyama faction.

Katayama cabinet in October, 1948, led to its replacement by the Liberals, now calling themselves the Democratic-Liberals, with Yoshida again assuming the premiership. This shift was stabilized by the January, 1949, general election, which resulted in a smashing victory for the government party and an equally decisive defeat for the centrist groups. It was also in this election that the far Left made substantial gains: the Labor-Farmer party, a far-left splinter party from the Social Democrats, received over half a million votes, and the Communists captured thirty-five Diet seats and nearly three million votes. A period of political stability followed this election as a result of the clear Liberal majority, but factionalism within the Liberal party gradually mounted and became the primary cause for Diet dissolution and the elections of October, 1952. Despite their internal problems, however, the Liberals again won a major victory, gaining nearly 50 per cent of the vote. In terms of their total vote the Socialists made gains over 1949, but now they were further divided, for the Social Democratic party had earlier split into two almost equal parts known as the right and the left wing, and these groups functioned as separate parties. The Communists suffered a very heavy loss in this election, failing to capture a single Diet seat. Continued disintegration within the Liberal party after the 1952 elections caused grave instability and led to another Diet dissolution and general election in April, 1953. This time the Liberals were split completely, but the Yoshida faction nevertheless polled nearly 40 per cent of the total vote, and the Hatoyama faction received about 9 per cent. The Progressives continued to decline, but various socialist groups scored some gains, while the Communists went down further in terms of popular vote, although they did elect one representa-

tive. For nearly two years longer the Yoshida government stayed in power, but the great breach within Liberal ranks was never healed, and anti-Yoshida conservative strength increased. The February, 1955, elections were preceded by the formation of a new party, the Democratic party, through the merging of the Progressives and the anti-Yoshida elements of the Liberal party under the leadership of Hatoyama. Conservative amalgamations under new labels had occurred before and with varied results. This time the Democratic party entered the 1955 elections with control of the government, Yoshida having given way to Hatoyama several months earlier. The elections were a victory for the party in power and a rather severe defeat for the Liberals; the Democrats got 37 per cent of the vote and one hundred and eighty-five seats in the Diet, while the Liberals slipped to 27 per cent of the vote and one hundred and thirteen seats. Again the socialists made moderate gains, but in this election they remained divided, although some joint strategies were devised and the usual pledge to seek unification was emphasized. The Communists made very minor gains and remained a small party with only 2 per cent of the vote and two seats in the lower house.

Behind all these election statistics and the trends which have determined them lie several factors of considerable importance. The first of these is that the conservative elements in Japanese politics have retained control in the postwar period up to date. There are numerous reasons for this. The conservative parties have been favored thus far by more experienced and professional leadership, by political roots previously established in the prewar era, by the weakness and divisive tendencies of the socialists, and, in the initial period, by SCAP. Postwar leadership in Japan was placed largely in the hands of conservative officials, who, in the absence of more logical candidates, were rendered acceptable by virtue of their antimilitarist record and their administrative experience. Men from the foreign office, like Shidehara, Yoshida, and Ashida, were placed in the forefront. Together with some seasoned veterans of the old Seiyukai and Minseito, these men were available as the cadre of conservative party leadership. These parties have thus been in a position to rely upon most of the old connections maintained by their predecessors, and this is particularly important in the rural areas, where men of local prestige continue to wield great political influence. It is also natural that the conservative elements should have, in general, greater access to financial backing, and election expenses have been exceedingly high. In addition, the weaknesses of the moderate Left have strongly contributed to their success. The socialists have been plagued by sharp ideological cleavages, leadership problems, and in recent years complete segmentation. During the occupation era, as we have seen, SCAP also served to assist the conservatives, especially after 1947. Despite its stated resolve to remain neutral in domestic politics, this was quite impossible; and in its own "suggestions" on political and economic policy, SCAP increasingly aided the conservatives. Certain world trends were also an asset, particularly the rising Communist threat in Asia, even though the long-range significance of this latter factor is much less clear. It should be emphasized, of course, that conservative dominance of Japanese party politics is in line with the prewar pattern, as is the gradual rise of a socialist challenge.

In addition to conservative strength, Japanese politics has also been marked in the postwar period by the existence of a multiparty system, yet one which seems always to offer some hope for de-

veloping into a system that would be essentially two-party in character. Here again the links with the prewar period are clear and the changes perhaps more developmental than radical in nature. Throughout most of the prewar period Japan had a system that was essentially two-party, with the two conservative parties the only serious contenders for power. Actually, however, this situation was not really representative of Japanese society; in considerable degree, it was artificial, sustained by limitations upon political activity and popular indifference to party politics, and, even so, there was the beginning of a challenge from the left-wing parties. In the initial postwar period, with Japan in the midst of social upheaval and a new political freedom at hand, the proclivities for party multiplicity were given free rein. These were abetted by a strong sectionalism and the continued force of factionalism based upon personal loyalty and group coalitions. We have described the importance of this factor in Japanese prewar politics, and it continues to be of great significance. It has surely been the greatest single barrier to a complete merging of the two conservative parties, although there have been numerous attempts to effect this coalescence since 1945. These will undoubtedly continue, for the policy differences between these parties are not major. The problem of the socialists is somewhat more complex, for here ideological as well as personal differences have obstructed the path of unity. In these respects it is easy to draw certain parallels between the Japanese socialist movement and the socialist movement in other parts of the contemporary world; many of the issues are basically the same. It is not difficult to understand, therefore, why Japan at present has a multiparty system and why there continue to be hopes that two unified groupings will eventually appear: a Liberal-Democratic union representing the conservatives and a Socialist party unified to speak for the socialists. It is generally taken for granted, of course, that, even if this were to develop, the Communists would continue to exist as a separate party and there might well be other minor fragments. The assumption is, however, that these elements would not be sufficiently strong even to act as a possible balance of power and that hence Japan could realize an essentially two-party system. But this has not come to pass, and it is certainly possible that the present multiparty system will continue, for, in addition to the problem of bitter personal factionalism, it cannot be denied that even within conservative circles there are certain gradations of political thought that are accommodated by the existing divisions. While it cannot be argued that the present Japanese party system is truly based upon as great a range of socioeconomic differences as those reflected in the French party system, it can be asserted that a considerable range of such differences does exist in Japanese society. Whether these will eventually produce a multiparty system of more differentiated character and more permanent form or whether a sufficient outlet to diverse interests will be given by two flexible and somewhat heterogeneous parties is a vital question that cannot be answered now. Under present conditions in Japan there is no doubt that the medium election district system, whereby three to five candidates are elected, with each voter having a single vote, abets the multiparty system to some extent. A single-district system would increase the pressure for greater party unity, but there is not likely to be any strong disposition for such a move until some progress has been made in meeting the more fundamental obstacles.

There is one final aspect of general party politics of the postwar period worthy of immediate notice. All the parties are still on trial in the eyes of the Japanese people. Mass affiliations are still quite loose in any conscious, reasoned sense, and the power of the political parties in Japanese society remains fluid. As any student of prewar Japanese politics could have predicted, every party has shown major weaknesses and malpractices. The continued strength of independent, nonparty candidates, especially at the prefectural levels, is one evidence of public uncertainty about the parties. While many independents are connected with one of the parties and a number of them actually join parties after the election, their proportion is substantially higher than in countries where the party system is relatively stable. Naturally, the parties continue to face collectively a strong challenge from the administrative bureaucracy; for while the legal power of the Japanese bureaucracy has been somewhat reduced and a series of reforms initiated to revise its personnel and philosophy, conditions have necessitated its retention of great legislative, administrative, and executive authority. And its attitude toward the parties remains marked by hostility and condescension. At the same time, the parties are closely tied to a portion of officialdom, especially the conservative parties, and this is reflected in their leadership and actions. With a military group gradually re-emerging in the public scene, another factor is being added to Japanese politics which will eventually affect the parties in a variety of ways. In summary, it must be said that democratic institutions in Japan are still very fragile and that therefore trends in party power must be described as tentative and uncertain in their implications for the future.

IV / AN ANALYSIS OF THE CONTEMPORARY PARTIES

Organization and Leadership

Japanese political parties remain strongly centralized, with the prewar organizational pattern still very largely intact. The conservative party structure, in particular, is dominated by the headquarters group, who formulate basic policies. Party general conventions are usually rather placid affairs, conflicts having been settled earlier at the headquarters level. Such control is facilitated by the extremely limited membership of the parties and by the character of subordinate party organs. The prefectural and local party branches are dominated by district politicians, often Diet or prefectural government officials who are closely affiliated with key party leaders and usually dependent upon party headquarters for financial support and political recognition during election campaigns. The absence of a primary system in Japanese elections allows central party authorities to exercise broad powers in the final determination of officially recognized candidates and, in general, to exercise a tighter control over branch organizations. This is partly offset, however, by the strong degree of factionalism which is so innate to Japanese society and which continues to operate in the highest party circles. The Japanese parties, especially the conservative parties, may still be described as clusters of leader-follower groups involved in continuously shifting alliances and with each group itself undergoing frequent changes. The conservative parties always have a small number of leaders struggling to build out of this situation a workable coalition within their party. Leadership competition affords subordinates a certain amount of choice and hence importance, conditioned, of course, by the particular pattern of social relationship characteristic of Japanese society. Certainly it makes the collective power of subordinates rather considerable, and this continues to operate behind the scenes in such a fashion as to curb individual leadership.

There is little difference in the organizational structure of the two conservative parties. In both cases the party is led by a president elected by the general party convention. The Liberal party has retained its tradition of fairly strong presidential powers. Certainly, Shigeru Yoshida exemplified this in the postwar period, and one of the major issues within the party revolved around the charges that he made policy without sufficient reference to party interest or information, that he was officious in his treatment of the rank and file, and that many of his close advisers were men outside the party. His opponents raised the cry of "secret diplomacy," referring to his domestic as well as to his foreign policies. Ultimately, the rivalry between the Yoshida and the Hatoyama factions of the Liberal party caused the latter to organize the Democratic party in combination with the Progressive party group, with Hatoyama the first party president and successor to Yoshida as premier. Hatoyama has had a reputation for "democratic leadership," meaning much closer rapport with various party spokesmen through the extensive use of inner-circle conferences. Struggles like those between Yoshida and Hatoyama and the similar ones that had taken place earlier in the Progressive party can also be connected with an element of conflict between "bureaucratic" and "professional politician" leadership in Japan. If this was an important factor in prewar conservative party politics, it has been almost equally important in the postwar period. SCAP, as was noted, actually aided the "bureaucratic" forces by purging most of the prewar professional politicians. Thus it removed

Hatoyama and Machida from their party presidencies and encouraged the rise of Yoshida, Kijuro Shidehara, and Hitoshi Ashida, all of them formerly foreign office officials, who were to become premiers in the postwar period and leaders of the conservative parties. Gradually the professionals have made a comeback, but both parties continue to have important "bureaucratic" wings in their leadership cadres. Co-operation as well as conflict has marked relations between these two elements, but it cannot be denied that in terms of supporters, administrative techniques, and even general attitude toward the idea of parties there have tended to be differences. Whatever their background, however, conservative party leaders thus far have been older men whose political experience was first established in the prewar period. Age, experience (though not necessarily political party experience), and access to funds continue to be primary qualifications for conservative leadership in Japan.

The headquarters organizations of the two conservative parties are very similar to each other and to the prewar structure except for the greater number of top party officials now nominally elected by the party general conference. Headquarters sections continue to be divided into various functional and socioeconomic group categories. Thus there are divisions on party affairs, organization, information, and elections, with an over-all secretary-general and a policy investigation committee; similarly, there are divisions or sections for youth, women, business, farmers, and labor, with certain special agencies for party publication and educational activities. A general policy committee, together with the party president, secretary-general, and senior councilors serves to co-ordinate headquarters actions. Members of headquarters are generally elected or confirmed by the party general conference, meeting annually and comprising representatives from the party branches.

The socialist parties have a somewhat different organizational structure. The titular leader of the party is the secretary-general, with the central executive committee of the party being the most important operating group. These, together with the senior councilors, are elected by and responsible to the general party conference. With a background of deep policy as well as personal differences, postwar socialist party conferences have often been exciting and even chaotic. Especially before the last split in the Social Democratic party in October, 1951, intensive rivalry between the right and left wings existed, as each sought to win grass-roots support from the district branches. The conferences produced many close votes on both platforms and party officials. With the major factions now existing as separate parties, general sessions and central executive committee meetings have recently been less stormy. It is doubtful whether one should consider socialist party branches as well-developed, important elements in the national party. Often, as in the case of the conservative parties, they have been essentially appendages of a leader or faction within the centralized hierarchy. Socialist party leaders have also been primarily older men who had connections with the prewar proletarian party movement. The names of men like Tetsu Katayama, Inejiro Asanuma, Mosaburo Suzuki, and Jotaro Kawakami have long been on the socialist roster.

Like all Communist parties, the Japanese Communist party has been organized according to the well-known principle of "democratic centralism," a system conducive to complete control from the top. A series of elections beginning with the smallest party cell is supposed to produce the party general congress. This group theoretically sets basic policy and selects the central executive committee, whose orders are then passed down to the various party units. As elsewhere, the Communist party in Japan is completely dominated by a small group of leaders, with ample evidence now available to show strong control from the U.S.S.R. and the Cominform. The party, however, has had serious factional and "deviationist" troubles dating back to its origins in prewar Japan and continuing down to the present. Both before and after the famous Nozaka affair, shortly to be discussed, a series of internal party struggles took place. Few of these have yet reached the full light of day, but even on the basis of limited information it is clear that the party has had serious difficulties in reaching complete agreement on basic policies.

Prior to its quasi-suppression by SCAP and the Japanese government in the summer of 1950, the Japanese Communist party had enjoyed some success in organizational activities at the grassroots level. In hard work and diligence on these matters it probably surpassed all other parties. Some of its mass meetings, demonstrations, and general rallies were reasonably effective and illustrated the weaknesses of the other parties in these things. The general purge which began in June, 1950, however, affected these activities as well as the general structure of the party. Most of the main leaders were scheduled for arrest, and almost all party publications were temporarily banned. Since that time the Japanese Communist party has sought to accommodate itself as best it can to its changed status. After the initial purges, when the top leaders went underground, party affairs were turned over to an executive committee of eight, headed by Etsuro Shiino, a relatively minor figure. Subsequently, throughout 1950 and 1951, other purges occurred, including that of Shiino and most of the committee. Open party leadership was put in the hands of a rump executive committee, at first consisting of three men. Since 1950, however, the real party has been underground and its major leaders' whereabouts unknown, although probably some of them are in Communist China. The new tactic of the party has become that of trying to combine legal and illegal action in such a fashion as to meet the new situation. A central bureau was established and Japan divided into eight regional bureaus. The regional bureaus were supposedly given fairly broad autonomous powers, so that they could continue to function independently in case of trouble. Also emphasized was the development of "Nuclear Self-defense Corps," the basic unit in an eventual military arm of the party. One Communist pamphlet describing these units is reported to have been camouflaged by using the title *How To Grow Flower Bulbs, No. 32!* The extent to which military or protomilitary cells of the Communist party have actually been formed within factories, schools, and other agencies is unclear. There has been no open commitment of these forces, of course, but the party policy envisages certain circumstances under which such units would become the nucleus for a "People's Liberation Army" patterned after the Chinese Communist model. The time is not ripe for any such maneuver, however, and it is doubtful whether great progress in these directions has as yet been achieved by the Japanese Communists. More important for the moment, as the Communists themselves recognize, is the tactic of infiltration into key left-wing organizations, the maximum use of propaganda permitted by the government, and pursuit of the "popular-front" thesis in the political arena. Red publications such as *Akahata*, or "Red Flag," the Communist newspaper, have reappeared, and the Japanese literary market is filled with pro-Communist writings, with major attention now being paid to the Chinese Communist movement. There is much evidence of Communist influence in some of the left-wing unions and student groups. Meanwhile, party organization is fashioned so as to combine legal and illegal tactics and to conduct diverse types of activities, including both those openly labeled with the Japanese Communist party trade-mark and those in which the Communist role is deliberately obscured. The ratio among these is to depend upon conditions, with flexibility considered highly important.

The leaders of the postwar Communist party in Japan have again been political veterans in the main. Secretary-General Kyuichi Tokuda joined the party at a very early stage and spent nearly twenty years in prison along with a few other comrades, who became the nucleus of the party upon its re-formation in the fall of 1945. Sanzo Nozaka also figured prominently in the prewar party and acquired much training in Russia and Communist China during his long period of exile from Japan. When he returned in January, 1946, he was immediately given considerable power. The Tokuda-Nozaka alliance has dominated the Japanese Communist party up to date, though not without challenge. It has generally been agreed that the party has had two main factions based upon both ideological and personal-geographic factors. The Tokuda-Nozaka element has been called the "central faction," "main school," or "national group"; and it has been estimated that this element has always controlled about 75 per cent of the party. Another group has been called the "Kansai faction" or "international group," having its central strength in the Osaka-Kobe area and led by Yoshio Shiga. Many aspects of this cleavage remain clouded, but it appears to have reached a climax dur-

ing the period around January, 1950, when Nozaka was attacked by the Cominform as being "petty bourgeois" and "anti-Marxist," for following a weak policy, and for asserting that socialism could make progress under the occupation. Some scholars believe that these charges were instigated by the Kansai faction. At any rate, in the aftermath of this explosion, charges and countercharges were openly hurled by leading Communists against one another. Tokuda was accused of "dictatorship" by the Shiga group, and the latter were castigated as "Trotskyites," a familiar Communist epithet. Despite the Russian-led attack upon them, the Tokuda-Nozaka forces held their own and even increased their control over the party. At one point in 1950 almost all of the Kansai faction had been expelled or removed from posts of party leadership. This was partly the result, however, of some "self-criticism" and alterations of policy in accordance with Cominform complaints. In the aftermath of the affair, moreover, foreign sources appear to have sanctioned the retaliation taken against the antileadership faction of the Japanese Communist party. It is possible that, with the purges and other forms of suppression, the Communists found unity more desirable and necessary. Present indications are that greater harmony within the ranks prevails, with some of the dissenters back in the good graces of the party. Shiga himself became the first important Communist party leader to re-emerge from obscurity when he came forth about a month before the 1955 elections and managed to be one of the two successful Communist candidates elected to the Diet. In view of the general history of the party, however, it would be most surprising if elements of tension and discord at the leadership level did not remain to some extent.

In any general survey of the Japanese party movement, the type of organization and the leadership remain vital, if essentially derivative, problems. Leadership weaknesses in the postwar period have been highlighted by a series of scandals implicating some top officials of the three leading democratic parties as well as many rank-and-file Diet members. These scandals have ranged over a wide field: complicity in the illegal sales of war materials, conspiracy to subsidize indiscriminately certain industrialists from government funds; and the acceptance of bribes to protect dubious companies or pass desired legislation—all of which are reminiscent of the prewar era. As usual, it is not always easy to separate authentic charges from those without foundation or to make a proper distinction between ethical and unethical action in the political arena. Nevertheless, corruption has been proved in a number of cases, and in some instances public attention has been focused for months upon newspaper headlines featuring one sensational revelation after another. The objectives, as usual, have varied from the desire to obtain large sums of money for party election expenses to the more personal need for individual living expenses; and opprobrium has fallen upon the Liberal, Democratic, and Social Democratic parties alike.

Many other factors enter into the problems of postwar Japanese leadership. The heavy burden of the past plays its full part, as we have already noted. The traditional leader—even of the so-called "liberal" parties—generally shunned the public forum and depended upon his success in manipulating private channels. Leadership was more a group than an individual prerogative, with most basic decisions arranged through the medium of secret negotiations, using go-betweens to smooth the pathway, protected by public indifference and ignorance. When the events after 1930 are related to these facts, the problems of current

party leadership become sharper. Under the odium of failure and the heavy pressure of more dynamic forces, the parties and the Diet failed to attract the younger generation, and party leadership was retained by default in the hands of a small group who moved from middle to old age. Since the war a few younger men, inspired by the spirit of public service or the idea of a new career, have entered the party movement, but their influence is still relatively minor. It is not easy for an older generation to change the accepted patterns of a lifetime, whatever new institutional arrangements may be made. There are some exceptions: a certain number of the older leaders, especially those from the "professional politician" category, have engaged in vigorous campaigning on a national level and placed increased emphasis upon general public relations work. It is also obvious that within a few years new men who are essentially products of the postwar ferment will begin to move into leadership positions in all the parties. The Japanese voter will then help to mold leaders, and he has already given some slight indication that he will reward publicly oriented leaders more than in the past. If this may well present new hazards to the Japanese parties, it may also present new opportunities.

Future trends in Japanese party organization will be greatly influenced by the leadership pattern and also by the question of whether or not a larger number of party workers at the local level can be recruited. Present party bylaws could accommodate a much less elite, centralized structure. Such a development, however, would have to take place in the context of similar trends within all Japanese associations and group relationships and be accompanied by a rising political consciousness on the part of a larger group of the people, although the group could still be small in terms of total population. Here it would be significant to turn to the question of popular affiliation with the postwar parties.

Membership and Affiliation

Today some forty-eight million Japanese are registered voters, but only an infinitesimal fraction of these are registered members of any political party. The parties are now required to register the number of their branch organizations and members with the attorney-general's office. Figures for 1950, for example, were as follows: Liberal party, 728 branches and 70,668 members; Democratic party, 293 organizations and 20,422 members; Social Democratic party, 1,336 organizations and 96,159 members; Communist party, 5,625 organizations and 108,593 members. The figures vary somewhat from year to year, and since 1950 there have been shifts with the changing fortunes of the parties: the Communist party statistics on file, for instance, show a sharp decline. Nevertheless, it can be seen that formal party registers do not reflect true party strength with the electorate. Low membership figures in comparison with the registered electorate are due chiefly to the fact that all the parties have membership qualifications of a fairly rigorous nature. And, since there are no primary elections in Japan and voters do not register by party affiliation, only those who live up to the formal requirements are considered party members. In the conservative parties prospective members must submit a request for entrance and be investigated and passed upon by the local party branch. In some cases sponsorship by two persons who are already party members is a necessity. The payment of dues is also required. Socialist party requirements are similar: candidates for membership must make written application, be sponsored by two party members, pay party dues, and agree to support party princi-

ples. The same general rules have applied in the Communist party, with the applicant being passed upon at a party meeting, accepted by a district committee, and finally approved by the central executive committee. Even though in practice these regulations are less rigorous than they appear on paper, still it is reasonable to compare them with rules governing admission to a club. But actually such formal requirements have been only one factor limiting party membership; it is at least equally important to recognize the weakness of party appeals to the average citizen and the long legacy of estrangement between him and the parties. Few party branches have made a concerted effort to organize sustained support from the public. While membership campaigns, public fund-raising activities, and similar ventures have received some attention from the parties on the Left, the figures attest to their general lack of success. The average Japanese voter does not think of himself as a member of any party and still tends to view parties as irrelevant to his own interests.

The immediate test of party strength, however, lies not in formal membership but in the proportion of the electorate supporting its candidates at election time. Certain generalizations pertaining to the current parties and their sources of support can be made, but many more detailed studies of voting behavior in Japan must be carried out before a detailed picture can be presented. The conservative parties have retained their hold over the upper and middle business groups for the most part and have generally continued to dominate the rural areas. The farmers' support of conservative party candidates has been an important factor in election results; nearly 50 per cent of the Japanese population can still be classified as agricultural in occupation, and a substantial majority of this social-economic category has stayed with the conservatives. Until the elections of 1955 the Liberals in particular could count upon a strong vote in most rural districts; the party split just prior to that election, however, produced at least temporary damage and enabled the Democrats to share a greater proportion than previously. Voting behavior in the rural areas continues to show the influence of established prewar patterns, with prominent families, district leaders, and village headmen providing guidance and direction. There are some socialist enclaves in the rural areas and indications of a general increase in the left-wing rural vote in recent elections, but the conservative parties still have a significant advantage in rural Japan as a whole. It must not be assumed, however, that these parties are without strength in the urban centers. Returns from the major Japanese cities in the postwar elections clearly indicate that the Liberals and the Democrats have drawn support from many classes in urban society, together consistently polling nearly two-thirds of the total vote. Many of the low-income people of Tokyo, Osaka, and the other large cities have been voting conservative. One may ascribe this to the popularity of name candidates, high-pressured and well-financed campaigning, the popularity of certain conservative symbols, the failure of the Left to satisfy these groups, or a lack of political consciousness.

The city vote, however, is naturally a primary source of such strength as the Left has been able to acquire. We have already noted the spectacular rise of organized labor in the postwar period. Recently the unions have suffered some reverses, but at present around five million workers, the great bulk of whom live in urban centers, retain union ties. In Japan the labor movement has always been essentially a political movement with very close ties to the political

parties of the Left. A great struggle to gain control of the major unions has been a constant feature of the postwar period. At first, the chief competitors were the more or less unified socialists and the Communists; since the Communist purges of 1950 and the socialist split of 1951, the most spirited open battles for control have been between the right- and the left-wing socialists, with the Communists concentrating on infiltration of the more leftist elements and planting its members under different labels. Political tides within organized labor have tended to swing in pendulum-like fashion, with the recent swing strongly toward the Left. At present, left-wing socialists and elements still further to the left are well intrenched in Sohyo, the major union federation. Sohyo, however, continues to give some official support to the right-wing socialists and urges that the Japanese socialist movement be reunited.

Organized labor is becoming increasingly important to the Left in terms of financial support. While the unions are financially weak, they have recently made some attempts to contribute election funds to the leftist parties. In the elections of 1955 Sohyo sought to collect a huge campaign fund by asking for a contribution of 100 yen per worker. It was hoped that 200,000,000 yen could be raised, of which 30,000,000 would be contributed to the left-wing, 10,000,000 to the right wing, 4,000,000 to the Labor-Farmer party, with the remaining 150,000,000 to be used by various unions to support individual candidates or groups on the Left. While no figures on this drive are yet available, it is very doubtful that any such sum was actually raised; but such a plan has great potential significance for the future of the socialist movement and Japanese politics in general. Japanese elections are very costly; despite the strict election laws limiting candidate expenditures to a relatively small sum, it is well known that many successful candidates spend millions of yen. Previously the conservatives had great advantages because of their access to business funds and also the independent wealth of some of their candidates. Conservative campaign war chests have dwarfed the meager funds of the Left, and this has enabled them not only to spend much more money per candidate but also to run many more candidates. It has proved as impossible to enforce satisfactorily the rigorous election laws in Japan as in most other countries, although in each election thousands of violations are reported and many individuals are prosecuted. Labor funds may redress the past imbalance in some degree, even though it is going to be difficult to get contributions from individual members when their livelihood is so precarious. At the same time as their financial importance to the left-wing parties increases, the unions can be expected to have an even greater power within party councils.

Despite the fact that the organized labor vote cannot be delivered intact to various parties on the Left and certainly not to any one party, there can be no doubt that the Japanese labor movement has a socialist orientation and has been moving in general in a leftward direction. In addition to organized labor, there are other important urban groups, such as the white-collar class (some of whom are unionized), the professional groups, and the small and medium business elements. As in most contemporary societies, these constitute a particular challenge to the competing parties. A considerable proportion of the socialist Diet members come from the professional and business categories, revealing the strength of the Japanese "middle class" in the socialist hierarchy. The right-wing socialists in particular undoubtedly get important support at the polls from such elements, offsetting to some extent their weakness vis-à-vis the left wing in most of the unions. Certainly, no party on the left has omitted any of the groups from its appeal. Even the Communists have emphasized the role which small and medium business would play in a "Democratic People's Republic" along lines similar to those used by the Chinese Communists. And while the conservatives have polled the bulk of this vote up to date, the socialists have gotten a very respectable percentage in the post-war elections.

The left-wing parties also count rather heavily upon support from the Japanese intellectuals. While not numerically large, this group is important because of its role in journalism, education, and general cultural activities. And there can be no doubt that the most articulate elements of the Japanese intelligentsia are firmly aligned with the Left. Evidence on this score can be obtained by reading the leading intellectual publications, noting the rosters of left-wing cultural associations, and observing some of the leading student intellectual organizations. If the Japanese conservatives have many advantages over the Left in terms of finances, well-established roots, and name leaders, the left-of-center has a certain advantage in the field of publications, especially those of a fairly high intellectual caliber, but not excluding an important proportion of the daily press. It is a common mistake to assume that all or nearly all of the Japanese intellectuals are on the Left. This is not true, however one defines the term "intellectual." For in any total tabulation the number of relatively conservative individuals in occupations generally equated with intellectual life would probably be surprisingly high, and the number of those affiliated with the Communists very low. It is correct, however, to assert that intellectual leadership in Japan is strongly dominated by the non-Communist Left; many of the most influential and active intellectuals of the younger age group can be counted on the side of the left-wing socialists, with their counterparts in the older age categories leaning more perhaps to the right-wing socialists. It would be wise to recall here the comments made earlier about the general role of the intellectuals in prewar Japanese politics, because many of the same circumstances and problems still apply. The leftist intellectual in Japan is appalled by what he considers the corruption and injustice of his society, remains in most cases committed to Marxism as the most correct general analysis of society and the most scientific methodology, and wrestles with the problems of how to synthesize this with certain liberal values which he holds and certain conservative patterns which dominate his personal life.

The larger industrial and commercial elements remain, of course, strongly committed to the conservative parties, provide the overwhelming proportion of their funds, and have great influence in determining their policies and personnel. The big business groups, however, are not without their political dilemma. Their primary interest continues to be in the kind of conservative unification which will promote political stability, for they have generally been sorely troubled by the factional disputes within conservative party ranks and the necessity for frequent and expensive elections. Various methods have been used to tackle these problems. Most recently leading industrial and financial circles established an Economic Reconstruction Council to provide the conservative parties with campaign funds. This may be viewed as both a defensive and an offensive measure: defensive in the sense of trying to establish some co-ordination and protect large-scale business against "excessive demands" for contributions, and offensive in the sense of bringing to bear maximum pressure for general business

programs and especially the unification of conservative forces. Each of the conservative parties has had certain long-established sources of funds from big business, as noted earlier, due to partisan and personal commitments. At the same time, however, a considerable number of business interests are able to shift their support or the proportions of that support, and this provides additional pressure upon the conservative party factions. No matter what their commitments, business interests have long been restive over the heavy cost of frequent elections, for they have often been squeezed for additional money until it hurt.

There continues to be some uncertainty as to how much change was produced by the occupation in the structure of Japanese industry, or perhaps one should say how little. The sharpest attack was, of course, upon the holding companies and cartels and upon a few prominent industrial families. In recent years, however, progress toward amalgamation of Japanese large-scale business and industry has taken place at an increasing rate, much of it strongly supported by government. The industrial structure, therefore, continues to present some of the same problems for Japanese democratic practice and theory as previously existed. There are ambivalence and uncertainty on these matters in the business community as in most other urban classes.

Indeed, in most respects, postwar Japanese society as a whole must be considered more fluid in its political commitments than at any time in the past. Even in the rural areas there are some signs that political affiliation is less fixed than was previously the case. Certainly, ideological commitment is weak, and that element of stability which derived from a deeply ingrained acceptance of hierarchy has been further threatened by events since 1945. While the conservative parties have retained, up to the present, most of their advantages, the task of holding these in the future may be more arduous. Again, both internal and world conditions will affect the result. It must not be forgotten that new generations of Japanese who have known only war and the occupation are now approaching maturity; and they have been subjected to a great variety of influences, some of them diametrically opposed to one another. The substantial degree of political confusion existing in Japanese society at present should therefore not be surprising. But, by the same token, party appeals to the vote based upon policy promises may influence an increasing number of the electorate. What are the parties offering the Japanese citizen in exchange for his vote, omitting those cases where candidates are offering cash on the spot?

Programs and Ideology

The policy declarations of the current Japanese parties provide keen insights into the dilemma of Japanese democracy, for each party faces its special problems in seeking to synthesize varying Western ideas with the structure of its own society. The conservative parties, especially the Liberals, have paid considerable homage to the tenets of classical liberalism. And in their numerous policy statements they have championed a "liberal economy," with the abandonment of public ownership wherever possible, assistance to private enterprise, and maximum scope for "private initiative." Under SCAP impetus, the Liberals while in office undertook a program of strict governmental economy, rigorous measures to halt inflation, and some general taxation reforms. These measures, however, were not entirely popular within Liberal party circles, and some subsequent modifications have been made in party platforms. The Liberals have increasingly backed amalgamation efforts

within Japanese industry and sought to move away from the stringent austerity program outlined by the Dodge plan. Their left-wing opponents have accused them of restoring the old *zaibatsu* and perpetuating economic inequities while working in close conjunction with the industrial-financial leaders. TheLiberals have defended themselves by pointing to industrial recovery in Japan and to generally improved markets.

In the political field the Liberals have used such Western slogans as "individualism," "limited government," and "curb the bureaucracy"—these were especially popular in the earlier days of the occupation, when conservative leaders were seeking to please SCAP officials. More recently the emphasis has been upon curbing leftist extremism, revising the constitution and other occupation legislation "ill-suited to Japanese society," and espousing a conservative nationalism which would help stabilize the country. The Liberals under Yoshida have strongly favored anti-Communist legislation curbing the leftists in labor unions and education. They have also been studying the questions of constitutional revision, favoring those changes which would bring fundamental law into line with Japanese practices. There has been no agreement within Liberal ranks on the precise nature of changes as yet, but many would like a document more closely modeled after the Meiji Constitution. The Liberals have also led the fight for a movement away from decentralization of governmental functions: the famous Police Bill providing for greater centralization of the Japanese police is one outstanding example. One of the issues arising out of all these actions and policy stands is how much of the old order do the Liberals want to reimpose? Or to put the question in another form: Where does one draw the line between "revising occupational excesses and impracticalities" and restoring most of the old order? There is a certain range of opinion on this type of issue within Liberal party ranks. An important group in the party has always held the conviction that with some added controls over the military the old political structure would have sufficed and that most of the occupational changes were both stupid and dangerous. Others would accept many of the changes or acknowledge them as a *fait accompli* and are presently willing to settle for more limited revisions. With constitutional revision difficult under present regulations, this latter position will probably prevail, especially since the Liberal party has shown itself sensitive to public opinion on some issues.

Whatever their position on domestic issues, the Liberal party in the field of foreign policy has tended to acquire the reputation of being the most "pro-American" party in Japan. In general, it has staunchly supported the inclusion of Japan in the Western camp, taken a rather jaundiced view of closer political and economic relations with the Communist bloc, and upheld American military commitments to Japan, including the military bases. Nevertheless, the Liberals have not been oblivious to increasing Japanese nationalist sentiment and the demands for greater independence—indeed, with certain connotations, they share these sentiments. They have been exceedingly cautious up to date in backing rearmament and have pledged themselves to a rather slow time schedule. They have also urged the return of certain former Japanese possessions, including Okinawa. And more recently they have supported political and economic explorations with the Communist nations. Their slogans have emphasized a more independent foreign policy along with alliance with the United States.

The Democratic party has often had considerable difficulty in differentiating itself from the Liberals in policy matters, especially when its leaders happen to be former Liberals, as is now in part the case. In the beginning of the postwar period the Progressive (Democratic) party sought to reflect a moderate conservatism and offer a "middle way" between the Liberals and the Social Democrats. And, despite leadership changes, there remains a strong element in the party still dedicated to this idea. Party platforms have often underlined *reformed* capitalism and emphasized welfare measures more than the Liberals. In addition there have been rather technical but nevertheless important issues between the two conservative parties in each election; sometimes these have related to questions of government fiscal policy. In general, however, the early occupation hope that the Democratic party would become a middle-of-the-road party has not materialized, at least up to the present.

In the field of foreign policy the Democrats used the nationalist issue rather earlier and more vigorously than the Liberals, partly, no doubt, because they were out of power. They have called for open rearmament and constitutional revision to make this possible without restrictions. One of their arguments has been that only with this development will true Japanese independence be possible. Probably the overwhelming number of Liberals agree with this position and will support it. The Democrats have also been somewhat more assertive in calling for trade with the Communist countries and an improvement in their political relations; many of them currently favor a "two Chinas" policy. But the Democratic leadership and the rank and file as well are at this time pledged to continued support of close ties with the United States, and the somewhat different tone taken recently by the Democrats in foreign policy as opposed to the Liberals can probably be ascribed more to political tactics than to basically different convictions. Both conservative parties will play upon certain nationalist themes and insist upon "an independent foreign policy" which looks toward the eventual importance of Japan in the councils of the world.

The socialist parties present real alternatives in domestic and foreign policies to those of the conservatives and, to some extent, to those of each other. The domestic programs of the major socialist parties, the right and the left wings, do not differ greatly except in the underlying matter of degree, which is not always spelled out in the respective platforms but is always present in the minds of socialist spokesmen. The essence of socialist domestic programs is, of course, the reduction or elimination of the capitalist system through an evolutionary process which would preserve parliamentary institutions and the basic requirements of a democratic society. Beginning steps involve the nationalization of basic and "monopolistic" industries, a strengthening of the land-reform program, and the backing of co-operatives both in agriculture and in industry. All elements within the socialist movement have insisted upon a rapid expansion of social welfare measures covering health, unemployment, and various other aspects of social policy; they have demanded increased governmental regulatory powers over many facets of the Japanese economy, with emphasis upon long-range planning.

The socialists have been intensely critical of the conservatives, particularly the Liberals. They have charged the latter with disregard for the welfare of the lower economic classes and policies benefiting the "privileged groups." They have sought to pin a number of major scandals upon the conservatives. There has also been a bitter attack upon conservative policy as it affects civil liberties, and laws relating to demonstrations, the unions, the press, and education have been vigorously denounced as assaults upon civil liberties that go far toward re-creating the atmosphere of prewar Japan. The overwhelming majority of socialists have long opposed any popular front with the Communists, but they have also opposed most anti-Communist legislation as dangerous and useless. Their argument has been that communism can be met only with basic reforms and that suppression not only will fail but will also jeopardize the whole structure of newly created Japanese civil rights.

As has been noted before, however, many of these positions involve a matter of degree. Since its inception the socialist movement in Japan has been influenced by diverse Western currents in seeking an approach to the "Japan problem." The inner recesses of nearly every Western socialist controversy have been explored, and the comparative merits of most socialist parties examined. Almost every European socialist leader and movement has had a group of supporters in Japan, and close agreement among these groups has always been short-lived. The occupation also presented a problem in connection with any socialist program. As previously outlined, the SCAP program ran increasingly counter to socialist necessities. Faced with a number of *faits accomplis,* the socialists could find no successful method of opposing SCAP power. Now they are cognizant of the fact that Japan has moved a considerable distance since 1945 and that certain trends adverse to them are deeply intrenched. How to meet this issue during the occupation and subsequently has contributed to the socialist division.

The issues of foreign policy, however, have been the most immediate causes for the major split in socialist ranks. When the Social Democratic party position was first stabilized in late 1949, it included a demand for the earliest possible conclusion of a peace treaty with all the wartime allies, the absolute neutrality of Japan in the cold war, and opposition to rearmament in any form or the continuation of American military bases in Japan. Subsequently, a division of opinion arose within the party concerning the first two propositions. Ultimately, the right wing supported the Peace Treaty of 1951, although they continued to oppose the Mutual Security Pact signed with the United States. The left wing continued vigorously to oppose both, and this was the central issue producing the party split in October, 1951. The Left has insisted upon a completely neutralist policy but one that frequently appears to emphasize anti-Americanism and to urge closer relations with the Communist powers. This is probably natural, however, given the trends of current conservative policies in Japan. The right wing is somewhat less neutralist, with indications that its basic values lie much closer to the Western democracies than to the Communist societies; but at the same time it has certainly not taken the position of the British Labour party in matters of foreign policy. One factor involved here is the very strong strain of pacifism present in the party and also the nationalist reaction to American power in Japan. The right wing still opposes rearmament and post-treaty American military bases, although some members within the party quietly support these in a limited way. The most recent principles agreed upon by the two wings as the basis for an attempt at reunification included opposition to rearmament, defense of the "Peace Constitution," realizing socialism through democratic and peaceful means, and establishing a clear distinction from the Communist party. Even if these latest attempts should be successful, however, the pathway of unification for the Japanese socialist movement is at least as hazardous as for that movement in certain Western nations.

The Japanese Communist party has had a long history of subservience to the U.S.S.R. and the Comintern-Cominform, which has been its international instrument. This continues to be demonstrated in terms of its current policies. In the first phases of the postwar period the Communists set forth a "moderate" policy. With Nozaka taking a prominent lead, the party soft-pedaled criticism of the occupation, strove to make communism compatible with Japanese attitudes and synonymous with democratic reform, and urged a popular front with all "democratic parties." This was the policy of making the party "lovable." The Chinese Communist movement obviously provided a model in shaping the general outlines of this approach. Primary emphasis was placed upon reforms in such fields as agriculture, labor, and industry that could find support from numerous non-Communists. This technique of superimposing appealing reforms over their basic goals and striking hard at certain legitimate grievances has always been a standard method of gaining voter strength. At no time, however, has the ultimate goal of complete collectivization under a party dictatorship been omitted from the program as a second phase, and orthodox Communist tactics in its achievement have been stoutly defended.

The "moderate" program was largely overthrown as a result of the Cominform attack upon Nozaka in January, 1950, which was discussed earlier. Although Nozaka's confession was not without a minor show of resistance, there followed a greatly sharpened assault upon the occupation and American policy in general; these were linked with the conservative parties as central targets of attack. The Communists began increasingly to play upon nationalism, a novel weapon for them in Japan but one that had done yeoman service for the Communists elsewhere in Asia. Words like *aikoku* ("patriotism") and *kokumin* (the "nation-people") seemed strange in Japanese Communist literature, but the recent campaign has been directed at "the liberation of the Japanese race from American slavery." Of course, the Communists have taken violent exception to recent conservative policies, both domestic and foreign. Their own foreign policy position does not need to be explained in detail, for it follows the general Communist line. Emphasizing "peace" and "democracy," it calls for the alignment of the Japanese people with "the peace-loving peoples of the world," led by "the great Soviet Union and our Asian brothers, the Chinese." Whatever may be true underneath, there have been no clear surface evidences as yet that Japanese Communist leadership is prepared to resist Russian demands or forced to make any choice between Russian and Chinese guidance.

Modern Japan is the product of a rather unique cultural heritage and a given timing of Western influence and modernization. As a result of this latter factor, Japan shares certain general political and economic phenomena in common with other "late-developing" nations, despite the obvious distinguishing features. The development and nature of the Japanese political parties can be understood only within this context. But it must be emphasized that it is a context which in its broader reaches includes the whole of the contemporary world. In the case of Japan, an explanation of the party system and party characteristics that hinges centrally upon some simple formula such as the electoral system is not satisfactory. Even if one grants that in certain respects and under certain conditions such matters have influenced or can influence the Japanese parties, it is far from sufficient as a basic explanation of the past and the present.

Party difficulties in Japan bear witness to the extraordinary problems of Western-style democracy in societies like those of modern Asia. It would seem unwise to attempt any long-range predictions at this time. Japan, however, will remain an important test case for the ideas of political competition and parliamentarism in a setting that is admittedly difficult but no more so than in many other areas of the world. The tutelage recently relinquished by the American occupation now rests to a considerable extent with the major political parties and particularly their leaders. It will be important to the West as well as interesting to see how they exercise this tutelage in the coming months and years in terms of both their individual appeals and their conduct when in power. The experiment will be valid, of course, only if the world can remain at peace.

Germany: Changing Patterns and Lasting Problems

SIGMUND NEUMANN
Wesleyan University

I / THE BASIC PATTERN

An aura of mystery has always surrounded the German party system. With its numerous groupings of unpronounceable names, undefinable aims, and constantly shifting composition, it seems to defy all classification. It has kept the wandering scholars at an awesome distance and has let popular prejudices take the field. Thus it has remained terra incognita until now. But this is an undeserved fate.

There is nothing mysterious about the German parties. Once their fundamental character is clearly detected, they present a simple pattern and a surprising continuity in program, personnel, and problems. If political parties are the lifeline of a nation—as no doubt they are—reflecting its persistent features, its changing historical forms, and its inner dynamics and dilemmas, Germany may indeed provide a perfect case study.

A careful check on the German party system can yield a twofold result —and doubly unexpected it may be. It shows the extraordinary persistence of the Reich's political forces, while at the same time it illustrates in the parties' drastic breaks the lasting crises of Germany's social order, reflecting the continuity and change in the body politic.

Weltanschauung

Two basic features of the German party system stand out: its emphasis on Weltanschauung (a fundamental philosophy of life) and its adherence to strong social-class alignments. They constitute the peculiar contribution, no less than the unresolved dilemmas of the Reich. Both factors also explain the relative stability of Germany's political fronts, despite their confusing temporary reshuffles and constantly changing nomenclature, climaxing in their complete submergence under the Nazis' totalitarian cover. While Germany underwent radical transformations from early small and separate states to Bismarck and the Wilhelmic Empire, to the Weimar Republic, and to the Third Reich, until it has come to the presently partitioned two Germanies, and while the wide world around it is living through this upsetting international civil war, the German parties seem to remain in repose in the midst of the shifting scene.

From the very outset they were parties of ideological orientation and class character. Both factors are rooted in the parties' fatal beginnings, from which they have not yet fully recovered. The German parties originated in an abnormal situation not at all conducive to the free unfolding of responsible, popular participation. The Prussian-German monarchy did not allow for such a necessary prerequisite of genuine party growth. At the same time the political upheavals in neighboring France aroused the aspirations and ambitions of awakened young Germans. They enthusiastically took sides for or against the "Grand Revolution." Thus long before the alert citizen could

354

test and balance his political acumen against pressing policy decisions (which he was not permitted to make), he had taken a stand in the battles of the mind. The result was that the ideological cleavages of the time were crystallized and (merged with traditional strands of long-standing and ever present German *Gründlichkeit*) soon petrified in the uncompromising world outlook of conservatism and liberalism. Ideologies existed before the parties, but they, in turn, did not mature into political movements to capture power.

This rigidity of political parties in the name of well-defined ideologies has remained a main feature of German politics. In consequence thereof, it has been difficult, if not impossible, to accept compromise as the appropriate technique for adjusting the divergent aims of the political contestants. Party programs were elevated to issues of political religions, over which one would fight to the bitter end, often in a political vacuum. Politics, the art of the possible, as the Anglo-American parties practice it, seemed a "compromising," a distasteful bargaining over constantly changing working platforms, when a fundamental, consistent stand was demanded. While a nascent appreciation of Western pragmatism may be noted in wider circles of the Second Republic, the Germans on the whole still take their politics religiously—if they take to them at all.

The interlude of military government, under whose aegis the German parties were reconstituted in 1945, may also have contributed to a renewed intransigence in the peoples' movements, which in critical formative years were relieved by the occupational powers from final practical decisions; they could thus fall back on "irresponsible" politics of absolute alternatives and demagogical demands. Ideological fronts could again be petrified along rigid lines of "principled" politics. Day-by-day deci-

sions of public concern might again be easily dismissed as "cheap maneuvers," below the dignity of educated men. The free flow between responsible leadership and mature public opinion—the prerequisites of effective party government—will always have hard going in an atmosphere of hardened programs of a fundamental world outlook.

Social Alignments

From the very outset, these difficulties of the German *Weltanschauungsparteien* were accentuated by a second peculiar element, namely, their close identification with specific social groups. Strict class alignments of political parties presage perilously inflexible politics. Moreover, the complex society of late nineteenth-century Germany encouraged the unfolding of a multiparty system—another complication for responsible government based on delicate majority-party coalitions.

A look at the burgeoning of political development gives a revealing indication of Germany's persistent troubles. The revolution of 1848 marks the official origin of the German parties. The promise of popular participation in a unified nation naturally aroused the desire for continuous political organizations.[1]

The beginning seemed to be simple enough. It is always the "opposition" that organizes itself first. Only in answer to its challenge do the powers of the status quo call on the conservative elements to rally behind the government. This was the case of that futile

1. They had found their forerunners in some southern German states, which, under the influence of neighboring France, had granted to their peoples a quasi-parliamentary regime "by the grace of God." It is not accidental that such earlier political experiences have given to southwestern Germany a greater sense of reality and more deeply rooted democratic attachments, which, down to the present, could be detected in the respective wings of their national parties.

revolution of 1848 in which a young, liberal middle class soon found itself confronted with a conservative ruling aristocracy that responded through the pressures of army, bureaucracy, and the Protestant church as defender of "Throne and Altar." A straight two-party system of the "ins" and the "outs," of conservative versus liberal, suggested itself as a natural political confrontation here as elsewhere.

In Germany, however, ideological discrepancies and social tensions soon made themselves felt in further party splits. The failure of the revolution had something to do with it. While at first it reunited the protagonists in their combined struggle against the oppressive reactionary regime, the enforced postponement of political responsibility allowed the opposition the luxury of ideological schisms between political sects. Moderate liberal constitutionalists were soon separated from the more radical democratic parliamentarians, and the shrewd political maneuvers of Bismarck fully exploited his antagonists' divisions, especially during the critical period of the constitutional conflict from 1862 to 1866.

The National Liberals, champions of the constitutional monarchy and national unification, became the staunch supporters of the Iron Chancellor, who had brought about—no matter how—the much-admired Second Empire, while the Progressives held on to their democratic ideal of parliamentary government which had been frustrated by Bismarck's "Blood and Iron" revolution from above. Moreover, this party schism, cutting right through the middle class, was reiterated by social differentiations. The National Liberals established themselves as the representation of the industrial society, and this party found itself fully rewarded by a working agreement with the ruling Junker class. In return for the support of high corn tariffs for the landed

aristocracy, the "barons of the factory chimneys" received a promise of protection for "infant" industries, a favorable fiscal policy, and the unreserved governmental support of ambitious aspirations for colonial markets. Bismarck's fluctuating party machinations notwithstanding, the National Liberals commanded powerful influence and always remained the proudest standard bearer of Germany's imperialistic drives and the unquestioning defender of the Second Empire's policies and institutions. Indeed, the Liberal party was the prototype of a feudalized bourgeoisie, which, according to the formula of the "Bismarckian Compromise," acquiesced in the political dictates of an experienced ruling caste, accepted its set of values and images, and had its middle-class sons share in the government's spoils as "lieutenant in reserve," as loyal civil servants and second-class aristocrats.

The unreconciled Progressives, on the other hand, comprised the proud self-conscious classes of commerce and banking in the traditionally world-minded Hansa cities of Hamburg, Bremen, and Lübeck and in the spreading new trade centers of central Germany. They embraced a policy of free trade and looked to the British parliamentary government as their ideal political image. As the years went by, this fratricidal strife among Germany's middle classes became more embittered. Political alignments clearly followed the lines of mounting economic divergencies. Such contrasts definitely established the Progressives as left-wing opponents of the regime and the National Liberals as a rightist party in support of the powers in being.[2]

2. The Conservative party itself had also attained a mass base below its customary ruling aristocracy by appealing to the *petite bourgeoisie* of craftsmen and small businessmen. Spokesman for this movement was Hermann Wagener, editor of the first conserv-

The Emergence of Socialism

This conservative turn of a large segment of the bourgeoisie was partly the result of a fearful reaction against the emerging socialist movement. These erstwhile allies of the revolution against feudalism were quickly stamped a threatening force of unwanted radical upheavals. The fateful year 1848 had brought forth the *Communist Manifesto,* the clarion call of a new, self-confident, and rapidly increasing proletariat. By the 1860's the working classes had found a powerful political organization, which, in less than half a century, had attracted a third of the electorate and had become the strongest party and the leading opposition of the empire.[3]

Naturally, such success gave cause for alarm to the politically still immature middle classes, which in large numbers sought protection against the "Red Peril" from the strong state that promised they would remain "boss at home." In return for such support in the economic sphere, the burgher gave up his political birthright to the feudal guarantors of law and order. The serious consequences of such surrender became fully obvious only when the middle class was belatedly called to political responsibility in the days of the Weimar Republic. Such was the

price paid for governmental backing in the Second Empire.

Equally tragic was the fact that the German monarchy did not allow for the growth of an equivalent to the British "His Majesty's Opposition." This made it difficult, if not impossible, for the Socialists to develop a responsible alternative government. Such a historical fate also had far-reaching effects on the party's inner development. Many deep-seated discrepancies between theory and practice, between class allegiance and national consciousness, throughout its tense party history can be derived from this abnormal exclusion of a major social class from political responsibility.

The proletariat did not want to be rejected as the party of *vaterlandslose Gesellen* and almost by a stroke of genius created, instead, a substitute world, a state within the state, a social habitat, an orderly organization of disciplined daily performance—indeed, next to the army and bureaucracy, the most Prussian institution of the empire. In this sense the Social Democratic party has always been a deeply national movement and, for better or for worse, has often "compromised" party principles for national concerns. This partisan sacrifice, painful though it be to its follower, and even treacherous in the eyes of a consistent international socialism, has made the movement a school for responsible statesmanship and in many ways the first genuine party in the German political system. It may not be surprising, therefore, that the SPD survived even the Nazi onslaught and reappeared in the Second Republic as the only "traditional" party of weight.

The Zentrum—a Stranger to the German Party System

There was another political group that, for almost a century, could claim equal, if not greater, success in its polit-

ative German newspaper, the *Kreuzzeitung* (1848), and founder of the *Preussische Volksverein* (1861) to counteract the liberal appeal among the middle classes. In their double fear of becoming victims of highly developed capitalism and proletarian socialism, the *Kleinbürger* allied themselves with the pre-capitalistic forces and, from then on, became a power to be reckoned with in modern mass society, until they emerged as the crucial stratum in the era of rising National Socialism.

3. In 1863 Ferdinand Lassalle founded his General Association of German Workers, to be followed in 1869 by Liebknecht-Bebel's International Workers' Association. Both groups merged in the German Social Democratic party at the Gotha party congress in 1875.

ical war. Significantly, this Zentrum was not based on any class orientation and in this sense was, from the very outset, different from all other parties. It constituted the political organization of the Catholic minority.[4] Threatened by the Protestant ruling class of the unitary new empire, the "Center" party remained the champion of a federalistic greater Germany that would include Catholic Austria and could thus redress the confessional balance. Bismarck's futile *Kulturkampf* (just as his fatal war on the Socialists enhanced the consolidation of his opposition forces instead of destroying them) was in this sense a continuation of the Austro-Prussian War of 1866 and definitely put the "ultramontane" Zentrum into the anti-Prussian camp.[5] This fact was not changed by the party's tactical *rapprochement* and temporary predominance in governmental coalitions. It only proved that the Zentrum soon attained, and always kept, the position of strategic center between the rightist and leftist wings.

This peculiar strength and amazing flexibility of the Zentrum had a good deal to do with its unique character, which differentiated it from the historical type of German party. Under the unifying, yet loose, bond of religious attachment, it combined seemingly divergent streams of conservatism, liberalism, and radical social reforms (bordering on socialism) and attracted members of heterogeneous social groups from landed aristocracy to small farmers, heavy industry to working class, tradesmen to handicraft workers.

Spanning the crosscurrents of ideas and social forces, the Zentrum purposely shunned the extreme and doctrinaire position. It was by no means an oversight that for almost fifty years the political platform of the short *Soester Wahlprogramm* (1870), with its mere nine directives, sufficed as a party program. In the words of leading centrist spokesmen, the party freely applied its basic principles, adjusted them to the changing ideas of the times, and thus realistically and continuously redefined its own position.[6]

It was the party of *Ausgleich,* aspiring to a dynamic redress of political forces in a daily restored balance and compromise. For this course it was often denounced by its opponents as an unscrupulous, unprincipled, opportunistic power group unfit for German politics.

In a way it was a stranger to the German party system and approached more the typical patterns and politics of Western constitutional parties. Attracting members from different social strata and divergent ideological leanings, it had to resolve basic conflicts within its own ranks and thus became a school of politics par excellence. No wonder that it has contributed such a remarkable share of statesman-like leadership from the days of its founder, Ludwig Windhorst, to its present personification in Adenauer. His Christian Democratic Union (CDU), as a careful structural analysis will show, can in some respects be regarded as a new party in a new

4. It had found a significant forerunner in the Katholische Fraktion (of 1852) which was organized in the fight against the anti-Catholic educational policies of Prussia's minister Von Raumer. This religious basis gave the party a unique stability of about 20 per cent of the electorate, which, incidentally, indicated that it comprised not more than about 60 per cent of the Catholic population.

5. It was a testimony to the chancellor's political instinct that he predicted an alliance between Zentrum and social democracy, after an eventual breakdown of the empire, as it actually materialized in the Weimar coalition.

6. It is equally interesting to note that not before 1911 did the party develop a unified organization, which seemed to be unnecessary in view of the persistent support from the Catholic church. This may be compared with similar delays in the development of the Christian Democratic machine after 1945.

political setting. Despite close threads of personnel and program, it does not even claim to be the Zentrum's legal successor.[7] Yet it perfectly illustrates the old Center's sensitivity to the changing demands of the times. In this sense it may again fill its historical position as a bridge in the radical transformations from the erstwhile Second Empire to

II / THE WEIMAR REPUBLIC

A study of the pattern and politics of the German party system during the Weimar period suggests three major aspects: (1) the new elements added to its traditional edifice; (2) the cause of its radical breakdown within the short span of hardly fourteen years; and (3) its lasting effects on the re-established

TABLE 1

PANORAMA OF MAJOR POLITICAL PARTIES IN THE SECOND EMPIRE

	PARTIES				
	Social Democrats (SPD)	Progressives (Fortschritts-partei) (Liberale Vereinigung)	Center Party Zentrum	National-Liberals (National-Liberale)	Conservatives (Conservative, Freiconservative)
Ideologies.........	Socialism	Democracy	Catholicism	Liberalism	Conservatism
Predominant social alignments......	Proletariat	Commercial middle class	Cross-section	Industrial middle class	Feudal aristocracy, Army, bureaucracy, Protestant church, small trade, and handicraft
Approximate percentage of electoral votes:					
1871...........	3.2	16.5	18.6	30.0	23.0
1912...........	34.8	12.3	16.4	13.7	12.2
Average.........	30	14	18	18	20
Political coalitions..	The Opposition Parties of July resolution during World War I Weimar coalition			The "Ruling" parties Fatherland's Front National opposition in Weimar	

the Second Republic. It must be essentially a different party, since the drastic development of the Weimar Republic and the Third Reich could not have been without a deep impact on a live movement.

Before recording these intervening experiences, a chart of the early German party system may serve as a recapitulation of its comparatively simple scheme and as a suggestive indication of its long-range effects (Table 1).

party government of the Second Republic. The November revolution of 1918 and, in its wake, the Weimar Constitution, confronted the German parties with a completely new and decisive

7. This claim has been raised with probably less justification by a splinter group, which under the old name of Zentrum attracted a segment of the Catholic workers' vote in the Rhineland until the September elections of 1953 nearly destroyed all small parties, including the Zentrum. It received only two representatives, by the grace of the CDU.

situation, even though the constitution never mentioned them as crucial forces in policy decisions.[8]

At first sight the outer appearance of the parties did not seem to change, even though they temporarily adopted new names, legitimizing the old and momentarily discredited imperial parties by affixing to their labels the attribute of "People's party," in order to prove to the young republic that within their domain, too, "the power of the state derives from the people" (Preamble to the Weimar Constitution). Unfortunately, the new nomenclature was soon forgotten, and the heritage and basic positions of the prewar parties were re-established.

Radical-Wing Parties: Left and Right

The only change in the traditional panorama was the addition of two wing parties to the right and left of the five major groups. Eventually, these radical outsiders were to seal the fate of the Republic by squeezing the historical parties in the middle out of their majority position. This was the irresponsible play of a negative majority combining forces in parliament while fighting each other in a life-and-death struggle in the streets of Berlin.[9]

8. The only reference made to political parties is a negative statement: "governmental officers are servants of the whole, not of a party" (Art. 13c). This lack of a positive definition is not accidental but illustrates the fundamentally liberal conception of the founders of the constitution, to whom a party was based on free competition and free representation without any institutional ties. Article 21 of the Weimar Constitution gave testimony of such an attitude, though the parliamentary practice was most certainly different from this proposition. The completely different treatment of political parties and the specific emphasis on their policy-making role in the Bonn document is most revealing for a new, realistic appraisal of these key forces in politics (compare Art. 21 of the Bonn *Grund-Gesetz*).

The rise of these intransigent radical factions spelled the end of the Weimar Republic and the beginning of the new era of the dictatorial party. Yet not before the attack on the republic became a two-front war (i.e., with the Nazi avalanche of 1930) did left-wing radicalism seriously threaten the established party system. In fact, the early appearance of the Communists hardly constituted a surprising phenomenon. In a way it was merely the belated organization of an inner conflict of long standing, that for decades had split the Social Democratic party between its revisionist and its radical wing. Now the outer necessities of the SPD demanded vital decisions, whether to turn to Weimar's parliamentary democracy or to accept the Communist alternative, which for the first time was concretized in the neighboring Soviet Union's bolshevism. Such inescapable choices brought the traditional ideological battle down to earth and forced the partisans to take a stand.

This parting found its prelude in the split-off of the Independent Socialists (USPD), who, rejecting war credits and Social Democratic support of the government during World War I, bolted the party as a separate parliamentary fraction (in 1916) and soon as an independent party (in 1917). Within this new group, however, the old contrasts prevailed. The revisionist Bernstein and the left-bourgeois Breitscheid were colleagues of radical Marxists like Wilhelm Ledebour and Otto Rühle. No wonder that after the original *raison d'être* for a separate party (the issue of war) had become obsolete

9. Such abuse of the parliamentary machinery by antiparliamentary forces led the fathers of the Second Republic to introduce the much-disputed Article 67, which permits the overthrow of a cabinet only if the vote of nonconfidence is effected by a majority ready and able to take over governmental power.

with the end of hostilities, the USPD was dissolved (at the party congress at Halle, 1920), letting its right wing return to the old SPD, while its left wing naturally found a home in the Communist party (which had been officially launched on January 1, 1919).

When the shock of the sudden collapse of the "invincible" empire was absorbed by the German people and the mist of their confusion was lifting, the traditional party system reappeared in its old structure. Even its numerical representation in the first regular parliamentary election of 1920 approximated the accustomed prewar distribution. Especially if one adds the larger

major shifts, from a first uneasy groping for their new role, to a self-confident position in the middle span, to the makeshift and final surrender of party government vis-à-vis extra-parliamentary forces and dictatorial power.[10]

The SPD—the National Liberals of the Republic

This fatal outcome notwithstanding, from the very beginning the parties understood their new position and possibly their perplexities too. This was especially true of the Socialists. The SPD had become the "National Liberals" of the democratic republic—a label which pointed at the party's his-

TABLE 2

VOTE (PERCENTAGES)

Elections	SPD	DDP	Zentrum	DVP	DNVP
1912	34.8	12.3	16.4	13.7	12.2
1920	21.7 (plus 17.9 USPD)	8.3	18.1	13.9	14.9

percentage of the USPD vote to the SPD, which the bulk of the Independents joined soon after the elections, the picture becomes quite conclusive (Table 2).

And yet a radical shift had occurred, dictated by the simple fact that the pseudo-parliamentary rule of the empire had made room for a political system that called for responsible parties. Did the parties recognize the signs of the times? Did they give the proper response to their historical challenge? Did they meet their first major test?

Theirs was, in truth, the story of the Weimar Republic. It unfolded in three poignant phases: the war-after-the-war period, the Locarno era of rehabilitation and reconstruction, and the mounting crisis leading up to the rise of Hitler's Third Reich. The political parties reflected and articulated these three

torical deeds, its inner discrepancies, and its fatal dilemmas. At the same time, more than any other party, the SPD epitomized the crucial stages of the Weimar Republic, its glory and its shame, its legacies of the past, its specific contributions as a live laboratory of radical party government, its early

10. The number of cabinets is indicative of this shifting stability of party government. Only six cabinet changes occurred between 1924 and 1929, while the first phase saw twice that number during a period of equal length. The artificial life of the four presidential cabinets (Brüning, Papen, Schleicher, and, finally, Hitler) in the last stage of the Republic, however, was no measure of the parties' strength. On the contrary, by that time they had, for all practical purposes, given up their parliamentary control and, through the machinery of "constitutional dictatorship" and its "enabling emergency legislation," had handed over the government to the executive and the powers "behind the throne."

crisis and collapse, and its forewarnings and forebodings of things to come.

The record of the First Republic is rich and worth recording. Its recurring themes, its lessons and lasting problems, may well be taken up in a discussion of the present parties of the Second Republic. Here only a few highlights should be mentioned, serving as pointers to the protagonists' fateful plight.

The beginnings indeed were not very promising. The parties, called to power, were charged with a heavy mortgage of the past regime which had gone down in defeat, yet had not allowed the growth of an alternative "shadow cabinet." Yet the so-called "Weimar coalition," jumping into the breach, comprised the same parties which had been the declared opposition factions of the empire; they had re-established their position during the war in the parliament's majority resolution of July, 1917, demanding "peace without annexation." There was continuity and persistence in this unofficial opposition to the Bismarckian-Wilhelminic Reich, and in the end there was even a "legalized" transfer of power from Prince Max von Baden (the last imperial chancellor) to Socialist Friedrich Ebert (leader of the strongest opposition party).

For all practical purposes, the Reich represented, underneath its bewildering multifarious groupings, a hidden two-party system. Again, as in its very beginnings in 1848, the challenge of the organized peace opposition was promptly met by the governmental forces through the creation of the Vaterlandspartei ("Fatherland's Front"), propagandizing far-reaching conquests. This policy found its last unhappy realization in the short-lived separate treaties of Brest-Litovsk with the Soviet Union and of Bucharest with Rumania (1918) —hardly six months before Ludendorff's arrogant military dictatorship, in a weak moment at least, had to confess its complete failure and the emperor

unheroically left the field to the utterly surprised parliamentary parties.

Their heritage from the imperial regime was the stigma of its defeat (with which they were soon identified in the peoples' mind) and a pathetic unpreparedness for the task to which the old masters had not admitted them. This double liability gave the nationalist parties the doubly unfair advantage of making themselves the guardians of Germany's national honor and of the traditional skills of the army and bureaucracy. Their good offices, though mostly offered with mere lip service, were needed by the new power-holders, who could never fully overcome their indebtedness and inferiority toward the more experienced.

DNVP—Loyal Opposition or Intransigent Party?

Despite those historical handicaps, the efforts of the parties to live up to their new role and the actual transformations they underwent were amazing. These shifts were not only visible within the new ruling republican majority but also within the opposition groups. It was more than a tactical move when the German National People's party (DNVP), in its original proclamation (*Gründungsaufruf*, November 22, 1918), declared the opposition's readiness to co-operate "on the basis of the parliamentary form of government which alone would be feasible after the latest events." The party, formed to organize the counterrevolution and to fight the Republic unrelentingly, thus agreed to "face facts" in order to serve its own vital social groups within the framework of the new state. Such a decision indicated deep inner conflicts within the DNVP between absolute opposition and active co-operation with the Republic—in this respect a fate similar to the inner tensions of the SPD within the empire.

So long as the Republic was a functioning political community, even its opposition forces tried to become an integrated part. By no mere accident was the new party leadership of the DNVP recruited not from the old-established and much discredited Junker caste (such as its prewar leader, Baron von Heydebrand) but from the relatively uncommitted imperial civil service (Dr. Delbrück, Count Posadovsky, Dr. Helfferich, Dr. Hergt, etc.). By their very nature, they could not remain in a persistently opposition position; neither could their mass following.

Moreover, with the loss of the old state machinery as a taken-for-granted basis of conservative party strength, it now became necessary to recruit a political following through a party apparatus for which the rightist parties had had no need before 1918 and which, in fact, they did not possess. The new postrevolutionary conservative parties did not develop a machine equal to that of the SPD, nor, no doubt, did they aspire to the latter's centralization. Until today, local and regional organizations have played a more significant part in the conservatives' organizations everywhere. Yet even in the DNVP the control of the party apparatus became the shibboleth of power, as a bitter conflict between the inner pary factions soon vividly illustrated.

These shifts were a barometer of the Republic's markedly improved status. While the DNVP kept aloof during the first period (although even then it rejected unmistakably radical "putschists," such as Kapp in 1920 and Hitler in 1923), its economic interests bound the party increasingly to the political center. The entrance of the neighboring German Peoples party (DVP) into a "great coalition" with Weimar's republican forces (Fehrenbach cabinet, June, 1920–May, 1921) gave an additional boost to this trend.

By the mid-twenties the DNVP had become a governmental party, participating in the Luther cabinet of 1925 and the Marx cabinet of 1927. It was always the economic force which pushed and threatened in this direction —the powerful industrial organizations, expecting an economic revival from the acceptance of the Dawes Plan; the Reichslandbund, fighting for agrarian tariffs; and the German National Organization of Trade Employees (DNHV), interested in social legislation. They all could not afford to remain outside the state. Moreover, psychological ferments came into play. In the long run, no vital force can live in resentment. (The waning of the dictators' opponents in a prolonged diaspora, abroad or at home, has presented telling examples in our time.) It was one of the most remarkable, though least noted, achievements of Gustav Stresemann, Weimar's foreign minister and mastermind of the Locarno period, that he freed (by his own complete turn from his monarchical past) a generation of young middle-class sons from such oppressing resentment and that he won them over to a positive stand for the Republic.[11]

This process of *rapprochement* was interrupted by the economic crisis of the late twenties, which ushered in the radicalization of German politics. Under the leadership of Dr. Hugenberg, the captain of industry and powerful newspaper magnate who gained control of the party (October, 1928), the DNVP made its fatal turn to the "National Opposition," which led it from the so-called "Harzburg Front" (initiating a plebiscite against the Young Plan) to Hitler's National Cabinet of January 30, 1933, and to the end of the German party system, including the DNVP.

11. This influence of Stresemann is a historical fact, whatever a new evaluation of his personality may reveal.

Splinter Parties—Ideological and Economic Interest Groups

There were, even at that late stage, forces at work within the German Reich which resisted this deadly drift, yet all they could master were insignificant splinter groups, reiterating the persistent fate of moderate conservatism throughout German history: the union of notable leaders without a crucial following.[12] They certainly could not stem the radical storm that was overwhelming the crisis-ridden land. Neither could the attempts at a political organization of economic interest groups, which were mushrooming in late Weimar's multiparty potpourri. Their numerical growth in parliament notwithstanding (rising from 1 per cent in 1919 to 8 per cent in 1930), they could not answer the needs of a sick society. In fact, they contradicted the essential function of political parties, whose major task is the integration of special interests into a political whole.

The questionable character of special-interest parties was exemplified *ad absurdum* in the Deutsche Wirtschaftspartei (German Business party), which, under the leadership of masterbaker Drewitz, attracted voters from the small bourgeoisie of impoverished craftsmen, shopkeepers, landlords, innkeepers, and *rentiers*, who had been the main victims of the money inflation. They remembered the better days of the past, which they tried to retrace in their one-track line of immediate needs. By necessity, theirs was more often than not a dead-end street.

The Wirtschaftspartei in parliament was helpless in the face of crucial political decisions, and frequently irresponsible too. What other orientation toward major issues of foreign politics could be gained from the price of bread but a tactical one? This did not have much to do with politics. Fundamentally, the followers of the Business party did not care for political decisions. They had resigned from politics or were prepolitical, but in any case they were apolitical. They were the typical nonvoters, pressed into political campaigns only by their economic plight. This very fact, however, gave them, with the help of proportional representation, a respectable strength and therefore at times a decisive position in the constantly shifting fronts of the unstable Brüning regime (1930–32). When the crisis reached its height (resulting partly from the activities of those parties which did not live up to their proper role), the Wirtschaftspartei was washed away by the great wave of popular unrest.

This was the hour of crisis for the entire German party system. Many elements entered into the making of this complete collapse. It should not be explained, or excused, or minimized by reference to any one of the great number of isolated elements: the technical shortcomings of the electoral system and obvious constitutional anomalies, the lack of dynamic leadership and petrifaction of the party apparatus, the programmatic saturation and disturbing ideological anemia. All these factors and many more doubtless played their part in the disintegration of the system.[13] Yet the deeper causes must be sought in the parties' inability to integrate and recruit large segments of the populace within their ranks.

It was a total crisis which was at the base of Weimar's breakdown. Only a comprehensive analysis of the plight of the major crucial strata could expose

12. The three major split-offs—the Konservative Volkspartei, the Landvolk, and the Christlich-sozialer Volksdienst—recruited in the elections of 1930 not more than 8 per cent of the electorate.

13. Even the fulfilment or general acceptance of its prior principles could lead to the rapid decline of a party which must represent a specific program and must always reach out for new aims. The fate of the DDP is a case in point.

Germany's alarming dilemmas, which were unscrupulously exploited by the rising Nazi movement. In turn the structure and strategy, the direction and final character, of the new radical movements of the left as well as of the right wing were largely defined by this total societal upheaval. It brought forward a new party, if such an emblem could properly be affixed to a totalitarian monolithic order.

III / THE TOTALITARIAN PHASE

The Lasting Significance of German National Socialism

The National-sozialistische Deutsche Arbeiterpartei (NSDAP) was the prototype of the modern totalitarian party. Its rise and fall suggest far-reaching comparisons and propositions in respect to its elder brother, fascism (which it soon outstripped), and its powerful precursor and conqueror, the Bolshevik party, which by now has become the chief concern, caveat, and contestant of the functioning democratic parties of the world. Despite the demise of the Third Reich, we are dealing with a vital issue of our time when we retrace the origin, staying power, and legacy of the Nazis.

The totalitarian party is the child and political articulation of permanent revolution. It feeds on *all* elements of unrest and therefore presents a most diversified panorama in each nation. Crisis strata may exist everywhere, yet they must be seen in their specific setting—historical, geographic, national. Caution is in order for any quick and easy transfer of totalitarian experiences. The theory of crisis strata underlying this interpretation has the advantage of allowing both for a general systematization and for its application to a peculiar one-party state.

The German case deserves a special hearing, but not so much on account of its characteristically painstaking plan-

ning, comprehensive coverage, and dire consequences. Although its complicated and clocklike machinery was, no doubt, most impressive to a horrified Western world while it was running at full speed, its sudden collapse revealed its basic flaws and made it, at best, a historical study. For this the contemporary state of the Soviet party might serve as a richer and more comprehensive mine of intelligence and direction for proper response.

What remains crucial in our concern about the Nazi interlude is, above all, the detection of the persistent breaks in German society which allowed such a radical revolution to originate—apart from an exposition of this one-party system, the stages of its development, its controls and tensions, and its lasting effects on Germany's political landscape.

Breaks in German Society and the Rise of the Crisis Strata

The breakdown of the German democratic party system was part and parcel of a total upheaval of German society. Reaching beyond, it was in fact the spearhead, articulation, and advanced stage of a wider European crisis. Whether this disintegration of a traditional society represented an irreversible trend can at the present only be surmised. Yet its lasting effects are serious enough to suggest a warning signal, despite the surprisingly vigorous recovery of the Second German Republic.

Such a watchful approach might be reinforced by recalling the equally amazing stabilization of the Weimar state in the mid-twenties, before it was overtaken by the break-through of undermining forces of long standing. So far as the German political parties were concerned, the seeming return to normalcy was effective even within the SPD, which had been the declared champion of a new society. The most perplexing phenomenon of the party during the Weimar days was the much-commented-on *Verbürgerlichung* ("process of becoming bourgeois-minded"), which made it a movement of workers who, differing from their prophet's prediction, had more to lose than their chains. The achievements of the Republic with its institutions of social security and economic improvement had something to do with it. No doubt, its continuing share in government responsibilities contributed to the change in the SPD's social structure, though an exact statistical breakdown of membership figures cannot be had.[14]

This shift in composition was furthered by developments within the SPD's neighboring parties, by the continuous decline of the DDP to its right, and the steady rise of the Communists to its left. Now the SPD became the party of the skilled workers and the lower officialdom of state and party. Unquestionably it had taken on a *petit bourgeois* outlook.

Such marked changes confronted the SPD with many new problems, some of which soon became central, such as the crucial matter of recruiting new leadership and a new social following. Most talked about was the related petrifaction of the party machine, which proved to be an effective issue in election campaigns against the "parties' state." *Kampf dem Bonzentum* became the battle cry of the non-Marxist parties (though they, in turn, aspired to possess the same organizational weapon, which in fact has become a "must" in

any mass society and a guarantor of party stability and growth). Indeed, in the name of popular antiparty and antimachine sentiment the Nazis set out to build their own superparty of the leviathan state—one of the many of its deceptive contradictions.

No doubt, hierarchical organization carried with it the dangers of depersonalized mechanization of a party, most apparent in the successful social democracy of the First Republic. This side of the process of *Verbürgerlichung* seemed to be almost unavoidable and did not remain unnoticed among the partisans.[15]

More surprising was the fact that the movement, even in its responsible quarters, did not fully recognize the fundamental changes within German society, especially the impact of the rising salaried classes. It was in this stratum that emerging National Socialism found its most ardent recruits.

The extraordinary quantitative growth of the white-collar man in modern industrial society led also to a qualitative change in his social prestige. His had become a static class position, if not a castelike predicament. At the same time, the discrepancy between his actual status and his now unfulfilled traditional aspirations of eventual independence and individual security made this group the frustrated class par excellence. This fate was re-emphasized in Germany by the specific experiences of a military defeat, money inflation, and radical economic depression, all of which hit the salaried employees the hardest. Thus a total crisis revolution-

14. Interestingly enough, even in the empire around one-fourth of the SPD electorate was recruited from nonproletarian sources. Neisser assumed in 1930 (that crucial year of the Nazi rise) a 40 per cent middle-class vote for the SPD, representing under a proportional system an even more direct declaration of sympathy on the part of the voters than in the prewar majority system, which, especially in the second ballot, forced the electorate to choose "the lesser evil."

15. The size of the bureaucracy, often inflated in the estimate of ardent opponents, amounted, in fact, to hardly more than 10,000; these succeeded in recruiting 1,000,-000 individual members and, more important, in preventing party fluctuation. More than 50 per cent of the SPD membership was organized within the party for more than five years.

ized this stratum, which could no longer expect the fulfilment of the middle-of-the-road parties' promise of "sharing the wealth" in an expanding economy. Neither was the salariat attracted by the Socialists' vague image of a planned society in which individual frustrations would be absorbed and sublimated by a rising class status.

National Socialism seemed to offer a satisfactory answer, with its simple solution of world conquest by the "master-race" which channeled desperate personal perplexities into outer drives of nationalist expansion. It satisfied emotional hungers, historical traditions, and activists' escapism from the bad dream of reality into the no man's land of utopia. This easy victory of demagoguery, in its strange combination of a romantic turn to a lost past and the claim of a social revolution for a "new order," was possible for a drifting middle class which was unprepared for daily public responsibilities and thus accepted short cuts of grandiose schemes.

This first mass layer of Nazi followers was reinforced by the equally uprooted unemployed, comprising more than one-fifth of the labor force and representing the political driftwood of the late Weimar Republic. They had this much in common with the thwarted *Kleinbürger:* in their craving for belonging they had also become the prisoners of this revolution of nihilism. Their masterminds were the irregulars, products of the war's chaos which they were not ready or able to forsake. They were truly the children of the war; it hit them in those formative years of life when man makes up his mind as to his lasting ties of friendship, love, profession, and social belonging. They chose the life of soldiers of fortune. They never returned home from World War I; they fought on wherever fighting was going on; and they finally succeeded in marching their own people into the bloodier battles of the second holocaust.

Every society is liable to harbor a certain percentage of irregulars, who do not fit its established agencies, patterns, and policies and who are in permanent conflict with its order. Wars and revolutions especially will bring such human flotsam to the surface. A nation's healthy institutions can usually control and check these outsiders. It is only when they find receptive mass strata whose own frustrations have uprooted them and have disintegrated their natural societal ties that the soldiers of fortune become a real menace to the state. This is their hour to strike. Now they usurp the role of the articulators of the masses' vague desires. And self-appointed new leaders put the people on the march to establish a new order. Such was the historical chance of the small band of Nazi leaders, who knew what they wanted in those depression days of the early thirties. They made themselves the proud challengers of the bourgeois world and the spokesmen for the middle class and their despair in a civic society.

It should be stated at the outset that these outsiders of society could succeed in conquering the state only by their shrewd alliance with the reactionary forces of Hugenberg, Seldte, Schacht, and Papen, who held crucial societal positions and who, in their pathetic misjudgment of the irregulars' revolutionary *élan,* deceived themselves in the naïve belief that they could control and streamline the revolution of the unscrupulous. Yet the "respectable experts" were appropriately used and dismissed as soon as they had served their usefulness to the usurpers. They in turn defined the rules of the game and established a one-party state.

Strategies of Conquest

The Nazi rise to power, different from Italian fascism—and, indeed, from the

Soviet seizure of power—did not succeed in a sudden coup d'état of a small band of aroused revolutionaries. The ill-famed Munich Putsch of November, 1923, frustrated the attempt to launch another march on the capital as Mussolini had staged his on Rome (in a sleeping car from Milan, to be sure, after being assured by phone that weak King Victor Emmanuel would become the throne behind the power of Il Duce). After their failure the Nazis had to try it the hard way, via the parliamentary route and routine.

This divergent strategy had a good deal to do with the different structure of the two fascistic parties. The development of a highly efficient and centralized party machine became a necessity for the NSDAP, and therefore the role of its lieutenants was tremendously enhanced.[16] It was no mere accident that they became definitely identified —Göring, Goebbels, Strasser, *et al.* There was no simple changing of the guards à la Mussolini or the popular wholesale liquidation of the Soviet brand. Moreover, in a highly stratified Germany the Nazi lieutenants represented and brought into the party their special clientele; thus they could command patronage and legitimately ex-

16. This fact, however, should not obscure the amazing fluctuations in personnel on the top level of Hitler's hierarchy. Leaving aside the turbulent times of the early days and the forgotten founders Harrer and Drexler, and beginning the chronology only after the movement was stabilized under the unchallenged leadership of Hitler, one could draw up the following list (in five-year intervals) of powerful henchmen:
1925—Gregor Strasser, Göring, Streicher, Feder, Rosenberg
1930—Gregor Strasser, Göring, Goebbels, Röhm, Frick
1935—Göring, Goebbels, Himmler, Schacht, Hess
1940—Göring, Hess, Himmler, Ribbentrop, Brauchitsch
1945—Bormann, Goebbels, Speer, Keitel (if in the turmoil of the last year of Hitler's tyranny any lineup was possible)

pect a share of the spoils. It was a feudal Third Reich, presided over by Hitler, the Overlord, who indeed took the personal loyalty of his vassals-in-chief most seriously.

The NSDAP started out as a conspiratorial movement, which it remained at its inner core, adding in its use of the parliamentary ruse a respectable mass following on its outer fringe. This was the only promising way to gain power among a people of law-abiding citizens. Yet it also created a deep dualism and the fatal division of the movement—between the revolutionary and the reactionary—even before the seizure of power. While such double standards of the leaders and the rank and file are characteristic of the intrenched totalitarian party, once it is in power, rising bolshevism had remained true to Lenin's dictum of a small elitist group of professional revolutionaries waiting for a "revolutionary situation" to activate the amorphous masses only for *one* crucial moment.

The democratic disguise of rising National Socialism was no doubt more complete, including all the paraphernalia of constitutionality and traditions through presidential appointment and Potsdam handshake. Yet the "parliamentary game" had been used by every totalitarian party in the preliminary stage of its seizure of power. Even the Bolsheviks did not neglect such a technique in their clever manipulation and channeling of the popular movements for peace, land, and national self-determination and in their original governmental coalition with the Mensheviks and Social Revolutionaries in the October Revolution of 1917. In fact, they have not forgotten these techniques in our time either, and it is only surprising that they can still succeed in using them in many places.

Fascists of all brands were even more successful in applying those strategies. During their initial period they tried to become respectable and, indeed, succeeded in reconciling many members of the national parties to those "wild radicals," whose emotionalism and exquisite fighting spirit the "well-experienced politicians" meant to use and to direct eventually into moderate channels. As a matter of fact, Nazi leaders often made their coalition partners believe that their radical talk was meant only for mass consumption and could be easily discarded when the hour of statesmanship arrived. So Hitler said to the captains of industry in 1931—and some of them believed him. And so did, in his time of success, a majority of the German people.

And yet a careful analysis of the inner party activities could have revealed the revolutionary character of the party even during this time of parliamentary respectability. From the outset, ruthless oppression of the opposition was the order of the day. Even the open party meetings were nothing but a staged demonstration of the new gospel and did not permit any dissenting vote. The storm troopers saw to its enforcement. Party purges were continuously going on within the dictatorial party (long before they received national and international prominence in the June purge of 1934). The relegation of Drexler, founder of the party, and the repudiation of Gottfried Feder, father of its twenty-five-point program, the suppression of the rebellion of Stennes and of the key lieutenants, the Strasser brothers—these are a few examples of the systematic molding of the party into a reliable weapon in the Fuehrer's hands. This stage was only preparatory to the final seizure of power. It showed the typical twofold technique of separate treatment for the insider and the outsider. While the party at this point was, above all, dictatorial within its own ranks, it still made conciliatory gestures in its relations to possible allies in the Reich.

After the seizure of power, the domain of totalitarianism was soon extended to include the whole nation, although the international world was still treated with some consideration in the hope of winning friends abroad. Within hardly a year[17] the last remnants of competing German parties were eliminated, and the sham coalition of the National Front cabinet of January, 1933, was transformed into the unchallenged one-party state and sealed by Hitler's succession to the presidency after Hindenburg's death.

In order to become a really total state, the complete *Gleichschaltung* ("enforced conformity") of all national institutions was imperative. This step took another four years, until even the most stubborn citadels, the army and the foreign office, surrendered in 1938, and Hitler was then ready to start his Napoleonic march to make the world his domain.

The One-Party State: Nature and Functions

The intrenched Third Reich is best described by four features: totalitarianism, institutionalization, the rule of the demagogue, and unlimited expansion. The Nazi party served as the enforcement agent of its fourfold functions. Originally the esoteric nucleus of the coming "New Order," it prepared itself for its first role as the recruiter of the ruling class, extending its totalitarian *Gleichschaltung* into all domains of human activity. This spelled the end of majority rule and minority rights, of spheres of personal privacy and respect for human dignity. Yet the continuity and efficiency of total power had to be bolstered by a second task: complete

17. This same transformation had taken Fascist Italy four long years. Fascism, however, never succeeded in attaining complete co-ordination of crucial state institutions such as the army and the foreign office. It never destroyed Italy's traditional social fabric; it never became fully totalitarian.

control and education of the masses. This involved the creation of a comprehensive net of organizations reaching from the top elite of the Fuehrer and his henchmen through the party nexus down to the lowest level of society—at home and in the neighborhood, in church and in school, at work and even in leisure time. Even these minute checks and controls did not suffice. Participation of the masses had to be assured in a postdemocratic dictatorship haunted by the peoples' democratic memories. Here is where the unique role of the demagogue came in. The "man of the people"—the "voice of the market place" in Mussolini's picturesque Mediterranean phrase, the "drummer" in Hitler's more robust and loud version —rising from the dark as an "unknown soldier," was their democratic chance of being powerful. The presumably "legal" seizure of power, through the unscrupulous employment of democratic institutions, the plebiscitary acclaim, established the myth of Goebbels' farcical "ennobled democracy."

The Nazi party was next charged with the vigilant maintenance of communication between state and society, to keep the powerful aware of the hidden popular grumblings and the people in line with government action—because, differing from historical forerunners, the Third Reich was dependent on mass acclaim. Popular participation was manipulated through three channels: institutions, violence, and propaganda. Apart from the all-pervasive positive ties of institutional controls, there was the negative check of enforced participation through terror. Government by fear was the very essence of the system. Yet it needed stronger assurances of popular support if it was to count on enduring popular backing.

This was the plan of comprehensive propaganda and public opinion control. In view of the ever present demagogic appeal to the emotional hungers of the aroused, distressed, and dispossessed, one should never underestimate Hitler's success on this score—so long as he *was* successful and could deliver the goods.

The elaborate efforts of propagandistic influence on the people were a necessity because of the fourth feature of naziism: its insatiable expansionism in order to preserve and justify its total hold on the people. Constant promises of peace to the contrary, the one-party state was fed by continuous belligerence. Its preservation and extension of power depended on the fulfilment of this last function. Originating in war, aiming at war, thriving on war, Hitler's Reich could redeem itself only in the unending battles of permanent revolution until this perpetual motion was stopped permanently by total defeat. As soon as it gave up fighting, it had to make room for a new conquering elite. The militant element not only was the driving force of the early fighting days but was predominant throughout the lifetime of the dictatorial government. It created all its essential attitudes and institutions: the readiness to battle, militancy, and discipline, the hierarchy of the party, and warlike obedience to orders from above. These features could not be removed from the dictatorial party which became the creator of the garrison state.

This enumeration of the party's services well proves its key position in the political edifice of modern totalitarianism. Yet to call such a dictatorial organization a "party" is a misnomer and often a conscious misconception, for the right to combine freely (the basic freedom of choice to participate in or to part from) is essentially denied. The dictatorial party's monopoly, which prevents the free formation and expression of opinion, is the precise antithesis of the party system.

What was the fundamental nature of a total party? It might, first of all, be defined as an *institution of public law*.

Not only did it achieve official standing and recognition, but the state defined its scope and function by specific legislation. The symbols of the party (the fasces, the hammer and sickle, the swastika) were adopted as the emblems of the state. But the fact of such a predominant and all-embracing position made it in the eyes of many critics extremely doubtful whether the party could be called an institution of public law such as municipalities, churches, and public utilities are. True, the dictatorial party received a charter from the state, signifying the latter's interest in its pursuits and therefore the right of control and inspection. But what could be the meaning of legal subordinacy in regard to an institution which, by its essence, claimed its identification with the state or even its irrefutable supremacy over the state? Such doubts pointed at the precarious dualism between state and party—one of the foremost problems of the one-party state. Its indissoluble contradictions could be seen within the institutional framework of every totalitarian state.

This much should be said here: while every dictatorship tries to strike a somewhat different balance between state and party, they all agree that to the dictatorial movement should be reserved the exclusive right of political volition, thus relegating to the state the mere execution of the will of the party. Whether such an interpretation still leaves to the state the sovereignty that is a precondition of its institutionalization of political agencies may be doubted. The party that merely makes use of the machinery of the state is sovereign. The concept of the party as an institution of public law thus becomes a legal fiction, important though it may be for winning over the conservative and neutral elements of the population and for creating a continuity of state loyalties.

In order to understand the reality of the dictatorial party, one should examine the nature of the dictatorial state. A second definition of the Fascist party as an *oligarchical fraternity* may answer such a query. The ruling class regarded itself as the creator of the revolutionary state, which, in turn, guaranteed the survival of the dictatorial minority. Its oligarchical character was basic for the dictatorial party. This became obvious in specific methods of co-optional self-renewal and regular membership purges. This fight of the elite for control against the outsiders of the party, against the nonparticipants in power, against the majority, and against the people created at the same time an inner-party democracy of the *Parteigenossen* (the party comrades). In fact, in spite of the pronounced social differentiation in the dictator's hierarchy, a democratic atmosphere of comradeship had to prevail among the insiders. The supreme leader set the tone for it, and the subleaders adopted it. The "community of trying experiences" created unity and loyalty, especially among the fighters of the "first hour." On those political battlefields thus arose a fraternity that could outlive many party crises and become the backbone of the party state. This political elite, fighting for the coming state and preconceiving its future existence, became the guardian of the new state when victory was won.

From such a concept, one has to proceed but one step to the definition of the party as the *nation in substance,* the awakened nation. According to such an analysis, the main function of the party was to represent the conscience of the nation, the true patriots, the trustees of the masses, the formative and driving force of the state, its organized minority—in short, the real state. "The Fascist party is the state." With this claim, it actually governed and administered the country and co-ordinated all the citizens' activities with its program. This characterization of the dictatorial party again led into hopeless contradictions between the "sovereign party" and the "strong state."

The Fascist party has been further called a *religious order.* "The party appears to us as a church, that is to say, a communion of faith, a union of wills and intentions loyal to a unique and supreme end," Panunzio stated. The inner driving forces of the modern dictatorial party are, no doubt, closely connected with this spiritual—one may almost say "semi-ecclesiastical"—character. The party is an asserter of faith, a faith that permeates all aspects of human destiny and reaches into the region of the absolute. Its totalitarian nature inevitably turns the party into a religious order, a theocracy. The faithful follow the party guide as the Jesuit Order made its followers ready for Christian service or Mohammed called upon his believers to fight the infidels.

The reality of the dictatorial party can be well described by this religious character. The party has its hierarchy, its rituals, its dogmas, its seminaries. It offers spiritual rewards and punishments. It prosecutes its mission also by administering material pain or pleasure. Fanaticism becomes the most significant feature of the zealous followers; heretics have to be converted, or they will be burned. To this end churches have always needed their militant orders and their missionaries. Institutions of propaganda were created to propagate the faith. Persuasion, stimulation, charitable works, public worship, and commemoration of saints and martyrs are consequential techniques of this new religious sect.

It is not a well-balanced program but a stirring myth that moves and possesses its followers. Georges Sorel (father of the most effective social myth and, in this respect, of fascism and bolshevism also) always stressed the religious origin

of the myth. Like religion, myth cannot be refuted. "We have created our myth. It is a belief, a passion. It does not matter whether it is reality. It becomes reality in us because it is faith and courage," Mussolini said shortly before he marched on Rome, inspired by the myth of the nation. Such secular revelation makes the movement as dogmatic, total, and intolerant as the *ecclesia militans.* It also helps to fill the empty space which has been created by the dissolution of basic religious concepts.

It was this quasi-religious character, above all, that made modern totalitarianism so great an object of suspicion to Japan, despite her otherwise autocratic tendencies. The radical social changes brought about in the Far East did not change the religious foundations of Japanese society. The Mikado-emperor remained the religious head of the nation. Prime ministers might be strong and military castes powerful; national movements might be created and strategic alliances with Axis powers played up—totalitarianism was still not acceptable to a nation which recognized "one sovereign over all, the Son of Heaven." In spite of the pronounced Westernization of Nippon, the secularization of the divine had certainly not progressed to the point of deifying political forces—a point which is the exact core of modern "faith movements" because the dictatorial party is, above all, the asserter of a new faith in an infidel world.

Finally, the Fascist party has been called a *civil militia.* In fact, the original meaning of *fascio* denoted a group of men armed for guerrilla warfare. The constitution of the fully intrenched movement defined the party along the same lines: "a civil militia under the order of Il Duce in the service of the Fascist state." Bolshevism is also "government by an armed sect," deriving far more from a wartime organization than from Marxist theory. The opening sentence of its new party statute (1952) characteristically reads: "The Communist Party of the Soviet Union is a voluntary militant union." For the NSDAP, the concept of the civil militia represented the most vital element of the dictatorial party.

Party Organization

These characteristic traits of the totalitarian movement naturally brought forward equally novel patterns of party organization. Military structure, hierarchical order, close-knit organization, and mass mobilization were the marked insignia of the party in power.

The belligerent nature of the dictatorial party found visible expression in its foremost feature: the *military structure*. Fascist parties centered around and crystallized in semi-military formations. In fact, the real life of the party began with the establishment of a "shirt" movement. Mussolini's Black Shirts and Hitler's Brown Shirts became the nucleus of the new movements. This is also true, though with some reservations, of Soviet Russia's Red army, the creation of the civil war. Indeed, a dictatorial party which does not succeed in organizing such a militant group does not establish totalitarian rule.

Because of a real or presumed danger, "defense organizations" were created which were called to "protect" the "peaceful" meetings of the rising party and "to free the street for the brown battalions." The fame of these *Saalschlachten* built up the myth of the party's defense corps. So did the Fascist punitive excursions into the "enemy's territory." Red villages and their Socialist mayors were "taught," with the help of castor oil during the small hours of the night, the fundamentals of a new heroic age. Burning trade-union buildings and destroying offices of the opposing parties spread the fame, fear, and repute of the rising movement, just as the Ku Klux Klan's night riders did in the restless South.

The military character of the party appealed especially to the crisis strata of shiftless irregulars. These first recruits of the movement became its most formative group. They owed everything to the party that took them back into society and gave them a stake in it. They became is most ardent fighters. They were fighters by profession.

The party in the hands of the legionnaires became basically a militant group. It preferred to call itself a fighting league (*Kampfbund*) instead of a party. It enrolled "military cadres" when it ventured a new orientation. Politics became a battlefield of two irreconcilable opponents who were out to win or to die. Military expressions became fashionable, and this turn toward a new and violent language was certainly more than a fashion. Captain Röhm of *Feme* murder fame and Balbo, a daring youth, became the prototypes of these novel movements. Followers were held in equally ruthless discipline; they had to follow the strict party line or face the party's purge.

The military nature of the dictatorial party was also seen in its second outstanding characteristic: its strict *hierarchical order*. Officers were appointed by their superiors, to whom alone they were responsible. They were beyond any control from below or outside. At the top of the pyramid would be found the general staff of the dictator: the Central Directorate of the National Socialist party, the Fascist Grand Council, the Politburo of the U.S.S.R. These are the "shadow cabinets" of modern autocracies and usually overshadow the official government as the actual power behind the power.

Here, again, the dualism between state and party became obvious, as it did throughout the whole political hierarchy down to local government, by a set of party offices paralleling the state bureaucracy. There was some unity of personnel in both hierarchies, more confusing overlapping of responsibilities, and always watchful control of official activities by the party officers enforcing the National Socialist world outlook everywhere. Constant interference to weaken the position of the state representatives was often only a preparation for the final storming of the "neutral" vestiges of the state. The shifts in key positions in the German ministries of economics and foreign affairs—from Schacht to Funk, from Neurath to Ribbentrop—were cases in question. The supreme party organ was the policy-making agency; thus the state offices were often degraded to the mere execution of policies decided in the party's inner circles.

The political hierarchy firmly established in a central body at the summit was carried through a whole set of regional organizations down to the smallest local party groups, from district leader to regional leader to local leader. National Socialism developed the system to perfection—and even beyond. Yet the undeniable frenzy of superorganization that no doubt contradicted the proverbial efficiency of modern dictatorships created an intricate system of checks and balances, which, though an artificial and costly substitute for democracy's open competition, strongly suggested the secret of dictatorship's efficacy.

This top-heavy mechanism, which draws practically every follower into a web of organizational controls from which there is no escape, at the same time manifests a third element of the political pattern: *close-knit organization*. It reflects dictatorial all-inclusiveness—the last step in a party's development from the loose and sporadic vote-getting organization to the totalitarian

order. A cell organization, taken over from the Bolshevik arsenal, is the partisan's keeper everywhere, especially in the sphere of his daily activities—at home, the watchful eye of the Blockwart; in the factory, the check of a circumspect Betriebszelle; during his leisure activities, the party's cultural organization, Kraft durch Freude. Thus a dictatorial hierarchy is fortified from below and made real by meeting and controlling its members in their day-to-day pursuits.

Dictatorships usually show a significant differentiation in their party mass mobilization between integral groups and affiliated associations, a differentiation which roughly corresponds to a separation between full-fledged members and mere followers. The first type represents the active core of the movement, specifically designated in National Socialism as the Storm Troopers (S.A.), the Elite Guard (S.S.), National Socialist Motor Corps (N.S.K.K.), Hitler Youth, National Socialist Student Association, and National Socialist Women's Organization. The second type enlarges the circle into wider areas of working organizations and professional groups—teachers, lawyers, physicians, technicians, public officials, etc. The German Labor Front in particular, with enforced membership for every working person of Aryan origin (employers included), reached down to the people.

Such expansion of the party's sway leads to a change of character on its periphery as well. Its actual composition shifts with an extension in space and time. Before the conquest of power the Fascist parties had an underrepresentation of farmers and manual workers and a prevalence of the typical crisis strata in the middle classes, as outlined earlier, especially among the hard-pressed white-collar employees and independent professionals.

Even more significant was the predominance of the younger age group and its continuous percentage rise before the seizure of power. Statistics for the total party membership in 1931 and 1932 show in this youngest set (eighteen to thirty years of age) an increase from 37.6 to 42.2 per cent. Compared with the age composition of the competing Social Democratic party, which had only 19.3 per cent of its membership in this age group, and with the age distribution of the country as a whole, where this same group represented only 31.1 per cent, the "youthfulness" of the National Socialists becomes obvious.

The victorious party showed a no less interesting change in its age composition. In 1935, only two years after the conquest of the state, a decrease to 35.4 per cent in the youngest age stratum was reported. This shift may reflect the typical fate of every revolutionary party grown big, old, and successful. The revolutionary has "arrived." Moreover, victory or imminent victory attracts the band-wagon followers—those less active, less daring, less revolutionary. It becomes safe to join.

Now the victorious movement has to ward off two opposite dangers at the same time. It may have to check the pretorian vanguard, which alone made victory possible but may thereafter endanger the stabilization of the new system. The victorious *condottiere* may thus accept Oswald Spengler's dictum: "The real master is known by the manner in which he dismisses them, ruthlessly and without thanks." Mussolini had done it; Hitler's June purge of 1934 seemed to suggest a similar move, though the following years brought a different course in Germany.

National Socialism was far more aware of the second danger: a weakening of the revolutionary spirit. Closing of the ranks, legalized privileges for the "old fighters," fanatical persistence on fighting strength, and a continuous acceleration of the revolutionary tempo—

these became acts of self-preservation. Hitler in his early writings proclaimed: "Thereafter solely the nucleus continues to lead." In fact, the entire leadership (with the significant exception of Hitler's personal confidants) was formed from "the basic stock of the old movement"; and even the few outsiders who had been taken in as experts by the victorious revolution were soon dropped, as the fates of Hjalmar Schacht, Karl Goerdeler, and Robert Schmidt so clearly prove.

The recruiting of party members after the party's seizure of power was almost exclusively reserved to special youth organizations. The party closed its ranks and admitted only new members who had risen through the recognized channels of its youth organization, membership in which was made compulsory for every child. The Hitler Jugend in the Third Reich, the Komsomols in Soviet Russia, the Balilla and Avantguardia in Fascist Italy not only guaranteed the future of the dictatorial party but at the same time served as a sifting process for bringing to the front reliable fighters for the cause. With this last link extended into the future, the political party became the nucleus and the training school for the ruling class.

Tensions, Breakdown, Aftermath

The seeming success in controlling the oncoming generation spelled at the same time one of the fundamental flaws of the dictatorial systems. It was easy to recruit little yes men, but the demands of complete submission were detestable to the independent minds among the best of the younger generation. They, in turn, developed a policy of outward conformity which covered up and concealed their detachment from, if not enmity to, the system ("emigrating at home"). In short, the party soon could not attract the enterprising and ingenious men of promise and thus could not really fulfil its crucial function: the selection of new leadership. Moreover, the petrifaction of the apparatus of the leviathan state brought out all the shortcomings of modern political bureaucratization.

These difficulties were accentuated by the fact that the total state, especially in its late stage of accelerated militant expansion reaching out for ever widening areas in bureaucracy, army, and the economic sphere, had to raise its claims on these executors. It had to borrow much-needed talents from the established services; and while they at first mutually profited from this alliance, the old servants of the New Order were soon deeply involved in the machinations of the political manager whom they had meant to direct; and he in turn became hopelessly enmeshed in the uncontrollable controls of a monolithic structure vis-à-vis the increasing complexity of its many tasks. Even in its heyday of success the party experienced basically irreconcilable tensions, as every dictatorial party must—between state bureaucracy and party machine, between the professional army and amateurish storm troopers, between captains of industry and party plenipotentiaries of the Four Year Plan— until the total state in the unspeakable inefficiencies of a top-heavy apparatus overreached itself in the unlimited drive toward world conquest. The breakdown of the Third Reich revealed the flagrant failure to bring about long-promised security, order, and peace to the people, who (in their great majority) had acquiesced in the rule of the functioning system and were equally eager to abandon the defeated Hitler. Such defeat from without left the world in uneasy inconclusiveness as to the true party loyalties of the German people in the aftermath of World War II. What fatal heritage did Hitler's one-party state leave to the New Republic?

IV / THE SECOND REPUBLIC
Uncertain Restoration

How new is the Bonn party system? Is it only a second and weaker edition of the First Republic? What are the basic patterns of the German political scene today? Which are the legacies of the Bismarck-Wilhelminic empire, of Weimar, of the Third Reich? Are today's two Germanies growing more apart day by day, or is unification in the offing? And if unification does come, what price will Germany's European neighbors have to pay for it? What are the promises, what the perils, of the political parties in the Second Republic?

There are more questions than answers about each party and the system as a whole. The miracle of Germany's renewed recovery leaves the interpreter hopelessly behind, always in arrears with his analysis and in deep doubt about the proper insight into the underlying forces of the outward mushroom growth. Says Theodore White, one of the keenest among our European observers: "Nobody knows which way Willi is going, not even Willi. But wherever he is going, he is moving fast." And White lets his key witness Willi Schlieker, conclude with the ominous note: "Everyone is waiting for a party." Such a widespread attitude suggests the question: How real is the existing party system of the Second Republic?

One might as well begin at the beginning. There was nothing but chaos in 1945 when the "Thousand Years' Reich" collapsed, after only twelve years of the total yoke, under the fatal blows of the Allied armies of the East and West. Gone were Hitler and his lieutenants, the one-party state, Germany altogether. The law of the land was that of the occupying powers, and they decreed the immediate restoration of the German political parties. Whether one might argue the wisdom of this decision (which was in a way forced on the Western powers by the early re-establishment of political life in the Soviet zone), it definitely gave direction to the original makeup of the re-established parties and left its mark on the ensuing development. Even today one may recognize zonal differences reflecting, within the regional parties, the preferences of the occupying powers. While such shadings have weakened and may eventually disappear altogether with the reassertion of the central party apparatus, the premature revival of the parties naturally fostered the restoration of the pre-Nazi system. Its old leaders, programs, and followings reappeared almost in the same way they had gone underground with the coming of the one-party state—only they were twelve years older by now. It was a bad omen for a fresh start. In view of this almost fatal handicap, it was surprising how many new faces, how many new ideas, and, in fact, how many new movements could be noticed in the party arena only half a decade later.

The nature and prospects of the German party system are by no means a foregone conclusion. Anything may be expected from its development. The risks may not even be calculable. And yet at least some of the basic difficulties of the unfolding political forces clearly derived from this hour of birth, which bound the parties to their past. In fact, it reasserted a basic feature and peril which had been characteristic of the pseudo-parliamentarism of the Bismarck empire, namely, political irresponsibility.

As the final say in crucial policy decisions rested with the Allied military governments, the party leaders were relieved of the full weight of responsible action. Any failure could easily be blamed on foreign authorities, and political demands could be raised without

consequences, just as had been the case in the Second Empire. While it should be stated in all justice that such a strategic bypass was not often used by the party leaders, it was significant that it hindered the entry of self-respecting parliamentarians into a system which seemed to make them liable for decisions beyond their actual control. They feared that this might make them "quislings" of the occupying powers. More important yet, the peoples' attitude toward political parties again took on the familiar pattern of playful non-commitment, allowing for irresponsible criticism and preposterous demagogical demands on their political spokesmen, who, through a kind of schizophrenia, were regarded both as pitiful puppeteers of foreign powers and as the responsible recipients of their own peoples' wrath. Political parties could not find a popular base—the absolute prerequisite for any functioning democratic party system.[18]

There are good reasons for such a reaction. The still fresh memories of the all-embracing total state and its omnipresent opinion control had made the people wise to propaganda, suspicious of the public domain, and craving for

18. If any statistical evidence is sought for such a fatal trend, which informally found its daily expression in newspapers and popular skepticism, one might mention the low percentage of party membership in a nation which is proverbially gregarious in its social affiliations. These are the available figures reported by the leading parties: SPD, 650,000; CDU/CSU, 350,000; FDP, 80,000; BHE, 200,000—all in all, less than 5 per cent of the voting population. According to F. A. von der Heydte, the percentage of members to party voters for the SPD is 8.2; for the FDP, 3.5; for the CD, 2.8. Compare these percentages, even for a "membership" party such as the SPD, with the other Socialist parties on the Continent, as reported by Maurice Duverger; and the contrast is surprising—with the Austrian Socialists leading with 37.9 per cent, closely followed by Sweden's Socialists with 35.5 per cent.

privacy. True, there have been notable shifts in recent years, due partly to a relaxed economic situation in which a fight for mere survival is no longer the only thing that matters. The high voting percentage in the election of 1953 shows a renewed popular interest in a nation awakening from the stupor of defeat and irresponsibility under foreign occupation. For the time being, however, this newly aroused public opinion may mean only further frustrations in a country unaccustomed to political participation, lacking proper institutional machinery, and incompetent to use it where it is available. Thus one hears sharp criticism against the powerful Chancellor Konrad Adenauer, who does not seek sufficient advice from cabinet, parliament, and the people, and may not even keep them fully informed. Our daily concern is naturally with the official policy-makers who alone speak up in councils and often do so effectively, like the chancellor. Yet one must not neglect popular reaction.

Fumbling, unsure, contradictory though public opinion still is in the Bonn Republic, it has become increasingly articulate. Yet the political parties are still left to a small group of old-time professionals. The people—skeptical, uncertain, restless—still keep out and may even succumb to the cunning of a demagogue who promises them quick solutions and a safe haven. Indeed, these many uncertainties reveal the necessarily provisional character of any study of present-day Germany—its frontiers, its leaders, its loyalties, and most certainly its political parties. An appraisal can be only tentative and, at best, only a preview of the promise and peril of its future destiny.

The facts seem to be familiar and are recorded in daily newspapers. A partitioned Germany is clearly divided into the Eastern party system, which hardly tries to conceal its total Soviet control, and the Western Bonn Republic, approximating a two-party system, with Adenauer's CDU and coalition partners in a predominant and stable power position and the SPD as "His Majesty's Opposition." Here democracy seems to face no serious competitor. A close examination, however, may reveal a more complex situation, a more open display of dynamic forces, and, at the same time, a surprising recovery of basic patterns of the traditional parties—in short, the familiar theme of continuity and change.

The Sozialdemokratische Partei Deutschlands (SPD)—the Traditional Party

Continuity finds its strongest support in the SPD. It is the traditional party par excellence; in fact, on close examination, it is the only one. This is its miracle and its malady. Miraculously, it survived the Nazi onslaught. Of its 650,000 dues-paying members, more than 90 per cent have been estimated to be of pre-Nazi vintage in age and in party adherence; 80 per cent of its leading officers suffered as Socialists in Hitler's prisons and concentration camps. This common background has created a unique solidarity and loyalty, paired with a distrust of any "outsiders," even within the party.

On the other hand, it was of crucial importance for the party to win over new followers from nontraditional strata if it were ever to expect to go beyond its traditional 30 per cent limit of the national electorate and thus reach a voting strength of majority proportions (at least in a feasible party coalition). This fact was fully recognized by the SPD's dynamic postwar organizer, Dr. Kurt Schumacher, who concentrated on broadening its social base far beyond its traditional rank and file by a synthesis of class and state in a newly structured working society. He correctly realized that such an aim would also presuppose a programmatic shift from previous Marxian doctrinairism. For this reason he emphasized a persistent drive for the middle-class vote, tied up with a powerful appeal to nationalist sentiment. That this turn was not merely an opportunist move on his part should not be doubted. Nor was such a policy altogether strange, in the light of the historical role played by the SPD. In fact, nationalism had been a living force and a liability of the party since Lassalle's days, highlighted and dearly paid for the moment it rose to political responsibility with the uneasy beginnings of the Weimar Republic.[19]

And yet the conclusion to be drawn after Schumacher's death in 1952 was his complete failure in this double task. The party had not recruited any appreciable new clientele, as the bitter experiences of the last elections proved. Nor has the widely felt shock and disappointment of these elections helped the programmatic reforms to get beyond a rather fruitless debating stage. A preliminary appraisal may in fact show a stiffening along old party lines and a frustrating failure of the forces of change within the leading councils, which were weakened by the untimely death of their stalwart Ernst Reuther, heroic mayor of Berlin. The party seems to have reached a stalemated position, which makes it increasingly difficult to muster new forces and to launch an effective attack on the intrenched governmental party. Such a frustrating plight becomes almost constitutionalized by Bonn's provisions against a negative vote of mistrust, which makes the governmental coalition, for all practical purposes, nearly invulnerable. In short, the SPD finds itself in the rather

19. How deeply these ideas represented a fundamental attitude of Dr. Schumacher may be illustrated by his Ph.D. thesis in the early 1920's, dealing with *Der Kampf um den deutschen Staatsgedanken in der deutschen Sozialdemokratie.* If this struggle had been successful, the rise of National Socialism might have been prevented altogether.

unfortunate position of being the official opposition party without being able to present an effective alternative government. If the situation is prolonged, it may completely handicap the party's future.

One of its unresolved problems, if not the key issue, centers around the succession to leadership and the recruitment of the younger generation. There is, first, the liability of an over-aged controlling elite whose concepts are superannuated and out of tune with present-day demands, yet whose enthusiastic loyalty is as unquestionable as it is overwhelming—especially in comparison to the reserve, if not apathy, of the restricted numbers of newly won youth. Beyond that, the difficulties of the restored party may have something to do with its main asset, the dynamic leadership of Dr. Schumacher—yesterday as a reality, and now as a heritage. The party had found in him a charismatic leader such as it had not possessed possibly since Lassalle's day. An extraordinary man, his moral stamina, political intelligence, and sincere integrity were beyond question. But he was also stubborn, tough, and uncompromising. He had the courage, background, and zeal of a martyr; he lost one arm in World War I and spent ten years in a Nazi concentration camp, emerging a physical wreck. His oratory was unequaled in present-day Germany, and his hatreds were reminiscent of the demagogue era. Although he antagonized many of his subordinates, he was still the unchallenged leader of the Social Democratic masses.

It was difficult, if not altogether impossible, for a new leader to grow up in his shadow. The man who took his place in name and position, Erich Ollenhauer—in fact, his closest collaborator and supporter and the head of the party's administration—was not accidentally the master of the machine. This is the natural succession in the leadership of any party. Moreover, it corresponds to the special character of the SPD. Its extensive apparatus has been the main strength of social democracy almost from the start; yet this has equally been its chief peril. The fight against the *Bonze,* as the caricatured functionary was increasingly described, had been an easy target of the party's powerful foes and was elevated to a major attack against the oligarchical tendencies of the modern party by one of the original sons of German social democracy, Robert Michels.

The regenerated SPD faces fundamentally the same basic problems as its pre-Nazi forerunner. The recurring characteristic weight and centralization of its party apparatus are shown by the prevalence of paid secretaries (a present estimate that they number 20 per cent of the leadership staff seems to be no exaggeration). This prevalence of the machine, demanding prolonged and loyal service from any aspirant to office, has long made it difficult for "young men in a hurry" to break into leading positions. It has also endangered the future of the SPD, which thus embraced a static credo and a stagnating apparatus instead of recognizing the growing and shifting needs of a political party aware of continuous electoral changes.

Such shortcomings might be fatal in a new Germany that in many ways seems to awaken to an appreciation of pragmatic politics. Certainly within the younger generation such a new "Western look" may be one of the most significant and promising signs in Bonn's political landscape.

The Christian Democratic Union (CDU)—a New Synthesis of Old Groups?

The CDU may well be a new phenomenon in the party lineup of the Second Republic—at least, that has been its claim since the beginning. No doubt,

it is not simply the revival and continuation of the old Catholic Center but is also a purposeful attempt at an interconfessional Christian party reaching out for the former followers of the Protestant CSVD (Christlichsozialer Volksdienst) and DNVP, as well as the Catholic Zentrum. The party could count on a wide appeal in a posttotalitarian society, eager to find in a common front against Nazi paganism a new center of traditional resurgence and social cohesion to overcome the spiritual vacuum of the disjointed dictatorial aftermath. The conscious bridging of the religious schism that had caused havoc throughout German history was foremost in the minds of the founders of the CDU in 1945, in their insistence upon approximate parity of Catholic and Protestant representation in the party councils.

One may question the success of the CDU/CSU in attaining this end, and its critics will point not only at the unchallenged predominance of Catholic Dr. Adenauer but also at the disturbing prevalence of party patronage according to confessional affiliation. On the other hand, the party can refer to numerous outstanding Protestant leaders among its key men, such as Minister of Interior Dr. Gerhart Schröder (the chancellor's "young man") and, above all, the former Protestant church dignitary and late speaker of the Bundestag, Dr. Hermann Ehlers, who had attained such a significant role as to make him a serious candidate for the succession to the chancellery until his premature death in 1954.[20] Even more sig-

20. Dr. Ehlers, this Pestalozzi among the parliamentary pedagogues, personifying strong fatherly authority and the party's conciliatory compromise, bridged the contradictions of its daily existence with wit, patience, and common sense. His youthful successor, Dr. Gerstenmaler, also a leader in the Protestant church, who on Adenauer's strong insistence was finally elected by a reluctant majority, will have to prove his prowess and power in parliament.

nificant may be the consistently high percentage of Protestants among the electorate and representatives in the Bundestag.[21]

No doubt the churches were the original focal point for the movement, which for this reason could forego the early establishment of a centralized apparatus. Such a postponement also furthered the inherent particularist tendencies within the party and allowed for the easy co-operation of divergent groups. Even the eventual development of an effective party machine based on eighteen active regions preserved these characteristic traits of decentralization, which distinguish its permanent staff (of around 250 members) from the highly centralized SPD.

The historical fate that made the CDU/CSU the governmental party emphasized further differentiations. Its leadership, largely constituted from the parliamentary representation, shows a prevalence of ministerial bureaucracy, while the SPD officials are still predominantly recruited from the functionaries of party and trade-unions. If there is any danger of petrification within the CDU, it does not derive so much from the inner party organization as from its official power position. Such a peril should not be minimized, especially after an overwhelming electoral victory. The party may misread its mandate (as probably its sister-organization in Italy did after De Gasperi's victory of 1948) and try to exploit its unique vantage point. It may then neglect its traditional role of protector of minority rights— a failure which in the long run has always been fatal to a political movement.

Such a policy, above all, would contradict some basic tenets of the party, founded on a genuine and continuously renewed compromise within its own

21. 38.5 per cent of the CDU/CSU representatives in the new Bundestag are Protestants (94 out of 244).

ranks and, based on the laboratory experiences of practical politics, in a pragmatic approach to the multiplicity of social and political forces within the nation as a whole.

Such a *vernunftsbetonte Tagespolitik* makes it difficult in fact to differentiate a right wing from a left wing within the party. Adenauer has often been identified with the conservatives and Rhenish heavy industry as distinct from the liberals, if not Christian Socialists, around Dr. Karl Arnold (prime minister of North Rhine Westphalia.) Yet the chancellor has always regarded as his primary task the bridging of the divergent forces. Thus he forestalled any weakening of the leftist groups and their eventual break with the party by supporting and even piloting aggressive social policies (for instance, in respect to economic codetermination and profit-sharing). Moreover, in international affairs Adenauer has become the most powerful spokesman of a sincere European Union, which involves him in frequent policy decisions which run counter to the traditional national conservative line. His handling of the Saar issue may turn out to be a case in question, as is his whole conciliatory attitude toward the French. If a bridge between the two neighbors and traditional antagonists is to be constructed, Adenauer may well be one of its architects.

In Germany's "sincere broker" the CDU has found a man who can formulate with precision and direct with purpose his nation's policies, internal and international. He commands confidence. One is sure of him, though not always of his ways and means. He has often been reproached for using the strategy of a fox, which he may have to apply in order to keep the disjointed factions of his party under control. Labor Lord Pakenham significantly said of Adenauer that he is possessed of the power to stand apart from his people like a father or, better yet, a grandfather. For this octogenarian, while he has an un-blemished record as a courageous, though cautious, fighter for democracy, represents a democracy of a special brand. His political foes accuse him of being an autocrat. He made his reputa-tion as lord mayor of Cologne, a posi-tion he held from 1917 to 1933 until the Nazis turned him out of office. When this lifelong civil servant started his great political career at the age of seventy in 1945, it was certainly shaped in terms of his impressive experiences as a pragmatic, down-to-earth adminis-trator ready to take on responsibilities and not without disdain for the dema-gogues and the irresponsible, abstract critics of the executive experts. For this reason, it is difficult to picture Adenauer as a leader of the opposition—a role which might very easily have been as-signed to him in the elections of 1949 and 1953 and an alternative position which his party should be ready to fill at any time. This indeed would be the true test of a democratic movement.

Adenauer knows how to rule with seigneurial dignity and peasant shrewd-ness. An air of impenetrable mystery surrounds this figure of ageless wisdom. He has no intimates. Naturally, his brand of democracy smacks of some autocratic tastes and of outspoken sus-picion of mob rule. The stability of the Bonn Republic is largely of Adenauer's doing. No doubt the ingenious Article 65 of the Bonn Constitution, outlawing the overthrow of the government by a negative majority, although it was bit-terly attacked by its opponents as a petrifaction of the system, gave Ade-nauer such an overwhelming power po-sition that his eventual disappearance may come as an irremediable upset of the seemingly secure Republic.

This issue touches upon a key prob-lem of the party and the nation as a whole. How stable is this democracy and its party system? The succession of Adenauer may spell out the crucial question of the party's future. Without a vigorous pace-setter, the neatly joined CDU may quickly fall apart and there-with its unifying links among the people. The restlessness of a nation, tamed by the experienced hand of the old sage, may break through again, and, underneath the thin veneer of its demo-cratic front, persistent forces of reac-tion and revolution may gather strength.

Much will depend on the accommo-dation of the party's political neighbors and coalition partners. No doubt, their number has shrunk and so has their numerical weight. Germany, for all practical purposes, has become a two-party democracy. Yet two movements, minor though they may be regarded vis-à-vis the two giants, must be con-sidered: the Free Democrats and the All-German Bloc.

The Free Democrats (FDP)—a "Split Personality"

The FDP in a way has served as a cushion between the two major parties and has justified its existence (and its defense of proportional representation, which has assured the party's preserva-tion) in terms of this bridge position. The party's most illustrious spokesman, federal President Theodor Heuss, has personified this role of the great bal-ancer throughout a rich life as teacher, scholar, publicist, and statesman. The presidential office is cut to his measure, and he, in turn, has made it grow in prestige and acumen. It is not the cen-ter of policy decisions, which rest large-ly with the federal chancellor, but it emanates "atmosphere" as its first in-cumbent has ingeniously perceived his role.

Even within his own party, leader-ship does not rest with Heuss but with Dr. Dehler, Dr. Euler, and Dr. Blue-cher. This definite ascendancy explains the increasing strength of right-wing forces of conservative big industry and big business and the steady decline of the liberal intelligentsia, of which the president is such a perfect representative.

The complex beginnings of the party may be significant for its ensuing fate and its lasting effects. The very fact that it was organized under different names in different parts of Germany (FDP in North Rhine–Westphalia; DVP in Baden and Württemberg-Hohenzollern; LDP in the Soviet zone and in Hesse) indicated the regional differentiations and, one might add in distinction from the SPD and CDU, the lack of a unifying idea. What brought about its creation was a negative reaction within a large segment of the population toward the economic policies of the SPD and the religious-cultural program of the CDU, apart from the generally prevalent rejection of any totalitarianism (in the words of one of the young adherents of the party: "I'm neither socialistic enough to vote for the SPD nor religious enough to vote for the CDU, thus I vote for the FDP").

The new party was anti-Marxist, anticlerical, and antiauthoritarian. If any positive tie could be conceived to unite the divergent factions, it was liberalism in a double sense: an undogmatic view of politics and heterogeneity of party members. Such a vague and in many ways merely negative definition points at the world-wide crisis of liberalism, lacking a positive creed. One should add, however, that the liberal idea in Germany has shown surprising strength. Far from reflecting the sheer romanticism of some old timers, it has seized upon the imagination even of many of the young and indeed has infiltrated all German democratic parties (which may well be one reason for the FDP's only limited success). Such a genuine revival is the natural reaction against the encroachments of the leviathan state of the Nazi past and the Soviet present. The strong reassertion of individualism can be seen in eco-

nomics, where Minister Erhard has proclaimed, with gusto, German *Gründlichkeit*, and undeniable success, a policy of complete laissez faire and the removal of all governmental controls. It has colored the much-discussed attitudes toward military revival and its dangers of regimentation. It has also affected the somewhat reserved reaction toward parties and their omnipotent threats of bureaucratization.

In this respect the Free Democrats could claim to be relatively free of a binding mass organization. In fact, if any party in the Bonn Republic be such, the FDP is not a "party of integration" but still and primarily a "party of representation" of the nineteenth-century type. It is not accidental that, like the French Radical Socialists, it is a party of committees whose main function is to select prominent citizens as spokesmen of the national movement. For this reason the local organization plays a greater part in the FDP than in the other mass parties.

The sociological definition of the Free Democrats, however, would not be complete if one overlooked the increasing power of industrial organizations and pressure groups in the party's councils. This development epitomizes, on the daily policy level, the fundamental tensions within the party—reminiscent of Weimar's Deutsche Volkspartei. The traditional liberal forces, emphasizing a strong stand for freedom above everything else and for unhampered educational policies, with increased concern about Catholic expansion and its threat to the party's Protestant views, are clashing with vigorous industrialists, who in the pride of their amazing economic recovery and accompanying self-confidence are increasingly dominating the party congresses and policy councils. While the daily conflicts within the party are tempered by participation in the federal and state governments, the FDP has definitely put itself to the right of the CDU,[22] although its participation in federal and state governments has tempered the daily conflicts within the party.

The Bloc of Expellees and Dispossessed/All-German Bloc (BHE/GB)—Successful Newcomer?

The same fact may also have its bearing on the BHE/GB. One might have suspected that this completely new creation among the parties, appealing to the ten million expellees from the East, would introduce a disturbing force into German politics by attracting the rootless *Neubürger*, who, with "nothing to lose but their chains" and without hope among the old *Besitzbürger*, would be open to demagogical enticements of a "promised land" beyond the Oder-Neisse line. The party, instead, became increasingly "respectable" and, finally, after the 1953 election, entered the government in Adenauer's coalition. Within four years it rose from an uneasy start of regional organizations within the states where expellees concentrated (above all, in Schleswig-Holstein and Lower Saxony) to participation in the government of four federal states and finally to a national party of considerable weight, polling 1.6 million votes (5.9 per cent) and achieving 27 Bundestag seats (out of a total of 487) in the September elections of 1953. In fact, it was the only successful smaller party which tried to compete in the parliamentary elections.

The party represented two amazing features. Its very creation in the midst

22. Orientation toward the Right becomes especially obvious in the predominant state of North Rhine–Westphalia, which has contributed more than two-thirds of the federal republic's finances and includes by far the greatest percentage of the FDP's membership. The elections of June 19, 1954, in this most heavily populated state, re-emphasized the FDP's strength, increasing the party's percentage to 11.5 (as compared with 8.5 per cent in the 1953 federal election).

of an already functioning party system (dominated by the SPD, CDU, and FDP) and a fully established constitutional setting seemed to meet an insurmountable handicap. And yet the BHE succeeded, and, in fact, by 1953 was the only successful aspirant among a host of five dozen competitors in achieving the stipulated 5 per cent of electoral votes necessary for parliamentary representation.

What was its *raison d'être*? Party leaders claimed two reasons for its existence: first and above all, the fact that the other parties did not understand the plight of the expellees and made no attempt to provide for their material and social betterment; second, that the old movements had become dogmatically petrified and did not give their citizens sufficient possibility of participation and freedom of political decisions.

Such a purposeful creation under the leadership of articulate spokesmen of German minority groups in the East, like the party leader Waldemar Kraft, pointed at the second feature of the party's significance. Here was a movement that seemed to be cut to measure for a party of interest groups, with all its political pitfalls, as illustrated by the fatal history of Weimar's Wirtschaftspartei. And yet the BHE escaped this dangerous trend. It might well be that the definite orientation toward *Lastenausgleich* as the main avenue of improving the expellees' plight forced the BHE to seek the co-operation of the established major parties, while these immediate purposes led the party members to make sacrifices for their movement. The BHE had never any electoral worries, as other parties did, and for this reason could take a noncommittal attitude in respect to all other issues of politics. That reaction brought about a refreshing pragmatic view among its leaders and followers, and since they covered all strata, their social concerns could easily embrace the whole nation.

While the problem of German reunification is foremost in the minds of the movement (the Brandenburg Gate, symbol of Berlin, is the party's emblem), it is the peaceful return of the expellees to their homeland that the BHE tries to achieve through a reorientation in international politics. It is interesting to note that the party leadership, after an initial rejection of such a policy at its first convention in September, 1952, later adopted the European Defense Community as a foreign-policy plank for a sovereign "United States of Europe."

The character and contribution of the party will not in the least depend on its ability to spell out for its members the farther-reaching national issues which at times may even run counter to the immediate interests of its adherents. At the same time, the more successful the BHE is in integrating the expellees into a new German nation, including their economic rehabilitation, the more it will foster its self-liquidation.

Whatever the long-range fate of the party may be, its very existence ought to contribute to a questioning and softening of established party lines and petrified clienteles. Whether the BHE can succeed in reaching out beyond the expellees proper (of whom an estimated 20–25 per cent voted for the party in 1953) and organize a wider segment of society (say, all those who have suffered property losses in war destruction and economic displacements) may well be questioned. Even more doubtful is the claim of a few among its intellectual spokesmen that the movement represents an altogether new ideology, displacing the self-satisfied and sleepy *Besitzbürger* by a dynamic *Neubürger* —a new crisis stratum of irregulars, of *déclassés*, of pariahs of the German fate, a truly fifth estate, which in fact may be heralding a new society in a post-Locarno second edition. Indeed, a most

explosive power could derive from this group if it succeeded in bringing together all elements of unrest in Germany, especially its least integrated group—the youth. Yet the dreams and expectations of a handful of hopeful ideologists who see in the party the seed bed of a reawakened class struggle and the basic force of a new morale are, to say the least, premature and probably entirely unrealistic.

In fact, by the middle of 1955, the prospects of the party seemed to have taken a turn for the worse. Deep conflicts within the leadership, breaking out in open quarrels in regional and national councils, finally led to the exodus of a third of the party's Bundestag representatives, including the founder of the party, Dr. Kraft, and its parliamentary chairman, Dr. Oberländer (both men the official representatives of the party in the Adenauer cabinet). The remaining rump faction is undoubtedly taking a more radical turn (even considering a new name for the organization) and may well move out of the government camp altogether. On the other hand, such a trend—momentarily disturbing though it may be for the Adenauer coalition—will hardly have any lasting effect on the national scene. It may well be surmised that in future parliamentary elections the party will be unable to gather the 5 per cent voting strength necessary to remain on the scene. Thus, after a promising beginning, the BHE seems to have lost its momentum and its specific place in German politics.

Where Is the Right Wing?

The same and an even more definite question can be raised in respect to the German party and its claim of representing a new vital conservatism. Confusing and controversial though this recently rediscovered favorite among the ideologies may be, it seems like stretching the terms too much to identify an insignificant and regionally limited movement with a basic political philosophy. Conservative the German party may be, in a negative sense, dating its antecedents back to the die-hard *Welfen* (Guelphs) who were still vainly fighting for the preservation of an independent Hanover after its forced incorporation into Bismarck's Prussia. As the German Hanoverian party, it had played some minor part on the right wing in the parliaments of the Second Empire and the Weimar Republic until it went under, together with all other parties, when the Nazis seized power.

The restored party quickly achieved its aim of an independent Hanover in the establishment of the state of Lower Saxony in 1946, but soon farther-reaching ambitions were fed by the influx of old-time rightist sympathizers, who, in lieu of a genuine conservative party, took temporary shelter within the German party (if not within the FDP). Yet neither its senior leader and erstwhile democrat, Wilhelm Heile, nor its younger cabinet ministers, passionate Guelph Heinrich Hellwige and ambitious Hans-Christoph Seebohm, can prevent its eventual demise—a fate similar to other regional parties such as the Bavarian party, which had enjoyed a short spurt in the first Bonn Bundestag and lost out under the 5 per cent rule in the second national elections.

The splinter parties altogether seemed to be doomed to failure, despite a complicated electoral system that allows them a qualified proportional representation.[23] Many careful observers have seen a healthy sign of a mature parliamentary system in this unexpected and yet consistently continued and recently accelerated process toward bipolarization of the German party system. The reasons for such a development are found (apart from the much-discussed constructive vote of nonconfidence, preventing diverse opposition forces from overthrowing the cabinet) in the *rap-prochement* of the governmental parties themselves, whose many years of experience of coalition have served as a cementing force. The very differentiation among the partners of the coalition may, however, prevent the unfolding of a true two-party system, which ought to confront the voters with the clear-cut issue of choosing the next prime minister. Instead, the prevailing electoral system deceives the citizen into believing that he is merely selecting preferences of ideological shadings and that he can transfer the hard policy decisions to the uncontrollable parliamentary and ministerial leadership. The peoples' last and proudest duty— of designating responsible leadership— is thus surrendered.

An even more serious peril may be hidden under the cover of Bonn's simplified party system. At first sight it presents the encouraging phenomenon of an overwhelming democratic bloc of about 90 per cent of the electorate, which seems to be unchallenged by any appreciable antidemocratic forces. This complete absence of radical-wing parties to the Right and the Left may, however, be deceiving. The outer contours of the party system are in no way indicative of the persistent tensions of its inner core. Neither the noisy appearance of the neo-Nazi Socialist Reich party (SRP), attracting, under the lead-

23. The chances of numerous splinter groups have been minimized by the new electoral law of June, 1953. Passed after a bitter debate even among the coalition partners, it aims at a qualified proportional representation by giving each citizen two votes— one to be applied directly to his electoral district, the other to be accounted for on a regional list. Only parties which succeed in winning a mandate in at least one district or which command 5 per cent of the national vote are permitted their proportional share on the regional lists. The result has been the elimination of practically all minor parties, with the exception of the German party and the Zentrum, which attained three seats through an electoral agreement with the CDU in a few constituencies.

ership of General Remer, Count Wolf von Westarp and Dr. Dorls, as many as 11 per cent of the votes in the Land elections of Lower Saxony in 1951, nor its effective outlawing in the summer of 1953 could give an adequate measure of the underlying trends in Germany.[24]

Important though the judicious attitude of the courts and the awakened responsibility of the administrations may be, what will count in the end will be the prevailing political climate within the nation. And here we can only state that it is still too early to tell whether a genuine democratic spirit has permeated Germany. The test will have to be fought out within each party. If anything is alarming in the inner political scene of West Germany, it is not so much the actual or prospective increase in the right-wing parties themselves as it is the continuous pressure that they exert on the predominant moderate parties. Eager to counteract their rivals and to compete with them for public support, they may even become the prisoners of a renewed radical, nationalist fervor. The numerous splinter groups, from Alfred Loritz' Wirtschaftliche-Aufbau Partei to the SRP and the National Union (of August Hausleiter), may be pushed aside by more purposeful, unscrupulous, and demagogical leaders and may thus appear in retrospect as a mere prelude to greater

24. It should be marked to the credit of the Bonn lawmakers that they tackled the delicate issue of the "limits of tolerance against tolerance," a measure which had been notoriously neglected by the Weimar Republic. "Whoever abuses freedom of expression of opinion . . . in order to attack the free democratic basic order . . . shall forfeit these basic rights," thus states the Bonn basic law (Art. 18); and it adds explicitly that parties which "according to their aims and their members' behavior are directed against the constitutional order or the concept of international understanding are illegal." Under this stipulation the SRP was outlawed in 1953 by the federal constitutional court.

threats to come for the young democracy.

What the final outcome of West Germany's party system may be will depend on the stability of the Bonn Republic itself. Its consolidation will be spelled out in terms of the genuine economic viability of the young nation, which alone could prevent the return of crisis strata that had once before wrecked a democratic party system.

The Socialist Unity Party (SED) and the Eastern Democratic Republic

In partitioned Germany the Bonn Republic is threatened not only from within but even more strongly from without, by the government of East Germany. True, the democratic leaders of the Western Republic may point with pride at the practical annihilation of the Communist party (which in the last elections did not even succeed in polling the necessary 5 per cent vote in order to place a single representation in the Bundestag), and this destruction of the challenger from the radical Left is not least due to intimate contact with the realities of Soviet overlordship in the Eastern zone. Yet this very proximity of the Soviet fatherland not only arouses fear this side of the Iron Curtain but also states a threatening alternative. The SED of the German Democratic Republic has thus become a not-so-silent, though indirect, partner in the functioning party system of Bonn.

One thing is sure, the Communist party (KPD) is no longer merely an internal national faction of West Germany but is primarily the militant arm of an international movement centered in Moscow. As an international force, it can almost be discarded—for the time being at least—for the Communists' Bonn story is a record of dismal failure. Starting out together with the Christian Democrats and Socialists as one of the big three parties in the revived western European party pattern of 1945, at no time has it pulled the political weight held by the Communists in France and Italy throughout the last decade. Nor has it gained a foothold in any of the Communists' customary auxiliary social institutions, such as the trade-unions, the police, and the armed forces.

To be sure, the KPD was the first party to appear in Berlin after Germany's collapse in 1945, under "ready-made" Soviet-trained leaders, who had fled to Moscow with the rise of the Nazis and were returned with the victorious Red army. Their password was the strict party line, and their only special task was to adjust it to the nation's peculiar lingo and circumstance. Part of their transfer of the true faith was the purging of a competing party elite that eventually returned from the West, where they had found a temporary haven and some unorthodox ideas. While this cleansing process was rigorously and, on the whole, successfully executed, the rank and file sobered in its early enthusiasm and high expectations of a revolution around the corner. From a voting record of about 9 per cent (close to the average KPD following in Weimar days) it has declined steadily to an almost negligible splinter group today.

This unique development (not even matched by the most stable Scandinavian party system, which had hardly any room for a revolutionary movement) is, first of all, a reflection of the simple fact that the revolutionary situation—if it had existed in this postwar Germany—had again passed, as it had thirty years before. Bonn's amazing economic recovery, lasting or temporary as it may be, had something to do with it. Full employment, a rising standard of living, and increasing confidence in the staying power of the prevailing economic system are no proper backdrop for revolutionary recruitment. The KPD's main contestant for the labor vote, the Western SPD, was in a pe-

culiarly favorable position. Not only did its persistent opposition stand in the Bonn Republic allow for the absorption of dissatisfied masses, but its noteworthy leadership in the developing Berlin crisis also served as a focus for militant elements which otherwise might have tended toward the KPD. The most significant factor in the decline of West German communism, however, was the polarization of national opinion in consequence of the all-pervasive East-West conflict, vis-à-vis a German Soviet zone that exemplified the somber expectations of a satellite state.

The fate of the West German KPD in more than one sense was a reflected glory—or, better, shame—of the phases of its Eastern partner. In quick succession the restored party moved from a Fatherland's Front strategy, appealing to all "anti-Fascist" factions (with special preference for the middle class and an appropriately moderate program as projected in the Moscow Manifesto of 1943) to a sudden advocacy of the originally rejected united front with the SPD to the final step of a forced merger of Eastern Social Democrats and Communists in the SED (April, 1946).

The SED's early pretense of the rule of parity was soon abandoned in favor of outright Bolshevist control. Minister President Otto Grotewohl, a former SPD leader, has quickly become a mere figurehead, as is the aged president of the German Democratic Republic, Wilhelm Pieck, a mere traditional relic from pre-Nazi communism. The real master of the SED, reaffirmed in this position at the Fourth Party Congress in the spring of 1954, is Secretary-General Walter Ulbricht, who, starting with his goatee, flatters himself that he is Lenin incarnated in person and strategy.

In a way the SED, losing all its trappings of a democratic movement, especially since the blow of the popular revolt of June 17, 1953, presents a repetition of the much-analyzed features, problems, and dilemmas of any totalitarian party, only in a more shopworn tradition.[25] For this reason it hardly deserves closer scrutiny. Yet what might be of interest is the disturbing transfer possibility of a Fascist-Nazi pattern to Soviet totalitarianism and, worse than that, the obvious attraction which the totalitarian doctrine holds for some confused though sincere people who see in it a haven of security, peace, and belonging. One should not underestimate (contrary to a widespread opinion abroad) the impact of a fully intrenched Communist dictatorship in the Eastern zone.

Here, as elsewhere, the movement must be divided into different spheres of numerical strength and ideological depth. From the large and loosely knit circle of sympathizers and possible voters, representing a fluctuating amorphous mass, to the truly indoctrinated party functionaries and, finally, to the inner core of a small band of policy-makers in the KPD, who claim to be the general staff of the future society, the party means different things to different people. Beyond that, it changes its structure and meaning at different times.

Above all, purging has become a part of any totalitarian party's definition, and the SED is no exception. The party is continuously cleansed of "Western-

tainted social-democraticism" among its membership of 1,230,000 (of whom 400,000 were formerly Social Democrats, according to Ulbricht's report to the Central Committee in 1953). Even without any dramatic mass expulsion in the near future, such a process must go on. Increase in the percentage of industrial and rural workers is an aim of the SED, in which government employees and other nonproletarian groups are believed to constitute more than half the membership.

At the same time, the SED must infiltrate larger segments of the East German democracy if it wants to have any chances for survival. One way to enlarge its basis was the permission given to the "bourgeois" parties, the CDU and LDP, to continue (in an Eastern version, to be sure) their sham existence. In addition, two new synthetic parties were created by the regime itself—the National Democratic party (NDP) and the Democratic Peasant party (DBP)—to activate the little Nazis and the predominant farming population. A so-called bloc system coordinates all these seemingly different groups. In order to gain support in the Soviet zone and, beyond that, in the Western non-Communist world, a smoke screen is created through the confusion of a unified ballot in the coalition government of a "national front." (Only 25 per cent of the slate of the Volkskammer were selected from the SED proper; 30 per cent came from the CDU and LDP and the rest from semi-independent organizations; but, in fact, all candidates were screened and selected by the almighty party). They all must participate in the government, i.e., must be subservient to the SED. Furthermore, its rule is extended into the daily life of the citizen through the agency of the Free German Trade-Union Federation (the FDGB, with more than 5,000,000 members), the Young Pioneers and the Free German

25. The new party statute passed by the latest party convention reflects this *rapprochement*, especially in its stress on the identity of party and state, with formulations completely paralleling the statute of the Soviet party in 1952. Similar statutes were recently passed by other satellite states, such as Poland and Bulgaria. "The Central Committee directs the work of the central state and social institutions through their inherent party cadres." In this connection it is interesting to note, as a new feature of this statute, that it explicitly decrees the erection of special party outfits within the peoples' police and the state organs of communication.

Youth (FDJ, claiming 3,000,000 members), and the Democratic League of Women (DFB with over 1,000,000 members).

The power and persistent threat is, however, not fully circumscribed by this political *Gleichschaltung*. In this repsect one may, in fact, be safe in saying that the regime has failed and, therefore, cannot face the test of a free election. Yet as long as the Soviet controls (including their tanks) can be maintained, a sufficiently disciplined minority of hardly 20 per cent may be all that is needed, and this number may well be recruited, especially among the impressionable youth. The real danger may be seen in the impact on the younger generation, hard to measure though it is. Here is the place where totalitarian education must be studied carefully in its far-reaching and possibly devastating effects, especially if the present enforced insulation from the outside world is preserved. Added to that, some improvement in living standards within the zone and complete co-ordination with the Council for Mutual Economic Assistance (the so-called Molotov Plan, September 29, 1950) and the Democratic Republic may be consolidated into the Soviet satellite system.

In the meantime, a highly developed propaganda campaign from the East is directed, with some measure of success, against the government of West Germany. In the guise of a campaign for German unification and world peace it denounces the Bonn Republic as a force of reaction, remilitarization, and neo-fascism. The SED beyond the Iron Curtain is in this sense the great antagonist and explosive element in an otherwise suspiciously tranquil West German party system, picking up the dormant forces of radicalism on the Left and even on the Right if and when the time seems ripe for the royal battle in an international civil war.

This East-West conflict as crystallized in the German party system shows that the struggle is not waged merely on a political, organizational level, but even more essentially reaches the inner core of each German's conscience—his loyalties, his beliefs, his hatreds, and his hopes. Here again—as throughout a long tragic history—Germany has become the testing ground of greater forces, domestic and international. The political parties are the reflection of fundamental social transformation, institutional changes, ideological reorientation, and international tensions; they are the mirror of a society in flux. And Germany, in the midst of this turmoil, presents the case in question.

TABLE 3a

THE WEIMAR REPUBLIC: PARTIES AND GOVERNMENTAL COALITIONS

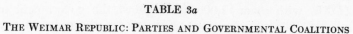

(Radical-Wing Parties: Left and Right)

(Pre–World War I Parties)

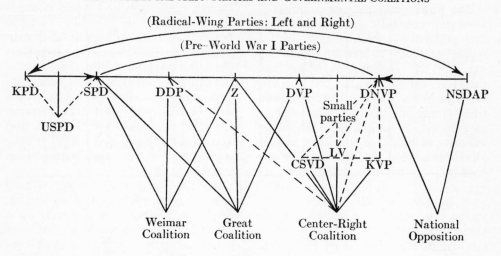

KPD SPD DDP Z DVP DNVP NSDAP

Small parties

USPD

LV

CSVD KVP

| Weimar Coalition | Great Coalition | Center-Right Coalition | National Opposition |

TABLE 3b

REICH CABINETS, 1919–33

Year	Weimar Coalition	Great Coalition	Center-Right	National Opposition
1919	(1) Scheidemann (S)			
	(2–3) Bauer (S)			
1920	(4) Müller (S)			
1921	(6–7) Wirth (Z)		(5) Fehrenbach (Z)	
1922			(8) Cuno	
1923		(9) Stresemann (V)	(10) Marx (Z)	
1925			(11/12) Luther	
1926			(13/14) Marx (Z)	
1928		(15) Müller (S)		
1930			(16/17) Brüning (Z)	
1932				(18) Papen
1933				(19) Schleicher
				(20) Hitler (NS)
Predominant in	1919–22	1923 / 1928–30	1923–28 / 1930–32	1932–33

TABLE 3c

REICHSTAG ELECTIONS, 1919–33 (PER CENT OF TOTAL VOTE)

Elections	KPD	USPD	SPD	DDP	Z	DVP	Small Parties	DNVP	NSDAP
NV Jan., 1919...	......	7.6	37.5	18.5	19.7	4.4	1.6	10.2	......
1. Jan., 1920....	2.1	17.9	21.7	8.3	18.1	13.9	3.1	15.1	......
2. May, 1924...	12.6	......	20.5	5.7	16.6	9.2	9.4	19.5	6.5
3. Dec., 1924....	9.0	......	26.0	6.3	17.3	10.1	7.2	20.5	3.0
4. May, 1928...	10.6	......	29.8	4.8	15.2	8.7	14.1	14.2	2.6
5. Sept., 1930...	13.1	......	24.5	3.5	14.8	4.9	14.0	7.0	18.3
6. July, 1932....	14.3	......	21.6	1.0	15.7	1.2	3.0	5.9	37.3
7. Nov., 1932...	16.7	......	20.4	0.9	15.0	1.8	3.0	8.5	33.1
8. March, 1933..	12.3	......	18.3	0.8	14.0	1.1	1.6	8.0	43.9

Weimar Coalition   Great Coalition   Center-Right Coalition   National Opposition

TABLE 4

THE BONN REPUBLIC: CONTINUITY AND CHANGE

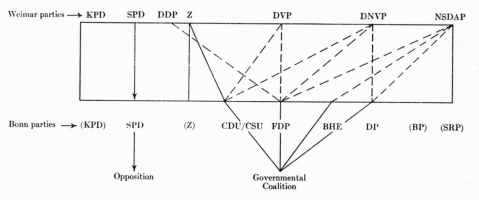

Weimar parties → KPD   SPD   DDP   Z   DVP   DNVP   NSDAP

Bonn parties → (KPD)   SPD   (Z)   CDU/CSU   FDP   BHE   DP   (BP)   (SRP)

Opposition   Governmental Coalition

BUNDESTAG ELECTIONS: PERCENTAGE OF VOTES AND SEATS

	(KPD)	SPD	(Z)	CDU/CSU	FDP	BHE	DP	(BP)	(SRP)
1949....	5.7 (3.7)*	29.2 (32.6)	3.1 (2.5)	31 (34.6)	11.9 (12.9)	....	4 (4.2)	4.2 (4.2)	1.8 (1.2)
1953....	2.2 (...)	28.8 (30.8)	0.8 (0.6)	45.2 (50.1)	9.5 (9.9)	5.9 (5.5)	3.2 (3.1)	1.7 (...)	1.1 (...)

* Number of seats in parentheses.

TOWARD A COMPARATIVE STUDY
OF POLITICAL PARTIES

Toward a Comparative Study
of Political Parties

SIGMUND NEUMANN

I / A Preliminary Definition

A definition of "party" might as well begin with its simple word derivation. To become a "party" to something always means identification with one group and differentiation from another. Every party in its very essence signifies *partnership* in a particular organization and *separation* from others by a specific program.

Such an initial description, to be sure, indicates that the very definition of party presupposes a democratic climate and hence makes it a misnomer in every dictatorship. A one-party system (*le parti unique*) is a contradiction in itself. Only the coexistence of at least one other competitive group makes a political party real. Still the fact remains that the term has been widely used by modern autocrats, and for a very obvious reason: to keep the semblance of a "peoples' rule" in their postdemocratic dictatorships. But it is also true that even the totalitarian party depends upon a functioning opposition. If one does not exist, it must still be assumed by the dictators, since under monolithic rule the dictatorial parties must constantly justify their existence in view of the ever present threat of a counter-revolution, hidden or imaginary though its organization may be. The opposition party is the *raison d'être* of the dictatorial movement and its all-pervasive controls through institutions, propaganda, and terror.

Thus parties must prevail under the total structure, too. Yet here again, as in all other strata of the political pyramid, divergent political systems are hidden behind the same nomenclature. Just as "leaders" and "lieutenants" carry different meanings in democracies and dictatorships, so do "parties" also.

Between the two extremes of "democracy" and "dictatorship" there are wide variations. The British, American, French, Indian, and Scandinavian democratic structures differ as greatly among themselves as do the totalitarian regimes of the Soviet Union, Fascist Italy, Nazi Germany, and Peronist Argentina. In short, the peculiar character of each party system must be defined in terms of the political order of which it is an integral part, if not its kingpin.

What is common to all parties, beyond partnership in a particular organization and separation from others, is their *participation* in the decision-making process, or at least the attempt at and a chance for such a mobilization for action. This ever present readiness alone makes them political in a genuine sense, for only in their fight for control and in their conscious influence on political forces, do parties gain meaning and importance. It is therefore not accidental that the beginning of modern political parties is closely tied up with the rise of a parliament. When political representation broadens and a national forum of discussion develops, providing a constant opportunity for political participation—wherever those conditions are fulfilled, political parties arise. This happened in England in the revolutionary seventeenth century; in France on the eve of the great Revolution of

1789; in Germany around 1848. Even where contingent influences may create political groups of an awakened intelligentsia, as in nineteenth-century tsarist Russia, they assume political dimensions only where some degree of participation is made possible.

While the hour of birth for the political party in every nation can well be defined by such a simple derivation from its original meaning, the same is true of the critical period of a party system. By its very definition, "party" connotes not only the coexistence of different competing entities, with their characteristic partnership, separation, and participation, but also a fourth feature, most significant and yet often forgotten—the essential inclusion of every separate group as *a part in a whole*. Only where the specific interests of parties are imbedded in a common whole does the political struggle not lead to disintegration of the entire group. Only when essentials uniting the political adversaries are constantly reaffirmed can differences be balanced. Just as children are ready to accept the rules of the gang only as long as they are willing to continue their group life, so can sacrifices be asked from each political opponent as long as the preservation of the community seems worth while. A common field of activity, a basic homogeneity, a common language, are presuppositions for a functioning party system. Such a common basis alone makes compromise, sacrifice, and even defeat bearable. Wherever this body politic becomes questionable, the crisis of parties seems the necessary result. The viability of a party system becomes a test for the stability of a social and political order. The strength of the Anglo-American party system is founded largely upon a basic national unity which makes the differentiations of political groups "differences in degree but not in kind."

This interdependence of the fate of political parties with the fate of the national whole is the very result of their "political" character; for political they are not only because of their claim to political power but even more so on account of their fulfilment of their political function of integration.

To summarize: we may define "political party" generally as *the articulate organization of society's active political agents, those who are concerned with the control of governmental power and who compete for popular support with another group or groups holding divergent views.* As such, it is *the great intermediary which links social forces and ideologies to official governmental institutions and relates them to political action within the larger political community.*

A party's concrete character can be spelled out only in time and space. What "this buckle" (to paraphrase Bagehot's description of the British cabinet) actually links up depends on a nation's specific constitution (i.e., the system of its correlated institutions) and its peculiar parallelogram of social forces. It is only in such a substantial situation that the functions, structure, and strategy of parties can be fully revealed.

II / FUNCTIONS OF POLITICAL PARTIES: DEMOCRATIC AND DICTATORIAL

It has often been stated that the primary task of political parties is to organize the chaotic public will. "They bring order out of the chaos of a multitude of voters" (Lord Bryce). They are brokers of ideas, constantly clarifying, systematizing, and expounding the party's doctrine. They are representatives of social interest groups, bridging the distance between the individual and the great community. They maximize the voter's education in the competitive scheme of at least a two-party system and sharpen his free choice. The coexistence of a competitor, therefore, is paramount to an effective democratic party system which presupposes that the final compromise will reflect the reasonable decision of a free electorate.

In fact, the basic assumption of democracy is the inevitability of differing views and the free operation of conflicting opinions. "The true democrat has a suspicion that he may not always be right," as W. Ivor Jennings remarked. Thus the opposition becomes the most important part of the parliament; its members are "critics by profession." It is not enough that Her Majesty's Opposition be highly respected by the ruling majority, but often its fruitful ideas are accepted—and, indeed, this is a wise course for the party in power to follow if it wants to remain there. Its political alternative represents not only the looming "Shadow Cabinet" but also an active participant in actual control.

The open forum of parliament becomes the clearinghouse for the policies that a state should follow. The political parties are the proper engine of such continuous plebiscite. They make the voters choose at least the lesser of two evils, thus forcing political differentiations into a few major channels. Yet important as such machinery of political concentration may be, the political services of the parties do not stop at that. What is even more essential, parties transform the private citizen himself. They make him a *zoon politikon;* they integrate him into the group. Every party has to present to the individual voter and to his powerful special-interest groups a picture of the community as an entity. It must constantly remind the citizen of this collective whole, adjust his wants to the needs of the community, and, if necessary, even ask sacrifices from him in the name of the community. Nor can even the so-called "class parties," which call upon only a specific part of the population, renounce this essential function. The outstanding example of such a class program, the *Communist Manifesto,* justifies its position with the claim that the united proletariat will represent the overwhelming majority and that its dictatorship will lead to a dissolution of all classes and therewith to the liberation of society as a whole. This second function differentiates the political party from a pressure group. Its specific interests must be fitted into the framework of the national collective. Wherever the policy-making parties do not succeed in this primary task, the modern state is in danger of deteriorating into a neofeudalism of powerful interest groups.

If the party in a democracy fulfils these two first functions of organizing the chaotic public will and educating the private citizen to political responsibility, then it can also lay claim to a third duty: *to represent the connecting link between government and public opinion.* Since democracies are pyramids built from below, the connection between leaders and followers becomes a necessity in the two-way traffic of democracy. It is the major function of the party to keep these lines of communication open and clear. Such a task makes the parties, if not the rulers, at least the controlling agencies of government in a representative democracy.

This crucial position is even more emphasized by the fourth function of a democratic party: *the selection of leaders.* Here as everywhere in a democracy, it is the competitive scheme, the choice between at least two oligarchies, which guarantees the quality of its leadership. Of course, such a selection presupposes an enlightened public, one qualified to make the right choice, and an intellectual climate appropriate to the functioning of democratic parties. Wherever these preconditions no longer prevail, the crisis of democracy is in the offing.

The crisis elements of democratic parties can be well perceived in the rise of dictatorial movements. In fact, dictatorial organizations often grow up within the democratic party system itself. They constitute a state within the state, alienated from its basic principles. And yet their rise is the expression of a basic lack within the society. They can recruit followers because there are those who no longer regard themselves as a part of the predominant society that does not seem to answer their essential desires and needs. No doubt every functioning group has and can bear some "outsiders" in its midst. So long as they do not represent a considerable number, they do not constitute a serious threat to the existing order. If, however, they succeed in recruiting an appreciable following, then the democratic process enters a critical stage. The rise of dictatorial parties within modern states is a storm signal for the democratic party system. From now on, the argument between parties concerns fundamentals and a fight over ultimate issues. For these integrated political groups compromise becomes increasingly difficult, and so does any coalition with another party.

The main purpose of the fully developed totalitarian parties becomes the fight for a new political order, for a new society. Speaking a different language and living according to a different set of values, the partisans have to be segregated from the political and social body of the ruling class and society, so the party leaders decree. Otherwise the partisans may be enchanted and taken in by the old order, the destruction of which is the essential purpose of the "guarantors" of the new morrow.

With the rise of the dictatorial party, its competitors in politics necessarily become more inflexible too. Struggle assumes the quality of a religious war; the only possible outcome for any contestant seems to be overwhelming victory or ultimate annihilation. Such a situation explains the revolutionary functions of a dictatorial party before its seizure of power: it is, above all, the *revolutionary vanguard* of the future state.

The functions of the dictatorial parties in power, outwardly at least, do not appear to be different from the four features of their democratic counterparts. They, too, have to organize the chaotic public will and integrate the individual into the group; they equally have to represent the connecting link between government and public opinion and, above all, guarantee the selection of leaders. Yet as their concepts of leaders and followers differ diametrically from democratic ideas, the meaning of these functions changes fundamentally. Organization of the chaotic will is fulfilled by a "monolithic control"; integration of the individual means "enforcement of conformity"; and, though these tasks are often directed by a "Ministry of Education and Enlightenment," the maintenance of communication between state and society is assured by a mere one-way propaganda stream from above. True, dictatorships also have to concern themselves with "public opinion." They must listen to the "voice of the people," especially since this is muted under the tyrant's rule. Thus the party serves through its secret agencies as a necessary listening post. Through such diverse services this leviathan apparatus, which claims at the outset to be the party to end all parties, becomes in fact the key instrument of modern totalitarianism.

All three functions, if successfully administered, secure the fourth and crucial purpose: the selection of leaders. Yet it is especially on this level of the creation, preservation, and extension of the ruling elite that the basic differences between the party systems become obvious.

Lenin's fight at the turn of the century for a small centralized revolutionary elite, as opposed to the Mensheviks' idea of a loose democratic mass organization, laid the foundation for a disciplined castelike order. He thus anticipated what revolutionary parties experienced a generation later when they had to choose between thoroughly revolutionist cadres and a mass following.

Only in a "revolutionary situation"—i.e., when complete victory or the prospect of impending success brings a rush of adherents to the revolutionary cause—is it possible for such a radical party to win and to hold the masses. Revolutionary parties reckoning with a long struggle can count on only a small elite of unrelenting fighters who do not care for rewards today and who are ready to make the revolution their life's calling. Masses are in need of visible rewards. If they cannot reap the fruits now—or at least have reasonable expectation of doing so in the near future—they will leave the ranks. This fact explains the extraordinary fluctuation in membership to be observed in radical parties everywhere. The Fascist followers of yesterday are turning up today as communism's most reliable fighters; and the reverse may be true tomorrow. Whoever delivers the spoils has the confidence of the fluctuating masses; but if he cannot do so by tomorrow, another liberator will be sought out.

How different from the rank-and-file reaction are the attitudes of the vanguard and the core members of the established movement, taking their orders from the central party organization, whether it means robbing a bank, organizing a party cell, or conceiving a new program. The revolutionary intellectual in his great flight into a future

morrow and the revolutionary "wire-puller" in his minute work, far apart though they be, have one thing in common: they do not expect rewards in this world. They have given their lives to the party, which in return becomes their own life. Discipline is the password of the movement. Said Lenin in 1900: "We must train men and women who will devote to the revolution not merely their spare evenings but the whole of their lives." This is the clarion call to the totalitarian party. It can appeal to the professional revolutionary at all times; yet to the masses it may be meaningful only during a revolutionary situation.

The Continental Communist parties in the interwar period opened their ranks to the masses partly because of their mistaken misapprehension of what they deemed a revolutionary situation (which had passed by 1920). They did not fare too well. In Soviet Russia, of course, they could offer their followers the spoils of the victor. In fact, many people joined the Bolshevik party for such reasons alone, and the early purges of the Soviet regime were partly to free the party from those "opportunists" (and more often from those whose services were originally useful but which now could be performed by newly recruited "reliable" followers).

The radical parties in the non-Communist countries did not have to eliminate "job-hunters" because there were no jobs to be distributed. As quickly as the prospects of revolutionary changes attracted the driftwood of a political reserve army, so did this army move quickly on to new shores which seemed more promising. The fate of the Communist parties outside Russia in the interwar period hinged on the dilemma between their revolutionary character and their aspirations for mass following, between their uncompromising attitude as a party which did not want to sell the revolution for a "mess of pottage" and the necessity of offering substantial results at once because the masses would not be satisfied with a promised millennium. They wanted higher wages, social security, political recognition—visible signs of success today. Thus they left the party that was preparing for a revolution not yet in sight.

A mass party cannot survive without foreseeable success. Its final fate becomes a race against time. The surprising staying power of the Communist parties in western Europe since 1945 seems to contradict such a statement; yet, as Charles Micaud's analysis convincingly shows, the left-wing radicals have learned some lessons from their earlier failures and have defined more realistically the function and place of the totalitarian party in what they regard as the preparatory stage of an oncoming revolution. In fact, the continued appeal of communism in France and Italy, despite the Marshall Plan and NATO, serves as a warning to the democratic powers in areas where they have not yet succeeded in reintegrating large segments of their national community. It is the claim of the Communist movements that they can give their followers a feeling of belonging, an active faith, and a promising direction for the future when the party will possess the whole community and seize the power of the state.

III / Toward a Classification of Parties

Since political parties are mainly concerned with the control of governmental power, the most obvious differentiation would be to distinguish the *in-group* from the *out-group*. Indeed, such a classification may point at some fundamental traits of political strategy and emphasize the advantage of a two-party system for clear-cut confronta-

tion. It would divide the "haves" and the "have-nots" in politics. Thus the insider at the controls would be often identified with the status quo, the conservative tendencies, while the challenging outsider would usually be the party of change and reform.

One may even go further and recognize in these two opposing camps a classification which has been frequently applied by Continental writers as the possessor's *party of patronage* versus the defiant's *party of principles* and thereby indicate the danger points of the two parties: the corruption of the "ins" by power and the irresponsible dogmatism of the "outs."

In a wider comparative approach, the degree of proximity to power may also explain interesting variations in national party systems. Wherever parties are called upon for political decision-making, as in the Anglo-American democracies, they may well emphasize the day-by-day *expediency interests*. On the other hand, in nations where the parties have played only a subordinate role or where they are purposely kept from political key positions by the government, as was the case during the greater part of German history, parties may easily retreat to the fundamental principles of an all-inclusive "faith movement" (*Weltanschauungs-* or *Glaubens-Parteien*).

These different national positions may also suggest a division of parties of *platform* and of *program*. One may, however, observe that such a strict cleavage has become less significant in recent decades. The more the German parties have been drawn into responsible politics, especially in the contemporary attempt at a democratic government, the more they are forced to make daily decisions along lines of concrete interests. Contrariwise, the Western democracies have been increasingly confronted with fundamental issues of international reorientation, national planning, and individual soul-searching—all of which demand a basic ideological outlook. This interesting *rapprochement* of seemingly contradictory systems will have far-reaching consequences and deserves our most careful consideration. At this point we must mention that the traditional lines of demarcation between the parties of expedient interests and those of fundamental principles have been blurred.

In the light of these developments another classification is losing its sharp contours, the suggestive division of *parties of personages* versus *parties of programs*. Although this dichotomy has reappeared today, but in a different version, in the contrast between dictatorial and democratic rule, between personal and institutional government—parties of personages are of the past. Max Weber's three stages of party development from aristocratic cliques to party of notables to plebiscitarian democracy point to a general trend in the Western world. The British party growth is a case in point, as Samuel Beer's careful study clearly shows. On the Continent, leaving aside preliminary aristocratic factions, the early period of parliamentary development, with its emphasis on local representation, was characterized by notables (*Honoratioren*) giving their name and decisive mark to political groups (as in the German parliament of 1848, the center and right-wing factions in the French Third Republic, and in pre-Fascist Italy). Yet today, when nation-wide public issues of class, religion, nationality, and international affairs constitute the dividing line of political parties, their leadership is forced to comply with the over-all program. Thus the parties became nationalized even in such traditionally decentralized structures as the United States, as E. E. Schattschneider's chapter pointedly describes (though personalities may still be crucial in making or breaking a party's hold on a nation, as the recent presidential elections in the United States abundantly testified).

The reality of modern politics represents a much more complex picture than is suggested by the simple array of insiders and outsiders, of parties of patronage and parties of principles, of expediency interests and Weltanschauung, of personages and programs. Such precise but utterly imaginary partitions fail to reveal the inner dynamics and tensions of a functioning democracy. In fact, it is the inexhaustible mixture of all these elements that comprises the life of modern political parties—and perhaps escapes any rigid classification.

A more modest attempt at systematization simply follows the number of contestants in the political field and speaks of one-, two-, or multiparty systems. But some important facts of political organization and control can be derived from such a classification.

A careful analysis of the causes and consequences of the two-party system versus the multiparty regime must probe into the historical circumstances, social structures, and institutional arrangements which underlie the divergent national political settings. While it is generally agreed that a two-party rule promises greater efficiency for the democratic process, as the British and American cases prove, it is equally obvious that such a political setting cannot be easily transplanted into national communities which do not meet its preconditions and which therefore, by no mere oversight or accident, possess a different political organization.

Historical precedents may suggest the following favorable circumstances for a two-party development: social homogeneity, political continuity, an early sanction of responsible political parties striving for political control, and their orientation at one elective office (the United States presidency, the British premiership) as the desired prize.

Wherever fundamental cleavages in social structure evolve and continue to exist because of differences in nationalities, regions, religion, or class which are often fostered by outside influences like *irredenta* movements and revolutionary internationals; wherever political revolutions coincide with great social transformations, as in France, central and eastern Europe, and the Near and Far East; wherever a controlling elite, through the divide-and-rule device, prevents parties from fulfilling their genuinely political functions of presenting clear-cut policy alternatives, as in Bismarck's strategies, for example; wherever the political machinery of a state diffuses the electorate's division by numerous choices —wherever any or all of these complicating factors enter the national political scene, a multiparty system finds its *raison d'être*. Obviously, it reflects in its more numerous groupings a fuller and more exacting picture of the peculiar features of a stratified society than a two-party system could ever present.

Once established, these different party systems have far-reaching consequences for the voting process and even more so for governmental decision-making. So far as elections go, in a two-party system both contenders will naturally compete for the shifting voter in the middle. Politics, therefore, will gravitate toward the center and the free-floating electoral bloc which is decisive for the winning or holding of a majority. The spectacle of a programmatic *rapprochement*, despite heated electoral campaigns, of the two main parties is not simply a trick of conniving politicians but a natural outcome of a party system that reflects a relatively stable order.

The double party has been called "a convenient system for contented peoples" who are agreed upon the general principles of the constitution and the policies of the government and feel not too intensely about measures over which they disagree. The fundamental cleavage over the slave issue broke for a time the efficacy of the American two-party system. The double party structure of modern England presupposed the reconciliation of the British Tories with the House of Hanover. Once the Glorious Revolution with its political institutions was recognized, they in turn could absorb the shock and major changes of the following social revolutions within their unchallenged political framework. Thus the miracle of British democracy in its combination of stability and progress was guaranteed. Once effectively established as a political institution, the two-party system reinforces and often perpetuates the trend toward conformity.

A multiparty system does not possess this unifying and centralizing order. On the contrary, yielding to its inability to produce a majority party in elections, its factions concentrate on the centrifugal forces of special-interest groups and may easily be directed at peripheral forces. Such diffusion of power, often emphasized by special electoral systems such as proportional representation (putting at high premium the true mirroring of all shades of public opinion), does not hold great promise for effective policy formation.

Policy-making in a two-party system is no doubt facilitated by its certain majorities and consequently its unmistakable party responsibilities. Yet even within the frame of the two major parties, a hidden multiparty system may often be detected with intra-party splits and factions or third parties, which may at times affect the crucial balance and enforce a break, new combinations, or compromises at the political front. In these critical moments the direct mandate of the people may be blurred by the parliamentary struggle for majorities until the voice of the electorate can be heard again.

What is exceptional in a two-party setting, however, becomes the rule under the procedures of a pluriparty system. By its very nature, it must transfer crucial decisions from a much-divided electorate to the parliament. This representative body in turn must content itself with a government by the formation of a coalition, attaining, after extended bickering, the compromise which in the two-party system is largely the voter's business to achieve within his own mind and political wisdom.

Even such a sketchy outline makes it obvious how much the character and policies of parties are defined by this formal division between two-party and multiparty systems. A classification along this line, therefore, proves to be quite suggestive and essential.

The differences are even more fundamental in the comparison of the one-party rule with the two-party and multiparty organizations. The character of the totalitarian rule indicates that a one-party system is a contradiction in terms. For clarity's sake it might be better to assign to this important contemporary phenomenon a different name, such as "political order." Modern usage, however, has coined the concept of the one-party state, and, if only for reasons of propagandistic appeal, the terminology has been accepted on the daily political fronts, both national and international. This being the case, one might recognize in the opposition of the one party versus the two and multi-parties the fundamental cleavage of our time: *dictatorship versus democracy.* Along this dividing line all basic tenets of modern parties must be redefined: their structure and strategy, their leadership, their apparatus, their following, their techniques of mass communication, their national policies, and their international ties. Through the organization and practices of these con-

trasting party systems, in turn, the two great contenders over political control in our society stand fully revealed. The essence of democratic and dictatorial rule is embodied in the daily life of their parties.

Essential though this sharp hiatus is for a classification of modern parties, such a crude black-and-white comparison cannot suffice for a substantial analysis of the political processes in our time. It leaves too much unsaid and unexplained: the shaded differentiation between existing political orders along the line of democracy and dictatorship, the twilight zones of their correlations, the conditions under which a transition from one to the other is facilitated, the inner complexities of the functioning institutions in both systems, and the shifting position occupied, in recent decades, by the modern parties in relation to the individual and the community at large.

The detailed analysis of dictatorial parties shows to what extent democracy is not only a symbol of aggression but also a claimed property of modern totalitarianism. The organization and incorporation of the people become the overwhelming concern of the seemingly independent autocracies. On the other hand, the effective democratic party has also radically changed its character and role in modern society, although this fact may not yet be fully recognized by its adherents.

Perhaps it is altogether impossible to try to put into systematic categories such an intricate and constantly shifting political process—but, at best, one might conceive a set of "emergent concepts" which would be highly significant. If one dared to measure at this point the long-range trends of party development, one might arrive at the following conclusions.

Modern parties have steadily enlarged their scope and power within the political community and have consequently changed their own functions and character. In place of a *party of individual representation,* our contemporary society increasingly shows a *party of social integration.*

This shift must be seen within the context of our changing society and its underlying philosophy. Three major stages can be observed in its development. Modern parties originated with the drive of a rising, self-conscious middle class that fought for liberation from the shackles of a feudal society and for representation to check monarchical absolutism. While the French Revolution officially proclaimed the end of this first phase of modern social development, the successful emancipation of rational man from the bonds of the *ancien régime* and its caste system proved to be only a transitional second stage. The individual, set free, was soon striving at reintegration into a new society. In fact, since the middle of the nineteenth century diverse claims for such a new orientation have been raised, promising to stop the fragmentation of a laissez faire society. The first and lasting challenge of rising socialism, the emergence and appeal of political irrationalism, and an awakening social liberalism gave contrasting answers to this key issue of our century. The dislocations caused by the sweeping industrialization, radical urbanization, and international migration, by world wars and total revolutions, gave substance to a planned search for a new social order. We are still in the midst of this third phase. It constitutes the crisis of modern society.

It is against this background of crisis that a new concept of party is evolving. Its emergence and persistence, in fact, may well depend on the momentous character of social crisis. The well-balanced communities of the Scandinavian states and the Anglo-American world seem to be least affected by this new type, while it has found its most complete expression within nations in the grip of revolutions. The islands of social equilibrium, however, have shrunk, and the party of integration has no doubt become a salient feature of our contemporary landscape.

The *party of individual representation* is characteristic of a society with a restricted political domain and only a limited degree of participation. Its membership activity is, for all practical purposes, limited to balloting, and the party organization (if existent at all) is dormant between election periods. Its main function is the selection of representatives, who, once chosen, are possessed of an absolutely "free mandate" and are in every respect responsible only to their own consciences. This conception of an ephemeral party as a mere electoral committee does not correspond to the political reality and practice of the modern mass democracy, a fact which in many countries has been recognized (though often most reluctantly) in the crucial controversy over party discipline and even in numerous court decisions codifying party regulations, responsibilities, and prerogatives. The fundamental concept of party, however, has hardly been challenged within democratic thinking.

Under the cover of such a persistent framework and rarely perceived even by circumspect political observers, a new type of party has emerged—the *party of integration.* The claim with which this party approaches its adherents is incomparably greater than that of the party of individual representation. It demands not only permanent dues-paying membership (which may be found to a smaller extent within the loose party of representation too) but, above all, an increasing influence over all spheres of the individual's daily life.

The first example of such a new party was presented by the Continental Socialists. Their organization has been jokingly characterized as extending from the cradle to the grave, from the workers' infant-care association to the atheists' cremation society; yet such a description articulates the intrinsic difference from the liberal party of representation, with its principle of "free recruitment" among a socially uncommitted, free-floating electorate (the bulk of which, in reality, may not be so independent). The following of the new movement is, indeed, much more clearly circumscribed by its permanent membership, the definite class alignment of its voting population, and its far-flung participation in over-all social affairs. The party can count on its adherents; it has taken over a good part of their social existence.

Despite such extensive organization and intensified ties of its partisans, the Socialist party (and in an even more limited way the Catholic movement and other democratic parties of integration) include only a small active core among its wider circle of mere dues-paying members and its even greater number of mere voters. In fact, this differentiation is at the base of the much-disputed "oligarchical" tendencies of modern mass parties which permit a relatively small group to decide the political fate of the disinterested and apathetic majority. Still, what is important is that the party in modern mass democracies has generally taken on an ever increasing area of commitments and responsibilities assuring the individual's share in society and incorporating him into the community. This is no mere usurpation of power by the politicians but the natural consequence of the extension of the public domain and the constantly increasing governmental functions in a reintegrated twentieth-century society.

In this sense the phenomenon of the *party of democratic integration* has become a matter of record. This fact makes it the more imperative to recog-

nize its basic variance from the *party of total integration,* which has found its prototype in bolshevism, fascism, and National Socialism. This all-inclusive party demands the citizen's unconditional surrender. It denies not only the relative freedom of choice among the voters and followers but also any possibility of coalition and compromise among parties. It can perceive nothing but total seizure and exercise of power, undisputed acceptance of the party line, and monolithic rule. The rise of this absolutist police state decrees the end of democracy, of constitutionalism, of communal self-government, of Western man and his inalienable rights, of political parties.

This radical juxtaposition should forewarn the responsible student of modern mass society against the threat of party petrifaction, but such a mortal peril cannot be met simply by a denial of the extended functions of modern parties and of their radically changing character—for the choice is not between the absolute state and the absolute individual or between autocracy or anarchy, as the great simplifiers and political demagogues make us believe. On the contrary, constructive thinking must concentrate on the much more difficult and urgent task of devising political institutions that allow for a new adjustment between the integrated society and the free individual. It is within such a realistic delineation of the fundamental prerequisites, present-day responsibilities, and necessary safeguards of a democratic society that the sociology of modern parties must be re-examined.

IV / Sociology of Political Parties

The study of the sociology of political parties has been completely dominated by Robert Michels' iron law of the oligarchical tendencies of social movements which he expounded with intense single-mindedness more than a generation ago in his *Political Parties.* While a standard work without doubt, it has shared the fate of so many classics—to be widely quoted and rarely read. Unfortunately, little empirical research has been done in the field of political sociology either in defining Michels' underlying assumptions or even in testing the validity of his thesis. In fact, it has become almost an undisputed axiom.

The first prerequisite for a more accurate appraisal of the intricate web of social relations within modern parties is an exacting theoretical framework. Without it, all the concrete investigations in the area will be meaningless, undirected, and just so much ballast in the scholar's bark. At this point only a few crucial concepts, issues, and hypotheses can be presented that may be suggestive for a proper orientation of future research. Key terms such as "leaders" and "followers," "participation" and "apparatus," need renewed clarification and a realistic differentiation in respect to the divergent political systems. Only an age corroded by the demagogical simplifiers of modern dictatorship could postulate the idea of a leaderless democracy. Only a naïve countermovement of overconfident democrats could overlook the weighty and often dangerous part played by aroused masses in present-day autocracies.

There are leaders and masses in democracies, just as in dictatorships. Leadership is a prominent theme of any political order. Yet every period, every society, every political system, establishes a different interrelation between leaders and followers. What is therefore important is to recognize clearly the divergent character, function, selection, and mobility, which vary in accordance with the whole structure of the prevalent political order. This social conditioning of modern leadership serves as a key to an understanding of the difference between democracies and dictatorships in our day.

Although differing greatly in time and space, two main types of political leadership can be distinguished: *institutional* and *personal.* These are types roughly corresponding to the contrasting political systems, democracy and dictatorship. The pre-eminent elements of leadership in a democracy are institutional. This fact, of course, leads to a difference in democratic leadership according to varying institutional structures. The unlike character of the British prime minister, the French president of the council, and the United States president are a reflection of different institutional setups of these democratic governments and their respective party systems. This institutional character defines the personal qualities of democratic authority, its functions, its rise to eminence, its continuation, and its fluctuation and limitations in power. Deference, which is no doubt a basic desideratum of any leadership, derives largely from the leader's skills, the extent of his knowledge, judgment, and foresight, his strength of conviction, his policies, his ability to attain social cohesion and to give direction to social forces. Balance of mind, distaste for violence of expression, a faculty for spreading conciliation on all sides, become highly valued qualities of democratic leadership. One should add, to enlarge upon Bagehot's famed remark, that the leader must be "an uncommon man of common opinions," which he articulates, intensifies, directs, and realizes through workable channels. This faculty of expressing the people's will points to a certain demagogical feature even in democratic leadership which is necessitated by the mass character of modern society. The pre-eminent elements of democratic authority, however, are institutional.

Dictatorial leadership is personal.

Here again will be found variations due to national traditions, historical circumstances, and personality patterns; but all modern dictators have this in common: they are anti-institutional. In fact, their very rise indicates the weakening or nonexistence of political institutions, of a ruling class, of an accepted code of rules, of a belief in a rational order. The modern dictator is the substitute for institutions in the mass age of political confusion and social disintegration. He is, above all, the demagogue—the leader of the people, who, rising from the dark as an unknown soldier, breaks through society's institutional barriers. He does not stand for a positive program but only for himself. He is responsible to no man but to God and the nation (who are conveniently removed from any direct interference), and in his very irresponsibility he is revered by the emotional, rootless, and amorphous masses seeking mystery, devotion, and the miraculous. He is the wonder-performing *charismatic* leader whose charm of personality conceals conflicts of policy. The "state of the masses" is indeed the key to the acceptance of his myth.

Charismatic leadership and bureaucracy may well accompany each other. Even though it may seem inconsistent with the emotional dynamics of this personal ruler, his power rests on a strong party organization, an apparatus. In fact, the guardians of his machine, the "lieutenants," reveal the true character of the one-party system, its daily life, its divided rule, its inner tensions, its chance for survival and succession. Generally speaking, it is on this second level of political control that the multifarious functions of modern parties become apparent, the differences in degree and kind between the democratic and dictatorial parties are manifest, and the resilience, flexibility, and deep antagonisms of contemporary political organizations are tested.

Bureaucratization is a categorical fate of modern society, involving equally government, business, and political parties. This fact may be deplored for its social strains and its often serious consequences of hampering spontaneity and free play in human affairs; it is still an indisputable necessity inherent in an efficient, highly developed mass organization. It implies stratification and hierarchy of office, specialization and fragmentation of the citizen's role, centralization of government. It has become "the organizational weapon" of modern dictatorship. Yet its perils are not met by denying its existence or by warning of the inevitable destruction of the democratic fiber by the spider of administration. What must be stated carefully, however, are the manifold expressions it has found, the conditions under which this necessary phenomenon may choke the basic forces of a free society, and the safeguards which can and must be erected against such constriction today and tomorrow.

As a preliminary investigation, an account should be given of the multifarious organizational forms within the diverse parties around the globe; possibly a comparison with developments in the adjacent trade-unions, business organizations, pressure groups, and social agencies would prove fruitful too. On the basis of these rich findings one might well arrive at some major qualifications of Robert Michels' glittering generalizations. They not only might be found to be an overstatement of the undeniable existence of oligarchical, hierarchic, and centripetal trends in every society but might be matched by data confirming the equally omnipresent democratic, leveling, and centrifugal forces encountered even within present-day totalitarian orders.

What is more important, Michels' emphasis may reveal a deeply imbedded bias in favor of the predominant bureaucratic, authoritarian values of his time. In this sense the initially socialist opponent of the Wilhelminic empire proves to be the latter's true child, who by no mere accident turns Fascist as a man. Such social conditioning may also be recognized in the crown witness of his inquiry—the German Social Democratic party, which, not without some justification, had been called one of the most Prussian institutions in the Reich. An analysis of other political movements growing out of a different social climate, such as the British Labour party, might have led Michels to very different conclusions.

Here is a random list of the multifactored determinants within the internal party organization which can help to define the conditions under which its complex relationship of leaders and followers may take a line different from that postulated by Michels.

First of all, variations in the character of those who are led are as important as those among those who lead, especially as the *concept of the masses* presents an even more elastic term. Leaving aside frequent moral connotations (such as "canaille," "the great unwashed," the "rebellious masses"), sharp distinctions should be made between the social variations of rural and urban groups, of scattered crowds and congregated mobs, of the latent and aroused masses, of the illiterate, numb, and untried and the educated, alert, skilled people. Different social classes invite a variety of stimuli and reactions. Political parties find an uneven appeal in various social strata, in accordance with their specific social experiences and historical conditions. Le Bon's influential school of crowd psychology, generalizing the experiences of the revolutionary upheavals in modern European capitals, identified the masses with the highly emotionalized and unstable character of the mob, thus stigmatizing mass action as devoid of individual self-control. While his simplifications still have

currency in popular thinking, highly sophisticated social research is beginning to uncover the much more complex interplay between the rational and irrational elements of modern mass reaction. Its findings will give a more adequate evaluation of mass participation in modern political movements.

Next to the specific character of the rank and file, the people's role in politics will depend on the *size of organization*. The transition from aristocratic factions to modern mass parties no doubt necessitated the development of bureaucracies, as in any other large-scale organizations. All other factors being equal, this must diminish the individual member's potential in policy-making. Moreover, time, continuous effort, and skills are increasingly demanded for adequate legislative decision and subsequent administration. Naturally, these prerequistics lead to the predominance of the permanent and party professional over the political amateur. The problem of political organization, however, is not solved by abolishing the experts but by finding methods of checks and controls by an alert citizenry. Danger spots for a dynamic democracy appear where an incumbent party administration has a permanent hold on the organizational machine, absolute control over financial resources, and monopoly of the internal channels of communication, thus stifling the voicing of counterpropaganda and alternative solutions and the rise of a substitute elite. The concrete situation in each nation and movement will depend on the complex of balances between party leadership and its apparatus, between parliamentary representation and national party conferences, between the executive core and peripheral membership.

Strength or weakness of the central authorities depends also on the *functions* to be performed. The single function of electioneering in the party of liberal representation will easily leave the power in the hands of "notables," just as trade-unions with an exclusive orientation toward labor contracts will not encourage wider membership participation. Not only do diffuse functions call for diverse leaders (efficient administrators and popular agitators, feudal confidants of the No. 1 man and reliable representatives of the interest groups, powerful masters of violence and political bosses, "ambassadors of the people," and informal holders of effective party patronage), but their consequent contradictions and controversies also offer the adherents alternative choices and increased influences. Even, and especially, the seemingly monolithic rule of modern dictatorships in their claim to total controls had to engage a multiple leadership that caused persistent tensions among the lieutenants, the inefficiency of secretly competing hierarchies within the party, and final disintegration of arbitrary government under the stress of supreme crisis. The failure of fascism and National Socialism might well be ascribed to the lack of open competition, of circulation of elites, and of free mass participation.

The *degree of participation* is a further key to the leader-followers relationship in political parties. Here again a preliminary exercise in definition is needed to clarify a politically charged and often purposely equivocal vocabulary. Ambiguity has become the secret weapon of modern autocrats. They will pride themselves on extending community enterprises as a genuine test of their "people's democracy." True, active involvement of a great number of party members can serve as a powerful counteracting force to oligarchical rule, yet democracy is not guaranteed by mere participation. If this means controlled and manipulated mass direction through the dictator's triple threat of all-embracing institutions, all-consuming fears, and

an all-pervading propaganda, it can in fact become the most potent instrument of his lasting power. Indeed, so far as his rule aspires to a radical change in the societal structure, effective mass participation seems to be a prerequisite for the successful breaking of the traditional patterns, for channeling the people's discontent, and for preventing a counterrevolution. In this sense modern autocracies are still children of a democratic age; they are postdemocratic dictatorships, and, because of that, they outdemonstrate any popular government in master-planned, minutely organized, mass meetings. Yet 100 per cent plebiscites are no demonstration of democracy, and true participation depends on more than "bread and circuses"; it demands political activation through free choice and decision. In order to assure such a democratic process it must, above all, keep its channels of communication clear and accessible to those who are ready to attend to their citizens' rights and duties.

A realistic appraisal of functioning democracies must, of course, take account of variations in popular participation in accordance with innate abilities, acquired skills, available time, and, above all, personal desires and aspirations. Negatively, the degree of apathy is indeed a most powerful and measurable factor in the failure of effective democracies. It is not the least conditioned by the promise of rewards in the sharing of power, although a careful analysis will also have to consider differentiations in popular participation in democracies without simplifying and unrealistic assumptions of equal sharing for *all* citizens in *all* actions at *all* times. The role of the expert, of the administrator, of the responsible policy-maker, will need a fresh evaluation.

The morale of the group depends largely on the extent of participation of its members. The degree of *fluctuation* in leadership, as enunciated by Mosca and Pareto in the suggestive theory of the *"circulation of elites,"* is a visible indication of the democratic chances of the party members. It gives a measure of the extent to which the controlling positions are open to free competition or monopolized by a closed group. It should also offer proof of the stability and longevity of the ruling class, although only isolated studies like Pontus Fahlbeck's classic on the Swedish aristocracy and similar works by Schott, Furlan, and Savorgnan on Continental development have so far presented the kind of exact material necessary for comprehensive comparative analyses.

Equally, if not more, important for democratic vitality is the party's ability to absorb and assimilate new social strata into the ruling class. Closely connected with this key problem is the much neglected phenomenon of the *succession in generations*. Many political revolutions have originated in this natural break between different political ages; the continuity of a political system, on the other hand, can well be measured in terms of its ability to guarantee a smooth and steady transition. This test of political wisdom and viability becomes manifest in the diverse selection and training of future leaders (and the mechanisms by which leaders can be retired). These procedures offer the most conclusive clue to the aims, character, and flexibility of the different party systems.

The usual *apprenticeship* of democratic aspirants through institutional channels of parliament, local government, and party organization is a selective process which tests particular qualifications: the capacity for effective statement, for framing legislation, for mastery in parliamentary debate, for teamwork, co-operation, and successful compromise. It offers a severe training and a slow rise to power—too slow for some young men in a hurry, who join extra-parliamentary move-ments that seem to promise a short cut to victory. The institutional path attracts certain personality types who may be groomed preferably by a definite educational system and who are more easily found in specific professions. The availability of trained political participants and, to use Max Weber's terminology, of "dispensable occupations" (lawyers, journalists, educators), which allow for career interruptions with even possible gains in skills and connections by such a political experience, will assure the filling of the necessary leadership reservoir. Equally important for the free flow of talent into political channels is a follow-up, a mechanism by which leaders can be retired and/or used for further advanced assignments without loss of craft and prestige. The rigidity of certain parties (and even more so, of many trade-unions) is often due to their petrified leadership which has no exit but oblivion.

While it is undoubtedly true, as Lasswell has stated, that stability of rule varies inversely with the degree of organization of a counterelite, the inner corruption of a power group is equally accelerated by the absence of an alternative challenge. And since the weakness of authority is often more significant for the breakdown of a system than is the strength of the opposition, one may perceive some chance for the disintegration of a monolithic rule, even if it has succeeded in destroying all articulate resistance.

Selection of leadership in modern autocracies meets with certain difficulties, despite the fact that conscious, long-range efforts are made for its preparation and for the master's succession. There is no natural competition in parliament or elsewhere to groom the dictator's lieutenants. Favoritism plays an important part in the selection, and especially in the higher brackets of the political hierarchy the leader's personal choice may even bring nonparty members into the inner council. The main channel, however is the party machine. Being a "charter member" of the party (the old guards of the first hour, the martyrs of the preceding "system's" prisons) is equivalent to a "safe" seat in a democratic parliament. These important qualities of the ardent fighters and trustworthy confidants may, however, at times become embarrassing after the seizure of power, and the "comrades of early and trying conspiracies" may be faced with purges and even the firing squad.

The composite structure of modern dictatorship in its all-embracing power requires varied types of leaders—demagogical, bureaucratic, militant, and feudal—and the party machine has to put forth the necessary material. This often discordant variety of functions creates, in fact, a hidden multiparty system within the monolithic regime, bringing about selection through partisan factions, victorious before the unpredictable court of the supreme potentate, where the sycophant wins a friendly hearing and qualified potential is discarded. Such arbitrary selection may in the end cost the dictator his effective rule, especially in a time of great trial, as the demise of fascism and National Socialism amply illustrates. As long as he lasts, the modern tyrant has, however, the audacity to bid for the perpetuation of his regime even beyond his life by usurping complete control over the mind of the nation's youth. This monopoly of training through state-controlled youth movements and a completely co-ordinated educational system may be modern dictatorship's most potent weapon. It is certainly too early to draw any definite conclusion as to whether it will succeed where its classical forerunners failed; yet certain prerequisites can be recorded.

Two preconditions for successful *perpetuation* of the dictatorial system seem to be indispensable: (1) the establish-ment of a well-functioning party machine and (2) the destruction or absorption of the traditional institutions. Success or failure will depend largely on the degree to which the system is internally consolidated. If the shots fired at Lenin in August, 1918, had killed him, the Soviet regime could easily have collapsed. When he did die in January, 1924, an integrated power system had grown up around him, and, after the short struggle between Stalin and Trotsky, the master of the party machine emerged as the victor. Similarly, the "heir apparent" of Stalin's regime had first been Kirov, and after his mysterious assassination Zhdanov took his place until he preceded his superior in death. If Khrushchev, following Malenkov, is destined to inherit Caesar's mantle, as has been widely assumed for a long time—the present transitional committee leadership notwithstanding—then the succession will adhere to the established procedures. The sequence of the list of "No. 2" men in Nazi Germany from Göring to Hess to Bormann indicated that Hitler followed similar succession plans. Apparently, Goebbels or Himmler never had a chance at the "line of succession" set down by Hitler. On the basis of our experience, which is extremely limited, we may surmise that the end of the political "glamour boys" of the revolution and the rise of the less conspicuous middle-of-the-road *apparatchik* may well describe the bureaucratizing pattern of dictatorial succession and—if it prove triumphant—the changing character of the revolutionary one-party regime.

V / THE PARTY IN A PLURALISTIC SOCIETY

This preliminary discussion of the sociology of political movements shows that a full definition of modern parties must include a clear understanding of the society of which they are a part and which they express. The nature and ethos of the ruling elite (military, managerial, intellectual, racial, religious, industrial, commercial, peasant, or proletarian, as the case may be), the status differentiation and degree of mobility (class or caste structure), the prevalent value system, the inner cohesion or crisis character of a nation—the complex interplay of these heterogeneous factors can alone indicate the extent of oligarchical trends or democratic participation within a political community.

Even the one-party state, with its seeming monolithic control by its dominant clique, cannot escape the intricacies of competing agencies in a highly developed society if it wants to survive. The purposely pluralistic democratic state must establish an ever renewed balance of society's divergent forces in order to assign the parties their proper place and function.

In fact, a high degree of diversity seems to create a favorable climate for a functioning democracy if it protects itself against the perils of castelike petrifaction and if it allows for a free interplay of its innumerable associations. And the varied parties serve as their forum.

Dictatorships, on the other hand, flourish among amorphous masses. If the natural groupings are not already pulverized, modern autocrats have to create a monolithic atmosphere, within which independent individuality and autonomous group life are submerged under the one-party rule and a "classless society" decrees "equality" before the tyrants. The fatal transformations in modern society—wars, inflation, depressions, and revolutions—prepared the ground and recruited the crucial strata of a dispossessed middle class, a propertyless peasantry, a rootless unemployed, and pugnacious partisans and perennial soldiers of fortune. Such constitute the social raw material of the rising autocracy, which systematically

dismantles all free agencies and reduces them to the level of enforced conformity. And this means the end of a functioning democratic party system.

The democratic process has to respect and integrate the numerous special interests within a live society. This creates the intricate and fascinating interrelations between *parties* and *pressure groups*, which are not identical and do not exclude each other; they coexist in continuous interdependence. Parties are not merely the sum of all pressure groups; nor can the public simply dismiss the interests' proper functions by muckraking exposés of lobby activities. For a long time parties and pressure groups have had a bad press, largely because of a mistaken classical approach, which judged politics from the isolated individual's point of view. Once the social group is recognized as a proper starting point, the balance between the representation of homogeneous pressure groups (seeking influence) and the decision-making activities of heterogeneous parties (seeking office and reconciling the diverse forces within the state) becomes a major theme of national politics.

The techniques of interrelations differ in time and space. Pressure groups may try to establish or conquer parties, as has been the case with a number of European parties with strict class alignments or straight nationality backing. They may play the role of a free-floating vote bloc, seeking out the highest bidder, as practiced in Anglo-American patterns; they may extend their influence through divided representation in different parties (*Querverbindungen*); or they may concentrate on minor parties, pressing their special interests.

Whatever their methods, the strength of the "invisible government," as William Allen White called this consequential agglomeration of more than a hundred thousand associations of all types in this country, should not be underestimated. Their power rests largely on their singleness of purpose and their great degree of centralization. This directed appeal to specific concerns has evoked a most active response from the people, as the effective mass organizations of the trade-unions and employers' organizations in the Western world testify, while a deep-seated skepticism concerning the political parties prevails. Unaccountable to the public at large, the economic pressure groups have often overshadowed the political parties and have, in fact, hindered them in their primary task of integrating the special interests into the framework of the national whole. A merely descriptive analysis of what is happening on the political scene is misleading. It seems to confirm the make-believe of politics as the sum total of pressure-group activities. Constructive leadership, while recognizing their claims, must guard against their aggressions and, in the knowledge of their essential role, must lift the demands of the specific interests to the level of national needs. This is where effective parties come in.

This crucial problem of rational integration is not solved by the creation of "economic parliaments." On the contrary, useful though such bodies may be as supplementary advisory councils for national legislation, wherever they are introduced in place of political parliaments, they decree the end of democracy. The "expert" character of occupational representatives limits their authority and naturally suggests the creation above them of a political apex which claims to represent the whole of the nation. Bismarck and Mussolini were not accidentally the champions of a chamber of corporations and the declared enemies of political parties. It is, indeed, through the network of political parties that the place and responsibilities of pressure groups must be circumscribed if the modern society is

not to deteriorate into a neofeudalism of powerful interest groups.

While the correlation of party and pressure groups decides the smooth flow of social forces, the political process is even more dependent on a proper delineation of *party and bureaucracy*. Here again the differences between democracy and dictatorship are obvious. It is equally true that the one-party state has in no way solved the dualism of the two forces; nor can democracies claim to have established an airtight distinction between the policy-making party government and the executive civil service. Theirs is a fluid relationship dependent on the continuous interplay of the agencies and, last but not least, on the incalculable informal contacts between the legislative and the executive branches.

The need for bureaucracy in the modern state is unquestionable, and so is the necessity for continuous checks on governmental agencies by the political parties in a democracy. How to combine the expert and the politician, administrative efficiency and democratic control, is a daily test of the ingenuity of political thinking. The British parliamentary rule of the responsible cabinet, the American presidential system, and the continuity of the French permanent civil service (vis-à-vis constant cabinet shifts in a multiparty system) —all suggest different solutions.

Leaving aside popular slogans of "the managerial revolution" and "the dictatorship of bureaucracy," one must recognize that policy formulation in the highly complex and time-pressured present-day state is done largely by the administrative bureaus, while the functions of the political organs are limited primarily to the control, articulation, and communication of public affairs. No simple formula can describe this intertwining process. Each nation has been trying in different fashions to adjust the tenuous relationship between bureaucracy and parties. Much spadework on this aspect of comparative administration is still needed to arrive at a fuller appreciation of possible solutions. To mention only a few outstanding problems: selection, training, ratings, and reforms of civil service; the extent and limitations of patronage appointments; the right of bureaucrats to participate in party politics and to accept political offices, parliamentary mandates, and cabinet positions; the actual influence of bureau chiefs and permanent undersecretaries in policy formation; the scope of delegated legislation; the administrative functions and control chances of political ministers; the changing attitudes of parties in power and in opposition to governmental agencies—all these much-discussed and controversial issues are indicative of the fact that it remains one of the major tasks of modern democracy to strike a new balance between executive and legislative power.

Confronted with such a challenge, the one-party regime finds itself in an insoluble conflict. The administration must be co-ordinated with the one and only political will and purged of all "undesirable" elements in a much more comprehensive fashion than the natural shift of political appointees indicates in the democratic range of government. (This "cleansing" from "party-book appointees," cynically termed a "restoration of civil service," is in fact a crude guise for securing promised rewards to "deserving partisans.") Yet the same dictators must show gratitude for the bureaucracy's service in bridging the old and the new order. The result is a discrepancy which reveals not only an inner party struggle between moderates and revolutionaries but the even more significant clash between state and party.

Dictatorial systems have varied in their attempts to meet these inherent contradictions. Fascist Italy alone went so far in at least posing the question of the self-dissolution of the Fascist party after its conquest of the state. This very suggestion may be proof of fascism's relative conservatism and state absolutism or of its utter failure to subdue Italy's bureaucracy.

Soviet Russia, on the other hand, decreed the complete abolition of the traditional bureaucracy; and the original Bolshevik theory even predicted the "withering-away" of the state altogether. In reality, Lenin outstripped Peter the Great, and Stalin outdid Ivan the Terrible, in establishing the mammoth totalitarian apparatus in a superplanned society. The results were wavering methods, continuous fluctuations between the radical purge of a managerial class and the creation of a huge amount of red tape, suspicion against the "experts," and unlimited power for the machine. The NEP, the calling of foreign specialists, the praise of the "shock workers" (Stakhanovites), the temporary independence of the Red army officers—all these measures, halfheartedly undertaken and repeatedly reversed, showed the indecision of the Soviet regime in respect to modern management and testified to the fatal failure of a party dictatorship to arrive at a *modus vivendi* with an efficient bureaucracy. Of course, the ruling party could also—and did, indeed—turn such a misfortune into an asset by making the resistant bureaucracy a welcome scapegoat for all the ills of the monolithic order.

The Nazis' seeming success in establishing a monolithic order turned out to be an even greater failure. More revolutionary than fascism and yet more loaded with traditional liabilities than bolshevism, Hitler's Germany tried a weird solution of an artificial separation of state bureaucracy and party machine —a "Dual State." This separation between the party and the state (the one free from official handicaps expressing the "boiling soul of the people," the other not responsible for this "spontaneous outburst") could be clearly played up in an intricate technique of legalizing revolutionary upheavals. It was a useful device to cover up irresponsible party action with "respectable" formal legislation and thus to calm legal-minded people. The master-plan to enrol the "neutral experts" in the strange combination of "arbitrariness and efficiency based on order" was the essence of the Third Reich. But it did not prevent continuous clashes between the two hierarchies of party and bureaucracy. The discrepancies were fully revealed in the critical years of the Nazis' war on the world. After the party's collapse the bureaucracy still had to pay for the insincerities of the "Dual State."

Another critical relationship, especially in dictatorial systems, is found between *party and armed forces*. Democratic parties, by definition, exclude the creation of private armies, recognize the monopoly of military force in the hands of the state, and exercise their power through ballots, not bullets. It is only in their resistance to modern aggressive movements that constitutional parties in Europe have half-heartedly considered the development of a para-military arm. These auxiliary forces, in fact, have not halted the attack against constitutional government but have only epitomized its loss in power and prestige.

The control of the armed forces is a question of survival for modern dictatorship. The military are usually the personification and last stronghold of traditional power, which must be crushed as the only serious threat to established totalitarianism. Moreover, their services are badly needed for a system directed toward war. This fact gives the professional soldier, especially in countries with a military tradition, a preferred position and a prestige far superior to that enjoyed in the "unsoldierly

bourgeois democracies." In the beginning the promise of promotion to career-bound, ambitious young officers and the semblance of seeming independence quickly flatter them into submission. Experts are often politically blind and usually raise no objections to having the policy-makers pass on to them the watchword in return for their "neutral services."

In most dictatorships, however, it does not take long, especially for the controlling military circles, to realize that their fundamentally rational institution is worlds apart from the irrational politics of the modern *condottiere* and his irregulars who cannot be held by the hard-and-fast rules of army discipline. They take the world by surprise and manifest the unpredictable daring of the amateur and restless adventurer. Partisan guerrilla warfare and total terror are their weapons, not the carefully calculated and purposely limited campaigns of the professional high command. There is no compromise possible between these two conflicting concepts of strategy in violence. The continuous clashes between the Nazi storm troopers and the Reichswehr, between the Fascist Blackshirts and the Italian army of Marshal Badoglio's brand, between the Soviet political commissars and Red army commanders, between the Peronisti and the Argentine army, all testify to the persistent difficulties of the one-party state in mastering the professional soldier. Success or failure entirely determines the striking power of the dictatorial regime and its persistence, for its militant character is at the roots of the modern totalitarian party.

The militant structure of the dictatorial party is indeed the strikingly novel element in modern political organization. From its beginnings it is, above all, a "fighting league," with its "shirt" movements to "protect" the peaceful meetings of the rising party, its punitive excursions against recalcitrant opponents, its strict hierarchical order and party discipline, its actual fighting of a civil war. Politics becomes a battle of two irreconcilable opponents who are out to win and thereby to destroy the nation's or the classes' archenemy.

This permanent revolution has to go on even after the state is conquered—opposition groups must be seized, the party must be kept in warlike preparedness and must be regularly purged. All this militancy at home is only a prelude to the march on the world of the revolutionary party. Every revolution which claims to be more than a mere change of government and which pretends to create a new social order must also stir up neighboring countries and awaken in them a spirit of deep unrest. This quasi-religious "missionarism" knows no frontiers and, with the services of world-shaking ideologies as a moving propaganda arm, tries to recruit soldiers of the new creed in an international civil war. This appeal brings into dramatic focus another element of the modern party—indeed its most critical feature—the international impact of political movements.

VI / The Internationals of Parties

Political parties, when fully unfolded, operate in three concentric circles. They are based on personal loyalties; they manifest themself through numerous groupings within a nation; and they reach out beyond state boundaries with their ideologies and their organized "Internationals." There is no Communist monopoly on world-wide planning, spectacularly and noisily though the Third International (Comintern or Cominform, as the case may be) has claimed a unique and unchallengeable position in this global battle of the minds. The color scheme runs the whole gamut of the spectrum. In fact, the basic char-

acter of any party may well be determined by its international behavior.

Little reliable material is available on these international ties and reactions; and the less is known, the more make-believe, rumor, and mystery enter the speculations of the troubled citizens. Yet in our time—when the frontiers between domestic and international affairs are blurred, and revolutionary upheavals, destroying the stability of a prevailing social structure, are reaching beyond national compounds—political parties have become international forces that must be studied, especially where they shun the broad daylight in their submerged activities and, like an iceberg, allow only a small portion of their power bloc to appear on the global surface.

These world-wide disturbances may be registered and measured through a threefold approach: (1) through an evaluation of prevailing political ideologies; (2) through an analysis of the changing social structures; and (3) through an appraisal of partisan strategies on an international plane.

In order to make them useful yardsticks in the present political labyrinth, ideologies must be reconsidered as to their real meaning. Such an examination will find that the accustomed classifications of political movements in terms of conservatism, liberalism, socialism, communism, etc., are misleading, to say the least. Not only have innumerable combinations (such as national bolshevism, liberal conservatism, conservative socialism, the peoples' democracy) confused the political fronts, but the fundamental concepts themselves have shifted their original meaning under the impact of a radically changing society. One may even doubt the simple contrast between right- and left-wing movements. Originally, "radical" groups, such as the Parti Radical Socialiste, have been pushed to the right under the pressure of newly appearing leftist movements. At the same time frequent attempts at bridging right- and left-wing radical organizations, insignificant though they may be in view of long-range developments, point at similar psychological attitudes even among deadly political opponents.

The proper recognition of these difficulties should not lead to the easy dismissal of the concept of ideology altogether, as is frequently suggested by shortsighted "realists" in politics. On the contrary, ideologies cannot be taken seriously enough in the vacuum of a spiritual crisis when the underlying unity of Christian European traditions is challenged by a counterchurch, when uncompromising conflicts along petrified political fronts are threatening, and when the drives for fundamental reorientation are of primary importance in the final lineup of the peoples—at least, wherever they still remain free to choose.

Ideologies are the key to an understanding of the long-range strategy behind the day-by-day tactics of political movements. The means of international tactics are subservient to the ends of the axiomatic political religion. In such a world setting ideologies have become the most powerful weapon in international politics, and even their ambiguity has proved to be a potent factor in the political orientation or misdirection of a confused world society.

This confusion is to a large extent due to the radical transformations of the major social classes, which naturally have transcended national frontiers. Shifting party lines the world over cannot be understood without a full realization of the crisis of the middle class. It represents as important a hiatus, especially in Western society, as formerly did the collapse of the feudal order which culminated in the French Revolution. The coinciding changes within the proletariat are equally remarkable, whether it takes a turn toward bour-

geois-mindedness or toward further class isolation.

The awakening of the peasantry, dormant for centuries, is another factor that may have far-reaching repercussions. The hesitant beginnings and sporadic appearances of a green International deserve careful watching. Last but not least, the rising crucial strata of all dimensions—the unemployed, the dispossessed, the militant irregulars—all have become international types and, as such, influence in some comparable fashion the political fronts in all nations.

In fact, the internationals of all colors have based their strategies on certain expectations of supra-national class behavior. The beginnings of an international Christian Democratic movement (whose support by adroit papal diplomacy and its popular arm, the Catholic Action, is difficult to appraise), the resurgence of world liberalism, neo-Fascist rumblings, the revival of the Socialist Second International, the gathering of latent forces among the erstwhile resistance movements, the first international party alignments at Strasbourg's Council of Europe—weak though all these attempts may still be, they can count on a certain response within different nations. These movements ought to be studied not only as potential powers of the future but also in their direct and indirect influence on national policy decisions at the present time. Political campaigns here and abroad have been deeply affected by their global connections. The strategy and outcome of the Italian elections of 1948 and 1952, the Papagos victory in Greece, the Saar vote, the United States presidential elections of 1952, the West German elections of 1953, and the British elections of May, 1955, might have been very different, had it not been for their international implications.

Even bolshevism, despite its watertight isolation, cannot escape the influence from without, especially if it wants to affect this outside world. In this light, the transition from the Comintern to the Cominform may reflect a shrewd and realisic reappraisal of the changing dynamics of modern society. This new strategy, while still insisting on Lenin's fundamental formula of class loyalty above national loyalty, seeks more than a mere proletarian base of recruitment and mobilizes instead—if only for short-run tactical purposes—all elements of unrest within the nations. Now the party appeals, above all, to powerful national ambitions. It is not altogether a new turn. Mao Tse-tung and Ulbricht may take their line from Borodin and Radek of a quarter of a century ago. Revolutionary activists of the war resistance, an awakened peasantry in the shadow of feudal southeastern Europe, China, and southeast Asia, and a deeply disillusioned middle class everywhere can be steered into a new "Fatherland Front" and might be united by the militant appeal of a grass-roots, partisan nationalism, by the fear of American "imperialism," and by the promise of "lasting peace." Indeed, peace becomes a most potent political weapon of Cominform propaganda in a war-weary world. But, while the new Communist combine of the U.S.S.R. with its ring of satellites, as compared with the old Comintern, seemingly allows for greater national autonomy and a more decentralized system of Red internationalism, its main purpose still remains the establishment of a strong arm of Soviet foreign policy. Wherever the new nationalism comes into conflict with Russian interests, it must be denounced in the name of the revolution as a nationalist deviation.

The world revolution has found a fatherland. It gives the Third International a tremendous striking power, which a revolutionary state does not hesitate to exploit unscrupulously. This very connection, however, creates all the liabilities under which communism as the international arm of Russian bolshevism suffers within every nation. The divided loyalty of its members has meant continuous setbacks to the Communist parties within other nations, purges among their leadership, and confusion for the following.

Red imperialism, by no mere accident, experiences increasing tensions within its own camp. Titoism is more than a peripheral phenomenon of an overexpanded superpower, although the fact of geography is not a minor item in this first defection from the Bolshevist creed. Geography may well be counted a deterrent to an extended defiance of Soviet rule among adjacent satellites which can be easily held under the sway of the Red army and of militant bolshevism. The "good neighbors" must present governments "friendly to the Soviet regime."

Indeed, in this age of *international civil war*—cold, lukewarm, or hot as it may be—between the superpower blocs of this bipolar world, political parties are aligned in the name of, or in opposition to, *revolution*. Commonly regarded as a mere internal upheaval, revolution has become a world phenomenon. Its significance is measured by its international effect. Radical upheavals, as all great revolutions are, must be played on an international stage. Every region has become sensitive to the developments of far-distant lands.

The very fact that areas far apart geographically and historically have been pushed together on this shrinking planet has created a revolution altogether different from the stereotypes found in story-books and even in more learned texts. The complexity of this new cataclysm must be fully comprehended in order to appraise the specific nature and aims, the spread and directions, of the contemporary upheaval.

Different ages and different revolutions have become strange contemporaries. They cannot be isolated in neat separate compartments—they fight, they influence, they imitate one another. The contemporary revolutions are inextricably mixed in structure and strategy, in patterns and politics. Still every era has its predominant type; the stronger revolution sets the style.

What is the character of the twentieth-century upheaval? It is neither an objective phenomenon outside human control, such as the interference of God or nature (in the definition of the Renaissance) within world affairs, nor is it the free, subjective human act of heroes standing up against and reversing the natural trend of objective phenomena, as the age of the barricades and the Romantic revolutions saw it. Now the "objective" march of events and the "subjective" deeds of heroic man are interwoven into a new revolution when "the time is ripe" for it and when dynamic leaders can articulate the "revolutionary situation" which otherwise may pass by. There is nothing accidental in its outbreak, no chance in its unfolding, no sudden whim in its success or failure. The modern revolution is a calculated, planned, long-range process and is executed almost to cold scientific exactness by the "professional revolutionaries." No longer can it trust to the appearance of the dynamic dilettante whom the spirit moves to enter meteor-like and to disappear when the excitement of the heroic battle is over. It summons the sober rationality of the patient expert. Organized political parties play a major role in preparing and continuing the permanent revolution. Like modern warfare, its outcome is often decided long before the actual declaration of hostilities. In fact, the carefully planned revolution may well be over but for the shouting at the time of the official outbreak, as the Czech coup of February, 1948, proved so tragically. Moreover, not a single soldier may be needed to move across national frontiers in order to win the major battles in this international civil war. A central revolutionary authority (under whatever name—Politbureau or Central Committee) can direct its orders across frontiers by remote control through the well-established revolutionary pipelines of the disciplined party and its organizational weapons.

Such an upheaval can be defeated by its opponents only if they recognize the changed character of modern revolutions and thus meet the long-range strategies of the Moscow manipulators by equally circumspect planning against the root causes of unrest—in time and with vigor.

The second feature of modern revolution—its confluence of different types of upheavals—is a case in question. Probably the most blatant example of this complex phenomenon is presented in southeast Asia and the Middle East today, where the democratic, the national, and the social revolutions coincide. While the first and the second kind have been the characteristic revolutionary expression of the great world in the nineteenth century, they are now finally evolving in the erstwhile colonial areas. Yet their belated appearance in the Far East, southeast Asia, the Near East, and southeastern Europe makes them contemporaries of the twentieth-century social revolution. And as in earlier upheavals a stronger nationalism had penetrated and conquered the weaker liberal forces, today the dynamic social revolutions easily take command of the budding democratic-national movements and direct them into the stream of the "coming world revolution." This may not be surprising in view of the difficult plight of these newcomers among nations (the effect of long-lasting foreign political and economic domination, of "imported" revolutions, of inexperienced leadership, and of a weak middle-class basis). Such a turn is quickly offered by the master-strategists of the Soviet revolution, who, in accordance with the Leninist-Stalinist theory of imperialism, attempt to co-ordinate both social revolt and colonial liberation and therewith raise the claim to revolutionary world leadership.

Marxism, which within a highly industrialized society has met with remarkable resistance among the "internal proletariat," to use Arnold Toynbee's suggestive phrase, may be more successful with the "external proletariat" of the poverty-stricken masses of agrarian feudalism in underdeveloped areas. (Incidentally, it is significant that Italy and France, least dynamic in their industrial development and still influenced by feudal traditions, have been the only Western powers where Soviet infiltration has made persistent and deep inroads.) Imperialism, until recently a mighty weapon in the hands of distant exploiters, may be turned by rising colonial peoples into an easy scapegoat for all the ills that have befallen them under imperial occupation. The dangerously vacillating game of passing demagogues, like Iran's Mossadegh or Egypt's Naguib and their fanatical "party gangs," must be seen against this sordid background of desperately impoverished economies. No doubt, revolutionary Marxism has been not without success in these areas of awakening nationalism, and this despite the fact that the drive for Westernization has been the clarion call for the "underdeveloped peoples," the U.S.S.R. included. The Point Four program is an attempt at mobilizing and recapturing the imagination of the colonial world and no less that of the United States,

which, we must remember, was also born of revolution.

Late may be the hour in this great competition for the support of the new protagonists just passing the threshold of their conscious history. Time is of the essence; yet it may not be ours. "The meeting of the East and West" has been a head-on collision brought about by wars and revolutions. This naturally means cultural dislocations and social tensions. To transplant complex production methods into a primitive economy and to telescope centuries of slow European growth into a short span of one generation presages serious perplexities. To direct the highly excited and equally immature masses will demand responsible leadership. Yet this individual sense of duty to the greater community may well be strange to oriental traditions. Besides, a germane political elite—one which has grown up in rebellion against imperial rule—may not be ready to take on the unaccustomed and different functions of governing. A new generation of leaders will be needed and may be wanting.

The development of a responsible party system could well be the secret of a successful transition from colonialism to political self-rule. India and Pakistan, despite their political "childhood diseases," show certain promising signs. The relatively smooth surrender on the part of the British, especially in the last critical stages, may have something to do with it.

These are but a few of the burning issues faced by the awakening nations and no less by their aged contemporaries. The peoples meet, clash, and conciliate their interests in the moves of organized parties on the international plane everywhere. They are often not sure of their own stand. Prelude or postlude, the intricate choices before them reflect the confluence of different streams of revolution and their consequent confusion. Hesitation and doubt also reflect widespread uncertainties as to the true nature and direction of the revolution in our time. Above all, however, this revolution challenges our ingenuity to articulate workable programs, to organize functioning movements, and to put them to constructive action —weighty responsibilities which rest primarily with the peoples' great intermediaries: the political parties.

FOR FURTHER STUDY

For Further Study

This extensive bibliographical appendix, selective and by no means comprehensive though it is, shows the extraordinary wealth of material available for further study. At the same time, it makes the researcher in the field fully aware of the necessary spadework still to be done in concrete field studies and the conceptual framework yet to be advanced. We are witnessing only the initial stages of a large-scale enterprise. The bibliography, therefore, is intended to be purposely tentative and suggestive and in no way definitive.

The proper answer to the many questions as to the nature, structure, and strategy of modern political parties must be sought empirically and in terms of the extraordinary diversity of historical circumstances, institutional traditions, and national characteristics. It is in a way amazing and promising for future developments that the study of political parties has suddenly found a refreshing start in different nations. Such case studies, using the newer techniques of quantitative and qualitative investigations, have been tackled simultaneously in various countries by pioneer workers in the field and by ambitious collective-research enterprises. To mention only a few impressive undertakings abroad, one may point to the exemplary studies of Nuffield College (Oxford), the French "Cahiers de la Fondation nationale des Sciences politiques," and the publications of the re-established Deutsche Hochschule für Politik (Berlin) and of the Vereinigung für politische Wissenschaften. The time may be near when attempts at a tentative drawing-together of such vast and diverse collections will provide valuable conclusions for a comparative analysis and thus establish a sound basis for an over-all new view of the democratic process. Such a rich harvest of research ought to be of the greatest significance for the developing field

of parties and political sociology in the United States as well as abroad.

To illustrate the breadth of the renewed attack on the study of political parties, the following group publications should be mentioned of the Nuffield studies: R. B. MacCullum and A. Readman, *The British General Election of 1945* (Oxford, 1947); H. G. Nicholas, *The British General Election of 1950* (London, 1951); D. E. Butler, *The British General Election of 1951* (London, 1952); and the equally impressive monograph by D. E. Butler, *Electoral System in Britain, 1918–1951* (Oxford, 1953), which, incidentally, gives valuable insights as to the possible effect that the much-discussed proportional representation would have had if it had been introduced into Great Britain.

The French "Cahiers de la Fondation nationale des Sciences politiques" (Paris: Librairie Armand Colin) has published, among others, the following: C. Moraze and others, *Études de sociologie électorale* (Paris, 1947); J. Cadart, *Régime électoral et régime parlementaire en Grande-Bretagne* (Paris, 1948); A. Siegfried, *Géographie électorale de l'Ardèche* (Paris, 1949); M. Duverger, F. Goguel, and others, *L'Influence des systèmes électoraux sur la vie politique* (Paris, 1950); A. Latreille and A. Siegfried, *Les Forces religieuses et la vie politique: Le Catholicisme et le protestantisme* (Paris, 1951); G. Dupeux and F. Goguel, *Sociologie électorale: Esquisse d'un bilan* (Paris, 1951); F. Goguel, *Géographie des élections française de 1870 à 1951* (Paris, 1951); and the classic controversy expressed in Maurice Duverger's study, *Les Partis politiques* (Paris, 1951), and G. E. Lavau, *Partis politiques et réalités sociales* (Paris, 1953).

See also "Schriften des Instituts für politische Wissenschaften": No. 1, *Wahlkampf und Machtverschiebung: Geschich-*

*te und Analyse der Berliner Wahlen vom
3. Dezember, 1950; No. 2, Faktoren der
Machtbildung: Wissenschaftliche Studien
zur Politik;* and the forthcoming studies:
*Die Auflösung der Weimarer Republik;
Analysen der Bundestagswahl 1953; Die
Monopolisierung der öffentlichen Meinung
in der Sovietischen Besatzungs-Zone.* Of
the promising series of the German Vereinigung für die Wissenschaft von der
Politik, edited by Dolf Sternberger, the
following studies should be mentioned:
Rudolf Wildenmann, *Partei und Fraktion,*
and Götz Roth, *Fraktion und Regierungsbildung* (both published by Meisenheim,
1954).

The American discussion has been
greatly furthered by the report of a committee of the American Political Science
Association, *Toward a More Responsible
Two-Party System* (New York, 1950), under the chairmanship of E. E. Schattschneider; see also the comprehensive survey edited by Paul T. David, *Presidential
Nominating Politics in 1952* (Baltimore,
1954). As a continuation of the 1952
study, the American Political Science
Association is presently sponsoring a comprehensive project on the 1956 elections.

For an over-all introduction, though
naturally dated as of two decades ago,
the essays on political parties written by
specialists for the *Encyclopaedia of the
Social Sciences,* XI (New York, 1933),
589–639, are still of great value, especially the bibliographies on the different
national party systems.

Valuable preparatory work has been
done by the Social Science Research
Council and its appointed committees on
comparative politics. See the symposium,
"Research in Comparative Politics," *American Political Science Review,* XLVII
(September, 1953), 641–75; for an earlier evaluation see Karl Loewenstein, "Report of the Research Panel on Comparative Government," *American Political Science Review,* XXXVIII (June, 1944),
542–43.

Among singlehanded attempts, the following books stand out as suggestive and
substantial contributions: C. J. Friedrich,
*Constitutional Government and Democ-
racy* (rev. ed.; Boston, 1950); Herman
Finer, *The Theory and Practice of Mod-*

ern Government (rev. ed.; New York,
1949); and Karl Loewenstein. *Political
Reconstruction* (New York, 1946). See
also the increasing discussion of the com-
parative method in neighboring fields and
disciplines, such as M. S. McDougal, "The
Comparative Study of Law for Policy
Purposes," *Yale Law Journal,* LXI (June–
July, 1952), 915–46; Harold D. Lasswell,
Daniel Lerner, and Ithiel de Sola Pool,
The Comparative Study of Symbols
("Hoover Institute Studies" [Stanford,
Calif., 1952]); and H. D. Lasswell, *The
Comparative Study of Elites: An Intro-
duction and Bibliography* ("Hoover Insti-
tute Studies" [Stanford, Calif., 1952]).
See also Chester Barnard's "Theory of
Comparative Systems," in his *The Func-
tions of the Executive* (Cambridge, Mass.,
1938); Marion Levy, *The Structure of
Society* (Princeton, 1952); A. R. Rad-
cliffe-Brown, *African Political Systems*
(1940) and *Structure and Function in
Primitive Society* (Glencoe, Ill., 1952).

The comparative approach is not altogether so new as some recent explorers
in the field seem to think. Without reaching further back, one may find pioneering
testimony in the works of the twentieth-
century masters: in Max Weber's *Wirtschaft und Gesellschaft* (Tübingen, 1923);
Alfred Weber's *Kulturgeschichte als Kul-
tursoziologie* (2d ed.; Munich, 1950); and
Émile Durkheim's *Les Règles de la mé-
thode sociologique* (rev. ed.; Paris, 1947).
For more recent studies along these lines
in the United States consult the writings
of H. D. Lasswell, Talcott Parsons, Robert
Merton, and others; see also F. X. Sutton,
"Social Theory and Comparative Politics"
(a paper presented at the Social Science
Research Council Conference on Comparative Politics, Princeton, June, 1955).

The following bibliography, consistent
with the organization of the book itself,
was prepared by the respective contributors.

I / Great Britain

General

M. I. Ostrogorski's *Democracy and the
Organization of Political Parties in the
United States and Great Britain* (1902)

is still indispensable; and the chapters in A. L. Lowell's *Government of England,* first published in 1908, are very useful. Deserving to rank with these standard works is a recently published book by R. T. McKenzie, *British Political Parties: The Distribution of Power within the Conservative and Labour Parties* (London, 1954).

Lists of books and articles on political parties will be found in many of the works given below. In particular should be mentioned the selected bibliography, compiled by Sydney D. Bailey and published in the special edition of *Parliamentary Affairs,* on the British party system (Vol. V, No. 1 [winter, 1951]), and the bibliography in McKenzie's *British Political Parties.*

For a yearly summary of political events see the *Annual Register.* Keezing's *Contemporary Annals* is useful in following events during the year. The best current commentary on party politics will be found in the *Observer* (Sunday). The *Times' House of Commons,* which is published after each general election and to which supplements are occasionally issued, includes biographies of all candidates, as well as a brief account of the campaign and summaries of election results in terms of votes and seats. For electoral statistics see also the *Constitutional Yearbook,* published by the Conservatives until 1938. The results of the surveys made by the British Institute of Public Opinion are published in the *News Chronicle.* Articles on parties and political behavior will be found in the *Political Quarterly, Political Studies* (the journal of the recently formed British Political Studies Association), the *British Journal of Sociology,* the *Manchester School,* and *Parliamentary Affairs.*

Party Publications

THE CONSERVATIVE PARTY.—The annual reports of the Executive Committee and Central Council and the verbatim report of the proceedings of the annual conference have been regularly published only since 1947. Full reports of party meetings, however, can also be found in the

London *Times.* Since 1893 the Central Office has published a periodical giving news of speeches and policy and party developments. Appearing weekly and, since 1946, under the name of *Notes on Current Politics,* this is indispensable not only because of its account of what is happening in the Conservative party but also because of its detailed analyses of events in the Labour party. Other important party publications include the eleven pamphlets in the "Organization Series"; the *Interim and Final Reports of the Committee on Party Organization* (1948 and 1949) (the Maxwell Fyfe report); and *Notes on Procedures for the Adoption of Conservative Candidates in England and Wales* (1953).

THE LABOUR PARTY.—The most useful of the party publications is the annual report, which includes the verbatim report of the party conference and the reports of the National Executive Committee and the parliamentary party as well as appendixes, such as the Constitution and Standing Orders of the party, the Standing Orders of the parliamentary party, and a list of affiliated members and constituency parties. These volumes go back to the first conference in 1901. Other important party publications are the *Model Rules* (sets A–E) for various types of constituency parties; H. Croft, *Party Organization* (rev. ed.; 1950); *Labour Year Book* (first put out in 1916); and the *Handbook: Facts and Figures for Socialists* (1950 and subsequent years). Monthly periodicals include the *Labour Press Service* and *Fact: The Labour Party Bulletin* (from 1941). A valuable list of party pamphlets, programs, reports, etc. (1914–47), is contained in the Bibliography of G. D. H. Cole's *History of the Labour Party from 1914.*

THE LIBERAL PARTY.—In addition to the *Constitution of the Liberal Party* (rev. ed.; 1952) and the reports of the Liberal party organization presented to the annual meetings of the assembly, there should be mentioned the pamphlets and programs issued by the publication department of the party, particularly the "Radical Programme Series."

Select List of Articles and Books on British Parties and Political Behavior

ATTLEE, C. R. *The Labour Party in Perspective—and Twelve Years Later.* London, 1949.

BEER, MAX. *History of British Socialism.* London, 1948.

BEER, S. H. "The Future of British Politics," *Political Quarterly,* January–March, 1955.

BENNEY, M., *et al.* "Social Class and Politics in Greenwich," *British Journal of Sociology,* December, 1950.

BIRCH, A. H., *et al.* "Voting Behavior in a Lancashire Constituency," *British Journal of Sociology,* September, 1950.

BURNS, J. M. "The Parliamentary Labor Party in Great Britain," *American Political Science Review,* Vol. XLIV, No. 4 (December, 1950).

BUTLER, D. E. *The British General Election of 1951.* London, 1951.

———. *The Electoral System in Britain, 1918–1951.* Oxford, 1953.

CAMPBELL, P., *et al.* "Voting Behavior in Droylsden in October, 1951," *Manchester School of Economics and Social Studies,* January, 1952.

COLE, G. D. H. *British Working Class Politics, 1832–1914.* London, 1941.

———. *A History of the Labour Party from 1914.* London, 1948.

CROSSMAN, R. H. S. (ed.). *New Fabian Essays,* New York, 1952.

FEILING, K. G. *A History of the Tory Party, 1640–1714.* Oxford, 1924.

———. *The Second Tory Party, 1714–1832.* London, 1938.

HEARNSHAW, F. J. C. *Conservatism in England.* London, 1933.

HOGG, QUINTIN. *The Case for Conservatism.* London, 1948.

JAY, DOUGLAS. *The Socialist Case.* London, 1947.

McCALLUM, R., and READMAN, A. *The British General Election of 1945.* Oxford, 1947.

MACCOBY, S. (ed.). *The Radical Tradition.* London, 1952.

McHENRY, D. E. *The Labour Party in Transition, 1931–38.* London, 1938.

MILNE, R. S., and MACKENZIE, H. C. *Straight Fight: A Study of Voting Behavior in Bristol North-East at the General Election of 1951.* London, 1954.

NICHOLAS, H. G. *The British General Election of 1950.* London, 1951.

Parliamentary Affairs. Vol. V, No. 1 (winter, 1951). Special issue on the British party system.

PELLING, HENRY (ed.). *The Challenge of Socialism.* London, 1954.

———. *The Origins of the Labour Party, 1880–1900.* London, 1954.

Political Quarterly, January–March and April–June, 1953. Special issues on the Labour party and the Conservative party.

ROSS, J. F. S. *Parliamentary Representation.* 2d ed. 1948.

SHAW, BERNARD, *et al. Fabian Essays.* First published 1889. Jubilee ed.; London, 1948.

SLESSER, SIR HENRY. *A History of the Liberal Party.* London, n.d.

ULAM, A. B. *Philosophical Foundations of English Socialism.* Cambridge, Mass., 1951.

WHITE, R. J. (ed.). *The Conservative Tradition.* London, 1950.

WILLIAMS, FRANCIS. *Fifty Years' March: The Rise of the Labour Party.* London, 1949.

Select List of Recent Biographies, Autobiographies, and Memoirs

AMERY, L. S. *My Political Life.* 2 vols. London, 1953.

ATTLEE, C. R. *As It Happened.* London, 1954.

BLACKBURN, F. *George Tomlinson.* London, 1954.

BROCKWAY, F. *Socialism over Sixty Years.* London, 1946.

DALTON, HUGH. *Call Back Yesterday: Memoirs, 1887–1931.* London, 1953.

FEILING, K. *The Life of Neville Chamberlain.* London, 1946.

JENKINS, ROY. *Mr. Attlee.* London, 1948.

JONES, T. *A Diary with Letters.* London, 1953.

———. *Lloyd George.* Cambridge, Mass., 1951.

MARTIN, KINGSLEY. *Harold Laski.* London, 1953.

NICHOLSON, H. *King George the Fifth: His Life and Reign.* London, 1952.

NORWICH, VISCOUNT. *Old Men Forget: The Autobiography of Duff Cooper.* London, 1953.

PETRIE, SIR CHARLES. *The Life and Letters of the Rt. Hon. Austen Chamberlain.* 2 vols. London, 1940.

POSTGATE, R. *The Life of George Lansbury.* London, 1951.

SAMUEL, VISCOUNT. *Grooves of Change.* (Memoirs.) London, 1946.

WEBB, BEATRICE. *Our Partnership.* Edited by B. DRAKE and M. I. COLE. London, 1948.

WILLIAMS, FRANCIS. *Ernest Bevin.* London, 1952.

WINTERTON, EARL. *Orders of the Day.* London, 1953.

YOUNG, G. M. *Stanley Baldwin.* London, 1952.

II / THE COMMONWEALTH OVERSEAS

Bryce's classic *Modern Democracies* analyzes political parties in Canada, Australia, and New Zealand, while Brady's *Democracy in the Dominions* gives an up-to-date, though relatively brief, description of parties in each of the four older Dominions. Hancock provides a brilliant account of developments after World War I, which Mansergh carries through the 1930's. The *Round Table* (London) provides quarterly summaries of events, while the *Journal of the Parliaments of the Commonwealth* brings digests and excerpts of the most important debates. In addition, there is much material to be found in the histories, analyses of governments, biographies, and specialized studies which are listed under the particular countries.

Canadian political parties have received relatively the greatest amount of consideration in books and articles. There is a thorough general account of their history and organization in Dawson's *Government of Canada*, while the articles by Frank Underhill are particularly illuminating. Oddly enough, the minor parties have received by far the more detailed attention. An outstanding work on the CCF is Lipset's *Agrarian Socialism;* McHenry's *Third Force in Canada* includes a comprehensive bibliography of primary and secondary material. Macpherson's *Democracy in Alberta* gives an individual interpretation of Social Credit. Hutchison's lively biography of Mackenzie King is a journalist's account and leaves one eager for the official biography to explain the reasons for his long political success.

The Australian party system has been treated fully by Louise Overacker, whose book also includes a comprehensive annotated bibliography. Crisp's *Parliamentary Government in Australia* provides a wealth of information, rooted in both study and personal experience. Lloyd Ross has written penetratingly on the Labour party. Evatts' *Australian Labour Leader* is a first-rate political biography. For New Zealand, Leslie Lipson's *Politics of Equality* provides the nearest equivalent to Crisp's work. A compact, comprehensive work on South Africa is provided by Leo Marquard, while Roberts and Trollip's *South African Opposition* is a brilliant, detailed study of Dr. Malan's Nationalist party during a significant, formative period. Roux's *Bunting* tells the early story of the Communist party in South Africa. Haigh gives a lively account of Parliament. In all cases the material on party programs and organization is widely scattered and must often be sought in newspapers or from party headquarters.

General

BRADY, ALEXANDER. *Democracy in the Dominions: A Comparative Study in Institutions.* Rev. ed. Toronto, 1952.

BRYCE, JAMES. *Modern Democracies.* 2 vols. New York, 1921.

HANCOCK, W. K. *Survey of British Commonwealth Affairs,* Vol. I: *Problems of Nationality, 1918–1936.* New York, 1937.

MANSERGH, N. *Survey of British Commonwealth Affairs,* Vol. I: *1931–1939.* New York, 1952.

Canada

BOOKS

BORDEN, HENRY (ed.). *Robert Laird Borden.* 2 vols. Toronto, 1938.

BROWN, G. W. (ed.). *Canada,* chap. xiv on "Political Parties and Ideas" by

F. H. UNDERHILL, pp. 331–52. Berkeley, 1950.

CLARK, S. D. *The Canadian Manufacturers' Association.* Toronto, 1939.

CLOKIE, H. M. *Canadian Government and Politics.* 2d ed. Toronto, 1950.

COLDWELL, M. J. *Left Turn, Canada.* New York, 1945.

CORRY, J. A. *Democratic Government and Politics.* Toronto, 1946.

CREIGHTON, D. G. *John A. Macdonald.* Boston, 1953.

DAWSON, R. M. *The Government of Canada.* 2d ed. Toronto, 1954.

HARDY, H. R. *Mackenzie King of Canada.* New York, 1949.

HUTCHISON, BRUCE. *The Incredible Canadian: A Candid Portrait of Mackenzie King, His Works, His Times, and His Nation.* New York, 1953.

LEWIS, D., and SCOTT, F. R. *Make This Your Canada.* Toronto, 1943.

LIPSET, S. M. *Agrarian Socialism: The Cooperative Commonwealth Federation in Saskatchewan: A Study in Political Sociology.* Berkeley, 1950.

LOGAN, HAROLD A. *Trade Unions in Canada.* Toronto, 1948.

McHENRY, D. E. *The Third Force in Canada: The Cooperative Commonwealth Federation, 1932–1948.* Berkeley, 1950.

MACPHERSON, C. B. *Democracy in Alberta: The Theory and Practice of a Quasi-party System.* Toronto, 1953.

MORTON, W. L. *The Progressive Party in Canada.* Toronto, 1949.

SHARP, P. F. *The Agrarian Revolt in Western Canada: A Survey Showing American Parallels.* Minneapolis, 1948.

SKELTON, O. D. *Life and Letters of Sir Wilfred Laurier.* Toronto, 1921.

STAPLES, MELVILLE H. (ed.). *The Challenge of Agriculture: The Story of the United Farmers of Ontario.* Toronto, 1921.

WADE, F. MASON. *The French Canadians, 1760–1945.* New York, 1955.

WARE, N. J., and LOGAN, H. A. *Labor in Canadian-American Relations.* New Haven, 1937.

WOOD, L. A. *A History of Farmers' Movements in Canada.* Toronto, 1924.

WOODSWORTH, J. S. *Toward Socialism: Selections from the Writings of J. S. Woodsworth.* Edited by EDITH FOWKE. Toronto, 1948.

ARTICLES

BURNET, J. "Town-Country Relations and the Problem of Rural Leadership," *Canadian Journal of Economics and Political Science,* August, 1947, pp. 395–409.

FERGUSON, G. V. "Parties of Protest," *Annals of the American Academy of Political and Social Science,* September, 1947, pp. 32–39.

FORSEY, E. "Mr. King and Parliamentary Government," *Canadian Journal of Economics and Political Science,* November, 1951, pp. 451–67.

IRVING, J. A. "The Evolution of the Social Credit Movement in Alberta," *Canadian Journal of Psychology,* March, 1947, pp. 17–27; June, 1947, pp. 75–86; September, 1947, pp. 127–40.

———. "The Evolution of the Social Credit Movement," *Canadian Journal of Economics and Political Science,* August, 1948, pp. 321–41.

———. "The Appeal of Social Credit," *Queen's Quarterly,* summer, 1953, pp. 146–60.

LEDERLE, J. W. "National Party Conventions: Canada Shows the Way," *Southwestern Social Science Quarterly,* September, 1944, pp. 118–33.

QUINN, H. F. "Parties and Politics in Quebec," *Canadian Forum,* May, 1944, pp. 32–34.

———. "The Role of the Liberal Party in Recent Canadian Politics," *Political Science Quarterly,* September, 1953, pp. 396–418.

REID, E. M. "The Rise of National Parties in Canada," *Proceedings of the Canadian Political Science Association* (1932), pp. 187–200.

———. "Canadian Political Parties: A Study of the Economic and Racial Bases of Conservatism and Liberalism in 1930," *University of Toronto Studies in History and Economics,* VI (1933), 7–39.

———. "Democracy and Political Leadership in Canada," *University of Toronto Quarterly,* IV (1933), 534–49.

———. "The Saskatchewan Liberal Machine before 1929," *Canadian Journal of Economics and Political Science,* February, 1936, pp. 27–40.

UNDERHILL, F. H. "The Party System in Canada," *Proceedings of the Canadian Political Science Association,* IV (1932), 200–212.

———. "The Development of National Political Parties in Canada," *Canadian Historical Review,* December, 1935, pp. 367–87.

———. "The Canadian Party System in Transition," *Canadian Journal of Economics and Political Science,* IX (1943), 300–316.

———. "Some Reflections on the Liberal Tradition in Canada," *Canadian Historical Association Annual Report* (1946), pp. 5–17.

———. "Canadian Election," *Contemporary Review,* October, 1953, pp. 211–16.

WARD, NORMAN. "The Bristol Papers," *Canadian Journal of Economics and Political Science,* February, 1946, pp. 78–87.

South Africa

BROOKES, EDGAR H. *South Africa in a Changing World.* New York, 1954.

CALPIN, G. H. (ed.). *The South African Way of Life.* New York, 1954.

———. *There Are No South Africans.* London, 1941.

CARTER, G. M. "Can *Apartheid* Succeed in South Africa?" *Foreign Affairs,* January, 1954, pp. 296–309.

———. "The Politics of White Supremacy," *Annals of the American Academy of Political and Social Science,* March, 1955, pp. 142–50.

CRAFFORD, F. S. *Jan Smuts.* New York. 1944.

DVORIN, EUGENE P. *Racial Separation in South Africa.* Chicago, 1952.

ENGELENBURG, F. V. *General Louis Botha.* London, 1929.

HAIGH, SCOTT. *Strangers May Be Present.* London, 1951.

HEEVER, C. M. VAN DEN. *General J. B. M. Hertzog.* Johannesburg, South Africa, 1946.

HOFMEYR, J. H. *South Africa.* New York, 1931. 2d ed., J. P. COPE (ed.). New York, 1953.

KEPPEL-JONES, A. *South Africa: A Short History.* 2d ed. New York, 1953.

LONG, B. K. *In Smuts' Camp.* London, 1945.

MARQUARD, LEO. *Peoples and Policies in South Africa.* New York, 1952.

MILLIN, S. G. *General Smuts.* 2 vols. Boston, 1936.

NEAME, L. E. *General Hertzog.* London, 1930.

ROBERTS, MICHAEL, and TROLLIP, E. A. G. *The South African Opposition, 1939–45: An Essay in Contemporary History.* New York, 1948.

ROUX, E. S. *P. Bunting: A Political Biography.* Cape Town, 1944.

SMUTS, J. C. *Holism and Evolution.* New York, 1926.

SPENDER, HAROLD. *General Botha.* New York, 1916.

WILLIAMS, A. F. BASIL. *Botha, Smuts, and South Africa.* New York, 1948.

Australia

CAIGER, G. E. (ed.). *The Australian Way of Life.* New York, 1954.

CAMPBELL, E. W. *History of the Australian Labour Movement: A Marxist Interpretation.* Sydney, 1945.

COWPER, N. L. "Australia Elects Her Parliament, December, 1949," *Australian Outlook,* March, 1950, pp. 3–12.

CRISP, L. F. *The Parliamentary Government of the Commonwealth of Australia.* 2d ed. New York, 1955.

———. *The Australian Federal Labour Party, 1901–1951.* New York, 1955.

DENNING, W. E. *Caucus Crisis: The Rise and Fall of the Scullin Government.* Sydney, 1937.

EGGLESTON, F. W. *Reflections of an Australian Liberal.* Melbourne, 1953.

EVATT, H. V. *Australian Labour Leader: The Story of W. A. Holman and the Labour Movement.* 3d ed. Sydney, 1945.

FITZHARDINGE, L. F., *et al. Nation Building in Australia: The Life and Work of Sir Littleton Groom.* Sydney, 1941.

FITZPATRICK, BRIAN. *A Short History of the Australian Labor Movement.* New enlarged ed. Melbourne, 1944.

GRATTAN, C. H. (ed.). *Australia,* chaps. vii and xvi, "Australian Party Politics," by Ross GOLLAN, pp. 105–18; and "The Role of Labor," by LLOYD ROSS, pp. 236–52. Berkeley, 1947.

GRATTAN, C. H. *Introducing Australia.* Rev. ed. New York, 1947.

HANCOCK, W. K. *Australia.* London, 1930.

HOWATT, G. "Australia Elects Senate by Hare System," *National Municipal Review,* July, 1953, pp. 354–58.

McCALLUM, J. A. "The Economic Basis of Australian Politics," in W. G. E. DUNCAN (ed.), *Trends in Australian Politics.* Sydney, 1935. Analysis of relation between unions and political parties at the state level.

MAYER, H., and RYDOR, J. *The Gwydir By-Election, 1953: A Study in Political Conflict.* Canberra, 1954.

MILLER, J. D. B. *Australian Government and Politics.* London, 1955.

OVERACKER, LOUISE. *The Australian Party System.* New Haven, 1952.

——. "Publications on Australia Useful to a Political Scientist: A Selective Survey," *American Political Science Review,* September, 1953, pp. 844–57.

PATON, G. W. (ed.). *The Commonwealth of Australia.* London, 1952.

ROSS, LLOYD. *William Lane and the Australian Labor Movement.* Sydney, 1938.

——. "The Philosophy of the Australian Labor Party," *Antioch Review,* spring, 1947, pp. 608 ff.

SAINSBURY, K A. F. "The Australian Elections of 1954," *Parliamentary Affairs,* autumn, 1954, pp. 401–8.

TURNBULL, CLIVE. *Bluestone: The Story of James Stephens.* Melbourne, 1945.

WEBB, LEICESTER. *Communism and Democracy in Australia: A Survey of the 1951 Referendum.* New York, 1955.

WEINER, H. E. "The Reduction of Communist Power in the Australian Trade Unions: A Case Study," *Political Science Quarterly,* September, 1954, pp. 390–412.

New Zealand

BELSHAW, HORACE (ed.). *New Zealand,* chapter on "Politics and Administration," by L. C. WEBB, pp. 263–91. Berkeley, 1947.

COLLIER, J. *Life of Sir George Grey.* Wellington, 1909.

CONDLIFFE, J. B. *New Zealand in the Making: A Survey of Economic and Social Development.* London, 1930.

DRUMMOND, J. *The Life and Work of Richard John Seddon.* Wellington, 1907.

HARE, A. E. C. *Industrial Relations in New Zealand.* Wellington, 1946.

LEE, JOHN A. *Socialism in New Zealand.* London, 1938.

——. *I Fight for New Zealand.* Auckland, 1940.

LE ROSSIGNOL, J. E., and STEWART, WILLIAM D. *State Socialism in New Zealand.* New York, 1910.

LIPSON, LESLIE. "Democracy and Socialism in New Zealand," *American Political Science Review,* April, 1947, pp. 306–13.

——. *The Politics of Equality.* Chicago, 1948.

LOUGHNAN, R. A. *A Biography of Sir Joseph Ward.* Sydney, 1929.

METIN, ALBERT. *Le Socialisme sans doctrine.* 2d ed. Paris, 1910.

MILLER, H. *New Zealand.* New York, 1950.

PAULING, N. G. "Labor and Government in New Zealand," *Southern Economic Journal,* January, 1953, pp. 365–76.

REEVES, W. P., and HARROP, A. J. *The Long White Cloud.* 4th ed. London, 1950.

ROBSON, J. L. (ed.). *New Zealand: The Development of Its Laws and Constitution.* London, 1954.

SIEGFRIED, A. *Democracy in New Zealand.* London, 1914.

STEWART, W. D. *Sir Francis H. D. Bell: His Life and Times.* Wellington, 1937.

——. *William Rolleston.* Christchurch, N.Z., 1940.

SUTCH, W. B. *The Quest for Security in New Zealand.* New York, 1942.

WEBB, L. C. *Government in New Zealand.* Wellington, N.Z., 1940.

WOOD, F. L. W. *Understanding New Zealand.* New York, 1944.

III / FRANCE

Background

IDEOLOGICAL BASES.—There is no systematic study of the impact of ideologies on French politics. The most convenient historical surveys are R. H. Soltau's *French Political Thought in the Nineteenth Century* (New Haven, Conn., 1931) and Shapiro's *Liberalism and the Challenge of Fascism* (New York, 1949). See also David Thomson's stimulating little essay, *The Democratic Ideal in France and England* (Cambridge, 1950), and his *Democracy in France: The Third Republic* (New York, 1946), as well as A. Thibaudet, *Les Idées politiques de la France* (Paris, 1932); "Alain," *Éléments d'une doctrine radicale* (Paris, 1925); and Robert de Jouvenel, *La République des camarades* (Paris, 1934), for a statement of the libertarian ideology. Leon Blum's *For All Mankind* (New York, 1946) and Vincent Auriol's *Hier—demain* interpret the *socialisme humaniste*, while Maritain's *Principes d'une politique humaniste* (Paris, 1945) gives the philosophical basis of Christian Democracy. See also *Church and State*, edited by Joseph Moody (New York, 1953). On the authoritarian Right see W. C. Buthnam, *The Rise of Integral Nationalism in France* (New York, 1939); and C. A. Micaud's *The French Right and Nazi Germany, 1933–1939* (Durham, N.C., 1943). For the extreme Left see A. Zevaès, *Histoire du socialisme et du communisme en France de 1871 à 1947* (Paris, 1948); and Paul Louis, *Histoire du socialisme en France* (Paris, 1946) and *Histoire du mouvement syndical en France* (2 vols.; Paris, 1948).

ECONOMIC AND SOCIAL BASES.—Since André Siegfried's pioneer work, *Tableau politique de la France de l'ouest* (Paris, 1913), the sociology of politics has been neglected until recently. A series of monographs published by the Fondation nationale des Sciences politiques (in Paris) is of special interest. Among them are: Charles Morazé *et al.*, *Études de sociologie électorale;* J. Gavarel, *Les Paysans de Morette;* A. Siegfried, *Géographie électorale de l'Ardèche;* P. George *et al.*, *Études sur la banlieue de Paris;* and Charles Bettelheim, *Auxerre in 1950.* The special issue of *Sondages* (No. 3 [1952]), "Les Attitudes politiques des Français," is most use-ful. See also the stimulating essay of G. E. Lavau, *Partis politiques et réalités sociales* (Paris, 1953).

A number of chapters in *Modern France,* edited by E. M. Earle (Princeton, 1952), are valuable contributions. So are Gordon Wright's chapter, "The Substructure of French Politics," in *European Political Systems,* edited by Taylor Cole (New York, 1953), and his "French Farmers in Politics," *South Atlantic Quarterly,* July, 1952. See also O. R. Gallagher, "Rural French Voting Habits," in *Social Research,* December, 1951; and Henry Ehrmann's "The French Peasant and Communism," in *American Political Science Review,* March, 1952; H. Ehrmann's *French Labor from Popular Front to Liberation* (New York, 1947) and Val Lorwin's *The French Labor Movement* (Cambridge, 1954) are the best recent analyses in English of the French labor movement.

On French economic problems the best surveys are: Charles Rist and G. Pirou, *De la France d'avant guerre à la France d'aujourd'hui* (Paris, 1939); C. Bettelheim, *Bilan de l'économie française* (Paris, 1946); Fourastié and Moutet, *L'Économie française dans le monde* (Paris, 1946); A. Sauvy, *Chances de l'économie française* (Paris, 1946); and Pierre Uri, "Les Problèmes économiques," in *Encyclopédie politique* (Vol. II [Paris, 1950]). See also S. B. Clough, "Retardation Factors in French Economic Development," *Journal of Economic History,* Vol. XCI, suppl. (1946).

On the social background see Michel Collinet, *Essai sur la condition ouvrière* and *Esprit du syndicalisme* (both Paris, 1951); Charles Morazé, *La France bourgeoise* (Paris, 1947); L. Chevalier, *Les Paysans* (Paris, 1946); A. Latreille and A. Siegfried, *Les Forces religieuses et la politique* (Paris, 1951). See also André Mayer, "La Crise de structure de la société française," *French Review* (offprint; New York, 1942); G. Gurvitch, "Social Structure of Pre-war France," *American Journal of Sociology,* Vol. XLVIII (1943); and several essays in E. M. Earle (ed.), *Modern France,* as well as the monographs published by the Fondation nationale des

Sciences politiques. Of the last, see especially *Partis politiques et classes sociales en France* (Paris, 1955), an important study directed by Maurice Duverger.

POLITICAL BACKGROUND.—The best political histories of the Third Republic are by D. W. Brogan, *France under the Republic* (New York, 1940); and J. P. T. Bury, *France, 1814–1940* (Philadelphia, 1949); while the most thoughtful interpretation of French politics is David Thomson, *Democracy in France: The Third Republic* (London, 1946). Also useful are Dorothy Pickles, *The French Political Scene* (London, 1943); Walter Sharp, *The Government of the Third Republic* (New York, 1938); W. C. Middleton, *The French Political System* (New York, 1933); and J. Barthélemy, *Le Gouvernement de la France* (3d ed.; Paris, 1939).

On the party system in the Third Republic the most useful book is F. Goguel, *La Politique des partis sous la troisième république* (Paris, 1946). Also important are A. Siegfried, *Tableau des partis en France* (Paris, 1930); R. H. Soltau, *French Parties and Politics, 1871–1930* (London, 1930); Bourgin, Carrère, and Guérin, *Manuel des partis politiques en France* (Paris, 1928). See also G. Lachapelle, *Les Régimes électoraux* (Paris, 1936); and A. Soulier, *L'Instabilité ministérielle sous la troisième république* (Strasbourg, 1939).

The Fourth Republic

The most useful and up-to-date work on the Fourth Republic is Philip Williams' *Politics in Post-war France* (New York, 1954). For the birth pangs of the Fourth Republic see Gordon Wright's *The Reshaping of French Democracy* (New York, 1948). A good essay on contemporary France is Herbert Lüthy's *A l'heure de son Clocher* (Paris, 1955); see also D. C. McKay, *France and the United States* (Cambridge, 1951). General treatments of the party system are to be found in F. Goguel, *France under the Fourth Republic* (Ithaca, N.Y., 1952), O. R. Taylor, *The Fourth Republic of France* (London, 1950), and Dorothy Pickles, *French Politics* (London, 1953). For a briefer treat-

ment of the party system see Gordon Wright, "France," in Taylor Cole (ed.), *European Political Systems* (New York, 1953). For the new institutional framework see R. K. Gooch, "The Government and Politics of France," in J. T. Shotwell (ed.), *Governments of Continental Europe* (New York, 1952).

In French the best accounts of the party system are by Jacques Fauvet, *Les Forces politiques en France* (Paris, 1951); and F. Goguel, *Les Partis politiques en France* (Paris, 1946). Maurice Duverger, *Les Partis politiques* (Paris, 1951), is an ambitious attempt at a systematic approach, of which G. E. Lavau, *Partis politiques et réalités sociales* (Paris, 1953), presents a brief criticism.

On the controversy over the new party system see Raymond Aron, *Le grand schisme* (Paris, 1948), and Michel Debré, *La Mort de l'état républicain* (Paris, 1947), and *La République et son pouvoir* (Paris, 1951).

On parties proper see several essays in E. M. Earle (ed.), *Modern France*.

On the MRP see Einaudi and Goguel, *Christian Democracy in Italy and France* (Notre Dame, 1952), and C. A. Micaud, "The Politics of French Catholics in the 4th Republic," in Joseph Moddy (ed.), *Church and State* (New York, 1953). On De Gaullism see Malraux and Burnham, *The Case for De Gaulle* (New York, 1948). On the Communist party see the contributions of Domenach in Einaudi *et al.*, *Communism in Western Europe* (Ithaca, N.Y., 1951); C. A. Micaud, "Organization and Leadership of the French Communist Party," *World Politics*, April, 1952; A. Rossi, *A Communist Party in Action* (New Haven, Conn., 1949), a shorter version of his *Physiologie du parti communiste français* (Paris, 1948); Monnerot, *Sociology and Psychology of Communism* (Boston, 1953); A. Brayance, *Anatomie du parti communiste français* (Paris, 1954); G. Walter, *Histoire du parti communiste français* (Paris, 1948); and Gabriel Almond, *The Appeals of Communism* (Princeton, 1954). On the Socialist party see E. D. Godfrey, Jr., *The Fate of the French Non-Communist Left* (New York, 1955), and C. A. Micaud, "Social Democracy in France," *World Politics*, July, 1955.

On electoral problems see Goguel, *Géographie des élections françaises de 1870 à 1951* (Paris, 1954); Dupeux and Goguel, *Sociologie électorale* (Paris, 1951); and M. Duverger, *L'Influence des systèmes électoraux sur la vie politique* (Paris, 1950), in addition to the monographs cited above.

For general reference see *Année politique* from 1945 to 1955. Of some interest are the special numbers of *Esprit*: "Le Régime des partis" (May, 1949) and "Pouvoir politique et pouvoir économique" (June, 1953); of *La Nef*: "Tableau politique de la France" (April, 1951) and "Le Socialisme français, victime du Marxisme" (June, 1950); and of *Les Temps modernes*: "La Gauche" (1955, Nos. 112–13). Of special interest is the number of *Sondages*, "Attitudes politiques des Français" (No. 3 [1952]), already mentioned.

IV / BELGIUM

GORIS, JAN ALBERT (ed.). *Belgium*, especially chap. viii, "Political Parties," by RENÉ HISLAIRE; and chap. ix, "The Flemish Movement," by SHEPARD B. CLOUGH. Berkeley and Los Angeles, 1945.

HERMENS, F. A. *Democracy or Anarchy? A Study of Proportional Representation.* Notre Dame, 1941. Chapter xii (pp. 301–11) deals with the influence of the Belgian P.R. system on party structure and alignments.

KALKEN, FRANS VAN. "Parties, Political, Belgium," in the *Encyclopaedia of the Social Sciences* (New York, 1933), XI, 613–15.

———. *Histoire de la Belgique.* Brussels, 1954.

OPPENHEIM, FELIX. "Belgian Political Parties since Liberation," *Review of Politics*, XII, No. 1 (January, 1950), 99–119.

SIMPSON, SMITH. "Belgium in Transition," *Annals of the American Academy of Political and Social Science*, Vol. CCXLVII (September, 1946). Contains articles by Belgian party and trade-union leaders on their respective political parties and labor unions.

V / SCANDINAVIA

For a fuller treatment of the historical development of Swedish parties and their role in the present political process, the reader is referred to Dankwart A. Rustow, *The Politics of Compromise: A Study of Parties and Cabinet Government in Sweden* (Princeton, 1955).

Brief references to Scandinavian parties will be found in the following books and articles in English.

ARNESON, BEN A. *The Demcoratic Monarchies of Scandinavia.* 2d ed. New York, 1949.

BELLQUIST, ERIC C. "Government and Politics in Northern Europe," in *Post-war Governments of Europe.* Edited by DAVID FELLMAN, Gainesville, Fla., 1946.

BRAATOY, BJARNE. *The New Sweden.* London, 1939.

FRIIS, HENNING (ed.). *Scandinavia between East and West.* Ithaca, N.Y., 1950.

HECKSCHER, GUNNAR. "Pluralist Democracy: The Swedish Experience," *Social Research*, XV (1948), 417–61.

HERLITZ, NILS. *Sweden: A Modern Democracy on Ancient Foundations.* Minneapolis, 1939.

SHIRER, WILLIAM L. *The Challenge of Scandinavia.* Boston, 1955.

SPENCER, RICHARD C. "Party Government and the Swedish Riksdag," *American Political Science Review*, XXXIX (1945), 437–88.

TINGSTEN, HERBERT. *The Debate on the Foreign Policy of Sweden, 1918–1939.* New York, 1950.

———. *Political Behavior.* London, 1937.

Further material will be found in the following works in the Scandinavian languages:

BJÖRNBERG, ARNE. *Parlamentarismens utveckling i Norge.* Uppsala, 1949.

FRISCH, HARTVIG, *et al.* (eds.). *Den danske rigsdagen.* 6 vols. København, 1949 ff.

HÅSTAD, ELIS. *Det moderna partiväsendets organisation.* 2d ed. Stockholm, 1949.

HÅSTAD, ELIS, *et al.* "Gallup" och den svenska väljarkåren. Stockholm, 1950.

HECKSCHER, GUNNAR, and HELTE, VER-NER. *De politiska åskådningår och partierna.* Stockholm, 1950.

HILDEBRAND, KARL, *et al.* (eds.). *Sveriges riksdag,* esp. Vol. XVII: *Riksdagspartierna,* by Edvard Thermænius. 17 vols. Stockholm, 1931–38.

HOLM, AXEL. *Rigsdagsvalgene i hundrede år.* København, 1949.

KOCH, HAL, and ROSS, ALF (eds.). *Nordisk demokrati.* Oslo, 1949.

NISSEN, BERNT A. *Idéen bak partierne.* Oslo, 1938.

——. *Politikk for alle.* Oslo, 1949.

Partierna i regering och riksdag. Stockholm, 1938.

ROSENKRANTZ, PALLE. *Den danske Regering og Rigsdag, 1913–1934.* København, 1934.

TINGSTEN, HERBERT. *Den svenska socialdemokratiens idéutveckling.* 2 vols. Stockholm, 1941.

ULRICHSEN, H. F. *Politisk Haandbog.* København, 1939.

Surveys of political events appear in the following scholarly journals:

Nordisk tidskrift för vetenskap, konst, och industri (monthly, Stockholm).

Økonomi og politik (quarterly, København).

Statsvetenskaplig tidskrift (quarterly, Lund).

Political debate on a high literary level is carried on in periodicals such as: *Svensk tidskrift* (monthly, Stockholm); and *Tiden* (monthly, Stockholm).

VI / UNITED STATES

Students of American politics will profit by a re-examination of a number of the classic treatises written at the turn of the century, especially the following: Woodrow Wilson, *Congressional Government* (Boston, 1885); Frank J. Goodnow, *Politics and Administration* (New York, 1900); Henry Jones Ford, *The Rise and Growth of American Politics* (New York, 1898); Moisei I. Ostrogorski, *Democracy and the Organization of Political Parties in the United States and Great Britain* (2 vols.; New York, 1902); and A. Lawrence Lowell, "The Influence of Party upon Legislation in England and America," *Annual Report of the American Historical Association for the Year 1901* (Washington, 1902).

The foregoing are summarized and commented upon by Austin Ranney in *The Doctrine of Responsible Party Government* (Urbana, 1954). The classics are now chiefly of historical interest but provide a kind of yardstick for measuring change in the party system in the first half of the twentieth century. Lincoln Steffens' *Autobiography* (New York, 1931) probably should be added to this list of classics, because Steffens, like Ford, Goodnow, and Ostrogorski, is deeply concerned with the problem of the corrupt political machine.

In the more recent literature of the field one important school of writers has tended to place great emphasis on the relative importance and influence of pluralist influences and special-interest group activity in American politics. Generally, this school tends to minimize the cohesion and strength of the parties. Illustrative of this point of view are Arthur N. Holcombe, *Our More Perfect Union* (Cambridge, Mass., 1950); Pendleton Herring, *The Politics of Democracy* (New York, 1940); Herbert Agar, *The Price of Union* (Boston, 1950); David E. Truman, *The Governmental Process* (New York, 1954); and Earl Latham, *The Group Basis of Politics* (Ithaca, N.Y., 1952).

A different point of view, generally tending to place a higher valuation on the importance of the party system, is to be found in E. E. Schattschneider, *Party Government* (New York, 1941); Samuel Lubell, *The Future of American Politics* (New York, 1951); James MacGregor Burns, *Congress on Trial* (New York, 1941); and *Toward a More Responsible Two-Party System: The Report of a Committee of the American Political Science Association* (New York, 1950).

An important contribution to the study of the American party system has been made by V. O. Key, Jr., in his *Southern Politics* (New York, 1949), and by Alexander Heard in *A Two-Party South?* (Chapel Hill, 1952). By implication, these studies of the "solid South" shed much light on the meaning of the two-party system elsewhere in the United States. In a very different line are Paul F. Lazarsfeld, Bernard Berelson, and Hazel Gaudet, *The People's Choice* (New York, 1944); Angus Campbell and Robert L. Kahn, *The People Elect a President* (Ann Arbor, 1952); Bernard R. Berelson, Paul Lazarsfeld, and William N. McPhee, *Voting* (Chicago, 1954); and Angus Campbell, Gerald Gurin, and Warren Miller, *The Voter Decides* (Evanston, 1954). These latter books provide a new interpretation of party conflict by examining the social cleavage which underlies it.

Presidential Nominating Politics in 1952, edited by Paul T. David, Malcolm Moos, and Ralph M. Goldman (5 vols.; Baltimore, 1954), deserves study because it is a comprehensive national survey of American politics in forty-eight states.

VII / The U.S.S.R.

English, French, and German Works

While it contains numerous titles, the following bibliography is suggestive rather than comprehensive. If used together with the bibliographies contained in Fainsod, Meissner, Moore, Seton-Watson, and Rostow, it will lead the reader to most of the significant work that has been done in Britain, the United States, and Germany on the Soviet system and Soviet foreign policy.

BOOKS

ACHMINOW, H. *Die Macht im Hintergrund.* Ulm, 1951. The best of the Soviet refugee books. Its thesis is that the Soviet system is eventually self-destroying. Available in French as *Le Fossoyeur du communisme.*

ALMOND, GABRIEL A. *The Appeals of Communism.* Princeton, 1954. Psychiatric, political science, and sociological techniques are combined in this very important study of Western communism. Strongest on the United States.

BARGHOORN, F. C. *The Soviet Image of the United States.* New York, 1950. A case study in Soviet ideology.

BAUER, RAYMOND A. *Nine Soviet Portraits.*

New York, 1955. Valuable living source material, presented in terms of scientific psychology.

BORKENAU, FRANZ. *European Communism.* New York and London, 1953. Valuable for brilliant insights but inadequately documented. To be used with caution.

CAREW HUNT, R. N. *The Theory and Practice of Bolshevism.* New York, 1951. A clear, concise account by a British Conservative. Sees Soviet communism as a consistent application of Marxism.

CARR, E. H. *The Bolshevik Revolution, 1917–1923.* 3 vols. New York, 1951–53. A solid and powerful work but cast in a Marxist determinist mold.

———. *The Interregnum.* New York, 1954. A brilliant account of the origins of Stalin's power.

CHAMBERLIN, WILLIAM HENRY (ed.). *Blueprint for World Conquest.* Chicago, 1946. Indispensable Comintern documents.

DENNETT, RAYMOND, and JOHNSON, JOSEPH E. (eds.). *Negotiating with the Russians.* Boston, 1951. Nine case studies and Philip E. Mosely's analytic article, "Some Soviet Techniques of Negotiation," which is the best introduction to the subject yet written.

DEUTSCHER, ISAAC. *Russia, What Next?* New York, 1953. Stimulating but speculative. The author's brand of Marxism clouds his vision.

———. *The Prophet Armed: Trotsky, 1879–1921.* New York, 1954. A brilliant biography, though with a "Trotskyite" Marxist bias.

DIXON, BRIGADIER AUBREY, and HEILBRUNN, OTTO. *Communist Guerilla Warfare.* New York, 1954. Partly fills an important gap on Communist use of unconventional methods of warfare.

FAINSOD, MERLE. *How Russia Is Ruled.* Cambridge, 1953. The outstanding work on Soviet political power, especially strong on the mechanisms of administration.

GRULIOW, LEO (ed.). *Current Soviet Policies.* New York, 1953. Indispensable translations of proceedings of the nineteenth party congress and other important material.

GURIAN, WALDEMAR (ed.). *Bolsehvism.* Notre Dame, 1952. A good brief introduction to Soviet doctrine from a liberal Catholic point of view.

——. *Soviet Imperialism.* Notre Dame, 1953. Six authors and several points of view on the nature of the problem posed to the free world by Soviet policy.

HAINES, C. G. (ed.). *The Threat of Soviet Imperialism.* Baltimore, 1954. Brief papers on most of the important aspects of Soviet foreign policy by academic and government experts. Useful as an introduction to further study of international communism.

INKELES, ALEX. *Public Opinion in Soviet Russia.* Cambridge, 1950. A scholarly study of Soviet communications media and theory.

KLIMOV, G. *The Terror Machine.* New York, 1953. An account of the Soviet occupation regime in Germany by a refugee officer.

KOLARZ, WALTER. *Russia and Her Colonies.* New York, 1952. The best, and a very good, book on Soviet nationality policy.

KULSKI, W. W. *The Soviet Regime.* Syracuse, 1954. A massive compendium. Useful supplement to Fainsod and Towster.

LEITES, NATHAN. *A Study of Bolshevism.* Glencoe, Ill., 1953. An analysis of Lenin's and Stalin's writings on the basis of psychological hypotheses. These often obscure the valuable political insights offered by Leites.

MEISSNER, BORIS. *Russland in Umbruch.* Frankfort, 1951. A substantial factual treatment of Soviet political institutions, brought closer to date in his *Die kommunistische Partei der Sowjetunion vor und nach dem Tode Stalins* (Frankfort, 1954).

MOORE, BARRINGTON, JR. *Soviet Politics: The Dilemma of Power.* Cambridge, 1950. This and the same author's *Terror and Progress* (Cambridge, 1954) represent the very best in Western scholarship. Profound, critical, and objective, but occasionally weakened by the author's lack of experience in the U.S.S.R.

NORTH, ROBERT C. *Moscow and Chinese Communists.* Stanford, 1953. Traces the interconnections between the Kremlin and Mao's movement.

OURALOV, ALEXANDRE. *Staline au pouvoir.* Paris, n.d. By a former Soviet functionary; interesting on the early thirties.

PLAMENATZ, JOHN. *German Marxism and Russian Communism.* London, 1954. A solid and brilliant book.

POSSONY, STEFAN. *A Century of Conflict.* Chicago, 1953. A historical study emphasizing the role of violence in Communist behavior.

RESHETAR, JOHN S., JR. *Problems of Analyzing and Predicting Soviet Behavior.* New York, 1955. A pioneer effort.

ROSTOW, W. W. *The Dynamics of Soviet Society.* New York, 1953. A collaborative work which attempts a "dynamic" analysis of the Soviet system.

ROYAL COMMISSION. *Report of Controller of Stationery.* Ottawa, 1946. Still the best documentary source on Soviet espionage and subversion.

SCHUELLER, G. K. *The Politburo.* Stanford, 1951. Valuable biographical data.

SELZNICK, PHILIP. *The Organizational Weapon.* New York and London, 1952. An attempt to apply the organizational theories of Robert Michels and others to Communist parties. Verbose and diffuse but useful and sometimes brilliant.

SETON-WATSON, HUGH. *From Lenin to Malenkov.* New York, 1953. Though elementary in idea content, this work is the soundest historical introduction to the study of world communism. Especially impressive for its range of sources in many languages and hence useful as a reference book.

STALIN, J. *Marxism and the National and Colonial Question.* New York, n.d.

——. *Problems of Leninism.* Moscow, 1940.

——. *The Great Patriotic War of the Soviet Union.* New York, 1945.

TOWSTER, JULIAN. *Political Power in the U.S.S.R.* New York, 1947. Superseded by Fainsod as a text but still a useful reference work, especially on formal institutional structure. Heavily documented.

WOLFE, BERTRAM D. *Three Who Made a*

Revolution. New York, 1948. A brilliant study of Lenin, Stalin, and Trotsky to 1914.

"Ypsilon," *Pattern for World Revolution.* Chicago, 1947. Valuable, if episodic, insights into Comintern and "Stalintern" policy.

MAGAZINE ARTICLES

BARGHOORN, F. C. "Stalinism and the Russian Cultural Heritage," *Review of Politics,* XIV, No. 4 (April, 1952), 178–203.

DANIELS, ROBERT V. "The State and Revolution: A Case Study in the Genesis and Transformation of Communist Ideology," *American Slavic and East European Review,* XII, No. 1 (February, 1953), 22–43. A brilliant study.

GARTHOFF, RAYMOND L. "The Concept of the Balance of Power in Soviet Foreign Policy," *World Politics,* IV, No. 1 (October, 1951), 85 ff. Valuable semantic analysis.

"HISTORICUS." "Stalin on Revolution," *Foreign Affairs,* XXVII, No. 2 (January, 1949), 175–214. A classic article.

NEMZER, LOUIS. "The Kremlin's Professional Staff: The 'Apparatus' of the Central Committee Communist Party of the Soviet Union," *American Political Science Review,* XLIV, No. 1 (March, 1950), 64–85.

———. "The Soviet Friendship Societies," *Public Opinion Quarterly,* XIII (1949), 265–84.

ZINNER, PAUL E. "The Ideological Bases of Soviet Foreign Policy," *World Politics,* IV, No. 4 (July, 1952), 488–511.

Russian Sources

Pravda, organ of the Central Committee of the Communist Party of the Soviet Union, is, by and large, the most important Soviet newspaper. Also very important are *Izvestiya,* organ of the Soviets, and *Trud,* organ of the All Union Central Council of Trade Unions.

Kommunist, the title of which was *Bolshevik* until after the nineteenth party congress of October, 1952, is the most important Soviet political magazine. It appears twice a month. Anyone who wishes to do research in the development of the Soviet Communist party will have to use, in addition to these, a wide range of periodicals and other materials. Perhaps most important are the reports of party and Comintern conferences and congresses. There have been nineteen party congresses (1898–1952) and seven Comintern congresses (1919–35). The stenographic reports, though difficult of access, are available in the United States; the best single source is the Library of Congress. *KPSS v rezolyutsiyakh i resheniyakh* (2 vols.; Moscow, 1953) is the most important recent collection of Soviet documents in Russian.

Miscellaneous

The Cominform publication, *For a Lasting Peace, for a Peoples' Democracy,* and the Soviet magazine, *New Times,* enable the English reader to follow the Kremlin's foreign propaganda line. *The Current Digest of the Soviet Press* has, since 1949, translated or excerpted important material from the Soviet press and is extremely useful. German readers will find valuable material in *Osteuropa,* a scholarly quarterly, and in *Ostprobleme,* an American government source, which publishes both original material and reprinted items from Communist and non-Communist sources.

Some congressional publications have been among the most illuminating studies of communism, particularly *The Strategy and Tactics of World Communism* (House Doc. No. 619 [80th Cong., 2d sess.]).

Refugees from Soviet totalitarianism, both "old" and "new" (mostly since 1941), contribute valuable material to the Menshevik organ *Sotsialisticheski vestnik* ("Socialist Courier") and to *Novy zhurnal* ("New Review"). *Posev* ("The Harvest"), organ of the NTS (or "Solidarist") group, is also worthy of mention. The Ukrainian émigré point of view on the Soviet nationality problem is represented in the *Ukrainian Quarterly.*

VIII / SATELLITE PARTIES IN EASTERN EUROPE

In the general field of eastern European political developments, materials of an analytical character are scattered and not always adequate. Several excellent British publications seem to be the main exceptions. Hugh Seton-Watson's *Eastern Europe between the Wars, 1918–1941* (Cambridge, 1946) and *The East European Revolution* (London, 1950) are valuable surveys of the interwar and postwar setting of political parties in this area. Under the title of *Southeastern Europe* (London, 1945), the Royal Institute of International Affairs has published comprehensive background studies of the political structure of individual countries. These were supplemented by *Central and South East Europe, 1945–1948*, edited by R. R. Betts (London, 1950), and by Stephen Clissold's *Whirlwind: An Account of Tito's Rise to Power* (London, 1949); Harry Hodgkinson's *Challenge to the Kremlin* (New York, 1952); and Doreen Warriner's *Revolution in Eastern Europe* (London, 1950). *Soviet Studies*, published by the University of Glasgow; *Fourth International*, sponsored by various Socialist parties; *World Today; International Affairs; International Journal; New Central European Observer;* and *East Europe* offer useful materials for the student of comparative parties and politics. *The Soviet-Yugoslav Dispute* (London, 1948) is an illuminating account of the origins and early development of Titoism. Of the documentary sources, the State Department's official collections, *Documents and State Papers*, the *Department of State Bulletin*, the *Reports of the United Nations' Special Committee on the Balkans*, and the *Calendar of Soviet Documents on Foreign Policy* (London, 1948) are the most valuable. Of eastern European materials, Tito's *Political Reports* to the annual congresses of the Communist party (Belgrade, 1947, 1948, and 1949); recent issues of *Borba, Glas,* and the *Yugoslav Fortnightly*, Hungary's *Társadalmi Szemle, Magyar-Szovjet Közgazdasági Szemle* ("Hungarian-Soviet Economic Review"), *Valóság,* and *Forum,* among the periodicals; and *Szabad Nép, Népszava, Világosság, Magyar Nemzet,* and *Kis Ujság,* among the daily newspapers, are particularly noteworthy. In Poland, *Nowe Drogi;* in Czechoslovakia, *Rude Pravo;* in Rumania, the Cominform journal *For a Last-*

ing Peace, for a Peoples' Democracy, now published weekly in Bucharest in eight languages; *Scanteia, Romania Libera, Frontul Plugarilor,* and the émigré paper *Courrier roumain* (Paris) offer interesting insights into the origins and activities of the new United Workers' parties, while in Bulgaria *Rabotnichesko Delo* and *Otechestven Front* are prominent in the faithful reporting of official Communist utterances. Among peripheral observers of satellite political developments, *Die Presse* and *Österreichische Volksstimme* (Communist) in Austria; *Pravda, Izvestiya, Komsomolskaya Pravda, Bolshevik,* and *New Times* in the Soviet Union; and *Revue politique et parlementaire* in France contain the most important source materials.

In the United States numerous accounts have been published in the past few years reviewing the life of political parties in eastern Europe and the impact of Titoism on the various satellite governments. Of the books, the most informative were written by Arthur B. Lane, *I Saw Poland Betrayed* (Indianapolis, 1948); Stanislaw Mikolajczyk, *The Rape of Poland: Pattern of Soviet Aggression* (New York, 1948); Ferenc Nagy, *The Struggle behind the Iron Curtain* (New York, 1948); Constantin Fotitch, *The War We Lost* (New York, 1948); Hamilton Fish Armstrong, *Tito and Goliath* (New York, 1951); Josef Korbel, *Tito's Communism* (Denver, 1951); Leland Stowe, *Conquest by Terror* (New York, 1952); Adam B. Ulam, *Titoism and the Cominform* (Cambridge, Mass., 1952); Henry L. Roberts, *Rumania: Political Problems of an Agrarian State* (New Haven, 1951); Dana Adams Schmidt, *Anatomy of a Satellite* (Boston, 1952); Oscar Halecki, *Borderlands of Western Civilization* (New York, 1952); Stephen D. Kertesz, *Diplomacy in a Whirlpool* (Notre Dame, 1953); and Samuel L. Sharp, *Poland: White Eagle on a Red Field* (Cambridge, Mass., 1953). Among periodicals, the *Review of Politics,* the *Political Science Quarterly,* the *Journal of Central European Affairs, Foreign Affairs,* the *Russian Review,* the *Ukrainian Quarterly,* and *World Politics* contain articles relevant to the postwar political development of eastern Europe. Particularly useful documentary surveys appeared in

"The Soviet Union since World War II," *Annals of the American Academy of Political and Social Science* (May, 1949); in "Soviet Satellites," published by the *Review of Politics* (Notre Dame, 1949); and in two translation projects sponsored by the Public Affairs Press (Washington, D.C.): G. F. Aleksandrov, *The Pattern of Soviet Democracy* (1948), and S. Kovalyov, *Ideological Conflicts in Soviet Russia* (1948).

IX / JAPAN

A full bibliography of materials on the Japanese parties would require many pages. Fortunately, most recent Japanese and English publications pertaining to this subject have included extensive listings of the major works. Here I shall select only a few items for those students who wish to explore further the Japanese party movement. Most of the studies available in English deal largely or wholly with the prewar parties. The following are some of those devoting considerable attention to this subject: Hugh Borton, *Japan since 1931: Its Social and Political Development* (New York, 1940); Nobutaka Ike, *The Beginnings of Political Democracy in Japan* (Baltimore, 1950); Walter W. McLaren, *A Political History of Japan during the Meiji Era* (London, 1916); E. Herbert Norman, *Japan's Emergence as a Modern State* (New York, 1940); Shigenobu Okuma (ed.), *Fifty Years of New Japan* (London, 1910); Harold S. Quigley, *Japanese Government and Politics* (New York, 1933); Edwin O. Reischauer, *Japan, Past and Present* (New York, 1953); Robert K. Reischauer, *Japan: Government—Politics* (New York, 1939); Robert A. Scalapino, *Democracy and the Party Movement in Pre-war Japan* (Berkeley, 1953); Rodger Swearingen and Paul Langer, *Red Flag in Japan* (Cambridge, 1952); George E. Uyehara, *The Political Development of Japan, 1867–1909* (London, 1910); Chitoshi Yanaga, *Japan since Perry* (New York, 1949); and A. Morgan Young, *Japan in Recent Times* (New York, 1929).

A few of the foregoing works include materials on the postwar parties as well, but, as yet, detailed research in English on this period is very limited. The reader should certainly consult such publications as *Contemporary Japan, Far Eastern Quarterly, Far Eastern Survey, Japan Quarterly*, and *Pacific Affairs* for analytical and factual articles on post-1945 developments. For serious study the voluminous SCAP materials, especially the monthly *Summation of Non-military Activities in Japan*, are most important. Already a number of general surveys of the occupation era have been written, with widely different points of view reflected. In most of these some interpretations of the Japanese parties and party system are presented. The following give different points of view: W. Macmahon Ball, *Japan: Enemy or Ally?* (New York, 1949); T. A. Bisson, *Prospects for Democracy in Japan* (New York, 1949); Russell Brines, *MacArthur's Japan* (Philadelphia, 1948); Robert A. Fearey, *The Occupation of Japan, Second Phase* (New York, 1951); E. M. Martin, *The Allied Occupation of Japan* (Stanford, 1948); and Robert B. Textor, *Failure in Japan* (New York, 1951). One general text, which includes up-to-date materials on the postwar Japanese parties, is *Far Eastern Governments and Politics—China and Japan*, by Paul M. A. Linebarger, Djang Chu, and Ardath W. Burks. In addition to the journals mentioned that regularly publish articles on Japanese parties and politics, one should also mention such scholarly journals as the *American Political Science Review* and publications devoted to general foreign affairs topics, like *Foreign Affairs, Foreign Policy Bulletin*, and the former *Foreign Policy Reports*.

When one turns to materials in Japanese the problem of choice becomes extremely complex. There are literally hundreds of works dealing with the Japanese parties, most of them from a historical point of view. The following are a limited number of important primary and secondary sources: Aono Kondo, *Nihon seito hensen shi* ("A History of Changes in Japanese Parties") (Tokyo, 1935); Arahata Kanson, *Nihon shakaishugi undo shi* ("A History of the Japanese Socialist Movement") (Tokyo, 1948); Hara Keiichiro (ed.), *Hara Takashi nikki* ("The Diary of Takashi Hara") (9 vols.; Tokyo, 1950–51); Harada Kumao, *Saionji-Ko to seikyoku* ("Prince

Saionji and the Political Situation") (9 vols.; Tokyo, 1950–52); Ichikawa Shoichi, *Nihon Kyosanto shoshi* ("A Short History of the Japanese Communist Party") (Tokyo, 1932; reprinted, 1947); Ito Masanori, *Kato Takaakira* (2 vols.; Tokyo, 1929); *Minseito soran* ("General Survey of the Minseito") (Tokyo, 1931); Oka Yoshitake, *Kindai Nihon no keisei* ("The Foundation of Modern Japan") (Tokyo, 1947); Osatake Takeshi, *Nihon kensei shi no kenkyu* ("A Study of Japanese Constitutional History") (Tokyo, 1943); Otsu Junichiro, *Dai Nihon kensei shi* ("A Constitutional History of Greater Japan") (11 vols.; Tokyo, 1927–28); Royama Masamichi, *Seiji shi* ("Political History") (Tokyo, 1940); also *Seito no kenkyu* ("Study of Political Parties") (Tokyo, 1948); Royama Masamichi (ed.), *Musanseito ron* ("Treatises on Proletarian Parties") (Tokyo, 1930); Suzuki Yasuzo, *Jiyuminken* ("Civil Rights") (Tokyo, 1948); Tanaka Sogoro, *Nihon shakai undo shi* ("History of the Japanese Social Movement") (Tokyo, 1949); Yoshino Sakuzo (ed.), *Meiji bunka zenshu* ("Collected Works of Meiji Culture") (24 vols.; Tokyo, 1928–30).

Students of modern Japanese politics will be familiar with three leading intellectual magazines: *Chuo Koron* ("The Central Review"), *Kaizo* ("Reconstruction"), and *Sekai* ("The World"). There are in these magazines a large number of articles written by scholars, most of them on the left wing, concerning both pre- and postwar party developments. Especially important articles are to be found in some of the postwar learned journals concerning the period since 1945. The Japan Political Science Association has published a journal and also a yearly volume that should be read. Historical and sociological journals are also most valuable. Many of these individual works have extensive references to additional materials. The postwar parties themselves are putting out a large volume of publications on their platforms, conventions, and general history.

X / GERMANY

The study of the German political parties, past and present, has received an ex-

traordinary impetus during the past decade or two, with more promising research in preparation in this country; yet no adequate study is available in English (or in German, for that matter) on the German party system as a whole. A general introduction to programs, progress, and problems of the major movements may be found in the representative textbooks on comparative governments, such as the contributions of Karl Loewenstein in J. T. Shotwell (ed.), *Governments of Continental Europe* (rev. ed.; New York, 1952); John Herz, in Ranney, Carter, and Herz, *Major Foreign Powers* (New York, 1952). John B. Mason, in Fritz Morstein-Marx (ed.), *Foreign Governments* (New York, 1949); Sigmund Neumann, in Taylor Cole (ed.), *European Political Systems* (New York, 1953); see also the article on "German Political Parties" in *Encyclopaedia of the Social Sciences*, XI (New York, 1933), 615–19.

For a first over-all view of the history of the German parties consult Ludwig Bergsträsser, *Geschichte der politischen Parteien in Deutschland* (7th ed.; Munich, 1952); Sigmund Neumann, *Die deutschen Parteien: Wesen und Wandel nach dem Kriege* (2d ed.; Berlin, 1932), with detailed bibliography; see also Rainer Barzel, *Die deutschen Parteien* (Geldern, 1952); Ossip Fleehtheim, *Die deutschen Parteien seit 1945* (Berlin, 1955); and Heinrich Striefler, *Deutsche Wahlen in Bildern und Zahlen* (Düsseldorf, 1946).

An exemplary collection of the historical programs of the German parties was presented by W. Mommsen and G. Franz, *Deutsche Parteiprogramme* (Leipzig, 1932), in continuation of the comprehensive three volumes of Felix Salomon. For a shorter up-to-date selection see W. Mommsen, *Deutsche Parteiprogramme* (Munich, 1951), and *Deutsche Parteiprogramme der Gegenwart* (Munich, 1954), and also Wolfgang Treue, *Deutsche Parteiprogramme, 1861–1954* (Göttingen, 1954).

Of major works on the pre–World War I history of the leading parties, the following are of special significance: Franz Mehring, *Geschichte der deutschen Sozialdemokratie* (4 vols.; Berlin, 1922); Karl Bachem, *Vorgeschichte, Geschichte und Politik der deutschen Zentrumspartei* (9 vols.; Cologne, 1927–32); Heyderhoff and Wentzke, *Deutscher Liberalismus im Zeitalter Bismarcks* (Bonn, 1925–26); Gerhard Ritter, *Die preussischen Konservativen und Bismarcks deutsche Politik* (Heidelberg, 1913); and Theodor Heuss, *Friedrich Naumann* (Tübingen, 1950).

Among the recent monographs on the empire special mention should be made of the following not only for their material wealth but also for their methodological contributions to the field: Carl Schorske, *German Social Democracy* (Cambridge, Mass., 1955); William O. Shanahan, *German Protestants Face the Social Question* (Notre Dame, 1954); Annelise Thimme, *Hans Delbrück als Kritiker der Wilhelminischen Epoche,* edited by the Kommission für Geschichte des Parlamentarismus und der politischen Parteien (Düsseldorf, 1955); Peter Gay, *The Dilemma of Democratic Socialism* (New York, 1952). For World War I and the transition period see A. J. Berlau, *The German Social Democratic Party, 1914–1921* (New York, 1949), and E. Prager, *Geschichte der U.S.P.D.* (2d ed.; Berlin, 1922).

The crucial issues of party organization and social composition are treated in Robert Michels, *Zur Soziologie des modernen Parteiwesens* (Leipzig, 1925); Herbert Sultan, "Zur Soziologie des modernen Parteiensystems," *Archiv für Sozialwissenschaft und Sozialpolitik,* LV (1926), 91–140. For the SPD specifically, see Theodor Buddeberg, "Das soziologische Problem der Sozialdemokratie," *Archiv für Sozialwissenschaft und Sozialpolitik,* XLIX (1922), 108 ff.; Wilhelm Schröder, "Geschichte der Sozialdemokratischen Parteiorganisation in Deutschland," *Abhandlungen und Vorträge zur sozialistischen Bildung,* Nos. 4–5 (Jena, 1912); Harry Marks, "The Sources of Reformism in the Social Democratic Party of Germany, 1890–1914," *Journal of Modern History,* IX (1930), 347 ff.; A. Schiffrin, "Parteiapparat und Parteidemokratie," *Die Gesellschaft,* Vol. VII (June, 1930); and "Kritik an der Organisation," *ibid.,* Vol. VIII (August, 1931). For leftist criticism see F. Bieligk *et al., Die Organisation im Klassenkampf* (Berlin, 1931), and for

rightist attack see the biting novel by F. Riemkasten, *Der Bonze* (Berlin, 1930). Among recent studies see J. Siemann, *Soziologie der sozialdemokratischen Führerschicht, 1918–1933* (Göttingen, 1954).

The party system of the Weimar Republic, in addition to the above-mentioned volumes by L. Bergsträsser and S. Neumann, is analyzed in the short monographs of the series, "Die geistige Struktur der politischen Parteien Europas," edited by K. O. Fr. Metzner (Berlin, 1937); see especially Fr. Dessauer, *Das Zentrum;* Freiherr von Freytagh-Loringhoven, *Deutschnationale Volkspartei;* Siegfried Marck, *Sozialdemokratie;* and Otto Moldenhauer, *Deutsche Volkspartei.* For a reassessment of the key figure Stresemann, on the basis of his now available papers, see Hans Gatzke, *Stresemann and the Rearmament of Germany* (Baltimore, 1954), and "The Stresemann Papers," *Journal of Modern History,* XXVI (1954), 49–59; see also Felix Hirsch, "Stresemann, Ballin, und die Vereinigten Staaten," *Vierteljahrshefte für Zeitgeschichte,* III (1955), 20–55. The Communist party is fully treated in Ossip K. Flechtheim, *Die KPD in der Weimarer Republik* (Offenbach a.M., 1948).

A remarkable regional case study on the province of Schleswig-Holstein is presented in Rudolf Heberle's *From Democracy to Nazism* (Baton Rouge, La., 1945).

For certain party aspects under the Weimar Republic see James K. Pollock, "An Area Study of the German Electorate, 1930–33," *American Political Science Review,* XXXVIII (1944), 89–95; and Sidney L. W. Mellen, "The German People and the Post-war World," *American Political Science Review,* XXXVII (1943), 601–25; Helga Timm, *Die deutsche Sozialpolitik und der Bruch der Grossen Koalition im März 1930* (Düsseldorf, 1953); and Armin Mohler, *Die konservative Revolution in Deutschland, 1918–1932* (Stuttgart, 1950). See also Werner Conze, "Die Krise des Parteien Staates in Deutschland 1929/30," *Historische Zeitschrift,* CLXXVIII (1954), 47–83; Karl Dietrich Erdmann, "Die Geschichte der Weimarer Republik als Problem der Wissenschaft," *Vierteljahrshefte für Zeitgeschichte,* III (1955), 1–19; and F. A. Hermens. *Democracy or Anarchy: A Study of Proportional Representation* (Notre Dame, 1941). The effect of the electoral reforms is critically analyzed in Johannes Schauff (ed.), *Neues Wahlrecht* (Berlin, 1929). See also Auguste Soulier, "Le Mode de scrutin sous la république de Weimar," in M. Duverger (ed.), *L'Influence des systèmes électoraux.*

For a strong stand against proportional representation in the Bonn Republic see the publication of the Deutsche Wählergesellschaft, *Der Wähler,* and its chief exponent Dolf Sternberger's "Das Schicksal der Parteien," *Der Wähler,* No. 7 (1951), pp. 263–73; see also the suggestive analysis of the federal elections of 1953 in the special number, *Das Deutsche Wahlwunder,* edited by Chr.-Claus Baer and Erwin Faul.

The militant, mostly antiparliamentarian groups preceding the Hitler Reich are analyzed in Ernst H. Posse, *Die politischen Kampfbünde* (2d ed.; Berlin, 1932); for the whole period see the comprehensive study by Dieter Bracher, *Die Auflösung der Weimarer Republik* (Berlin, 1955).

The critical history of the National Socialist party is still to be written. For the official Nazi interpretation see Gottfried Neesse, *Partei und Staat* (Stuttgart, 1935); see also H. P. Ipsen, "Vom Begriff der Partei," *Zeitschrift für die gesamte Statts-wissenschaft,* C (1940), 309–36, 447–510. On the concept of the totalitarian party see Sigmund Neumann, *Permanent Revolution* (New York, 1942). Also see Hans Gerth, "The Nazi Party: Its Leadership and Composition," *American Journal of Sociology,* XLV (1940), 517–41; A. V. Boerner, "The Position of the NSDAP in the German Constitutional Order," *American Political Science Review,* XXXII (1938), 1059–81; John B. Mason, "The Judicial System of the Nazi Party," *American Political Science Review,* XXXVIII (1944), 96–103; and suggestive articles in C. J. Friedrich (ed.), *Totalitarianism* (Cambridge, Mass., 1954). For the place of the party in the whole Hitler regime see also the relevant studies of A. Bullock, William Ebenstein, Ernst Fraenkel, Karl Lowenstein, Franz Neumann, James K. Pollock, and J. S. T. Roberts. It is equally interesting in this connection to recall the

extended discussion among fascist theorists; see Guido Bortolotto, *Lo Stata e la dottrina corporativa* (Bologna, 1930); B. Liuzzi, *Il Partito nazionale fascista nel diritto* (Rome, 1930); Sergio Panunzio, *Lo Stato fascista* (Bologna, 1924) and *Il Sentimento dello stato* (Rome, 1929).

The nature, appeal, and staying power of totalitarianism in modern mass society are far from a merely academic concern. The issue remains doubly significant to present-day Germany not only in view of latent Nazi forces and their potential revival but also because of the Soviet predominance in the Eastern zone with its possible effects on the German federal republic. With these possible repercussions in mind, the significant contributions of recent Russia interpreters must be consulted, among them Boris Meissner, *Russland im Umbruch: Der Wandel in der Herrschaftsordnung und Sozialstruktur der Sowjetunion* (Frankfort, 1951); G. F. Achminow, *Die Macht im Hintergrund* (Ulm, 1950); and Reinhart Maurach, *Handbuch der Sowjetverfassung* (Munich, 1955).

See also the intensive discussion of developments in the Eastern zone, such as M. G. Lange, *Totalitäre Erzichung* ("Schriften des Instituts für politische Wissenschaft" [Frankfort, 1954]); Otto Stammer, "Gesellschaftsstruktur und politische Dynamik in der Sowjetzone," *Gewerkschaftliche Monatshefte,* III (1952), 330–34; M. G. Lange, Ernst Richert, and Otto Stammer, "Das Problem der neuen Intelligenz in der sowjetischen Besatzungszone," in *Festschrift Veritas, Justitia, Libertas* (Berlin, 1954); and Ernst Richert, "Aus der Praxis totalitärer Lenkung: Die politische Entwicklung im Kreise Schmalkalden, 1945–1949," in A. R. L. Gurland, *Faktoren der Machtbildung* ("Schriften des Instituts für politische Wissenschaft" [Berlin, 1952]). Of the limited literature on the SED, the following give pertinent information: Carola Stern and Kurt Walter Freiberg, *The SED: Construction, Character, Situation* (Köln, SBZ-Archiv, 1954); H. O. Lewis, "The Socialist Unity Party of Germany," *American Perspective,* II (1949), 523–31; Otto Kirchheimer, "The Government of Eastern Germany," in Hans J. Morgenthau (ed.), *Germany and the Future of Europe* (Chicago, 1950). On the significant cadre organization of the SED see E. E. Müller, *Die Kaderbildung in der sowjetischen Besatzungszone Deutschlands* (Berlin, 1954); L. Slepor, *Die Auslese der Kader* (Berlin, 1953); and J. Schultz, *Die Kader in der sowjetischen Besatzungszone Deutschland* (Berlin, 1953); see also Otto Stammer, *Der kleine Mann als Object der manipulierten Meinungsbildung in der Sowjetzone* (Berlin, 1953), and Martin Drath, *Verfassungsrecht und Verfassungswirklichkeit in der sowjetischen Besatzungszone* (Bonn, 1954).

The political parties in the Second Republic are still too much in flux to permit a definite delineation, yet the renewed concern at home and abroad about German democracy has brought forward a flood of literature. Among the numerous publications, the following may be singled out: James K. Pollock, "The Electoral System of the Federal Republic of Germany," *American Political Science Review*, XLVI (December, 1952), 1056–68, and "The West-German Electoral Law of 1953," *ibid.*, XLIX (March, 1955), 107–30; Hans J. Morgenthau (ed.), *Germany and the Future of Europe* (Chicago, 1951), especially Gabriel A. Almond's "German Political Parties," pp. 89 ff.; Edward H. Litchfield (ed.), *Governing Postwar Germany* (Ithaca, N.Y., 1953), especially Richard M. Scannon's "Political Parties" and "Post-war Elections and Electoral Processes," pp. 471–533; Kirchheimer, "Notes on the Political Scene in Western Germany," *World Politics*, VI (April, 1954), 306–21; and "The Composition of the German Bundestag," *Western Political Quarterly*, III (1950), 590–601. See also Dolf Sternberger, "Berufs-Politiker und Politiker-Berufe: Zur Soziologie des deutschen Bundestages," *Die Gegenwart*, V, No. 22 (1950), 9–11; Otto Kirchheimer and Arnold H. Price, "Analysis and Effects of the Elections in Western Germany," *Department of State Bulletin*, XXI (October, 17, 1949), 563–73; Harry L. Bretton, "The German Social Democratic Party and the International Situation," *Proceedings of the American Political Science Association*, XLVII (December, 1953), 980–96; Tay-

lor Cole, "Neo-fascism in Western Germany and Italy," *American Political Science Review*, XLIX (March, 1955), 131–43; Hans Speier, "German Rearmament and the Old Military Elite," *World Politics*, VI (January, 1954), 147–68; Richard K. Ullmann, "The Struggle for Representative Institutions in Germany," *Parliamentary Affairs*, II (1950), 361–77; Heinz Gollwitzer, "Parteien und Weltanschauung," *Internationales Jahrbuch der Politik*, II (1954), 219–30; Otto Kirchheimer, "Parteistruktur und Massendemokratie in Europa," *Archiv für öffentliches Recht*, LXXIX (1954), 301 ff.; and G. Rabus, "Die innere Ordnung der politischen Parteien in gegenwärtigen deutschen Staatsrecht," *Archiv für öffentliches Recht*, LXXVIII (1952), 163 ff.

Representative monographs of promising field research are Rudolf Wildenmann, *Partei und Fraktion: Ein Beitrag zur Analyse der politischen Willensbildung und des Parteiensystems in der Bundesrepublik* (Meisenheim, 1954); Hans Georg Wieck, *Die Entstehung der CDU und die Wiedergründung des Zentrums im Jahre 1945* (Düsseldorf, 1953); Stephanie Munke, *Wahlkampf und Machtverschiebung: Geschichte und Analyse der berliner Wahlen, 1950* ("Schriften des Instituts für politische Wissenschaft" [Berlin, 1952]); H. Hund, *Der BHE in Koalition und Opposition* (Heidelberg, 1953); and Götz Roth, *Fraktion und Regierungsbildung: Eine monographische Darstellung der Regierungsbildung in Niedersachsen* (Meisenheim, 1954).

For suggestive contemporary discussions see Wilhelm Grewe, "Parteienstaat—oder was sonst?" *Der Monat*, XXXVI (September, 1951), 563–87, and F. R. Allemann, "Das deutsche Parteiensystem," *Der Monat*, LIII (January, 1953), 365–88. For the programmatic debate see also Carlo Schmid, *Die sozialdemokratische Partei Deutschlands vor der geistigen Situation dieser Zeit* (Hamburg, 1950).

The place and position of the major parties have been largely determined by their leaders. For the late SPD spokesman Schumacher see the comprehensive biography edited by Arno Scholz and W. G. Oschilewski, *Turmwächter der Demokra-*

tie (Berlin, 1953); see also F. Wesemann, *Kurt Schumacher: Ein Leben für Deutschland* (Frankfurt a.M., 1952). On Adenauer see Joachim Peck, *Dr. Konrad Adenauer* (Berlin, 1954), and Edgar Alexander's forthcoming biography; see also C. Jacobi, "Germany's Great Old Man," *Foreign Affairs*, XXXIII (January, 1955), 239–49, and K. Adenauer, "Germany: The New Partner," *Foreign Affairs*, XXXIII (January, 1955), 177–83.

The unique and representative position of the first Bundespräsident, Theodor Heuss, has been well evaluated in Hans Bott (ed.), *Begegnungen mit Theodor Heuss* (Tübingen, 1954), and Margaret Boveri, *Theodor Heuss: Die literarische Gestalt* (Stuttgart, 1954); see also H. H. Welchert, *Theodor Heuss: Ein Lebensbild* (Bonn, 1953). Of Heuss's numerous publications, the following may be most revealing of his personality: *Vorspiele des Lebens: Jugenderinnerungen* (Stuttgart, 1953); *Friedrich Naumann* (2d ed.; Stuttgart, 1949); *Deutsche Gestalten: Studien zum 19. Jahrhundert* (Stuttgart, 1949); *1848: Werk und Erbe* (Stuttgart, 1948); and *Verfassungsrecht und Verfassungspolitik vom monarchischen Konstitutionalismus zum demokratischen Parlamentarismus* (Krefeld, 1950).

Among recent contributions to the theory of political parties and their place in the modern state and constitution are: Ernst Forsthoff, Karl Loewenstein, and Werner Matz, *Die politischen Parteien im Verfassungsstreit* (Tübingen, 1950); Wilhelm Grewe, "Zum Begriff der politischen Partei," in *Kaufmann Festschrift: Um Recht und Gerechtigkeit* (Stuttgart, 1950); Gerhard Leibholz *et al.*, *Verfassungsrechtliche Stellung und innere Ordnung der Parteien* ("Verhandlungen des 38. deutschen Juristentages" [Tübingen, 1951]); F. A. von der Heydte and Karl Sacherl, *Soziologie der deutschen Parteien*

(Munich, 1955); O. H. von der Gablentz, *Politische Parteien als Ausdruck gesellschaftlicher Kräfte* (Berlin, 1952); Klemens Kremer, *Der Abgeordnete zwischen Entscheidungsfreiheit und Parteidisciplin* (Munich, 1952); S. Barbarino, *Staatsform und politische Willensbildung* (Munich, 1949); Otto Stammer, "Das Elitenproblem in der Demokratie," *Schmollers Jahrbuch*, LXXI (1951), 513–40; Karl Loewenstein, "Über die parlamentarische Parteidisciplin im Ausland," *Deutsche Rechtszeitschrift*, Vol. V (1950); Eugen Kogon, "Formen und Funktionen der Opposition," *Zeitschrift für Politik*, N.F., I (December, 1954), 365–72. For material sources see Klaus Mehnert, *Deutschland Jahrbuch 1953* (Essen, 1953); and the yearbooks of the leading parties: *Politisches Jahrbuch der CDU/CSU*, Vol. I (Frankfort, 1950); *Jahrbuch der Sozialdemokratischen Partei Deutschlands* (Hanover, 1946 ff.); as well as the protocols of their party congresses.

For further bibliographical material see A. R. L. Gurland, *Political Science in Western Germany* (Washington, 1952); also Hochschule für politische Wissenschaften, *Literaturverzeichnis der politischen Wissenschaften* (Munich, 1952); and representative periodicals, such as *Zeitschrift für Politik, Die Gegenwart, Der Wähler, Der Monat, Politische Studien* (formerly *Politische Bildung*), *Schmollers Jahrbuch, Europa Archiv, Das Parlament, Deutsche Universitätszeitung*, and *Vierteljahrshefte für Zeitgeschichte*.

For a systematic approach see also earlier treatises, such as Heinrich Triepel, *Die Staatsverfassung und die politischen Parteien* (Berlin, 1928); Von Calker, *Wesen und Sinn der politischen Parteien* (Tübingen, 1930); and, above all, Max Weber, *Wirtschaft und Gesellschaft* (Tübingen, 1923), and his "Politik als Beruf," in *Gesammelte politische Schriften* (Munich, 1921).

INDEX

Index